P9-BYR-274

ADMINISTRATION OF WILLS, TRUSTS, AND ESTATES

TITLES IN THE DELMAR PARALEGAL SERIES

Ransford C. Pyle, *Foundations of Law for Paralegals: Cases, Commentary, and Ethics,* 1992.

Peggy N. Kerley, Paul A. Sukys, Joanne Banker Hames, *Civil Litigation for the Paralegal,* 1992.

Jonathan Lynton, Donna Masinter, Terri Mick Lyndall, *Law Office Management for Paralegals,* 1992.

Daniel Hall, *Criminal Law and Procedure,* 1992.

Daniel Hall, *Survey of Criminal Law,* 1993.

Jonathan Lynton, Terri Mick Lyndall, *Legal Ethics and Professional Responsibility,* 1993.

Michael Kearns, *The Law of Real Property,* 1993.

Angela Schneeman, *The Law of Corporations, Partnerships, and Sole Proprietorships,* 1993.

William Buckley, *Torts and Personal Injury Law,* 1993.

Gordon W. Brown, *Administration of Wills, Trusts, and Estates,* 1993.

Richard Stim, *Intellectual Property: Patents, Copyrights, and Trademarks,* 1993.

ADMINISTRATION OF WILLS, TRUSTS, AND ESTATES

Gordon W. Brown

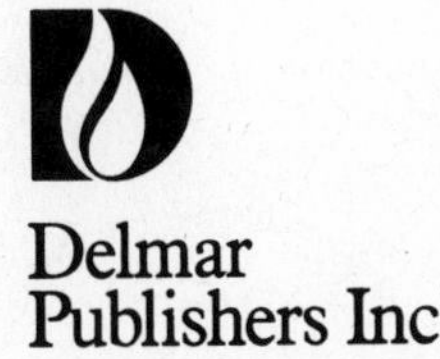

Delmar
Publishers Inc.

NOTICE TO THE READER

Publisher does not warrant or guarantee any of the products described herein or perform any independent analysis in connection with any of the product information contained herein. Publisher does not assume, and expressly disclaims, any obligation to obtain and include information other than that provided to it by the manufacturer.

The reader is expressly warned to consider and adopt all safety precautions that might be indicated by the activities described herein and to avoid all potential hazards. By following the instructions contained herein, the reader willingly assumes all risks in connection with such instructions.

The publisher makes no representations or warranties of any kind, including but not limited to, the warranties of fitness for particular purpose or merchantability, nor are any such representations implied with respect to the material set forth herein, and the publisher takes no responsibility with respect to such material. The publisher shall not be liable for any special, consequential or exemplary damages resulting, in whole or in part, from the readers' use of, or reliance upon, this material.

Cover photo by Mike Gallitelli
Cover design by John Orozco

Delmar Staff

Administrative Editor: Jay Whitney
Developmental Editor: Christopher Anzalone
Editing Supervisor: Judith Boyd Nelson
Production Supervisor: Larry Main
Design Coordinator: Karen Kunz Kemp

For information, address

Delmar Publishers Inc.
3 Columbia Circle, Box 15-015
Albany, New York 12212

Printed in the United States of America

2 3 4 5 6 7 8 9 10 XXX 99 98 97 96 95 94

Library of Congress Cataloging-in-Publication Data

Brown, Gordon W., 1928–
Administration of wills, trusts and estates / Gordon W. Brown.
p. cm.
Includes index.
ISBN 0–8273–5053–8
1. Wills—United States. 2. Probate law and practice—United States
3. Trusts and trustees—United States. I. Title.
KF755.B76 1993
346.7305'4—dc20
[347.30654] 92–33816
CIP

CONTENTS

APPENDICES

DEDICATION

This book is dedicated with thanks and love to Jane.

AM JUR PLEADING AND PRACTICE FORMS, REV: MODEL PRACTICE FORMS FOR EVERY STAGE OF A LEGAL PROCEEDING.

AM JUR PROOF OF FACTS: A SERIES OF ARTICLES THAT GUIDE THE READER IN DETERMINING WHICH FACTS ARE ESSENTIAL TO A CASE AND HOW TO PROVE THEM.

AM JUR TRIALS: A SERIES OF ARTICLES DISCUSSING EVERY ASPECT OF PARTICULAR SETTLEMENTS AND TRIALS WRITTEN BY 180 CONSULTING SPECIALISTS.

UNITED STATES CODE SERVICE: A COMPLETE AND AUTHORITATIVE ANNOTATED FEDERAL CODE THAT FOLLOWS THE EXACT LANGUAGE OF THE STATUTES AT LARGE AND DIRECTS YOU TO THE COURT AND AGENCY DECISIONS CONSTRUING EACH PROVISION.

ALR AND ALR FEDERAL: SERIES OF ANNOTATIONS PROVIDING IN-DEPTH ANALYSES OF ALL THE CASE LAW ON PARTICULAR LEGAL ISSUES.

U.S. SUPREME COURT REPORTS, L ED 2D: EVERY REPORTED U. S. SUPREME COURT DECISION PLUS IN-DEPTH DISCUSSIONS OF LEADING ISSUES.

FEDERAL PROCEDURE, L ED: A COMPREHENSIVE, A–Z TREATISE ON FEDERAL PROCEDURE—CIVIL, CRIMINAL, AND ADMINISTRATIVE.

FEDERAL PROCEDURAL FORMS, L ED: STEP-BY-STEP GUIDANCE FOR DRAFTING FORMS FOR FEDERAL COURT OR FEDERAL AGENCY PROCEEDINGS.

FEDERAL RULES SERVICE, 2D AND 3D: REPORTS DECISIONS FROM ALL LEVELS OF THE FEDERAL SYSTEM INTERPRETING THE FEDERAL RULES OF CIVIL PROCEDURE AND THE FEDERAL RULES OF APPELLATE PROCEDURE.

FEDERAL RULES DIGEST, 3D: ORGANIZES HEADNOTES FOR THE DECISIONS REPORTED IN FEDERAL RULES SERVICE ACCORDING TO THE NUMBERING SYSTEMS OF THE FEDERAL RULES OF CIVIL PROCEDURE AND THE FEDERAL RULES OF APPELLATE PROCEDURE.

FEDERAL RULES OF EVIDENCE SERVICE: REPORTS DECISIONS FROM ALL LEVELS OF THE FEDERAL SYSTEM INTERPRETING THE FEDERAL RULES OF EVIDENCE.

FEDERAL RULES OF EVIDENCE NEWS

FEDERAL PROCEDURE RULES SERVICE

FEDERAL TRIAL HANDBOOK, 2D

FORM DRAFTING CHECKLISTS: AM JUR PRACTICE GUIDE

GOVERNMENT CONTRACTS: PROCEDURES AND FORMS

HOW TO GO DIRECTLY INTO YOUR OWN COMPUTERIZED SOLO PRACTICE WITHOUT MISSING A MEAL (OR A BYTE)

JONES ON EVIDENCE, CIVIL AND CRIMINAL, 7TH

LITIGATION CHECKISTS: AM JUR PRACTICE GUIDE

MEDICAL LIBRARY, LAWYERS EDITION

MEDICAL MALPRACTICE — ALR CASES AND ANNOTATIONS

MODERN APPELLATE PRACTICE: FEDERAL AND STATE CIVIL APPEALS

MODERN CONSTITUTIONAL LAW

NEGOTIATION AND SETTLEMENT

PATTERN DEPOSITION CHECKLISTS, 2D

QUALITY OF LIFE DAMAGES: CRITICAL ISSUES AND PROOFS

SHEPARD'S CITATIONS FOR ALR

SUCCESSFUL TECHNIQUES FOR CIVIL TRIALS, 2D

STORIES ET CETERA — A COUNTRY LAWYER LOOKS AT LIFE AND THE LAW

SUMMARY OF AMERICAN LAW

THE TRIAL LAWYER'S BOOK: PREPARING AND WINNING CASES

TRIAL PRACTICE CHECKLISTS

2000 CLASSIC LEGAL QUOTATIONS

WILLISTON ON CONTRACTS, 3D AND 4TH

FEDERAL RULES OF EVIDENCE DIGEST: ORGANIZES HEADNOTES FOR THE DECISIONS REPORTED IN FEDERAL RULES OF EVIDENCE SERVICE ACCORDING TO THE NUMBERING SYSTEM OF THE FEDERAL RULES OF EVIDENCE.

ADMINISTRATIVE LAW: PRACTICE AND PROCEDURE

AGE DISCRIMINATION: CRITICAL ISSUES AND PROOFS

ALR CRITICAL ISSUES: DRUNK DRIVING PROSECUTIONS

ALR CRITICAL ISSUES: FREEDOM OF INFORMATION ACTS

ALR CRITICAL ISSUES: TRADEMARKS

ALR CRITICAL ISSUES: WRONGFUL DEATH

AMERICANS WITH DISABILITIES: PRACTICE AND COMPLIANCE MANUAL

ATTORNEYS' FEES

BALLENTINE'S LAW DICTIONARY

CONSTITUTIONAL LAW DESKBOOK

CONSUMER AND BORROWER PROTECTION: AM JUR PRACTICE GUIDE

CONSUMER CREDIT: ALR ANNOTATIONS

DAMAGES: ALR ANNOTATIONS

EMPLOYEE DISMISSAL: CRITICAL ISSUES AND PROOFS

ENVIRONMENTAL LAW: ALR ANNOTATIONS

EXPERT WITNESS CHECKLISTS

EXPERT WITNESSES IN CIVIL TRIALS

FORFEITURES: ALR ANNOTATIONS

FEDERAL LOCAL COURT RULES

FEDERAL LOCAL COURT FORMS

FEDERAL CRIMINAL LAW AND PROCEDURE: ALR ANNOTATIONS

FEDERAL EVIDENCE

FEDERAL LITIGATION DESK SET: FORMS AND ANALYSIS

PREFACE

It is said that two things are certain in life—death and taxes. Although those two things are the subject of this book, more importantly, this book is directed toward giving paralegal students the knowledge to be able to assist lawyers in this most certain field.

A paralegal with knowledge of the law of wills, trusts, and estates is an extremely valuable asset to an attorney. The vast majority of law offices draw wills as a matter of course. Trusts are now more popular than ever, and more and more people every day are realizing the importance of estate planning. Many law firms have become highly dependent upon the use of skilled paralegals in this important field.

Administration of Wills, Trusts, and Estates was written with the student in mind. Each chapter begins with an outline, followed by a law office scenario that captures the student's interest at the very beginning. The scenario is followed by a discussion of the law, written in a lively, nonthreatening, easy-to-understand, straightforward fashion, making the book enjoyable to read. Legal jargon and unnecessary verbiage are avoided, and essential legal terms are defined when they are first presented.

Because this subject matter is governed exclusively by state law, which differs from state to state, it is important for students to be exposed to the law of their own states. For this reason, the book contains a wealth of legal forms from a variety of states. Similarly, up-to-date appellate court cases and statutes from many states are used to illustrate points of law. Cases are presented in an analytical style, with the facts summarized, the legal issue identified and answered, and the reason given for the court's decision. Maps and tables are used to pinpoint states that have adopted particular rules of law.

The book is filled with motivating features that help to reinforce learning. Charts, diagrams, cartoons, and illustrations are sprinkled generously throughout the text, making the subject matter interesting and easier to understand. Sample clauses found in wills and trusts are illustrated when they are discussed, and many documents are reproduced in their entirety. A highlight of the book is the *celebrity feature,* found in each chapter, containing an interesting, true article about the will, trust, or estate of a well-known personality.

Administration of Wills, Trusts, and Estates contains a wealth of end-of-chapter features designed to provide classroom activity and realistic student projects. They include chapter summaries, numbered to correlate with the beginning outline and major chapter heads; questions for review; provocative cases to discuss; and assignments geared to sharpen students' skills as paralegals in this important field.

The author wishes to thank Mary McGarry, Senior Editor, Delmar Publishers Inc., for bringing this book into being; Ellen O'Donnell, Director of Paralegal Studies at North Shore Community College, for her initial guidance in the text's development; Sandra Knight, a paralegal student at North Shore Community College, for assisting with research; Thomas Scanlon for aiding in the production of our computer generated features; Dr. Marsha Gadzera, Professor at North Shore Community College, for assistance in preparing the appendices; and Richard Adamo, Librarian of the Essex County Law Library, Salem, Massachusetts, for making the library and its materials so readily accessible. Special thanks to Cynthia Entwistle, Reference Librarian at North Shore Community College, for researching and obtaining photographs, writing many of the celebrity features, and helping to bring the entire book together under a tight deadline.

I also express my appreciation to the reviewers whose thoughtful commentary has made this a better book:

Richard Glasner
University of San Diego
San Diego, CA

Peggy Kerley
Southeastern Paralegal Institute
Dallas, TX

Karen Schwartz
Woodbury College
Montpelier, VT

Jay Wolek
Lansing Community College
Lansing, MI

Ruth Ellen Post
Rivier College
Nashua, NH

Gordon W. Brown

ABOUT THE AUTHOR

Gordon W. Brown is a college professor with 35 years of teaching experience. He presently teaches business law and real estate law at North Shore Community College in Beverly, Massachusetts, where he serves as a member of the paralegal advisory board. He is author of *Legal Terminology* and coauthor of *Understanding Business and Personal Law* and *Business Law with UCC Applications*. In addition, he is a speaker at workshops and conferences on methods of law instruction. Mr. Brown is a practicing attorney and a member of the Massachusetts Bar.

SECTION ONE

Wills

bituaries

P. Predich, 45; executive vice

S VALLEY—James P. Predich, 45, son Avenue, died Thursday in Hospital of coronary disease.

include Mr. Predich's wife, Anna is two sons, Gerald and Peter; and daughters, Grace, Tanya, and Ellen, ders Valley. Also surviving are his Belinda Predich, of Enterston; two Carl Predich of Helteren and Kenneth of New York City; and a sister, Carrington of Burnsville.

will be held at 11 a.m. Monday in ingstar Funeral Home, 567 Newton Penders Valley, with burial in the Cemetery, Richmond.

y requests that contributions be made erican Heart Association or the choir e Penders Valley Alliance Church.

W. Brookes, 39, graphic

ELD—Danny W. Brookes, 39, died of head injuries sustained in a le accident late Thursday night.

okes graduated Magna Cum Laude San Francisco School of Graphic Arts ving two consecutive tours as a r pilot in the Vietnam War. He opened design studio soon after returning to l.

okes is survived by his wife, Wendy avis) Brookes, and four daughters, Marlene, Mariah and Melody, and ents William and Helen Brookes, and William Brookes, Jr., of Chicago.

rial candlelight service will be held at Monday in the chapel of the Whitfield Home, 368 Auburn Lane. Services held at 10 a.m. Tuesday at the d Funeral Home, with burial in the n Cemetery, Richmond.

okes was a veteran of the Vietnam War family requests donations be sent to erican M.I.A./P.O.W. Agency, 9612 Boulevard, Washington, D.C., in lieu rs.

e an announcement in the Obituary

9934 Oak Park Street, with burial in Lawnhome Cemetery immediately thereafter.

Consuela T. Martinez, 79; retired physician

MOUNTVIEW—Dr. Consuela "Connie" T. Martinez, age 79, died Monday of injuries sustained in an automobile accident. She retired from private practice only four years ago, and was a frequent volunteer at the Mountview Children's Shelter.

Dr. Martinez is survived by her daughter, Teresa Shillibaugh of Albany, and six grandchildren.

In addition to her service with the Children's Shelter, Dr. Martinez was active in Our Lady of Sorrows Church Symphony Associatio made to any of those o

Robert Thomas assistant manager, Rob

MOUNTVIEW—Mr. of the University of So

Survivors include hi Barbara Joan (Beck brothers, Andrew and

Visitation will be from 10 a.m. to noon Tuesday at Swan Lake Funeral Home, 1841 West Grace Street. Private family interment is planned.

Memorial contributions may be made to the M.A.D.D. (Mothers Against Drunk Drivers) organization in lieu of flowers.

Arlene Meghan Fullerton, 50, registered nurse

GEORGETOWN—Arlene Meghan (Gibson) Fullerton, 50, of Iroquois Avenue, died Sunday after a short illness. Mrs. Fullerton worked at General Hospital for 26 years and volunteered at the women's shelter.

Mrs. Fullerton is survived by her husband of 27 years, James Douglas, daughter Katherine Elizabeth Ryan, two sons, Alexander James and Michael Thomas, two sisters, Meghan Colleen Amble and Sarah Janette Hamilton, and a brother, Brian Michael Gibson.

No services are scheduled. The family requests that contributions be made to the American Lung Association or the American Cancer

Dinah Z. Norton, 67; Allied G retiree

GREATER HILLTOWN—Dinah "Dinnie Norton, a resident of the Bellemar Apartm died Friday in St. Mary's Hospital, Richm after a brief illness.

She was born in New York City and mov Hilltown as a teenager. She was gradua Jefferson High School. She retired two ago from Allied Global, after 23 yea service.

She lived in Greater Hilltown for all o working life, and was a resident of Bellemar Apartments at the time of her d She was active in the Bellemar Apartn Tenants' Association and the First U

Calling hours will be 3-5 and 7-9 p.m. M in the Smith Funeral Home. Contribution be made to the American Heart Associati the Bellemar Tenants' Association.

Hallibert M. Nowell, 68; forme employee

TENSGROVE—Hallibert (Bert) M. Nov retired railroad worker, died Monday at t of 68, after a long illness.

Mr. Nowell is survived by his wife Roseanne (Marshall) Nowell, his two John (Jack) Patrick and Kevin Norri daughter, Rose Marie Patterson, and grandchildren.

Mr. Nowell, who spent most of his w career in the Tensgrove Switching Statio a member of the Tensgrove United Chur was certified as a master gardener.

A memorial service will be held Tensgrove United Church on Wednes 11:00 a.m. Private inurnment will be Jackson Memorial Shrine.

Contributions may be made to the Ten

CHAPTER 1
Where There's a Will

"Most good lawyers live well, work hard, and die poor."

Daniel Webster

OUTLINE

LAW OFFICE SCENARIO

Marie Perez, a paralegal, was the first to arrive at the law office on Monday morning. Although she was not due in the office until 8:30, she usually arrived about 15 minutes early. A woman was waiting near the office doorway.

"Good morning," Marie said to the woman as she unlocked the door.

"Good morning," the woman replied. "Will Attorney Pierce be in this morning?"

"He has to be in court at 9:00," Marie answered. "He usually goes directly to court without stopping here first. Can I help you with anything?"

"Well, my father passed away last week, and I need to talk to Mr. Pierce about his estate."

"Oh, I'm sorry. Why don't you come in?" Marie responded. "Perhaps I can make an appointment for you."

"He was elderly, and he didn't leave a will," the woman continued. "I'm afraid that everything he owned will go to the state."

Marie showed the woman to a chair and took out a yellow legal pad. "What was your father's name?" she asked.

"Vincent Marino," the woman replied, holding up a pillow case. "He was a wonderful father. Look what he wrote on his hospital pillow case before he died. 'I leave all of my property in equal shares to my daughter, Pearl, and my son, Vito.' "

"He signed it, too," Marie observed. "And those look like the signatures of two witnesses."

"Yes," the woman replied, "he had two nurses sign the pillow case. He didn't know that my brother, Vito, died two days before he did. We just didn't have the courage to tell him."

"Oh, I'm so sorry," Marie answered. "Will you be free this afternoon to see Attorney Pierce? I'll make an appointment for you."

1.1 WHERE THERE'S A WILL . . .

A pillow case may seem like an unusual legal document, but wills come in a fascinating variety of shapes, sizes, and sorts. They have been written on the backs of envelopes, restaurant place mats, prescription blanks, hospital charts, tractor fenders, and jailhouse walls. A Philadelphia housewife wrote the following will on a page of her handwritten book of kitchen recipes:

CHILI SAUCE WITHOUT WORKING

4 quarts of ripe tomatoes, 4 small onions, 4 green peppers, 2 teacups of sugar, 2 quarts of cider vinegar, 2 ounces ground allspice, 2 ounces cloves, 2 ounces cinnamon, 12 teaspoons salt. Chop tomatoes, onions and peppers fine, add the rest mixed together and bottle cold. Measure tomatoes when peeled. In case I die before my husband I leave everything to him.

Even without witnesses, the will was proved and allowed by the probate court in 1913. Pennsylvania statutes allow wills written entirely in the deceased's handwriting to be proved without any witnesses.

A PERSONAL TOUCH

Photo courtesy of Ford Motor Co.

Henry Ford II, wealthy member of the Ford Motor dynasty, was so intent on maintaining family harmony that he left a videotape to be shown after his death. The 15-minute video provided a personal message to his (third) wife and three children (by his first marriage) that explained the rationale behind the distribution of his $325-million estate. Unfortunately, even his extra effort could not prevent a feud between his wife and children. But perhaps his expectations were too high, since his daughters had already demonstrated their animosity by boycotting the couple's wedding seven years before his death.

Another unusual form for a will was used by William Taylor at a bon voyage party held in his honor. When a guest at the party asked Taylor if he had a will, Taylor replied "no," took a dance invitation from his pocket, and wrote his will on the back of the invitation. When he died several years later, long after returning from the voyage, the 29-word will on the back of the dance invitation was allowed by the probate court.

In a similar situation, George W. Hazeltine had no paper available when he wanted to make his will. One of his nurses lifted her dress and allowed Mr. Hazeltine to write his will on her petticoat. Among other gifts, the will left $10,000 to each of his two nurses as a reward for their devotion. The Los Angeles court disallowed the "petticoat will," however, not because it was written on a petticoat, but because the same two nurses who inherited under it also signed the will as witnesses.

Just as wills may appear in different formats, their lengths vary greatly. The shortest known will, dated January 19, 1967, was written by Karl Tausch of Langen, Hesse, Germany. The will read: "Vse zene," which is Czechoslovakian for "All to wife." A similar will was written by an Englishman at the turn of the century. The will contained three words: "All to mother." The will went to litigation, however, over the meaning of the term *mother,* and the court held that "mother" meant not his mother but his wife.

The longest known will was that of Frederica Evelyn Stilwell Cook. The will was probated in London in 1925 and consisted of 4 bound volumes containing 95,940 words on 1,066 pages. Cook's estate totaled $100,000.

There Is Motivation

In 1927, a Canadian lawyer named Charles Miller left his estate "to the Mother who has given birth in Toronto to the greatest number of children" during the 10 years following his death. A competition, referred to as the "Stork Derby," took place, and $568,000 was eventually divided among 4 mothers who had each produced 9 children within the 10-year period.

There Is Kindness

Remembering what it was like to be without a job and having worn-out shoes, an actor named Conrad Cantzen, who died in 1945, left $226,608.34 "for the people who can't buy shoes, even if they are not paid-up members of Equity. Many times I have been on my uppers, and the thinner the soles of my shoes were, the less courage I had to face the managers in looking for a job." Today, professional actors and actresses who are making the rounds, looking for work in worn-out shoes, can "do the shoe bit." Thanks to Conrad Cantzen, they can obtain money for a pair of shoes from Actors Equity, 226 West 47th Street, New York City.

There Is Decision Making

Henry Durrell could not decide which of his three nephews should inherit his stately property located on the shore of Hamilton Harbor, Bermuda. To solve the problem, he stated in his will that the choice should be made by a throw of the dice. On March 15, 1921, dice were thrown by the three nephews, and one of them, Richard Durrell, became the sole owner of the property.

There Is Retribution

The German poet Heinrich Heine wrote a will leaving all his assets to his wife on the condition that she remarry, "[b]ecause then there will be at least one man to regret my death."

In contrast, Patrick Henry, famous for the statement, "Give me liberty or give me death," provided generously for his wife in his will, "But in case my said wife shall marry again . . . I revoke and make void every gift, legacy, authority, or power herein mentioned and order, will and direct, She, my said Wife, shall have no more of my estate than she can recover by law." His widow decided to marry again and take the share that the law provided to wives.

There Is Surprise

A New Yorker, who died in 1880, wrote in his will: "I own seventy-one pairs of trousers, and I strictly enjoin my executors to hold a public sale at which these shall be sold to the highest bidder, and the proceeds distributed to the poor of the city. I desire that these garments shall in no way be examined or meddled with, but be disposed of as they are found at the time of my death." The executors did as they were instructed. Following the sale, each pair of trousers was found to contain $1,000 sewn into the lining.

There Is Appreciation

Famous for the prizes awarded each year in his honor, Joseph Pulitzer left much of his fortune to employees when he died in 1911. His "faithful valet" received $25,000 (equal to over $325,000 today); his "chief" secretary received $20,000 (over $260,000). He also instructed the executors of his estate to confer with management at the two newspapers he owned and divide $40,000 among "the oldest and most faithful employees . . . giving a special preference on account of loyalty and length of service and to employees receiving salaries of less than $100 a week."

In a similar fashion, when the financier, J. P. Morgan, died in 1913, his will provided one year's salary to each employee of J. P. Morgan and Company.

1.2 THE PRIVILEGE OF HAVING A WILL

This brief overview of the more entertaining aspects of wills does not diminish the significance of making a will. The right to leave property by will is not an inherent right, but a privilege permitted by law. Each state has its own laws, passed by its legislature, setting forth precise rules for the disposition of property by will. Without such laws, one could not make a valid will. Massachusetts Gen. Laws. ch. 191, § 1 is an example of a state statute permitting the making of a will:

> Every person eighteen years of age or older and of sound mind may by his last will in writing, signed by him or by a person in his presence and by

> his express direction, and attested and subscribed in his presence by two or more competent witnesses, dispose of his property, real and personal . . . .

Wills are not cast in stone. They are **ambulatory**; that is, they are movable or subject to change. They can be revoked or changed at any time before death. People may change their wills as often as they wish, and it is not uncommon for people to have several wills during their lifetime. People should review their wills about every five years to consider changes in their assets. They may also need to change guardians, executors, and trustees as their circumstances in life change. In addition, it is often necessary, especially in view of today's high divorce rate, to change one's **beneficiaries**—those who inherit under the will.

1.3 RISKS IN WRITING ONE'S OWN WILL

Ensuring that beneficiaries receive their intended shares of an estate requires the thoughtful and deliberate preparation of a legally sound will. Writing one's own will can be risky for a lay person, because the law of wills is highly technical and differs widely from state to state. Lay people who write their own wills are often not aware of the many rules that apply to the writing of a will. In addition, they are not familiar with the true meaning of some of the terms that are commonly used in wills. The trained paralegal can provide the knowledge that the average person lacks. Without proper professional assistance, people may die assuming their wills are clear and straightforward when, in fact, the opposite is true.

The *DeLong* case illustrates this possible confusion. In deciding the *DeLong* case, the court of appeals said, "The problems encountered with the will in this case illustrate how treacherous it is to rely on preprinted form wills. At the time the decedent executed the will, she may have saved herself the expense of a lawyer, but in the end, her presumed devisees lost it all to intestacy."

LEGAL TERMS

ambulatory
Movable or subject to change.

beneficiary
A person who receives a gift under a will. A person holding equitable or beneficial title of a trust (also called *cestui que trust*).

MATTER OF ESTATE OF DELONG
788 P.2d 889 (Mont. 1990)

FACTS: Doris I. DeLong wrote her own will, using a preprinted form. Following the printed words, "I give, devise and bequeath to," she originally wrote in her own handwriting, "James E. DeLong and Helen DeLong." Thereafter, she lined out the word "and" and substituted the word "or," so that the sentence read, "I give, devise and bequeath to James E. DeLong or Helen DeLong."

LEGAL ISSUE: Does a will that states "I give, devise and bequeath" to one party "or" another party provide enough information to determine the intent of its maker?

COURT DECISION: No.

REASON: By lining out the word "and" and by inserting the word "or," the will does not adequately identify what is to be bequeathed or devised, nor who is to inherit. The will simply does not leave any property to anyone. Because the real and personal property of the decedent were not effectively allocated by her will, that property passes under the laws of intestate succession.

Wills must be executed precisely in accordance with the law of the state where they are made, and state laws are not the same. For example, some states require wills to be signed at the end; others do not. Some states require witnesses to sign in each other's presence; others do not. Some states require two witnesses except for wills written in the maker's own handwriting, which require none; other states always require two witnesses, and a few states require three. Because lay people are not usually familiar with these rules, they can easily make a mistake when executing a will without an attorney. The requirements for executing wills are discussed in chapter 4.

Other rules of law relating to the interpretation of wills are also not usually known by lay people. For example, if a child is unintentionally omitted from a parent's will, that child may be able to inherit from the parent's estate. Similarly, in some states, if a gift is made in a will to a relative who dies before the person who made the will, the deceased relative's children take their parent's share of the estate. Language can be used in drafting a will to prevent these situations from occurring. Unaware of such technicalities, lay people who write their own wills may end up leaving their property to unintended heirs. These and other rules of law are discussed more fully in the chapters that follow.

1.4 FINDING THE TESTATOR'S INTENT

The importance of proper legal advice in the preparation of a will cannot be overstated. The language used in a will becomes particularly significant when a court tries to interpret the meaning of a will and determine the intention of the man (**testator**) or woman (**testatrix**) who made the will. The testator's intention must be ascertained from the particular words used in the will itself, from the context in which those words are used, and from the general scope and purposes of the will, read in light of the surrounding and attending circumstances. Elvis Presley's will provides an illustration of the importance and implications of precise wording.

LEGAL TERMS

testator
A man who has made a will.

testatrix
A woman who has made a will.

issue
Lineal descendants; all persons who have descended from a common ancestor.

PRESLEY V. HANKS
782 S.W.2d 482 (Tenn. 1989)

FACTS: Elvis Presley's will contained a testamentary trust directing the trustee, among other things, to pay for the support and maintenance of "my daughter, Lisa Marie Presley, and any other lawful issue I might have." Deborah Delaine Presley filed a petition alleging that she is the illegitimate daughter of Elvis A. Presley and is entitled to a share of the estate under this clause. (Determining that it was beyond the scope of the proceeding, the court in this case did not rule on the question of whether Deborah Delaine Presley was the illegitimate daughter of Elvis Presley.)

LEGAL ISSUE: Do the words "lawful issue" in a will include children born outside of wedlock?

COURT DECISION: No.

REASON: The court noted that Elvis Presley had been involved in a paternity case and was aware of claims placed against him for children born out of wedlock. At the time the will was executed, Presley had one child from his only marriage. The provision for the child is coupled with the provision "and any other lawful issue I might have." There was no doubt in Mr. Presley's mind that Lisa Marie was his child (**issue**), nor was there any question that she was born in lawful wedlock. With this knowledge of the status of his daughter, he explicitly describes the other objects of his bounty as "any other lawful issue." The clause provides for issue the testator "might have," indicating his intent to provide for those coming into existence after the execution of the will. The intent of the testator to provide for only legitimate children becomes even more clear when we consider his disposition of the corpus of the trust. Here again, he utilizes the descriptive word "lawful" when referring to his children who should receive his bounty. A will should be construed to give effect to every word and clause contained therein. We are compelled to believe that the word "lawful" was used to denote those born in lawful wedlock.

1.5 WHERE THERE'S NO WILL . . .

When someone dies without a will, his or her property passes according to a specific scheme that has been adopted by the state legislature. The scheme, known as *the law of intestate succession,* may or may not carry out the wishes of the decedent. **Intestate succession** is the legal name for the process of an heir's becoming beneficially entitled to the property of one who dies without a will. In general, **real property** (the ground and anything permanently affixed to it) passes according to the law of intestate succession in the state where the property is located. In contrast, **personal**

property (everything that can be owned that is not real property) passes according to the law of intestate succession in the state where the decedent was **domiciled** at the time of death. State laws of intestate succession are not identical. People often die thinking their property will pass one way, when in fact it passes in a different way altogether. The law of intestate succession is discussed thoroughly in chapter 3, but the major implications of dying without a will are highlighted in this section.

There Are No Named Heirs

Without a will, specific individuals or institutions cannot be designated as the appropriate inheritors of an estate. The state, not the deceased, determines who receives the estate and in what proportion they receive it. Some people believe that a will is unnecessary if they own little or no property. What such people overlook is that their financial status may change before they die. For example, a friend or relative may die shortly before them, leaving them sizeable estates. A simple will would have left the unforeseen inheritance according to their wishes rather than according to the scheme developed by the state legislature.

There Is No Named Guardian

Without a will, a guardian for minor children will not be chosen by the deceased; instead, the court will appoint a guardian. A **guardian** is a person appointed to care for and manage the person, property, or both of a minor. The law makes a distinction between the guardianship of a minor's person and the guardianship of a minor's property. The two parents or the one surviving parent are the natural **guardians of a child's person**. They are not, however, the natural **guardians of a child's property**.

State laws provide for the division of property among the surviving spouse and the surviving children of a person who dies without a will. If a minor child inherits real or personal property, the surviving spouse loses control of the portion of the property inherited by those young children, because the appointed guardian will oversee the minor's property. In many family situations, it is more desirable to have the surviving spouse inherit the entire estate of a deceased spouse, rather than split the estate with minor children. And this can be done only if the deceased spouse leaves a will.

There Is No Named Personal Representative

Without a will, a personal representative will not be chosen or appointed by the deceased. The **personal representative** is the person who carries out the terms of the will. He or she gathers together the assets, pays the debts and taxes, and distributes the remainder according to the terms of the will. The various types of personal representatives and their duties are discussed in detail in chapter 11.

LEGAL TERMS

intestate succession
The process of an heir's becoming beneficially entitled to the property of one who dies without a will.

real property
The ground and anything permanently affixed to it.

personal property
Everything that can be owned that is not real property.

domicile
One's principal place of abode to which, whenever one is absent, one has the present intent of returning with no present purpose to depart.

guardian
Person who is appointed to care for and manage the person, property, or both of a minor or incompetent.

guardian of the person
One who has the care and custody of a child.

guardian of the property
One who has the responsibility of caring for a child's property until the child becomes an adult.

personal representative
Person who carries out the terms of a will or administers an estate; an executor or administrator.

ONE OF THE MANY HOWARD HUGHES WILLS

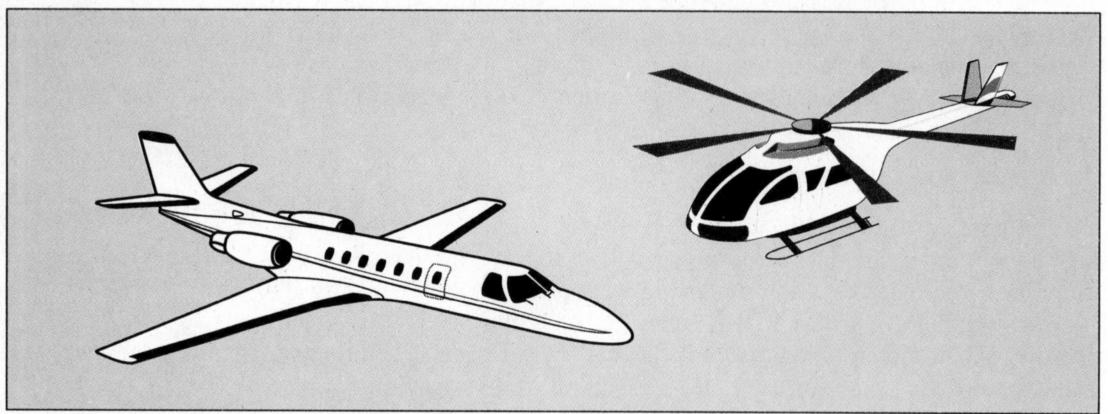

I Howard R. Hughes being of sound and disposing mind and memory, not acting under duress, fraud or other undue influence of any person whomsoever, and being a resident of Las Vegas, Nevada declare that this is to be my Last Will and revoke all other Wills previously made by me.

After my death my estate is to be divided as follows:

first: one forth of all my assets to go to "Hughes Medical Institute of Miami.

second: one eight of assets to be divided among the University of Texas—Rice Institute of Technology of Houston—the University of Nevada and the University of Calif.

third: one sixteenth to Church of Jesus Christ of Latterday Saints—David O. Makay

Forth: one sixteenth to establish a home for Orphan Children

Fifth: one sixteenth of assets to go to Boy Scouts of America

sixth: one sixteenth to be divided among Jean Peters of Los Angeles and Ella Rice of Houston

seventh: one sixteenth of assets to William R. Loomis of Houston, Texas

eighth: one sixteenth to go to Melvin DuMar of Gabbs, Nevada

ninth: one sixteenth to be divided among my personal aids at the time of my death

tenth: one sixteenth to be used as school scholarship fund for entire country

the spruce goose is to be given to the City of Long Beach, Calif.

the remainder of My estate is to be divided among the key men of the companys I own at the time of my death

I appoint Noah Dietrich as the executor of this will

signed the 19 day of March 1968

□ □ □

Over 30 wills that were submitted to courts in various states claimed to be that of Howard Hughes, the mysterious and reclusive American billionaire. The famous "Melvin Dummar/Mormon Church" version printed here inspired the film *Melvin and Howard,* starring Jason Robards as Hughes. The will seems too rough and simplistic to be that of so wealthy and worldly a businessman as Hughes. However, only after a long legal battle was the will finally rejected by the courts. None of the thirty wills was ever admitted to probate. The massive Hughes fortune passed by intestacy to distant relatives whom he hardly knew.

When a person dies without a will, the personal representative is appointed by the court following a priority list set by state statute. Generally, surviving spouses are given first priority, followed by **next of kin** (those most nearly related by blood). Next in line, however, are strangers to the decedent, including creditors and **public administrators** (officials appointed by the court to administer estates). Most people would probably not want strangers going through their personal belongings and making decisions about their property, even though they are not around to witness it. Yet that is what can happen when a person dies without a will.

There Is No Testamentary Trust

Without a will, a trust that takes effect upon death cannot be established. A **trust** is an arrangement whereby property is held by one person for the benefit of another. Legal title is held by a **trustee**, who holds the property in trust for the benefit of a beneficiary. Property may be placed in trust in two ways: (1) by creating a **living trust**, that is, a trust that becomes effective while the person is alive, or (2) by creating a **testamentary trust**, which is a trust within the body of a will. Without a will, a testamentary trust cannot be created and a trustee cannot be named. Estate planners consider a will to be a necessity even when a living trust is used as part of the estate plan. Estate planning, taxes, and trusts—important areas of concern to the paralegal—are discussed thoroughly in later chapters, but a primer by an expert in financial planning is appropriate for this introduction.

SUMMARY

1.1 Wills have been written on many kinds of strange materials, including the backs of envelopes, restaurant place mats, and recipe books. Wills often cause surprise and may motivate people to take certain courses of action. Wills can also embody acts of kindness, appreciation, gratitude, and retribution.

1.2 The right to leave property by will is a privilege permitted by law rather than an inherent right. Each state has its own statutes setting forth precise rules relating to the disposition of property by will. Wills can be revoked or changed at any time before death.

1.3 Because the law of wills is highly technical and differs widely from state to state, it is risky for one to write one's own will. Lay people are usually not aware of the many rules that apply to the writing of a will and may not be familiar with the true meaning of legal terms commonly used in wills.

1.4 A will must be executed with the intent to dispose of one's property upon one's death. The language of the will provides the court with the means to determine the intention of the person who made the will.

LEGAL TERMS

next of kin
Those persons who are nearest of kindred to the decedent; that is, those who are most nearly related by blood.

public administrator(-trix)
An official appointed to administer the estate of an intestate decedent when no one appears who is entitled to act as administrator.

trust
Arrangement under which title to property is divided into two parts, legal title and equitable title.

trustee
Person who holds legal title in trust for the benefit of a beneficiary.

living trust (also called inter vivos trust)
Trust that becomes effective during the settlor's lifetime.

testamentary trust
A trust within the body of a will.

GUEST EDITORIAL

Excerpted with permission from James Publishing, Legal Assistant Today *(September/October 1990).*

WEALTH BUSTERS

Howard M. Sachs, J.D.

During One's Lifetime, Impediments to the Accumulation of Wealth Include: Income Taxes, Inflation, Probate and Estate Taxes

Where there is wealth, there will be taxes. And where there are taxes, there will be inspired attempts to avoid them.

So, assuming that it is generally desirable to minimize taxes and preserve wealth—for family members or others—let's see what can be done under current law to do just that.

WEALTH BUSTERS

During one's lifetime, impediments to the accumulation of wealth include:

1. Income Taxes: Presently as high as 31 cents of every dollar earned (plus state taxes for those liable).

2. Inflation: Even a moderate annual rate of 4.5 percent could cause prices of goods and services to increase by 100 percent over a 16-year period.

Death brings about further, potentially more onerous, threats to family wealth retention:

3. Probate: Fees and costs levied during this court-supervised process can easily absorb 5–10 percent of the value of one's net asset base. Probate can be time-consuming—depriving beneficiaries of your largesse for years.

4. Estate Taxes: Just the federal portion of these marginal tax rates can reach as high as 60 percent of the fair market value of your assets. Because these levies are based on the *value* of your assets and not merely on the income produced therefrom, they are especially burdensome.

HOW TO SURVIVE PROBATE

Probate is actually the process of "proving a will"—ensuring the validity of its provisions and terms, and the distribution of assets thereunder.

Remember: only assets passed under a will are subject to probate.

Assets not subject to probate:

1. Assets owned jointly with right of survivorship.

If one of the joint owners dies, the property automatically passes to the survivor. Virtually any asset may be owned in this fashion, including stocks, bonds, mutual funds and real estate.

Remember: When either of the joint owners dies, the survivor will own those assets individually.

2. Assets assigned to a beneficiary by contract.

Insurance policies, annuity contracts, IRA accounts, some retirement plan accounts, 403(b) plans and the like normally afford this opportunity.

Bonus: This is the simplest, most efficient and generally the most cost-effective method of transmitting wealth.

3. Assets "Gifted" outright to another during one's lifetime.

You may make an unlimited number of gifts to an unlimited number of people each year during your lifetime with no gift tax consequence. But these gifts must not exceed $10,000 per year per person. A gift from husband and wife to an individual may total $20,000 with no gift tax (but a gift tax return must be filed with the IRS).

4. Assets passed via a trust to its beneficiaries upon the creator's death.

Caveat: In order for assets to be passed "extra," or outside, the probate process, they must be registered as owned by the trustee prior to the creator's death.

Note: Be sure to register a trust with your CPA, estate planner, lawyer, etc.

Stocks, bonds, bank accounts, mutual funds, money market accounts, real estate—all must be properly registered as owned by the named trustee(s), or such assets may first be subject to probate *before* the trust terms and provisions become operative. This is generally not a desirable result.

Should you pass away *without* a will, the laws of intestacy in your state of domicile will stipulate how and to whom your assets are to pass.

Should you create a trust within your will, to take effect upon your death, assets will be subject to probate prior to the trust's terms and provisions prevailing over them.

Assets registered to a trust created during your lifetime will pass to your beneficiaries without the intervening step of probate.

Master these basics:

- Assets to pass under a will must first be probated.
- A will becomes effective only upon the occurrence of one event—death.
- At almost any age, the statistical probability of a term of disability or period of incapacity to manage one's affairs is more likely than death.
- A trust can anticipate and provide for substitute management; a will cannot.
- A power of attorney (durable and general) can also comprehend such an occurrence. However, such a document *does not* address the disposition of assets upon death.
- Trusts can be irrevocable—permanent in nature; or revocable—subject to change at any time prior to death.
- Wills are similarly revocable.
- A revocable trust created during one's lifetime can comprehend and describe the management and control of one's affairs given any eventuality during life. It can also program the distribution of assets upon death. This "Intervivos" (living) trust provides for flexible and comprehensive wealth management.

Note: Concerned parties should consult their own tax and legal counsel prior to taking any action.

ESTATE TAXES—THE BIG BITE

To get a feel for just how intrusive and exacting federal estate taxes can be:

1. Add up the value of everything you own in *today's dollars* (including face amount of life insurance policies and IRA accounts).

2. Subtract any debts, liabilities or outstanding payments due to creditors (including mortgages and loans on insurance policies, or from retirement plans).

3. Allow $25,000 for funeral costs and final expenses. Disregard any possible transfers to one's spouse, charitable contributions or other transfers one might make to reduce the estate's value.

If the amount calculated above exceeds $600,000, your wealth could be subject to taxes ranging from 37 to 60 percent, depending upon the size of your estate.

MINIMIZING ESTATE TAXES

The Unified Credit Exemption Equivalent (UCEE) of $600,000 is the single most important estate planning tool available to *everyone.* It must, however, be used properly. For example:

Husband and wife each have available to them the opportunity to reduce their taxable estates by up to $600,000—thereby protecting up to $1,200,000 of their assets from federal estate taxation. But, if husband or wife dies, leaving his/her entire assets to the other, one $600,000 UCEE is lost forever and will result in up to $235,000 of additional federal estate tax liability.

For better results:

Each party must stipulate in his/her trust or will that up to the first $600,000 of individual assets will not be left to the spouse directly, but instead to children or other heirs, or better yet in a subsequent trust for the eventual benefit of these heirs. This trust, commonly referred to as a credit shelter trust or bypass trust, may be structured to allow income and limited use of principle for the benefit of the spouse. Only upon the surviving spouse's death are assets passed to the final beneficiaries. This protects the spouse from loss of benefit during his/her lifetime.

By structuring this strategy through specific language in your trust or will, you can save up to $235,000 in taxes.

POTENTIAL DANGER ZONES

1. Life Insurance Policies.

If you or your spouse die owning a life insurance policy, then its value—the face amount of the policy—is includable in your estate for federal estate tax purposes. A $1,000,000 life insurance policy might suffer as much as 60 percent taxation, leaving only $400,000 net proceeds for heirs.

What to Do:

If the policy is no longer necessary to pay off debts, ensure the education of children or provide comfort and customary lifestyle for your family, transfer ownership to children or other heirs for whom the proceeds are intended. Even better—transfer the policy to an irrevocable trust established for the benefit of your intended. Certain technicalities must be adhered to in order to ensure the trust's validity and tax status. Also, you must survive the transfer of the trust by three years to avoid its inclusion of the proceeds in your estate.

2. Retirement Plans.

Great for wealth accumulation, but in 1986 Congress enacted provisions that could subject these assets to an extra 15 percent penalty tax *(in addition to any estate tax)* for "excess accumulations."

What to Do:

If you have accumulated in excess of $1,000,000 in your various retirement plans (including IRAs), it may be in your interest to see if this extra tax may be applicable to you. You may choose to discontinue contributions to these plans.

Those with sizable retirement plan accounts may want to consider splitting the beneficiary designation so that some portion of these accounts goes directly to beneficiaries and some is directed to your bypass trust to reduce tax liability.

Also, it is imperative that you regularly review your beneficiary designations on all of your retirement plans. Named beneficiaries should be updated to comport with current wishes/intentions.

Remember: a named beneficiary takes precedence over any arrangements made in a will or trust. Be certain that beneficiary designations and intentions as reflected in your will or trust are consistent, compatible and up to date.

3. Too Much Jointly Held Property.

While husband or wife may pass unlimited assets to each other, owning a significant portion of one's estate in joint fashion may create a tax nightmare.

If husband and wife own 100 percent of their assets jointly, the survivor will receive title to all assets on the death of the first. This plan would effectively eliminate the benefit of one UCEE, as no assets will pass from the first to die to someone other than the surviving spouse.

What to Do:

Be certain that husband and wife own at least $600,000 of assets in his/her own name (beware of divorce!), then utilize the plan discussed earlier for maximization of both UCEEs.

A similar sequence should be undertaken where husband and wife have elected to leave their respective assets to each other via will or trust. Current law allows for an unlimited marital deduction between husband and wife. This means no estate tax (or gift tax) is levied on transfers between them. But maximizing the use of both UCEEs will require the redrafting of each will or trust.

4. Do You Have a Will?

A yes answer indicates probate, but if this document was drafted prior to 1981, you need an update. Laws passed in 1981 (effective in 1982) and subsequent legislation may have rendered your plan obsolete and may not afford you full advantage of wealth retention opportunities.

5. Consider "Gifting."

The winds of change have been swirling around the $600,000 UCEE for several years—with Congress threatening to eliminate it, reduce it, cut it in half—the outcome remains uncertain.

Since this credit is also available during your life for gifts you may make, consider gifting up to $600,000 of assets that are likely to appreciate and perhaps do not provide you with current income—e.g., real estate or growth stocks. Not only are such gifts free of gift taxes (and eventually estate taxes) but any appreciated future value also escapes any such taxation.

An asset worth $600,000 today may be worth $1,200,000 in roughly 10 years at 7 percent annual inflation. If your death occurred at that time, your estate would be taxed at $1,200,000 fair market value. A gift today to children or other heirs will be tax-free since its value is $600,000 or less.

Not only will this benefit attach, but you will create the certainty of receiving the *full* benefit of the (current) $600,000 UCEE.

Howard M. Sachs, J.D., is Vice President of Financial Planning at Raymond James & Associates, Inc., Member NYSE-SIPC, Belleair Bluffs, FL.

SUMMARY (Continued)

1.5 When people die without a will, their property passes according to the law of intestate succession, which varies from state to state. People who die without a will lose the opportunity to name heirs, guardians, personal representative, or trustees.

QUESTIONS FOR REVIEW

1. Generally, how does property pass when someone dies without a will?
2. What are four advantages of having a will?
3. What is meant by the statement, "The right to leave property by will is not an inherent right."
4. How often may people change their wills? How often should people review their wills?
5. In construing the meaning of a will, what does the court seek to determine?
6. Give an example of how state laws differ in their requirements for executing a will.
7. Why can writing one's own will be risky for a lay person?
8. What can happen in some states if a gift is made in a will to a relative who dies before the person who made the will?

CASES TO DISCUSS

1. In anticipation of extended travels, Claude Rogers (who was 78 years old and unmarried) and Maxine Robinson invited Maxine's daughter, Judee Dunn, son-in-law, Bill, and a friend, Ina Witherspoon, to dinner. During the evening, Maxine wrote out a two-and-a-half-page will in her own handwriting, at the end of which she signed her name. Beneath her signature she wrote: "Judee Dunn: Claude & I give you full power to do & take care of all our Business & do as you wish with, with it, with no problems from anyone. You can sell or dispose of all property & monies." This was signed by both Claude and Maxine and witnessed by Bill and Ina. Later, Claude died. Is the instrument the will of Claude? Explain. *Dunn v. Means,* 803 S.W.2d 542 (Ark. 1991).
2. Father Paul Thomas Quinn executed a will containing the following bequest: "To my housekeeper of many years, Judy Crowe, I give, devise and bequeath an undivided eight per cent share of all the rest and residue of my estate if she be in my employment at the time of my death. If she is not in my employment at the time of my death then this gift to her shall lapse and the same shall be distributed in accordance

with the provisions of paragraph Third, part F of this my Last Will and Testament." Later, Father Quinn's health deteriorated. He was hospitalized in September and spent the remainder of his life either in the hospital or a nursing home. During his stay in both places, he told Judy that he wanted her to work for him since he planned to return to his apartment when possible. Judy performed her last duties as housekeeper the following January, when Father Quinn's lease of the apartment was terminated. Father Quinn died in March. Did Judy Crowe inherit under Father Quinn's will? Why or why not? *Matter of Estate of Quinn,* 450 N.W.2d 432 (S.D. 1990).

3. Joseph Forti's will stated, "I am married to LUCIA M. FORTI, who is referred to in this Will as 'my wife.' We presently have two children, KENNETH J. FORTI and DENISE A. FORTE who together with any other children of mine born or adopted after the execution of this Will, are referred to in this Will as 'my children.'" Another clause in the will said, "Reference to 'child' and 'children' means lawful descendants in the first degree, whether by blood or adoption." His will left his property to Lucia in trust and upon her death to "each of my children then living." Before making the will, Joseph had committed adultery and become the father of Stephanie, whom he acknowledged as his child. In deciding whether Stephanie should inherit from Joseph's estate, how must the court determine Joseph's intention? *Bell v. Forti,* 584 A.2d 77 (Md. 1991).

SHARPENING YOUR PROFESSIONAL SKILLS

1. Refer to the opening law office scenario and answer the following questions: (a) How might Marie have responded to the woman's statement that everything her father owned will go to the state because he died without a will? (b) What would you have told the woman about the words written on the pillow case? (c) What further information would you need to have about the woman's brother, Vito?
2. Look up your state statute that permits a person to make a will, write down the statutory reference, and photocopy the statute for your notebook.
3. How many witnesses to a will are required under the law of your state? Give the statutory reference where the provision is found.
4. Think of a member of your family whom you believe has no will. Write some disadvantages that would result if that person should die at this time without a will.

CHAPTER 2
A Bundle of Rights

"You want someone who has tasted many different situations, who struggled, who raised a family, who lived in a neighborhood all their [sic] lives rather than a penthouse on Sutton Place."

Mario Cuomo, on lawyers

OUTLINE

LAW OFFICE SCENARIO

The phone rang at the desk of Maude Vickers, a paralegal in the office of Wittenhagen & Cooper. "Good morning," Maude answered.

"Good morning, Maude." The receptionist was on the line. "Ms. Ryan is here. She wants to see an attorney, and there's no one here. Can you talk to her?"

"Sure. I'll come right out." Maude went out to the waiting room, greeted Ms. Ryan, introduced herself, and ushered Ms. Ryan into her office.

"My brother passed away last week, and his wife wants everything that was in my brother's safe-deposit box," Ms. Ryan sputtered angrily.

"Oh, I'm sorry to hear that," Maude replied in a comforting tone. "Were they married long?"

"Three weeks," Ms. Ryan replied. "My brother was a bachelor for 65 years. He died on his honeymoon at a campground on St. John in the Virgin Islands."

"How terrible!"

"His wife's trying to get everything he owned, and it was all joint with me," Ms. Ryan continued. "The house, all the bank books, the stock certificates—they were all in my name and his."

"Do you have a key to the safe-deposit box?" Maude asked.

"No. That's the only thing that was not joint. He didn't want me to know what was in that. He always said it was personal."

"Did he have any life insurance?"

"Yes. But my mother was the beneficiary of the policy, and she died five years ago."

"Did he leave a will?" Maude inquired.

"Yes," Ms. Ryan answered, "I have his will, but I know he didn't know what he was doing when he wrote it. He made it out just before they went on the honeymoon, and he left everything to her. I have a good mind to tear it up."

"You had better not do that," Maude counseled. "I'll make an appointment for you to see Attorney Wittenhagen as soon as possible. Are you free at 4:00 this afternoon?"

2.1 A BUNDLE OF RIGHTS

Paralegals need a basic understanding of property in its various forms—bank accounts, stock certificates, life insurance, etc.—because property is the basic element underlying wills, estates, and trusts. Without property, there would be nothing to give anyone in a will, nothing to plan about, and nothing to put in trust.

Property is generally considered anything that people own, such as houses, cars, furniture, bank accounts, stocks, bonds, and money. Indeed, property is sometimes defined as everything that is the subject of ownership. In a legal sense, however, property is not considered to be the item itself. More correctly, it consists of the various rights or interests that people have in the item. Thus, property, in the eyes of the law, is considered to be a "bundle of rights."

The bundle of rights can be considerable and can be spread among various people. For example, many people may have rights to a house and the land that goes with it. The owner (there is often more than one) has the exclusive right to possess the property unless it is leased to someone else, along with the right to bring a trespass action against a trespasser. If someone else has a life estate in the property (discussed later), that person has the exclusive right to possession for his or her lifetime, and a third person may have a future interest—the right to possession when the life tenant dies.

The bank that holds a mortgage on the property has the right to prevent the person in possession from committing waste, that is, damaging the property. The bank also has the right to take the property or sell it if the owner does not pay the mortgage. An attaching creditor who wins a suit against a property owner may have the right to have the property sold by a sheriff in order to obtain the amount of the judgment. Cities and towns have similar rights to sell private property to satisfy liens for overdue taxes.

If the property is leased to a tenant, the tenant has the exclusive right to possession as well as the sole right to bring a trespass action against a trespasser—even against the landlord who owns the property. However, the landlord regains the right to possession once the lease terminates. The holder of an easement over the property has the right to use the property according to the terms of the easement. The holder of a license given by the owner has the right to do whatever the license allows, such as the right to place an advertising billboard on the property. The holder of a **profit à prendre** has the right to go on the property and extract minerals or timber.

Traditionally, things such as wild animals in their natural state, air, running water, and sunlight could not be the subject of ownership and were not considered property, because no one had the exclusive right to possess them. In modern times, however, with increased water shortages and the expanded use of solar energy, state laws give certain property rights even in these areas.

These varied rights that people may have make up the bundle of rights that is usually referred to as real property. Similar rights relating to personal property are also applicable. When people die owning such rights, the rights pass to others according to the law that you are about to study.

2.2 PROBATE PROPERTY

When an estate is settled, the probate court deals only with what is commonly referred to as **probate property** or the **probate estate**. This is real and personal property that was owned either solely by the decedent or with others as a tenant in common (discussed later). Title to real property owned by a decedent **vests** in (accrues to) the decedent's heirs immediately upon death, but is subject to **divestiture** (being taken away) in order to pay debts of the estate. The probate process is necessary to prove the heir's title. In contrast, title to personal property owned by a decedent passes to the executor or administrator of the decedent's estate; the probate process is necessary to have the executor or administrator appointed and to safeguard the rights of all interested parties.

Real Property

Real property is the ground and anything permanently affixed to it. Land, buildings on the land, and trees and perennial plants growing on the land, as well as the airspace above the land, are all considered to be real

LEGAL TERMS

profit à prendre
Right to take part of the soil or produce of another's land.

probate property (also called probate estate)
Property belonging to the decedent that is subject to administration by the executor or administrator. Among other things, it includes real and personal property that was owned either solely by the decedent or with others as a tenant in common.

probate estate (also called probate property)
Property belonging to the decedent that is subject to administration by the executor or administrator.

vest
Accrue to.

divest
Take away.

real property
The ground and anything permanently affixed to it.

property. People can own real property either solely or concurrently with others as tenants in common, joint tenants, or, in some states, as tenants by the entirety. To determine the type of ownership that a decedent had in real property, it is necessary to examine the decedent's deed to the property. If the decedent inherited the property, it is necessary to examine the probate court records to determine the decedent's extent of ownership.

Real property that was owned **severally**, that is, apart from others or solely by the decedent, is part of the probate estate and must be included in the list of probate assets. Similarly, the decedent's interest in real property that was owned with others as a tenant in common is also part of the probate estate. **Tenants in common** are two or more persons who own an undivided interest in property in such a way that each owner's interest passes to his or her heirs upon death rather than to the surviving co-owners. Thus, if a decedent and one other person owned a parcel of real property as tenants in common, the decedent's one-half undivided interest in the property would be included among the assets of the decedent's estate. If, instead, a decedent and five other people owned a parcel of real property as tenants in common, the decedent's one-sixth undivided interest in the property would be included among the assets of the decedent's estate. People become tenants in common when they are deeded or willed property in that manner (see figure 2-1) or when they inherit property under the law of intestate succession.

As the *Evans* case illustrates, when co-owners of real property are tenants in common, they have *unity of possession.* This means that each co-tenant is entitled to the possession of the entire premises.

LEGAL TERMS

severally
Apart from others; solely.

tenants in common
Two or more persons who own an undivided interest in property in such a way that each owner's interest passes to his or her heirs upon death rather than to the surviving co-owners.

EVANS V. COVINGTON
795 S.W.2d 806 (Tex. 1990)

FACTS: When J. R. Scott died, his surviving spouse inherited a one-half undivided interest and his children inherited a one-half undivided interest in his real property. James Evans purchased the children's interest, took possession of the property, enclosed it with a chain-link fence, and used it for many years. Scott's surviving spouse conveyed her interest in the property to Roberta Covington. Evans claims that Covington was not a tenant in common with him because she did not use the property during the years that he possessed it.

LEGAL ISSUE: Does a person who purchases several co-tenants' interests in property become a tenant in common with the remaining co-tenant?

QUITCLAIM DEED

I, ELIZABETH L. HOLLAND, surviving spouse of EZRA S. HOLLAND, deceased, of Salem, Essex County, Massachusetts, for consideration paid, and in full consideration of $118,300.00

grant to PEARL M. KLINE and WALTER P. MARINO, both of 34 Gallows Hill Rd., Salem, Massachusetts, as tenants in common, with QUITCLAIM COVENANTS

the land with the buildings and improvements thereon, located at 34 Gallows Hill Rd., Salem, Massachusetts, described as follows:

That certain parcel of land on Gallows Hill Rd. in said Salem and shown as Lot One Hundred Seventy-Eight (178) on a plan of land entitled "Plan of Land of Gallows Hill, Salem, Mass.," dated December, 1913, and recorded with Essex South District Registry of Deeds in Plan Book 21, Plan 42; said Lot 178 being more fully described as follows:
Bounded

SOUTHWESTERLY and SOUTHERLY on a curved line by said Gallows Hill Rd., ninety-one (91) feet;
NORTHWESTERLY by Lot 177 as shown on said plan, seventy-seven and 20/100 (77.20) feet;
NORTHEASTERLY by Lot 186 as shown on said plan, twenty-four and 83/100 (24.83) feet; and
EASTERLY by Lot 179 as shown on said plan, seventy-two and 15/100 (72.15) feet.

Being the same premises conveyed to my late husband and me by my deed dated December 9, 1981 and recorded with Essex South District Registry of Deeds in Book 7763, page 129.

Witness my hands and seal this 3rd day of January, 1993.

____

Elizabeth L. Holland

COMMONWEALTH OF MASSACHUSETTS

Essex, ss. January 3, 1993

Then personally appeared the above-named Elizabeth L Holland and acknowledged the foregoing instrument to be her free act and deed before me

____

Notary Public
My commission expires

Pearl M. Kline and Walter P. Marino each own a one-half undivided interest in the property as tenants in common. If either one dies, his or her share passes to his or her heirs rather than to the surviving co-owner.

FIGURE 2-1
Quitclaim deed

COURT DECISION: Yes.

REASON: When a party claims title under a deed that conveys an interest in an existing co-tenancy relationship, he or she becomes a tenant in common with the other co-owners. The surviving spouse and children became co-owners of the property when Mr. Scott died. Thus, when Evans purchased the undivided interest of the children, he entered into an existing co-tenancy, first with Mrs. Scott and later with Roberta Covington. Each co-tenant has a right to enter upon the common estate and a corollary right to possess and use the entire estate.

Personal Property

Personal property is everything that can be owned that is not real property. Coins and paper currency, for example, are personal property. **Tangible personal property** is property that has substance and can be touched. Motor vehicles, household furniture, jewelry, silverware, china, crystal, books, televisions, personal effects, tools, and coin and stamp collections are examples of tangible personal property that are commonly part of decedents' estates. Certificates of title must usually be examined to determine the decedent's title to automobiles, boats, and motor homes.

Intangible personal property is property that is not susceptible to the senses and cannot be touched. Such things as stocks, bonds, negotiable instruments (checks, drafts, and promissory notes), patents, copyrights, and trademarks are examples of intangible personal property. They are evidence of the right to property but not the property itself. For example, a stock certificate is evidence of one's ownership in a corporation, and a promissory note is evidence of the right to receive money from a debtor. It is interesting to note that a lease of real property is considered to be an item of intangible personal property.

The legal name for an item of intangible personal property is a **chose in action.** This is a personal right not reduced to possession but recoverable by a suit at law. Other examples of choses in action that are sometimes owned by estates are lawsuits that survive death that were initially brought by the decedent; rights to collect money due for debts or damages; royalty rights; and the proceeds of life insurance policies and pension benefits when the decedent's estate is named as the beneficiary. Documents such as stock certificates, bond certificates, promissory notes, bank books, insurance policies, and written contracts may be used to prove title to intangible personal property.

FROM THE DETAILED WILL OF LILLIAN HELLMAN

. . . to MIKE NICHOLS, the Toulouse Lautrec poster in the hall of my New York apartment . . .

. . . to MAX PALEVSKY, the Spanish table presently in the study of my New York apartment . . . the framed Russian altar cloth presently over the fireplace in the living room, given to me by Pudovkin, the movie director, as it was executed by a member of his family in 1796 . . . and the two chairs against the wall near the sofa in the living room of my New York apartment, made by unknown cabinet makers in Bohemia or possibly France and exchanged by these amateurs one to the other in the early nineteenth century . . .

. . . to ROBERT POIRIER . . . the three-step library ladder in the study of my New York apartment; the three (3) Russian china doves, the French secretary and two electrified brass lamps with tulip bulbs in the living room of my New York apartment; and the rare 18th century Biblio bookcase in the bedroom of my New York apartment . . .

. . . to HOWARD BAY, the Forain drawing and the wooden birdcage hanging from the ceiling in the living room of my New York apartment . . .

. . . to WILLIAM ABRAHAMS, the box in the guest bathroom of my New York apartment that has the little foxes on it . . .

□ □ □

In her will, writer Lillian Hellman provided precise descriptions of the items designated for her friends. Her will reads like an inventory of personal property.

2.3 NON-PROBATE PROPERTY

Some things that people own are not part of their estates when they die. Such non-probate property includes jointly owned property, community property, life insurance with named beneficiaries, money in Totten trust accounts (discussed in chapter 7), property that is held in a living trust, pension plan distributions, and individual retirement accounts (IRAs) with named beneficiaries. Although these items pass outside of probate directly to the surviving joint owner or beneficiary, they are part of the decedent's gross estate for estate tax purposes.

As part of their work, paralegals often assist the attorney in gathering the information needed to settle an estate and to complete tax returns. A detailed list of non-probate property, together with its value, must be obtained by the personal representative of the estate to determine whether the estate is large enough that an estate tax return must be filed. If the gross estate (total of all taxable items) is $600,000 or more, a federal estate tax return must be filed. The varied tasks that the paralegal may perform when assisting the personal representative are discussed in chapter 11.

LEGAL TERMS

personal property
Everything that can be owned that is not real property.

tangible personal property
Personal property that has substance and can be touched.

chose in action (also called intangible personal property)
A personal right not reduced to possession but recoverable by a suit at law.

Jointly Owned Property

Real property that was owned by a decedent and another as joint tenants is not part of the decedent's probate estate. Joint property remains the property of the surviving joint owner or owners when one of the owners dies (figure 2-2). **Joint tenants** are two or more persons holding one and the same interest, accruing by one and the same conveyance, commencing at one and the same time, and held by one and the same undivided possession.

AFFIDAVIT—DEATH OF JOINT TENANT

STATE OF CALIFORNIA,)
) ss.
County of ________________)
______________________________)

________________, of legal age, being first duly sworn, deposes and says:

That ______________, the decedent mentioned in the attached certified copy of Certificate of Death, is the same person as ________________ named as one of the parties in that certain __________ dated__________, executed by ______________ to ______________________, as joint tenants, recorded as Instrument No. ________, on __________, in Book/Reel ____, Page/Image ____, of Official Records of ____________ County, California, covering the following described property situated in the __________, County of __________, State of California:

That the value of all real and personal property owned by said decedent at date of death, including the full value of the property above described, did not then exceed the sum of $__________.

Dated______________________ ____________

SUBSCRIBED AND SWORN TO before me __________

this ____ day of __________

Signature ____________________

(This area for official notarial seal)

Title Order No. ______________ Escrow or Loan No.

FIGURE 2-2
Affidavit—death of joint tenant

This affidavit is filed at the county recorder's office to establish proof of the death of a joint owner of real property.

This form of ownership is sometimes referred to as **joint tenants with the right of survivorship.** A similar form of ownership, but which can be held only by a husband and wife, is a tenancy by the entirety. **Tenants by the entirety** are a husband and wife who hold title as joint tenants, modified by the common law doctrine that gives the husband the exclusive rights of possession and profits with protection against attachment and alienation (conveying away) by one spouse alone. This form of ownership is popular because of its protection against attachment by creditors, and some states have modernized the law to give husbands and wives equal rights to possession and profits in property owned as tenants by the entirety.

Under the law of some states, such as Massachusetts, ownership of real property by a husband and wife as joint tenants or as tenants by the entirety automatically changes to ownership as tenants in common if the couple is divorced. Thus, after a divorce in Massachusetts, if one marriage partner dies before changing the title to the property, the decedent's interest in the property passes to his or her heirs rather than to the former spouse automatically. Other states do not follow this rule. In Montana, for example, a divorce does not change a joint tenancy into a tenancy in common.

Another form of ownership that causes property to pass outside of probate is tenancy in partnership. **Tenancy in partnership** is a form of co-ownership of property belonging to members of a partnership. Like a joint tenancy, when one partner dies, the surviving partners, rather than the estate of the decedent, own the partnership property.

Bank accounts, stocks, bonds, and automobiles are commonly owned by two or more people as joint tenants. Unless it can be shown that a bank account was opened in joint names only for convenience purposes, the account will pass to the surviving depositor when one depositor dies, and will not be part of the decedent's estate. The *Parker* case illustrates this point.

LEGAL TERMS

joint tenants (also called joint tenants with the right of survivorship)
Two or more persons holding one and the same interest, accruing by one and the same conveyance, commencing at one and the same time, and held by one and the same undivided possession.

tenants by the entirety
A husband and wife who hold title as joint tenants, modified by the common law doctrine that gives the husband the exclusive rights of possession and profits with protection against attachment and alienation by one spouse alone.

tenants in partnership
Form of co-ownership of property belonging to members of a partnership.

PARKER V. PEAVEY
403 S.E.2d 213 (Ga. 1991)

FACTS: In addition to establishing certificates of deposit in his own name, Bennie Parker established one in the amount of $86,887 jointly with his wife of one year, Sallie Parker. When he died two years later, his first wife, to whom he had been married 49 years, and his two adult children (who were named in his will) claimed that the joint certificate of deposit was part of his estate.

LEGAL ISSUE: Does a certificate of deposit that is in the name of two people jointly belong to the estate of the first to die?

COURT DECISION: No.

REASON: Sums remaining on deposit at the death of a party of a joint account belong to the surviving party as against the estate of the decedent, unless there is clear and convincing evidence of a different intention at the time the account is created. This right of survivorship vests at the death of a party to a joint account.

Some states have statutes providing that money in a joint bank account belongs to the joint depositor only when both depositors have signed an agreement to that effect. For example, the Texas Probate Code ch. 11, § 439(a) provides:

> Sums remaining on deposit at the death of a party to a joint account belong to the surviving party or parties against the estate of the decedent if, by a written agreement signed by the party who dies, the interest of such deceased party is made to survive to the surviving party or parties. A survivorship agreement will not be inferred from the mere fact that the account is a joint account.

Sometimes the question arises as to whether the contents of a safe-deposit box held in joint names belongs to the surviving joint owner when one owner dies. Some courts hold that unless there is an express written agreement saying that the contents of the box belong to the joint owner, the contents of the box belong to the estate of the decedent. The *Kulbeth* case provides an example of such an agreement.

KULBETH V. PURDOM
805 S.W.2d 622 (Ark. 1991)

FACTS: Ivan C. Wright leased a safe-deposit box jointly with Pearl Purdom. When Wright died, the box was opened and found to contain $266,150 in cash. The special administrator of Wright's estate claimed the money as an asset of the estate, pointing out that Wright's will bequeathed $100,000 to Purdom. Wright and Purdom had signed the following joint-tenancy agreement when they initially obtained the safe-deposit box: "In addition to agreeing to the foregoing provisions of safe deposit box lease which are hereby made a part of this paragraph, the undersigned agree that each, or either of them is joint owner of the present and future contents of said box and said Bank is hereby authorized to permit access to said box by either of the undersigned and that in the event of the death of either of the undersigned the survivor shall have the right to withdraw said contents and upon said withdrawal said Bank shall be automatically relieved of any further obligation or responsibility to the heirs, legatees, devisees or legal representatives of the deceased."

LEGAL ISSUE: Do the contents of a jointly owned safe-deposit box pass to the co-owner's estate when a co-owner dies when an agreement has been signed by the co-owners that either may withdraw the box's contents?

COURT DECISION: No.

REASON: The clause clearly and unequivocally denotes a joint tenancy agreement with right of survivorship between the lessees, as it contains specific references to the joint ownership of the contents of the box and the right of withdrawal of the contents after the death of either party. The money in the safe-deposit box is not an asset of Wright's estate; it belongs to the co-owner, Purdom.

Frequently, husbands and wives put all of their property in joint names except an automobile, and the estate of the first spouse to die must be probated for the sole purpose of clearing the title to the automobile. Massachusetts has addressed the issue by enacting Gen. Laws ch. 90D, § 15A., which treats a solely owned automobile as joint property of the husband and wife, avoiding the need for probate:

> Upon the death of a married resident of a motor vehicle registered as a pleasure vehicle in the Commonwealth, and unless otherwise provided in a will, said motor vehicle, if used for such purposes shall be deemed to have been jointly held property with right of survivorship and the interest of said decedent shall pass to the surviving spouse . . . .

A STINGY PRESIDENT?

What is striking about the will of President Lyndon B. Johnson is his apparent lack of concern for his wife. After generously providing for his children and siblings, he designates only minor items—kitchen furniture, musical instruments, books, and jewelry—for his wife. The explanation is that the will was written in the "community state" of Texas: by law a wife is recognized as 50-percent owner of a couple's entire community property. Therefore, Johnson could not will his wife what was legally hers: in this case, half of his more than $10-million estate.

Lyndon Baines Johnson (1908-1973), 36th President of the United States. Courtesy LBJ Museum, Austin, Texas.

Community Property

A form of ownership by spouses, called community property, is used in nine states in the United States (see figure 2-3). **Community property** is property (except a gift or inheritance) that is acquired by the personal efforts of either spouse during marriage and which, by law, belongs to both spouses equally. In community property states, a spouse can leave his or her half of the community property by will to whomever he or she chooses.

Provision in Will for Community Property
[20 AM. JUR. *Legal Forms* 2d 266:413]

I confirm to my husband his one-half share of our community property. All the remainder of my one-half share of our community property not specifically disposed of above I give, devise, and bequeath to my son, Joseph.

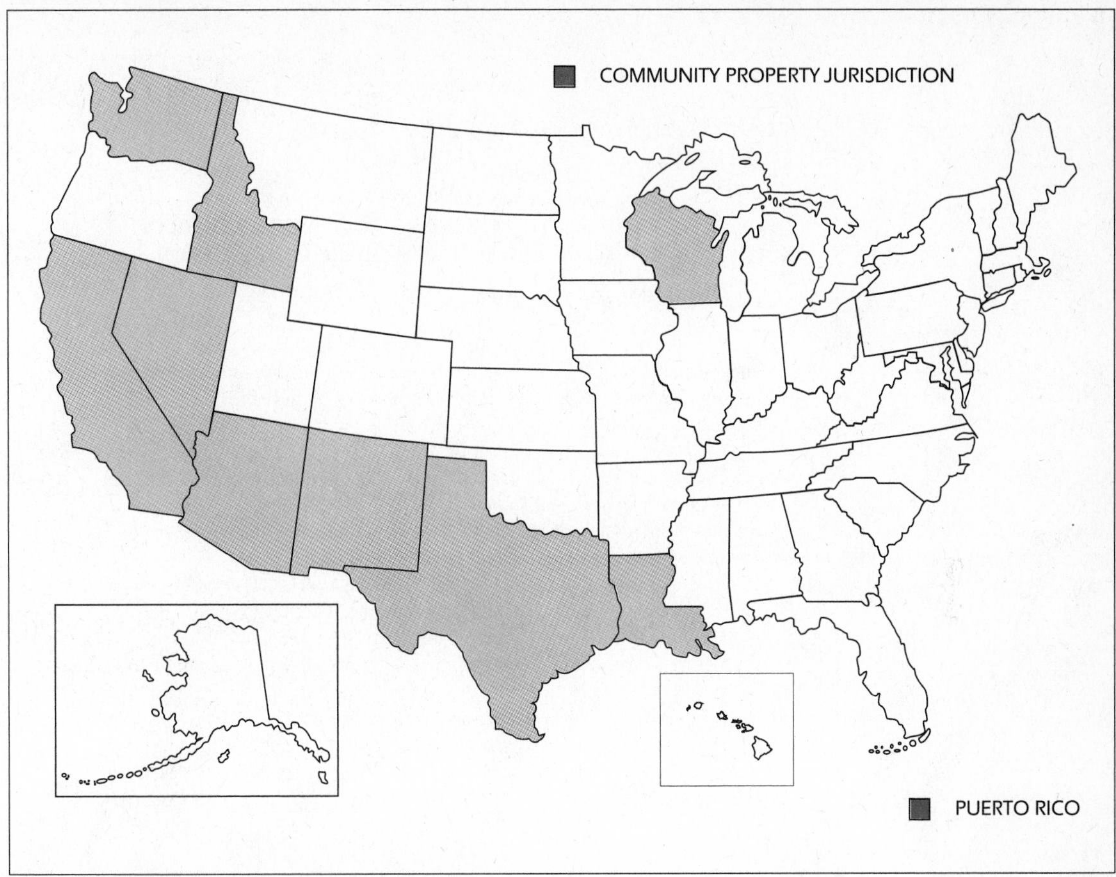

FIGURE 2-3

Community property jurisdictions

In some community property states, when a spouse dies intestate, all of the community property passes to the surviving spouse. (See figure 2-4.) In such a situation, the surviving spouse retains his or her half-interest and inherits the deceased spouse's half-interest, obtaining full title to the entire property.

The following are not considered to be community property: (1) property owned by either spouse before marriage; (2) property either spouse received as a gift or inherited during marriage; and (3) income, such as rents or interest, earned from the separate property of either spouse. If they wish to do so, spouses can agree to treat separately owned property as community property or vice versa.

LEGAL TERMS

community property
Property (except a gift or inheritance) that is acquired by the personal efforts of either spouse during marriage and which, by law, belongs to both spouses equally. Community property is recognized in Arizona, California, Idaho, Louisiana, Nevada, New Mexico, Texas, Washington, and Wisconsin.

RECORDING REQUESTED BY:

AND WHEN RECORDED MAIL TO:

____

AFFIDAVIT OF SURVIVING SPOUSE
SUCCEEDING TO TITLE TO COMMUNITY PROPERTY
(CALIFORNIA PROBATE CODE SECTION 13500)

I, the undersigned, declare that:

1. The real property described below is the community property of the undersigned and __________________, having been acquired during the period of our marriage while residing in California, and not having been acquired by gift or inheritance;

2.____________________ died on __________, 19___, as evidenced by the attached certified copy of the decedent's death certificate;

3. I am the surviving spouse of __________________, and title to the real property described below devolved to me under the provisions of Section 13500 of the California Probate Code;

4. I have not filed in any court of competent jurisdiction an election under Section 13502 of the California Probate Code to subject the real property described below to administration;

5.____________________is the person named in that certain deed, dated ___________, 19___, executed by ______________________ to ________________, recorded as Instrument No. ______, on ________, 19___, in Book No. _______, Page No. ______, of Official Records of ________________ County, California, covering the property described below, which is situated in the City of __________________, County of __________________, State of California:

I certify (or declare) under penalty of perjury under the laws of the State of California that the foregoing is true and correct.
Dated: ______________________, 19___

____

STATE OF CALIFORNIA)
) ss.
COUNTY OF __________)

On __________, 19___, before me, a notary public for the State of California, personally appeared __________________, personally known to me (or proved to me on the basis of satisfactory evidence) to be the person whose name is subscribed to this instrument, and acknowledged that (he/she) executed the same.

WITNESS my hand and official seal.

____

Notary Public

FIGURE 2-4

Affidavit of surviving spouse (community property jurisdiction)

This affidavit is filed at the county recorder's office to establish title to community property following a spouse's death.

Life Insurance with Named Beneficiary

A life insurance policy with a named, living beneficiary is not part of the probate estate of the decedent. The proceeds of the policy are paid directly to the beneficiary, bypassing probate altogether. Like jointly owned property, however, life insurance owned by a decedent is part of the decedent's gross estate for estate tax purposes, and must be included on the estate tax return.

In contrast, when decedents name their estate as their beneficiary on life insurance policies, or when the named beneficiary predeceases the insured, the proceeds of the life insurance policy are part of the probate estate and must be listed on the probate inventory.

Pay-on-Death Accounts

A **pay-on-death (POD) account**, also known as a **Totten trust** (see chapter 7) is a savings account in the name of the depositor as trustee for another person called a **beneficiary**. The depositor may withdraw money from the account at any time during the depositor's lifetime. When the depositor dies, however, the money in the account belongs to the beneficiary. If the beneficiary dies before the depositor, the trust terminates and the money belongs to the depositor. Totten trust accounts are not part of the depositor's estate. Instead, they pass directly to the beneficiary, not to the estate of the depositor, unless there was a revocation of the trust by the depositor prior to the depositor's death.

Living Trusts

A **living trust,** also known as an **inter vivos trust**, is a trust that becomes effective during the lifetime of the person who establishes it. A living trust is not under the control and supervision of the probate court, and property held by such a trust is not part of a decedent's probate estate.

Many people advocate the use of living trusts to avoid probate; however, estate taxes are not avoided by the use of a living trust unless the trust is irrevocable. Moreover, although probate may be avoided by using a living trust, in small estates the costs necessary to establish and administer the trust may be more than those required to probate the estate. Trusts are discussed in more detail in chapters 6 and 7.

Life Estates

A **life estate** is an ownership interest that is limited in duration to either the life of the owner or the life of another person. When the life tenant dies, the property belongs to whoever owns the remainder interest, without the necessity of probate. Life estates have become popular in recent years as a device to save capital gain taxes. This is because the donee of a

LEGAL TERMS

pay-on-death (POD) account (also called a Totten trust)
A savings account in the name of the depositor as trustee for another person.

Totten trust (also called a pay-on-death (POD) account)
Savings account in the name of the depositor as trustee for another person.

beneficiary
Person who receives a gift under a will; person holding equitable or beneficial title of a trust (also called *cestui que trust*).

living trust (also called inter vivos trust)
Trust that becomes effective during the settlor's lifetime.

inter vivos trust (also called living trust)
Trust that becomes effective during the settlor's lifetime.

life estate
Ownership interest that is limited in duration to either the life of the owner or the life of another person.

gift of real property must use the donor's basis (cost plus improvements) when the property is sold, often resulting in a large capital gain. However, if the donor retains a life estate in the property, the donee's basis is the value of the property at the time of the donor's death, usually resulting in a much smaller capital gain. The life tenant's estate, however, will be subject to the federal estate tax if the estate reaches the amount of $600,000 including the life estate property. Estate taxes are discussed in more detail in chapter 13.

SUMMARY

2.1 In its legal sense, property is the foundation of wills and consists of a bundle of rights—the various rights or interests that people have in the item.

2.2 Probate property is real and personal property that was owned either solely by the decedent or with others as a tenant in common. Tangible personal property is property that has substance and can be touched. Intangible personal property is not susceptible to the senses and cannot be touched.

2.3 Non-probate property includes jointly owned property, community property, life insurance with named beneficiaries, money in Totten trust accounts, property that is held in a living trust, pension plan distributions, and individual retirement accounts with named beneficiaries.

QUESTIONS FOR REVIEW

1. Why is it essential for paralegals working in the field of wills, estates, and trusts to have a fundamental understanding of the meaning of property, the various kinds of property, and how it relates to this specialized area of law?
2. In the eyes of the law, what is property considered to be? Why is this so?
3. Name some rights that different persons have to a house and the land that goes with it.
4. When property is leased to a tenant, who has the sole right to bring a trespass action? Against whom may the action be brought?
5. Traditionally, what could not be the subject of ownership and were not considered property? How has this changed?
6. When does title to real property owned by a decedent vest in the decedent's heirs?
7. To whom does title to personal property owned by a decedent pass?
8. What real property owned by a decedent is included among the probate assets?
9. What is the difference between tangible and intangible personal property?
10. What are five kinds of property that are not part of the probate estate?

CASES TO DISCUSS

1. In the course of settling an estate, the probate court ordered that costs of administration be paid out of assets, which included a Totten trust account. Is a Totten trust account an asset of the depositor's estate from which costs of administration may be paid? Explain. *Nahar v. Nahar,* 576 So. 2d 862 (Fla. 1991).
2. Laura Mitchell's will left all of her property to her illegitimate son. When she died, however, Mitchell's attorney did not think the will was valid in form and decided not to present the will to the court. Instead, the attorney began an intestate succession proceeding. Was the attorney correct in making that decision? Explain. *Succession of Mitchell,* 574 So. 2d 500 (La. 1991).
3. Howard and Mary Sander, who were married to each other, purchased land in Montana as joint tenants. They were later divorced but did nothing about the Montana property. Ten years later, when Howard died, his then wife, Jean, claimed the Montana land as an asset of Howard's estate. Mary claimed that it belonged to her after Howard died. How would you decide? Why? *Matter of Estate of Sander,* 806 P.2d 545 (Mont. 1991).

SHARPENING YOUR PROFESSIONAL SKILLS

1. Refer to the law office scenario at the beginning of this chapter and answer the following questions:
   a. Who will have access to the safe-deposit box?
   b. Who will be the beneficiary of the life insurance policy?
   c. Are the house, the bank books, and the stock certificates part of the decedent's estate?
   d. Why did Maude counsel Ms. Ryan against tearing up the will?
2. Obtain a copy of the deed to your house or that of your parent, relative, or friend. Attach to it a statement as to how the property is owned (either severally, or as tenants in common, joint tenants, or tenants by the entirety). Then state who will own the property if the sole owner or one of the co-owners dies.
3. Under the law of your state, does the dissolution of a marriage change the couple's ownership of real property as joint tenants into ownership as tenants in common? When you find the answer, write down the reference to the statute or the citation to the case in which it is found.

4. Assume that a client has placed a solar energy water heater on the roof of her house and that her next-door neighbor is about to build an additional story onto his house that will block the client's sunlight. Look up your state statute, if there is one, on a property owner's right to sunlight. Photocopy the statute and give the statutory reference where it can be found.

CHAPTER 3
Intestate Succession

"The body is the chief witness in every murder."

G. K. Chesterton

OUTLINE

LAW OFFICE SCENARIO

Diane Sherman, a paralegal intern, had been given the task of closing the office and was just about to leave for the day when an obviously upset woman appeared in the waiting room looking for Attorney McKay.

"Mr. McKay has left for the day," Diane told her politely. "May I make an appointment for you to see him?"

"Yes," the woman responded excitedly. "Make it as soon as possible, please. I buried my husband, Will, today and everything we owned was in his name—the checkbook, our bankbooks, the car, even the house."

"Oh, I'm sorry," Diane replied, reaching for a note pad. "What is your name?"

"Gertrude Nullius. You probably read about my husband in the paper. He was murdered by his own son."

"Oh, my heavens. What a tragedy!"

"I still can't believe it! He wasn't my son, thank God. He told me he was going to use the inheritance from his father to hire a good defense lawyer. Can you imagine that? How much do you think he'll inherit?"

"Did your husband have a will?" Diane asked.

"No. He kept putting it off. He was always going to have one made but never got around to it."

"How many children did you have?"

"My husband and I were both married before. I had a daughter by my first husband, and Will had a son—that no-good murderer—by his first wife. We were very happy until this happened. My husband loved my daughter. He treated her just like one of his own. He often said that when he died, he wanted her to share in his estate along with his own children."

"Did your husband have other children?"

"Will and I, we, uh, also had a son of our own who was born a year before we were married. We never told anyone that Will was the real father, you know, because I was still married to my first husband. But Will and I knew the child was ours. In fact, I named him Phil because it rhymes with his father's name, Will. Phil turned out to be a wonderful boy. He can sure use his father's inheritance, too."

"Let me look at Mr. McKay's calendar, Mrs. Nullius. Maybe we can squeeze you in for an appointment early tomorrow morning."

3.1 INTESTACY

Paralegals usually learn early in their careers that people often delay making wills. Reasons for postponing the preparation of a will are numerous. Some people may want to avoid the expense of consulting a lawyer. Others may dread any discussion of death or may assume that their assets are not worth enough to require a will. Still others may be well intentioned, but too busy or too preoccupied with the responsibilities of daily life.

As discussed in chapter 1, an individual is entitled to make a will at age 18; however, at so young an age, few are motivated to do so. Not until assets increase, or families are formed, or loved ones die, does the need to prepare a will become more apparent to the average person.

When people die without a will, it is said that they die **intestate**. The law of the state where the decedent is domiciled determines how his or her personal property will pass. In contrast, the law of the state where the property is located will determine how real property will pass. Thus, because state laws differ, it is possible for an intestate's real property that is located within the state to pass differently from real property that is located outside the state.

In the past, the rules determining the passing of intestate property were known as the law of *descent and distribution.* Technically, **descent** refers to the passage of real property, and **distribution** refers to the passage of personal property. Although the words "descent and distribution" are still in use today, the more commonly used terminology to describe how intestate property passes is the law of **intestate succession** or **intestacy**. Paralegals who work in the probate field will use these terms frequently.

3.2 THE PASSING OF INTESTATE PROPERTY

It is important for paralegals to know how intestate property passes. This knowledge will be useful when assisting the law firm in settling testate estates as well as intestate estates. This is because in all estates, whether testate or intestate, the **heirs** (those who would have inherited under the law of intestate succession) must be listed on the court petition for probate of a will or administration of an estate. In addition, the heirs must be notified of the court procedure and given an opportunity to appear if they wish to do so. This is explained further in chapter 12.

Probate property, as discussed in the previous chapter, passes according to the law of intestate succession when the owner dies without a will. In contrast, non-probate property passes directly to the joint owner or owners and does not pass according to the law of intestate succession.

Even when someone dies with a will, some property may not be included under the terms of the will. That property passes as intestate property according to the state law of intestate succession. This occurs, for example, when a will is drawn without a residuary clause, which distributes all of the testator's property that is not disposed of in other clauses of the will. The *Jackson* case involves a will that did not include such a clause.

LEGAL TERMS

intestate
To die without a will. Also, a person who dies without a will.

descent
Passage of real property by inheritance from an intestate.

distribution
Passage of personal property by inheritance from an intestate.

intestate succession
The process of an heir's becoming beneficially entitled to the property of one who dies without a will.

intestacy
The state of dying without having made a valid will.

heirs
Those persons, including the surviving spouse, who are entitled under the statutes of intestate succession to the property of a decedent. In its broadest sense, persons who inherit property from a decedent's estate.

IN RE ESTATE OF JACKSON
793 S.W.2d 259 (Tenn. 1990)

FACTS: Dorothea Jackson's will established a system for relatives to select desired items of tangible personal property and stated that relatives were to receive nothing more. The will also read: "In the event there is any of said personal property remaining, my Executor is directed to sell the remaining property at public or private sale, as deemed most appropriate by my Executor, and the proceeds therefrom shall be paid to the Eastminster Presbyterian Church, hereinabove referred to." The will contained no residuary clause. A $102,000 certificate of deposit, not specifically bequeathed, was included among the assets of the estate.

LEGAL ISSUE: How will property not specifically bequeathed pass when a will has no residuary clause?

COURT DECISION: According to the law of intestate succession.

REASON: When a will contains no residuary clause, the will makes no disposition of the personal property of the estate other than that which is specifically bequeathed. When there is no residuary clause, property not specifically bequeathed in the will passes as if the deceased had died intestate. A testator can disinherit heirs only by giving his or her property to others; instructions to exclude the heirs will not be enough to disinherit them unless others are named as the recipients of the property.

Property may also pass by intestacy when the persons named in the residuary clause of a will die before the testator. The residuary clause is explained more fully in chapter 5. Similarly, as will be discussed in chapter 9, children who are omitted unintentionally from their parent's will may be able to take the share they would have received had their parent or grandparent died intestate. The *Dorn* case involves a granddaughter omitted from her grandmother's will.

MATTER OF ESTATE OF DORN
787 P.2d 1291 (Okla. 1989)

FACTS: Laura Mae Dorn's will stated: "I am a widow and my family consists of my son, Richard D. Dorn, presently residing at Oklahoma City, Oklahoma." The will further provided: "I give and bequeath all of my estate, real property, personal or mixed property of whatever character and wheresoever situated of which I die seized or possessed, or which I may own to Richard D. Dorn, my son, to be his forever." The will made no mention of Laura's two deceased children, Kenneth and Jacqueline, nor did it mention her granddaughter, Lynn Mark, the daughter of Jacqueline, who was alive.

LEGAL ISSUE: May the daughter of a testator's deceased child, who is not named in the will, take the share she would have taken had the testator died intestate?

COURT DECISION: Yes.

REASON: Under the Oklahoma statute: "When any testator omits to provide in his will for any of his children, or for the issue of any deceased child unless it appears that such omission was intentional, such child, or the issue of such child, must have the same share in the estate of the testator, as if he had died intestate, and succeeds thereto as provided in the preceding section." Okla. Stat. tit. 84, § 132 (1981). Thus, as the pretermitted heir of the testator, Lynn Mark was entitled to the same share in the estate of the testatrix as if she had died intestate—that is, one-half of the estate.

Property can also pass by intestacy when someone named to receive a gift in a will refuses to accept it. This may seem strange, but death taxes can sometimes be reduced when property passes to a family member other than the one who is named in the will to receive it. The gift is renounced or disclaimed and passes by intestacy to other family members in a way that results in a tax savings to the family as a whole. Such tax-saving maneuvers and other techniques are discussed in chapter 8 under the subject of postmortem (after death) planning, and illustrate how the laws of intestate succession can be used as an estate planning tool.

Simultaneous Death

Sometimes a husband and wife, a parent and child, or other relatives die in a common disaster, and it is impossible to determine who died first. The Uniform Simultaneous Death Act, which has been adopted by almost every state (see table 10-1 in chapter 10), allows the property of each person to be distributed as if he or she had survived, unless a will or trust provides otherwise. For example, if a husband and wife die together in a car accident and each owns separate property, (1) the husband's property will pass to his heirs as though his wife were not living at the time of his death, and (2) the wife's property will pass to her heirs as though her husband were not living at the time of her death.

In the case of property owned jointly by both decedents, the property is distributed equally. Thus, in the preceding example, half of the jointly owned property of the husband and wife will pass to the husband's heirs as though his wife were not living at the time of his death, and the other half will pass to the wife's heirs as though her husband were not living at the time of her death.

When the beneficiary of an insurance policy dies simultaneously with the insured, the proceeds of the policy are payable as if the insured had survived the beneficiary. Thus, if a parent names a child as the beneficiary of a life insurance policy, and the parent and child die together in an accident, the child will be regarded as deceased at the time of the parent's death. The proceeds of the policy will go to the parent's heirs unless an alternate beneficiary is named in the policy. The Uniform Simultaneous Death Act is discussed in more detail in chapter 10.

In states that have adopted the Uniform Probate Code (see figure 3-1), a specific time period must pass to establish that someone has "survived" an intestate. If someone does not survive the intestate by 120 hours (5 days), he or she is considered to have died *before* the intestate. UPC § 2-104

Homicide by Heir or Devisee

A murderer inheriting from his or her victim is a repulsive thought. To ensure that people do not benefit from their own wrongdoings, state laws provide that one who is convicted of murdering another cannot inherit from the victim's estate. In the opening law office scenario, Gertrude's stepson would not be able to inherit from his father.

Some states, including those which have adopted Uniform Probate Code § 2-803, have passed laws, called **slayer statutes**, to this effect. Other states reach the same conclusion through court decisions. Some courts use a **constructive trust** theory to prevent killers from inheriting from their victims. Under this theory, an heir who murders an intestate takes the inheritance as trustee for the benefit of the persons who would have been heirs if the murderer had died before the victim.

3.3 RIGHTS OF SURVIVING SPOUSE

The amount that a surviving spouse inherits from a spouse who dies without a will differs widely from state to state. Some states give only dower or curtesy rights; others merely allow a life estate in real and personal property; still others give property to the surviving spouse and children during widowhood and afterward to children. Some states give the

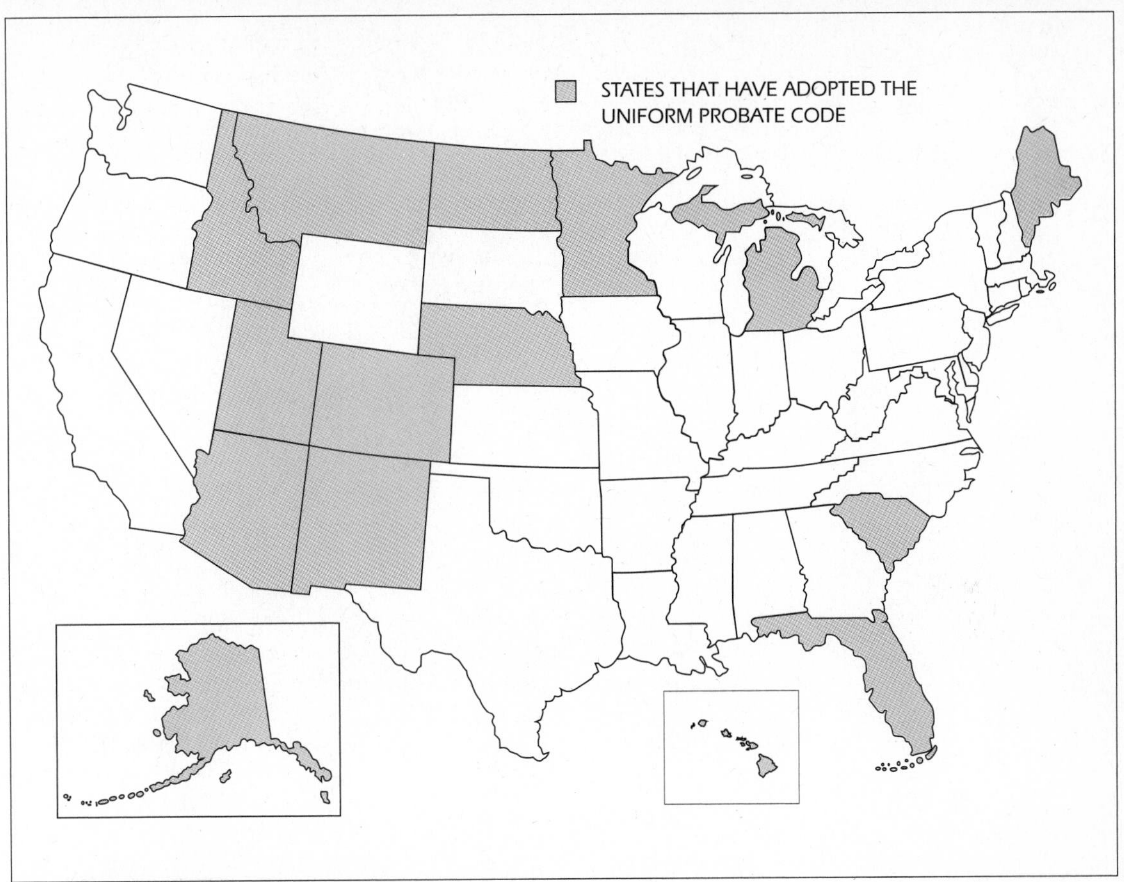

The Uniform Probate Code (UPC), which has been adopted by the states shown on this map, was drafted by the National Conference of Commissioners on Uniform State Laws in 1969 with the aim of modernizing and standardizing the laws relating to the affairs of decedents. The original version has undergone several amendments, and many states adopting it have made their own changes as well. Article II of the UPC (see appendix D) underwent a major change in 1990. The UPC is often referred to in the text and is discussed in more detail in chapter 10.

FIGURE 3-1
States that have adopted the Uniform Probate Code

surviving spouse an absolute interest in the property up to a specified amount; other states deduct an amount from the surviving spouse's share, depending upon the extent of his or her separately owned assets.

The portion of the estate given to a surviving spouse depends upon who else is alive; that is, if parents, children, grandchildren, or other descendants of the deceased are still living. States adjust the amount given to the surviving spouse according to the existence or absence of parents, children, grandchildren, and descendants of the deceased spouse. Table 3-1 demonstrates the varied approaches to what is considered an appropriate share for the surviving spouse when other relatives are taken into account.

LEGAL TERMS

slayer statutes
State laws providing that one who is convicted of murdering another cannot inherit from the victim's estate.

constructive trust
Trust created by operation of law when someone obtains legal title to property through fraud or other wrongdoing.

This general summary of state laws illustrates the wide differences among the states in the laws of intestacy. The summary does not include all variations in every state. Because of the tendency of these laws to change, up-to-date statutes must be checked when looking up a state's intestacy law.

If the Deceased is Survived by	A Surviving Spouse Receives	In These States
Children of the marriage	All*	AZ, IA, MT, VA, WI
	\$100,000 + ½*	CT
	\$ 70,000 + ½*	MN
	\$ 60,000 + ½*	MI
	\$ 50,000 + ½*	AL, AK, ID, ME, NE, NH, NJ, ND, NY, UT
	\$ 30,000 + ½	OH**, PA*
	\$ 25,000 + ½*	CO
	\$ 20,000 + ½*	FL, MO
	\$ 15,000 + ½	MD, NC**
	\$ 5,000 + ½	DE+
	½	CA**, HI, IL, IN**, KS, KY+, MA, NV**, OK, OR, RI+, SC, SD**, VT#**, WA, WY
	⅓	AR+, TX, VT+, WV
	¼	NM
	Life estate + ⅓	AR#, KY#
	Life estate	DE#, IN#, RI#
	Equal with children	GA, MS
	Homestead + 1 yr. allow.	TN
No children but by parents	All	AZ, AR++, CO, FL, GA, IL, IA, KS, MN, MS, MT, NM, NY, OH, OK, OR, SC, TN, VA, WI, WV, WY
	\$200,000 + ½	MA
	\$100,000 + ¾	CT
	\$100,000 + ½	AL, SD, UT
	\$ 60,000 + ½	MI
	\$ 50,000 + ½	DE+, ID, ME, NE, NH, NJ, ND, RI+
	\$ 30,000 + ½	PA

TABLE 3-1
Rights of a Surviving Spouse of One Who Dies Intestate

	$ 25,000 + ½	NC, VT
	$ 20,000 + ½	MO
	$ 15,000 + ½	MD
	$ 5,000 + ½	AK
	¾	IN, WA
	½	CA, HI, KY, NV, TX
	Life estate + $75,000	RI#
	Life estate	DE#
No children and no parents but by brothers or sisters	All	AL, AK, AZ, AR++, CO, CT, DE+, FL, GA, HI, ID, IL, IN, IA, KS, MD, MI, MN, MS, MO, MT, NE, NC, ND, NM, NH, NJ, NY, OH, OK, OR, PA, SC, TN, UT, VA, WI, WV, WY
	$200,000 + ½	MA
	$100,000 + ½	SD
	$ 50,000 + ½	ME, RI+
	$ 25,000 + ½	VT
	¾	WA
	½	CA, KY, NV, TX
	Life estate + $75,000	RI#
	Life estate	DE#
No children, parents, brothers, or sisters	All	In many states

**The surviving spouse receives half when the deceased is survived by children who are not of the marriage, except in Virginia, where the surviving spouse receives one-third.*
***One-third when the deceased is survived by two or more children.*
+Personal property.
++If married three years.

TABLE 3-1
(Continued)

Because a divorce ends a marriage, a divorce also terminates the right of a former spouse to inherit under the laws of intestate succession. (*See* UPC § 2-802.) This rule does not generally apply when a divorce is held to be void or when the parties to a divorce remarry. Because a decree of separation (sometimes called a divorce from bed and board) does not terminate a marriage, the right of either spouse to inherit from the other spouse is not affected.

LEGAL TERMS

next of kin
Persons who are nearest of kindred to the decedent; that is, those most nearly related by blood.

consanguinity
Kinship; blood relationship.

lineal consanguinity
Relationship between people who are related in a direct line, either downward, as between child, grandchild, and great-grandchild, or upward, as between parent, grandparent, and great-grandparent.

collateral consanguinity
Relationship between people who have the same ancestors but who do not ascend or descend from each other, such as one's brothers and sisters, aunts and uncles, nieces and nephews, and cousins.

3.4 RIGHTS OF OTHER HEIRS

The terms *heirs* and *next of kin* have different meanings. Years ago, under common law, when someone died intestate, the "heirs" were those who inherited the real property, and the "next of kin" inherited the personal property. Modern laws have largely eliminated that distinction, but the two terms are still uniquely different. In most jurisdictions today, *heirs* are defined as those persons, including the surviving spouse, who are entitled under the statutes of intestate succession to the property of a decedent (UPC § 1-201(17)). Sometimes the term *heirs* is used in an even broader sense, referring to anyone who inherits property, whether by will or by intestate succession. In contrast, **next of kin** are those persons who are nearest of kindred to the decedent; that is, those most nearly related by blood. Spouses are not related by blood and are therefore not considered next of kin.

Consanguinity and Affinity

Kindred—people related by blood—are said to be related by **consanguinity**, which means kinship or blood relationship. The relationship may be either lineal or collateral. **Lineal consanguinity** is the relationship between people who are related in a direct line either downward, as between child, grandchild, and great-grandchild, or upward, as between parent, grandparent, and great-grandparent. **Collateral consanguinity**, on the other hand, is the relationship between people who have the same ancestors but

ART OBJECTS GALORE

When he died without a will in 1973 at age 91, artist Pablo Picasso had produced an astounding number of artworks, making him one of the world's richest men. His estate included 1,885 paintings, 1,228 sculptures, 7,089 drawings, 30,000 prints, 150 sketchbooks, and 3,222 ceramic works, as well as 5 homes, cash, gold, and bonds. Settling the estate involved an intricate network of lawyers, appraisers, catalogers, government-appointed art experts, officials of several government ministries, and even the President of France. After six years of wrangling among Picasso's six heirs, the estate was finally settled—at a cost of over $30 million. The six heirs were: Jacqueline Roque Picasso, the artist's widow (30% or $70 million); Marina and Bernard (20% or $47 million each), the children of Paulo, who was the only one of Picasso's four children born in wedlock; Maya Picasso Widmaier (10% or $23.4 million); and Claude and Paloma (10% or $23.4 million each), the children of Françoise Gilot.

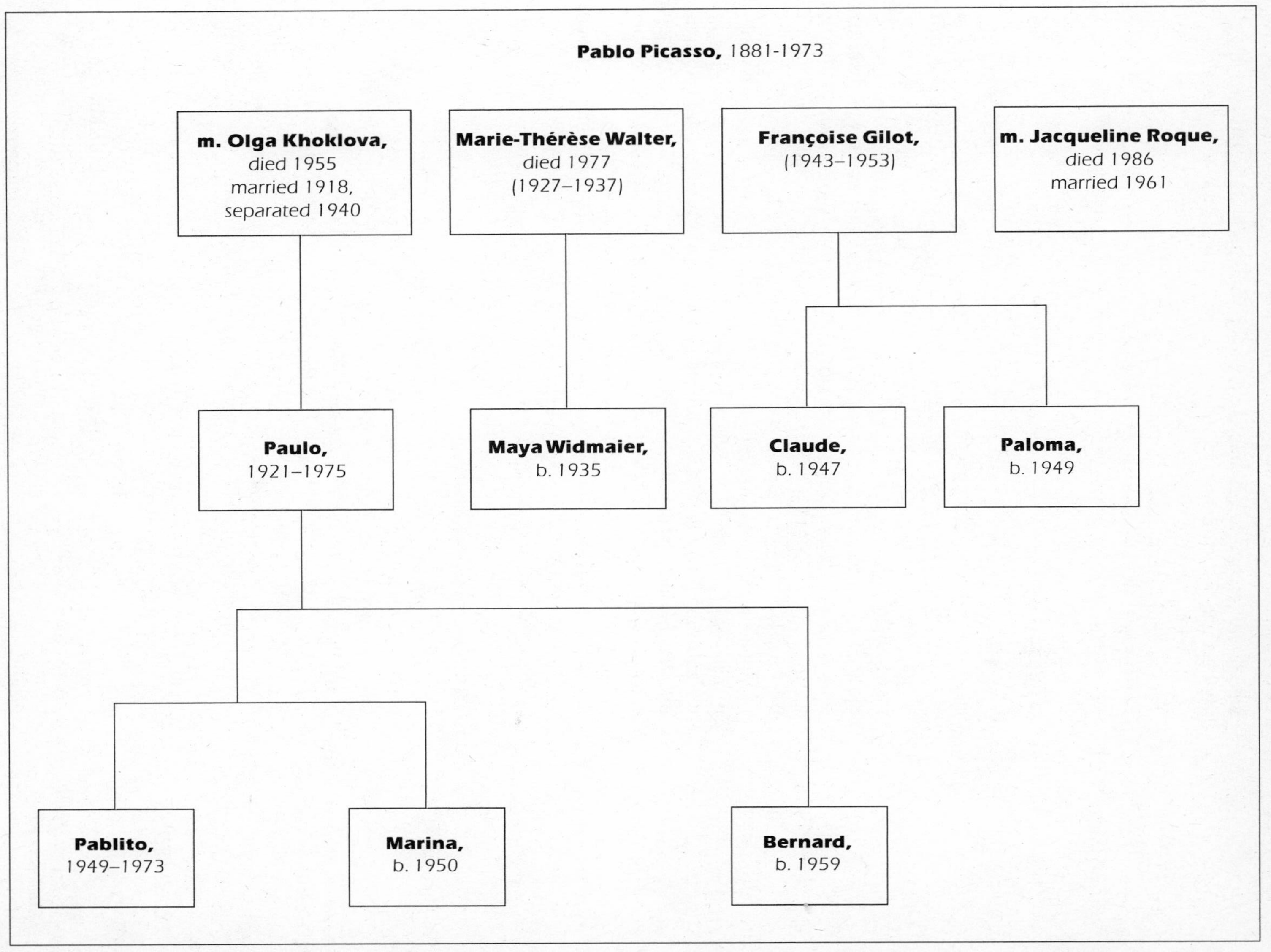

Pablo Picasso, 1881-1973
m. Olga Khoklova, died 1955 married 1918, separated 1940
Marie-Thérèse Walter, died 1977 (1927–1937)
Françoise Gilot, (1943–1953)
m. Jacqueline Roque, died 1986 married 1961
Paulo, 1921–1975
Maya Widmaier, b. 1935
Claude, b. 1947
Paloma, b. 1949
Pablito, 1949–1973
Marina, b. 1950
Bernard, b. 1959

who do not ascend or descend from each other. Collateral relatives include brothers and sisters, aunts and uncles, nieces and nephews, and cousins.

People who are related by marriage are said to be related by **affinity**. They include stepparents, stepchildren, parents-in-law, and daughters- and sons-in-law. Because they are not related by blood to a decedent, they do not inherit from the decedent under the laws of intestate succession.

Half Blood

People who are related by **half blood**, such as a half-brother or half-sister, have the same mother or father in common, but not both parents. The laws of intestate succession differ among the states as to relatives of the half blood. Many states allow half-blood kindred to take equally with whole-blood kindred. For example, the Massachusetts statute reads: "the kindred of the half blood shall inherit equally with those of the whole blood in the same degree." Mass. Gen. Laws Ann. ch. 190, § 4 (West 1990) Similarly, Uniform Probate Code § 2-107reads: "Relatives of the half blood inherit the same share they would inherit if they were of the whole blood."

Some states permit brothers and sisters of the half blood to inherit only if there are no brothers or sisters of the whole blood. Other states give to the half blood only half as much as is given to the whole blood. For example, the Florida Probate Code, Fla. Stat. Ann. § 732.105 reads: "When property descends to the collateral kindred of the intestate and part of the collateral kindred are of the whole blood to the intestate and the other part are of the halfblood, those of the halfblood shall inherit only half as much as those of the whole blood; but if all are of the halfblood they shall have whole parts."

Degrees of Kindred

Determining how closely people are related by blood can be a complex process. The method most commonly used in the United States to determine the relatives who are most nearly related by blood is the civil law method. Under this method, each relationship to the decedent is assigned a degree (see figure 3-2). The degree of kinship of a relative is calculated by counting upward from the decedent to the nearest common ancestor, then downward to the nearest relative. Each generation represents one degree. For example, parents and children of a decedent are related to the decedent in the first degree. Grandparents, grandchildren, brothers, and sisters are related to the decedent in the second degree. Uncles, aunts, nephews, nieces, and great-grandparents are third-degree relatives. First cousins, great-uncles, great-aunts, and great-great-grandparents are fourth-degree relatives.

A few states follow the common law, or canon law, method of computing degrees of kinship. Under this method, the degree of kinship is determined by counting the nearest common ancestor down to the decedent, and then by taking the longer of the two lines when they are unequal.

LEGAL TERMS

affinity
Related by marriage.

half blood
Relation between persons having only one parent in common.

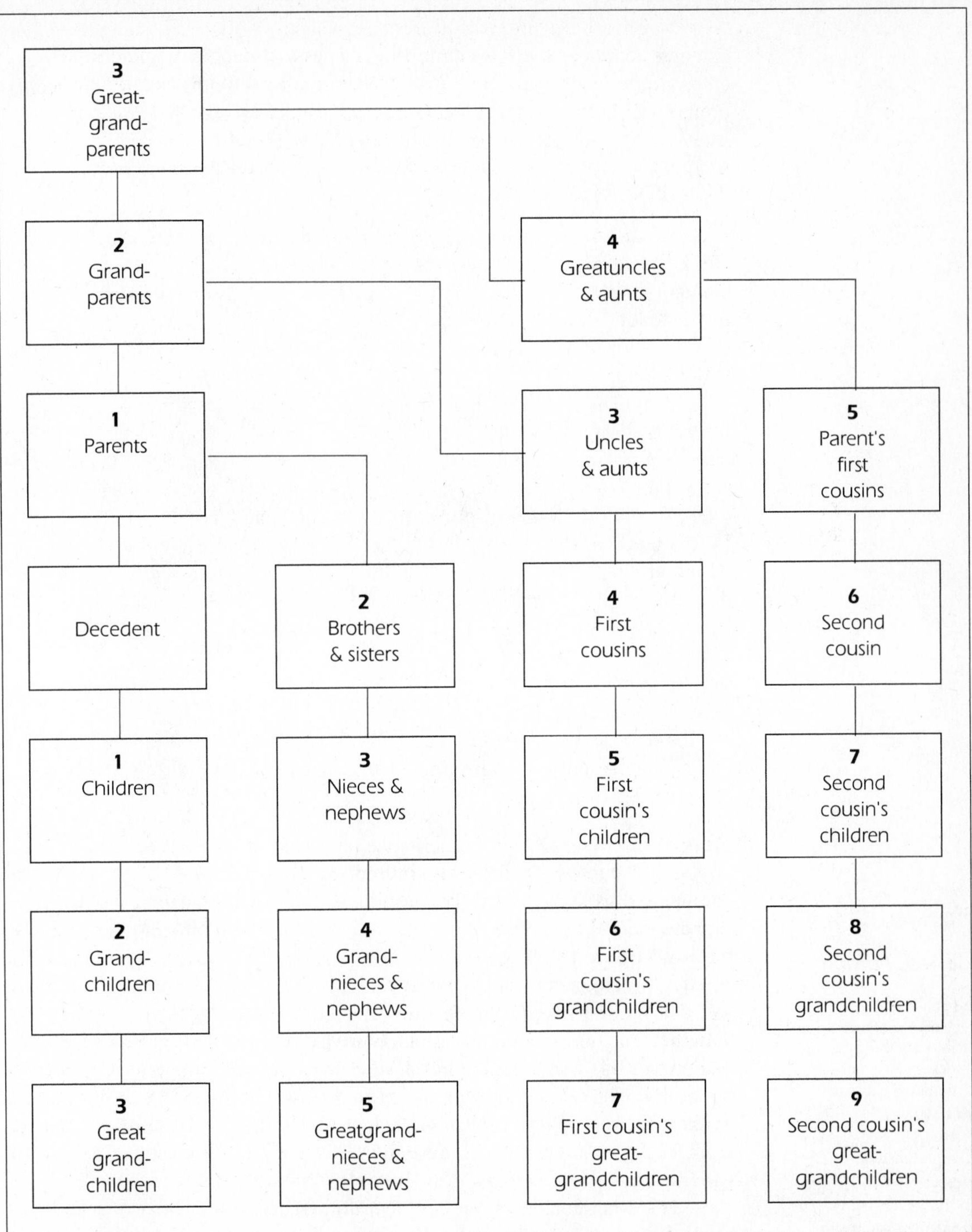

FIGURE 3-2
Degrees of kindred

Within the degrees of kindred, certain priorities are recognized. For example, the decedent's children receive preference over the decedent's parents, although they are both in the same degree. Similarly, the decedent's brothers and sisters are favored over the decedent's grandparents.

Lineal Descendants

As discussed earlier, a "lineal" relationship exists between a person's children, grandchildren, and great-grandchildren. They all descend from a common ancestor and are referred to as **issue**. When someone dies intestate, the decedent's children receive what remains after the surviving spouse receives his or her share. If no surviving spouse exists, the children share the entire estate.

Grandchildren take their parent's share **per stirpes**, that is, by right of representation, when their parents are dead; children stand in place of their deceased parents for purposes of inheritance. (See figure 3-3.) Under some state laws, when all of the intestate's children have predeceased the intestate, grandchildren inherit **per capita** (by the heads) rather than per stirpes. In this method, the number of grandchildren are counted and each receives an equal share. For example, the Massachusetts statute reads, "if all such descendants are of the same degree of kindred to the intestate, they shall share the estate equally; otherwise, they shall take according to the right of representation." Mass. Gen. L. ch. 190, § 3.

The law also provides for issue who are not yet alive at the time of the decedent's death. Lineal descendants who are conceived before, but born after, the decedent's death are called **posthumous issue** and inherit as if they had been born during the lifetime of the decedent. UPC § 2-108.

Adopted Children. For inheritance purposes, modern state statutes generally treat adopted children as kindred or blood relatives of the adopting parents and as strangers to their former blood relatives. Under the Uniform Probate Code, for the purposes of intestate succession, an adopted person is the child of an adopting parent and not of a natural parent. When a child is adopted by the spouse of a natural parent, the relationship between the child and that natural parent remains the same. UPC § 2-109. Thus, if Alice, the daughter of Janis Akerson, is adopted by Mr. and Mrs. Babson, Alice (adopted child) will inherit from Mr. and Mrs. Babson (adopting parents), not from Janis Akerson (natural mother). If instead Janis Akerson (natural mother) marries John Burns and he adopts Alice, Alice will be able to inherit from both her natural mother, Janis, and her adoptive father, John. The *Carlson* case illustrates this distinction.

The Massachusetts statute regarding the rights of an adopted child reads: "A person shall by adoption lose his right to inherit from his natural parents or kindred, except when one of the natural parents of a minor child has died and the surviving parent has remarried *subsequent to* such parent's

LEGAL TERMS

issue
Lineal descendants; all persons who have descended from a common ancestor.

per stirpes
By right of representation.

per capita
By the heads.

posthumous issue
Issue conceived before the decedent's death but born afterwards.

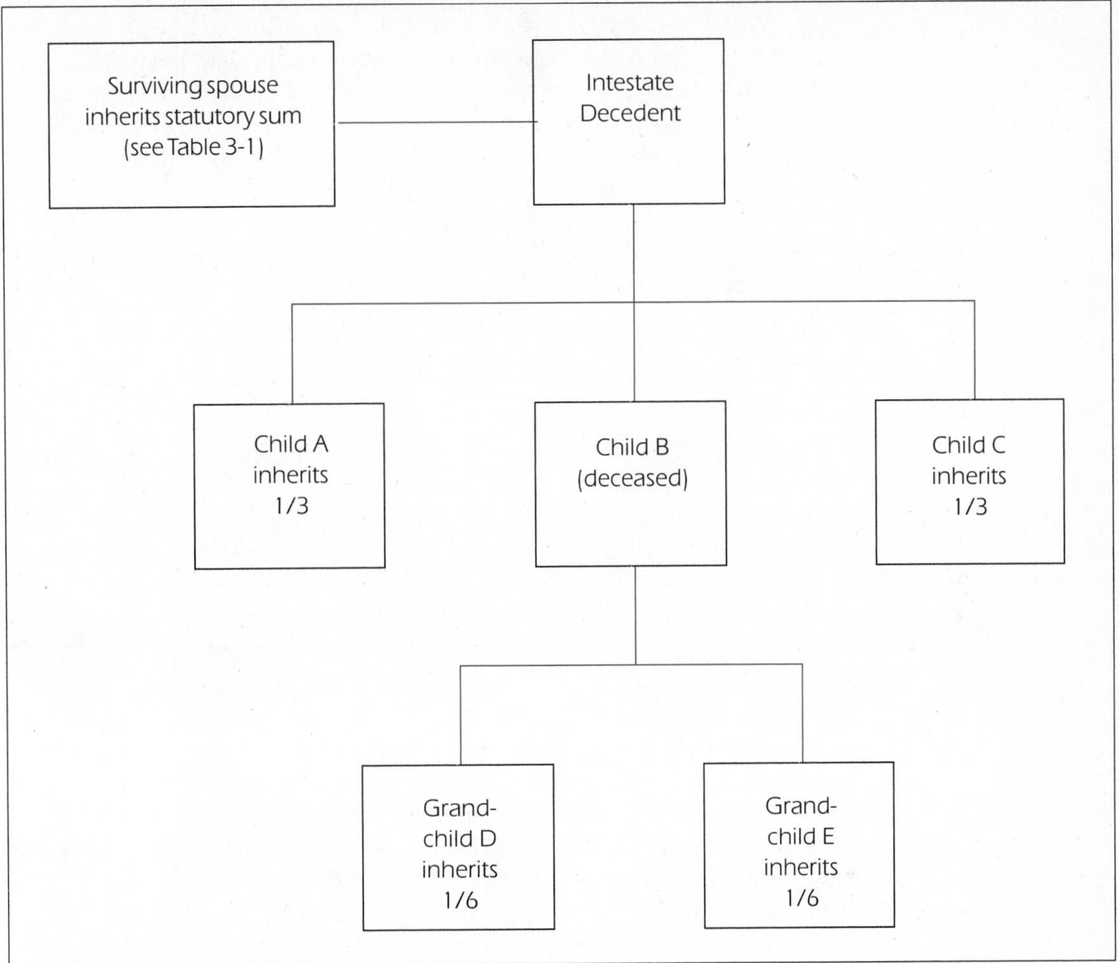

When someone dies intestate and is survived by issue, the part of the estate not passing to a surviving spouse passes to the decedent's issue by right of representation.

FIGURE 3-3
Rights of children and grandchildren of intestate decedent

IN RE ESTATE OF CARLSON
457 N.W.2d 789 (Minn. 1990)

FACTS: Russell Carlson was four years old when he and his two younger brothers were placed in an orphanage after the death of their parents in 1920. Russell went to live with the Klug family but was never adopted. Both of his brothers, however, were adopted by the families with whom they lived. Over the years, the brothers maintained contact with one another through telephone calls, letters, and visits. Russell never married and was childless when he died intestate in 1988. A first cousin once removed claims to be Russell's closest relative for inheritance purposes.

LEGAL ISSUE: Are adopted-out brothers entitled to inherit from a natural brother's estate?

COURT DECISION: No.

REASON: The statutes explicitly provide that adoption eliminates the rights of inheritance from natural relatives. The only exception is when a child is adopted by a spouse of a natural parent.

death, subsequent adoption of such child by the person with whom such remarriage is contracted shall not affect the right of such child to inherit from or through the deceased parent or kindred thereof." Mass. Gen. L. ch. 210, § 7. In the *Lockwood* case, the court held that the Massachusetts adoption statute applies only when a person dies intestate, not when a person leaves a will.

LOCKWOOD V. ADAMSON
566 N.E.2d 96 (Mass. 1991)

FACTS: William P. Wharton executed a will leaving a certain amount of money in trust to his nephew, Dr. Smith, "or his issue by right of representation if he is not living on the date of distribution." Dr. Smith was not living on the date of distribution, but he was survived by four children and one grandchild who was the son of a deceased fifth child. The fifth child divorced his wife and died shortly after his wife remarried. The grandchild was later adopted by her new husband. The exception in the adoption statute [quoted in the text] did not apply because the natural mother remarried *before* the natural father's death.

LEGAL ISSUE: Does the statute, which states that a person shall by adoption lose the right to inherit from natural parents or kindred, apply to testate cases?

COURT DECISION: No.

REASON: General Laws ch. 210, § 7 applies only to the inheritance of property through intestate succession. The word "inherit," as a legal term of art, though not necessarily in its popular sense, has been defined as referring to intestate succession by an heir and not to transfers of property by will or trust. The Massachusetts Uniform Statutory Will Act provides that "an individual adopted by the spouse of a natural parent is also the child (or issue) of either natural parent" for purposes of construing those terms in wills. Thus, the grandchild is entitled to take his natural father's share of the trust.

Illegitimate Children. The terminology and rights relating to illegitimate children have changed greatly over time. Under the English common law, children who were born out of wedlock, known as **bastards**, could not be anyone's heir or have any heirs of their own except the heirs of their own body. In those early days, a child born out of wedlock was referred to as a **filius nullius**, which means a child of nobody. Today, such children are referred to as **illegitimate children**, or **nonmarital children**.

In contrast to the English common law, most states in the United States have traditionally had statutes allowing illegitimate children to inherit from their mothers and their maternal ancestors. The rationale was that it is unjust to "visit the sins of the parents upon their unoffending offspring." The right of illegitimate children to inherit from their fathers, however, was not widely acknowledged until 1977. In that year, the United States Supreme Court held that an Illinois law allowing children born out of wedlock to inherit by intestate succession only from their mothers, and not their fathers, violated the equal protection clause of the Fourteenth Amendment to the United States Constitution. Since then, most state laws allow nonmarital children to inherit from and through their fathers who have either acknowledged paternity or have been adjudicated to be their fathers in paternity proceedings, as well as from and through their mothers.

LEGAL TERMS

bastard
A child born out of wedlock.

filius nullius
A child of nobody.

illegitimate children
Children born out of wedlock.

nonmarital children
Children born out of wedlock.

MATTER OF ESTATE OF SCHNEIDER
441 N.W.2d 335 (Wis. 1989)

FACTS: David was born to Mary Ann while she was married to Jack Seng. The birth certificate listed his name as Seng. A few years after David's birth, Mary Ann eloped with Arthur Schneider, taking David with her. David, who now goes by the last name of Schneider, is seeking to inherit Arthur Schneider's estate as a nonmarital child who has been acknowledged as Arthur's son in writings signed by Arthur.

LEGAL ISSUE: Is a husband presumed to be the natural father of his wife's child who is born or conceived during their marriage?

COURT DECISION: Yes.

REASON: This presumption is one of the strongest presumptions known to law. The evidence offered tended to show a strong emotional bond between David and Arthur, but no absence of a biological bond between David and Jack Seng. The evidence was insufficient to rebut the presumption that David is a marital child. David cannot inherit from Arthur's estate as a nonmarital child.

Under the Uniform Probate Code, a person born out of wedlock is a child of the mother, and also a child of the father if (1) the natural parents participated in a marriage ceremony before or after the birth of the child, or (2) the paternity is established by an adjudication before the death of the father or is established thereafter by clear and convincing proof. The paternity is ineffective, however, to qualify the father or his kindred to inherit from or through the child unless the father has openly treated the child as his, and has not refused to support the child. UPC § 2-109. The treatment of nonmarital children by federal statutes is summarized in table 3-2.

Lineal Ascendants

We have learned that lineal descendants "descend" from the individual and include a person's children, grandchildren, great-grandchildren, etc. In the same way, lineal ascendants "ascend" from the individual, include parents, grandparents, and so on, and have their own distinctive inheritance

A COUNTRY MUSIC LEGEND

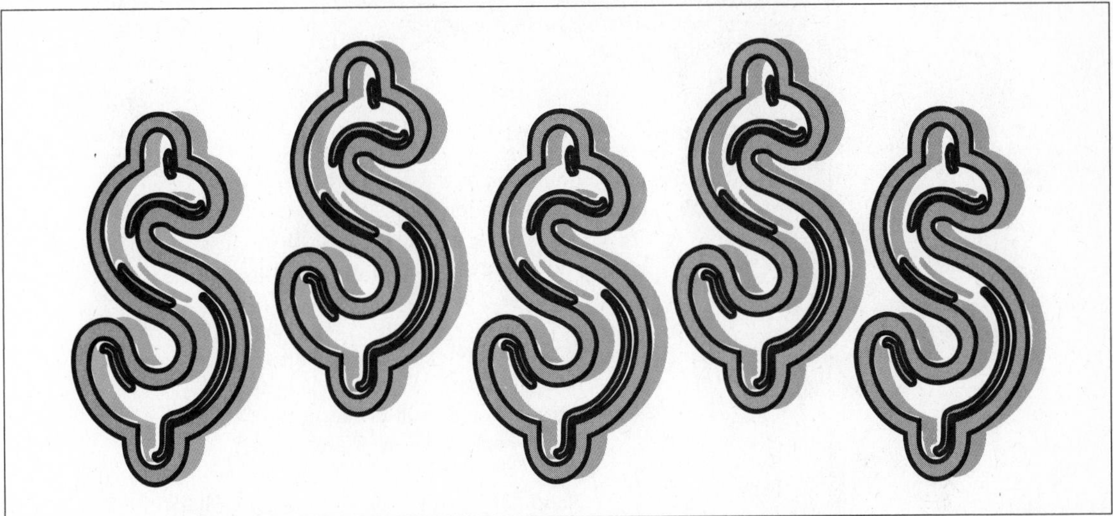

Jett Williams, the illegitimate child of country music legend Hank Williams, Sr., finally inherited a share of her father's estate in 1990, but only after a long, difficult battle to prove her identity. In 1952 Hank signed an agreement with the birth mother, Bonnie Webb Jett, that allowed Lillian Stone, Hank's mother, to assume custody of the baby for two years. Thereafter, Hank would take control. Instead, Hank died days before the child's birth. Until her death in 1955, Mrs. Stone took care of the baby, who was then put up for adoption. Only when Jett turned 21 and inherited $2,000 from Mrs. Stone did the details of her birth and early childhood surface. Hank's estate still receives over $1 million a year from song royalties; despite her illegitimacy and her father's untimely death without a will, Jett is entitled to a portion of those substantial proceeds.

rights under intestate succession. When no issue of an intestate are alive, both parents, or the surviving parent if one is deceased, inherit what remains after the surviving spouse receives his or her share (figure 3-4). Parents are entitled to inherit from their child's estate whether or not the parents supported or cared for the deceased child during the child's minority. Even a mother who abandons her infant is entitled to inherit under the laws of intestate succession, as demonstrated by the *Hotarek* case.

Acceptance of the idea that justice requires nonpunitive treatment of nonmarital children is reflected in numerous federal statutes. A representative list of such statutes was compiled in *Matter of Hoffman,* 53 A.D.2d 55, 385 N.Y.S.2d 49 (1976):

Statute	Purpose	Effective Date
33 U.S.C. § 902(14)	Longshoremen's and Harbor Workers' Compensation Act. Defines a child as including an acknowledged illegitimate child dependent upon the deceased.	1927
42 U.S.C. § 416(h)(3)(A)	Social Security. Defines a child of an insured individual as one who[m] the insured person has acknowledged in writing as his child or has been decreed by the court to be the father of such child.	1935
8 U.S.C. § 1409	Nationality and Citizenship. Children born out of wedlock. A child born out of wedlock of a service parent is also to be considered a national and citizen of the United States at birth.	1952
8 U.S.C. § 1432	A child born out of wedlock to an alien mother may become a citizen in certain circumstances when such mother is naturalized prior to the sixteenth birthday of said child.	1952
38 U.S.C. § 101(4)(C)	Veterans Benefits Act. Defines a child as including an illegitimate if the father has acknowledged the child in writing or has been judicially decreed to be the father of such child.	1958
38 U.S.C. § 765	Payment of servicemen's life insurance under group policy. Benefits may be made to certain specified persons and defines "child" in the following manner: "An illegitimate child as to the mother, or an illegitimate child as to the alleged father" if he has acknowledged said child in writing or has been judicially decreed to be the father of such child.	1971

TABLE 3-2
Federal Statutes Relating to Nonmarital Children

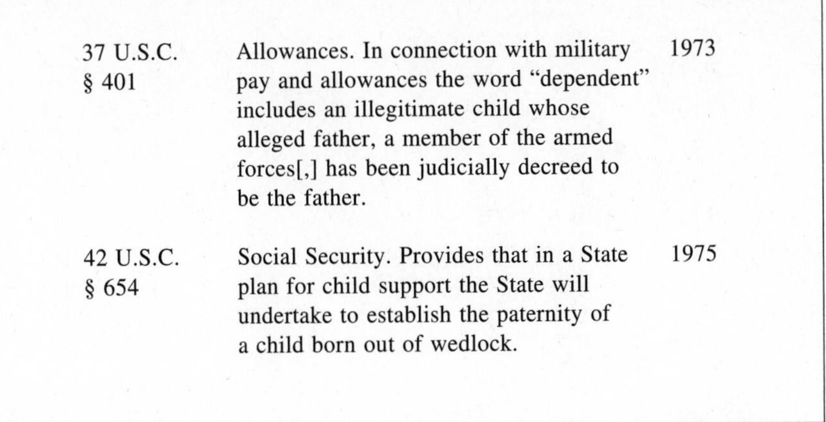

37 U.S.C. § 401	Allowances. In connection with military pay and allowances the word "dependent" includes an illegitimate child whose alleged father, a member of the armed forces[,] has been judicially decreed to be the father.	1973
42 U.S.C. § 654	Social Security. Provides that in a State plan for child support the State will undertake to establish the paternity of a child born out of wedlock.	1975

TABLE 3-2
(Continued)

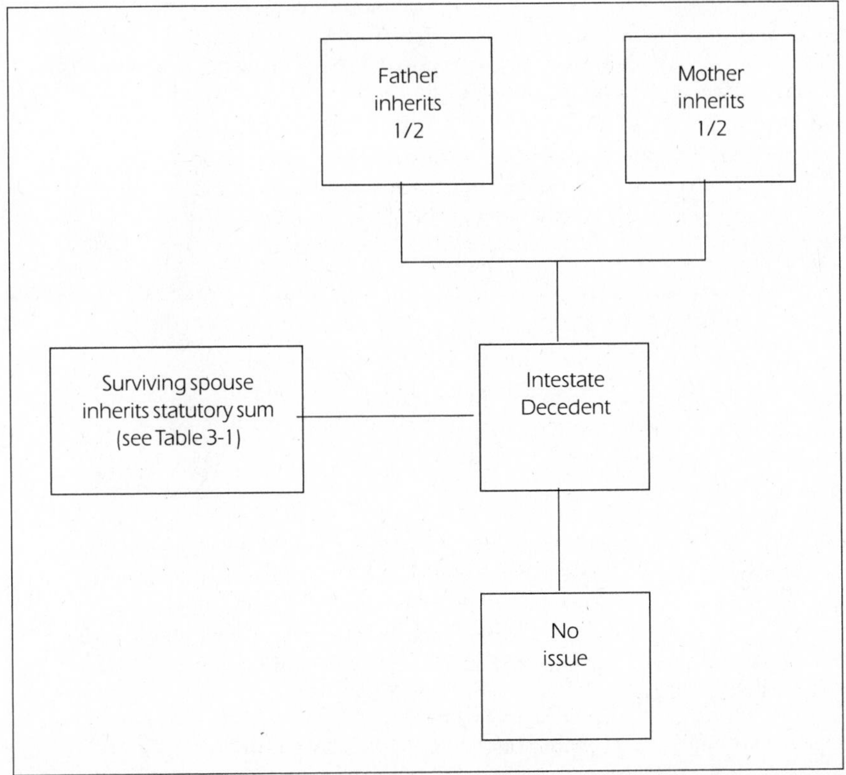

FIGURE 3-4
Rights of parents of intestate decedent

When someone dies intestate survived by no issue, the part of the estate not passing to a surviving spouse passes to the decedent's father and mother equally or to the survivor of them.

HOTAREK V. BENSON
557 A.2d 1259 (Conn. 1989)

FACTS: Paul Hotarek's parents were divorced when he was two years old. His mother abandoned him at the age of three, allegedly having no contact with him after that time. At the age of 15, Paul was killed in a motor vehicle accident. His estate received $300,000 in damages. Seventeen months after Paul was killed, his mother was located in a small town in Utah by a private investigator and told of her son's death. She claimed half of his estate.

LEGAL ISSUE: Is a parent who abandons a three-year-old child entitled to inherit from the child's estate under the laws of intestate succession?

COURT DECISION: Yes.

REASON: By statute, if a person dies intestate leaving no spouse or children, the residue of the intestate's estate shall be distributed equally to the decedent's parent or parents. In the absence of statutory provisions to the contrary, the fact that a parent has abandoned and neglected a deceased minor child does not bar the right of that parent to inherit from the child's estate under the statutes governing descent and distribution.

Some states do, however, have laws that prohibit parents from inheriting from their children if the parents have neglected to support those children. For example, the Pennsylvania statute, 31 Pa. Cons. Stat. § 2106(b), reads:

> Any parent who, for one year or upwards previous to the death of the parent's minor or dependent child, has willfully neglected or failed to perform any duty of support owed to the minor or dependent child or who, for one year, has willfully deserted the minor or dependent child shall have no right or interest . . . in the real or personal estate of the minor or dependent child.

Although many state statutes give the decedent's entire estate to the parents or surviving parent when no surviving spouse, child, or descendant of a child exists, some states divide the estate among parents and brothers and sisters.

Brothers and Sisters

When someone dies intestate survived by no issue and no father or mother, the part of the estate not passing to the surviving spouse usually passes to the decedent's brothers and sisters equally. The children of deceased brothers and sisters (i.e., nieces and nephews) take their parent's share by right of representation (figure 3-5). To illustrate, the Uniform Probate Code provides, "if there is no surviving issue or parent, to the issue of the parents or either of them by representation." UPC § 2-103(3).

As in the case of grandchildren, some state laws provide that when all of the intestate's brothers and sisters have predeceased the intestate, their issue inherit per capita rather than per stirpes. The number of nieces and nephews are counted and each receives an equal share.

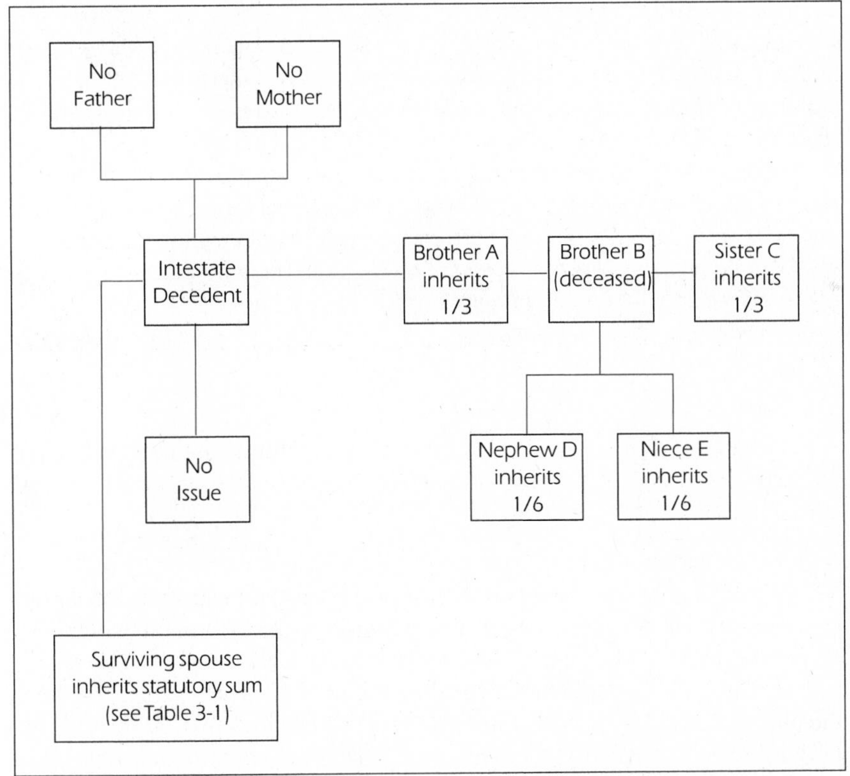

When someone dies intestate survived by no issue and no mother or father, the part of the estate not passing to a surviving spouse passes to the decedent's brothers and sisters, with the children of any deceased brothers and sisters taking their parent's share by right of representation.

FIGURE 3-5
Rights of siblings of intestate decedent

Next of Kin

When someone dies intestate survived by no issue, no father or mother, and no brothers or sisters or children of deceased brothers or sisters, the part of the estate not passing to the surviving spouse passes to the decedent's closest kindred. These include grandparents, aunts and uncles, and cousins. (See figure 3-2.)

Grandparents. Existing grandparents usually inherit to the exclusion of aunts, uncles, and cousins because they are more closely related to the intestate. In some states, grandparents inherit equally. In others, if a distribution is to be made to grandparents, the estate is divided into halves and one-half passes to the maternal side and the other half to the paternal side. If there are no grandparents, some states allow great-grandparents to inherit; others do not.

Aunts, Uncles, and Cousins. If no grandparents are living, aunts and uncles are the next in line to inherit, and cousins follow them. Some state statutes provide that intestate property passes to the lineal descendants of the intestate's grandparents by right of representation. Under these statutes, the children of deceased aunts and uncles—that is, cousins—take their parent's share by right of representation.

Other state statutes provide that intestate property passes to the next of kin "in equal degree." Under these statutes, because aunts and uncles are third-degree relatives, they take the entire estate to the exclusion of all others. No one takes by right of representation. Cousins, who are fourth-degree relatives, inherit only when no aunts and uncles are alive when the intestate passes away. (See figure 3-6.)

3.5 ESCHEAT

When people die intestate survived by no spouse and no ascertainable kindred, their property **escheats**, that is, passes, to the state. Some state laws provide that personal property escheats to the state in which the deceased was domiciled, and real property escheats to the state in which the property is located. Other state laws provide that both real and personal property escheat to the state in which the property is located.

Some state laws provide that an inheritance escheats to the state when the beneficiary under a will cannot be located. For example, a Florida statute provides that when the lawful owner of an inheritance is unknown or cannot be located, the inheritance must be given to the state treasurer to the credit of the state school fund. Under the law, the lawful owner has 10 years to claim the money, after which it escheats to the state for the benefit of the school fund. Fla. Stat. Ann. § 733.816

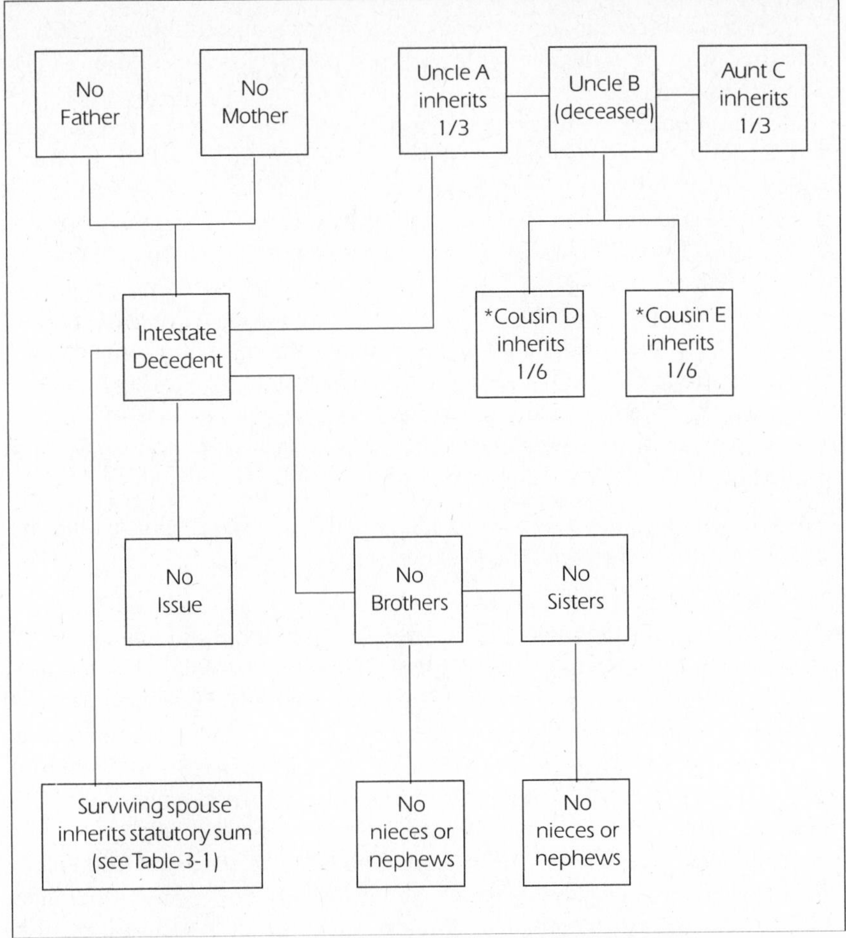

FIGURE 3-6
Rights of extended family of intestate decedent

When someone dies intestate survived by no issue, no mother or father, no brothers or sisters, and no children of deceased brothers or sisters, the part of the estate not passing to a surviving spouse passes to the decedent's uncles and aunts. In some states, the children of any deceased uncles and aunts (i.e., cousins) take their parent's share by right of representation. In other states, uncles and aunts take to the exclusion of all others; cousins inherit only when there are no uncles or aunts.

**In some states, cousins inherit only when no uncles or aunts are alive.*

SUMMARY

3.1 When someone dies intestate, the law of the decedent's domicile determines how personal property will pass. In contrast, the law of the place where the property is located determines how real property will pass.

3.2 All property that does not pass under a will passes as intestate property, according to the state law of intestate succession.

LEGAL TERMS

escheat
The passing of property to the state.

When people die simultaneously, so that it is impossible to determine who died first, each person's solely owned property is disposed of as if he or she had survived. In the case of property owned jointly by both decedents, the property is distributed one-half as if one had survived and one-half as if the other had survived. When the beneficiary of an insurance policy dies simultaneously with the insured, the proceeds are payable as if the insured had survived the beneficiary. Any person who fails to survive the intestate by 120 hours is deemed to have predeceased the intestate, under the UPC.

Anyone who is convicted of murdering another cannot inherit from the other's estate. In addition, a divorce terminates the right of a former spouse to inherit from an intestate. People who are related by affinity, such as stepchildren, do not inherit from an intestate. In contrast, half-blood relatives often inherit the same share they would inherit if they were of the whole blood.

3.3 The amount that a surviving spouse inherits from a spouse who dies without a will differs from state to state.

3.4 The balance remaining after the surviving spouse receives his or her share passes to the decedent's children equally, with the children of any deceased children taking their parent's share by right of representation. If there are no children or grandchildren, the decedent's parents inherit the estate. If there are no parents, the decedent's brothers and sisters inherit equally, with the children of any deceased brothers and sisters taking their parent's share by right of representation. If there are no brothers, sisters, nieces, nephews, uncles, or aunts, cousins inherit, depending on the state law.

Modern state statutes treat adopted children as strangers to their former relatives and consider adopting parents as though they were legitimate blood relatives to their adopted children. However, adoption of a child by the spouse of a natural parent has no effect on the relationship between the child and that natural parent.

Illegitimate children, under most state laws, inherit from and through their fathers who have either acknowledged paternity or have been adjudicated to be their fathers, as well as from and through their mothers.

3.5 When people die intestate survived by no spouse and no ascertainable kindred, their property escheats to the state.

QUESTIONS FOR REVIEW

1. What law determines the passing of an intestate's: (a) out-of-state personal property? (b) out-of-state real property?
2. When a husband and wife are killed at the same time in an accident, how does the wife's solely owned property pass? How does the husband and wife's jointly owned property pass?

3. What is the rationale for state laws providing that one who is convicted of murdering another cannot inherit from the other's estate?
4. In states that have adopted the Uniform Probate Code, how do relatives of the half blood inherit? How do stepchildren inherit?
5. How does the term *heirs* differ from the term *next of kin?*
6. Under the civil law method, how is the degree of kinship of a relative calculated?
7. Give examples of priorities that are recognized within the degrees of kindred.
8. For inheritance purposes, how do modern state statutes treat adopted children?
9. Since the United States Supreme Court decision in 1977, in what way may nonmarital children inherit from their father and mother who die intestate?
10. When does the property of one who dies intestate pass to the state?

CASES TO DISCUSS

1. Mary Holliday was brutally murdered in her home during the evening hours. A grand jury returned an indictment against her son, Craig Holliday, on the charge of murder with the use of a deadly weapon. Holliday was subsequently tried by a jury and acquitted of all charges. Later, a district court determined that Holliday could not inherit from his mother's estate because of the murder. Do you agree? Why or why not? *Holliday v. McMullen,* 756 P.2d 1179 (Nev. 1988).
2. One year before Delynda was born, her mother, Princess Ann Ricker, and her father, Prince Rupert Ricker, were ceremonially married. The marriage, however, was not valid, because Prince Rupert's divorce from his first wife had not been finalized. Prince Rupert died intestate when Delynda was 18 years old. The Texas court refused to allow her to inherit from her father's estate. A Texas statute prohibited an illegitimate child from inheriting from her father unless her parents had subsequently married, which Delynda's parents had not done. Is the Texas statute valid under the United States Constitution? Explain. *Reed v. Campbell,* 476 U.S. 850 (1986).
3. Helen Russell died in the state of Florida, leaving a will that left one-half of her estate to her son, Kenneth Smith, and the other half to her stepchildren, Robert, Ronald, and Patricia Russell. The three stepchildren could not be located. Had Helen died intestate, her only child, Kenneth, would have inherited the entire estate. Kenneth argued that because the stepchildren could not be located, he was entitled to the entire estate. Do you agree? Why or why not? *In re Estate of Russell,* 387 So. 2d 487 (Fla. 1980).

SHARPENING YOUR PROFESSIONAL SKILLS

1. In the opening law office scenario, how should Diane Sherman respond to: (a) Gertrude Nullius's question about how much the son who murdered his father will inherit? (b) Gertrude's statement that her husband wanted her daughter to inherit from him? (c) Gertrude's statement that her son, Phil, can use his father's inheritance?
2. Look up your state statute that sets forth the right of inheritance of the surviving spouse of a person who dies intestate. Write down the statutory reference, and give the fraction the spouse will inherit (a) if the decedent is survived by issue; (b) if the decedent is survived by no issue but kindred; and (c) if the decedent is survived by no issue and no kindred.
3. A person died intestate. After all debts, taxes, and expenses of administration were paid, the amount remaining to be distributed was $400,000. Under the laws of your state, how will the $400,000 be divided and to whom will it be given if the decedent is survived by: (a) a spouse and two children; (b) a spouse and a father and mother; (c) a spouse but no blood relatives; (d) four children; (e) a brother and two children of a deceased sister; (f) a spouse and a 95-year-old aunt; and (g) no blood relatives and no surviving spouse.
4. (a) List the people who are related to you by lineal consanguinity. (b) List the people who are related to you by collateral consanguinity. (c) List the people who are related to you by affinity. (d) List the people who would inherit from you, and the fractional share each would receive, if you were to die intestate today.
5. In case number 3 of the Cases to Discuss, how would Helen Russell's estate have passed if she had been domiciled in your state when she died? Provide state statutory references or case citations to back up your answer.

CHAPTER 4
The Last Will and Testament

"The foolish and the dead alone never change their opinions."

James Russell Lowell

OUTLINE

LAW OFFICE SCENARIO

Angela Clark, a paralegal in the office of Dillon & Harvey, was given the assignment of interviewing an elderly client in a nursing home for the purpose of drafting the client's will. The client, Mrs. Frothmeyer, acted friendly and smiled pleasantly when she was introduced to Angela by a nursing home attendant. The moment the attendant left, however, Mrs. Frothmeyer whispered to Angela that she needed a will because the people in the nursing home were planning to kill her. Mrs. Frothmeyer said that a bomb had been placed under her bed and was timed to go off at midnight that night; the patient in the next room was scheming to steal all of her furniture. She knew this because she had heard people plotting against her in the middle of the night.

When Angela asked for the names of her children, Mrs. Frothmeyer replied that she had no children. She said that she wanted a new will leaving everything she owned to an aide at the nursing home who had been especially kind to her.

After leaving Mrs. Frothmeyer, Angela inquired at the desk for the name of Mrs. Frothmeyer's guardian and discovered that it was her daughter, Vivian.

4.1 WILLS AND TESTAMENTS

Paralegals need good judgment and interpersonal skills when interviewing clients for the preparation of the clients' wills. A testator must be of sound mind at the time of execution of the will in order for the will to be valid. As discussed later in this chapter, being able to assess whether a client is of sound mind becomes crucial when the paralegal is asked to witness the will: witnesses may later be asked to vouch for the mental stability of the testator if the will is contested.

Besides dealing with the person behind the will, paralegals must be familiar with specific requirements of the legal document itself: for example, that wills must be in writing in most cases; that specifically two witnesses must be present; that witnesses must sign in each other's presence or in the presence of the person making the will; that real estate is treated differently from personal property. Understanding the rationale behind these details requires a brief look at history.

The law of wills, estates, and trusts of today has its roots in the feudal system that prevailed in England in the eleventh, twelfth, and thirteenth centuries. In those days, it was considered a disgrace to die without a *testament,* which was a will of personal property; wills of real property were not generally allowed. Until the Reformation, the Church, rather than the state, had jurisdiction over the law of testaments of personal property in England. Testaments were received orally by a priest as part of the last confession; the Church frequently received gifts of personal property when people died. In fact, much of the law relating to testaments was developed by the Church.

In the fourteenth century, a method evolved whereby landowners could bypass the law against making wills of real property. Under this rather ingenious procedure, X (a landowner) would give real property to Y "to the use of X for life and then to the use of X's will." X would then draft a will declaring a use in favor of Z. Since X still had the use of the property and therefore benefited, X was considered the beneficial owner. Y, however, was the legal owner until X died, and then Z became the owner. This arrangement was the forerunner of our present-day trust, discussed in chapter 6.

To regain revenues and reduce fraud, England enacted the Statute of Uses in 1536. Under the statute, when X conveyed land to Y "to the use of Z," the use in the hands of Y was destroyed, and full ownership to the property went immediately to Z. Thus, it once again became impossible to dispose of real property by will.

The inability to leave real property by will caused such outrage that England passed the Statute of Wills in 1540, allowing wills of real property to be made "in writing" by most landowners. When feudalism ended in 1660, all land could be disposed of by a written will.

In 1677, more formal requirements were imposed upon wills by the passage of the English Statute of Frauds. That statute declared that a will of real property "shall be in writing, and signed by the party so devising the same, or by some other person in his presence and by his express direction, and shall be attested and subscribed in the presence of the said devisor by three or four credible witnesses."

A will of personal property under the English Statute of Frauds could be oral unless the value exceeded 30 pounds; in that case, the will was not valid unless: (1) it was proved by the oath of three witnesses present when it was made, (2) the testator made the persons present bear witness to the will, (3) the will was made in the last sickness of the testator, and (4) the testimony was given within six months or committed to writing within six days after the will was made.

Technically, the term **will** refers to an instrument that disposes of real property and the term **testament** refers to an instrument that disposes of personal property. A **will and testament** refers to an instrument that disposes of both real and personal property. (See table 4-1 for other terms.) This distinction is not made, however, in practice in the United States today.

LEGAL TERMS

will
Under early English law, a will of real property.

testament
Under early English law, a will of personal property.

will and testament
Under early English law, a will of real and personal property.

beneficiary	A person who receives a gift under a will. Known as a **devisee** under the Uniform Probate Code (UPC).
bequeath	To give personal property by will.
bequest	A gift of personal property in a will. Known as a **devise** under the UPC.
decedent	One who is deceased.
devise	A gift of real property in a will. Under the UPC, a gift of real or personal property in a will.
devisee	A person who receives a gift of real property under a will. Under the UPC, a person who receives a gift of real or personal property.
devisor	A person who makes a gift of real property in a will.
execute	To perform or carry out.

TABLE 4-1
Legal Terms Relating to Wills

intestate	The state of having made no valid will; also, a person who dies without a valid will.
legacy	A gift of personal property in a will.
legatee	A person who receives a gift of personal property under a will.
legator	A person who makes a gift of personal property in a will.
testate	The state of a person who has made a will.
testator	A man who has made a will.
testatrix	A woman who has made a will.
testamentary	Relating to a will or testament.

TABLE 4-1
(Continued)

4.2 STATE STATUTORY FORMALITIES

Paralegals who work in the field of wills, estates, and trusts must become familiar with their own state statutes governing the formalities of executing a will. This is because each state in the United States has passed its own statutes setting forth the requirements for executing a will. Except for states that have adopted the Uniform Probate Code, the laws are not uniform. State statutes follow either the requirements of the English Wills Act, or the English Statute of Frauds, or a combination of the two. Some differences in the two English statutes are listed here.

1. The English Wills Act required the signature of the testator "at the foot or end thereof." This was not required under the English Statute of Frauds. As you will learn, some states, such as New York, still require a will to be signed by the testator at the end of the will.
2. The English Wills Act required two witnesses, whereas the English Statute of Frauds required three witnesses. Until recently, some states in the United States required two witnesses to a will; others required three. Most states today, however, require only two witnesses to a will.
3. The English Wills Act required that the witnesses be present at the same time, whereas the English Statute of Frauds allowed witnesses to attest separately. Some states today follow the English Wills Act; others follow the English Statute of Frauds relative to the presence of witnesses to the signing of a will.
4. Both statutes required that witnesses attest in the presence of the testator.

Age Requirements

Under the laws of most states, a person must have reached the age of 18 to make a will. People reach the age of 18 on the day before their 18th birthday, because people are considered to have lived the entire day on which they are born. Since the first day of life is counted, infants are 365 days old on the day before their first birthday, and are actually one year and one day old on their first birthday.

Some state variations exist on the general age requirement of 18. For example, in Oregon and Texas, married people under the age of 18 may also make wills; in Idaho, emancipated minors may do so as well. Members of the armed forces and the Merchant Marines may make a will at any age in the states of Indiana and Texas.

LEGAL, BUT . . .

Even before his daughter became a movie star and Princess Grace of Monaco, John ("Jack") B. Kelly, Jr., was a prominent figure in Philadelphia, having risen from bricklayer to millionaire contractor. In his unorthodox yet legal will, Kelly replaces legal jargon with personality and wit. He speaks for himself from the beginning:

> For years I have been reading Last Wills and Testaments and I have never been able to clearly understand any of them at one reading. Therefore, I will attempt to write my own Will in the hope that it will be understandable and legal. Kids will be called "kids" and not "issue," and it will not be cluttered up with "parties of the first" . . . and a lot of other terms that I am not sure are only used to confuse those for whose benefit it is written.

After allocating his property, he speaks to his family:

> In this document I can only give you things, but if I had the choice to give you worldly goods or character, I would give you character. The reason I say that, is with character you will get worldly goods because character is loyalty, honesty, ability, sportsmanship and, I hope, a sense of humor. If I don't stop soon, this will be as long as *Gone With the Wind,* so just remember, when I shove off for greener pastures or whatever it is on the other side of the curtain, that I do it unafraid and, if you must know, a little curious.

Philadelphia businessman and millionaire John "Jack" B. Kelly, father of actress-turned-princess Grace and grandfather of Princess Caroline, Princess Stephanie, and Prince Albert of Monaco. Courtesy of AP/Wide World Photos.

With characteristic flair, Kelly signed the will in Kelly green ink.

Testamentary Capacity

For a will to be valid, the person making the will must have **testamentary capacity**. This means that he or she must be of **sound mind** at the time of execution of the will. There is a four-part test to determine soundness of mind. Testators must:

1. Know, in a general way, the nature and extent of their bounty (i.e. riches)
2. Know, in a general way, who would be the natural objects of their bounty (although they need not leave anything to them)
3. Know that they are making a will; and
4. Be free from delusions that would influence the disposition of their property.

In the opening law office scenario, Mrs. Frothmeyer would not pass the test of soundness of mind. Apparently she was having delusions about a bomb being placed under her bed, and she did not know that she had a daughter—a natural object of her bounty.

As suggested earlier, paralegals are often called upon to witness wills, so they may have to determine if an unfamiliar testator is "of sound mind." Conversation is the natural way to explore someone's mental capabilities, especially when dealing with elderly clients. Asking questions about the testator's family, occupation, places of residence, travels, and leisure-time activities can be an effective way to get to know the testator in the short time available.

The burden of proving the soundness of mind of the testator falls on the **proponent** of the will—that is, the person presenting the will to the court. Establishing the testator's soundness of mind is usually done by offering the will itself, the affidavits of subscribing witnesses, and the judgment admitting the will to probate. In a will contest, witnesses and the testator's physician are usually asked to testify as to the testator's mental capacity. Therefore, the paralegal's role in witnessing wills is a serious responsibility. The paralegal must evaluate the testator's mental capacity exclusively at the time of execution of the will. The *Hedges* case demonstrates that lapses of mental ability in an elderly person do not invalidate the required soundness of mind on the day a will (or codicil) is executed.

LEGAL TERMS

testamentary capacity
Having the ability to make a will; being of sound mind.

sound mind
Having the ability to make a will.

proponent
One who proposes or offers something.

nuncupative will
An oral will.

holographic will (sometimes spelled olographic)
A will written entirely in the handwriting of the testator(rix) and signed by the testator(rix) but not witnessed.

MATTER OF HEDGES
473 N.Y.S.2d 529 (N.Y. 1984)

FACTS: On the eve of her 102d birthday, Nelly Hedges executed a will in which she devised her residence to her long-time friend, Halsey Brower. Seven months later, she signed a codicil to the will revoking the devise to Brower and leaving the residence to her church. After her death, Brower objected to the allowance of the codicil, claiming that Hedges lacked testamentary capacity. Brower offered testimony to indicate that at various times before and after signing the codicil, Hedges had suffered delusions and was irrational and forgetful. No evidence was offered to contradict the testimony of the subscribing witnesses, which established that at the time the codicil was executed, the testatrix was of sound mind and capable of understanding the nature of her action.

LEGAL ISSUE: Is evidence that an elderly testator suffered delusions and was irrational and forgetful before and after signing a codicil, when witnesses testified that she was of sound mind, sufficient to establish lack of testamentary capacity?

COURT DECISION: No.

REASON: It has long been recognized that old age, physical weakness, and senile dementia are not necessarily inconsistent with testamentary capacity as long as the testatrix was acting rationally and intelligently at the time the codicil was prepared and executed. Furthermore, evidence relating to the condition of the testatrix before or after the execution is significant only insofar as it bears upon the strength or weakness of mind at the exact hour of the day of execution. Thus, the evidence adduced at trial was entirely insufficient to establish lack of testamentary capacity at the exact time of the codicil's execution.

Necessity of a Writing

With the exception of certain **nuncupative** (oral) wills allowed by many states, wills must be in writing. Many states recognize nuncupative wills of personal property made by soldiers in military service and mariners at sea. Some states also recognize nuncupative wills of very small amounts of personal property and nuncupative wills of personal property made during a last illness when witnesses are present.

A **holographic will** (sometimes spelled **olographic**) is a will that is entirely in the handwriting of the testator and signed by the testator but not

olographic will (also called holographic will) A will that is entirely in the handwriting of the testator(rix) and signed by the testator(rix) but not witnessed.

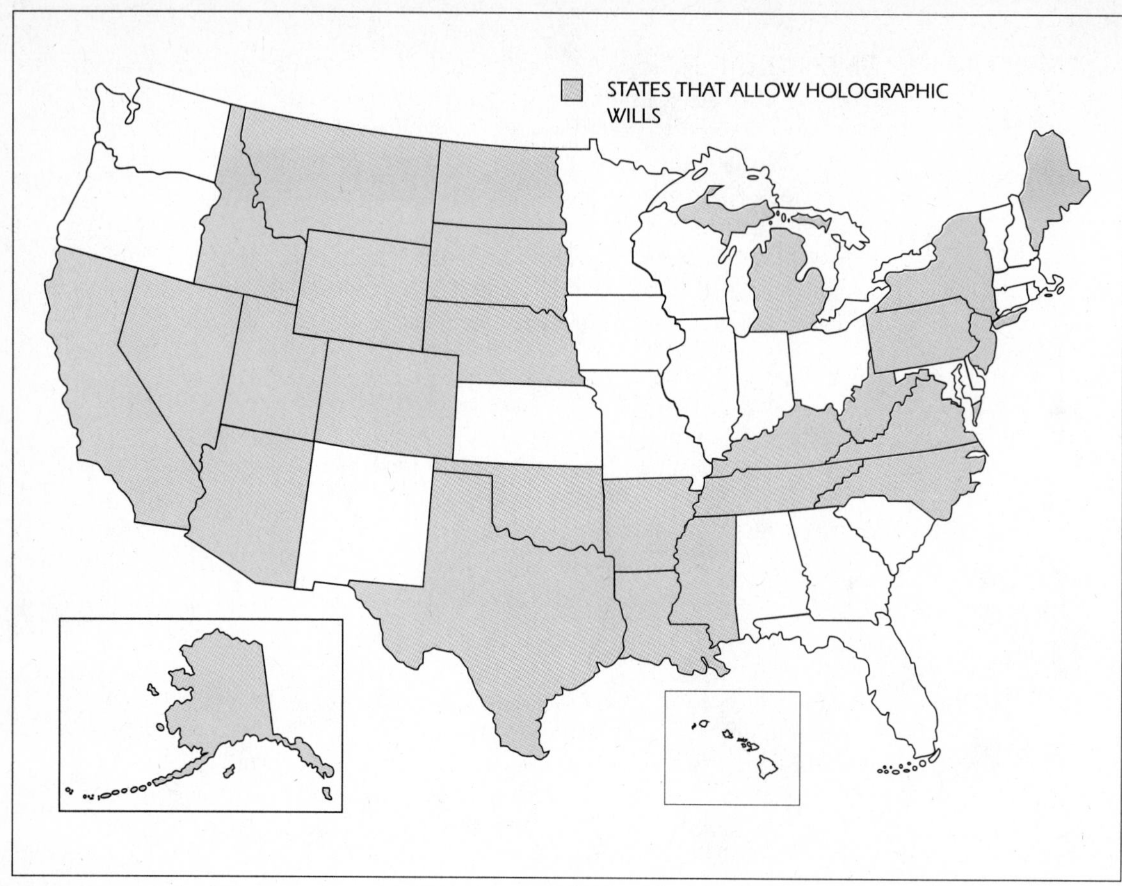

FIGURE 4-1
States that allow holographic wills

witnessed. About half of the states in the United States recognize holographic wills as being valid (see figure 4-1). The rest of the states do not allow them because of the lack of witnesses. Under the UPC, a holographic will is valid if the signature and the material (i.e., important) portions of the document are in the testator's handwriting. UPC § 2-502.

The courts have held that an audiotape recording does not meet the requirements of a holographic will, as illustrated by the *Reed* case.

The Will's Execution

Paralegals working in law offices often play key roles in the execution of wills. It is important that they be thoroughly familiar with their state law on signing and witnessing requirements, because wills can be contested if they are not properly executed. Wills must be signed, attested, and witnessed

MATTER OF ESTATE OF REED
672 P.2d 829 (Wyo. 1983)

FACTS: Robert G. Reed died without a formally drawn will. However, a sealed envelope was found among his belongings on which was written in his handwriting, "Robert G. Reed To be played in the event of my death only! Robert G. Reed." The envelope contained an audiotape recording of Mr. Reed's directions for the distribution of his assets when he died. The court recognized that the voice-recorded statement did resemble a nuncupative will, but noted that nuncupative wills are not valid in the state of Wyoming.

LEGAL ISSUE: Does an audiotape recording that is placed in a sealed envelope with handwritten instructions that it be played only in the event of death amount to a holographic will?

COURT DECISION: No.

REASON: The envelope notation, standing alone, has no testamentary consequence and cannot be considered a will. Moreover, the statute is not complied with even if the tape and writing are considered together, because no part of the alleged will could be considered to be in the testator's handwriting.

in accordance with the precise rules of the state in which the will is executed. This is one of the reasons why it is dangerous for lay persons to make their own wills. Most lay persons are not aware of the technical rules that must be followed when executing a will.

Signature Requirements. Written wills must be signed either by the testator or by someone else in the testator's presence who is directed to do so by the testator. A signature may be any mark that the testator intends to be a signature. Thus, a barely discernible signature written by an elderly person's shaking hand, or an *X* made by someone who cannot write, are accepted as signatures if the intent of the person writing it was to authenticate the instrument.

In the states indicated in figure 4-2, the testator's signature must be written at the end of the will. To illustrate, the Pennsylvania statute states, "Every will shall be written and be signed by the testator at the end thereof." The *Hopkins* case points out the danger of making a will without obtaining sound legal advice.

Most states, however, do not require the testator's signature to be at the end of the instrument. For example, in Illinois, "Every will shall be in writing, signed by the testator or by some person in his presence and by his direction and attested in the presence of the testator by two or more credible witnesses." Ill. Rev. Stat. ch. 110 ½, para. 4-3 (1985). This statute was referred to by the Illinois court in deciding the *Carroll* case.

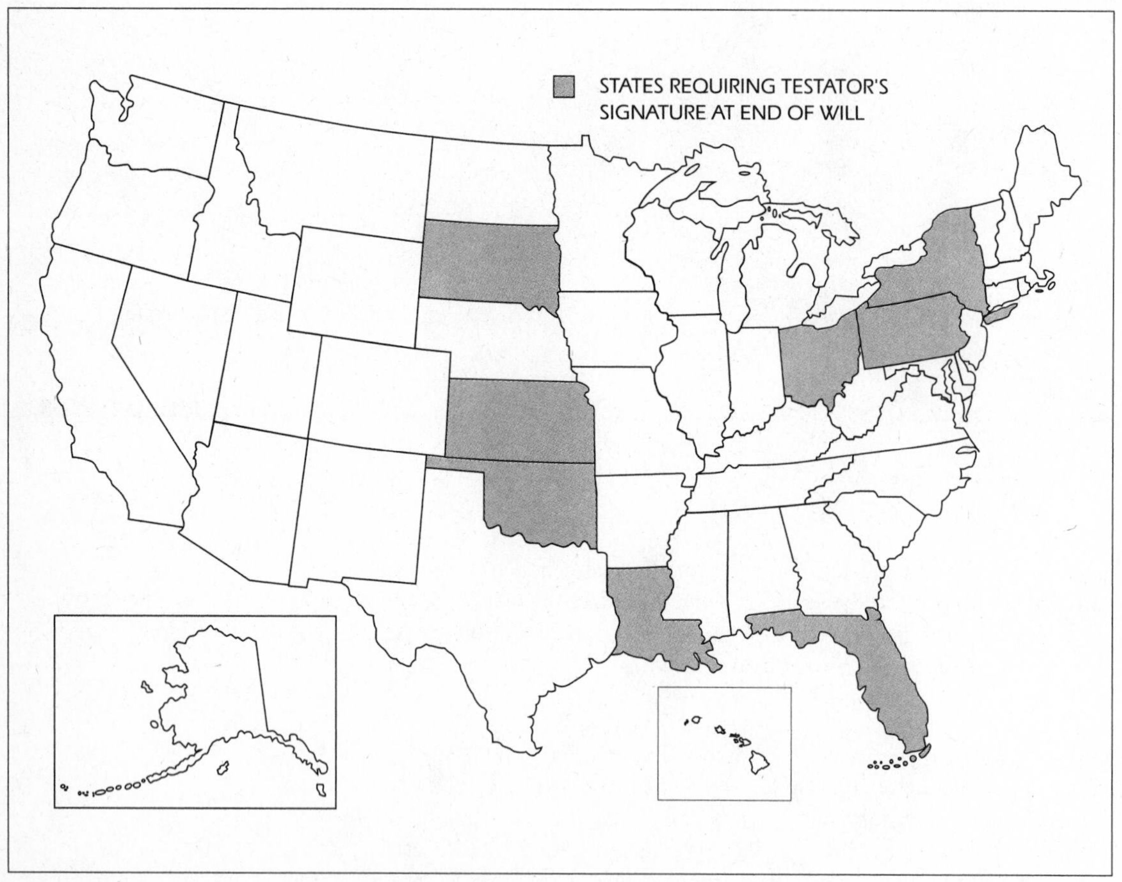

FIGURE 4-2
States that require testator's signature at the end of a will

IN RE ESTATE OF HOPKINS
570 A.2d 1058 (Pa. 1990)

FACTS: A four-page document that had been handwritten on lined notepad paper was introduced in court as the will of Edna A. Hopkins. Hopkins had signed her name vertically along the margin of each page, but she failed to sign the document at the end.

LEGAL ISSUE: In Pennsylvania, must a will be signed by the testator at the end of the instrument?

COURT DECISION: Yes.

REASON: The Pennsylvania statute requires that a will be signed by the testator "at the end thereof." This requirement was enacted to prevent the probate of unfinished papers and mere expressions of intent. By signing at the end of a document, the writer has expressed that he or she has decided on a testamentary scheme and that the writing is not half-formed thoughts never intended to be operative. The will was not allowed, causing Hopkins's property to pass by intestacy.

IN RE ESTATE OF CARROLL
548 N.E.2d 650 (Ill. 1989)

FACTS: Genevieve B. Carroll filled out a printed form and signed it on the first line in a sentence declaring the document to be her last will and testament. Near the end of the document, she inserted the date and year in the blank spaces in a line reading: "IN WITNESS WHEREOF I have hereunto set my hand and seal this ___________ day of _________, 19____." She did not sign the will a second time. The will was properly witnessed.

LEGAL ISSUE: In Illinois, must a will be signed by the testator at the end of the instrument?

COURT DECISION: No.

REASON: The Probate Act does not require that the testator's signature appear at the end of the will. It is immaterial where in the will the signature of the testator is placed, if it was placed there with the intention of authenticating the instrument. The way the will was filled in suggests that the deceased intended her signature at the beginning of the will to be her authoritative signature.

Witness Requirements. Non-holographic wills must be witnessed in the presence of the testator by competent witnesses. With the exception of Louisiana and Vermont (which require three witnesses), all states in the United States require two witnesses to a will. Some state laws stipulate that the witnesses be in each other's presence when they sign as witnesses to a will. The map in figure 4-3 indicates the states with this requirement. Paralegals who work in one of these states must be aware of the rule, because a violation can cause a will to be invalidated. Most states do not have this particular requirement, however.

"THE GREAT ONE"

Comedian Jackie Gleason, the "Great One," is probably best known for his role as bus driver Ralph Kramden in the television series "The Honeymooners." His will is straightforward, but the codicil is unusual. Executed the day before he died, the codicil quadrupled the gift to his secretary from $25,000 to $100,000. The debilitating effects of his cancer made Gleason unable to sign his own name on the codicil. He instructed someone else to sign his name for him, in the presence of two witnesses.

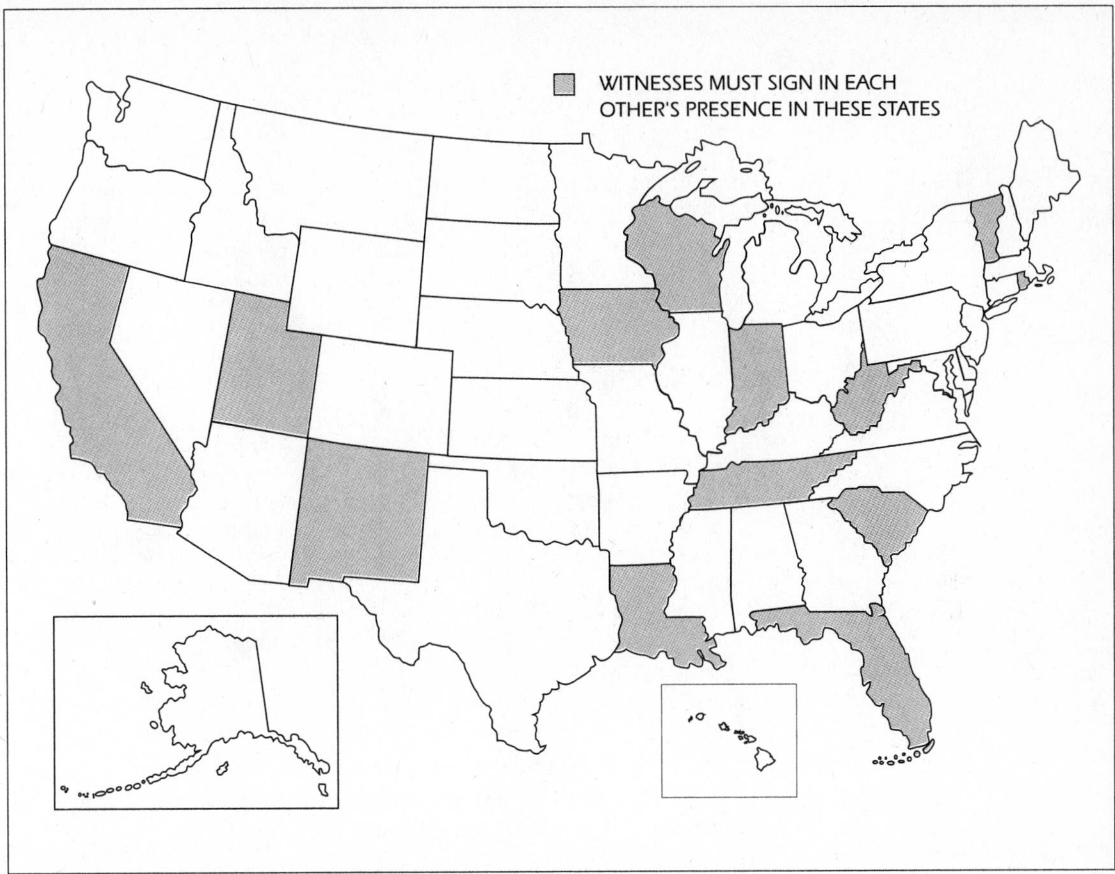

FIGURE 4-3
States that require witnesses to a will to sign in each other's presence

The act of witnessing a will consists of two parts, attesting and subscribing. To **attest** means to see the signature or take note mentally that the signature exists as a fact. To **subscribe** means to write beneath or below. Usually courts hold that witnesses to wills must do both. Thus, some cases have held that a will was improperly executed—and therefore void—when the testator refused to allow the witnesses to see his signature, which he had previously written.

Some states avoid this problem with attestation by the use of suitable language in their statutes. For example, the Virginia law states that a testator's signature "shall be made or the will acknowledged by him in the presence of at least two competent witnesses, present at the same time; and such witnesses shall subscribe the will in the presence of the testator, but no form of attestation shall be necessary." The *Robinson* case illustrates that the courts do not interpret the word *subscribe* literally.

LEGAL TERMS

attest
To see a signature or take note mentally that the signature exists as fact.

subscribe
To write beneath, below, or following.

ROBINSON V. WARD
387 S.E.2d 735 (Va. 1990)

FACTS: When Joane G. Tannehill became ill, she told her very good friend, Katherine D. Ward, to get a legal pad and "Write exactly what I say, and do not interrupt me." As Tannehill dictated, Ward wrote:

> To *Katherine D. Ward* I leave everything I own for her life time. She is to maintain the farm & provide employment for Penny Guin for as long as Penny cares to stay. I would hope that Katherine can maintain the farm & herself with the income from the farm & interest on my principal. At her death, the principal that is left is to be used as an endowment as maintaining this farm, which I wish to go to Covington Boys Home. The farm is to be used by them as a teaching facility. If they do not wish to use it that way then the entire request is to go to VPI to be used in the same manner.

After Ward finished writing the will, Tannehill read it over, signed her name, dated it, and placed it on a bedside table. Shortly thereafter, George A. Knudson, a member of the rescue squad, arrived. Tannehill told Knudson that she had dictated her will to Ward and asked him to read and witness it. He read the will, dated it, wrote "Witness" and signed it in the presence of Tannehill and Ward. Tannehill died that day. The next day, on the advice of an attorney, Ward signed the will below Knudson's signature.

LEGAL ISSUE: Is the signature of a witness on the first line of a will a satisfactory subscription by that witness?

COURT DECISION: Yes.

REASON: Ward did not intend to act as a witness when she wrote her name in the first line of the document. Yet, she was a subscribing witness to the execution of the will within the meaning of the statute. Although the testatrix never formally asked Ward to be a witness to the will, the evidence establishes that Tannehill expected her to act as a witness and treated her as one. (Three judges dissented, saying that Virginia's statutory language requires "signing a will *with the intention of acting as a witness.")*

In some states, witnesses who are named as beneficiaries under the will lose the inheritance unless there are two other witnesses who inherit nothing under the will. If the case of *Robinson v. Ward* had occurred in Massachusetts, for example, Ward would not have inherited, because she was a witness to the will and two other witnesses were not present. Even spouses of witnesses often lose their inheritances, unless there are extra witnesses who do not inherit under the will. Many states, however, protect witnesses who make the mistake of witnessing a will under which they are also beneficiaries. Their laws provide that if the witness would have inherited had the testator died intestate, the witness may inherit the amount in the will, but not more than the intestate share.

The 1990 revision of the UPC goes even further, by giving full protection to witnesses when they inherit under the will. The revised law states that the signing of a will by an interested witness does not invalidate the will or any provision of it. UPC § 2-505. The map in figure 4-4 indicates

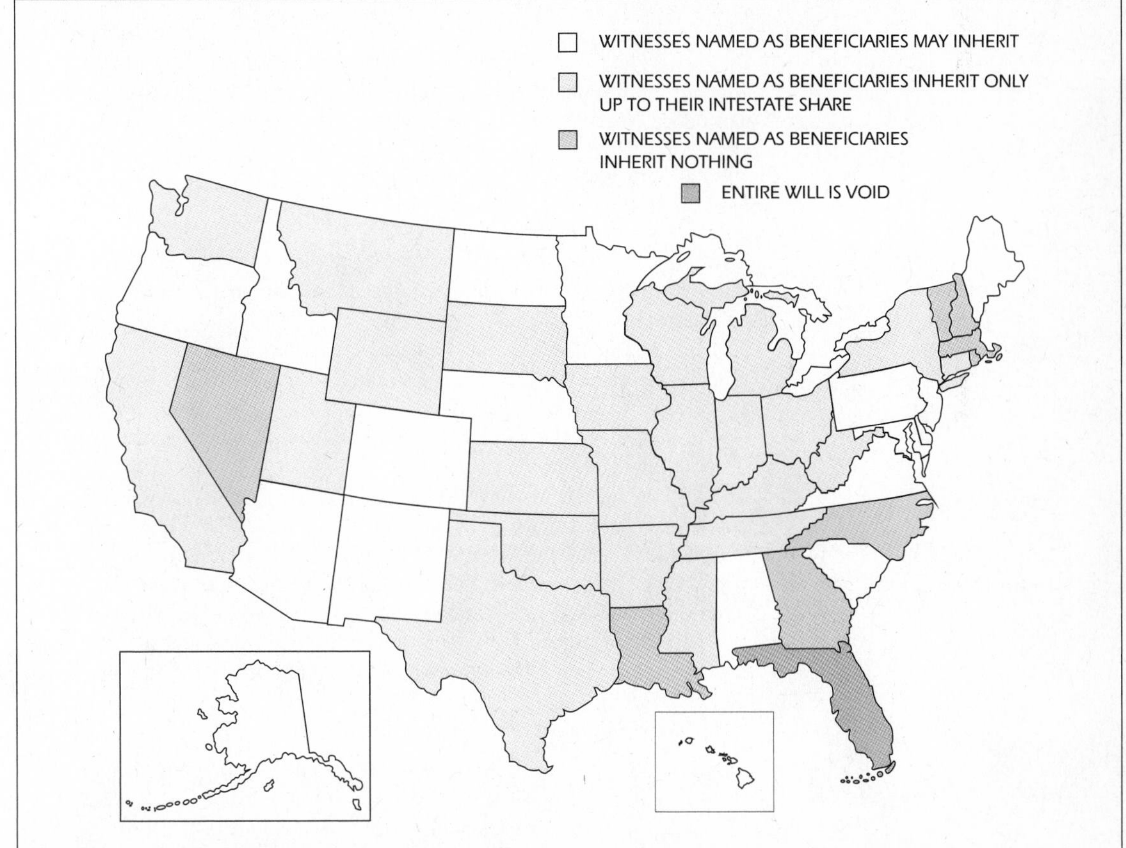

FIGURE 4-4
Effect of witnesses' being beneficiaries of wills

the states that follow these rules when a witness to a will is also a beneficiary under that will.

Witnesses to a will must be competent. In general, this means competent to be a witness in a court of law. Massachusetts has defined *competency* as being of "sufficient understanding," meaning that the witness understands what a will is and what is taking place when the will is executed. Although most states have no age requirements for witnesses to wills, Arkansas and Utah require witnesses to be at least 18 years old, Iowa requires them to be at least 16 years old, and Texas requires them to be at least 14 years of age.

Relaxation of Formalities. The 1990 revision of the UPC contains a section that relaxes the strict, formal requirements relative to executing wills if the proponent of the document establishes by clear and convincing evidence that the decedent intended the document to be a will. UPC § 2-503.

Professional Guidelines

To avoid the pitfalls of an improperly executed will, this procedure is recommended:

1. The testator is asked to read the will carefully, being certain that it is accurate, that it expresses the testator's will, and that all aspects of the will are understood.
2. The proper number of witnesses are brought into the room, introduced to the testator, the door is closed, and the group should not be interrupted.
3. The testator declares to the witnesses that the instrument before them is his or her will and requests them to act as witnesses to its execution. The witnesses do not read the will.
4. The testator signs the will at the end, making sure that all witnesses observe the signature.
5. The testator initials or signs the margin of each page of the will for purposes of authenticity.
6. One witness reads the attestation clause (the clause preceding the witness's signature) aloud. The witnesses then sign their names and write their addresses while the testator and other witnesses observe.
7. If a self-proof clause is used, a notary public, who must also be present, takes the oaths and acknowledgments of the testator and the witnesses.

4.3 CHANGING AND REVOKING WILLS

Just as making a will involves technicalities, changing or revoking a will also requires certain formalities. Paralegals should encourage testators to seek competent legal advice whenever they want to alter their wills in any way.

Changing a Will

Altering the terms of a will is most effectively done through a **codicil**, which is a separate instrument with new provisions that change the original will in some way. A codicil must refer specifically to the will being changed and must be executed with the same formalities as are required for the execution of a will. (See figure 4-5.) A properly executed codicil has the effect of **republishing**, that is, reestablishing, the will. It is said that a codicil breathes new life into a will. Thus, a will with only one witness or a will that has been revoked is reestablished with a properly executed codicil.

LEGAL TERMS

codicil
A separate instrument with new provisions that change a will in some way.

republish
Reestablish.

AN EXAMPLE OF A
CODICIL TO A LAST WILL AND TESTAMENT

I, SANDRA M. DOE, of Anytown, Essex County, Massachusetts, make this the first codicil to my last will and testament executed by me on April 19, 1992.

I revoke ARTICLE VII of my said will and substitute the following in its place:

> I nominate and appoint my husband, JAMES T. DOE, as executor of this will. If he shall fail to qualify or cease to serve, I nominate and appoint my son, DAVID K. DOE, and my brother, ARTHUR X. SMITH, to serve as co-executors in his place.

In all other respects I ratify and confirm all of the provisions of my said will dated April 19, 1992.

I, the undersigned testator, do hereby declare that I sign and execute this instrument as my first codicil to my last will, that I sign it willingly in the presence of each of said witnesses, and that I execute it as my free and voluntary act for the purposes herein expressed, this 8th day of February, 1993.

____
Sandra M. Doe

We, the undersigned witnesses, each do hereby declare in the presence of the aforesaid testator that the testator signed and executed this instrument as the first codicil to her last will in the presence of each of us, that she signed it willingly, that each of us hereby signs this codicil as witness in the presence of the testator, and that to the best of our knowledge the testator is eighteen (18) years of age or over, of sound mind, and under no constraint or undue influence.

(Witness)	(Address)
(Witness)	(Address)

FIGURE 4-5
Example of a codicil

COMMONWEALTH OF MASSACHUSETTS
COUNTY OF ESSEX

Subscribed, sworn to and acknowledged before me by the said testator and witnesses this 8th day of February, 1993.

____
Notary Public
My commission expires:

FIGURE 4-5
(Continued)

Unfortunately, people often choose to avoid the expense of a lawyer and decide to cross out words or sections of their wills on their own. Such deletions may be accepted without being witnessed if evidence exists that the deletions were done intentionally by the testator. However, proving who made the markings and whether the changes were intended is difficult. Cross-out marks on wills cause confusion, invite contests, and can lead to costly litigation.

Additions to a will following its execution have no legal effect unless the will is re-signed by the testator and reattested by the proper number of witnesses. As discussed earlier, paralegals should encourage testators to seek proper legal expertise when considering changes to their wills. Making a new will or adding a codicil to the existing will is an effective way to avoid future problems.

Either task can be performed easily and speedily through the use of a word processor. Computerized systems allow documents to be easily retrieved and updated. Personal data may have to be changed, as in the case of a marriage, divorce, death, or adoption; a condition or clause in a will (or trust) agreement may no longer be valid. With word-processing software, these changes require a few keyboard strokes and little time. Standardized forms may be retrieved on the computer and then customized for the client. Whole paragraphs may be reworked, deleted, or rearranged with minimal effort and time.

Revoking a Will

State statutes set forth precise methods for **revoking** (canceling) a will. The act of revoking a will must be accompanied by the testator's intent to revoke the will. There are four principal methods of revoking a will.

1. The English Statute of Frauds declared that a will could be revoked by "burning, canceling, tearing, or obliterating." (See sample in figure 4-6.)

CODICILS BY J. PAUL GETTY TO THE WILL DATED SEPTEMBER 22, 1958

1st Codicil: June 18, 1960
2nd Codicil: November 4, 1962
3rd Codicil: December 20, 1962
4th Codicil: January 15, 1963
5th Codicil: March 6, 1963
6th Codicil: September 16, 1965
7th Codicil: March 11, 1966
8th Codicil: January 5, 1967
9th Codicil: November 3, 1967
10th Codicil: February 24, 1969
11th Codicil: March 28, 1969
12th Codicil: June 26, 1970
13th Codicil: March 8, 1971
14th Codicil: July 29, 1971
15th Codicil: March 20, 1973
16th Codicil: June 14, 1973
17th Codicil: October 9, 1973
18th Codicil: July 4, 1974
19th Codicil: January 21, 1975
20th Codicil: August 27, 1975
21st Codicil: March 11, 1976

The number of codicils added to the will of oil magnate J. Paul Getty seems excessive: why a new, updated document was never drafted is anyone's guess. In a time before computerized revisions with word-processing programs, perhaps retyping the entire will required too much time and inconvenience. Or maybe Getty chose the method of adding codicils to show beneficiaries exactly when he no longer approved of them or their actions. For example, in the 5th codicil, signed in 1963, Getty's youngest son loses the right to share in his father's personal effects and receives a meager $500; but then, 12 years later, he reappears in the 19th codicil as an executor and trustee of the will with another brother—apparently "approved" once again by his father.

The English Wills Act prescribed "burning, tearing, or otherwise destroying." Most American statutes use the language of one of these acts.

2. In general, the execution of a new will revokes a prior will. To revoke a prior will in some states, however, the new will must either expressly state that it revokes an earlier will or be inconsistent with the old will; otherwise, the new will is treated as a supplement (like a codicil) to the old will. The 1990 revision of the UPC attempts to clarify this rule with the following language:

> The testator is presumed to have intended a subsequent will to replace rather than supplement a previous will if the subsequent will makes a complete disposition of the testator's estate [UPC § 2-507(c)]. The testator is presumed to have intended a subsequent will to supplement rather than

LEGAL TERMS

revoke
Cancel.

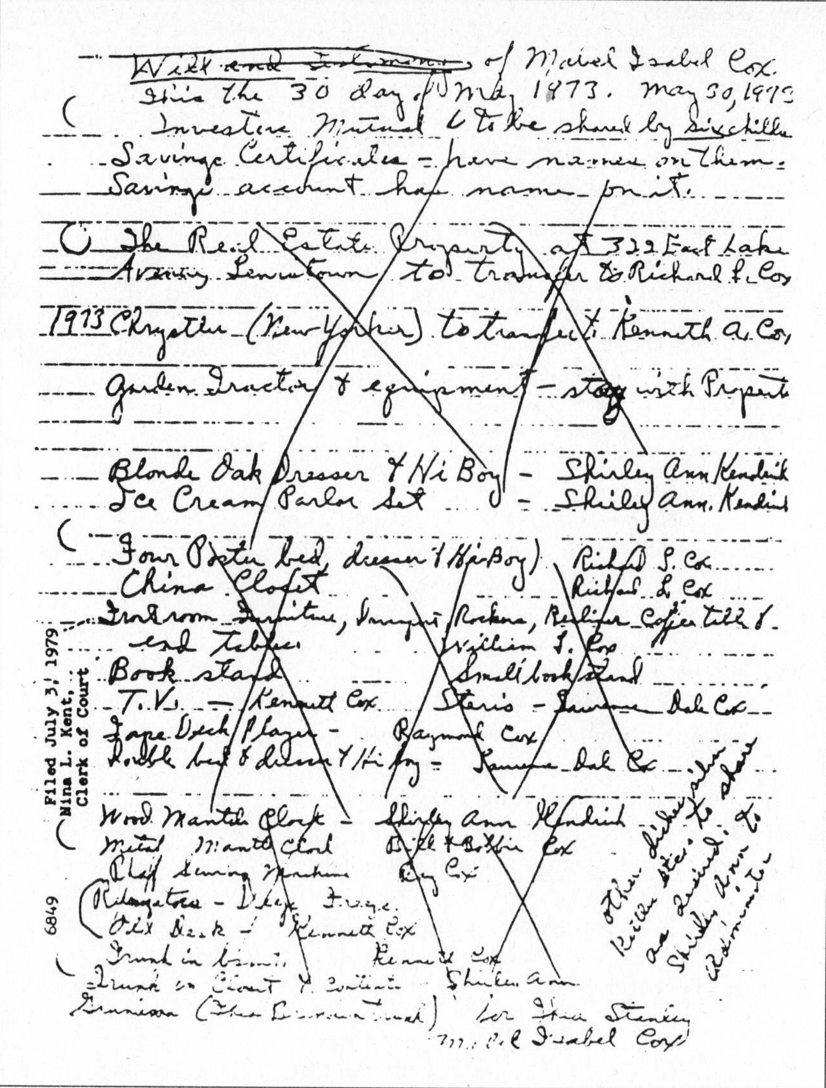

~~Will and Testament~~ of Mabel Isabel Cox.
This the 30 day of May, 1973. May 30, 1973
Investors Mutual to be shared by six children
Savings Certificates - have names on them.
Savings account has name on it.

The Real Estate Property at 322 East Lake Avenue Lewistown to transfer to Richard L. Cox

1973 Chrysler (New Yorker) to transfer to Kenneth A. Cox

Garden Tractor & equipment - stay with Property

Blonde Oak Dresser & Hi Boy - Shirley Ann Kendrick
Ice Cream Parlor Set - Shirley Ann Kendrick
Four Poster bed, dresser & Hi-Boy) Richard L. Cox
China Closet Richard L. Cox
Front room furniture, Davenport Rocker, Recliner, Coffee table & end tables William L. Cox
Book stand Small book stand
T.V. - Kenneth Cox. Stereo - Lawrence Dale Cox
Tape Deck Player - Raymond Cox
Double bed & dresser & Hi Boy - Lawrence Dale Cox

Wood Mantle Clock - Shirley Ann Kendrick
Metal Mantle Clock Bill & Bobbie Cox
[illegible] Sewing Machine Ray Cox
Refrigerator - Deep Freeze
Old Desk - Kenneth Cox
Trunk in basement Kenneth Cox
Trunk in Closet & contents - Shirley Ann
[illegible] for [illegible]
Mabel Isabel Cox

Other dishes silverware kitchen stuff to share as desired. Shirley Ann to Administrate

Filed July 31 1979
Nina L. Kent,
Clerk of Court
6849

FIGURE 4-6
Sample of cancelled holographic will

This holographic will, found among Mabel Isabel Cox's belongings, was held by the court to be cancelled. Matter of Estate of Cox, *621 P.2d 1057 (Mont. 1981).*

replace a previous will if the subsequent will does not make a complete disposition of the testator's estate [UPC 2-507(d)].

Sometimes the act of destroying a will does not revoke it. This occurs when a testator cancels a valid will after making a new one, and the new will turns out to be void. Under a rule known as the doctrine of *dependent relative revocation,* the cancelled will is held to be effective in order to avoid intestacy. The reasoning behind the rule is that the testator's intent was to cancel the will only if the new will became effective. If the new will is not effective, the cancelled will is revived.

3. The subsequent marriage of a person who has made a will revokes the will in some states unless the will declares that it is made in contemplation of marriage to a particular person. In a small number of jurisdictions, subsequent marriage revokes a will only when a child is born of that marriage. In Louisiana, the birth or adoption of a child itself revokes a will unless the child is provided for in the will. In a few states, instead of revoking a will completely, subsequent marriage revokes only gifts made in a will to a former spouse. The map in figure 4-7 indicates the effect of subsequent marriage under the laws of different states.
4. Under the laws of many states, a divorce or dissolution of marriage revokes bequests and devises to a former spouse—but not the will itself—unless the will specifically provides otherwise. In addition, a divorce revokes the appointment of the former spouse as an executor or trustee under the will. See table 4-2.

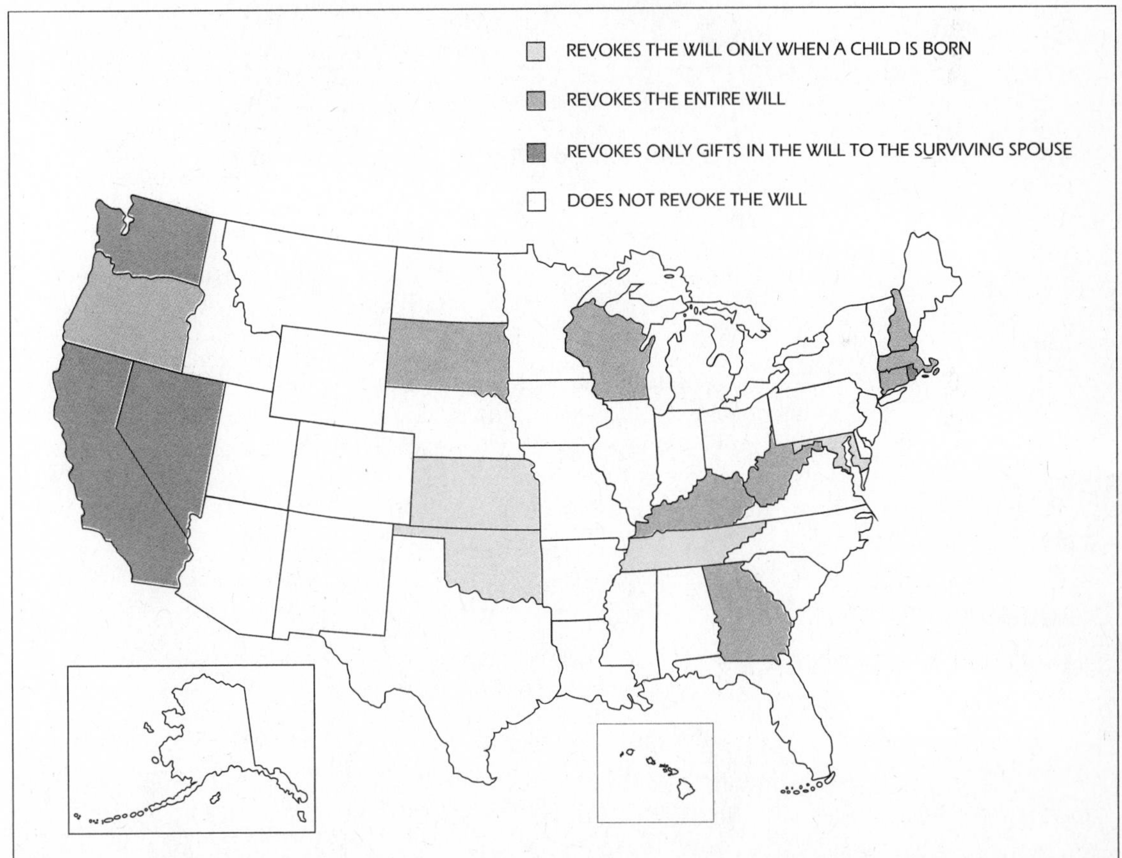

FIGURE 4-7
Effect of subsequent marriage upon will

A divorce revokes all bequests and devises made in a will to a former spouse in these states:

Alabama	Maine	Oklahoma
Alaska	Maryland	Oregon
Arizona	Massachusetts	Pennsylvania
Arkansas	Michigan	Rhode Island
California	Minnesota	South Carolina
Colorado	Missouri	South Dakota
Delaware	Montana	Tennessee
Florida	Nebraska	Texas
Hawaii	Nevada	Utah
Idaho	New Jersey	Virginia
Illinois	New Mexico	Washington
Indiana	North Carolina	Wisconsin
Kansas	North Dakota	Wyoming
Kentucky	Ohio	

A divorce revokes an entire will in these states:

Connecticut	Georgia	West Virginia

A divorce has no effect on a will in these states:

Iowa	Mississippi	New York
Louisiana	New Hampshire	Vermont

TABLE 4-2
Effect of Divorce on Bequests to Former Spouse

State statutes differ with regard to the annulment of a marriage. An annulment revokes the entire will in Maryland and West Virginia. In many states, however, instead of revoking the entire will, an annulment revokes only gifts in the will to a former spouse. The *Knott* case illustrates the Kentucky rule as to the effect of an annulment on a will.

KNOTT V. GARRIOTT
784 S.W.2d 803 (Ky. 1990)

FACTS: Following his wife's death, Wilbert Martin executed a will. Four years later, Martin married Barbara Mattingly. That marriage was annulled shortly thereafter because of Martin's incapacity to consent to marriage.

LEGAL ISSUE: Does a marriage, subsequently annulled, revoke a will made prior to the marriage?

COURT DECISION: No.

REASON: A decree annulling a marriage is a declaration that no valid marriage ever existed. An annulled marriage is void *ab initio* (from the beginning) and cannot operate to invalidate a will made prior to the marriage.

Sometimes, a testator will leave his or her entire estate to a particular person without mentioning in the will that he or she intends to marry that person. Shortly thereafter, the testator marries that person, and the question arises as to whether the subsequent marriage revoked the will. Courts have held, in recent cases, that the will is not revoked in this situation because there is clear and convincing evidence that the will was made in contemplation of the marriage, even though that fact was not mentioned in the will itself.

4.4 JOINT AND MUTUAL WILLS

A **joint will** is one instrument that serves as the will of two or more people. The instrument is **probated** (proved and allowed by the court) each time a co-testator dies. Generally, it is not good practice to draw joint wills: the parties may separate; one of them, rather than both, may have custody of the will and the other may not know its whereabouts; one of them may destroy the will without the other's knowledge or consent. It is better to draw a separate will for each testator, even if the wills are identical.

Mutual wills (also called **reciprocal wills**) are separate, identical wills for each testator containing reciprocal provisions accompanied by an agreement that neither testator will change his or her will after the death of the other. The *Johnson* case involved a will that was both joint and mutual and contained a provision requiring mutual agreement for the will to be changed.

A written contract to provide for another by will is enforceable in most states; an oral contract is not. However, to prevent unjust enrichment, anyone who furnishes services to another based on the other's oral promise to leave a gift by will can recover the fair value of those services from the other's estate.

LEGAL TERMS

joint will
One instrument that serves as the will of two or more persons.

probate
To prove and allow by the court.

mutual wills (also called reciprocal wills)
Separate, identical wills by two testators containing reciprocal provisions and accompanied by an agreement that neither testator will change his or her will after the death of the other.

reciprocal wills (also called mutual wills)
Separate, identical wills by two testators containing reciprocal provisions and accompanied by an agreement that neither testator will change his or her will after the death of the other.

IN RE ESTATE OF JOHNSON
781 S.W.2d 390 (Tex. 1989)

FACTS: Soon after being married, Emma and James Johnson executed a joint will. Both had been previously married and had several children by their prior marriages. The will, among other things, provided for Emma's son and contained the following provision: ". . . this is our joint and mutual will made by each in consideration of the other so doing and shall be irrevocable excepting by the mutual agreement of both." Four years later, unbeknownst to Emma, James executed a new will, revoking the earlier will and providing for his son instead of Emma's son. Emma learned of the new will when James died seven years later.

LEGAL ISSUE: May a joint and mutual will stating that it is irrevocable except by mutual consent be revoked by one co-testator without the consent of the other?

COURT DECISION: No.

REASON: The express provisions of the earlier will alone constituted sufficient evidence to show a joint and mutual will containing contractual provisions, mutual consideration, irrevocability except by mutual agreement, and a comprehensive plan for the disposition of both testators' estates. Contracts not to revoke wills are governed by § 59A of the Texas Probate Code, which provides, "A contract to make a will or devise, or not to revoke a will or devise . . . can be established only by provisions of a will stating that a contract does exist and stating the material provisions of the contract."

4.5 GROUNDS FOR CONTESTING A WILL

To be able to contest a will, a person must have *standing*—that is, have some beneficial interest that will be lost if the will is allowed. This usually means that the person contesting would either inherit under an earlier will or under the law that is applied when someone dies without a will. As mentioned earlier, wills may be contested on the grounds of improper execution and unsound mind. Other grounds for contesting a will are fraud and undue influence.

To successfully contest a will on the ground of fraud, it must be shown that the testator relied on false statements when making the will. To contest a will on the ground of undue influence, it must be shown that the testator's free will was destroyed and, as a result, the testator did something contrary to his or her true desires. The burden is on the person alleging fraud or undue influence to prove that those conditions existed. When there is fraud or undue influence, the court may disallow only part of the will, instead of the entire will, as in the case of improper execution and unsound mind.

SUMMARY

4.1 The law of wills, estates, and trusts has its origins in early England. Wills of real property were not always allowed in England, until the end of feudalism in 1660. The Church, rather than the state, had jurisdiction over the law of testaments, which were often made orally to a priest as part of the last confession.

4.2 In general, a person must be 18 years old and of sound mind to make a will. With limited exceptions for personal property, wills must be in writing and signed either by the testator or by someone else in the testator's presence who is directed to do so by the testator. A signature may be any mark that the testator intends to be a signature. Some states require a testator's signature at the end of the instrument; others do not. Non-holographic wills must be witnessed in the presence of the testator by either two or three competent witnesses, depending on state law.

4.3 When items are crossed out of a will and there is evidence that the deletion was done intentionally by the testator, the deletion will be accepted even though it was not witnessed. In contrast, when additions are made to a will following its execution, the additions have no legal effect unless the will is re-signed by the testator and reattested by the proper number of witnesses. A codicil must refer specifically to the will being changed and must be executed with the same formalities as are required for the execution of a will. A properly executed codicil has the effect of republishing a will. Wills may be revoked by: (1) burning, cancelling, tearing, or obliterating; (2) the execution of a new will; (3) subsequent marriage, unless the will declares that it is made in contemplation of marriage to a particular person; and (4) in some states, divorce or annulment with regard to gifts made in a will to a former spouse (but not the will itself), unless the will specifically provides otherwise. A divorce or an annulment also revokes the appointment of the former spouse as an executor or trustee under the will.

4.4 A joint will is one instrument that serves as the will of two or more persons. Mutual or reciprocal wills are separate, identical wills for each testator that contain reciprocal provisions accompanied by an agreement that neither testator will change his or her will after the death of the other.

4.5 A person must have standing to contest a will. The most common grounds for contesting a will are (1) improper execution, (2) unsound mind, and (3) fraud or undue influence.

QUESTIONS FOR REVIEW

1. What is the technical difference between a will and a testament?
2. Under the law of most states, how old must a person be to make a will? When does a person reach that age?
3. What is the four-part test that determines soundness of mind to make a will?
4. When are nuncupative wills recognized?
5. How may wills be signed by testators?
6. How must non-holographic wills be witnessed?
7. The act of witnessing a will consists of what two parts?
8. Why should testators be discouraged from crossing things out of and adding things to their wills?
9. In what ways may a will be revoked?
10. Name the most common grounds for contesting a will.

CASES TO DISCUSS

1. William Cole made a will leaving his entire estate to Catherine Jackson and naming her executrix. The will stated, "I hereby cut off from this will and testament my brothers . . . my only heirs-at-law." Nothing in the will mentioned that it was made in contemplation of marriage to Jackson. Six months later, Cole married Jackson. Did the marriage to Jackson revoke Cole's will? Why or why not? *D'Ambra v. Cole,* 572 A.2d 268 (R.I. 1990)
2. Shortly before her death, Anita P. Clardy, a 79-year-old widow, executed a will leaving her property to various friends and relatives. She left only one dollar to each of her two adopted children "because of their vile attitude towards me since 1953 and the vile names they have called me." The children contested the will on the ground that Mrs. Clardy lacked testamentary capacity. They claimed that Mrs. Clardy became irrational and experienced false delusional beliefs regarding them and their treatment of her. In finding against the children, the trial court held that the burden of proof rests with the contestants and that the contestants failed to meet that burden. Was the court's decision correct? Explain. *Clardy v. National Bank,* 555 So. 2d 64 (Miss. 1989).

3. Margaret C. Mergenthaler's will consisted of four pages. Just before the will was executed, the pages were incorrectly stapled together so that page four, on which the testator signed, came before the residuary clause on page three. The law of that state requires that the testator sign the will "at the end" and provides that matter, other than the attestation clause, following the testator's signature is ineffective. Was the residuary clause in this case ineffective? Why or why not? *Will of Mergenthaler,* 474 N.Y.S.2d 254 (N.Y. 1984).

SHARPENING YOUR PROFESSIONAL SKILLS

1. Look up your state statute that permits a person to make a will, write down the statutory reference, and look for the answers to the following questions: (a) How old must a person be to make a will? (b) Is a holographic will recognized as valid? (c) How must a will be signed? (d) How must a will be witnessed?
2. Under your state statute, how may a will be revoked? Give the statutory reference where the provision is found.
3. Select a friend or someone in your family who needs a will and obtain as much information as you can about that person that would be necessary to draft the will. If you have access to a law library, the checklist in 20 AM. JUR. *Legal Forms 2d* 266:62 would be helpful.
4. Join a discussion group with three other members of the class to discuss the predicament Angela Clark faced in the opening situation of this chapter. What does the group conclude as to Mrs. Frothmeyer's testamentary capacity? How should Angela Clark handle the situation? How should the attorneys in the office of Dillon & Harvey handle the situation?

CHAPTER 5
Structure of a Model Will

"The confession of evil works is the first beginning of good works."

St. Augustine

OUTLINE

LAW OFFICE SCENARIO

Angela Clark introduced herself to Jack Russell, who sat nervously in the waiting room in the office of Dillon & Harvey. Angela apologized for Mr. Dillon's absence, saying that he had been held up in court but should return shortly. She explained that she would begin taking down information that Attorney Dillon would need in drafting a will. Angela ushered Mr. Russell into her office.

After making Mr. Russell feel comfortable by talking with him about how everyone postpones making a will, Angela asked, "May I have your full name?"

"Everybody calls me Jack, but my real name is John. Actually, John is my middle name. My full name is Edward John Russell. I never use Edward, though, except on formal papers, because that was my Dad's first name. Sometimes I go by E. John Russell, sometimes just John Russell, but my friends call me Jack."

"Do you ever use the name Edward J. Russell?" Angela asked.

"Maybe on a few stock certificates, but that's about all."

"What is your address?"

"Well, I live six months in Fort Myers, Florida, and six months on the Jersey shore. Which address do you want?"

"Why don't you give me both addresses, just to be sure." Angela wrote down the Florida and New Jersey addresses.

"I love warm weather, and I love the beach! In fact, I've never told anybody this, but I want to be cremated and have my ashes dropped in the sea at one of my favorite beaches. And I want that to be in my will. My wife won't like it, though. She's already got a spot picked out for both of us in a cemetery where she grew up in Paramus, New Jersey, but I don't want to be buried there."

"Okay, I'll make a note of that."

"And another thing, while I think of it, I want two copies made of my will—one to keep in Florida and one to keep at the shore. I'll sign both of them. That way there'll be a will nearby wherever I die."

At that moment, Attorney Dillon arrives and joins the conference that Angela is having with Mr. Russell.

BOLD BUT BLAND

Theodore Roosevelt, America's first "cowboy" president, was a bold and vigorous figure, the former head of the Rough Riders who fought in the Spanish-American War. Roosevelt left a strikingly dull will, however. Earlier presidents had written testaments that revealed personal beliefs, feelings, and sentiments. In contrast, Roosevelt's more "modern" will reveals little of the person, but focuses on the legal terminology necessary to prevent lawsuits. The terms *issue* and *testator* now appear; and beginning with Roosevelt, a president's will is no longer "signed" but "subscribed, sealed, published, acknowledged, and declared by the Testator."

Theodore Roosevelt (1858-1919), 26th President of the United States. Courtesy of the National Portrait Gallery, Washington, DC/Art Resource, NY

5.1 COMMON ELEMENTS

Names, addresses, burial directions—these are among the many details that paralegals will discuss with clients when preparing their wills. No required form for a valid will exists, other than the placement of the signature in some states. However, carefully drawn wills often follow a similar pattern.

Wills and trusts are drafted with the aid of a computer or word processor in the modern law office. Most of the clauses in wills and trusts are stored in the computer's memory for use when needed. Then they are pulled up and tailored to fit the particular situation at hand. Paralegals today must be computer-literate and able to create documents when called upon to do so.

Common elements of a will include: (1) opening paragraphs, (2) the main body, (3) fiduciary and tax provisions, and (4) ending paragraphs. See figure 5-1.

5.2 INTRODUCTORY PARAGRAPHS

The introductory paragraphs of a will often include the exordium clause, directions for funeral arrangements, and instructions to pay debts.

Exordium Clause

The opening paragraph of a will is called the **exordium clause** or the **publication clause**. Its purposes are: (1) to identify the testator, (2) to state the testator's domicile or residence, (3) to declare the instrument to be the testator's last will, and (4) to revoke all prior wills and codicils made by the testator.

LEGAL TERMS

exordium clause (also called publication clause)
The opening paragraph of a will.

EXORDIUM CLAUSE

I, (name of testator), also known as [other names if any], [or formerly known as (maiden name)] of [street address], City of _________,

California Statutory Will

Without Trust Provisions

Notice to the person who signs this will:

1. It may be in your best interest to consult with a California lawyer because this statutory will has serious legal effects on your family and property.

2. This will does not dispose of property which passes on your death to any person by operation of law or by any contract. For example, the will does not dispose of joint tenancy assets or your spouse's share of community property, and it will not normally apply to proceeds of life insurance on your life or your retirement plan benefits.

3. This will is not designed to reduce death taxes or any other taxes. You should discuss the tax results of your decisions with a competent tax advisor.

4. *You cannot change, delete, or add words to the face of this California Statutory Will.* You may revoke this California Statutory Will and you may amend it by codicil.

5. If there is anything in this will that you do not understand, you should ask a lawyer to explain it to you.

6. The full text of this California Statutory Will, the definitions and rules of construction, the property disposition clauses, and the mandatory clauses are contained in the probate code of California.

7. The witnesses to this will should not be people who may receive property under this will. You should carefully read and follow the witnessing procedure described at the end of this will. All of the witnesses must watch you sign this will.

8. You should keep this will in your safe-deposit box or other safe place.

9. This will treats most adopted children as if they are natural children.

10. If you marry or divorce after you sign this will, you should make and sign a new will.

11. If you have children under 21 years of age, you may wish to use the California Statutory Will with trust or another type of will.

FIGURE 5-1
Sample will without trust provisions. Courtesy Forms Inc., La Jolla, CA

CALIFORNIA STATUTORY WILL OF

____

Insert Your Name

ARTICLE 1. DECLARATION

1.1. This is my will and I revoke any prior wills and codicils.

ARTICLE 2. DISPOSITION OF MY PROPERTY

2.1. PERSONAL AND HOUSEHOLD ITEMS

I give all my furniture, furnishings, household items, personal automobiles and personal items to my spouse, if living; otherwise they shall be divided equally among my children who survive me.

2.2. CASH GIFT TO A PERSON OR CHARITY

I make the following cash gift to the person or charity in the amount stated in words and figures in the box which I have completed and signed. If I fail to sign in the box, no gift is made. If the person mentioned does not survive me, or the charity designated does not accept the gift, then no gift is made. No death tax shall be paid from this gift.

____

Full Name of Person or Charity to Receive Cash Gift • Please Print • Name One only

____ $__________

Amount of Gift Written Out and in Numbers

____

Signature of Testator

2.3. ALL MY OTHER ASSETS

I adopt only one Property Disposition Clause in this paragraph 2.3 by writing my signature in the box next to the title of the Property Disposition Clause I wish to adopt. I sign in only one box. I write the words "not used" in the remaining boxes. If I sign in more than one box or if I fail to sign in any box, the property will go under Property Disposition Clause (c) and I realize that means the property will be distributed as if I did not make a will.

PROPERTY DISPOSITION CLAUSES

Select One

(a) To my spouse if living; if not living, then to my children and the descendants of any deceased child.	(b) To my children and the descendants of any deceased child. I leave nothing to my spouse, if living.

(c) To be distributed as if I did not have a will.

ARTICLE 3. NOMINATIONS OF EXECUTOR AND GUARDIAN

3.1. EXECUTOR

(Name at Least One.)

I nominate the person or institution named in the first box of this paragraph 3.1 to serve as executor of this will. If that person or institution does not serve, then I nominate the others to serve in the order I list them in the other boxes.

First Executor.	Second Executor.	Third Executor.

FIGURE 5-1
(Continued)

County of ____________, State of ____________, declare this to be my last will and testament, hereby revoking all wills and codicils heretofore made by me.

____

Identification of Testator. When naming the testator in a will, it is important to include all names that the testator uses in the ownership of all types of property, including real property, personal property, securities, and bank

3.2. GUARDIAN

If you have a child under 18 years of age, you should name at least one guardian of the child's person and at least one guardian of the child's property. The guardian of the child's person and the guardian of the child's property may, but need not, be the same. An individual can serve as guardian of either the person or the property, or as guardian of both. An institution can serve only as guardian of the property.

If a guardian is needed for any child of mine, then I nominate the individual named in the first box of this paragraph 3.2 to serve as guardian of the person of that child, and I nominate the individual or institution named in the second box of this paragraph 3.2 to serve as guardian of the property of that child. If that person or institution does not serve, then the others shall serve in the order I list them in the other boxes.

First Guardian of the Person.	First Guardian of the Property.
Second Guardian of the Person.	Second Guardian of the Property.
Third Guardian of the Person.	Third Guardian of the Property.

3.3. BOND

My signature in this box means that a bond is not required for any individual executor or guardian named in this will. If I do not sign in this box, then a bond is required for each of those.

I sign my name to this California Statutory Will on ____________ at ____________, ____________.
Date City State

____
Signature of Testator

STATEMENT OF WITNESSES

You must use two adult witnesses and three would be preferable.

Each of us declares under penalty of perjury under the laws of California that the testator signed this California statutory will in our presence, all of us being present at the same time, and we now, at the testator's request, in the testator's presence, and in the presence of each other, sign below as witnesses, declaring that the testator appears to be of sound mind and under no duress, fraud, or undue influence.

Signature ____________________ Residence Address: ____________________
Print Name
Here: ____________________ ____________________

Signature ____________________ Residence Address: ____________________
Print Name
Here: ____________________ ____________________

Signature ____________________ Residence Address: ____________________
Print Name
Here: ____________________ ____________________

FIGURE 5-1
(Continued)

Some states, such as California, have legislated a precise form that may be used to make a valid will. It is important to read the instructions on the form carefully before executing this type of instrument.

accounts. This is often done by writing the words "also known as . . ." after the testator's name. In the interviewing process, the paralegal may need to jog the client's memory so that all variations of names used by the client will be recorded. Failure to list all names used by the testator can cause confusion and lead to the need to obtain court authorization to collect or transfer assets. This process can be expensive and can cause delays in settling the estate.

Domicile of Testator. The testator's domicile establishes the court in which the estate will be settled. The probate court in the place where the testator was domiciled at the time of death has primary jurisdiction to administer the decedent's estate. One's **domicile** is one's principal place of abode. It is the place to which one intends to return whenever one is absent. A person can have several residences, but only one domicile at any particular time. Once a domicile is established, it continues until a new one is actually acquired. To effect a change of domicile, there must be an actual abandonment of the first domicile, coupled with an intent not to return to it. In addition, physical presence must be established in the other place with the intention of making the last-acquired residence one's permanent home. The *Elson* case clarifies these distinctions concerning a "domicile."

IN RE ESTATE OF ELSON
458 N.E.2d 637 (Ill. 1983)

FACTS: Natalie Elson studied recreation and equine sciences at Southern Illinois University. She completed an equestrian internship, taught horseback riding to handicapped children, and trained horses in Illinois. After living her entire life in Illinois, she moved to Pennsylvania to study dressage and to train for the Olympic Games. She took her horse and most of her belongings with her, closed out her bank accounts, and opened new accounts in banks near her new residence. Five days later, she died in an automobile accident at the age of 27. In an unmailed letter she had penned the day before her death, Natalie wrote that she had "moved to Pennsylvania."

LEGAL ISSUE: May a new domicile be established by residing five days in one state after living one's entire life in a different state?

COURT DECISION: Yes.

REASON: The question of domicile is largely one of intention. In this case, there is sufficient evidence to establish that Natalie intended to abandon her Illinois domicile permanently and acquire a new domicile in Pennsylvania. Natalie had changed the focus of her life in a permanent manner from Illinois to Pennsylvania in pursuit of her equestrian career.

When a will is made in a place other than the testator's domicile, the exordium clause of the will should state "presently residing in" rather than "of" a certain place. This will help to clarify the fact that the testator is domiciled in another place and may prevent litigation when the will is probated.

Revocation of Earlier Wills. As discussed in chapter 4, one way to revoke a will is to make a new will. In some states, for a revocation to be effective, it is necessary to mention in the new will that it revokes the old one. In other states, a later will revokes an earlier one even though nothing is mentioned in the new will about revocation. By stating in a will that it revokes all prior wills, there can be no questions about the testator's intent when wills with different dates are found after the testator's death.

In some states, the subsequent marriage of a person who has made a will revokes the will unless the will declares that it is made in contemplation of marriage to a particular person (see figure 4-7 in chapter 4). This sentence may be added to the exordium clause to make such a declaration: "I declare that I am contemplating marriage to [name] and that I have made provision in this will for said [name] if my contemplated marriage to [him or her] is consummated."

Exordium Clause for a Joint Will
[AM JUR. *Legal Forms* § 266:216]

We, [name of one spouse] and [name of other spouse] husband and wife, of [street address], City of ____________, County of ____________, State of ____________, both being of sound mind and disposing memory and desiring to make disposition of our property so that no contention may arise concerning the same when we or either of us are dead, do each mutually in consideration of the other making a will, and of the provisions made herein in each other's behalf, make this our last will and testament and agree that the same cannot be changed or varied by either without the consent in writing of the other, and that the same cannot be changed or varied by the survivor of us.

Funeral Arrangements

Including funeral and burial arrangements or cremation instructions in a will is not always advisable; such matters must be taken care of immediately, and the will may not be found or allowed by the court for several weeks. In addition, the courts in some states do not treat the testator's wishes regarding funeral and burial arrangements as binding, deferring instead to the wishes of the surviving spouse or next of kin. Clients, however, often request that their preferences concerning their funeral, burial, or cremation be placed in their wills. In those cases, a brief statement is usually sufficient:

LEGAL TERMS

domicile
One's principal place of abode to which, whenever one is absent, one has the present intent of returning with no present purpose to depart.

Funeral and Burial Directions

I direct that my funeral be held at [name and address of place of funeral], City of ____________, County of ____________, State of __________, that it be conducted according to the rites of the [church], and that my remains be buried in my lot in the [cemetery] at [address], City of ____________, County of ____________, State of __________.

Statements such as the following are commonly used in wills:

Funeral Directions
[Am. Jur. *Legal Forms* § 266:322]

I direct that my funeral and burial is to be conducted in accordance with my written instructions therefor which are on file at [name and address of funeral director] at [address], City of ________________, County of ______________, State of ____________. The said written instructions are hereby incorporated into and made a part of this will.

Directions for Cremation
(usually included in introductory paragraphs)

I direct that on my death my remains be cremated, and that the ashes be placed in an urn with my name, my date of birth, which is _________,

NOVELS BY CHARLES DICKENS

A Christmas Carol
David Copperfield
A Tale of Two Cities
Great Expectations
Our Mutual Friend
Oliver Twist
Hard Times
Little Dorrit
Dombey and Son
The Pickwick Papers

Charles Dickens, the famous author of these familiar novels, wanted little fanfare when he died. In his will, he was specific and forceful: "I emphatically direct that I be buried in an inexpensive, unostentatious, and strictly private manner." He further demanded that "no public announcement be made of the time or place of my burial; that at the utmost not more than three plain mourning coaches be employed." He also ordered that mourners "wear no scarf, cloak, black bow, long hat-band, or other such revolting absurdity." All of Dickens's wishes were disregarded: he was eulogized publicly and profusely, with a long cortege, and by a massive audience dressed in the full trappings of mourning.

"Isn't that cute? He wants to bury you in the sand."

and the date of my death inscribed thereon, and that the urn be placed [in the grave of ________________, or deposited in the mausoleum in the ________________ cemetery].

Attorneys sometimes advise their clients to write a separate letter of instructions about funeral arrangements rather than to include them in a will. The letter can be placed in the envelope with the will, with copies given to close family members and to a funeral director.

Some people find it desirable to make their funeral arrangements in advance and to pay for the arrangements in advance as well (figure 5-2). Funeral directors often agree to a preestablished price for conducting a funeral, even though the date of death is unknown; the payment for the funeral is held in trust until the time for the funeral arrives. If older clients can be persuaded to make funeral arrangements in advance, the remaining relatives will be spared this added burden while grieving the loss of their loved one.

Instructions to Pay Debts

Because the executor is required by law to pay the debts of the decedent, it is not necessary to put a clause in the will instructing the executor to do so. In fact, it can be dangerous to include such a clause, because it might

Furber Funeral Home, Inc.

2925 Main St., P.O. Box 498
North Conway, N.H. 03860

(603) 356-5561

TRUST AGREEMENT FOR PREPAID FUNERAL ARRANGEMENTS

I, ______________________________ OF ______________________________
hereby transfer unto Furber Funeral Home of North Conway, New Hampshire, the sum of $____________ to hold the same in trust, nevertheless, upon the following terms and conditions, viz:

1. That said money be deposited at the highest interest rate available in the ______________________ of ______________________ in the name of my said trustee.

2. That my said trustee is instructed not to withdraw the whole or any part of the funds held by said bank or trust company until after my death and then only for the purpose of paying my funeral expense.

3. The transfer of said monies is expressly irrevocable so that I shall no longer have any power or authority to withdraw any of the funds held by said Bank.

4. A copy of this agreement is to become a permanent record of the banking institution referred to herein and said bank is hereby ordered and directed not to permit the withdrawal of said sum, or any part thereof, except upon certification by said Trustee that the funds are being withdrawn to pay funeral expenses related to my death.

5. The settler hereby reserves the right at any time to change the name of the Trustee above named by notification in writing to said Trustee or his legal representative and notification to the Bank or Trust Company above named, which later notice shall contain a statement of agreement and acceptance by the successor Trustee in substantially the same form as is contained below.

6. The settler may make future deposits under this trust agreement and said sums shall become subject to the terms and conditions thereof.

7. All interest accrued shall become part of the trust.

Bank Account No. ______________________

Account name: Furber Funeral Home, Inc., Trustee, under written agreement for

____

______________________ Witness

______________________ Settler

______________________ Date

____

I, ______________________, Trustee named above, hereby accept said Trust and agree to abide by the terms and conditions thereof.

______________________ Witness

______________________ Date

____
Trustee-Furber Funeral Home, Inc.
North Conway, NH 03860

FIGURE 5-2
Trust agreement for prepaid funeral arrangements. Form courtesy of Furber Funeral Home, Inc., North Conway, NH, and Charles Sutton

Many people plan and pay for their funerals before they die, relieving relatives of the unpleasant task. Often the money is held in trust by the funeral director until the time of death.

require the payment of otherwise uncollectible debts (such as debts that were extinguished by bankruptcy or a statute of limitations), as well as the payment of mortgages on the decedent's real property. Without such a clause, real property will pass to the devisees subject to any existing mortgages on the property. With such a clause, the executor might have to pay off existing mortgages from other assets of the estate so that the real property will pass to the devisees free and clear of all debt.

Instructions to Pay Debts
[Use with caution]

I direct that all of my just debts, including the expenses of my last illness, funeral and burial expenses, and expenses of the probate of my will and administration of my estate be paid as soon as possible after this will has been admitted to probate.

5.3 MAIN BODY

The main body of a will consists of the dispositive provisions, the residuary clause, and sometimes other miscellaneous clauses.

Dispositive Provisions

The **dispositive provisions** of a will are the provisions that dispose of the testator's property. These provisions vary considerably, as they are drafted to meet the needs of the individual client. Gifts under a will may be specific, general, or demonstrative.

Specific Legacies. In states that have not adopted the Uniform Probate Code (UPC), a **specific legacy** (often called a specific bequest) is a gift in a will of an identifiable item of property (other than real estate), such as a car, a diamond ring, a bank account, or a stock certificate. In states that have adopted the UPC, a legacy or bequest is referred to as a **devise**.

Specific Legacies

I give and bequeath the following items of personal property if owned by me at the time of my death to the individuals listed below:

(a) To my daughter, [name], if she shall survive me, the portrait of my husband's grandmother.
(b) To my daughter, [name], if she shall survive me, my diamond-ruby-sapphire ring, my Korean satsuma vase, and all pieces of my Friendly Village china.
(c) To my daughter, [name], if she shall survive me, my blue-and-gold vase, and my opal-and-diamond brooch.
(d) To my son, [name], if he shall survive me, my carved marble-top table and my large Chinese platter.

I may leave a memorandum stating my wishes with respect to the disposition of other articles of tangible personal property, but such memorandum will be simply an expression of my wishes and shall not create any trust or obligation, nor shall it be offered for probate as a part of this will.

One advantage of a specific legacy is that it is used for the payment of debts only after the general legacies (money from the general assets of the

LEGAL TERMS

dispositive provisions
The provisions of a will that dispose of the testator's property.

specific legacy (also called specific bequest)
A gift in a will of an identifiable item of property other than real estate.

devise
A gift of real property in a will.

estate) have been depleted. On the other hand, a specific legacy is subject to **ademption** (extinction; not being owned). If the testator does not own the item at the time of death, the person named to receive it receives nothing. A common type of specific legacy is a gift of all of one's **tangible personal property** (personal property that can be touched).

Bequest of
All Tangible Personal Property

I give to my [relationship], [name], all articles of tangible personal property which I own at the time of my death and not otherwise specifically bequeathed by this will, including but not limited to, personal effects, household goods, furniture and furnishings, automobiles, clothing, and jewelry, but not including currency, and securities. If my said [relationship] does not survive me, I give and bequeath the aforesaid property to my [relationship], [name].

Specific Devises. A gift of real property in a will is known as a *devise.* A **specific devise** is a gift in a will of an identifiable parcel of real property. The term includes personal property in states that have adopted the UPC.

When a person dies owning real property solely, or with others as a tenant in common, title to the decedent's share passes to his or her heirs at the moment of death. This contrasts with title to personal property, which passes to the **personal representative** (executor or administrator), who then distributes it to the heirs after paying the estate's debts, taxes, and expenses. Real property can, however, be taken from the heirs and sold by the executor, under a power-of-sale clause in the will or under a license to sell from the court, to pay debts of the estate. Unless a will provides otherwise, real property is usually the last asset to be used for the payment of estate debts.

Devise of Real Property

To my [relationship], [name], I give my real property consisting of a residence and lot located at [street address], City of ___________, County of _______________, State of _______________, and more particularly described as follows: [insert full description], if [he or she] survives me; but if [he or she] fails to so survive me, I give the above-described property to [relationship], [name], if [he or she] survives me.

General Legacy. A **general legacy** is a gift of money from the general assets of the estate. Gifts given under a residuary clause in a will (discussed later in this section) are also considered to be general. A gift of money in a will, in addition to being a general legacy, is known as a **pecuniary bequest.**

Pecuniary Bequest

I give to [name], of [address], City of ____________, County of ____________, State of ____________, the sum of __________ Dollars ($____), if [he or she] survives me.

Demonstrative Legacy. A **demonstrative legacy** is a gift of a specific sum of money with a direction that it be paid out of a particular fund. It differs from a specific legacy in that the gift is not taken away, i.e., adeemed, if there is no money in the fund. Instead, the general assets of the estate are used to fund the gift. Thus, a demonstrative legacy is a special kind of general legacy.

Demonstrative Legacy

I give to [name], of [address], City of ____________, County of ____________, State of ____________, if [he or she] survives me, the sum of ____________ Dollars ($____), to be paid out of the funds on deposit in my savings account No. ____________, in the [name of bank], at [address], City of ____________, County of __________, State of ____________.

Residuary Clause

A will should be written so that it allocates all of the testator's property. To do this, a will must contain a residuary clause. As described in chapter 3, the **residuary clause** distributes all of the testator's property that is not disposed of in other clauses of the will. It is a crucial clause because it acts as a safety net, catching any property that falls through the cracks or that is inadvertently omitted from the will. The *Jones* case demonstrates the importance of including a residuary clause.

LEGAL TERMS

ademption
Extinction; not being owned.

tangible personal property
Personal property that has substance and can be touched.

specific devise
A gift in a will of an identifiable parcel of real property.

personal representative
A person who carries out the terms of a will or administers an estate; an executor or administrator.

general legacy
A gift of money from the general assets of an estate.

pecuniary bequest
A gift of money in a will.

demonstrative legacy
A gift in a will of a certain sum of money with a direction that it be paid out of a particular fund.

residuary clause
The clause in a will that distributes all of the testator's property not disposed of in other clauses of the will.

MATTER OF ESTATE OF JONES
341 N.E.2d 565 (N.Y. 1975)

FACTS: The subject matter of this litigation was a collection of antique, rare, and original books left to the decedent by her father. The lower-court judge held that the rare book collection passed under Article Eleventh of the will. The appellant argues that the collection should pass under Article Fourteenth. The two articles follow:

> ELEVENTH. I give and bequeath all my personal property, consisting of furniture, carpets, curtains, china, linen, miscellaneous prints and pictures, antique chandeliers, Louis XVI mantel, mirror and fireback installed in drawing room in my residence, and miscellaneous bric-a-brac to said Harriet C. Weed to be held and enjoyed by her during the period of her natural life. . . . Upon the death of said Harriet C. Weed I give and bequeath to the Minneapolis Institute of Arts . . . .
>
> FOURTEENTH. All the rest, residue and remainder of my estate, both real and personal and wheresoever situate, not herein otherwise disposed of, I give, devise and bequeath to said Harriet C. Weed.

LEGAL ISSUE: Does a bequest of all of one's personal property followed by the words "consisting of" limit the bequest to only the items that follow?

COURT DECISION: Yes.

REASON: Nowhere in the detailed provisions of Article Eleventh is there to be found any reference to books or to the decedent's library. Nor is there any general language susceptible of the interpretation that Article Eleventh was intended as a catch-all paragraph designed to blanket in all tangible personal property not otherwise specifically described. The opening words of the paragraph, "all my personal property," standing alone, would have supported such an interpretation, but these words are then immediately limited by the particularizing phrase, "consisting of," followed by the detailed listing. The diction here was not, for instance, "all my personal property, including, etc.," in which event it could have been argued that the list of specified articles was not intended as an exclusive schedule.

Some situations in which a gift would pass according to the instructions in a residuary clause include:

1. When a gift is void (e.g., in some states when a gift is given to a witness to the will).
2. When a gift is revoked (e.g., when crossed out by the testator).
3. When a gift lapses (e.g., when the legatee or devisee dies before the testator), unless an anti-lapse statute (discussed in chapter 9) is available.

Without a residuary clause in such situations, the failed gift would pass according to the law of intestacy, as explained in chapter 3. Property (real and personal) would also pass according to the law of intestacy if a residuary clause is not included in a will.

No particular language is necessary for a residuary clause in a will. The clause may begin, "I give, devise, and bequeath the rest, residue, and remainder of my estate to . . . " or it may simply say, "I give the residue of my estate to . . . ." Similar variations are acceptable as well.

Residuary Clause

I direct that all the rest, residue, and remainder of my estate, real, personal, and mixed, of whatever kind and wherever situated, of which I may die seized and possessed, or in which I may have any interest or to which I may be entitled or over which I may have any power of appointment, including any lapsed or deemed legacies (herein called my "residuary estate"), shall be divided into [number] equal shares, to be disposed of as follows: ____________.

Miscellaneous Clauses

Wills are drawn to meet the particular needs of individuals, so there is no limit to the variety of clauses that can be included in a will. Also, new clauses are continually written to keep up with changes in state inheritance laws and federal tax laws. A few miscellaneous clauses that are sometimes found in wills are discussed here.

Adopted Children. As was discussed in chapter 3, modern statutes generally treat adopted children as strangers to their former relatives and consider adopting parents as though they were legitimate blood relatives to their adopted children. However, defining the terms *child* or *children* in a will helps to avoid any possible confusion.

Adopted Child
[20 AM. JUR. *Legal Forms* 2d § 266:278]

The word "child" or "children," as used in this will, includes any child or children lawfully adopted by me at any time before or after the execution of this will.

Community Property. **Community property** is property (except a gift or inheritance) acquired by either a husband or a wife during marriage. In community property states (see the map in figure 2-3), such property belongs to both spouses equally. When making a will in a community property state, it is often advisable to clearly state how the testator would like to distribute his or her share of community property.

LEGAL TERMS

community property
Property (except a gift or inheritance) acquired by the personal efforts of either spouse during marriage and which, by law, belongs to both spouses equally.

Community Property

I declare that all of the property of my estate which is hereby bequeathed and devised is my one-half interest in the community property of myself and my [wife or husband], [name].

Disinheritance. Some states have laws protecting certain heirs who are omitted from a will. For example, children and certain grandchildren who can prove that they were unintentionally disinherited by a parent may be able to inherit their intestate share from that parent or grandparent. This subject is discussed in detail in chapter 9. When family members are intentionally disinherited, it is recommended that an explicit declaration be made in the will reinforcing the testator's intention to disinherit those heirs who are not mentioned. A clause to that effect is as follows.

Disinheritance
[20 AM. JUR. *Legal Forms* 2d § 266:371]

I have, except as otherwise provided in this will, intentionally and with full knowledge, omitted to provide for my heirs who may be living at the time of my death, including any person who may become my heir by reason of marriage or otherwise after the date of the execution of this will.

No-Contest Provision. Sometimes testators believe that one or more disgruntled relatives might attempt to contest the provisions of the will. One way to address this possibility is to provide for such people in the will, and then to stipulate that anyone who contests the will shall lose all interests he or she would otherwise have under the will. A provision eliminating a will contestant from being a beneficiary under the will is called a **no-contest** or **in terrorem** (in terror or warning) **clause.**

No-Contest Clause

Every heir, legatee, devisee, or beneficiary under this will who shall contest in any court any provision of this instrument shall not be entitled to any devises, legacies, or benefits under this will or any codicil hereto or any trust created hereby, and any and all devises, legacies, and portions of the income or corpus of my estate otherwise provided to be paid to such person shall lapse and shall be paid, distributed, and passed in accordance with the residuary clause of this will.

In states that have adopted the UPC, the no-contest provision set forth here would be ineffective. Under the UPC, a provision in a will purporting to penalize any interested person for contesting the will or instituting other proceedings relating to the estate is unenforceable if probable cause exists for instituting proceedings. UPC § 3-905.

Incorporation by Reference. Occasionally it is desirable to refer in a will to another existing document and to make the other document a part of the will itself. This is known as **incorporation by reference** and may be done only if the other document is in existence at the time the will is executed.

Incorporation by Reference
[20 AM. JUR *Legal Forms* 2d § 266:301]

I hereby declare that it is my intention to, and I hereby, incorporate by reference into this will that certain document dated [date], which is now in existence, is located at [address], City of ________________, County of ________________, State of ____________, and is described as follows: ________________.

5.4 FIDUCIARY AND TAX PROVISIONS

Wills commonly have provisions naming fiduciaries, giving them special powers, and allowing them to serve without furnishing a surety on their official bond. In addition, many wills contain a clause that establishes the source for payment of death taxes.

Appointment of Fiduciaries

Paralegals will have many opportunities to deal with fiduciaries in the course of their work, because the nature of a fiduciary's responsibility often requires working with a law firm. **Fiduciaries** are persons appointed to oversee property that belongs to others and who, therefore, serve in a position of trust. In the case of a will, fiduciaries include executors, guardians, and trustees.

Executor. An important advantage of having a will is that the testator is allowed to select the person who will eventually settle the testator's estate. An **executor** (male) or an **executrix** (female) is a person who is named in a will to serve as the personal representative of the estate. His or her principal task is to gather the assets, pay the debts (including taxes and expenses of administration), and distribute the remainder according to the terms of the will.

Appointment of Executor or Executrix

I nominate and appoint my [relationship], [name], as executor of this will. If he [or she] shall fail to qualify or cease to serve, I nominate and appoint my [relationship], [name], to serve as executor in [his or her] place.

A testator should consider the items on this list when appointing an executor in a will (8 AM. JUR. *Legal Forms* 2d § 104:14):

LEGAL TERMS

no-contest clause (also called in terrorem clause)
A provision in a will eliminating a will contestant from being a beneficiary under the will.

incorporation by reference
A reference in a will to another existing document that makes the other document a part of the will itself.

fiduciary
A person who is appointed to serve in a position of trust, including an executor, administrator, guardian, and trustee.

executor
A male nominated in the will of a decedent to carry out the terms of the will.

executrix
A female nominated in the will of a decedent to carry out the terms of the will.

1. Individual or corporate executor
2. Willingness of appointee to serve
3. Competency of appointee
4. Familiarity of appointee with estate
5. Residency of appointee
6. Compensation
7. Bond requirement
8. Compatibility of appointee with heirs.

Guardian. Another advantage of having a will is that parents can name one or more guardians for their children in the event they die while their children are minors. There are two kinds of guardians: a guardian of the person and a guardian of the property. A **guardian of the person** has the care and custody of the child. This is given as a natural right to parents unless they are found to be unfit. In contrast, a **guardian of the property** has the responsibility of caring for the child's property until the child becomes an adult. Such a guardianship is not a natural right of a parent and may be given by a court to someone other than a parent. Language in a will naming a surviving spouse as guardian of the person and property of minor children, however, is usually followed by the court.

Appointment of Guardian

I appoint my spouse, [name], as guardian of the person and property of my minor children. If for any reason my spouse fails to qualify or ceases to serve as guardian of the person of any minor child of mine, I appoint my friend [or other relationship], [name], as such guardian in my spouse's place. If for any reason my spouse fails to qualify or ceases to serve as guardian of the property of any minor child of mine, I appoint my friend [or other relationship], [name], as such guardian in my spouse's place. No guardian of the person or property appointed in this will need furnish any surety on any official bond.

Trustee. When a will contains a trust, the trust is known as a **testamentary trust** (see chapter 6). The will appoints one or more trustees to administer the trust and often provides for the appointment of successor trustees in the event the first-named trustees are unable to serve. The subject matter of trusts is treated in depth in chapters 6 and 7.

Appointment of Trustee

I nominate and appoint [name] and [name] as trustees of all trusts created hereunder. If any trustee is unwilling, unable, or ceases to serve as trustee, [name] shall serve as successor trustee, and if the successor trustee or any other trustee is unwilling, unable, or ceases to serve as trustee, [name] shall serve as successor trustee.

If there is a vacancy in a trusteeship for which no successor has been appointed under the preceding paragraph, the adult beneficiaries entitled to receive a majority of the income may appoint in writing a successor trustee.

Powers of Fiduciaries

The power of a fiduciary to act without court approval is somewhat limited. Unless the will provides otherwise, fiduciaries must seek court approval to do what is necessary for proper administration of the estate. The way to eliminate the need for fiduciaries to seek court approval and thereby to reduce administration costs is to include a powers clause in the will.

Powers of Executor

My executor shall have full power of management and authority to sell, either at public or private sale, or to exchange, lease, pledge, or mortgage, in such manner and on such terms as such executor deems advisable, any or all property, real or personal, in my estate and to execute all deeds, assignments, mortgages, leases, or other instruments necessary or proper for these purposes; to compromise claims in favor of or against my estate on such terms as such executor deems advisable; to retain any securities or other property owned by me at the time of my death, although the same may not be considered a proper investment; to make distribution of property in kind, and for such purposes to determine the value of such property; and generally to do any and all such acts and things and execute any and all such written instruments with respect to such property as if the absolute owner thereof.

No Surety on Bond

Executors are required to post a bond before they can be appointed. By doing so, they become personally liable up to the amount of the bond in the event the estate is mishandled. In some states, unless the will provides otherwise, there must be a surety on the bond. A **surety** is either an insurance company or one or more individuals who stand behind the executor by agreeing to pay the amount of the bond in the event the executor becomes liable on the bond. The cost of a surety can be saved by providing in the will that the executor be exempt from giving surety on his or her bond.

No Surety on Bond

I direct that any executor be exempt from giving surety on his or her official bond. The word "executor" shall include any administrator of this will.

LEGAL TERMS

guardian of the person
One who has the care and custody of a child.

guardian of the property
One who has the responsibility of caring for a child's property until the child becomes an adult.

testamentary trust
A trust within the body of a will.

surety
One who stands behind a fiduciary by agreeing to pay the amount of the bond in the event the fiduciary becomes liable to pay it.

Tax Provision

The purpose of the tax provision in a will is to establish the source for payment of death taxes. The tax clause apportions the burden of federal and state death taxes among the estate assets.

In some states, if a tax clause is not used, taxes imposed on the probate property are paid from the residuary estate and taxes imposed on the non-probate property are paid from the non-probate property. Thus, the money to pay the taxes on legacies and devises would come from the residuary clause, the money to pay the taxes on jointly owned property would come from the joint property, and the money to pay the taxes on life insurance would come from the life insurance proceeds. A tax clause is included in a will when payment of estate taxes from a different source is preferable.

When everything in an estate goes to the same person or equally to a group of people, a direction to pay all death taxes from the residuary estate is usually appropriate. However, when items of vastly different value are given to different people, or when there is jointly owned property, life insurance, a pension plan, or a trust, the residuary estate may be an inappropriate source from which to pay death taxes.

Tax Clause

All inheritance, estate, and other taxes in the nature of death taxes, whether state or federal, with respect to any property passing under this Will shall be paid by my Executor out of the residue of my estate, and, in addition, my Executor may in his or her discretion pay from my residue all or any part of such taxes attributable to property not passing under this Will. My Executor shall have full power and authority to pay, compromise, or settle any or all such taxes at any time whether on present or future interests.

5.5 ENDING PARAGRAPHS

The ending paragraphs of a will include the testimonium clause, the attestation clause, and the self-proof clause.

Testimonium Clause

The **testimonium clause** (sometimes called the **signature clause**) is the clause that comes immediately before the testator's signature. It is used to establish the end of the will, to introduce the testator's signature, and to fix the date of execution of the instrument. Some attorneys like to have the testator read the testimonium clause out loud to the witnesses before signing it as a declaration that the instrument being signed is the testator's will.

Testimonium Clause

In Witness Whereof, I, the undersigned [name of testator or testatrix], do hereby declare that I willingly sign and execute this instrument as my last will, in the presence of each of the witnesses, who also sign below, and that I execute it as my free and voluntary act for the purposes herein expressed, this __________ day of __________, 19___.

Besides signing on the signature line below the testimonium clause, the testator should either sign or initial all of the other pages of the will. Although not a requirement, signing every page helps to prevent the substitution or loss of pages that come before the testimonium clause.

Only the original of a will should be signed. A will should never be executed in duplicate or triplicate. When more than one signed copy of a will is in existence, the court may require that all copies be produced for probate. If a copy cannot be produced, it may raise a presumption that the testator destroyed the copy with the intention of revoking the will. In the opening law office scenario, what seemed convenient to the client, Mr. Russell—having a signed copy of his will at both of his residences—could prove dangerously confusing.

LEGAL TERMS

testimonium clause (also called signature clause)
The clause in a will that falls immediately before the testator's signature.

A PRESIDENTIAL NEATNIK

George Washington, a man obsessed with neatness and meticulous detail, prepared his will without any legal assistance. He penned his 15-page will on both sides of watermarked parchment with strict adherence to a justified right margin. The document looks almost computer-produced: the lines are precisely spaced and identical in length; dashes or curved strokes fill any empty spaces; words at the end of lines are hyphenated improperly if necessary to maintain the justified margin; each page is signed directly below the center of the last line. No witnesses were necessary, because a handwritten testament without them was legally binding in the 1790s in that state.

George Washington (1732-1799), first President of the United States

Attestation Clause

The **attestation clause** is the clause that follows the testator's signature and precedes the witnesses' signatures. The clause is not required, but is customary and helps to ensure compliance with the law of executing a will. A will is usually executed properly when the directions in the attestation clause are followed precisely.

Attestation Clause

On this __________ day of __________, 19___, at [address], City of __________, County of __________, State of __________, the above-named testator signed the foregoing instrument in our presence, and at the same time declared it to be his last will and testament, and we do now at his request, and in his presence and in the presence of each other, hereto subscribe our names as witnesses hereof.

After the testator has signed the will in the witnesses' presence, it is customary to have one of the witnesses read the attestation clause aloud. When this is done, the witnesses sign below the attestation clause and write their home addresses beside their signatures. Witnesses may have to be contacted after the testator has died in order to prove the will. Neither the testator nor the witnesses should leave the room until all witnesses have finished signing the will in the testator's and each other's presence.

Attestation Clause (alternate form)

We, the undersigned witnesses, each do hereby declare in the presence of the aforesaid testatrix that the testatrix signed and executed this instrument as her last will in the presence of each of us, that she signed it willingly, that each of us hereby signs this will as witness in the presence of the testatrix, and that to the best of our knowledge the testatrix is eighteen (18) years of age or over, of sound mind, and under no constraint or undue influence.

Self-Proof Clause

In many states, if all of the heirs at law of a decedent do not assent to the allowance of a will, the testimony (or sworn affidavit) of one of the witnesses is required for the will to be allowed. This condition sometimes creates problems: heirs at law cannot always be located; witnesses may have moved or died. To alleviate these complications, some states have enacted a statute that allows a will to be proved without testimony if it is self-proved by affidavits of the testator and the witnesses made before an officer authorized to administer oaths (usually a notary public). The clause, located at the end of the will, is called a **self-proof clause**.

Self-Proof Clause

I, [name], the testator, sign my name to this instrument this _____ day of _________, 19____, and being first duly sworn, do hereby declare to the undersigned authority that I sign and execute this instrument as my last will and that I sign it willingly (or willingly direct another to sign for me), that I execute it as my free and voluntary act for the purposes therein expressed, and that I am eighteen (18) years of age or older, of sound mind, and under no constraint or undue influence.

____
Testator

We, _____________, ____________, the witnesses, sign our names to this instrument, being first duly sworn, and do hereby declare to the undersigned authority that the testator signs and executes this instrument as his last will and that he signs it willingly (or willingly directs another to sign for him), and that each of us, in the presence and hearing of the testator, hereby signs this will as witness to the testator's signing, and that to the best of our knowledge the testator is eighteen (18) years of age or older, of sound mind, and under no constraint or undue influence.

____
Witness

____
Witness

State of ___________________
County of _________________

Subscribed, sworn to, and acknowledged before me by _________, the testator, subscribed and sworn to before me by ___________, and _________, witnesses, this _________ day of ___________, 19____.

____
(Seal) Notary public

5.6 PROFESSIONAL GUIDELINES

Table 5-1 summarizes the principal clauses to be included in a will. Figure 5-3 shows each clause in a sample will. The paralegal should use

LEGAL TERMS

attestation clause
The clause in a will that follows the testator's signature and precedes the witnesses' signatures.

self-proof clause
A clause in a will containing affidavits of the testator and witnesses that allow a will to be proved without testimony.

Clause	Function
Exordium Clause	To identify the testator, state the domicile, declare the instrument to be a will, and revoke prior wills.
Funeral Directions	To specify the funeral and burial conditions.
Instructions to Pay Debts	To instruct the executor to pay debts (use cautiously).
Dispositive Provisions	To dispose of specific property.
Residuary Clause	To distribute all property not otherwise disposed of.
Appointment of Fiduciaries	To appoint the executor, guardian, and trustee.
Powers of Fiduciaries	To provide special powers to the fiduciaries.
No Surety on Bond	To avoid a surety on the bond.
Tax Clauses	To establish the source for payment of death taxes.
Testimonium Clause	To establish the end of the will, introduce the testator's signature, and fix the date of execution of the instrument.
Attestation Clause	To introduce the witnesses' signatures and insure compliance with the law of execution of wills.
Self-Proof Clause	To prove the will without testimony.

TABLE 5-1
Principal clauses in a will

these examples and the following list of considerations for guidance when assisting with drafting a client's will.

LAST WILL AND TESTAMENT
OF
STANLEY P. GOODCHILD

I, STANLEY P. GOODCHILD, of Rockport, County of Essex, Commonwealth of Massachusetts, make this my Last Will and Testament, hereby revoking all earlier wills and codicils.

Exordium clause

ARTICLE I

I direct that all of my funeral expenses and the cost of the administration of my estate be paid out of my residuary estate as soon as practicable after my death.

Funeral expenses and cost of administration clause

ARTICLE II

I give, devise, and bequeath all my estate, real, personal, and mixed, and wherever situated to my wife, GERALDINE R. GOODCHILD, if she is living on the thirtieth day after my death.

Dispositive provisions using a residuary clause

ARTICLE III

If my wife, GERALDINE R. GOODCHILD, is not living on the thirtieth day after my death, I give and devise all of my property of every kind and wherever located which I own at the time of my death or to which I am then in any way entitled in equal shares to my children, LUCINDA E. GOODCHILD and DANIEL H. GOODCHILD. If either of the foregoing beneficiaries shall predecease me, his or her share thereof shall pass to his or her issue then living by right of representation, and in default of such issue then his or her share shall pass to the surviving beneficiary, if living, and if not, to the surviving beneficiary's issue then living by right of representation.

Alternate residuary clause

ARTICLE IV

I may leave a memorandum stating my wishes with respect to the disposition of certain articles of tangible personal property, but such memorandum will be simply an expression of my wishes and shall not create any trust or obligation nor shall it be offered for probate as a part of this will.

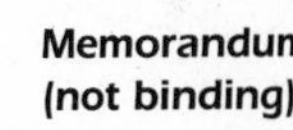

ARTICLE V

I nominate and appoint my wife, GERALDINE R. GOODCHILD, as executrix of this will. If she shall fail to qualify or cease to serve, I nominate and appoint my brother, CONRAD T. GOODCHILD, to serve as executor in her place.

Nomination of executor and alternate

ARTICLE VI

I direct that any executor be exempt from giving surety on his or her official bond. The word "executor" shall include any administrator of this will.

No surety on bond clause

FIGURE 5-3
Sample will with clauses defined

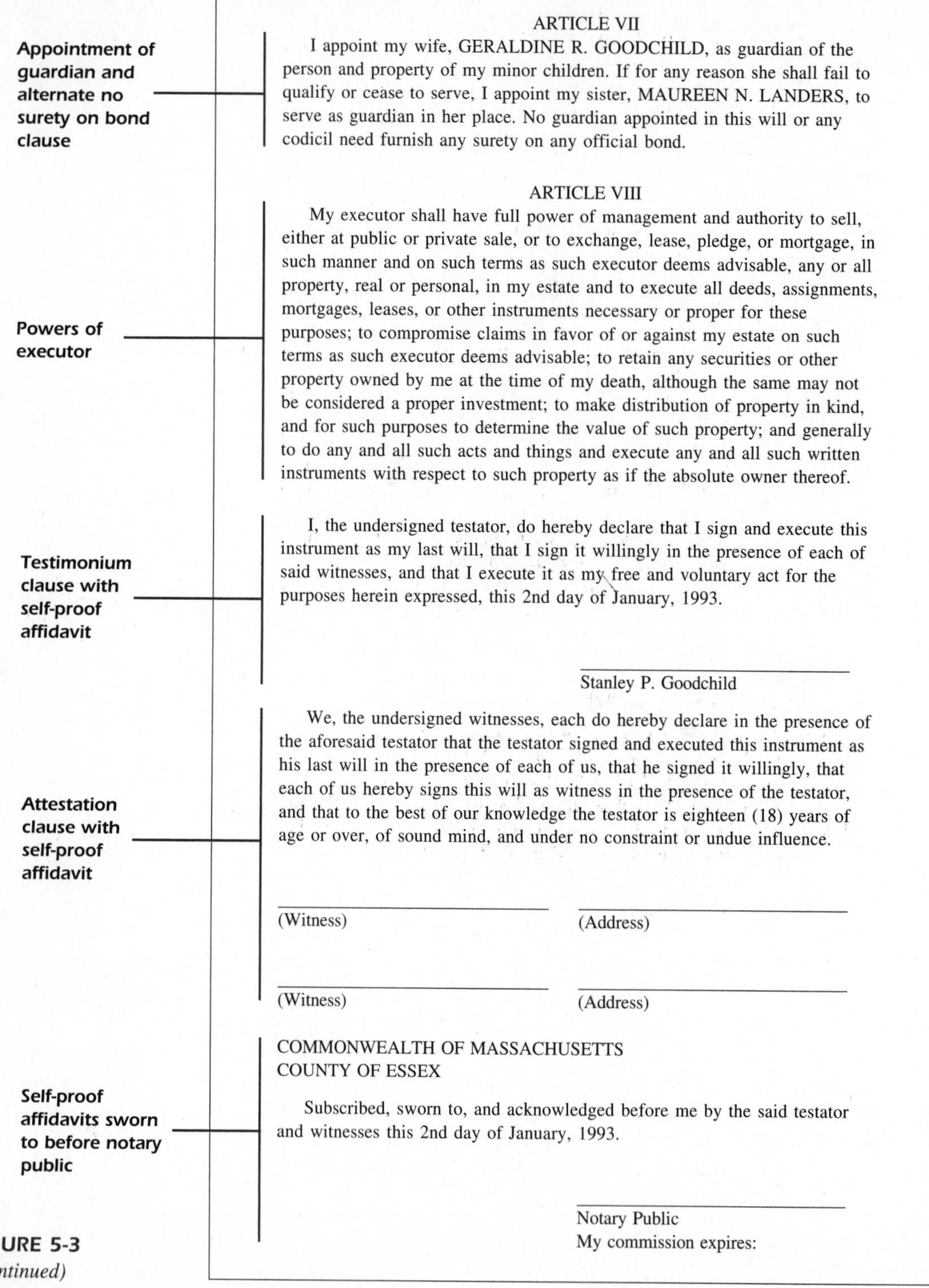

ARTICLE VII

I appoint my wife, GERALDINE R. GOODCHILD, as guardian of the person and property of my minor children. If for any reason she shall fail to qualify or cease to serve, I appoint my sister, MAUREEN N. LANDERS, to serve as guardian in her place. No guardian appointed in this will or any codicil need furnish any surety on any official bond.

ARTICLE VIII

My executor shall have full power of management and authority to sell, either at public or private sale, or to exchange, lease, pledge, or mortgage, in such manner and on such terms as such executor deems advisable, any or all property, real or personal, in my estate and to execute all deeds, assignments, mortgages, leases, or other instruments necessary or proper for these purposes; to compromise claims in favor of or against my estate on such terms as such executor deems advisable; to retain any securities or other property owned by me at the time of my death, although the same may not be considered a proper investment; to make distribution of property in kind, and for such purposes to determine the value of such property; and generally to do any and all such acts and things and execute any and all such written instruments with respect to such property as if the absolute owner thereof.

I, the undersigned testator, do hereby declare that I sign and execute this instrument as my last will, that I sign it willingly in the presence of each of said witnesses, and that I execute it as my free and voluntary act for the purposes herein expressed, this 2nd day of January, 1993.

____
Stanley P. Goodchild

We, the undersigned witnesses, each do hereby declare in the presence of the aforesaid testator that the testator signed and executed this instrument as his last will in the presence of each of us, that he signed it willingly, that each of us hereby signs this will as witness in the presence of the testator, and that to the best of our knowledge the testator is eighteen (18) years of age or over, of sound mind, and under no constraint or undue influence.

______________________ ______________________
(Witness) (Address)

______________________ ______________________
(Witness) (Address)

COMMONWEALTH OF MASSACHUSETTS
COUNTY OF ESSEX

Subscribed, sworn to, and acknowledged before me by the said testator and witnesses this 2nd day of January, 1993.

____
Notary Public
My commission expires:

FIGURE 5-3
(Continued)

Considerations When Drafting a Will

1. A carefully drawn will must be tailored to the individual and personal needs of the testator.
2. Provisions in a will that meet the needs of one testator are often inappropriate and sometimes dangerous for use in another testator's will.
3. Generic forms that meet the laws of one state are not always appropriate under the laws of other states.
4. A carefully drawn will minimizes death taxes to the fullest extent. For this reason, detailed information about the testator's family, assets, liabilities, business, and personal affairs must be obtained and examined by a attorney skilled in estate tax law.
5. As state laws and federal tax laws change, wills drawn under earlier laws must be reevaluated.
6. Because circumstances change in people's lives, testators are well advised to review their wills at least every five years or so to determine whether changes need to be made.

SUMMARY

5.1 The common elements of a will include opening paragraphs, the main body, fiduciary and tax provisions, and ending paragraphs.

5.2 When naming the testator in the exordium clause of a will, it is important to use all names that the testator uses in the ownership of all types of property. The probate court in the place where the testator was domiciled at the time of death has primary jurisdiction to administer the decedent's estate. A later will generally revokes an earlier will unless the later will states otherwise. Including funeral and burial arrangements or cremation instructions in a will is not recommended because such matters must be taken care of immediately, and the will may not be found or allowed by the court for several weeks. In addition, the courts in some states do not treat as binding the testator's wishes regarding funeral and burial arrangements. It might be dangerous to put a clause in a will instructing the executor to pay debts because it might require the payment of otherwise uncollectible debts as well as the payment of mortgages on the decedent's real property.

5.3 Gifts under a will may be specific, general, or demonstrative. An advantage of a specific legacy is that it is used up only after the general legacies have been depleted for the payment of debts. However, a specific legacy is subject to ademption. When people die owning real property solely, title passes to their heirs at the moment of death; personal property passes to the personal representative of the estate. The residuary clause is very important because it acts as a safety net, covering any property that is otherwise omitted from the will.

5.4 Wills often contain clauses that appoint executors, guardians, and trustees, and allow them to serve without furnishing a surety on their bond.

Wills often contain clauses that establish the source for payment of death taxes. A powers clause in a will helps to reduce the cost of administration by eliminating the need for the fiduciary to seek court approval when taking certain actions.

5.5 The testimonium clause falls immediately before the testator's signature. Only the original of a will should be signed—it should never be executed in duplicate or triplicate. The attestation clause precedes the witnesses' signatures. A will is usually executed properly when the directions in the attestation clause are followed precisely. In some states, a will may be proved without testimony if it contains a self-proof clause.

5.6 A carefully drawn will is tailored to an individual's needs, minimizes death taxes, and follows specific state laws. In addition, it is kept up to date to reflect changes in the law and changes in family circumstances.

QUESTIONS FOR REVIEW

1. Why is it important, when drafting a will, to use all the names that the testator uses in the ownership of real and personal property?
2. What court has primary jurisdiction to administer a decedent's estate?
3. What words can be written in a will to prevent a subsequent marriage from revoking the will?
4. Why is it not necessarily preferable to include funeral and burial arrangements in a will?
5. What is one advantage and one disadvantage of a specific legacy?
6. When and to whom does title to real property pass when a sole owner dies?
7. How does a demonstrative legacy differ from a specific legacy?
8. When a decedent dies testate and there is no residuary clause in the will, who receives property that is omitted from the will?
9. What is the difference between a guardian of the person and a guardian of the property?
10. Why is a clause giving powers to a fiduciary helpful?

CASES TO DISCUSS

1. Article SIXTH of Barnett's codicil provided: "I direct that all the rest, residue and remainder of my estate, including my home and its contents, of whatsoever nature and wheresoever situate, be sold and liquidated and I give and bequeath such remainder, including any legacy which may have lapsed or otherwise not be distributable, to the Federation of Jewish Philanthropies of New York." Did this language

create a specific, demonstrative, or residuary gift to the Federation? Explain. *In re Estate of Barnett,* 408 N.Y.S.2d 295 (N.Y. 1978).

2. In her will, Helen Nesmith left all of her tangible personal property to Frederic T. Greenhalge, II, except those items which she designated by a memorandum to be given to others living at the time of her death. Before executing two codicils to her will, she had drafted a "memorandum" which listed 49 specific bequests of tangible personal property to be made upon her death. She had also written in a notebook entitled "List to be given," the following words: "Ginny Clark farm picture hanging over fireplace. Ma's room." Ginny Clark, a neighbor and close friend, had admired the picture, and Nesmith had told two nurses that the picture would go to Clark. Will Clark receive the farm picture under Nesmith's will? Why or why not? *Clark v. Greenhalge,* 582 N.E.2d 949 (Mass. 1991).
3. Hanna LeSueur had lived for at least 50 years in Lakewood, Cuyahoga County, Ohio. At the age of 96, after being diagnosed as having chronic dementia, she was moved to a Lucas County nursing home, where she died in less than three months. Her will declared her to be a resident of Lakewood, and her funeral services and burial were there also. Her niece, Marjorie, who lived in Fulton County, filed the will for probate in the Fulton County Court of Common Pleas. Does that court have jurisdiction to settle the estate? Explain. *LeSueur v. Robinson,* 557 N.E.2d 796 (Ohio 1988).

SHARPENING YOUR PROFESSIONAL SKILLS

1. Refer to the law office scenario at the beginning of this chapter and draft the initial part of an exordium clause identifying Jack Russell.
2. Refer to the opening law office scenario and answer the following questions: (a) What further questions might Angela Clark ask Jack Russell to determine his domicile? (b) What might Angela Clark tell Jack Russell about his desire to be cremated? (c) How should Angela Clark respond to Mr. Russell's request to sign two copies of his will?
3. Draft an exordium clause for a person who plans to be married and wishes to leave a gift in the will to the future spouse.
4. Obtain a copy of a deed to someone's real property. Using the property description in the deed, draft a clause for a will that devises the specific property to another person.
5. Jack Russell has $15,000 in Account No. 007 64 329 at the Ocean City Savings Bank. (a) Draft a clause for his will leaving a specific legacy of $10,000 to his daughter, Mildred F. Russell. (b) Draft a clause for his will leaving a demonstrative legacy of $10,000 to his son, Michael S. Russell.

6. Jack Russell wishes to leave the residue of his estate in equal shares to his two children, Mildred and Michael. Mildred is adopted. Look up your state statute on adopted children. (a) Cite the statutory reference where it is found. (b) Determine whether it would be necessary to include in the will the clause about adopted children discussed in this chapter.
7. Draft a testimonium clause and an attestation clause for the will of Jack Russell, using the information found in the opening vignette of this chapter.
8. Does the law of your state provide for the self-proving of a will? If so, (a) give the statutory reference where the provision is found, and (b) draft a self-proof clause following your state statute.

SECTION TWO

Trusts

CHAPTER 6
Trusts

"Don't worry, I'm going to outlive those bastards."

Thurgood Marshall

OUTLINE

LAW OFFICE SCENARIO

Lisa Brewer, a legal secretary, entered the office of Tiffany Casey, a paralegal in the law firm of Knight and Francis.

"Hi, Tiffany," Lisa said. "Have you got a minute?"

"Sure. Come on in!"

"I'm working on a living trust for Attorney Fitz, that new attorney who just started Monday . . . "

"Oh, yes, the young one who's working with Muriel Knight, right?"

"Yes. He's just out of law school," Lisa replied. "He went to court today with Attorney Knight, so I can't ask him about this trust."

"What's the problem?"

"Well, our client is naming his son as the sole trustee, and, according to the file, the son is a minor. I don't know if Mr. Fitz knows that."

"Who is the beneficiary?" Tiffany asked.

"The same son." Lisa answered. "He's the sole trustee and the sole beneficiary."

"It sounds like there may be a problem there," Tiffany countered. "You had better ask Mr. Fitz about it."

"I think I'll set it up the way Mr. Fitz told me to and print out a draft copy for him to look over tomorrow."

"That's a good idea," Tiffany agreed.

"You look busy today," Lisa observed.

"I am busy. Our client wrote his own will before he died. Listen to this: 'I leave $20,000 to my brother, Carl, and I desire that Carl take care of my sister, Diane, until she reaches the age of 25.' Attorney Knight wants me to research this to see if it creates a trust."

"It sounds interesting," Lisa observed.

"When I'm through with that, I have to go back to a trust that one of our clients had prepared years ago by another firm. The client wants to revoke it, and Attorney Francis put it on my desk with a note to go through the trust with a fine-tooth comb to see if it can be revoked."

"Do you think it can be?" Lisa queried.

"I've read it through once, and there is nothing that says that it's irrevocable," Tiffany responded, "but I haven't found anything that says it can be revoked, either."

"Good luck, and enjoy your reading!"

6.1 THE TRUST ARRANGEMENT

Paralegals who work with trusts will need to be familiar with terminology that reflects the varied complexities of trust arrangements. Simply stated, a trust is an arrangement whereby a person called the **settlor** gives property to a **trustee** (one or more individuals) who holds the property in trust for the benefit of the **beneficiary** (one or more individuals) according to the terms of the trust instrument. (See figure 6-1.) The property held in

LEGAL TERMS

settlor (also called donor, grantor, and trustor)
Person who establishes a trust.

trustee
Person who holds legal title in trust for the benefit of a beneficiary.

beneficiary (also called cestui que trust)
Person holding equitable or beneficial title of a trust.

trust is known by different names including the **trust res**, the **trust corpus**, the **trust principal**, the **trust property**, and the **trust fund**, and may include cash, securities, real estate, etc.

LEGAL TERMS

trust res (trust corpus, trust principal, trust property, trust fund)
Property that is held in trust.

trustor (donor, grantor, settlor)
Person who establishes a trust.

cestui que trust
The beneficiary of a trust.

6.2 PARTIES TO A TRUST

The parties to a trust are the **settlor** (also known as the **trustor**, the **grantor**, or the **donor**), the trustee, and the beneficiary (or **cestui que trust**).

The Settlor

To be a settlor of a trust, a person must be competent. This means, generally, that the person must be capable of making a will or entering into

CALIFORNIA STATUTORY WILL
WITH TRUST PROVISIONS

Notice to the person who signs this will:

1. This form contains a trust for your descendants. If you do not want to create a trust, do not use this form.

2. It may be in your best interest to consult with a California lawyer because this statutory will has serious legal effects on your family and property.

3. This will does not dispose of property which passes on your death to any person by operation of law or by any contract. For example, the will does not dispose of joint tenancy assets or your spouse's share of community property, and it will not normally apply to proceeds of life insurance on your life or your retirement plan benefits.

4. This will is not designed to reduce death taxes or any other taxes. You should discuss the tax results of your decisions with a competent tax advisor.

5. *You cannot change, delete, or add words to the face of this California statutory will.* You may revoke this California statutory will and you may amend it by codicil.

6. If there is anything in this will that you do not understand, you should ask a lawyer to explain it to you.

7. The full text of this California statutory will, the definitions and rules of construction, the property disposition clauses, and the mandatory clauses are contained in the probate code of California.

8. The witnesses to this will should not be people who may receive property under this will. You should carefully read and follow the witnessing procedure described at the end of this will. All of the witnesses must watch you sign this will.

9. You should keep this will in your safe-deposit box or other safe place.

10. This will treats most adopted children as if they are natural children.

11. If you marry or divorce after you sign this will, you should make and sign a new will.

FIGURE 6-1
Sample will with trust provisions. Form courtesy of Forms Inc., La Jolla, CA

a contract. A minor or someone who is insane, for example, would not have the capacity to be the settlor of a trust. In addition to being competent, a settlor must own the property that is to be placed in trust. When property is already held in trust, only the beneficiary has the power to establish another trust in the property.

CALIFORNIA STATUTORY WILL WITH TRUST PROVISIONS OF

____
Insert Your Name

ARTICLE 1. DECLARATION

1.1. This is my will and I revoke any prior wills and codicils.

ARTICLE 2. DISPOSITION OF MY PROPERTY

2.1. PERSONAL AND HOUSEHOLD ITEMS

I give all my furniture, furnishings, household items, personal automobiles and personal items to my spouse, if living; otherwise they shall be divided equally among my children who survive me.

2.2. CASH GIFT TO A PERSON OR CHARITY

I make the following cash gift to the person or charity in the amount stated in words and figures in the box which I have completed and signed. If I fail to sign in the box, no gift is made. If the person mentioned does not survive me, or the charity designated does not accept the gift, then no gift is made. No death tax shall be paid from this gift.

____
Full Name of Person or Charity to Receive Cash Gift • Please Print • Name One only

______________________________ $__________
Amount of Gift Written Out and in Numbers

____
Signature of Testator

2.3. ALL MY OTHER ASSETS

I adopt only one Property Disposition Clause in this paragraph 2.3 by writing my signature in the box next to the title of the Property Disposition Clause I wish to adopt. I sign in only one box. I write the words "not used" in the remaining boxes. If I sign in more than one box or if I fail to sign in any box, the property will be distributed as if I did not make a will.

PROPERTY DISPOSITION CLAUSES
Select One

(a) To my spouse if living; if not living, then in one trust to provide for the support and education of my children and the descendants of any deceased child until I have no living child under 21 years of age.	(b) To my children and the descendants of any deceased child in one trust to provide for their support and education until I have no living child under 21 years of age. I leave nothing to my spouse, if living.

ARTICLE 3. NOMINATIONS OF EXECUTOR, TRUSTEE, AND GUARDIAN

3.1. EXECUTOR
(Name at Least One.)

I nominate the person or institution named in the first box of this paragraph 3.1 to serve as executor of this will. If that person or institution does not serve, then I nominate the others to serve in the order I list them in the other boxes.

First Executor.	Second Executor.	Third Executor.

FIGURE 6-1
(Continued)

3.2. TRUSTEE

Name at least one.

Because it is possible that after I die my property may be put into a trust, I nominate the person or institution named in the first box of this paragraph 3.2 to serve as trustee of that trust. If that person or institution does not serve, then the others shall serve in the order I list them in the other boxes.

First Trustee	Second Trustee	Third Trustee

3.3. GUARDIAN

If you have a child under 18 years of age, you should name at least one guardian of the child's person and at least one guardian of the child's property. The guardian of the child's person and the guardian of the child's property may, but need not, be the same. An individual can serve as guardian of either the person or the property, or as guardian of both. An institution can serve only as guardian of the property.

If a guardian is needed for any child of mine, then I nominate the individual named in the first box of this paragraph 3.2 to serve as guardian of the person of that child, and I nominate the individual or institution named in the second box of this paragraph 3.2 to serve as guardian of the property of that child. If that person or institution does not serve, then the others shall serve in the order I list them in the other boxes.

First Guardian of the Person.	First Guardian of the Property.
Second Guardian of the Person.	Second Guardian of the Property.
Third Guardian of the Person.	Third Guardian of the Property.

3.4. BOND

My signature in this box means that a bond is not required for any individual (a) executor, (b) trustee, or (c) guardian named in this will. If I do not sign in this box, then a bond is required for each of those persons as set forth in the Probate Code.

I sign my name to this California Statutory Will on ______________ at ______________, ______________.
Date City State

____
Signature of Testator

FIGURE 6-1
(Continued)

The Trustee

A valid trust must have a provision for the office of trustee, but it is not necessary that someone be nominated for that position. The court will not allow a trust to fail for lack of a trustee. When no one is nominated or the nominee is deceased, incompetent, or declines the position, and no provision for a replacement is provided, the court has the power to appoint a trustee.

STATEMENT OF WITNESSES

You must use two adult witnesses and three would be preferable.

Each of us declares under penalty of perjury under the laws of California that the testator signed this California statutory will in our presence, all of us being present at the same time, and we now, at the testator's request, in the testator's presence, and in the presence of each other, sign below as witnesses, declaring that the testator appears to be of sound mind and under no duress, fraud, or undue influence.

Signature ______________ Residence Address: ______________
Print Name
Here: ______________ ______________

Signature ______________ Residence Address: ______________
Print Name
Here: ______________ ______________

Signature ______________ Residence Address: ______________
Print Name
Here: ______________ ______________

FIGURE 6-1
(Continued)

This form, established by the California state legislature, contains a testamentary trust.

Generally, anyone having the capacity to manage his or her own affairs can be a trustee. This usually excludes someone under a legal disability, such as a minor, a mentally ill person, or a person under guardianship. It is interesting to note, however, that a minor could serve as a trustee and, upon reaching full age, ratify all acts done during minority. A trustee must also be a fit person to perform that task. Whether or not someone is fit to be a trustee lies in the discretion of the court. Banks often serve as trustees because of their investment expertise and probability of continued existence.

The sole trustee of a trust cannot be the sole beneficiary of that trust. However, a trustee can be a beneficiary by combining with other trustees or other beneficiaries. For example, a sole trustee can be a beneficiary if one or more additional beneficiaries are included. Similarly, a trustee can be a sole beneficiary if an additional person serves as a co-trustee. Table 6-1 summarizes these conditions.

Duties of Trustee. Trustees have a **fiduciary relationship** with their beneficiaries. This is a relationship of trust and confidence requiring the exercise of a high degree of honesty and good faith. Trustees must be loyal to their trust at all times: they cannot profit personally from the trust property; they cannot commingle trust property with their own property; they must treat their beneficiaries fairly; and they cannot delegate the management of the trust to others. Trustees must also keep accurate accounts, showing receipts and disbursements of principal and income. In addition, trustees must exercise reasonable care and prudence in the management of the trust property.

Powers of Trustee. Although trustees have some implied powers and various powers provided by state statutes, the principal powers of a trustee are found in the "powers clause" of the instrument that created the trust. For this reason, trustees should be familiar with the trust instrument that created

LEGAL TERMS

fiduciary relationship
A relationship of trust and confidence requiring the exercise of a high degree of honesty and good faith.

WHO MAY BE A TRUSTEE

	Trustee	Beneficiary
One may be a sole trustee for another.	A*	B**
One may be a trustee with another for a third person.	A and B	C***
One may be a sole trustee for oneself and another.	A	A and B
One may be a trustee with another for oneself alone.	A and B	A
One may be a sole trustee for oneself for life if the trust property goes to another at death.	A	A for life; then B
One may be a sole trustee for another for the other's life with the trust property going to oneself at the other's death.	A for B's life	A at B's death

WHO MAY NOT BE A TRUSTEE

	Trustee	Beneficiary
One may *not* be a sole trustee for oneself alone.	A	A

**Oneself*

***Another person or persons*

****A third person*

TABLE 6-1
Conditions for Trusteeship

the trust under which they operate. Similarly, persons dealing with trustees may wish to examine the trust instrument to determine the extent of the trustees' power, especially when purchasing real property from a trustee.

The purposes of a trust can sometimes be thwarted by putting limitations on trustees, so some attorneys and estate planners recommend that settlors select their trustees carefully and then give them very broad powers to perform their duties. The following is an example of a broad powers clause that could be used in a testamentary trust.

> **[17 AM. JUR. *Legal Forms* 2d § 251:665]**
>
> Trustee shall have the power to do all acts, institute all proceedings, and exercise all rights, powers, and privileges that an absolute owner of the trust property would have, subject always to the discharge of trustee's fiduciary obligations.

Co-trustees must usually join in all fiduciary activity unless a state statute or the trust instrument allows individual trustee action. This is because trustees' powers, like their title, are held jointly by co-trustees.

The Beneficiary

A beneficiary is an essential party to a trust. Without one, a trust cannot exist. It is not necessary that a particular person be named as beneficiary; it is merely necessary that a beneficiary be capable of being identified and ascertained. At all times during the life of the trust, it must be possible to determine the person or persons for whose benefit the trust was created. The beneficiary need not be in existence when the trust is created. Thus, trusts for the benefit of unborn children are valid.

Any person who is capable of owning property may be a beneficiary of a trust. Individuals of any age or capacity, corporations, and governmental bodies fall into that category. In some states, unincorporated associations may be beneficiaries; in other states, they may not because they are not legal entities. Beneficiaries are not always human beings. Trusts for the benefit of animals and for the upkeep of cemetery lots have been allowed by the courts.

A sole beneficiary of a trust may be a co-trustee with others, but may not be the sole trustee of that trust. When an instrument is drawn naming the sole trustee as the sole beneficiary, the trust fails, and the named trustee becomes the owner of the property outright. The reason for this outcome relates to the crucial distinction between legal title and equitable title, discussed in § 6.3.

6.3 CREATION OF A TRUST

When a trust is established, the trustee receives the **legal title** to the property—that is, full and absolute ownership, but without a beneficial interest (i.e., without any personal gain or profit). The beneficiary, on the other hand, holds what is designated as the **equitable title** (also known as **beneficial title**), which is the right to profit or benefit from the property.

LEGAL TERMS

legal title
Full, absolute ownership without a beneficial interest.

equitable title (also called beneficial title)
The right to the beneficial enjoyment of trust property.

beneficial title (also called equitable title)
The right to the beneficial enjoyment of trust property.

"TO MY BELOVED DOG, ROVER . . . "

Although guppies, ferrets, pythons, and cockatoos have been named, dogs and cats are the usual beneficiaries in the unusual bequests of pet lovers. Perhaps the largest canine inheritance was that from Eleanor Ritchey, heiress to the Quaker State Refining Corporation, who willed $4.5 million to her 150 dogs in 1968. By the time an agreement was reached with family members who had contested the will, the escrow estate had increased to $14 million. Seventy-seven of the dogs had died, but the remaining dogs were awarded $9 million, or $123,287.69 each for food, grooming, and housing. Two million dollars went to family members; the remainder served as legal fees.

A trust can be created either by a conveyance in trust or by a declaration of trust. In a conveyance in trust, the legal title moves away from the settlor to the trustee. In a declaration of trust, the legal title is retained by the settlor, who becomes the trustee.

Conveyance in Trust

When a trust is created by a **conveyance in trust**, the settlor transfers legal title to someone else—a trustee. The settlor may either retain the equitable title to the property or transfer it to someone else. By definition, whoever has equitable title is the beneficiary of the trust. A conveyance in trust is usually created by a trust agreement (a contract) between the settlor and the trustee. The trust agreement describes the trust property, gives directions for distribution of the principal and income, and spells out the duties and powers of the trustee.

Declaration of Trust

A **declaration of trust** is a trust in which the settlor transfers the equitable title to the trust property to someone else and retains the legal title. (See figure 6-2.) It is often referred to as a *one-party trust.* The settlor declares that he or she is now holding the property in trust for the benefit of someone else—the beneficiary. The settlor thus becomes the trustee.

LEGAL TERMS

conveyance in trust
Trust created by a settlor transferring legal title to trust property to a trustee for the benefit of either the settlor or someone else.

declaration of trust
Trust in which a settlor transfers equitable title to trust property to someone else and retains legal title.

DECLARATION OF TRUST
[17 AM. JUR. *Legal Forms* 2d § 251:21]

This declaration of trust made on ________, 19___, by __________, of [address], City of ______________, County of ______________, State of ____________, hereinafter referred to as trustor.

Section One
Declaration of Trust

I, ______________, as trustor, have assigned myself as trustee and hereby declare that I hold in trust the securities described in Schedule A attached hereto and incorporated herein by this reference, and that I and my successor trustee will hold such securities, and all substitutions therefor and additions thereto, as the trust estate, for the use and benefit of _________, of [address], City of ____________, County of ____________, State of __________, hereinafter referred to as beneficiary, for the following purposes and on the following terms and conditions:

FIGURE 6-2
Sample declaration of trust

Section Two
Purpose of Trust

Trustee shall receive and collect the income, profits, interest, and dividends from the trust estate and, after first deducting all taxes, commissions, and other charges against the same, shall pay the income to beneficiary during the period of his [or her] natural life up to _________, 19___.

Section Three
Termination of Trust

On ___________, 19___, or on the death of beneficiary, whichever shall first occur, the trust hereby created shall terminate and the principal of the trust estate shall be paid to _________, of [address], City of _______, County of ___________, State of ___________, absolutely and free from any claim hereunder.

Section Four
Successor Trustee

On my death, resignation, or inability to act as trustee, I name _______, of [address], City of _____________, County of _____________, State of _____________, as successor trustee hereunder, and such successor trustee shall have all the powers and discretions herein given trustee without any further conveyance or transfer of the trust estate.

Any determination of my inability to act as trustee hereunder shall be made (a) by an adjudication of my incompetency by a court of competent jurisdiction, or, in the absence of such adjudication, (b) by the delivery to successor trustee of a written certificate stating that for mental or physical reasons I am incapable of properly managing my business affairs, and executed by any physician currently attending me and by my [spouse and children] who are then living and legally competent. Successor trustee may rely conclusively on any such certificate.

Section Five
Powers and Duties of Trustee

1. *Resignation.* Any trustee may resign by giving ____ days' written notice to me or, if I am not then living or legally competent, by giving such notice to beneficiary. If no successor trustee has been appointed or designated by me hereunder, then beneficiary may appoint any bank or trust company as successor trustee.
2. *Acceptance of Accounts.* With my consent, or with beneficiary's consent if I am not then living or legally competent, any successor trustee may accept without liability the accounts rendered and the assets delivered to it by any predecessor trustee, and any such consent shall discharge the predecessor trustee.
3. *Statement of Receipts and Disbursements.* Trustee shall render a statement of its receipts and disbursements to me, whenever requested by me, and at least [annually] to beneficiary. After my death, beneficiary may approve at any time such statements with the same

FIGURE 6-2
(Continued)

effect as their approval by a court of competent jurisdiction would have.

4. *Compensation.* The successor trustee herein named shall be entitled to reasonable compensation for services performed by him [or her], and shall be entitled to reimbursement for expenses incurred by him [or her] in the administration of the trust estate.
5. *Court Approval; Bond.* No trustee shall be required to obtain authority from, or the approval of, any court in the exercise of any power conferred upon him [or her] unless such authority or approval is specially required by law and may not be hereby waived.
   No trustee, in the absence of an overriding statute or order, shall be required to furnish any bond or other security, or make any reports or accountings to any court.
6. *Specific Powers of Trustee.* Subject to the foregoing, trustee shall have the following specific powers with respect to the trust estate, in addition to the powers herein and by law conferred upon him [or her]: [enumerate specific powers].

Section Six
Powers Reserved to Trustor

I shall have the right from time to time during my lifetime, by written instrument delivered to the then-acting trustee, to amend or revoke this declaration of trust in whole or in part. However, if a trustee other than myself is serving hereunder, no amendment may change his, her, or its powers, duties, and discretions without such trustee's consent.

If, while I am acting as trustee, any asset of the trust estate is sold and the proceeds are not put in my name as trustee, or if any asset of the trust estate at any time is in my individual name, any such asset shall be conclusively deemed to have been withdrawn from the trust estate.

So long as I am living and legally competent, I shall have the right and power at any time to appoint any additional trustee or trustees, and to remove any trustee with or without the appointment of a successor.

If this declaration is revoked in whole or in part, the trust estate subject to such revocation shall be delivered to me or on my order.

Section Seven
Governing Law

This declaration of trust shall be governed by, and interpreted in accordance with, the laws of the State of ____________.

IN WITNESS WHEREOF, I have executed this declaration of trust at [designate place of execution] on the day and year first above written.

[Signature of Trustor]

[Signature of Witness]

FIGURE 6-2
(Continued)

Trust Formalities

Although trusts are usually created by some written document, such as a deed, a will, a trust agreement, or some other instrument, a writing is not always necessary to create a trust. **Parol** (oral) trusts dealing with personal property are generally enforceable. Some states require that notice be given to the beneficiary by the grantor when an informal, oral declaration of trust for personal property is made in order to establish the intent necessary to create a trust.

In contrast, trusts dealing with real property must be in writing under many state laws. For example, the Massachusetts statute reads: "No trust concerning land, except such as may arise or result by implication of law, shall be created or declared unless by a written instrument signed by the party creating or declaring the trust or by his attorney." Mass. Gen. L. c. 203, § 1.

Marilyn Monroe. Photo courtesy of AP/World Wide Photos.

"GOODBYE, NORMA JEAN. . . "

Before she died in 1962 at age 36 from an overdose of sleeping pills, the legendary actress Marilyn Monroe carefully provided for those closest to her. She established a trust of $100,000 to maintain the institutional care of her mentally ill mother. Neither of her famous ex-husbands (baseball star Joe DiMaggio or playwright Arthur Miller) were named in her will, nor did she have any children to endow. Instead, the major portion of her estate went to her acting mentor, Lee Strasberg; her psychiatrist, Marianne Kris, also inherited a share. Monroe's estate continues to receive more than $1 million a year in licensing fees for use of her image, etc. The beneficiaries of the original inheritors receive the proceeds: Kris's share goes to a children's psychiatric institute in London, and Strasberg's portion goes to his surviving widow . . . whom he married six years *after* Monroe's death.

6.4 EXPRESS TRUSTS

Express trusts, sometimes referred to as **voluntary trusts**, are trusts that are created in explicit terms, either oral or written. No particular words, such as "trust" or "trustee," are required to create an express trust. However, the intent to create a trust by the settlor is essential and must be evident. The intention that the legal title be vested in one person, to be held in some manner or for some purpose on behalf of another, must be apparent. To be valid, an express trust must include the following elements: (1) a competent settlor, (2) the provision for a trustee, (3) a trust res, and (4) one or more designated beneficiaries. The testamentary trust and the living trust are the most common forms of express trusts.

Testamentary Trusts

A **testamentary trust** is a trust in which the trust property is bequeathed or devised in a will to a trustee for the benefit of a beneficiary. (See figure 6-3.) It is a conveyance in trust created by will and has no effect until the testator(rix) dies. The will must clearly express the testator(rix)'s intent to create a trust by separating the legal title from the equitable title and by conveying the legal title to a trustee for the beneficiary's benefit.

Like the will itself, a testamentary trust is under the control and supervision of the probate court after the death of the testator(rix). The trust becomes a matter of public record, open for anyone to see once the testator dies, and the trustee is required to file annual accounts with the probate court.

LEGAL TERMS

parol
Oral.

express trust (also called voluntary trust)
Trust that is created in explicit terms, either oral or written.

testamentary trust
Trust within the body of a will.

TESTAMENTARY TRUST
FOR SUPPORT, MAINTENANCE,
AND EDUCATION OF CHILDREN
[17 AM. JUR. *Legal Forms* 2d § 251:239]

I give the residue of my estate, in trust, to [name of trustee], of [address], City of _______________, County of _______________, State of ___________. If [he or she] should fail or refuse to serve, or cease to serve, as trustee, then to [name of alternate or successor trustee], of [address], City of ___________, County of ___________, State of ___________. The trust hereby created shall be held, administered, and distributed in the following manner:

1. *Trustee's Discretionary Payment among Beneficiaries.* I direct trustee to pay or apply so much of the net income [if desired, add: and principal] of this trust to the support, maintenance, and education of any of my children who have not reached twenty-two (22) years of age as in the discretion of trustee seems necessary for the proper support, maintenance, and education of such children.

FIGURE 6-3
Sample testamentary trust

In making any payment or application, I direct that trustee take into consideration other resources and income of my children. I direct trustee to accumulate all undistributed net income of the trust property and add it to the principal.

In exercising [his or her] discretion in making such payments of net income [if appropriate, add: or principal], trustee is not limited to making equal distribution to all the beneficiaries, but may make such distributions, considering the balance remaining in the trust and the estimated future requirements of the beneficiaries, as appear necessary under the circumstances.

Trustee shall charge support payments made under this provision against the trust estate, rather than against the ultimate distributive share of the beneficiary for whose benefit the support payments are made.

2. *Division of Trust Estate When All Children Have Reached Twenty-two Years of Age.* When all my children have either attained twenty-two (22) years of age or died prior thereto, I direct trustee to divide the trust estate into a number of shares equal to the number of my living children and deceased children having surviving issue. I direct trustee to divide the shares, giving one share to each living child, and one share to the surviving issue of each deceased child, per stirpes.
3. *"Education" Defined.* The term "education" as used in the trust provisions of this will includes both college and post-graduate study by the beneficiary concerned at an accredited institution of his or her choice. Distribution by trustee from the trust of amounts for "education" shall include reasonable living and travel expenses of the beneficiary concerned.
4. *Disposition of Trust Principal When All Beneficiaries Die Before Time Prescribed for Distribution.* If when I die, or if at any time before distribution of my trust estate as herein otherwise provided, my [wife or husband] and all my issue are deceased, and no provision has been made in this will governing the disposition in such case of the trust estate herein established, I direct that such trust, or whatever portion of it remains, be distributed to those who are at that time my heirs.
5. *Saving Clause Avoiding Rule Against Perpetuities.* Each trust provided for in this will shall in any event terminate 21 years after the death of the last to survive of [my wife or my husband or other named beneficiaries] and my issue living at the time of my death. On such termination, the trust estate, both income and principal, shall be distributed among the income beneficiaries of the trust in the proportions in which they are entitled to receive the income. If the respective amounts of income which the beneficiaries are at that time entitled to receive are not definite, I direct trustee to distribute the trust estate to such of my issue as are entitled to receive income at that time, per stirpes. If at that time I have no issue surviving, the trust estate shall be distributed to the beneficiaries then entitled to the trust income, in equal shares.

FIGURE 6-3
(Continued)

For a testamentary trust to become operative, the will must first be proved and allowed, and letters testamentary must be issued by the court. Next, the assets of the estate must be gathered by the executor(rix), and the debts, taxes, and costs of administration paid. Meanwhile, the person named in the will as trustee, or someone else if none is named, files a petition with the court to be appointed trustee. Many states require the filing of a bond when the trustee is appointed. Finally, the executor(rix) makes distribution of the estate assets. He or she turns over to the trustee the property that is to be held in trust according to the directions given in the will. Thus, when there is a testamentary trust, the trustee's job begins when the executor(rix)'s job ends.

Sometimes a testator(rix) will leave money to someone in a will accompanied by a wish or desire that the legatee use the money in a particular way or for a particular purpose. When this happens, the question arises as to whether a trust was created by the *precatory* words: words of entreaty, request, or desire. If a trust was created, the "wish or desire" of the testator(rix) must be carried out; if a trust was not created, the request need not be carried out. A **precatory trust** is a trust that is created by words of entreaty, request, desire, or recommendation rather than by direct command.

A woman, for example, left a will which read:

> I give and bequeath unto my husband the use, income, and improvement of all the estate for and during the term of his natural life, in the full confidence that upon my decease, he will, as he has heretofore done, continue to give and afford my children such protection, comfort and support as they may stand in need of.

In holding that there was a trust for the children, the court said:

> If the objects of the supposed trust are certain and definite, if the property to which it is to attach is clearly pointed out, if the relations and situation of the testator and the supposed cestuis que trust are such as to indicate a strong interest and motive on the part of the testator in making them partakers of his bounty, and above all, if the recommendatory or precatory clause is so expressed as to warrant the inference that it was designed to be peremptory on the donee, the just and reasonable interpretation is that a trust is created which is obligatory and can be enforced in equity as against the trustee by those in whose behalf the beneficial use of the gift was intended.

Although words such as "wish," "request," and "desire" have been held to be commands creating a precatory trust in some wills, in other cases (like the *McReynolds* one) these same words have been considered only recommendations.

Living Trusts

A **living trust**, also known as an **inter vivos trust**, is a trust that becomes effective during the settlor's lifetime. It is created by either a conveyance in trust or a declaration of trust (see figure 6-2). A living trust may be funded or unfunded while the settlor is alive. Unlike a testamentary trust, a living trust is not under the control and supervision of the probate court and is not a matter of public record, unless the trust must be recorded to establish title to real property. The lack of court supervision and the

LEGAL TERMS

precatory trust
Trust created by words of entreaty, request, desire, or recommendation rather than by direct command.

living trust (also called inter vivos trust)
Trust that becomes effective during the settlor's lifetime.

ESTATE OF McREYNOLDS
800 S.W.2d 798 (Mo. 1990)

FACTS: Stanley Hope McReynolds's will left all of his estate in trust for the support of his father and, upon his father's death, to "Rev. Herbert W. Armstrong . . . and I request that said legatee shall use the money so received by him in the promotion and furtherance of his Radio Ministry and the spreading of the Gospel as he may see fit, and the Trust shall terminate." Mr. McReynolds's father and the Rev. Armstrong both died before the testator. The will contained no provision for the disposition of the trust property in the event both beneficiaries predeceased the testator. The church contended that the language used in the will created a charitable trust for the church rather than a gift to Rev. Armstrong for his own personal use.

LEGAL ISSUE: Does the word "request" standing alone in a will create a precatory trust?

COURT DECISION: No.

REASON: A trust is not lightly imposed on mere words of recommendation and confidence when property is given absolutely. A testator's use of the word "request" does not necessarily create a precatory trust, and it never does unless a plain intention appears to create a trust in other parts of the will. Similarly, a charitable trust is created only if the testator manifests an intention that the property be held subject to a legal obligation to devote it to purposes that are charitable. Because both beneficiaries predeceased the testator, the gift in trust lapsed, and the trustee held the trust property in a "resulting trust" for the testator's heirs under the law of intestate succession.

element of privacy are considered to be important advantages of a living trust. Living trusts may be either revocable or irrevocable.

Revocable Living Trust. A **revocable living trust** is a living trust in which the settlor retains the right to alter, amend, or revoke the trust during the settlor's lifetime. When the settlor dies, the dispositive provisions of the trust take effect, and the trust then becomes irrevocable. The right to revoke a trust does not survive the settlor's death. Because of its flexibility, a revocable living trust is a commonly used device by estate planners. Such a trust has no tax-saving advantages, however, and is therefore not used for that purpose.

A trust can be altered, amended, or revoked only if the power to do so is expressed in the trust instrument. For that reason, a clause such as the following is essential to make a living trust revocable.

Revocation and Amendment of Trust
[17 AM. JUR. *Legal Forms* 2d § 251:105]

> Trustor reserves the power to revoke this agreement in whole or in part, or to alter or amend the terms of this agreement, and to free any sums of money, securities, or other property from the terms of the trust created hereby, at any time during trustor's lifetime, upon written notice to that effect duly executed by trustor and delivered to trustee. On receipt of such written notice, trustee shall pay and surrender to trustor such sums of money, securities, or other property theretofore belonging to the trust estate as are described in such notice.

Settlors can put all of their property into a revocable living trust, receive the income during their lifetime, and give the principal, through the trust instrument, to whomever they designate upon their death. Property that is held in trust does not belong to the settlor's estate; it is owned by the trust, as the trustee has legal title to it. By using trusts, in some states, people can avoid homestead awards and prevent other types of family allowances from being taken from their estate. Homestead awards and family allowances are discussed in chapter 9.

When the settlor of a revocable living trust wishes to revoke the trust, he or she should notify the trustee in writing to that effect. Although no special words are necessary, a letter such as the one in figure 6-4 may be used to notify the trustee of the settlor's intention to revoke the trust.

Irrevocable Living Trust. An **irrevocable living trust** is a living trust that cannot be revoked or amended by the settlor once it has been established. A trust is irrevocable unless the trust instrument contains a statement that it can be revoked. To make the intent of the settlor clear, however, practitioners usually put the following clause in an irrevocable trust.

[17 AM. JUR. *Legal Forms* 2d § 251:122]

> This trust shall be irrevocable and shall not be revoked or terminated by trustor or any other person, nor shall it be amended or altered by trustor or any other person.

The principal advantage of an irrevocable trust is the elimination of the trust property from the settlor's gross estate for federal estate tax purposes. In addition, income from trust property may be shifted from the settlor to the trust itself, which may be in a lower tax bracket than the settlor.

LEGAL TERMS

revocable living trust
Living trust in which the settlor retains the right to alter, amend, or revoke the trust during the settlor's lifetime.

irrevocable living trust
Living trust that cannot be revoked or amended by the settlor once it has been established.

[17 AM. JUR. *Legal Forms* 2d § 251:932]

To: [name of trustee]
[address of trustee]

I, [name of trustor], of [address], City of ______________, County of ____________, State of ______________, as trustor in a trust agreement dated ___________, 19___, wherein you are designated as trustee, do hereby revoke the powers and trusts created and conferred by trustor in that trust instrument, pursuant to and in exercise of the right to revoke reserved to trustor in Section [number] of that trust instrument. I hereby direct you, as trustee, to turn over and deliver to me all property held by you subject to the terms and provisions of the trust instrument, together with all accumulations of interest and income.

In witness whereof, I have executed this instrument at [designate place of execution] on ____________, 19___.

[Signature of trustor]

I, [name of trustee], received the foregoing revocation of trust on ___________, 19___.

[Signature of trustee]

FIGURE 6-4 Sample revocation-of-trust letter

The principal disadvantage of an irrevocable trust is that it cannot be changed once it has been established.

Pour-Over Trust. A **pour-over trust** is a provision in a will in which the testator leaves a gift (often the residue of the estate) to the trustee of an existing living trust (figure 6-5). When the testator(rix) dies, the assets of the estate pour into the existing trust, and are distributed according to the directions contained in the living trust. Although a pour-over trust receives its assets from a will after the death of the settlor, such a trust is considered to be a living trust rather than a testamentary trust because the trust comes into existence while the settlor is alive. In addition, the details of the trust, including the trustee's rights and duties, are contained in the trust instrument rather than in the will.

Some years ago, a legal problem existed when a living trust was amended after the execution of a will containing a pour-over provision. Some courts held that the pour-over provision was invalid because the living trust had been amended but the will had not. Other courts took an opposite viewpoint. To avoid the conflict, many states have adopted the Uniform Testamentary Additions to Trusts Act.

PROVISION IN WILL
FOR POUR OVER TO TRUST
[Harris, *Family Estate Planning Guide* § 48 (3d ed., Hoops, 1992)]

I GIVE, DEVISE, and bequeath all of the rest, residue, and remainder of my estate, real, personal, and mixed, whatsoever and wheresoever situated, of which I may die possessed, or which I may have the power to dispose of at my death, to that person or to those persons, including any corporation or corporations, that at the time of my death are serving as Trustee or Trustees under that instrument of Trust executed by me on ____________, 19___, at [city and state], and entitled TRUST AGREEMENT BETWEEN [name of settlor] and [name of trustee], INITIAL TRUSTEE. This gift, devise, and bequest is to be added to the property then held in that Trust and shall become part of the corpus thereof. It is to be held in accordance with the terms and conditions of that trust as now written and as hereafter amended, and to that end I direct this gift, devise, and bequest to be interpreted by reference to that Trust instrument.

IF FOR ANY REASON THAT TRUST is not in force at the time of my death, or if this gift, devise, and bequest to the then Trustee of that Trust is held invalid, then I direct that this gift, devise, and bequest shall be held and managed in exactly the manner described in the instrument of Trust now in existence and by the same Trustee, and for that purpose only, I hereby incorporate that instrument of Trust, as it now stands, by reference to this my LAST WILL AND TESTAMENT.

FIGURE 6-5
Sample provision for pour-over trust

Uniform Testamentary Additions to Trust Act [Mass. Gen. L. ch. 203, § 3B]

A devise or bequest, the validity of which is determinable by the laws of this state, may be made to the trustee or trustees of a trust established or to be established by the testator or by the testator and some other person or persons or by some other person or persons, including a funded or unfunded life insurance trust, although the trustor has reserved any or all rights of ownership of the insurance contracts, if the trust is identified in the will and the terms of the trust are set forth in a written instrument executed before or concurrently with the execution of the testator's will or set forth in the valid will of a person who has predeceased the testator, regardless of the existence, size or character of the corpus of the trust. The devise or bequest shall not be invalid because the trust is amendable or revocable, or both, or because the trust was amended after the execution of the will or after the death of the testator. Unless the will provides otherwise, the property so devised or bequeathed (a) shall not be deemed to be held under a testamentary trust of the testator, but shall become a part of the trust to which it is given and (b) shall be administered and disposed of in accordance with the provisions of the instrument or will setting forth the terms of the trust including any amendments thereto made before or after the death of the testator. A revocation or termination of the trust before the death of the testator shall cause the devise or bequest to lapse.

LEGAL TERMS

pour-over trust
Provision in a will in which the testator(rix) leaves a gift to the trustee of an existing living trust.

6.5 IMPLIED TRUSTS

Implied trusts, also called **involuntary trusts**, come about by operation of law rather than by the express terms of the settlor. Sometimes, an implied trust comes into existence when an express trust cannot. For example, an express trust for real property requires a writing; an implied trust for real property has no writing requirement. There are two kinds of implied trusts: resulting trusts and constructive trusts.

LEGAL TERMS

implied trust (also called involuntary trust)
Trust that comes about by operation of law rather than by the express terms of the settlor.

Resulting Trusts

A **resulting trust** is a trust that is implied from the intentions of the parties that the person holding legal title is holding it for another's benefit. One of the most common ways that a resulting trust occurs is when one person pays for something and title is placed in another's name.

RAINEY V. RAINEY
795 S.W.2d 139 (Tenn. 1990)

FACTS: William J. Rainey and John R. Rainey, who were brothers, agreed to buy a farm, each agreeing to pay half the purchase price and each owning a one-half interest in the farm. Notwithstanding the agreement, title to the property was taken in the names of J. R. Rainey and Tommy Ray Rainey (John's son). In addition, John paid the entire purchase price for the property. When John died, a dispute arose over the ownership of the farm.

LEGAL ISSUE: Does a resulting trust arise when property is purchased with the money of one person and title is taken in the name of another person?

COURT DECISION: Yes.

REASON: When property is purchased with the money of one person but the title is taken in the name of another, a resulting trust arises. The title holder becomes a trustee for the payor. John supplied the consideration necessary to create a resulting trust in Tommy Ray as his trustee. As a result, John's heirs owned the property when John died.

Resulting trusts also occur when express trusts fail for some reason, or when a fiduciary uses fiduciary funds to buy something and takes title in his or her own name individually. A resulting trust does not occur when the present intent of the person paying for the property is to make a gift of it to the person in whose name the property is placed.

resulting trust
Trust that is implied from the intentions of the parties that the person holding legal title to property is holding it for another's benefit.

constructive trust
Trust created by operation of law when someone obtains legal title to property through fraud or other wrongdoing.

Constructive Trusts

A **constructive trust** is a trust that is created by operation of law when someone obtains legal title to property through fraud or other wrongdoing. To avoid unjust enrichment, the court imposes a trust on the person holding legal title, declaring that title is held for the benefit of the one to whom title should belong. In general, the elements that are necessary to establish a constructive trust are: a confidential or fiduciary relationship, a promise by one of the parties, a transfer by the other party in reliance on the promise, and unjust enrichment.

HALBERSBERG V. BERRY
394 S.E.2d 7 (S.C. 1990)

FACTS: David Halbersberg entered into an oral partnership with William and Catherine Berry to manufacture and sell neon t-shirts and to share the expenses and profits equally. The parties agreed to lease land on Myrtle Beach, build a building on it to use as a retail outlet, and to rent part of it out. Halbersberg paid the contractor $10,000 toward the construction cost of the building. William Berry paid the contractor the balance and took the lease in his own name. Berry then excluded Halbersberg from the partnership, leased the property out but shared no income with Halbersberg, and made no attempt to return the $10,000.

LEGAL ISSUE: Does a constructive trust arise when one partner leases property and excludes the other partner from partnership income?

COURT DECISION: Yes.

REASON: A constructive trust arises against one who, by fraud, duress, abuse of confidence, commission of a wrong, or any form of unconscionable conduct, either has obtained or holds the right to property which he ought not in equity and good conscience hold and enjoy. Constructive trusts are resorted to in equity to vindicate right and justice or to frustrate fraud. The court held that the partnership agreement had been breached by Berry. The court imposed a constructive trust on the lease income for the benefit of Halbersberg.

SUMMARY

6.1 A trust is an arrangement whereby a person called the settlor gives property to a trustee, who holds the property in trust for the benefit of the beneficiary according to the terms of the trust instrument.

6.2 To establish a trust, a person must be competent and own the property that is to be placed in trust. The court will not allow a trust to fail for lack of a trustee. Generally, anyone having the capacity to manage his or her own affairs can be a trustee. Trustees have a fiduciary relationship with their beneficiaries and must exercise a high degree of honesty and good faith. The principal powers of a trustee are found in the trust instrument. Without a beneficiary, there can be no trust, and the beneficiary must be capable of being identified and ascertained at all times, even though it need not be in existence. A sole beneficiary may not be a sole trustee; however, a sole beneficiary may be a co-trustee with others.

6.3 When a trust is established, legal title is held by one person for the benefit of another person who holds equitable title. In a conveyance in trust, the settlor transfers legal title to a trustee and either retains the equitable title or transfers it to someone else. In a declaration of trust, the settlor transfers the equitable title to someone else and retains the legal title. Except for real property, a writing is not always necessary to create a trust.

6.4 No particular words are necessary to create an express trust; however, the intent to create a trust by the settlor is essential. A testamentary trust is under the control and supervision of the probate court, whereas a living trust is not. A trust can be altered, amended, or revoked only if the power to do so is expressed in the trust instrument. An irrevocable living trust has tax-saving advantages; however, it cannot be changed once it has been established. Although a pour-over trust receives its assets from a will after the death of the settlor, it is considered to be a living trust rather than a testamentary trust.

6.5 A resulting trust occurs when one person pays for real or personal property and title is placed in another's name. A constructive trust occurs when someone obtains legal title to property through fraud or other wrongdoing.

QUESTIONS FOR REVIEW

1. What happens to legal title to the trust property when a trust is created (a) by a conveyance in trust? (b) By a declaration of trust?
2. In what way do the requirements for trusts dealing with personal property differ from those dealing with real property, in many states?
3. To be valid, what elements must an express trust include?
4. Describe the process that must occur for a testamentary trust to become operative and receive trust assets.
5. What three words have been held to create a precatory trust in some wills, but only recommendations in others?
6. In what two ways may a living trust be created?
7. When may a trust be altered, amended, or revoked?
8. What is the principal advantage of an irrevocable trust?
9. How does a resulting trust differ from a constructive trust?
10. When may a trustee also be a beneficiary?

CASES TO DISCUSS

1. Maude Keyes paid the full purchase price for a Chevrolet Monte Carlo, but was unable to obtain liability insurance in her name. For that reason, the certificate of title named her son, George W. Keyes, as the owner of the car, and Maude was listed as a lienholder. The car was insured in George's name. When George died, his estate claimed the car. Was his estate entitled to it? Why or why not? *Keyes v. Keyes,* 392 S.E.2d 693 (W.Va. 1990).
2. Before his death, Paul Overmire transferred all of his separate property into a revocable living trust. A bank was named trustee and Paul was to receive the income of the trust during his life. Upon his death, $100,000 of the trust funds were to remain in trust for the benefit of his son by a previous marriage. The balance of the fund was to remain in trust, with the income going to his wife, Sadie, and upon her death, the principal to the Red Cross. Sadie petitioned the court for an award in lieu of homestead of $25,000 and asked that it be charged to the trust, because there were apparently no other funds in the estate. Was Sadie entitled to the $25,000 from the trust? Why or why not? *Estate of Overmire v. Red Cross,* 794 P.2d 518 (Wash. 1990).
3. Larry Mendal, a 38-year-old college graduate with a degree in economics, lived and worked on his parents' farm. He was befriended by the Hewitts, who were also farmers, and with whom he had transacted farming business. After the death of his parents, Mendal looked to the Hewitts for advice and guidance, and a relationship akin to that of parent and child developed. Mendal alleges that he acceded to the

Hewitts' advice to sell his family farm and transfer a large amount of money to the Hewitts to invest in the purchase of another farm as a joint venture with them. Later, Mendal learned that title to the other farm had been conveyed solely to the Hewitts. On what legal grounds might Mendal obtain relief? Explain. *Mendal v. Hewitt,* 555 N.Y.S.2d 899 (N.Y. 1990).

SHARPENING YOUR PROFESSIONAL SKILLS

1. Refer to the law office scenario at the beginning of this chapter, and answer the following questions:
   (a) Why did Tiffany say to Lisa, "It sounds like there may be a problem there," when Lisa asked her about the trust?
   (b) What might Tiffany learn when she researches the problem of the testator leaving money to his brother with the desire that his sister be taken care of until she reaches the age of 25?
   (c) With the information Tiffany has discovered thus far, can the trust she was reading be revoked?
2. Does the law of your state require trusts dealing with real property to be in writing? If so, give the statutory reference or case citation where the provision is found.
3. If you have access to a law library, use 17 AM. JUR. *Legal Forms* 2d § 251:201-338 as a guide in drafting the following testamentary provisions:
   (a) A trust providing income to someone for life with a reversion to the residuary estate.
   (b) A pour-over to an inter vivos trust.
   (c) A trust for a former spouse pursuant to a property settlement.
   (d) A gift of $50,000 in trust for the care, maintenance, and support of a pet cat.
4. Draft a revocable trust agreement in general form. (If you have access to a law library, use 17 AM. JUR. *Legal Forms* 2d § 251:91-194 as a guide.)

CHAPTER 7
Specialized Trusts

"I've never killed anybody, but I frequently get satisfaction reading the obituary section."

Clarence Darrow

OUTLINE

LAW OFFICE SCENARIO

Tiffany Casey, a paralegal in the office of Knight & Francis, is called into Attorney Knight's office, where she is introduced to Mr. and Mrs. DeNunzio, a middle-aged couple.

"We're going to do some estate planning for the DeNunzios, and I'd like you to help them with the estate-planning questionnaire," Attorney Knight explains to Tiffany.

"I'll be glad to," Tiffany replies. "The questionnaire is quite complicated."

"Our lives are quite complicated, too," Mrs. DeNunzio interrupts. "We just won the state lottery!"

"Congratulations!" Tiffany exclaims.

"We've only been married for two years, but we were both married before," Mrs. DeNunzio volunteers. "I have six children from my first marriage, and Angelo has eight children from his first marriage."

"That is some family!"

"If I die first, I want Angelo to have enough to live comfortably, but I want my own children to inherit my money. Angelo wants his children to inherit his money, too," Mrs. DeNunzio continues as Angelo looks on quietly.

"We might consider using a special type of trust that will qualify for the marital deduction and save a considerable amount of taxes for your estate," Attorney Knight suggests.

"Good," Mrs. DeNunzio answers. "Right now I have a bank account for each of my children in my name in trust for each child. Will the children get that money if I die?"

"We'll review your bank accounts when we have all the information together and develop a plan that will be suitable for both of you," Attorney Knight answers.

"Good," Mrs. DeNunzio answers, "Angelo has a daughter who goes through money like water over a dam. If she inherits from Angelo, it won't last very long."

"Tiffany," Attorney Knight suggests, "why don't you take Mr. and Mrs. DeNunzio into your office and go over the estate-planning questionnaire with them? Then you can set up an appointment for us to meet again when we have the information we need."

"Fine," Tiffany replies, ushering Mr. and Mrs. DeNunzio to her office.

7.1 TOTTEN TRUST

Paralegals who work with trusts must be familiar with a variety of trusts so that they will know what type of trust is most suitable in a particular situation. As in the case of Mrs. DeNunzio, people may open bank accounts in their own names "in trust" for someone else, without signing any other trust instrument. The trust that is created when this happens is known as a **Totten trust** (from a 1904 New York case, *In re Totten,* 71 N.E. 748 (N.Y. 1904)). A Totten trust is a savings bank account in the name of the depositor as trustee for another person. The depositor may withdraw money from the account at any time during the depositor's lifetime. When the

LEGAL TERMS

Totten trust (also called a pay-on-death (POD) account)
Savings account in the name of the depositor as trustee for another person.

depositor dies, the money in the account belongs to the beneficiary, as shown in the *Adams* case. If the beneficiary dies before the depositor, however, the trust terminates; the money belongs to the depositor, not the beneficiary's estate.

IN RE ESTATE OF ADAMS
587 A.2d 958 (Vt. 1990)

FACTS: Bertha Mae Adams deposited her own money in her own name in the Troy Savings Bank "as trustee for Evelyn Lindquist," her daughter. Adams died without making any changes to the bank account.

LEGAL ISSUE: Does a bank account opened by a depositor in trust for another belong to the depositor's estate when the depositor dies?

COURT DECISION: No.

REASON: A deposit of one's own money in one's name as trustee for another is a tentative trust only, revocable at will, until the depositor dies. When the depositor dies before the beneficiary, there is a presumption that an absolute trust was created. This was a valid Totten trust. Evelyn Lindquist was entitled to the balance in the account, not Adams's estate.

7.2 SPECIAL PURPOSE TRUSTS

There are many types of trusts that are used for special purposes. Among them are spendthrift trusts and sprinkling or spray trusts.

Spendthrift Trusts

A **spendthrift** is a person who spends money profusely and improvidently. A **spendthrift trust** is a trust containing a provision that protects the assets of the trust from creditors and from the beneficiary's reckless spending. With such a provision in a trust, the principal and interest of the trust cannot be reached by creditors until it is received by the beneficiary, and the beneficiary cannot assign the principal and interest before receiving it. Without such a provision, a beneficiary for whom money is being held in

spendthrift
Person who spends money profusely and improvidently.

spendthrift trust
Trust containing restrictions on the voluntary and involuntary alienation of the trust's principal and interest.

trust could take the trust instrument to a bank, borrow on it, and assign the rights to the money to the bank as collateral for the loan.

The restrictions imposed by the spendthrift trust are described in the following provision.

Spendthrift Trust Provision
[16A AM. JUR. *Legal Forms* 2d (Rev.) § 237:17]

It is the purpose of this trust to secure Marilyn Doe from want or her own mismanagement and improvidence and to provide Marilyn Doe with a reasonable means of support free from the claims or interests of any other person. The interest of Marilyn Doe in the trust estate and the income therefrom shall not be liable for her obligations or debts, and shall not be assignable in any manner. No part of the income from this trust estate shall be anticipated, pledged, encumbered, hypothecated, or in any way disposed of by beneficiary, nor shall any part be taken on execution, received by creditor's bill, garnished, or subject to any other process or writ by any person having, or alleging to have, a claim against beneficiary. All payments for which provision is made in this trust shall be paid directly to Marilyn Doe, and to no other person or entity.

Sprinkling Trusts

A **sprinkling trust**, which is also known as a **spray trust**, gives the trustee the power to determine how the trust's income or principal or both are to be allocated among a group or class of beneficiaries. This type of trust is also called a **discretionary trust**, because trustees are allowed to use their own discretion in distributing principal and income to the beneficiaries. Trustees have the power to "sprinkle" or "spray" the trust income and principal among the people who are most needy or in a way that will save taxes.

An advantage of this type of trust is that when the trust is established, the settlor does not have to decide specifically who will receive the income and principal. The trustee makes that decision at a later time when the circumstances of potential beneficiaries are better known. Funds can be distributed according to need. The trustee can also take advantage of the tax brackets of the different beneficiaries when distributing income, and thereby save income taxes. In addition, estate taxes can often be reduced. Another important advantage of a sprinkling trust is that the spendthrift provision is built in: the trustee can control allotments to a beneficiary who spends money profusely and improvidently.

A disadvantage of a sprinkling trust is that the trustee has ultimate control. Before choosing to use a sprinkling trust, a settlor should trust and respect the prospective trustee greatly: the trustee, not the settlor, will decide exactly who will benefit from the trust within the general group or class of people that the settlor chooses. The use of a provision like the following in a trust instrument creates a sprinkling trust.

Sprinkling Trust Provision
[17A AM. JUR. *Legal Forms* 2d (Rev.) § 251:234]

Trustee shall hold, manage, invest, and reinvest the trust estate, and shall apply and distribute the income and principal of the trust as follows:

(a) *Distribution of income.* Trustee shall pay to or apply for the benefit of my children, herein referred to as income beneficiaries, at least annually, and in such proportions as trustee in its absolute discretion may from time to time determine, all of the net income of the trust estate.

(b) *Invasion of principal.* At any time and from time to time and notwithstanding any other provision of this agreement, trustee may, in its absolute discretion, in addition to any other payments provided for in this agreement, pay to or apply for the benefit of income beneficiaries such amounts as trustee may, in its absolute discretion, elect from the principal of the trust estate.

(c) *Further disposition of trust estate.* Income beneficiaries' interests in the trust estate, as provided in subparagraphs (a) and (b) hereof, shall terminate when the youngest beneficiary reaches the age of 30 years. The trust estate shall thereupon be paid and distributed as follows: In equal shares to my issue then living by right of representation.

(d) *Shares of income beneficiaries.* Payments made to each of income beneficiaries pursuant to this section need not be equal.

7.3 MARITAL DEDUCTION TRUSTS

Under federal estate tax laws, property passing from a decedent to a surviving spouse is not taxable. Instead, it is deductible from the decedent's taxable estate and is known as the **marital deduction**. A trust that is designed to make optimal use of the marital deduction is called a **marital deduction trust**. A marital deduction trust may distribute property to a surviving spouse in various ways, including: (1) an outright gift; (2) a life estate with a general power of appointment; (3) a credit-shelter trust; and (4) a QTIP trust.

Distribution Outright

Sometimes settlors wish to give the entire trust corpus outright to a surviving spouse when they die. This can be done through a simple clause in the trust:

> Upon the settlor's death, the trustee shall distribute all principal and income, outright and free of trusts, to the settlor's surviving spouse.

The surviving spouse thereby receives full access to and control of the trust property and qualifies for the full estate tax marital deduction. However, choosing this option makes the entire trust property part of the surviving spouse's estate, which may be subject to probate when the surviving spouse dies and taxable at that time. In addition, the surviving spouse, not the

LEGAL TERMS

sprinkling trust (also called spray trust and discretionary trust)
Trust that gives the trustee the power to determine how the trust's income or principal or both are to be allocated among a group or class of beneficiaries.

marital deduction
Under federal estate tax law, property passing from a decedent to a surviving spouse. It is not taxable.

marital deduction trust
Trust that is designed to make optimal use of the marital deduction.

settlor, will have the power to decide who will be the ultimate beneficiaries of the trust property.

Life Estate with Power of Appointment

Another way to qualify for the marital deduction is to leave property in trust to the surviving spouse for life and, upon the spouse's death, to whomever the surviving spouse appoints in a will. This can be done with either a living trust or a testamentary trust.

Testamentary Trust Provision for Spouse with Limited Power of Appointment [17 AM. JUR. *Legal Forms* 2d (Rev.) § 251:231]

I give the residue of my estate to the trustee herein named, in trust, to be administered, paid, or applied as follows:

A. The net income of such trust shall be paid to my wife for her life. If my wife does not survive me, the property shall be distributed to my then living children or the issue of any deceased child, per stirpes, but if none survive me then to [name].

B. Following the death of my wife, trustee shall pay and divide the principal and income of the trust estate among my children and the issue of any deceased child, per stirpes, in such share as my wife shall by will appoint and subject to such provisions as are set forth in her will. In default of such appointment, and so far as any such appointment extends to persons other than my children living at my death and the issue of any deceased child of mine, the principal and income of such trust shall be paid, in equal shares, to my children. The issue of any deceased child of mine shall take per stirpes such share as such child of mine would have taken if then living.

In the preceding trust provision the husband's will leaves the residue of his estate in trust for his wife to receive the income from the trust for her life. Upon her death, the trust ends, and the principal of the trust is distributed among the husband's children in whatever fractions his wife sets forth in her will. To qualify for the marital deduction, the trust, however, must meet specific requirements found in the Internal Revenue Code. I.R.C. § 2056(b)(5).

Credit-Shelter Trust

In a **credit-shelter trust**, also known as an **A-B trust**, a **bypass trust**, or an **exemption equivalent trust**, a deceased spouse's estate passes to a trust rather than to the surviving spouse. This strategy reduces the possibility of the surviving spouse's estate being taxable (a drawback noted earlier in the discussion of an outright distribution).

Assume, for example, that a married couple's total assets are $1.2 million. The husband dies, leaving everything to his wife. There will be no federal estate tax because of the 100-percent marital deduction. However, when the wife subsequently dies, the amount in her estate that exceeds \$600,000 (\$600,000 in this example) will be subject to the estate tax, which could be as high as \$235,000. The tax can be avoided by using a credit-shelter trust.

Under a credit-shelter trust, the will of the first spouse to die leaves \$600,000 (or the amount that is exempt from the federal estate tax) to an irrevocable credit-shelter trust called Trust A. Trust A provides income for the surviving spouse for life; upon that spouse's death, the corpus of Trust A passes to other named beneficiaries, such as children or grandchildren. In addition, the will of the first spouse to die leaves \$600,000 to Trust B for the benefit of the surviving spouse, allowing it to qualify for the marital deduction and, therefore, not be taxable. When the second spouse dies, the amount in Trust A is not part of his or her estate and, therefore, is not subject to the estate tax. The only item that is subject to the estate tax is the money in Trust B, but it also is not taxable because it does not exceed \$600,000.

A-B Trust
[17A AM. JUR. *Legal Forms* 2d (Rev.) § 251:353]

If my wife survives me, I direct that trustee shall divide the entire trust estate into two separate trusts, which are herein referred to as "Trust A," the marital trust, and "Trust B," the residuary trust.

(1) The following shall be placed in Trust A: An amount equal to one-half of the value of my adjusted gross estate as that term is defined for purposes of the marital deduction under the Internal Revenue Code. The amount of Trust A, as so determined, shall be reduced by the value, to the extent includable in my gross estate under the Internal Revenue Code, of all assets or interests that pass or have passed to my wife other than by the terms of this paragraph and that are eligible to satisfy the marital deduction.

(2) Trust B shall be equal in amount to the balance of my residuary estate after deducting the amount allocated to Trust A.

QTIP Trust

A third type of trust that qualifies for the marital deduction is a QTIP trust. This type of trust is used when the settlor wants to pass the entire principal of the trust to someone other than the surviving spouse, but wants the spouse to have the income from the trust for life. A **qualified terminable interest property (QTIP) trust** is a trust that gives all trust income to the surviving spouse for life, payable at least annually. During the surviving spouse's lifetime, no one can appoint the trust property to anyone other than the surviving spouse. This type of trust must also meet specific requirements found in the Internal Revenue Code. I.R.C. § 2056(b)(7).

Suppose, for example, that a woman has three children by her first husband and no children by her second husband to whom she is still

LEGAL TERMS

credit-shelter trust (also called A-B trust, bypass trust, and exemption-equivalent trust)
Trust under which a deceased spouse's estate passes to a trust rather than to the surviving spouse, thereby reducing the possibility of the surviving spouse's estate being taxable.

QTIP trust (qualified terminable interest property trust)
Trust that gives all trust income to the surviving spouse for life, payable at least annually, and which meets the requirements of I.R.C. § 2056(b)(7).

married. She wants her children to inherit her property if she dies before her husband, but also wants her husband to live comfortably for the rest of his life. If the estate is large enough to produce sufficient income, a QTIP trust would be appropriate, because the husband would benefit, but would be restricted to the income from the trust for his life. Upon his death, the principal would pass intact to the three children.

An interesting aspect of a QTIP trust is that the decision to actually use the QTIP provision is made *after* the death of the decedent, even though the trust is created before death. The decedent's executor elects to treat the property as qualified terminable interest property on the estate tax return. Otherwise, the property does not qualify as QTIP. The executor has the option to either elect or not elect to have the QTIP trust qualify for the marital deduction. The estate planner can look at the circumstances that exist at death, rather than at the time the trust is executed, to make the final decision. Such flexibility makes the QTIP trust an advantageous option in postmortem planning.

7.4 CHARITABLE TRUSTS

A **charitable trust**, sometimes called a **public trust**, is a trust in which the property held by the trustee must be used for public charitable purposes. A charitable trust is created for the benefit of a part of the general public rather than for an individual or designated group of individual persons. In a charitable trust, the actual beneficiaries are indefinite and unascertainable. Such trusts are established for religious, charitable, scientific, or educational purposes, or the like. Because no particular individual can benefit from a charitable trust, no one person can bring suit to enforce the trust. For this reason, charitable trusts are enforced by the attorney general of the state where they are established. Gifts to charities, in general, are exempt from the federal estate tax; however, to be exempt, the recipient of the gift must qualify as a charity under the rules found in I.R.C. §§ 2055 and 2106(a)(2).

Cy Pres Doctrine

When money or property is left in trust to a charity, and the charity ceases to exist, does the trust also end? Under the doctrine of **cy pres**, which means "as near as possible," if the court finds that the settlor had a *general* charitable intent, the trust fund will be turned over to another closely related charity. (See figure 7-1.) If instead the court finds that the settlor had a *specific* intent to benefit one charity exclusively, and that charity ends, the trust will also be discontinued, and the trust property will revert to the settlor's heirs. In the *Crawshaw* case, the use of cy pres was considered appropriate, and the court allowed a substitution.

LEGAL TERMS

charitable trust (also called public trust)
Trust in which the property held by the trustee must be used for public charitable purposes.

cy pres ("as near as possible")
Doctrine which dictates that, if a charity receiving trust funds discontinues existence and the court finds that the settlor had a general charitable intent, the trust fund will be turned over to another closely related charity; otherwise, the trust fund will revert to the settlor's estate.

Charitable Beneficiaries

		N/A	To be Done	Done	By Whom
.01	Verify the identity of each charitable beneficiary named in the will or revocable trust agreement, to make sure that it was the organization that the decedent intended to benefit.	( )	( )	( )	______
.02	Determine the validity of any charitable disposition made in the will or revocable trust agreement.	( )	( )	( )	______

Annotations: 6 ALR4th 603, 25 ALR3d 736, 41 ALR3d 833, 75 ALR3d 877

		N/A	To be Done	Done	By Whom
.03	Resolve whether any unsatisfied charitable pledge made by the decedent is enforceable.	( )	( )	( )	______
.04	Ascertain the validity of any charitable trust created by the will or revocable trust agreement.	( )	( )	( )	______

Annotations: 6 ALR4th 903

FIGURE 7-1
Checklist of charitable beneficiaries.
Excerpted from *Tennessee Post Mortem Estate Planning Checklist* (Lawyers Cooperative Publishing)

This checklist provides some guidance on how to administer a Tennessee will or trust with charitable beneficiaries. The annotations refer to American Law Reports.

MATTER OF ESTATE OF CRAWSHAW
806 P.2d 1014 (Kan. 1991)

FACTS: After making specific bequests totaling $350 to family members, Chester D. Crawshaw's will left 15 percent of the residue of his estate to the Salvation Army and 85 percent in trust to Marymount College in Salina, Kansas, for school loans to nursing students and other students. If for some reason Marymount College could not accept and administer the trust, the will provided that the bequest go in trust to "the official Board or Association of said college having the legal capacity to accept and administer the herein created trust." One month after Crawshaw died, Marymount College terminated its existence. The Marymount Memorial Educational Trust Fund was established by the college and the Roman Catholic Bishop to administer this and other scholarship funds.

LEGAL ISSUE: Does the doctrine of cy pres apply when a testator leaves the bulk of his estate to a named college to provide loans to nursing and other students and the college ceases operation?

COURT DECISION: Yes.

REASON: Under Kansas law, the doctrine of cy pres permits a court to implement a testator's intent and save a testamentary charitable gift by substituting beneficiaries only when these conditions are met: First, the gift must be to a charitable organization for a charitable purpose. Second, it must be impossible, impractical, or illegal to carry out the donor's stated charitable purpose. Finally, it must appear that the donor had a general charitable intent. All three requisites are met in this case, and the use of cy pres is appropriate.

LEGAL TERMS

rule against perpetuities
Rule providing that every interest in property is void unless it must vest, if at all, not later than 21 years after some life in being at the time of creation of the interest.

Rule Against Perpetuities

One feature of a charitable trust is that the rule against perpetuities does not apply: this means that charitable trusts can exist indefinitely, unlike private trusts. Under the **rule against perpetuities**, every interest in property is void unless it must vest, if at all, not later than 21 years after some life in being at the time of creation of the interest. For example, if a settlor left money in trust for the settlor's children and then for the lives of the settlor's grandchildren, the rule would be violated, because the grandchildren

A BENEVOLENT BUSINESSMAN

There is a natural law, a Divine law, that obliges you and me to relieve the suffering, the distressed and the destitute. Charity is a supreme virtue, and the great channel through which the mercy of God is passed onto mankind. It is the virtue that unites men and inspires their noblest efforts.

"Love one another, for that is the whole law"; so our fellow men deserve to be loved and encouraged—never to be abandoned to wander alone in poverty and darkness. The practice of charity will bind us, will bind all men in one great brotherhood.

Courtesy Conrad N. Hilton Foundation, Reno, Nevada

Conrad N. Hilton was not only an astute businessman who built a worldwide hotel empire; this gentle-looking man was also a compassionate philanthropist, as shown by this excerpt from his will, which was addressed to the directors of the Hilton Foundation. Hilton began the Foundation in 1944 as a trust, then later transferred its assets to a nonprofit corporation. When Hilton died in 1979, the Foundation received much of his wealth (over $180 million) to support his philanthropic ideals: "to alleviate human suffering," particularly among disadvantaged children, and to promote the human services activities of the Catholic Sisters worldwide.

could include children of an as-yet-unborn child of the settlor, and this may occur more than 21 years after the death of all currently living beneficiaries. Thus, the trust would be void. If, instead, the settlor left money in trust to a charitable institution, there would be no time limit and the trust could continue for many generations.

Charitable Remainder Trusts

A **charitable remainder trust** is a trust in which the settlor, or a beneficiary, retains the income from the trust for a period of time (usually for life), after which the trust principal is given to a charity. Settlors can use part of such gifts as deductions on their federal income tax returns, thereby

charitable remainder trust
Trust in which the settlor or a beneficiary retains the income from the trust for a period of time (usually for life), after which the trust principal is given to a charity.

A TRUST FOR THE ARTS

The J. Paul Getty Museum
The Getty Center for the History of Art and the Humanities
The Getty Conservation Institute
The Getty Art History Information Program
The Getty Center for Education in the Arts
Museum Management Institute
Program for Art on Film, a Joint Venture with the Metropolitan Museum of Art, New York

The J. Paul Getty Trust, endowed by oil magnate Getty, currently operates the seven programs listed here as well as a grant program to promote the visual arts and humanities. The Trust began in 1953 with the creation of the J. Paul Getty Museum as a California charitable trust. (The Museum was located in Getty's ranch house in Malibu at the time.) When the Trust inherited a large portion of Getty's fortune in 1982, its purposes and projects expanded to further Getty's goal of "the diffusion of artistic and general knowledge."

increasing their total earning power. In addition, the gift to charity may be deducted from the settlor's federal estate tax. Charitable remainder trusts may be in the form of an annuity trust or a unitrust.

Annuity Trusts. A **charitable remainder annuity trust** is a trust in which a fixed amount of income is given to a beneficiary at least annually, and the entire remainder is given to charity. Under Internal Revenue Service (IRS) regulations, the beneficiary must receive annually at least 5 percent of the amount that was initially given to the trust. The amount can never change, regardless of the needs of the beneficiary or economic inflation. If the income of the trust is insufficient to meet the required annual payment, the difference must be paid from the principal of the trust. If the income of the trust is more than the required payment, the difference remains in the trust. When IRS requirements are met, the settlor receives an income tax deduction for the contributions made to the trust, based on an IRS formula.

Unitrusts. A **charitable remainder unitrust** is similar to an annuity trust, but does not require the payment of a fixed amount each year to an income beneficiary. Instead, the income beneficiary must receive a fixed percentage—not less than 5 percent—of the value of the trust property, which is determined annually. (See figure 7-2.) A unitrust is in effect a type of variable annuity: it offers protection against inflation because the beneficiary's income increases as the value of the trust property increases. Figures 7-3 and 7-4 show sample unitrusts.

LEGAL TERMS

charitable remainder annuity trust
Trust in which a fixed amount of income is given to a beneficiary at least annually, and the entire remainder is given to charity.

charitable remainder unitrust
Trust in which a percentage—not less than 5%—of the value of the trust property is determined annually and given to a beneficiary, with the entire remainder going to charity.

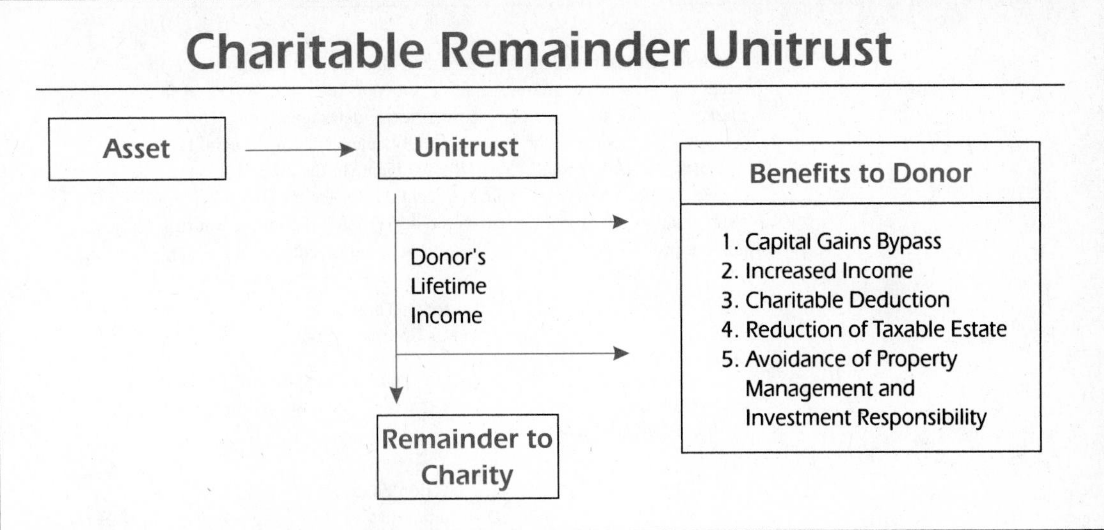

FIGURE 7-2
Charitable remainder unitrust structure

CHARITABLE REMAINDER UNITRUST
[4A AM. JUR. *Legal Forms* 2d (Rev.) § 55:21]

I, [name of settlor] (hereinafter referred to as "the donor"), desiring to establish a charitable remainder unitrust, within the meaning of Rev. Proc. 89-20 and § 664(d)(2) of the Internal Revenue Code, hereby create the [name] Charitable Remainder Unitrust and designate [name] as the initial trustee.

Section One
Funding the Trust

The donor transfers to the trustee the property described in Schedule A, [not included in this sample], and the trustee accepts such property and agrees to hold, manage, and distribute such property of the trust under the terms set forth in this trust instrument.

Section Two
Payment of Unitrust Amount

The trustee shall pay to a living individual (hereinafter referred to as "the recipient") in each taxable year of the trust during the recipient's life a unitrust amount equal to ten percent (10%) of the net fair market value of the assets of the trust valued as of the first day of each taxable year of the trust (the "valuation date"). The unitrust amount shall be paid in equal quarterly amounts from income and, to the extent that income is not

FIGURE 7-3
Charitable remainder unitrust provision

sufficient, from principal. Any income of the trust for a taxable year in excess of the unitrust amount shall be added to principal. If the net fair market value of the trust assets is incorrectly determined, then within a reasonable period after the value is finally determined for federal tax purposes, the trustee shall pay to the recipient (in the case of an undervaluation) or receive from the recipient (in the case of an overvaluation) an amount equal to the difference between the unitrust amount properly payable and the unitrust amount actually paid.

Section Three
Proration of Unitrust Amount

In determining the unitrust amount, the trustee shall prorate such amount on a daily basis for a short taxable year and for the taxable year of the recipient's death.

Section Four
Distribution to Charity

Upon the death of the recipient, trustee shall distribute all of the then principal and income of the trust (other than any amount due recipient or recipient's estate, under Sections Two and Three, above) to [name of charity] (hereinafter referred to as the Charitable Organization). If the Charitable Organization is not an organization described in §§ 170(c), 2055(a), and 2522(a) of the Internal Revenue Code at the time when any principal or income of the trust is to be distributed to it, then the trustee shall distribute such principal or income to one or more organizations described in §§ 170(c), 2055(a), and 2522(a) which trustee shall select in its sole discretion.

Section Five
Additional Contributions

If any additional contributions are made to the trust after the initial contribution, the unitrust amount for the year in which the additional contribution is made shall be the same percentage as in Section One.

Section Six
Prohibited Transactions

The income of the trust for each taxable year shall be distributed at such time and in such manner as not to subject the trust to tax under § 4942 of the Internal Revenue Code. Except for the payment of the unitrust amount to the recipient, the trustee shall not engage in any act of self-dealing, as defined in § 4941(d), and shall not make any taxable expenditures, as defined in § 4945(d). The trustee shall not make any investments that jeopardize the charitable purpose of the trust, within the meaning of § 4944, or retain any excess business holdings, within the meaning of § 4943.

Section Seven
Successor Trustee

The donor reserves the right to dismiss the trustee and to appoint a successor trustee.

FIGURE 7-3
(Continued)

Section Eight
Taxable Year

The taxable year of the trust shall be the calendar year.

Section Nine
Governing Law

The operation of the trust shall be governed by the laws of the State of ______________. However, the trustee is prohibited from exercising any power of discretion granted under such laws that would be inconsistent with the qualification of the trust under § 664(d)(2) of the Internal Revenue Code and the corresponding regulations.

Section Ten
Limited Power of Amendment

The trust is irrevocable. However, the trustee shall have the power, acting alone, to amend the trust in any manner required for the sole purpose of ensuring that the trust qualifies and continues to qualify as a charitable remainder unitrust within the meaning of § 664(d)(2) of the Internal Revenue Code.

Section Eleven
Investment of Trust Assets

Nothing in this trust instrument shall be construed as restricting the trustee from investing the trust assets in a manner possibly resulting in the annual realization of a reasonable amount of income or gain from the sale or disposition of trust assets.

IN WITNESS WHEREOF, [donor] and [trustee] by its duly authorized officer have signed this trust instrument on [date].

____
Donor

Trustee

by ______________________________

FIGURE 7-3
(Continued)

7.5 LIFE INSURANCE TRUSTS

If carefully prepared, a life insurance trust may be used to pass money to heirs tax-free. First, an irrevocable trust is established; then the trustee purchases a life insurance policy on the settlor's life. The settlor contributes a certain amount of money each year to the trust, which is used by the trustee to pay the premiums on the policy. When the settlor dies, the proceeds of the insurance policy are paid to the trust. If the trust contains Crummey

CHARITABLE REMAINDER UNITRUST

I give, bequeath and devise all the rest, residue and remainder of my estate, real, personal and mixed to . . . ., in trust, nevertheless, to invest and reinvest the same upon the following terms and conditions:

(a) I direct my trustee to keep said trust property invested in income producing property.

(b) I direct my trustee, beginning as of the date of my death and continuing until the date of the death of my son, ..., to pay to him, not less than quarter-annually, a unitrust amount equal to 5% of the net fair market value of the trust assets valued as of the first day of each taxable year of the trust, and pro-rata for a part of a year.

(c) I direct that such unitrust amount shall be paid from trust income to the extent that they are not in excess of trust income and from trust principal to the extent they exceed trust income.

(d) I direct that any income for any taxable year which shall be in excess of such payment shall be added to trust principal.

(e) I direct that the said trust shall be funded as expeditiously as possible after my death, and that all payments of income from the date of my death shall thereupon be paid to my said son with interest on all deferred payments at 6% per annum, compounded annually.

(f) If the net fair market value of the trust assets shall be incorrectly determined by the trustee for any taxable year, I direct that my said trustee shall, within a reasonable period after the final determination of the correct value, pay to my said son, in the case of an undervaluation, or shall receive from my said son, in case of an overvaluation, an amount equal to the difference between the unitrust amount which should have been paid and the unitrust amount which was actually paid.

(g) I direct that no additional contributions shall be made to the trust after the original contribution hereinabove provided and prior to the time herein fixed for termination.

(h) The trust hereby created is intended to qualify as a charitable remainder trust under the Internal Revenue Code. I direct that my trustee shall, at all times, conform to the requirements imposed upon such trusts by the Internal Revenue Code, Regulations and Revenue Rulings, as they presently exist or may hereafter be amended.

(i) Upon the death of my said son, or if he shall not survive me, I give, bequeath and devise all the rest, residue and remainder of my estate, real, personal and mixed, to *(charitable organization)* provided that, if it is not an organization described in Sections 170(c) and 2055(a) of the Internal Revenue Code (or any corresponding provisions of subsequent federal tax laws) I direct my trustee to distribute the principal to one or more other organizations, selected by said trustee in its sole discretion, each of which is engaged in activities similar to those now being performed by said *(charitable organization)* and is then described in Sections 170(c) and 2055(a) of the Internal Revenue Code.

FIGURE 7-4
Charitable remainder unitrust provision. Courtesy of *Estate Planning and Administration in Illinois* (2d ed., Lawyers Cooperative Publishing, 1991)

To obtain the charitable deduction for the federal estate tax, when a trust creates a life estate in one or more persons and the remainder is given to a charitable organization, the testator should use a properly drawn charitable name in the unitrust.

powers (described later), the settlor's spouse may receive the income from the trust for life; upon the spouse's death, the principal passes tax-free to the settlor's heirs.

Crummey powers (named from the case of *Crummey v. Commissioner,* 397 F.2d 82 (9th Cir. 1968)), give one or more of the trust beneficiaries the right to withdraw each year the money that is contributed to the trust. The withdrawal amount is usually the amount of the contribution to the trust or the amount of the annual gift tax exclusion ($10,000 per donee), whichever is less. Because the contribution may be withdrawn, it is considered a present interest and qualifies for the gift tax annual exclusion. Without these special Crummey powers of withdrawal, the payment of insurance premiums to a trust would normally be considered a taxable gift, not a gift of present interest, and not eligible for the annual $10,000 exclusion.

Crummey Withdrawal Provision in Irrevocable Trust
[17A AM. JUR. *Legal Forms* 2d (Rev.) § 251:168]

The beneficiary shall have the right during each calendar year, upon making written demand upon the trustee therefor, to receive from the trustee outright and free from this trust all or any part of any property transferred or added to such trust by way of inter vivos gift during such calendar year. The trustee shall give the beneficiary notice of any such transfer within 10 days of such transfer. However, in no event shall the trustee honor any such demand which exceeds the sum of Ten Thousand Dollars ($10,000) per donee in one calendar year. The trustee shall honor any such demand in cash or in kind, in the discretion of the trustee, immediately upon receipt by the trustee of the written demand of the beneficiary. Such payment shall be made from the property transferred to the trust by each donor during that year.

Trust funds must be sufficient to allow for the Crummey withdrawals. Therefore, gifts to an otherwise unfunded trust to pay insurance premiums should be held in trust until the demand period has elapsed. Of course, with this type of trust, the settlor and the beneficiaries would probably want the withdrawal power to lapse each year so that the money could be used to pay the insurance premiums.

SUMMARY

7.1 A Totten trust is a savings account in the name of the depositor as trustee for another person. The depositor may withdraw money from the account at any time during the depositor's lifetime. When the depositor dies, the money in the account belongs to the beneficiary. If the beneficiary dies before the depositor, the trust terminates and the money belongs to the depositor.

7.2 Spendthrift trusts are used to prevent beneficiaries who spend money profusely or unwisely from having access to trust funds until they are due.

LEGAL TERMS

Crummey powers
Powers in a life-insurance trust that give one or more beneficiaries the right to withdraw each year the money that is contributed to the trust.

Sprinkling trusts give the trustee, rather than the settlor, the power to decide who will receive the trust income and principal.

7.3 Property passing to a surviving spouse, called marital deduction property, is not taxable under federal estate tax laws. The deduction may be obtained by an outright gift to the surviving spouse; however, when that spouse dies, his or her estate may be large enough to be taxable. Another way to obtain the deduction is by giving a life estate to the surviving spouse and allowing that spouse to determine who will inherit when he or she dies. This is called a power of appointment. A third way to use the marital deduction is to establish a credit-shelter trust, which passes the deceased spouse's property to a trust for the spouse's benefit (using the $600,000 regular exemption) and any balance to the spouse outright, qualifying for the marital deduction. A QTIP trust gives the income of the trust to the surviving spouse for life, tax-free, payable annually, with the balance left intact for whomever the settlor designates.

7.4 Charitable trusts are created to benefit a part of the general public rather than individuals and are free of federal estate taxes. Under the doctrine of cy pres, if a charity comes to an end and the settlor had a general charitable intent, the trust fund will be turned over to a similar charity. Charitable trusts, unlike private trusts, can exist indefinitely, as exceptions to the rule against perpetuities. A charitable remainder annuity trust provides a fixed amount of income annually to a beneficiary, with the corpus going ultimately to a charity. In contrast, a charitable remainder unitrust offers protection against inflation by providing a percentage (not less than 5 percent) of the value of the trust property each year to a beneficiary, with the corpus going ultimately to a charity.

7.5 A life insurance trust may be used to pass money to heirs tax-free if the trust contains Crummey powers, that is, powers given to beneficiaries to withdraw the money that is contributed to the trust.

QUESTIONS FOR REVIEW

1. In a Totten trust, who is entitled to the money when the depositor dies before the beneficiary? When the beneficiary dies before the depositor?
2. When would a settlor use a spendthrift trust?
3. Why is a discretionary trust also called a sprinkling or spray trust?
4. What are one advantage and one disadvantage of a sprinkling trust?
5. What is an advantage of leaving the entire corpus of a trust outright to a surviving spouse at one's death? What can be a disadvantage?
6. When a surviving spouse is left property in trust for life with a power of appointment, who receives the trust property when the surviving spouse dies?

7. What type of trust is used when the settlor wants to pass the entire principal of the trust on to someone other than the surviving spouse, but wants the spouse to have the income from the trust for life?
8. What is the rule against perpetuities and when does it not apply?
9. How does a charitable remainder annuity trust differ from a charitable remainder unitrust?
10. What are Crummey powers and why are they used?

CASES TO DISCUSS

1. Joseph Berson deposited $73,544.51 with the Metropolitan Savings Bank in an account entitled "Joseph Berson in Trust for New York City Jewish Defense League." Berson made no further deposits to or withdrawals from the account. When Berson died, the administrator of his estate claimed that the money belonged to the estate. Is the administrator correct? Explain. *In the Matter of Joseph Berson, Deceased,* 170 A.D. 2d 504, 566 N.Y.S.2d 74 (N.Y. 1991).
2. Dorothy A. Hewlett left part of the residue of her estate to the New Canaan Inn, Inc. The Inn describes itself as a "non-profit corporation" in its certificate of incorporation. The average age of the inn's residents is 83. The facility provides recreation, health services, housing, and related facilities suited to the special needs and living requirements of the elderly occupants, three meals a day, bed linen, towels, and maid service. Although residents pay monthly, expenses exceed income by $4,000 per resident per year. The additional expenses are paid for by contributions. The residence agreement states, "Once admitted, no resident who has fulfilled all the other elements of this Agreement shall be asked to leave the Inn for inability to pay beyond his or her control." Did Hewlett's gift to the Inn qualify as a gift to charity? Why or why not? *Bannon v. Wise,* 586 A.2d 639 (Conn. 1990).
3. Robinson's will established a trust for the benefit of his wife for life, with the remainder to their daughter. The executor of the estate did not make an election on the estate tax return to treat the trust property as qualified terminable interest (QTIP) property. Does the amount in the trust qualify for the marital deduction on the estate tax return? Why or why not? *Robinson v. United States,* No. CV489-273, 90-2 U.S.T.C. (S.D. Ga. 1990).

SHARPENING YOUR PROFESSIONAL SKILLS

1. Refer to the law office scenario at the beginning of this chapter and answer the following questions:

(a) What type of trust might be considered to give the survivor of Mr. and Mrs. DeNunzio a suitable income, while retaining the principal for the children?
(b) What is the answer to Mrs. DeNunzio's question about the bank accounts in her name in trust for each child?
(c) What might Attorney Knight consider as a way to handle the problem of Angelo's daughter, who spends money "like water over a dam"?

2. In your law library, look up and write a brief of the case that decided the current law on Totten trusts, *In re Totten,* 71 N.E. 748 (N.Y. 1904). Then Shepardize the case to find a recent reference to it in your state, and brief the latest case you find.
3. Describe a factual situation for which you believe an attorney would recommend the use of:
   (a) a spendthrift trust
   (b) a sprinkling trust
   (c) a credit-shelter trust
   (d) a QTIP trust.

SECTION THREE

Estates

CHAPTER 8
Estate Planning

"During one's lifetime, impediments to the accumulation of wealth include: income taxes, inflation, probate, and estate taxes."

Howard M. Sachs

OUTLINE

LAW OFFICE SCENARIO
8.1 PURPOSE OF ESTATE PLANNING
8.2 THE PLANNING TEAM
8.3 GATHERING INFORMATION
- Domicile
- Property
- Beneficiaries
- Objectives
- Planning Checklist

8.4 ESTATE PLANNING TOOLS
- Wills
- Trusts
- Gifts
- Powers of Appointment
- Insurance

8.5 POST-MORTEM PLANNING
SUMMARY

LAW OFFICE SCENARIO

Tiffany Casey, a paralegal in the law firm of Knight & Francis, was discussing a client's estate with Attorney Knight.

"Mrs. Bradbury is coming in at 2:00 this afternoon," Attorney Knight said. "She's still quite despondent about the death of her husband, but we need to begin the probate work."

"It must be hard for her. I'll get the file out right away," Tiffany responded. "Didn't they live in a lot of different states?"

"Yes. If I remember correctly, they owned property in New Mexico, Oregon, and Connecticut, among other places. While I think of it," Attorney Knight continued, "you had better check to see if any of those states are community property states."

"Okay," Tiffany replied, jotting down some notes.

"We could have a domicile problem with this estate," Attorney Knight thought out loud. "When you go through the file, look for evidence of Mr. Bradbury's domicile."

"There might be an estate planning questionnaire in the file," Tiffany suggested.

"I don't think so," Attorney Knight countered. "Mr. Bradbury found it hard to talk about death and didn't want to do much more than make out a will when he came in to see us. We did a trust for him, though, and gave Mrs. Bradbury a power of appointment, among other things."

"Oh, that's good. Maybe now that he's gone we can do some post-mortem planning for his estate," Tiffany offered.

"You can bet on that," Attorney Knight responded. "And we'll see what we can do for Mrs. Bradbury before she dies, too."

"That's a good idea. I'll get her file out so that you can review her will while she's here."

"Thanks, Tiffany," Attorney Knight replied. "If you're free at 2:00, it would be helpful if you could join us."

"Fine. I'll plan on it."

8.1 PURPOSE OF ESTATE PLANNING

Paralegals need to know the general purpose of estate planning in order to appreciate their specific role and tasks in the process. **Estate planning** is the positioning of a person's assets to maintain and protect the family most effectively, both during and after the person's life. The main purpose of all family estate planning is to obtain the maximum benefits of principal and income for the family and to pass on the family property intact (i.e., without any losses). Also important is the disposition of the property according to the client's desires, while maintaining family harmony at the same time.

The general goal of estate planning is to protect the family unit and provide financial and psychological security. The proper positioning of a person's assets may even make a larger proportion of after-tax income available for the family to save or spend. A thoughtful insurance program can help to create a cash reserve and an estate that would otherwise be nonexistent. Assets that might be depleted or reduced in value can be preserved by appropriate planning. Gifts, trusts, marital deductions, powers of appointment, pension and profit-sharing plans, and other business arrangements are

LEGAL TERMS

estate planning
Arrangement of a person's property and estate in the manner best calculated to maintain and protect the family, both during the client's lifetime and after the client's death.

additional devices used by the estate planning team to insure the family's financial and psychological security and to maximize the assets ultimately shared by the beneficiaries (see table 8-1).

	No will or trust	Will only	Living trust	Estate tax trust
Can I avoid probate?	No	No	Yes	Yes, if funded during your life
Can I reduce/ avoid federal estate taxes?	No	No	No	Yes
Will my estate stay private when I die?	No	No	Yes	Yes, if funded during your life
Can I keep inheritance from my heirs until they reach age 30 or older?	No	No	Yes	Yes
Can I arrange to have funds managed for the benefit of an heir who is handicapped or otherwise unable to handle funds?	No	No	Yes	Yes
Can I make sure my grandchildren will receive my estate after my children die, excluding spouses of my children?	No	No	Yes	Yes

TABLE 8-1

Estate plans compared. Reproduced with permission by Armond D. Budish, Michael Gilfix, Dennis Clifford, all contributors to *Modern Maturity*

Can I leave assets to children from an earlier marriage, cutting out my present spouse?	No	No	Depends on the state	Depends on the state and how trust is set up
How long should it take after my death until all assets are distributed and the estate is closed, assuming all goes well?	6 mo.–2 yr.	6 mo.–2 yr.	2–9 mo.	9 mo.–2 yr.
Can I retain control over my assets while I'm alive?	Yes	Yes	Yes	Depends on how trust is set up
Can I change/revoke the plan?	N/A	Yes	Yes	Depends on how trust is set up
Does the plan provide for someone to handle my finances if I become disabled?	No	No	Yes	Yes, if funded during your life
What is the cost for a simple plan?	0	$50–$200	$300–$2,500	$1,000–$3,000

TABLE 8-1
(Continued)

8.2 THE PLANNING TEAM

Individuals with different training and abilities, including the paralegal, form the estate planning team. An attorney who specializes in estate planning plays a key role, because many legal issues have to be addressed. The client's accountant can provide information about the client's income taxes, details of assets and liabilities, and realistic appraisals of those assets.

A life insurance underwriter can determine the client's need for life insurance, suggest the type and amount required, and prepare an overall, cost-effective life insurance plan for the client.

If a bank is appointed as an executor or trustee, a trust officer of the bank will also be a team member. The trust officer provides advice on how specific investments are to be used in an estate plan. Based on his or her experience with administrative details, the officer may be able to suggest easier and more economical ways to administer the trust or estate.

An important member of the estate planning team is the well-trained paralegal, who can provide much-needed assistance to the attorney. Paralegals can relieve the attorney of many of the routine details of the estate planning process and thereby reduce the costs and time involved in the process. With proper training, paralegals can assist the attorney in many ways, including the following:

- Working with clients to assure that necessary estate planning information is gathered
- Assisting with the preparation of estate planning questionnaires
- Analyzing client assets and financial information
- Drafting legal documents, such as deeds, wills, and trusts
- Preparing summaries of provisions of wills and trust agreements
- Preparing tax calculations
- Monitoring state statutes to ensure that estate plans conform to state law
- Reviewing and analyzing insurance policies
- Preparing change-of-beneficiary forms
- Recording instruments at appropriate registries.

8.3 GATHERING INFORMATION

Paralegals are frequently involved in the first, and probably most important, step of the estate planning process: gathering facts. Without these facts the process cannot proceed. Obtaining all the necessary data requires persistence and is the basis for all other procedures. The needed facts can be classified into four categories: (1) domicile, (2) property, (3) beneficiaries, and (4) the individual's objectives.

Domicile

As discussed in chapter 5, the probate court in the place where the testator was domiciled at the time of death has primary jurisdiction to administer the decedent's estate. This is also where the estate is taxed, and this state's law is followed to determine the distribution of personal property. Thus, the estate planner must establish and make clear the client's domicile.

A person can have several residences, but only one domicile at any given time. It is not always easy to determine whether someone has acquired a new domicile. For a new domicile to be established, the person must reside in the new place of residence and, at the same time, have the intent to establish a principal residence there. As the *Winkler* case illustrates, a person's intention regarding domicile is determined by the person's conduct and all the surrounding circumstances. When there is a dispute over domicile, the burden of proving a change of domicile is on the person claiming that it has been changed. So long as a reasonable doubt remains, there is a presumption that the domicile has not been changed.

APPLICATION OF WINKLER
567 N.Y.S.2d 53 (App. Div. 1991)

FACTS: When Frederick E. Winkler died, the question arose as to the location of his domicile. He owned a home in Seaview, Fire Island, Suffolk County, New York, where he lived for seven months of the year. He spent the other months in his two other homes in New York County. His voting records, passport, marriage certificate, and driver's license listed Seaview as his residence, and witnesses' testimony indicated that he intended the home in Seaview to be his domicile.

LEGAL ISSUE: Is a person's intention to be domiciled in a particular location determined by that person's conduct?

COURT DECISION: Yes.

REASON: The intention of one's domicile is determined by the conduct of the person and all the surrounding circumstances which may be proven by acts and declarations. The documentation in this case, as well as witnesses' testimony, were sufficient to show that it was the decedent's intention that his home in Seaview, Fire Island, was to be his domicile.

Property

All property should be listed in detail, including automobiles, household effects, objects of art, stamp collections, books, and similar possessions. The estate planner must determine the location of all real estate, the form in which title is held, its cost, fair market value, and the amount of all mortgages on the property. All insurance must be listed, with cost, age, present value, face value, cash surrender value, type of policy, and beneficiaries noted. Balance sheets and income statements of all businesses and partnerships must be reviewed. Stocks, bonds, and bank accounts should all be listed individually, and pension plans, profit-sharing plans, and stock option agreements should also be noted. All jointly owned property must be listed, as well as information about gifts made during the client's lifetime.

Beneficiaries

A family tree is a helpful device to visualize a family and all its members. Such a diagram makes concrete the often complex lineal relationships discussed in chapter 3. (See figure 8-1.) Besides this visual aid, however, detailed information about all family members is essential to acknowledge or locate all heirs.

Objectives

The individual objectives of the client are the main focus of estate planning. The client's desires must be clarified and fulfilled in whatever way the client determines. The client may wish to endow the surviving spouse primarily or to favor one child, despite possible family resentment. The legal ramifications of such decisions must be discussed, but ultimately the client's personal preferences are what determine the specific aspects of the estate plan.

Planning Checklist

These four categories of facts—domicile, property, beneficiaries, objectives—point to general kinds of information needed in the estate-planning process. The following checklist is a helpful guide to the more specific information required.

Family Estate Plan Checklist
[Harris, *Family Estate Planning Guide* § 20 (2d ed., Lawyers Co-operative Publishing Co., 1971)]

1. Name in full—other names or initials
2. Residence—domicile
3. Age and medical history
4. Family tree
5. Is there a safe-deposit box? Where? Where is key? Form in which held?
6. Is there a will? Where kept?
7. Is there an antenuptial agreement?
8. Has there been a divorce or separation?

9. Beneficiaries—names, addresses, relationship, age, marital status, financial status, financial needs, prospects, character traits
10. Personal property—auto, boat, airplane, objects of art, jewelry, household effects, stamp or coin collection, library
11. Real estate—domestic, foreign, record owner
12. Insurance—cost, value, age, amount, kind, beneficiary
13. Business interest—sole proprietor, partner, shareholder
14. Securities—bonds, mortgages, stock, cost, present market values, ownership
15. Trading accounts—broker, securities, balance, cost, present market value, ownership
16. Pledged property—value, cost, amount due, agreement
17. Joint property
18. Trust accounts
19. Custodian accounts
20. Pension rights
21. Profit-sharing plan rights
22. Stock options
23. Deferred compensation agreement
24. Social Security benefits
25. Power of appointment
26. Possible testamentary benefits
27. Settlor of trust
28. Beneficiary of trust
29. Previous gifts—dates, amounts, donees, income tax returns
30. Cash, savings accounts, checking accounts, accounts receivable
31. Patents
32. Copyrights
33. Wasting assets
34. Contract rights
35. Liabilities—secured, unsecured, contingent
36. Community property

Even more detailed is the questionnaire that experienced family estate planners normally request clients to complete before the initial interview with the attorney (see figure 8-2). Completion of the questionnaire in advance reduces the attorney's time and legal fees. Many items in the questionnaire may not apply to a particular client; however, using so detailed a questionnaire insures that all facts will be considered when formulating the best plan for the client.

8.4 ESTATE PLANNING TOOLS

Estate planning is sometimes called an art rather than a science. It involves a considerable amount of creativity. Every client's unique situation requires a creative approach by the estate planner. The tools available to the estate planner are limitless, but the principal ones used are wills, trusts, gifts, powers of appointment, and insurance.

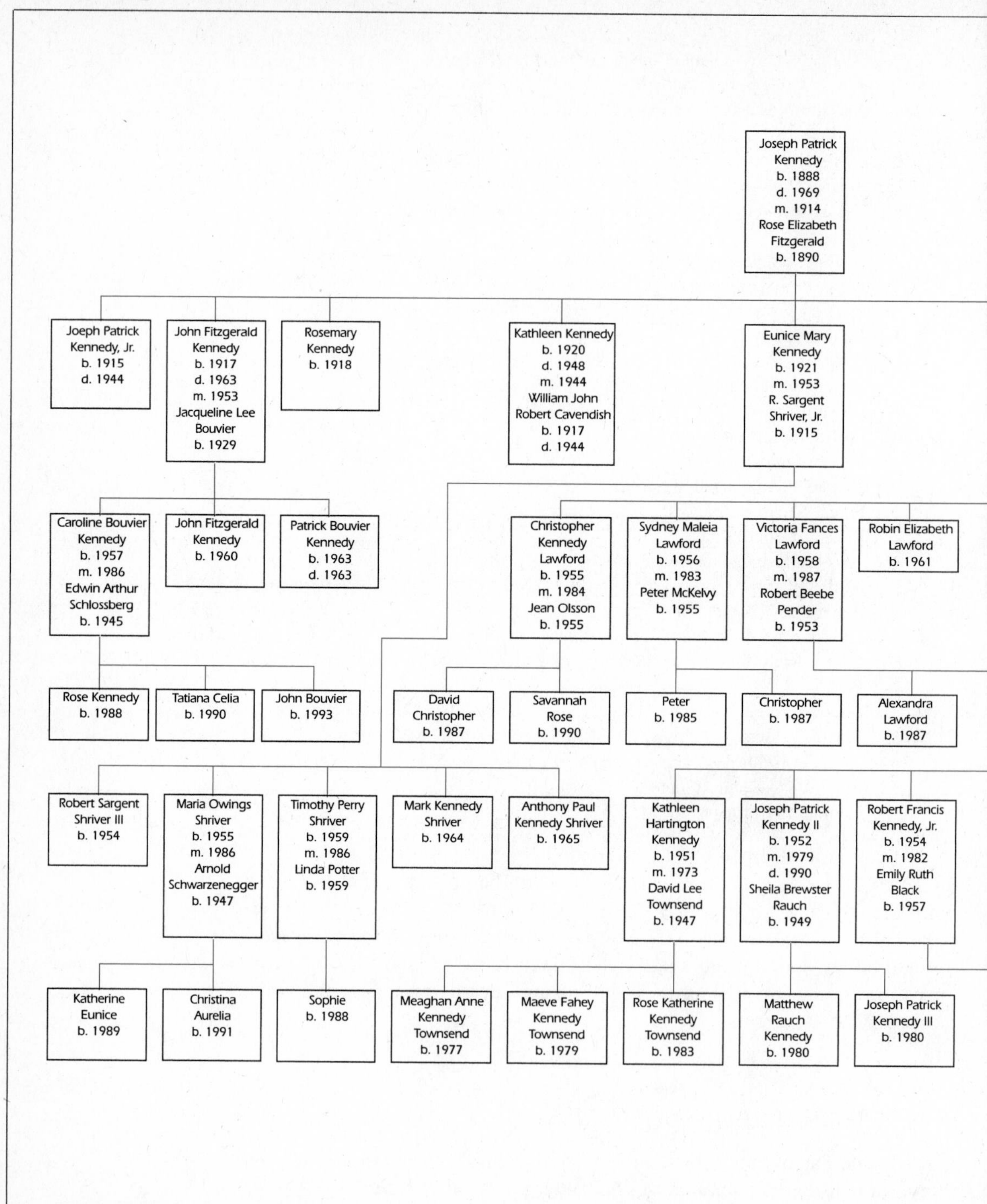

FIGURE 8-1
Kennedy family tree

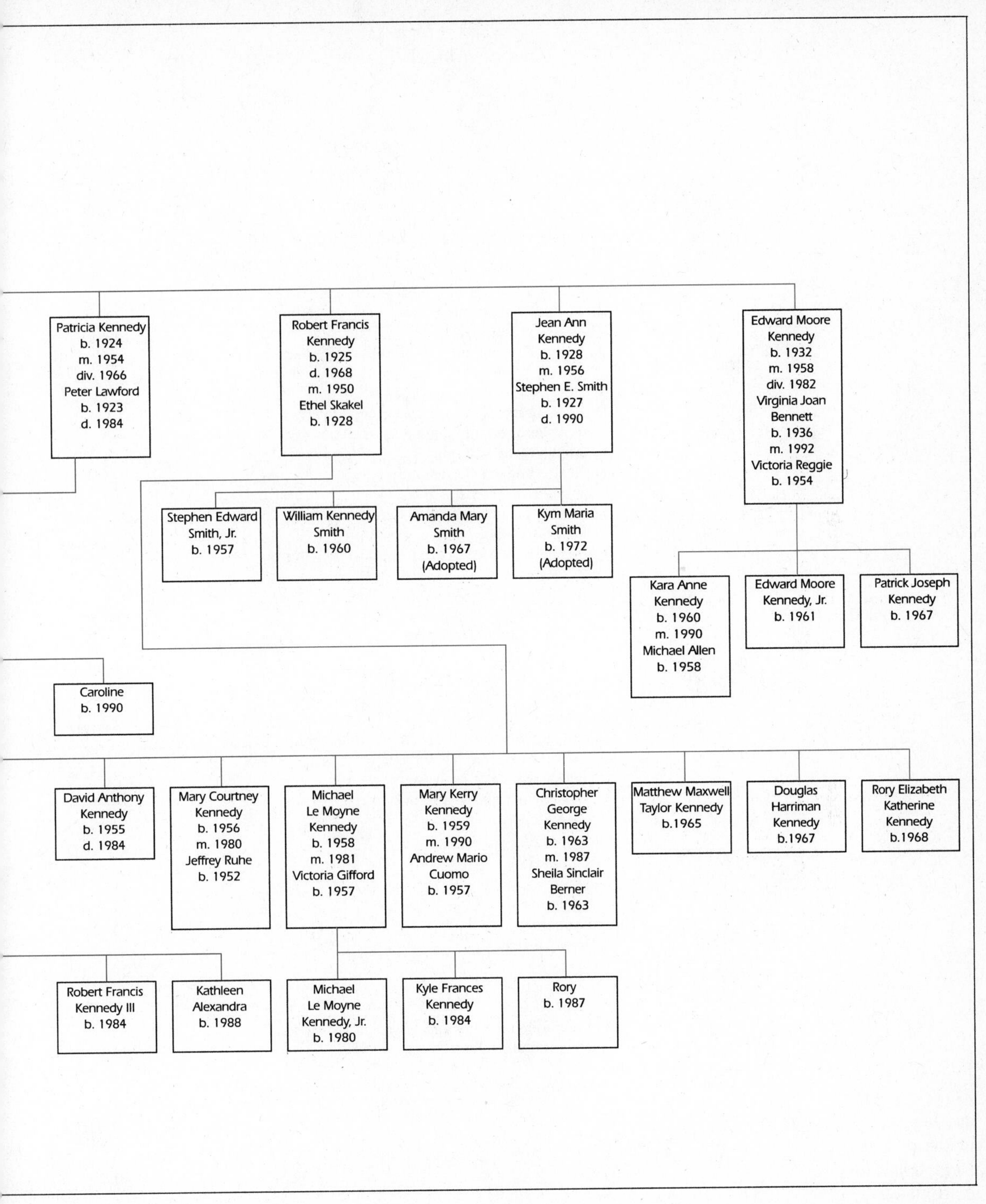

Patricia Kennedy b. 1924 m. 1954 div. 1966 Peter Lawford b. 1923 d. 1984
Robert Francis Kennedy b. 1925 d. 1968 m. 1950 Ethel Skakel b. 1928
Jean Ann Kennedy b. 1928 m. 1956 Stephen E. Smith b. 1927 d. 1990
Edward Moore Kennedy b. 1932 m. 1958 div. 1982 Virginia Joan Bennett b. 1936 m. 1992 Victoria Reggie b. 1954
Stephen Edward Smith, Jr. b. 1957
William Kennedy Smith b. 1960
Amanda Mary Smith b. 1967 (Adopted)
Kym Maria Smith b. 1972 (Adopted)
Kara Anne Kennedy b. 1960 m. 1990 Michael Allen b. 1958
Edward Moore Kennedy, Jr. b. 1961
Patrick Joseph Kennedy b. 1967
Caroline b. 1990
David Anthony Kennedy b. 1955 d. 1984
Mary Courtney Kennedy b. 1956 m. 1980 Jeffrey Ruhe b. 1952
Michael Le Moyne Kennedy b. 1958 m. 1981 Victoria Gifford b. 1957
Mary Kerry Kennedy b. 1959 m. 1990 Andrew Mario Cuomo b. 1957
Christopher George Kennedy b. 1963 m. 1987 Sheila Sinclair Berner b. 1963
Matthew Maxwell Taylor Kennedy b.1965
Douglas Harriman Kennedy b.1967
Rory Elizabeth Katherine Kennedy b.1968
Robert Francis Kennedy III b. 1984
Kathleen Alexandra b. 1988
Michael Le Moyne Kennedy, Jr. b. 1980
Kyle Frances Kennedy b. 1984
Rory b. 1987

ESTATE PLANNING WORKING INFORMATION

____
CLIENT

____
DATE

____
INTERVIEWED BY

COPIES OF DOCUMENTS THAT MUST BE REVIEWED

	Obtained	Returned
1. Existing wills of both spouses.	_______	_______
2. All gift tax returns ever filed by client and/or spouse.	_______	_______
3. Individual income tax returns for past five (5) years.	_______	_______
4. Insurance policies in effect.	_______	_______
5. Existing pension, profit-sharing, deferred compensation or similar type plans and employment agreements.	_______	_______
6. Real estate deeds and mortgages.	_______	_______
7. Trust instruments.	_______	_______
8. Personal and business financial statement for past years.	_______	_______
9. Business income tax returns for past five (5) years.	_______	_______
10. Buy-sell or stock redemptions agreements.	_______	_______
11. Partnership and/or joint venture agreements.	_______	_______
12. Powers of appointment.	_______	_______
13. Divorce, separation and pre-marital agreements.	_______	_______
14. Instruments showing basis of assets held.	_______	_______
15. Instruments creating spouses' joint tenancies or tenancies by entirety.	_______	_______
16. Has client ever lived in any of the following states:		
Arizona	_______	_______
California	_______	_______
Idaho	_______	_______
Louisiana	_______	_______
Nevada	_______	_______
New Mexico	_______	_______
Texas	_______	_______
Washington	_______	_______
Puerto Rico	_______	_______
17. Purchase contracts and leases of property bought and/or leased.	_______	_______

* This form prepared and utilized by C. Douglas Miller, Esq., Professor of Law at the University of Florida Graduate Tax Program; Member of the Florida Bar and practicing attorney with the firm of Miller and Honigman in Orlando, Florida.

FIGURE 8-2

Estate planning questionnaire. Courtesy of Harris, *Family Estate Planning Guide* 3d ed. (Hoops, ed., Lawyers Cooperative Publishing, 1992)

ESTATE PLANNING—FAMILY INFORMATION

Estate Owner__________ D/B__________ Place__________

Spouse__________ Maiden Name__________ D/B__________ Place__________

Former Marriages?__________

If Previous Marriage, Any Problems?__________

Residence Address__________ Years__________

Former Address__________ Years__________

Office Address__________ Occupation __________

Name of Employer__________

CHILDREN (& SPOUSE)	D/B	PLACE	GRANDCHILDREN NAME	D/B

Any adopted or by a previous marriage?__________

Others Dependent upon you or Spouse for Support__________

Name__________ Age__________ Monthly Income Required

Are you a Veteran?__________ Dates of Active Duty__________ Serial No.__________

Are you, or did you ever receive Veteran's Disability Benefits?__________

Nature of Disability__________

Are you in the National Guard or Reserves?__________

Any unusual health problems? Self__________ Spouse__________

Children__________

Have you ever had insurance disability claims?__________ Date__________

Reason__________

Aviation Activities?__________

Who is taxed under Social Security?__________

ADVISORS

	NAME	ADDRESS
Attorney		
Accountant		
Trust Officer		
Other Bank Officer		
Investment Advisor		
Stock Broker		
Tax Advisor		
Gen. Ins. Broker		
Physician		
Other		

FIGURE 8-2
(Continued)

Wills

A will is considered to be the single most important estate planning instrument. Without a will, state law rather than the wishes of the decedent

SUMMARY

DATE: ____________

ASSET DATA

	Husband		Wife		Joint		Husband's Percentage Contribution
	A/B	FMV	A/B	FMV	A/B	FMV	
Cash	$____	$____	$____	$____	$____	$____	________
Personal effects	____	____	____	____	____	____	________
Life insurance	____	____	____	____	____	____	________
Stocks	____	____	____	____	____	____	________
Bonds and treasury notes	____	____	____	____	____	____	________
Real estate/limited partnerships	____	____	____	____	____	____	________
Other tangible assets	____	____	____	____	____	____	________
Business ownership	____	____	____	____	____	____	________
Retirement benefits	____	____	____	____	____	____	________
Other business and investment assets	____	____	____	____	____	____	________
Total Assets	$____	$____	$____	$____	$____	$____	________
Aggregate appreciation of assets over basis	$____	$____	$____	$____	$____	$____	________

LIABILITIES

	Husband A/B	Husband FMV	Wife A/B	Wife FMV	Joint A/B	Joint FMV	Husband's Percentage Contribution
Real estate mortgages and contracts payable	$____	$____	$____	$____	$____	$____	________
Other liabilities	____	____	____	____	____	____	________
Total Liabilities	$____	$____	$____	$____	$____	$____	________
NET WORTH	$____	$____	$____	$____	$____	$____	________

CASH AND PERSONAL EFFECTS

	Bank	Amount	Income	Form of Ownership With Whom*	Husband's Percentage Contribution
Bank Accounts:					
Certificates of Deposit:					
Total		$____	$____		

FIGURE 8-2
(Continued)

will determine the disposition of the decedent's property. A will has no effect until the testator(rix) dies and may be changed or revoked by the testator(rix) at any time prior to death.

	Fair Market Value	Income	Form of Ownership With Whom*	Husband's Percentage Contribution
Automobiles				
Household furnishings				
Jewelry				
Collections (Art, etc.)				
Others (describe)**				
Total	$	$		

* If held in joint ownership with spouse, indicate whether created after 1976 or before 1977.

** Such as accounts, notes and mortgages receivable, patents, royalties, etc.

LIFE INSURANCE POLICIES AND ANNUITIES*

Life Insurance Provided by Employer

	Policy #1	Policy #2	Policy #3
Company			
Policy #			
Type			
Insured			
Owner			
Beneficiary			
Contingent Beneficiary			
Face Value			
Amount of Loan			
Employee's Contribution			

Other Life Insurance

	Policy #1	Policy #2	Policy #3
Company			
Policy #			
Type			
Insured*			
Owner			
Beneficiary			
Contingent Beneficiary			
Face Value			
Current Cash Surrender Value			
Amount of Loan			
Annual Premium			

* Include policies on life of spouse and children

FIGURE 8-2
(Continued)

A well-organized will should be outlined before it is drafted. An outline forces the drafter to think through the entire document before focusing on specific details. It provides an overview of what has to be done and helps

STOCKS

Company & Type	Ownership*	Number of Shares	Date of Purchase or Acquisition	Basis	Current Market Value
			Total	$	

* Indicate restrictions on transfer, if any.

BONDS AND TREASURY NOTES

			Total	$	

* List if securities are marketable only.

MUTUAL FUNDS

			Total	$	

REAL ESTATE/LIMITED PARTNERSHIPS

	Property 1	Property 2
Legal Description	Please Attach	
Location		
Personal Residence?		
Owned in Names of:		
Form of Ownership		
Date of Acquisition		
How acquired (Gift, Purchase, etc.)		
Cost Basis		
Accumulated Depreciation*		
Current Market Value		
Encumbrances:		
Names of mortgagees, lienors, etc.		
Amount		
Monthly payments (principal & interest)		
Interest rate		
Remaining period of loan		
Annual interest		
Annual taxes		
Annual income (gross)*		
Annual depreciation*		

FIGURE 8-2
(Continued)

ensure that the final document includes all necessary provisions. An outline also helps weed out potential inconsistencies in the document and furnishes a fail-safe checklist to make sure that everything required has been included.

Annual costs
(maintenance, etc.)* ________ ________
Annual net income* ________ ________

* Income-producing property only

CLOSELY HELD BUSINESS INTERESTS

(Use separate sheet for each business interest)

Name________
Type of Entity: Corporation ____ Partnership ____ Sole Proprietorship____
Percentage of Ownership: Self:____ Spouse:____
Others:____ Children:____
Buy/sell or redemption agreement? Yes ____ No ____ Details:____

Client's wishes on disposition of interest____
Key-man insurance:

EMPLOYEE	FACE VALUE	CASH VALUE

Most recent transfer of ownership equity by any other:
Price____ Percentage or number of shares____
Date of transfer____
Corporate obligations guaranteed by client____
Estimate of fair market value per your analysis____
Estimate of fair market value per client____
Basis of securities held____ Date acquired____

REMARKS

LIABILITIES

(Not previously listed)

Debtor	Creditor	Secured By	Interest Rate	Due Date	Repayment Schedule	Current Balance

HUSBAND/WIFE

EMPLOYMENT

Current employer____
Date employed____
Annual compensation____ Projected retirement date____

FIGURE 8-2
(Continued)

It is recommended that any handwritten notes taken by the attorney and the legal assistant during the client interview be retained in the client's

CASH FLOW

	Currently	Projected After Client's Death	Projected for Retirement
Sources of cash:			
Compensation	$______	$______	$______
Dividends	______	______	______
Interest	______	______	______
Cash Flow from rental property	______	______	______
Business interests:			
______	______	______	______
______	______	______	______
Miscellaneous:			
Trusts	______	______	______
______	______	______	______
______	______	______	______
Pension benefits	______	______	______
Social security	______	______	______
______	______	______	______
______	______	______	______
______	______	______	______
Total	______	______	______
	______	______	______

CASH FLOW

	Currently	Projected After Client's Death	Projected for Retirement
Expenditures:			
Standard of Living:	$______	$______	$______
Food	______	______	______
Mortgage payments or rent	______	______	______
Real estate taxes	______	______	______
Entertainment	______	______	______
Miscellaneous (clothing, utilities, etc.)	______	______	______
Other:			
Income taxes	______	______	______
Savings and investment	______	______	______
Other loan payments	______	______	______
Education	______	______	______

FIGURE 8-2
(Continued)

file. These notes are useful in refreshing the attorney's and the legal assistant's recollection in the event of a will contest after the client dies.

Life insurance premiums	____	____	____
Keogh	____	____	____
IRA	____	____	____
Unusual expenditures	____	____	____
____	____	____	____
____	____	____	____
____	____	____	____
Total			
Excess (deficit)	$____	____	____

TYPE OF PLAN

	Pension*	Profit-Sharing*	Individual Retirement Account	Deferred Compensation
Company____**				
Retirement benefits				
Amount currently vested				
Death benefits				
Disability benefits				
Beneficiary at death				
Amount excludible Under IRC 2039(c)				
Employee contributions to date				
Years in plan to date				
Name and address of plan administrator(s)				

* Indicate if either are Keogh plans

** If more than one, attach separate sheet.

STOCK OPTIONS

	Date of Grant	Option Price	Number of Shares	Type of option	F.M.V. at Date of Grant
Option 1	____	$____	____	____	____
Option 2	____	$____	____	____	____

	Expiration Date	How Long Exercisable by Estate	Present F.M.V.	Value: Number of Shares × (F.M.V. Option Price)
Option 1	____	$____	____	____
Option 2	____	$____	____	____

FIGURE 8-2
(Continued)

Trusts

Trusts are used by estate planning specialists to reduce problems created by joint ownership, avoid the expense and publicity of probate, and

RESTRICTED PROPERTY

Description of property subject to restriction	Nature of Restriction	Expected Date Such Restriction Will Lapse	Section 83(b) Election in Effect
________	________	________	________
________	________	________	________

GIFTS

Lifetime Gift Tax Exemptions

	Federal*	State
Husband has used:	$________	$________
Wife has used:	________	________

Lifetime Use of Unified Estate and Gift Tax Credit

Husband has used:	$________	$________
Wife has used:	________	________

Cumulative Taxable Gifts Per Latest Gift Tax Returns

	Federal*	State
Husband:	$________	$________
Wife:	________	________

GIFT DATA:

A. Trusts created (grantor, beneficiaries, powers and rights retained, value of gift, trustee, term, reversion, present value].
____
____

B. Existing custodial accounts under Uniform Gift to Minors Act (donor, date, custodian, minor (age), value of gift, present value):
____
____

*Applicable only for pre-1977 gifts using federal lifetime exemption.

LOCATION OF ASSETS AND DOCUMENTS

1. Safe deposit box (location of box, who has access, who has keys):
____
____
2. Original current wills:________________
3. Life, health and accident insurance policies:________________
____
____
4. Pass books (location):________________
____
5. Securities:________________
____
6. Trust agreements:________________
____
7. Tax returns: years covered:________________
____
8. Contracts and business agreements:________________
____

FIGURE 8-2
(Continued)

reduce death taxes. Trusts are also used to pass assets on to future generations, provide income for people during their lives, and prevent family assets from being mismanaged or spent unwisely.

9. Real Estate and condominiums: ______
   a. Location and how owned: ______
   b. Deed and title policy: ______
   c. Leases: ______
10. Custody and other managed accounts: ______
11. Jewelry and other valuable tangibles: ______
12. Cancelled checks and stubs; period covered: ______
13. Cemetery plot (location of plot and deed; care arrangements): ______
14. Birth certificates: ______
15. Marriage certificates: ______
16. Divorce papers: ______
17. Employee benefit statements: ______
18. Employee benefit plan copies: ______
19. Military discharge papers: ______
20. Naturalization papers ______
21. Passports: ______
22. Adoption papers: ______
23. General insurance policies: ______
24. Private safe (location, who has access): ______
25. Firearms and registration requirements: ______
26. Funeral direction: ______

POWERS OF ATTORNEY outstanding including bank accounts and safe deposit access. Give dates and names (obtain copies; show: attorney in fact; address; description of power; date): ______

MEDICAL AND DISABILITY INSURANCE

	Company	Benefits	Beneficiary
Medical	______	______	______
Surgical	______	______	______
Hospital	______	______	______
Disability	______	______	______

FIGURE 8-2
(Continued)

As was discussed in chapter 5, trusts may be created so that they come into effect when one is alive, or they may be created in the body of a will so that they come into effect after one passes away. Living trusts may be revocable or irrevocable. Trusts may be funded by life insurance. Spray, or sprinkling, trusts allow the trust principal and income to be distributed in a manner determined by a trustee rather than by the person who created the trust. Spendthrift trusts can be created to protect the interests of beneficiaries who might spend trust funds unwisely. Charitable trusts, credit-shelter trusts, and QTIP trusts are often used to reduce death taxes.

Gifts

The use of gifts during one's lifetime is an important estate planning device that offers tax-saving advantages. Death taxes can be reduced by giving property away while one is alive, but the gift must be completed. A *completed gift* is a donation that is placed beyond the dominion and control of the **donor** (one who makes a gift). "Dominion and control" means the retention by the donor of power to direct the disposition or manner of enjoyment of the property that was given away.

A donor can give $10,000 a year to each of any number of **donees** (people who receive gifts) without any tax consequences. Under the **split-gift provision** of the Internal Revenue Code, spouses may consent to treat gifts of one spouse as if made one-half by each spouse, and double the amount that may be given away tax-free each year. For example, one parent of three children can give as much as $30,000 annually to the children ($10,000 to each) without filing a gift tax return, and both parents, by consenting, could increase the amount to $60,000.

Except for a $10,000-per-donee-per-year exclusion, the federal government taxes all gifts made during one's lifetime, as part of estate tax law. Gifts to the donor's spouse and to charitable institutions are exempt from the tax, as are gifts for tuition and medical care. Gifts over $10,000 in any one year per donee, other than to a spouse, must be reported to the Internal Revenue Service (IRS) on Form 709 (figure 8-3). Form 709A may be used to report split gifts. Because the federal gift and estate tax has a combined exemption of $600,000, no gift tax is payable on gifts reported on Form 709 until the amount exceeds $600,000, or $1.2 million for split gifts of husbands and wives. When the donor dies, the total gifts exceeding $10,000 per donee made during the donor's life are subtracted from the $600,000 allowance on the federal estate tax return.

LEGAL TERMS

donor
Person who makes a gift or creates a power of appointment.

donee
Person who receives a gift or who has the right to exercise a power of appointment.

split-gift provision
Provision in the Internal Revenue Code under which spouses may consent to treat gifts of one spouse as if made one-half by each spouse, thereby doubling the amount that may be given away tax-free each year.

Advantages of Intervivos Gifts
[Harris, *Family Estate Planning Guide* 3d ed. 189 (Hoops, ed., Lawyers Cooperative Publishing 1992)]

1. $10,000 per donee per year is excluded from the federal estate and gift tax
2. Lifetime gifts reduce the assets which would otherwise pass through probate, thereby reducing the delays and expenses incidental to probate administration
3. Removal of assets from the jurisdiction of the probate court serves also to remove such assets from public scrutiny
4. A testamentary expression of intent can be challenged and successfully attacked more easily than a completed lifetime gift
5. The donor may be relieved of the responsibilities of managing assets
6. A gift in trust may furnish skilled investment advice to an inexperienced investor, although the same result could be achieved by retention of an investment counsellor

Form **709** (Rev. October 1990)
Department of the Treasury Internal Revenue Service

United States Gift (and Generation-Skipping Transfer) Tax Return
(Section 6019 of the Internal Revenue Code) (For gifts made after December 31, 1989, and before January 1, 1993)
Calendar year 19 _____
▶ **See separate instructions. For Privacy Act Notice, see the Instructions for Form 1040.**

OMB No. 1545-0020
Expires 8-31-93

Part 1.—General Information

1 Donor's first name and middle initial	2 Donor's last name	3 Social security number
4 Address (number, street, and apartment number)		5 Domicile
6 City, state, and ZIP code		7 Citizenship

	Yes	No
8 If the donor died during the year, check here ▶ ☐ and enter date of death ________________, 19 _____.		
9 If you received an extension of time to file this Form 709, check here ▶ ☐ and attach the Form 4868, 2688, 2350, or extension letter.		
10 Enter the total number of separate donees listed on Schedule A—count each person only once . . . . ☐		
11 If you (the donor) filed a previous Form 709 (or 709-A), has your address changed since the last Form 709 (or 709-A) was filed?		
12 Gifts by husband or wife to third parties.—Do you consent to have the gifts (including generation-skipping transfers) made by you and by your spouse to third parties during the calendar year considered as made one-half by each of you? (See instructions.) (If the answer is "Yes," the following information must be furnished and your spouse is to sign the consent shown below. If the answer is "No," skip lines 13–18 and go to Schedule A.).		
13 Name of consenting spouse — 14 SSN		
15 Were you married to one another during the entire calendar year? (See instructions.)		
16 If the answer to 15 is "No," check whether ☐ married ☐ divorced or ☐ widowed, and give date (see instructions) ▶		
17 Will a gift tax return for this calendar year be filed by your spouse?		

18 **Consent of Spouse**—I consent to have the gifts (and generation-skipping transfers) made by me and by my spouse to third parties during the calendar year considered as made one-half by each of us. We are both aware of the joint and several liability for tax created by the execution of this consent.

Consenting spouse's signature ▶ **Date** ▶

Part 2.—Tax Computation

1	Enter the amount from Schedule A, Part 3, line 15	1	
2	Enter the amount from Schedule B, line 3	2	
3	Total taxable gifts (add lines 1 and 2)	3	
4	Tax computed on amount on line 3 (see Table for Computing Tax in separate instructions)	4	
5	Tax computed on amount on line 2 (see Table for Computing Tax in separate instructions)	5	
6	Balance (subtract line 5 from line 4)	6	
7	Maximum unified credit (nonresident aliens, see instructions)	7	192,800 00
8	Enter the unified credit against tax allowable for all prior periods (from Sch. B, line 1, col. C) .	8	
9	Balance (subtract line 8 from line 7)	9	
10	Enter 20% (.20) of the amount allowed as a specific exemption for gifts made after September 8, 1976, and before January 1, 1977 (see instructions)	10	
11	Balance (subtract line 10 from line 9)	11	
12	Unified credit (enter the smaller of line 6 or line 11)	12	
13	Credit for foreign gift taxes (see instructions)	13	
14	Total credits (add lines 12 and 13)	14	
15	Balance (subtract line 14 from line 6) (do not enter less than zero)	15	
16	Generation-skipping transfer taxes (from Schedule C, Part 3, col. H, total)	16	
17	Total tax (add lines 15 and 16)	17	
18	Gift and generation-skipping transfer taxes prepaid with extension of time to file	18	
19	If line 18 is less than line 17, enter BALANCE DUE (see instructions)	19	
20	If line 18 is greater than line 17, enter AMOUNT TO BE REFUNDED	20	

Please attach check or money order here

Under penalties of perjury, I declare that I have examined this return, including any accompanying schedules and statements, and to the best of my knowledge and belief it is true, correct, and complete. Declaration of preparer (other than donor) is based on all information of which preparer has any knowledge.

Donor's signature ▶ Date ▶

Preparer's signature (other than donor) ▶ Date ▶

Preparer's address (other than donor) ▶

For Paperwork Reduction Act Notice, see page 1 of the separate instructions for this form. Form **709** (Rev. 10-90)

FIGURE 8-3
Internal Revenue Service Form 709

7. A gift in trust could provide for management and preservation of the assets in the event of the donor's incompetency, without necessity for judicial intervention
8. A gift in trust can fend off importuning relatives
9. Speculatively inclined donors can protect their families against their own business reverses and assure themselves of future financial security
10. If accumulation is prohibited by the law of the donor's domicile, a gift in trust permits the donor to select the law by which the trust will be governed

Form 709 (Rev. 10-90) Page 2

SCHEDULE A Computation of Taxable Gifts

Part 1.—Gifts Subject Only to Gift Tax. *Gifts less political organization, medical, and educational exclusions—see instructions*

A Item number	B Donee's name, relationship to donor (if any), and address and description of gift. If the gift was made by means of a trust, enter trust's identifying number below and attach a copy of the trust instrument. If the gift was securities, enter the CUSIP number(s), if available.	C Donor's adjusted basis of gift	D Date of gift	E Value at date of gift
1				

Part 2.—Gifts Which are Direct Skips and are Subject to Both Gift Tax and Generation-Skipping Transfer Tax. You must list the gifts in chronological order. *Gifts less political organization, medical, and educational exclusions—see instructions. (Also list here direct skips that are subject only to the GST tax at this time as the result of the termination of an "estate tax inclusion period." See instructions.)*

A Item number	B Donee's name, relationship to donor (if any), and address and description of gift. If the gift was made by means of a trust, enter trust's identifying number below and attach a copy of the trust instrument. If the gift was securities, enter the CUSIP number(s), if available.	C Donor's adjusted basis of gift	D Date of gift	E Value at date of gift
1				

Part 3.—Gift Tax Reconciliation

1	Total value of gifts of donor (add column E of Parts 1 and 2)	1	
2	One-half of items ________ attributable to spouse (see instructions)	2	
3	Balance (subtract line 2 from line 1)	3	
4	Gifts of spouse to be included (from Schedule A, Part 3, line 2 of spouse's return—see instructions). If any of the gifts included on this line are also subject to the generation-skipping transfer tax, check here ► ☐ and enter those gifts also on Schedule C, Part 1.	4	
5	Total gifts (add lines 3 and 4)	5	
6	Total annual exclusions for gifts listed on Schedule A (including line 4, above) (see instructions)	6	
7	Total included amount of gifts (subtract line 6 from line 5)	7	
	Deductions (see instructions)		
8	Gifts of interests to spouse for which a marital deduction will be claimed, based on items ________ of Schedule A . . . 8		
9	Exclusions attributable to gifts on line 8 . . . 9		
10	Marital deduction—subtract line 9 from line 8 . . . 10		
11	Charitable deduction, based on items ____ to ____ less exclusions . 11		
12	Total deductions—add lines 10 and 11	12	
13	Subtract line 12 from line 7	13	
14	Generation-skipping transfer taxes payable with this Form 709 (from Schedule C, Part 3, col. H, Total)	14	
15	Taxable gifts (add lines 13 and 14). Enter here and on line 1 of the Tax Computation on page 1	15	

(If more space is needed, attach additional sheets of same size.)

FIGURE 8-3
(Continued)

11. A gift may create financial maturity and independence among the family members.

Powers of Appointment

When making a will or a trust, people sometimes do not know who their beneficiaries should be. They cannot predict which family members will be most needy at the time of the testator's death. A power of appointment in a will or trust allows flexibility in determining who will inherit

Form 709 (Rev. 10-90) Page 3

SCHEDULE A Computation of Taxable Gifts (continued)

16 Terminable Interest (QTIP) Marital Deduction. (See instructions.)

☐ ◄ Check here if you elected, under the rules of section 2523(f), to include gifts of qualified terminable interest property on line 8, on page 2. Enter the item numbers (from Schedule A) of the gifts for which you made this election ►

17 Election out of QTIP Treatment of Annuities

☐ ◄ Check here if you elect under section 2523(f)(6) to **NOT** treat as qualified terminable interest property any joint and survivor annuities that are reported on Schedule A and would otherwise be treated as qualified terminable interest property under section 2523(f). (See instructions.) Enter the item numbers (from Schedule A) for the annuities for which you are making this election ►

SCHEDULE B Gifts From Prior Periods

Did you (the donor) file gift tax returns for prior periods? (If "Yes," see instructions for completing Schedule B below.) ☐ Yes ☐ No

A Calendar year or calendar quarter (see instructions)	B Internal Revenue office where prior return was filed	C Amount of unified credit against gift tax for periods after December 31, 1976	D Amount of specific exemption for prior periods ending before January 1, 1977	E Amount of taxable gifts
1 Totals for prior periods (without adjustment for reduced specific exemption)		1		
2 Amount, if any, by which total specific exemption, line 1, column D, is more than $30,000			2	
3 Total amount of taxable gifts for prior periods (add amount, column E, line 1, and amount, if any, on line 2) (Enter here and on line 2 of the Tax Computation on page 1.)			3	

SCHEDULE C Computation of Generation-Skipping Transfer Tax

Note: *Inter vivos direct skips which are completely excluded by the GST exemption must still be fully reported (including value and exemptions claimed) on Schedule C.*

Part 1.—Generation-Skipping Transfers

A Item No. (from Schedule A, Part 2, col. A)	B Value (from Schedule A, Part 2, col. E)	C Split Gifts (enter ½ of col. B) (see instructions)	D Subtract col. C from col. B	E Nontaxable portion of transfer	F Net Transfer (subtract col. E from col. D)
1					
2					
3					
4					
5					
6					
If you elected gift splitting and your spouse was required to file a separate Form 709 (see the instructions for "Split Gifts"), you must enter all of the gifts shown on Schedule A, Part 2, of your spouse's Form 709 here. In column C, enter the item number of each gift in the order it appears in column A of your spouse's Schedule A, Part 2. We have preprinted the prefix "S-" to distinguish your spouse's item numbers from your own when you complete column A of Schedule C, Part 3. In column D, for each gift, enter the amount reported in column C, Schedule C, Part 1, of your spouse's Form 709.		Split gifts from spouse's Form 709 (enter item number)	Value included from spouse's Form 709		
		S-			
		S-			
		S-			
		S-			
		S-			
		S-			
		S-			
		S-			

(If more space is needed, attach additional sheets of same size.)

FIGURE 8-3
(Continued)

from a decedent's estate. It allows someone besides the decedent to decide, after the decedent's death, who will be the beneficiaries and to what extent.

A **power of appointment** is a right created in a will, trust, or other instrument which allows the holder (the donee) to direct the disposition of property. The testator(rix) or other person who creates the power is known as the *donor*. The person to whom the power is given—that

LEGAL TERMS

power of appointment
Right created in a will, trust, or other instrument which allows the holder to direct the disposition of property.

Form 709 (Rev. 10-90) Page 4

Part 2.—GST Exemption Reconciliation (Code section 2631) and Section 2652(a)(3) Election

Check box ▶ ☐ if you are making a section 2652(a)(3) (special QTIP) election (see instructions)
Enter the item numbers (from Schedule A) of the gifts for which you are making this election ▶ ....

1 Maximum allowable exemption	1	$1,000,000
2 Total exemption used for periods before filing this return	2	
3 Exemption available for this return (subtract line 2 from line 1)	3	
4 Exemption claimed on this return (from Part 3, col. C total, below)	4	
5 Exemption allocated to transfers not shown on Part 3, below. You must attach a Notice of Allocation. (See instructions.)	5	
6 Add lines 4 and 5	6	
7 Exemption available for future transfers (subtract line 6 from line 3)	7	

Part 3.—Tax Computation

A Item No. (from Schedule C, Part 1)	B Net transfer (from Schedule C, Part 1, col. F)	C GST Exemption Allocated	D Divide col. C by col. B	E Inclusion Ratio (subtract col. D from 1.000)	F Maximum Estate Tax Rate	G Applicable Rate (multiply col. E by col. F)	H Generation-Skipping Transfer Tax (multiply col. B by col. G)
1					55% (.55)		
2					55% (.55)		
3					55% (.55)		
4					55% (.55)		
5					55% (.55)		
6					55% (.55)		
7					55% (.55)		
8					55% (.55)		
					55% (.55)		
					55% (.55)		
					55% (.55)		
					55% (.55)		
					55% (.55)		
					55% (.55)		
					55% (.55)		
					55% (.55)		
Total exemption claimed. Enter here and on line 4, Part 2, above. May not exceed line 3, Part 2, above		**Total generation-skipping transfer tax.** Enter here, on line 14 of Schedule A, Part 3, and on line 16 of the Tax Computation on page 1					

(If more space is needed, attach additional sheets of same size.)

FIGURE 8-3
(Continued)

IRS Form 709, U.S. Gift (and Generation-Skipping Transfer) Tax Return, is used to report gifts over $10,000 in any one year per donee, other than to a spouse. Making gifts while one is alive is an important estate planning device to save estate taxes.

LEGAL TERMS

appointee
Person for whose benefit a power of appointment is made.

appointment
The act of executing a power of appointment.

appointive property
Property subject to a power of appointment.

general power of appointment
Power of appointment that gives the donee the right to appoint the property to any desired appointee, including the donee or the donee's estate.

is, the power holder, the one who has the right to exercise the power—is called the *donee*. The person for whose benefit the appointment is made is known as the **appointee**. The act of executing the power is called the **appointment**. The property that is subject to the power is known as the **appointive property**.

Powers of appointment may be either general or special. A **general power of appointment** gives the donee the right to appoint the property to any appointee he or she desires, including the donee or the donee's estate. In contrast, a **special power of appointment** limits the appointment of the property to a specified class of persons named by the donor. The following is an example of a special power of appointment in the body of a trust:

> On the death of the donor's wife, the remaining trust property shall be paid over as the donor's wife may in her last will and by express reference to this instrument appoint to any of the donor's issue. Insofar as the donor's wife fails to exercise this power of appointment, the remaining

> trust property shall be distributed to the donor's then living issue by right of representation.

In view of the language used in this sample power of appointment, the donor's wife must select the appointees from among the donor's issue. The following is an example of a provision that could be used in the wife's will to exercise the power:

> I am the donee of a power of appointment under a declaration of trust dated ___________, 19___, wherein the settlor is my late husband. I hereby expressly exercise such power by appointing the appointive property thereunder as follows: 50% to my husband's daughter Karen; 25% to my husband's daughter Cynthia; and 25% to my husband's son Charles.

Insurance

Insurance performs many roles in a family estate plan. Most important is its ability to furnish liquidity to an estate. As part of an integrated business plan, insurance may be used to finance the sale of a business interest, thereby guaranteeing sufficient cash to prevent a forced liquidation and the accompanying losses. Insurance may also create an estate that would otherwise be nonexistent.

Broadly speaking, life insurance is divided into three general classes: (1) term, (2) whole life, and (3) endowment. **Term insurance** furnishes maximum protection for the period of coverage at minimum cost, but has no cash surrender value and offers no protection after the expiration of the term.

Whole life insurance, also called **ordinary life insurance** and **straight life insurance**, provides lifetime protection and builds up a cash surrender value, but payments continue for life. If the policy is cancelled, the policyholder can receive the cash surrender value of the policy, making the insurance a form of savings. **Limited-payment life insurance** requires a greater annual premium, but need only be paid for the limited period required by the policy, such as 10, 20, or 30 years. After that period, the policy is paid up. Like ordinary life insurance, limited-payment life insurance has a cash surrender value.

> The endowment policy requires a larger premium but provides both protection and a fund available during the insured's lifetime if the insured survives to the end of the policy period. The endowment policy is really a kind of forced saving.
>
> Several types of insurance are available to the client through an employer. Group term life insurance and split-dollar insurance are common types.
>
> Group term life insurance is term life insurance protection provided under a master policy, or group of individual policies, which form part of a plan of group insurance as defined by the U. S. Treasury Regulations. The insurance supplied under such a plan must provide for general death benefits.

special power of appointment
Power of appointment that limits appointment of the property to a specified class of persons named by the donor.

term insurance
Type of insurance that furnishes maximum protection at minimum cost but has no cash surrender value and offers no protection after expiration of the term.

whole life insurance (also called ordinary life and straight life)
Insurance that gives lifetime protection and builds up a cash surrender value, with the payment of premiums continuing for the insured's life.

limited-payment life insurance
Insurance for which premiums are paid only for the limited period required by the policy, such as 10, 20, or 30 years. After that period, the policy is paid up.

endowment insurance
Kind of insurance providing protection for a stated time—20 to 30 years. The face value of the policy is paid to the insured at the end of the agreed period, or, if the insured dies during that period, the face value is paid to the beneficiary.

group term life insurance
Term life insurance protection provided under a master policy, or group of individual policies, which form part of a plan of group insurance as defined by U.S. Treasury Regulations.

Under a split-dollar insurance policy, the employee pays only that part of the annual premium which is the difference between the annual increase in the cash surrender value of the policy and the annual premium. The employer pays that part of the premium which equals the annual increase in the cash surrender value. If the employee dies, the employer receives the amount of the cash surrender value which the employer has paid, and the employee's beneficiary receives the balance of the maturity value.

As stated earlier, the insurance underwriter plays an important role on the family estate planning team. The selection of the proper form of insurance to be acquired, the use of annuities, and the coordination of pension, profit-sharing, and social security benefits contributes an important share to an effective family estate plan.

Harris, *Family Estate Planning Guide* 3d ed. § 16 (Hoops, ed., Lawyers Cooperative Publishing Company, 1992)

8.5 POST-MORTEM PLANNING

As unusual as it may seem, estate planning does not end when someone dies; rather, it continues until all possible benefits are identified, explained to heirs, and claimed if possible. Estate planning after a person dies is known as **post-mortem planning** and can sometimes be advantageous, especially in saving taxes. An instrument such as a will or a trust cannot be changed or discarded after the death of a decedent; however, decisions can be made and actions taken that can produce tax-saving benefits.

Sometimes estate taxes can be saved by disclaiming an inheritance. For example, suppose a person dies intestate, survived by an elderly mother and a sister. Under many state laws, the elderly mother inherits and the estate is subject to estate taxes. Soon thereafter, the mother passes away, leaving everything to her daughter. Like her son's estate, the mother's estate is subject to estate taxes, even though some of it was just taxed. This double taxation could have been avoided if the elderly mother had disclaimed the inheritance from her son and allowed the property to pass to her daughter initially. A **disclaimer** is a formal renunciation of a gift under a will, a trust, or the law of intestate succession. Under federal tax law, a **qualified disclaimer** is defined as an irrevocable and unqualified refusal by a person to accept an interest in property, but only if it is: (1) in writing, (2) received within a specified time, (3) received prior to the acceptance of any benefits, and (4) legally effective to pass the disclosed interest to another person without direction from the person making the disclaimer. See figure 8-4.

Sometimes taxes can be saved if a spouse exercises elective rights (discussed in chapter 9). For example, suppose a wife died with a will that left everything to her son. In order to reduce the estate tax liability on his wife's death, her husband elected to take his intestate share, which under state law qualified for the estate tax marital deduction. The husband's actions resulted in an estate tax savings of approximately $22,000. The

LEGAL TERMS

split-dollar insurance policy
Insurance policy in which the employee pays only that part of the annual premium which is the difference between the annual increase in the cash surrender value of the policy and the annual premium. The employer pays that part of the premium which is equal to the annual increase in the cash surrender value. If the employee dies, the employer receives the amount of the cash surrender value which the employer has paid, and the employee's beneficiary receives the balance of the maturity value.

post-mortem planning
Estate planning after a person dies.

disclaimer
Formal renunciation of a gift under a will, a trust, or the law of intestate succession.

qualified disclaimer
Under federal tax law, an irrevocable and unqualified refusal by a person to accept an interest in property. It is effective only if it is in writing, received within a specified time, received prior to the acceptance of any benefits, and legally effective to pass the disclosed interest to another person without direction from the person making the disclaimer.

husband then made a gift of his elective share directly to his son's children, incurring a gift tax liability of only $5,000 and reducing the estate taxes ultimately payable upon his son's subsequent death. (This example is drawn from Harris, *Family Estate Planning Guide* 533 (Hoops, ed. 3d ed., Lawyers Cooperative Publishing, 1992).)

Other devices used in post-mortem planning are the release of a power of appointment and the selection of optional provisions in life insurance policies. Also considered are the selection of the tax year for income tax purposes and whether to file a joint return on the decedent's final return.

TRANSFER AND DISCLAIMER OF INTESTATE SHARE

I, [name], [relationship] of [decedent], who died on [date], do hereby transfer, disclaim, renounce and refuse to accept any and all interests in the Estate of [decedent] to which I might otherwise have been entitled under the provisions of the intestate succession laws of the State of ___________.

It is my intention that by executing this transfer and disclaimer that any interests which I might have otherwise have had in the Estate of [decedent] be terminated as completely as if I had predeceased her [or him]. I hereby transfer all of the interests in the Estate of [decedent] to which I might otherwise have been entitled to [names of persons designated under local law to receive the disclaimed property].

I affirm that I have not accepted any interest in or benefit from the property interests hereby transferred and disclaimed, and that I have not received and I will not receive any consideration in money or money's worth for making this transfer and disclaimer.

It is my intention that this transfer and disclaimer constitute a qualified disclaimer as defined in Section 2518(c)(3) of the Internal Revenue Code, as amended, or the corresponding provisions of any subsequent federal tax law.

In witness whereof, I have executed this transfer and disclaimer on the ___________ day of ___________, 19___.

____
Signature of Disclaimant

State of _____________
County of _____________

On this ___________ day of ___________, 19___, [name of disclaimant], known to me to be the individual described in and who executed the foregoing instrument, personally appeared before me and acknowledged the execution thereof.

____
Signature of Notary Public

FIGURE 8-4
Sample disclaimer provision. Courtesy of Harris, *Family Estate Planning Guide* 3d ed. (Hoops, ed., Lawyers Cooperative Publishing, 1992)

Other strategies include delaying the administration of the decedent's estate and distributing estate assets over a period of time to beneficiaries rather than giving them out all at one time.

SUMMARY

8.1 The primary purpose of all family estate planning is to arrange the affairs of the family unit to obtain the maximum benefits of principal and income for the family and, to the fullest extent possible, pass on the family property without any loss. The overall goal is to protect the family unit and achieve financial and psychological security to the maximum extent possible.

8.2 The first step in planning an estate is to gather the facts, which fall into four categories: (1) domicile, (2) property, (3) beneficiaries, and (4) the individual's objectives. A questionnaire should be completed by the client and returned to the lawyer before any discussion of specific family estate planning proposals. The individual objectives of the client cannot be overlooked in planning an estate.

8.3 An attorney who specializes in estate planning, an accountant, and a life insurance underwriter are members of the estate planning team. If a bank is a fiduciary, a trust officer is also included. An important member of the estate planning team is the well-trained legal assistant.

8.4 The principal tools used by an estate planner are wills, trusts, gifts, powers of appointment, and insurance. A will is considered to be the single most important estate planning instrument. Trusts are used by estate planners to pass assets on to a future generation, provide income for people during their lives, and prevent family assets from being mismanaged or spent unwisely. Trusts also help to reduce problems created by joint ownership, avoid the expense and publicity of probate, and reduce taxes. Gifts are important to reduce death taxes. Powers of appointment allow flexibility in determining who will inherit from a decedent's estate. Insurance can create an estate where otherwise there would be none. It can also furnish liquidity, thus preventing a forced sale of estate property.

8.5 Estate planning does not end when a person dies. Post-mortem planning can often save estate taxes. Devices such as disclaiming inheritances and exercising a spousal election can sometimes reap tax-saving benefits for beneficiaries.

QUESTIONS FOR REVIEW

1. What is the primary purpose of all estate planning?
2. Name six members of an estate planning team.

3. What is the first step in estate planning? List the four categories into which the needed facts can be classified.
4. Why is the determination of domicile important?
5. What are the principal tools used by estate planners?
6. Why are trusts used by estate planners?
7. How can the use of gifts as an estate planning device reduce death taxes?
8. Why might someone use a power of appointment in a will or trust?
9. Give two reasons for using insurance in a family estate plan.
10. Describe two post-mortem estate planning devices.

CASES TO DISCUSS

1. John L. Lauricella, Jr., died while living in a house that was owned by his son and located in St. Tammany Parish, Louisiana. Three months before he died, in a codicil to his will, Lauricella declared himself to be a resident of St. Tammany Parish. He also had a checking account there. However, in his last will and testament, executed seven years earlier, Lauricella had declared himself to be a domiciliary of Jefferson Parish. In at least three real estate transactions conducted a month before he died, and in a trust agreement executed 10 days before his death, Lauricella identified himself as a resident or domiciliary of Jefferson Parish. He was a registered voter in Jefferson Parish, and his driver's license, income tax records, and death certificate all identified him as a Jefferson Parish resident. His son stated that his father lived in the St. Tammany Parish house for insurance purposes. Who has the burden of proving a change of domicile? Was Lauricella domiciled in St. Tammany Parish or in Jefferson Parish? Explain. *Succession of Lauricella*, 571 So. 2d 885 (La. 1990).
2. Mr. Macklem made a donation to the Church of the Adamic Communion, a religious enterprise founded by Mr. Macklem. Mr. Macklem was the sole member of the church, which was located at his residence. No regular worship services were conducted by or at the church. The church operated to disseminate Mr. Macklem's personal religious views and to proselytize others to his views. Was the gift to the church a completed gift? Why or why not? *Macklem v. United States*, 757 F. Supp. 6 (D. Conn. 1991).

SHARPENING YOUR PROFESSIONAL SKILLS

1. Refer to the vignette at the beginning of this chapter, and answer the following questions:

(a) Are New Mexico, Oregon, and Connecticut community property states?
(b) Why did Attorney Knight say, "We could have a domicile problem with this estate"?
(c) Why is an estate planning questionnaire important?
(d) When and by whom should an estate planning questionnaire be completed?
(e) What could Mrs. Bradbury do with a power of appointment?
(f) What are some possibilities with regard to post-mortem planning for Mr. Bradbury's estate?

2. Using the estate planning questionnaire in figure 8-2:
   (a) Prepare the asset and liabilities data section for yourself.
   (b) Complete the real estate section for your home (or your family's home).
   (c) Write out for a bewildered client the meaning of the terms relating to "life insurance policies and annuities."
3. Draw a diagram of your family (a family tree).

CHAPTER 9
Family Protection, Lapses, and Ademption

"The safety of the people shall be the highest law."

Marcus Tullius Cicero

OUTLINE

LAW OFFICE SCENARIO

The office of Dillon & Howard was relatively quiet at four o'clock on the warm Friday afternoon in July. Angela Clark, the legal assistant, was one of the few people remaining in the office when Despina Papadakis walked in, accompanied by her two young children, Nick and Christo. Angela noticed that Mrs. Papadakis looked extremely troubled, greeted her with a sense of concern, and told her that none of the attorneys were in at the moment. Mrs. Papadakis related to Angela that her husband, Vasillios, had recently drowned in a boating accident and that she had no money to support her two children because the bank accounts were in her husband's name.

Angela ushered the distraught woman and her children to a conference room, made them comfortable, and started writing down the facts. Mrs. Papadakis told Angela that, although they owned their own home, they owed many creditors, and she was afraid that she would lose the house to the creditors. Tears ran down her cheeks as she handed Angela a wrinkled legal document and said that her husband had left her out of his will completely. Her grief turned to anger as she mentioned that the will left a large sum of money and a boat to her husband's secretary. The anger turned to rage as she pointed out that the children were also omitted from the will.

Angela tried to calm Mrs. Papadakis down while, at the same time, listening to her and taking notes. She made an appointment for Mrs. Papadakis to see Attorney Dillon on Monday morning. Mrs. Papadakis laughed as she left the office, saying, "At least she won't get the boat! It sank along with my husband! It was covered by insurance, though."

9.1 PROTECTION OF WIDOWS AND CHILDREN

Paralegals may need to calm clients like Mrs. Papadakis whose security and actual survival are threatened by the death of a spouse or income provider. Knowledge of the protection provided by state laws enables paralegals to offer reassurance to fearful clients. Attorneys can provide specific suggestions to address their needs. Some available options include a family allowance, homestead protection, exempting property from creditor's claims, dower and curtesy, a spouse's elective share, and pretermitted children laws.

Family Allowance

To provide for the immediate support of the family when a breadwinner dies, state laws generally contain a mechanism for immediate access to money from the decedent's estate. Probate courts have authority to grant an allowance from the estate to the widow or widower and surviving children to provide for their immediate needs after the death of the decedent (see figure 9-1). The allowance is known as the **family allowance** or **widow's allowance**. The amount of the allowance is discretionary with the court depending on the size of the estate, the debts of the estate, and the needs of the surviving spouse and children. To illustrate, the Uniform Probate Code (UPC) contains the following provision for a family allowance, in § 2-404:

> (a) In addition to the right to homestead allowance and exempt property, if the decedent was domiciled in this state, the surviving spouse and minor children whom the decedent was obligated to support and children who were in fact being supported by him are entitled to a reasonable allowance in money out of the estate for their maintenance during the period of administration, which allowance may not continue for longer than one year if the estate is inadequate to discharge allowed

LEGAL TERMS

family allowance (also called widow's allowance)
Allowance from a decedent's estate to a widow or widower and surviving children to provide for their immediate needs after the death of the decedent.

AC70

COMMONWEALTH OF MASSACHUSETTS

To the Honorable the Judges of the Probate Court in and for the County of Essex:

RESPECTFULLY represents ....

of .... in the County of ....

that .... late of ....

in said County, whose estate is in course of settlement in said Court, died possessed of personal estate appraised at $ .... and real estate appraised at $ ....;

that she is his widow and has under her charge a family consisting of

....

....

....

and she further represents that the personal property is insufficient to afford her proper allowance.

Wherefore, she prays that the Court will allow her—all—part—of the personal estate of said deceased as necessaries for herself and family under her care, in addition to the provisions and other articles by law belonging to her—*and a further sum to be derived from the sale—mortgage—of real property of the deceased.*

Dated this .... day of .... 19 .

....

COMMONWEALTH OF MASSACHUSETTS

Essex, ss. Probate Court

At a Probate Court held at .... *in and for said County of Essex, on the* .... *day of* .... *in the year of our Lord one thousand nine hundred* ....

ON the petition of .... representing that she is the widow of ....

late of .... in said County, deceased, whose estate is in course of settlement in said Court, and praying to be allowed—all—part—of the personal estate of said deceased as necessaries for herself and family under her care—*and a further sum to be derived from the sale—mortgage—of real property of the deceased.*

It appearing that she is the widow, and entitled to an allowance as aforesaid; all—part—of the personal estate of said deceased to the amount of ....

.... dollars,—

and a further sum of .... *dollars*

to be derived from the sale—mortgage—or real property—is hereby allowed to her as necessaries for herself and family under her care, in addition to the provisions and other articles by law belonging to her.

.... *Judge of Probate Court*

FIGURE 9-1
Sample petition for widow's allowance (Massachusetts)

In Massachusetts, a widow or widower may file this petition for an allowance from the estate to provide for the immediate support of the family. If the personal property is insufficient, the court may order the real property to be sold or mortgaged to provide the necessary support.

claims. The allowance may be paid as a lump sum or in periodic installments. It is payable to the surviving spouse, if living, for the use of the surviving spouse and minor and dependent children; otherwise to the children, or persons having their care and custody; but in case any minor child or dependent child is not living with the surviving spouse, the allowance may be made partially to the child or his guardian or other person having his care and custody, and partially to the spouse, as their

Courtesy of the Historical Department of the Church of Jesus Christ of Latter-Day Saints. Used by permission

MANY WIVES, MANY CHILDREN

Mormon leader Brigham Young was survived by 17 wives and 48 children when he died in 1877. His carefully drawn will provided: "To avoid any question, the words 'married' or 'marriage' in this will shall be taken to have become consummated between man and woman, either by ceremony before a lawful magistrate or according to the order of the Church of Jesus Christ of Latter-Day Saints, or by their cohabitation in conformity to our custom." The will divided family units into three classes: (1) those with wives with children, (2) those with wives with no children, and (3) those with children of deceased wives. Among other things, each family inherited the house in which it was living. Until all wives died or until the youngest child came of age, the income from the undistributed properties went into a trust to be divided among the various mothers for the support of their children.

needs may appear. The family allowance is exempt from and has priority over all claims but not over the homestead allowance.

(b) The family allowance is not chargeable against any benefit or share passing to the surviving spouse or children by the will of the decedent unless otherwise provided, by intestate succession, or by way of elective share. The death of any person entitled to family allowance terminates his right to allowances not yet paid.

The period of time covered by the family allowance coincides with the period that estate assets are frozen for the protection of creditors, which is usually not more than one year. In Texas, the court may not make an allowance for the surviving spouse when the survivor has separate property adequate for his or her maintenance. However, as shown by the *Churchill* case, the family allowance must be made in consideration of the whole condition of the estate during the first year after the spouse's death, and for the necessities of the surviving spouse and the circumstances to which he or she has been accustomed.

CHURCHILL V. CHURCHILL
780 S.W.2d 913 (Tex. 1989)

FACTS: Richard Churchill's will made ample provision for his wife, Marian, and other family members. Marian's separate property at the time of her husband's death consisted of jewelry and a residence valued at $51,000. Marian testified that she had annual expenses of $34,161 and that she was accustomed to spending an additional $18,000 to $24,000 per year on golf tournaments with her husband. The trial court awarded Marian a family allowance of $30,000.

LEGAL ISSUE: Is a surviving spouse entitled to a family allowance when adequate provision was made for her by will and there was no evidence that the spouse's separate property was inadequate for her maintenance?

COURT DECISION: Yes.

REASON: The family allowance is to be made in consideration of the whole condition of the estate during the first year after the spouse's death, and of the necessities of the surviving spouse and the circumstances to which he or she has been accustomed. The evidence was sufficient to show that Marian's separate property was not adequate to her maintenance. In addition, given the testimony showing that Marian's need for maintenance greatly exceeded her income, the court was unable to conclude that the allowance in the amount of $30,000 was excessive.

Homestead Protection

An important protection for families who own their own residences is the **homestead exemption**. This exemption is available under many state laws whether or not there is a death in the family, and is designed to place the family residence beyond the reach of creditors. The exemption allows the head of a family to keep the family home regardless of the amount of family debt.

In states that have adopted the Uniform Probate Code, a surviving spouse is entitled to a homestead allowance up to a certain amount of money; if there is no surviving spouse, minor children qualify for the allowance. The homestead allowance is exempt from and has priority over

LEGAL TERMS

homestead exemption
Law that places the family residence beyond the reach of creditors, allowing the head of a family to keep the family home regardless of the amount of family debt.

all claims against the estate and is in addition to any share passing to the surviving spouse or minor children by will of the decedent, intestate succession, or by way of an elective share. UPC § 2-401.

In states that have not adopted the Uniform Probate Code, the person who is entitled to the homestead exemption is the **head of household** or the **householder**. In the past, this was the husband. Today, however, many states recognize either a husband or a wife as a head of household. Some states allow only married persons (including widows and widowers) to claim the exemption.

Generally, householders are entitled to the homestead exemption only when they are residing with someone whom they have an obligation to support or who is dependent upon them for support. In a few states, persons who have attained a certain age are entitled to a homestead exemption whether or not they are the head of a household.

Although the homestead exemption applies in most states only to real property, a few states allow a homestead exemption on personal property as well. Some states put a limit on the value of the homestead exemption; others have no limitation on the exemption.

The laws of some jurisdictions provide for an automatic homestead exemption; other jurisdictions require the signing and recording in a public place of a written declaration of homestead (see figure 9-2). The written declaration names the homestead owner, describes the homestead property, and states that the homestead is the owner's principal residence. See figure 9-3.

The owner of a homestead may convey the property to someone else free of the homestead restriction. In some states, this is done simply by signing an ordinary deed; in other states, a statement in the deed specifically releasing the homestead is necessary (see figure 9-4). Most jurisdictions require that both spouses consent to the conveyance of a homestead. The following clause may be used in a deed to release the right of homestead.

Clause in Deed Releasing Homestead Rights
[9A AM. JUR. *Legal Forms* 2d (Rev.) § 135:53]

Grantor hereby expressly waives and releases any and all right, benefit, privilege, advantage, and exemption under or by virtue of any and all statutes of the State of ______________________________, providing for the exemption of homesteads from sale on execution or otherwise.

Exempt Property

Under the laws of some states, certain property of a decedent, called **exempt property**, passes to the surviving spouse or children and is not subject to the claims of general creditors. (See figure 9-5.) For example, in states that have enacted the Uniform Probate Code, a surviving spouse is

LEGAL TERMS

head of household (also called householder)
Person who is entitled to the homestead exemption.

RECORDING REQUEST BY

____

AND WHEN RECORDED MAIL TO

____

____

_______________ SPACE ABOVE THIS LINE FOR RECORDER'S USE

DECLARATION OF HOMESTEAD

STATE OF ARIZONA, } SS
County of_____________

____

being first duly sworn upon oath, deposes and says that:

1. Declarant(s) is (are)

NOTE: CHECK ONE OF THE FOLLOWING

☐ Single Person

☐ Married couple claiming community property or jointly owned property as a homestead.

☐ Married person claiming separate property as a homestead.

2. Declarants(s) actually reside in Arizona.

3. Declarant(s) hereby select(s) and designate(s), pursuant to A.R.S. § 33-1101 as amended, as a homestead exempt from attachment, execution and forced sale the following property having an equity value of $_______________:

NOTE: YOU ARE TO CHECK ONE OF THE FOLLOWING AND FURNISH A DETAILED DESCRIPTION OF THE PROPERTY

☐ Real Property in one compact body upon which exists a dwelling house in which the declarant resides. (Furnish legal description of land.)

____

____

☐ Land in a compact body. (Furnish legal description of land.)

____

____

FIGURE 9-2
Sample declaration of homestead for recording (Arizona). Form courtesy of Forms, Inc., La Jolla, CA

entitled to $3,500 worth of personal property comprising any combination of household furniture, automobiles, furnishings, appliances, and personal effects. UPC § 2-402. If there is no surviving spouse, children of the decedent are entitled jointly to the same value. These rights are in addition to the homestead allowance, as well as any benefits or share passing to the surviving spouse or children by the will of the decedent, by way of an elective share, or by intestate succession.

exempt property
Certain property of a decedent that passes to the surviving spouse or children without being subject to the claims of general creditors.

☐ A mobile home in which the declarant resides. (Furnish description, including make, model, year and serial number.)

____

____

☐ A mobile home in which the declarant resides and the land upon which the mobile home is located. (Furnish description of mobile home, including make, model, year and serial number and legal description of land.)

____

____

____

____

SUBSCRIBED and sworn to before me this _____day of _____________, 19____

by ______________________________________

____
Notary Public

My commission expires:_____________

NO.________

DECLARATION OF HOMESTEAD
(Husband of Wife)

of

Claimant.

Dated

STATE OF ARIZONA }
County of } SS

I hereby certify that the within instrument was filed and recorded at request of ________

Book________

In Docket________

on Page________.

Witness my hand and official seal the day and year aforesaid.

County Recorder.

By________ Deputy Recorder.

FIGURE 9-2
(Continued)

In Arizona, this form may be filled out and recorded at the county recorder's office to obtain homestead protection.

LEGAL TERMS

dower
Under English law, a right that a widow had, upon the death of her husband, to a one-third life estate in all real property owned by the husband during the marriage.

Dower and Curtesy

The rights of dower and curtesy originated in early England to provide surviving spouses with a means of support upon the death of a spouse. **Dower**, under English law, was the right of a widow to a one-third life estate in all real property owned by the husband during the marriage. **Curtesy** was the right of a widower to a life estate in all real property owned by the wife during the marriage, but only if issue of the marriage were born alive.

Declaration of Homestead by Spouse
[9A AM. JUR. *Legal Forms* 2d (Rev.) § 135:16]

I, _____________, hereby declare:

I am the head of a family, I am married, and my spouse's name is ____________. My family consists of my spouse and ____________ children.

At the time of making this declaration of homestead, I actually reside with my family on the premises located in the County of ____________, State of ____________, more particularly described as follows: [set forth legal description].

I claim and declare the premises, with the dwelling house [and outbuildings] on it, and its appurtenances, as a homestead for the joint benefit of myself and my spouse and family.

No former declaration of homestead had been made by me or by my spouse, either jointly or separately.

I estimate the actual cash value of the premises to be ____________ dollars ($____).

Executed on ____________, 19____.

____
(Signature)

(Acknowledgment)

FIGURE 9-3
Sample declaration of homestead by spouse

In this day and age, partial interests in real estate can be a hindrance rather than a source of support for a surviving spouse. Many states (including those that have adopted the Uniform Probate Code) have abolished the rights of dower and curtesy altogether. UPC § 2-113. Other states have changed the early English rules of dower and curtesy to their own liking, making dower and curtesy rights different in each state. The *Del Guercio* case illustrates the New Jersey law, applying the right of dower in 1985.

Dower and curtesy rights arise only upon the death of the other spouse. In addition, these rights do not apply to real property owned by the deceased spouse as a joint tenant with someone else, or to property to which the surviving spouse has released the right of dower or curtesy. In addition,

curtesy
Under English law, a right that a widower had, upon the death of his wife—but only if issue of the marriage were born alive—to a life estate in all real property owned by the wife during the marriage.

IN RE DEL GUERCIO ESTATE
501 A.2d 1072 (N.J. 1985)

FACTS: Janet and Fred Del Guercio took title to their residence on September 24, 1970, as tenants by the entireties. On October 24, 1971, Janet

"THE JOINT IS JUMPIN' "

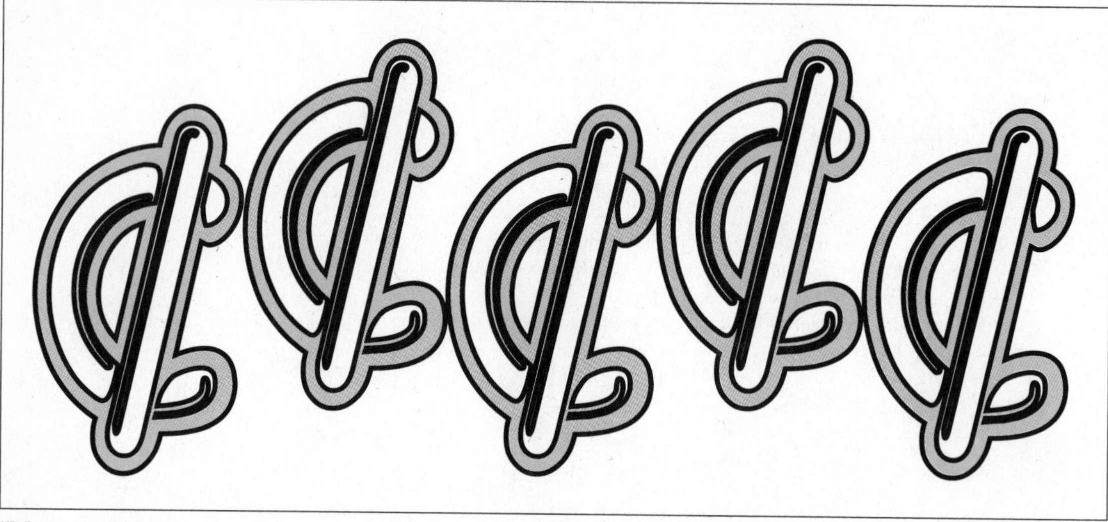

"Money can't buy me love" was a marital theme of jazz great Fats Waller long before the Beatles sang their hit tune.

In his will, Thomas ("Fats") Waller, the celebrated jazz pianist and composer of the 1930s, left one dollar to his wife "for reasons best known to her." Instead, a dower right established by law provided her with one-third of the estate.

conveyed her interest in the property to Fred by bargain and sale deed. Some years later, marital difficulties arose between the couple. Janet left the marital residence in 1984 and instituted a divorce action. Fred died before being served with process in that action.

LEGAL ISSUE: Is a widow entitled to a dower interest in real property held initially with her husband as a tenant by the entireties but which was solely owned by the husband at the time of his death?

COURT DECISION: Yes.

State of Arizona
County of } ss.

I hereby certify that the within instrument was filed and recorded

on

in Docket at Page

at the request of

In witness whereof I have hereunto set my hand and seal.

When recorded mail to:

County Recorder

Deputy County Recorder

Fee No.

Compared

Photostated

Fee

ABANDONMENT OF HOMESTEAD

STATE OF ARIZONA
County of } ss.

The undersigned have heretofore filed a Declaration of Homestead on the ________ day of ________________, 19____ which Homestead is recorded in ________________________ County, Docket ______________, Page ____________.

The Declaration homesteaded the following described property:

The undersigned do hereby abandon, vacate and revoke the above described Declaration of Homestead.

Dated this ________ day of ________________, 19____.

____

____

Subscribed to and sworn before me a Notary Public this ________ day of ________________,

19____, by ______________________________.

____
Notary Public

My Commission Expires:

FIGURE 9-4
Sample abandonment of homestead for recording (Arizona). Form courtesy of Forms, Inc., La Jolla, CA

This form may be filled out and recorded at the county recorder's office in Arizona when someone who has recorded a homestead wishes to revoke it.

REASON: Under the New Jersey statute, "[t]he widow . . . of a person dying intestate or otherwise, shall be endowed for the term of her . . . natural life of the full and equal half part of all real property of which the

AOC-835
Rev. 12-84

Commonwealth of Kentucky
Court of Justice

KRS 391.030, 395.455, 396.090

PETITION FOR TRANSFER OF EXEMPTION AND TO DISPENSE WITH ADMINISTRATION (Surviving Spouse)

Case No. ______
Court ______
County ______

In re Estate of ______, who died on the ______ day of ______, 19____, a legal resident at ______ Street, ______ Kentucky.

(This procedure may be used in both testate and intestate cases.)

(If surviving spouse also claims as preferred creditor, add words to heading "and as preferred creditor." Also fill in the parenthetical statement below.)

Petitioner ______, who resides at ______ states that petitioner is the surviving spouse of ______, who died leaving no estate to be administered with the exception of ______

(Complete this statement if claim is also made as preferred creditor. Otherwise leave blank.)

(Petitioner states that petitioner has paid the funeral and/or hospital expenses of said decedent to ______ in the amount of $______.) (Attach receipts.)

Petitioner further states that there has been no previous administration in said decedent's estate in Kentucky or elswhere.

WHEREFORE, Petitioner demands that administration of the estate of the above decedent be dispensed with, and that the above personal property be set aside and transferred to petitioner as part of petitioner's exemption as allowed by law (and as preferred creditor.)

(Strike out "and as preferred creditor" if inapplicable.)

______
Petitioner

(Petitioner is the surviving spouse.)

Subscribed and sworn before me by petitioner this ______ day of ______, 19____. My commission expires ______

______
Notary Public, ______ County, Ky.

(Continued on Back)

FIGURE 9-5
Sample petition for transfer of exemption (Kentucky)

decedent . . . was seized of an estate of inheritance at any time during coverture prior to May 28, 1980 to which the widow . . . shall not have relinquished her right of dower . . . by deed duly executed and acknowledged in the manner provided by law to record deeds.

AOC-835: Page 2
Dispense with Administration (Spouse)

In re estate of ____________________, decedent; case no. __________ .

ORDER

(The ORDER should be completed by petitioner.)

Upon verified petition filed by ____________________

and it appearing to the Court that the statements contained in the above petition are true and that petitioner is the surviving spouse of ____________________ , who died testate/intestate a resident of ____________________ County on ____________________, 19____, leaving no estate to administer with the exception of ____________________

____

____

____

(Strike out last three lines if inapplicable.)

and that the petitioner has paid the funeral and/or hospital expenses of the decedent to ____________________ in the amount of $__________ (receipts filed herewith),

(If less than all personal property is designated to another, please specify.)

IT IS HEREBY ORDERED, that administration of the estate of the above decedent be dispensed with and that the above mentioned personal property be transferred to petitioner or to ____________________ (a party designed by the petitioner to receive it in whole or part) as part of the exemption allowed by the law to the surviving spouse (and as preferred creditor).

(Strike out "and as preferred creditor" if inapplicable.)

(A copy of this order should be obtained for presentation to each holder of the property.)

Date ____________________ ____________________
Judge

This certifies that the within petition was prepared or subscribed by the undersigned in accordance with the meaning and tenor of Kentucky Civil Rule No. 11.

____________________ ____________________
Attorney for Petitioner Address

FIGURE 9-5
(Continued)

When an estate consists of a small amount of personal property, this form may be used in Kentucky to ask the court to transfer the exempt property to the surviving spouse and children without probating the estate.

in many states, such rights are subject to **purchase money mortgages** (mortgages given to purchase the property on which the mortgage is placed), whether or not the surviving spouse signed the mortgage. Despite such limitations, dower and curtesy rights have preference over the rights of creditors and can thereby provide protection to surviving spouses in the case of insolvent estates. (See figure 9-6.)

LEGAL TERMS

purchase money mortgage
Mortgage given to purchase the property on which the mortgage is placed.

Spouse's Elective Share

To protect surviving spouses from being disinherited, state laws allow surviving spouses to renounce the provisions made for them in their

AC66A

G. L. (Ter. Ed.) c. 189, § 1.

TO THE HONORABLE THE JUDGES OF THE PROBATE COURT IN AND FOR THE COUNTY OF ESSEX:

RESPECTFULLY represents ....

....

of .... in the County of .... that he is ....
the widow—*husband*—of ....

....

late of .... in the County of Essex, deceased; that on
the .... day of .... 19 , the bond of
the execut —administrat .... —of the
estate—will—of the deceased was approved by this Court, and that he hereby elects and
claims dower—*curtesy*— .... in the estate of the deceased, instead of the
interest in real property of the deceased given in section one of chapter one hundred and ninety of the
General Laws.

And he also hereby waives any provisions that may have been made in the will of the deceased for h and claims such portions of the estate of the deceased as he would have taken if the deceased had died intestate.

Dated this .... day of .... 19 .

FIGURE 9-6
Sample form to elect the right of dower (Massachusetts).

This form is used in Massachusetts by a surviving spouse to claim the right of dower.

deceased spouse's will. Instead of inheriting under the terms of the will, surviving spouses may elect to take against (i.e., waive) the will and inherit an amount that is set forth in their state's statute. This is often referred to as a **forced share** or an **elective share**.

In some jurisdictions, the forced share is tied to the amount that the survivor would have received if the deceased spouse had died without a will. In the *Spencer* case, a widow opted for the share provided by state statute rather than the amount designated in her husband's will.

LEGAL TERMS

forced (elective) share
Share of a deceased spouse's estate which a surviving spouse may elect instead of inheriting under the terms of the deceased spouse's will.

SPENCER V. WILLIAMS
569 A.2d 1194 (D.C. 1990)

FACTS: Loy Henderson died at the age of 93. Among other things, his will left $200,000 in trust for the benefit of his wife, Elise, and upon her death to beneficiaries named by Mr. Henderson. If she renounced the will and took the amount provided by statute, Mrs. Henderson would receive $160,000 outright, instead of $200,000 in trust, and be able to name her own beneficiaries upon her death.

LEGAL ISSUE: May a surviving spouse renounce his or her deceased spouse's will and take a different share of the estate?

COURT DECISION: Yes.

REASON: An individual who is predeceased by his or her spouse, and whose spouse leaves a will, may either take the property left him or her in the will or, alternatively, take the share provided for by statute—in this jurisdiction, an amount equal to that which the individual would have received had the spouse died intestate, up to a maximum of one-half the net estate.

In other states, a different formula is used to determine the amount of inheritance when a surviving spouse decides to renounce the provisions of a will and become a **forced heir**. Alabama lists specific amounts in its statute, as shown in the *Barksdale* case.

forced heir
Surviving spouse who elects to renounce the provisions of a deceased spouse's will and, instead, to take a forced share.

BARKSDALE V. BARKSDALE
551 So. 2d 1006 (Ala. 1989)

FACTS: In his will, Elton Barksdale left certain property outright to his wife, Ruby, and the remainder to her for her life. Instead of taking her share under the will, Ruby filed a petition for an elective share of the estate in addition to claims for homestead and an exempt property allowance.

ISSUE: In Alabama, may a surviving spouse take an elective share in addition to a homestead and exempt property allowance?

COURT DECISION: Yes.

REASON: The homestead and exempt property allowances are awarded irrespective of a surviving spouse's decision to take an elective share of the spouse's estate. The amounts to be distributed are stated clearly in the Alabama statute: one-third of the estate for the elective share, $3,500 for exempt property, and $6,000 for the homestead allowance.

There is a time limit, ranging from six to nine months, within which a surviving spouse may renounce a deceased spouse's will. (See figure 9-7.) An election to do so must be made while the surviving spouse is still alive, as illustrated by the *Dahlmann* case.

ESTATE OF DAHLMANN V. DAHLMANN
668 S.W.2d 520 (Ark. 1984)

FACTS: William F. Dahlmann died on April 14, 1982. His will acknowledged his wife of 30 years, but left her nothing. Mrs. Dahlmann died two months after her husband without electing to take against his will.

ISSUE: May the estate of a woman who died two months after her husband elect to take against her husband's will?

COURT DECISION: No.

REASON: When a spouse dies testate, the surviving spouse must exercise the option to take against the will in his or her lifetime. Otherwise, the right is forfeited, because it is personal and does not survive the surviving spouse.

Prob. 105-H

PROBATE COURT OF ______________ COUNTY, OHIO

ESTATE OF ______________________________, DECEASED

Case No. ______________ Docket ______________ Page ______________

CITATION TO SURVIVING SPOUSE TO ELECT TO TAKE UNDER OR AGAINST WILL

Revised Code, Sec. 2107.39

To ______________ (Surviving Spouse) ______________ (Address)

As decedent's surviving spouse, Ohio law permits you to choose whether to take under decedent's Will, or to take against the Will.

If you elect to take under the Will, you must take under it alone as to property governed by it, unless it plainly appears from the Will that the provisions in it for you are in addition to an intestate share of the estate.

If you elect to take against the Will, you are entitled to one-half of decedent's net estate, unless there are two or more of decedent's children or their lineal descendants surviving, in which case you are entitled to one-third of decedent's net estate.

Whichever choice you make, you will not be barred from your rights to purchase or to remain in the family home for one year, to receive an allowance for support, or to receive an automobile owned by decedent, as and to the extent you may have such rights under the law.

Before making your election, you are entitled to file a complaint in this Court asking that the Will be construed in your favor.

You have one month from the date of service of this citation in which to make your election to take under or against the Will, or to file a complaint for construction of the Will. The Court may extend such time for good cause. If you take no action within the one-month period, it will be conclusively presumed that you elect to take under the Will.

If you elect to take under the Will, you may do so in writing if you wish, but you may also do so merely by taking no action, as explained in the preceding paragraph.

If you elect to take against the Will, you must come to this Court and do so in person. Before accepting your election to take against the Will, the Judge or Referee must explain decedent's Will, your rights under the Will, and your rights in case of your refusal to take under the Will.

It is recommended that you consult your attorney if you are in any doubt as to your rights, as to how to claim them, or as to which course of action would be to your best advantage.

______________ (Date) ______________ (Probate Judge/Clerk)

FORM 8.0 - CITATION TO SURVIVING SPOUSE TO ELECT TO TAKE UNDER OR AGAINST WILL

FIGURE 9-7 Sample citation to surviving spouse (Ohio). Form courtesy of Barrett Brothers, Publishers, Springfield, Ohio

This form is issued by the court in Ohio to inform surviving spouses of their right to take either under or against the deceased spouse's will.

In states that have adopted the Uniform Probate Code, the subsequent marriage of a testator does not revoke a will. UPC § 2-301. However, an omitted spouse who married the testator after the execution of the will takes the share he or she would have taken had the decedent died intestate, unless (1) it appears from the will that the omission was intentional, or

(2) the testator provided for the surviving spouse outside the will in lieu of a testamentary provision. The *Groeper* case involves a clarification of an "omitted spouse."

Divorce ends a marriage, so a person who is divorced from a decedent is not a surviving spouse and does not have the right to an elective share of the decedent's estate. In addition, some states, such as New Jersey, do not allow a surviving spouse to receive an elective share if, at the time of the spouse's death, they were living apart while a divorce was pending and had ceased to cohabit as man and wife. In some states, a spouse who is living in adultery at the time of a spouse's death or who has abandoned a spouse without just cause is prevented from taking any part of the spouse's estate. The *Oliver* case addresses the issue of adulterous cohabitation.

ESTATE OF GROEPER V. GROEPER
665 S.W.2d 367 (Mo. 1984)

FACTS: On the day that Walter H. Groeper's first wife, Meta, died, he executed a will leaving his property in equal shares to his five brothers and sisters and Meta's five brothers and sisters, including Melinda, who at the time was the widow of Meta's brother, Hugo. Shortly thereafter, Walter married Melinda. He continued to be married to her until he died, without making a new will.

LEGAL ISSUE: Is a surviving spouse who was a beneficiary under her husband's will as a member of a class (in this case a sister-in-law) considered to be an omitted spouse and thus able to take an intestate share of her husband's estate?

COURT DECISION: Yes.

REASON: When a will that is executed before marriage contains a provision for a named individual who later becomes the testator's spouse, the surviving spouse has the burden of proving that the provision was not made in contemplation of marriage. Because Melinda was the testator's sister-in-law at the time, and the remainder of the class were either brothers, sisters, or in-laws, there is no question that the testator did not contemplate Melinda as a future spouse at the time he executed the will.

OLIVER V. ESTATE OF OLIVER
554 N.E.2d 8 (Ind. 1990)

FACTS: Dorothy Oliver, who was suffering from physical ailments associated with diabetes, entered a nursing home. While she was there, her husband, Warren Oliver, began residing in a trailer with another woman. There was evidence that he took the other woman to dinner parties and was living with her at the trailer at the time of his wife's death.

LEGAL ISSUE: May the trial court infer adulterous cohabitation from circumstantial evidence when applying the statute that prevents a surviving spouse who is living in adultery from taking from the estate?

COURT DECISION: Yes.

REASON: Although, admittedly, the circumstantial evidence offered here would have been insufficient to sustain a criminal conviction of adultery, this is a civil case, in which the degree of proof necessary is the lesser preponderance of the evidence standard. Oliver is likewise not aided by a presumption of innocence. The fact of carnal intercourse must in almost every case of adultery be inferred from the circumstances, because direct proof of sex acts between the parties is virtually impossible to produce.

Pretermitted Children

Generally, parents may disinherit children as long as they do so intentionally. If a **pretermitted child** (a child omitted from a parent's will) can prove that the omission was unintentional, the omitted child may be able to inherit an intestate share of the parent's estate. This rule also applies to the **issue** (lineal descendants) of deceased children who are omitted from a parent's will. In the *Birman* and *Uliscni* cases, the intention of the testator to omit a child is maintained despite a contest.

LEGAL TERMS

pretermitted child
Child omitted from a parent's will.

issue
Lineal descendants; all persons who have descended from a common ancestor.

BIRMAN V. SPROAT
546 N.E.2d 1354 (Ohio 1988)

FACTS: Constance Birman, the illegitimate child of Vearl Sproat, contested her father's will. Sproat's will gave $500 each to his son, four stepdaughters, and the Friedens Lutheran Church. The residue was bequeathed to Sproat's wife, Frances. Constance Birman was not mentioned in the will.

LEGAL ISSUE: Can a parent disinherit a child by not mentioning the child in a will?

COURT DECISION: Yes.

REASON: If the testator makes no mention of one of his children in his will and by such will disposes of all his property, such child is as completely disinherited as if the testator had specifically so provided. The specific bequests made by Sproat to his natural son and stepdaughters necessarily imply he meant to exclude Constance Birman from a similar bequest under his will.

In states that have adopted the Uniform Probate Code, the following rules apply to pretermitted children (UPC § 2-302):

> (a) If a testator fails to provide in his will for any of his children born or adopted after the execution of his will, the omitted child receives a share in the estate equal in value to that which he would have received if the testator had died intestate unless:
> (1) it appears from the will that the omission was intentional;
> (2) when the will was executed the testator had one or more children and devised substantially all his estate to the other parent of the omitted child; or
> (3) the testator provided for the child by transfer outside the will and the intent that the transfer be in lieu of a testamentary provision is shown by statements of the testator or from the amount of the transfer or other evidence.
>
> (b) If at the time of execution of the will the testator fails to provide in his will for a living child solely because he believes the child to be dead, the child receives a share in the estate equal in value to that which he would have received if the testator had died intestate.

MATTER OF ESTATE OF ULISCNI
372 N.W.2d 759 (Minn. 1985)

FACTS: Michael Uliscni died testate, survived by his only child, Holly Nakari, who was born out of wedlock. Uliscni's will left his entire estate to his nephew. The will contained the following clause: "I do hereby specifically disinherit any and all persons who are or who claim to be my heirs at law except as herein provided." Uliscni's lawyer testified that he had a conference with Uliscni prior to drafting the will and that Uliscni told him that he had no children. After Uliscni died, however, the lawyer found in his file a copy of a will he had drawn for Uliscni five years earlier, in which Holly Nakari was specifically named and excluded.

LEGAL ISSUE: Was the evidence sufficient to establish an intentional omission of a child from a will?

COURT DECISION: Yes.

REASON: In Minnesota, a testator's intent to disinherit need not appear on the face of the will. The evidence is not limited to the will itself. The specific words in a will must be interpreted in light of the circumstances and extrinsic evidence offered in each individual case. Here, the earlier unexecuted will specifically names and disinherits Nakari. There was no evidence of any change in Uliscni's and Nakari's relationship between the making of the two wills that would indicate that Uliscni had decided to provide for Nakari in his will.

Clauses in a will such as the following help to make clear the testator's intention as to omitted children.

Will Clauses Pertaining to Omitted Children
[20 AM. JUR. *Legal Forms* 2d § 266:375]

My failure to provide in this will for my son, John, is intentional and not occasioned by accident or mistake.

I have intentionally made no provision in this will for any future children which might be born to or adopted by me and my present spouse or any future spouse, other than as otherwise specifically provided herein.

9.2 LAPSED LEGACIES AND DEVISES

It is common for testators to outlive some or all of the individuals to whom they leave gifts in their wills. When legatees or devisees die before the testator, gifts to them in the testator's will are known as **lapsed legacies** or **lapsed devises**. With some exceptions, such gifts become part of the residuary estate and are inherited by the residuary legatees and devisees named in the residuary clause of the will.

Many states have statutes, known as **antilapse statutes**, that minimize the effects of such lapses. The typical antilapse statute provides that if a gift is made to a relative of the testator who dies before the testator and leaves issue surviving the testator, the issue will receive the gift. Some state antilapse statutes apply only to gifts given to children; some apply to gifts given to anyone at all. In states that have adopted the Uniform Probate Code, the antilapse statute applies to gifts given to grandparents and lineal descendants of a grandparent. UPC § 2-605.

Quite often testators do not want the antilapse statute to go into effect. The use of the words, "if he or she shall survive me" accomplishes that result. The clause shown here would prevent the issue of Natalie I. Nichols from inheriting the $50,000 gift if Natalie predeceased the testator.

> I give the sum of Fifty Thousand Dollars ($50,000) to my sister, Natalie I. Nichols, if she shall survive me.

9.3 ADEMPTION

Frequently, property that is specifically bequeathed or devised in a will is not owned by the testator at death. Either the testator disposed of property after executing the will or the property became extinct. A specific legacy or devise is **adeemed** (extinguished or taken away) if the property is not in existence or does not belong to the testator at the time of death. The item is said to adeem by **extinction**. When an item of property adeems, the legatee or devisee of that property simply does not receive it. In addition, he or she receives nothing in its place, as is pointed out by the *Opperman* case.

Ademption can also come about by a method known as **satisfaction**. This occurs when a gift of property or money is given by the testator, while alive, to a legatee with the intent that the gift or payment be in lieu of the legacy. The *Wolff* case illustrates this method.

9.4 CHECKLIST AND GUIDELINES

Use the list on page 224 to be sure that you have all the required information for your client's homestead declaration.

LEGAL TERMS

lapsed legacies (also called lapsed devises)
Gifts of personal or real property in a will that fail because the legatee predeceased the testator.

antilapse statutes
Statutes that minimize the effects of lapse in a will. Typically, they provide that gifts in a will made to relatives who die before the testator but leave issue surviving the testator pass to the relative's issue.

adeem
Extinguish; take away.

extinction
Act of extinguishing or putting to an end.

satisfaction
The giving by a testator, while alive, of property or money that was provided by will, with the intent that the gift or payment be in lieu of the legacy.

OPPERMAN V. ANDERSON
782 S.W.2d 8 (Tex. 1989)

FACTS: Among other things, Ethel M. Ramchissel's will left one-half of her stock in the Pabst Brewing Company to a named individual and all of her stock in the Houston Natural Gas Corporation to six named individuals "if owned by me at the time of my death." All of the Pabst Brewing stock and all but 65 shares of the Houston Natural Gas stock were converted to cash before the testatrix died. The remaining 65 shares of stock were redeemed for cash after she died.

LEGAL ISSUE: Do the proceeds from shares of stock sold before death pass to the legatee of those specific shares of stock?

COURT DECISION: No.

REASON: Mrs. Ramchissel clearly intended that the gifts of stock be specific bequests subject to ademption. The will was carefully worded to make the bequests of stock operative only in the event that the shares were on hand at her death.

MATTER OF ESTATE OF WOLFF
349 N.W.2d 33 (S.D. 1984)

FACTS: Jacob Wolff, who had three sons, executed a will providing that in the event his wife should predecease him, his estate should pass to his sons "equally, share and share alike." A year later, he and his wife deeded 1,000 acres of land to their son, Arthur, and 1,040 acres of land to their son, Erwinn, for "$1.00 and other good and valuable consideration." Prior to deeding the two tracts of land, Wolff wrote a letter to his third son, Jacob, Jr., telling him of the two deeds and saying, "From now on they did not have to send any more rent from the land that is deeded to them, and about your land, I don't know yet. See how it is turning out. Erwinn can buy it or rent for cash, from now on. Or what did you think? I thought if Erwinn buys it I can make the Deed to him. If he rents for cash I make the Deed to you." Nothing further was done before Jacob died.

LEGAL ISSUE: In South Dakota, may a general legacy adeem by satisfaction?

COURT DECISION: Yes.

REASON: Although there is authority that ademption applies only to specific legacies, a South Dakota statute (S.D. Codified Laws § 29-6-14) allows for ademption of general legacies if an intention to adeem is expressed by the testator in writing. The testator's letter to his son, Jacob, Jr., satisfied the writing requirement of the statute.

Information Required in a Declaration of Homestead
[9A AM. JUR. *Legal Forms* 2d (Rev.) § 135:16]

- Name of the declared homestead owner.
  If state law permits, a husband and wife both may be named as declared owners in the same declaration, if each owns an interest in the dwelling selected as the declared homestead.
- Description of the declared homestead.
- Statement that the declared homestead is the principal dwelling of the declared homestead owner or such person's spouse.
- Statement that the declared owner or such person's spouse actually resides in the declared homestead on the date the declaration is recorded.
- Statement that the facts stated in the homestead declaration are known to be true as of the personal knowledge of the person executing and acknowledging the declaration.
- If executed and acknowledged by a guardian or conservator or a person acting under a power of attorney, a statement that the person has authority so to act on behalf of the declared homestead owner or the spouse of the declared homestead owner, and the source of that person's authority.
- A statement as to whether a former declaration of homestead has been made; if so, a statement that it is abandoned.
- Actual cash value of premises.

Also, keep in mind the following professional guidelines when drafting a formal declaration of homestead [9A AM. JUR. *Legal Forms* 2d (Rev.) § 135:14]:

1. Local law must, of course, be checked to determine if a formal declaration of homestead is required by statute to be executed and recorded. In order that a claim of homestead may be sustained, the claimant must show that there has been substantial compliance with the provisions of the statute, and the declaration of homestead must have been executed and filed exactly as therein provided. Ordinarly, such a declaration must show that the claimant is the head of a family. In general, the claimant's right to select a homestead and to exempt it from forced sale must appear on the face of the declaration, and its omission cannot be supplied by extraneous evidence. Under some states, a declaration of homestead may be made by the owner or by his or her spouse.

2. A description of the premises claimed in a declaration of homestead, if required by statute, need not be more particular than is required in an ordinary conveyance. If the statute requires that the declaration state an actual cash value of the premises, substantial compliance with this requirement is sufficient; and it is satisfied where an estimate is entered even though it does not properly reflect the true cash value of the premises. Generally, the declaration must also contain a statement that the person making the declaration is residing on the premises.

SUMMARY

9.1 State laws give various kinds of protection to surviving family members when an income provider or spouse dies. With variations from state to state, types of protection include a family allowance, homestead protection, exempting property from creditors' claims, dower and curtesy, a spouse's elective share, and pretermitted children laws.

9.2 Gifts in a will to a devisee or legatee who dies before the testator lapse and fall into the residuary part of the estate, pursuant to the residuary clause of the will, unless they are prevented from doing so by an antilapse statute and pass to the issue of the deceased legatee or devisee.

9.3 A specific legacy or devise that is not owned by the testator or was given to the legatee or devisee while the testator was alive is said to have adeemed, and the legatee or devisee receives nothing in its place.

9.4 When preparing a declaration of homestead, it is necessary to examine the statutes of the state in which the property is located and to include in the declaration all information that the law requires.

QUESTIONS FOR REVIEW

1. What mechanism is provided by state laws to provide for the immediate support of family members when a breadwinner dies?
2. What is the purpose of the homestead exemption, and what does it do?
3. In states that have adopted the Uniform Probate Code, what kind and how much property is considered to be exempt property, and from what is it exempt?
4. What was the difference between dower and curtesy under early English law?
5. Describe generally the provisions of state laws that protect spouses from being disinherited.
6. Under what circumstances may a pretermitted child inherit from a parent's estate?
7. In general, who inherits a gift in a will to a legatee who dies before the testator?
8. What does a typical antilapse statute provide?
9. When a specific legacy or devise in a will is not owned by a testator at death, what does the legatee or devisee receive in its place?
10. How does ademption by satisfaction occur?

CASES TO DISCUSS

1. George A. Magoon filed a complaint for divorce in the family court on August 12, 1986, and a decree of divorce was entered on March 4, 1987. The court, however, reserved issues related to support and property division for further hearing. Mr. Magoon died on June 6, 1987, before the court was able to conduct a further hearing. Was Mrs. Magoon entitled to receive an elective share of Mr. Magoon's estate? Why or why not? *Magoon v. Magoon*, 780 P.2d 80 (Haw. 1989).
2. Thomas and Trudy Veit owned real property as tenants by the entireties. The holder of a mortgage on the property brought a foreclosure action for nonpayment of the mortgage. Mrs. Veit argued that, although her husband was still alive, she had a dower interest in her husband's property that prevented the mortgage from being foreclosed. Do you agree with Mrs. Veit? Explain. *Jones v. Veit*, 453 N.E.2d 1299 (Ohio 1982)
3. After 17 years of marriage, Thomas Carr left his wife, Joyce. A year later, Joyce Carr filed a complaint for divorce on the grounds of desertion. While the case was pending and the parties were living apart, Thomas Carr died, leaving his entire estate to his children from a prior

marriage. Is Joyce Carr entitled to an elective share of her husband's estate? Why or why not? *Carr v. Carr,* 576 A.2d 872 (N.J. 1990).

SHARPENING YOUR PROFESSIONAL SKILLS

1. Refer to the opening law office scenario and answer the following questions:
   a. Is there any way that Mrs. Papadakis can obtain money from her husband's estate for the immediate support of her family?
   b. Is any protection available to Mrs. Papadakis to prevent the loss of her house to creditors?
   c. Can Mrs. Papadakis do anything about being left out of her husband's will?
   d. Can the children do anything about being left out of their father's will?
   e. Will Mr. Papadakis's secretary inherit the insurance from the boat that sank?
2. Look up your state statute, if there is one, relating to each of the following protective devices:
   a. Family allowance
   b. Homestead protection
   c. Exempt property
   d. Dower and curtesy

   Write down the statutory reference and make a photocopy of each statute you find.
3. What rights do disinherited surviving spouses have in your state? Give the statutory reference where the provision is found.
4. What rights do disinherited children have in your state? Give the statutory reference where the provision is found.
5. Obtain an actual deed to a family member's or friend's property and draft a declaration of homestead following the form in figure 9-3. Before doing this assignment, look up your state's homestead statute to be sure that the form complies with your state's requirements.

CHAPTER 10
Probate Courts and Uniform Laws

"Laws are a dead letter without courts to expound and define their true meaning and opinion."

Alexander Hamilton

OUTLINE

LAW OFFICE SCENARIO

Claude Vickers, a paralegal, had just returned from his lunch break when he was called into the office of Attorney Zielinski.

"Did you hear about that car accident that happened last night on the Interstate, Claude?" Attorney Zielinski inquired.

"Do you mean that head-on collision with a drunk driver that killed two people?" Claude replied.

"Yes. That's the one. The man who was killed had signed an organ donor card but it wasn't witnessed," Attorney Zielinski continued. "Will you see what our state statute says about that?"

"Right away," Claude responded. "I heard that the couple died instantly."

"That's right. They were both dead when the ambulance arrived at the scene. We have their estates to settle, and I'm on my way over to their house now to talk with the children's grandparents."

"How many children did they have?" Claude asked.

"The man who died, his name was Kenneth Blake, had a three-year-old daughter from a former marriage. The woman's name was Leslie Johnson. She had a seven-year-old son from a former marriage. They were living together but weren't married," Attorney Zielinski explained.

"What a shame. Those poor children."

"Neither parent had a will," Attorney Zielinski continued. "They owned a house together as joint tenants, and they had a joint bank account. I've written some details here in the file. Kenneth owned his own car and a large amount of AT&T stock. Leslie owned her own car and quite a few U.S. Savings Bonds. Leslie was the beneficiary of Kenneth's life insurance policy. I'd like you to check the simultaneous death statute to see who will inherit their property."

"Okay," Claude replied as Attorney Zielinski put on her coat, preparing to leave the office.

"And while you're at it, see if our statute allows an estate to transfer money to minors," Attorney Zielinski said as she walked out of her office. "Those children are going to inherit quite a bit of property."

"I'll look into that, too," Claude replied, thinking about where he would begin his research.

10.1 PROBATE JURISDICTION

In their research, paralegals must often locate state statutes that apply to specific situations and determine what court has jurisdiction. **Jurisdiction** is the power or authority that a court has to hear a case and to make a decision. Without jurisdiction, any decision by a court would be meaningless.

Federal Courts

Federal courts have no jurisdiction to probate a will or to administer an estate. Federal court cases are usually cases involving **in personam jurisdiction** (jurisdiction over the person), whereas probate court proceedings are **in rem proceedings** (proceedings that are directed against property rather than against persons). The purpose of the proceedings is to determine title to, or the extent of people's interests in, specific property located within a state court's jurisdiction.

Federal courts cannot appoint or control executors, administrators, or guardians. However, once an executor or administrator has been appointed by a state court, a claim against the estate may be brought in a federal court,

LEGAL TERMS

jurisdiction
The power or authority that a court has to hear a case and to make a decision.

in personam jurisdiction
Jurisdiction over the person.

in rem proceedings
Proceedings directed against property rather than against persons.

but only under these specific conditions: when the parties are citizens of different states and the claim exceeds $50,000.

State Courts

Specific state courts have jurisdiction to probate a will or to administer an estate. This jurisdiction derives from either the state constitution or acts of the state legislature. Many states have established a separate court and empowered it with **probate jurisdiction** (i.e., the authority to probate wills and to administer estates). In most states, this separate court is referred to as the **probate court**. However, some states designate this same court as the **court of chancery**, the **surrogate court**, or the **orphan's court**. States that have not established separate courts give the authority to probate wills and to administer estates to courts of general jurisdiction, such as superior courts, district courts, circuit courts, county courts, and courts of common pleas. Some of these courts of general jurisdiction have separate divisions, one of which is empowered to probate wills and to administer estates.

10.2 PROBATE RECORDS

In some states, the records of all probate activities are kept in an office called the **Registry of Probate**. In these states, an official, called the Register of Probate, is either elected or appointed to administer the office. The Register of Probate is responsible for the care and custody of all books, documents, and papers filed with the probate court. He or she must maintain the probate records, compile indexes, and make the records available to the public upon request. In other states, this recordkeeping function is performed by the clerk of court.

The register or clerk keeps a docket of all cases that come before the court and, in general, handles all clerical matters necessary for the court's operation. The Uniform Probate Code contains the following provision relative to court records:

> The [Clerk of Court] shall keep a record for each decedent, ward, protected person or trust involved in any document which may be filed with the Court under this Code, including petitions and applications, demands for notices or bonds, trust registrations, and of any orders or responses relating thereto by the Registrar or Court, and establish and maintain a system for indexing, filing or recording which is sufficient to enable users of the records to obtain adequate information. Upon payment of the fees required by law the clerk must issue certified copies of any probated wills, letters issued to personal representatives, or any other record or paper filed or recorded. Certificates relating to probated wills must indicate whether the decedent was domiciled in this state and whether the probate was formal or informal. Certificates relating to letters must show the date of appointment.

UPC § 1-305.

LEGAL TERMS

probate jurisdiction
Authority to probate wills and to administer estates.

In some states, the Registry of Probate is housed in the same building as the **Registry of Deeds**, which is the office that retains deeds, mortgages, and other instruments affecting title to real property. A search of the title to real property often requires the use of both offices. When property is transferred by deed, the Registry of Deeds records the deed. When property is transferred by will or intestacy, no deed is used; the probate records must be examined to determine who has title to the property. Having the two offices in the same building allows title examiners conveniently to examine both types of records.

probate court (also called court of chancery, surrogate court, orphan's court) A court with probate jurisdiction.

Registry of Probate An office where the records of all probate activities are kept.

Registry of Deeds An office where deeds, mortgages, and other instruments affecting title to real property are kept.

uniform laws (also called model acts) Laws that have been proposed by the National Conference of Commissioners on Uniform State Laws for adoption by state legislatures.

10.3 UNIFORM LAWS

Uniform laws, sometimes called **model acts**, are laws that have been proposed by the National Conference of Commissioners on Uniform State Laws (a body with representatives from every state) for adoption by state legislatures. These recommendations are not a requirement: states may adopt the uniform laws or pass their own laws. Some uniform laws have been adopted, either in whole or in part, by many state legislatures; others have been adopted by only a few state legislatures. The version adopted by a state is often amended by the state legislature, thereby making the "uniform law" no longer uniform. Table 10-1 lists the uniform laws relating to wills,

Name of Uniform Act	States That Have Adopted Uniform Act
Absence as Evidence of Death and Absentees' Property Act	TN, WI
Anatomical Gift Act (1987 Act),	AR, CA, CT, HI, ID, MT, NV ND, RI, UT, VT, VA, WI
(1968 Act)	AL, AK, AZ, CO, DE, DC, FL, GA, GU, IL, IN, IA, KS, KY, LA, ME, MD, MA, MI, MN, MS, MO, NE, NH, NJ, NM, NY, NC, OH, OK, OR, PA, SC, SD, TN, TX, VT, VI, WA, WV, WY
Ancillary Administration of Estates Act	WI
Disclaimer of Property Interests Act	AL, IL, ME, MD, VT, WV

TABLE 10-1
Uniform laws relating to wills, trusts, and estates

Disclaimer of Transfers by Will, Intestacy or Appointment Act	DE, IL, KS, KY, ME, MN, NJ, NC, OR
Disclaimer of Transfers Under Nontestamentary Instruments Act	DE, KS, KY, ME, ND, OR
Disposition of Community Property Rights at Death Act	AK, AR, CO, CT, HI, KY, MI, MT, NY, OR, VA, WY
Disposition of Unclaimed Property Act (1966 Act)	AL, AR, DC, IL, IN, IA, KS, MN, MS, MO, NE, NV, OK, OR, SD, TN
(1954 Act)	MD, VT, WV
Durable Power of Attorney Act	AL, AZ, CA, CO, DE, DC, HI, ID, IN, KS, KY, ME, MA, MI, MN, MO, MT, NE, NM, ND, OK, PA, SC, TN, UT, WV, WI
Estate Tax Apportionment Act (1964 Act)	HI, ID, MD, ND, OR, RI, VT, WA
(1958 Act)	AL, MI, MT, NH, WY
Gifts to Minors Act (1966 Act)	CT, DE, MS, NE, NJ, NY, PA, SC, TN, TX, VT, WA
(1956 Act)	MI, VI
Guardianship and Protective Proceedings Act	AL, AZ, CO, DC, HI, ID, ME, MI, MT, NE, NM, ND, SC, UT
Interstate Arbitration of Death Taxes Act	CA, CO, CT, ME, MD, MA, MI, MN, NE, PA, SC, TN, VT, WV, WI
Interstate Compromise of Death Taxes Act	CA, CO, CT, ME, MD, MA, MI, MN, NE, NH, NJ, NY, PA, SC, TN, VT, WV

TABLE 10-1
(Continued)

Multiple-Person Accounts Act	CO
Probate Code	AL, AZ, CO, FL, HI, ID, ME, MI, MN, MT, NE, NM, ND, SC, UT
Probate of Foreign Wills Act	TX, WI
Simultaneous Death Act	All states except LA, MT, and OH
Statutory Form Power of Attorney Act	CA
Statutory Rule Against Perpetuities	CT, FL, GA, MA, MI, MN, MT, NE, NV, OR, SC
Statutory Will Act	MA
Testamentary Additions to Trusts Act	All states except AL, LA, RI, VA, and WI
TOD Security Registration Act	CO, WI
Transfers to Minors Act	AL, AK, AZ, AR, CA, CO, DC, FL, GA, HI, ID, IL, IN, IA, KS, KY, LA, ME, MD, MA, MN, MO, MT, NV, NH, NJ, NM, NC, ND, OH, OK, OR, RI, SD, UT, VA, WV, WI, WY
Unclaimed Property Act	AL, AZ, CO, HI, FL, GA, ID, IA, LA, ME, MD, MN, MT, NV, NH, NJ, NM, ND, OR, RI, SC, TN, UT, VT, VI, VA, WA, WI
Veterans' Guardianship Act	AR, CO, IN, KY, LA, MO, NC, OH, OK, RI, SD, TN, VT, VI, WA, WI

TABLE 10-1
(Continued)

estates, and trusts and the states that have adopted them. Using the index to your state's statutes will help you find your own state's version of any of these uniform laws.

Uniform Probate Code

The **Uniform Probate Code (UPC)** is a law designed to modernize and standardize the laws relating to the affairs of decedents, minors, and certain others who need protection. The law developed in response to growing dissatisfaction with the high cost, long delays, and unnecessary formalities involved with the old-fashioned probate procedure. Some people resented judicial control and interference by the court in what they considered to be family matters. For some states, the UPC offered welcome changes.

For example, the UPC gives heirs and devisees the option of selecting supervised or unsupervised administration. **Supervised administration** occurs under the continuing authority of the court. In contrast, **unsupervised administration** occurs without court action, unless requested by an interested person. Although there is no court supervision, the Registrar of Probate is given the authority to process any necessary documents and to decide whether they are complete. In unsupervised administration, an interested person can petition the court to resolve a question, such as the validity of the will or the appointment of the personal representative. The court does not become involved unnecessarily—only to settle controversies or doubts.

The purposes of the Uniform Probate Code are:

1. to simplify and clarify the law concerning the affairs of decedents, missing persons, protected persons, minors, and incapacitated persons;
2. to discover and make effective the intent of a decedent in the distribution of his or her property;
3. to promote a speedy and efficient system for liquidating the estate of the decedent and making distribution to its successors;
4. to facilitate use and enforcement of certain trusts; and
5. to make uniform the law among the various jurisdictions.

UPC § 1-102. Table 10-2 lists the eight articles and contents of the Uniform Probate Code.

In 1990, major changes in Article II of the UPC were made in response to the following developments in society:

1. Fewer formalities exist today than in the past.
2. The use of living gifts, jointly owned property, and trusts have increased so much that they constitute a major form of wealth transmission.
3. The advent of a multiple-marriage society, wherein a significant portion of the population marries more than once and has stepchildren and children by previous marriages and wherein a partnership theory of marriage has gained acceptance.

LEGAL TERMS

Uniform Probate Code (UPC)
Uniform law designed to modernize and standardize the laws relating to the affairs of decedents, minors, and certain other persons who need protection.

Article I	General provisions, definitions and probate jurisdiction of court
Article II	Intestate succession and wills
Article III	Probate of wills and administration
Article IV	Foreign Personal Representatives; Ancillary administrations
Article V	Protection of persons under disability and their property
Article VI	Nonprobate transfers on death
Article VII	Trust administration
Article VIII	Effective date and repealer

TABLE 10-2
Uniform Probate Code articles and contents

Uniform Simultaneous Death Act

When two people die at the same time, as in an automobile accident, plane crash, boating accident, gas poisoning, or house fire, it is often impossible to determine who died first. The **Uniform Simultaneous Death Act** is a uniform law, adopted by most states, that sets forth rules to be followed when the passage of property depends upon the time of death, and no sufficient evidence can establish which person died first.

Before the development of this uniform law, the individual states addressed the issue of simultaneous death in different ways. Some states followed the common law rule that required a claimant to prove that one person died before the other, an almost impossible task. Other states developed presumptions that could not be rebutted, many of which were unrealistic. For example, in some states it was conclusively presumed that an adult in good health always survived a minor child. Realistically, however, a parent might very well die attempting to save a child's life.

The following rules apply under the Uniform Simultaneous Death Act when two or more persons die at the same time:

1. When title to property depends upon priority of death, and there is insufficient evidence that the persons died other than at the same time, the property of each person shall be disposed of as if he or she had survived. Thus, when a mother's will leaves her entire estate "to my daughter, Kathleen, if living, but if not, to Kathleen's children equally,"

supervised administration
Process in which an estate is settled under the continuing surveillance of the court from beginning to end.

unsupervised administration
Method of administering an estate, under the UPC, without court action unless it is requested by an interested person.

Uniform Simultaneous Death Act
Uniform law, adopted by most states, that sets forth rules to be followed when the passage of property depends upon the time of one's death, and there is no sufficient evidence that the persons died other than at the same time.

and the mother and daughter die at the same time in a car accident, the mother's estate will pass directly to the daughter's children.

2. When two or more beneficiaries are designated to take successively or alternatively by survivorship under another person's will or trust, and there is insufficient evidence that they died other than simultaneously, the property shall be divided into as many equal portions as there are successive or alternate beneficiaries and a share distributed to each.
3. When there is no evidence that joint tenants or tenants by the entirety died other than simultaneously, half shall be distributed to each. When there are more than two joint tenants in the same situation, the property is distributed among them all equally.
4. When an insured and a beneficiary of a life insurance policy have died, and there is insufficient evidence that they died other than simultaneously, the proceeds are payable as if the insured had survived the beneficiary.

The law does not apply when there is competent evidence that one person died before the other person, as in the *Villwock* case.

MATTER OF ESTATE OF VILLWOCK
418 N.W.2d 1 (Wis. 1987)

FACTS: Roy and June Villwock, critically injured but alive and conscious after a head-on car crash, were transported together to a hospital. All five emergency medical technicians on board agreed that Roy suffered cardiopulmonary failure minutes before June similarly failed. Upon arrival at the hospital, each was taken to a separate treatment room, where CPR was continued, but both were soon pronounced dead. After hearing testimony of physicians, the court found that Roy died in the ambulance while his wife was still alive and conscious and that she died a few minutes later. There were no children born to their marriage. Roy's will left everything to June, and June's will left everything to specific members of her family. Roy's daughter by a previous marriage inherited nothing.

LEGAL ISSUE: Do the provisions of the Simultaneous Death Act apply when the victims of an automobile accident die minutes apart?

COURT DECISION: No.

REASON: The Villwocks did not die simultaneously. The statute's nontechnical words, if not specifically defined, will be given their ordinary and accepted meaning, which may be ascertained from a recognized dictionary. *Webster's Third New International Dictionary* defines *simultaneous* as "occurring at the same time."

Uniform Gifts (Transfers) to Minors Act

Before the mid-1950s, the only legal way to transfer property to a minor was through a trust or by having a guardian appointed for the minor. Both methods were time-consuming and expensive. The **Uniform Gifts to Minors Act (UGMA)** was formulated in 1956 to provide an inexpensive, easy method to transfer property to minors. This uniform law eliminated the need to create a trust or appoint a guardian by allowing a custodian to receive and administer gifts of securities and cash for the benefit of a minor. A **custodian** is a person who is entrusted with property belonging to a minor. Although the property vests in the minor when the gift is made, the custodian retains possession and control.

The UGMA was revised in 1966. The revision (1) expanded the number of institutions that could serve as depositories of custodial funds, (2) provided for the designation of successor custodians, and (3) added life insurance policies and annuities to the types of property that could be made as gifts. Many states adopted the 1966 revision, but many others chose to retain the 1956 version. At the same time, many states revised their versions of the UGMA even further. Such diversity of the Act in the various states jeopardized its uniformity.

To reestablish the Act's uniformity, the National Conference of Commissioners on Uniform State Laws approved a new act in 1983, called the **Uniform Transfers to Minors Act (UTMA)**. This Act revises and restates the Uniform Gifts to Minors Act, and has been adopted by 38 states and the District of Columbia. Besides money and securities, the UTMA allows any kind of property, whether real or personal, tangible or intangible, to be transferred to a custodian for the benefit of a minor. Transfers may be made from trusts, estates, and guardianships as well as from living donors. To be consistent with Internal Revenue Service policy, the UTMA uses the age of 21, rather than 18, to determine when custodianship ends and the former minor receives the property.

LEGAL TERMS

Uniform Gifts to Minors Act (UGMA)
Uniform law that provides an inexpensive, easy mechanism for transferring property to minors.

custodian
Person who is entrusted with property that belongs to a minor.

Uniform Transfers to Minors Act (UTMA)
Uniform law that revised and restated the Uniform Gifts to Minors Act.

Under the uniform law, a transferor (or donor) can register a stock certificate or other security in the name of the transferor (or donor), other adult person, or trust company "as custodian for [name of minor] under the [name of state] Uniform Transfers to Minors Act." Similarly, a transferor (or donor) can open a bank account in the name of the transferor (or donor), other adult person, or trust company "as custodian for [name of minor] under the [name of state] Uniform Transfers to Minors Act." An interest in real property is recorded in the name of the transferor, an adult other than the transferor, or a trust company, followed in substance by the words: "as custodian for [name of minor] under the [name of state] Uniform Transfers to Minors Act."

Each transfer may involve only one minor, and only one person may be the custodian. The minor's Social Security number is used to identify the account, and the income from the securities or bank account is usually taxable to the minor. A gift to a minor under the Uniform Transfers (or Gifts) to Minors Act is considered to be a completed gift, making it subject to the federal gift tax discussed in chapter 8.

A custodian must keep custodial property separate and distinct from all other property and must maintain records of all transactions relating to the custodial property. When investing funds, the UTMA requires the custodian to "observe the standard of care that would be observed by a prudent person dealing with the property of another."

A gift made under the Act is **irrevocable**: that is, it cannot be taken back. The *McLaughlin* case demonstrates this point of law. Gifts made under the UTMA must be held by the custodian and used only for the minor's support, maintenance, education, and benefit. When the minor becomes 21 years old (18 in some states), the balance of the property held by the custodian must be given to the minor outright.

MATTER OF ESTATE OF McLAUGHLIN
483 N.Y.S.2d 943 (N.Y. 1985)

FACTS: Rose McLaughlin established two separate $20,000 bank accounts under the Uniform Gift to Minors Act, one for each of her two daughters. A year later, she closed the accounts and placed the money in two Totten trust accounts in joint names, each naming one of her daughters as a Totten trust beneficiary. When Rose died, the creditors of her estate claimed that the bank accounts should be included as assets of her estate.

LEGAL ISSUE: Can money that is placed by a donor in a custodial account under the Uniform Gifts to Minors Act be returned to the donor?

COURT DECISION: No.

REASON: A gift under the Uniform Gifts to Minors Act is irrevocable and indefeasibly vests title in the donee. The discretionary powers granted to the custodian do not authorize the dissipation of the minors' interest in such property for the purpose of returning the gift to the donor. The custodian in this case wrongfully administered the custodial accounts by restructuring them in the form of joint-Totten trusts. The funds in the accounts are neither estate assets nor within the reach of estate creditors. They belong to the children.

Uniform Anatomical Gifts Act

The **Uniform Anatomical Gifts Act (UAGA)** provides an easy way to make a testamentary donation of vital organs for medical research or transplant. All 50 states and the District of Columbia have now adopted either the 1968 or the 1987 version of the Act.

Although the 1968 version was adopted by many states, few people participated. Over the years, the demand for organ donations continued to exceed the supply. A Gallup poll taken in 1985 reported that 93 percent of Americans surveyed knew about organ transplantation; of these, 75 percent approved of the concept of organ donation. However, only 27 percent indicated that they would be very likely to donate their own organs, and only 17 percent had completed donor cards. Also in 1985, the Hastings Center assessed the Uniform Anatomical Gifts Act and described the main problems that hindered organ donation:

1. Failure of persons to sign written directives.
2. Failure of police and emergency personnel to locate written directives at accident sites.
3. Uncertainty on the part of the public about circumstances and timing of organ recovery.
4. Failure on the part of medical personnel to recover organs on the basis of written directives.
5. Failure to systemically approach family members concerning donation.

LEGAL TERMS

irrevocable
Cannot be taken back.

Uniform Anatomical Gifts Act (UAGA)
Uniform law that provides a simplified manner of making a testamentary donation of vital organs for medical research or transplant.

Every state has enacted the Uniform Anatomical Gifts Act, which regulates the gift of a body or parts of a body to be made after the death of a donor. Reprinted by permission of Tribune Media Services.

6. Inefficiency on the part of some organ procurement agencies in obtaining referrals of donors.
7. High wastage rates on the part of some organ procurement agencies in failing to place donated organs.
8. Failure to communicate the pronouncement of death to next of kin.
9. Failure to obtain adequate informed consent from family members.

To help eliminate these obstacles to organ donation and to help narrow the gap between supply and demand for organs and tissues, the Uniform Anatomical Gifts Act was revised in 1987. Under the 1987 Act, no witnesses are required on the document used to make an anatomical gift, such as a donor card or driver's license. In addition, the consent of the next of kin after death is not required. Identifying actual donors became easier because hospital admissions personnel must search for a document of gift or inquire about the patient's interest in donating organs. Other provisions of the 1987 Act include the following:

1. A donor may revoke the offer of an anatomical gift without advising any specified donee.
2. The designation of a gift of one organ—for example, eyes or a heart—does not restrict the use of other organs as donations after death unless otherwise indicated by the decedent.
3. Hospitals rather than the attending physicians are the donees of anatomical gifts.
4. The sale or purchase of organs and tissue are prohibited.
5. People who act in good faith in accordance with the terms of the Act cannot be liable in any civil or criminal action relating to the transplant.

Anatomical gifts are discussed further in chapter 14.

SUMMARY

10.1 Federal courts have no jurisdiction to probate wills or to administer estates. Probate proceedings are in rem, their purpose being to determine title to specific property located within the state. Specific state courts have probate jurisdiction, their authority coming from state constitutions or statutes. Each state has either a separate court or a court of general jurisdiction with jurisdiction over probate matters.

10.2 In some states, probate records are kept in the Registry of Probate and are the responsibility of an official known as the Register of Probate. Other states give the responsibility to a clerk of court. Some states house the Registry of Probate in the same building with the Registry of Deeds to facilitate the examination of records in both offices.

10.3 Uniform laws are laws that have been proposed by a national committee for adoption by state legislatures. Some uniform laws have been adopted by many states; others have been adopted by only a few states. States sometimes amend uniform laws after adopting them, making them no longer uniform.

The Uniform Probate Code, adopted by 15 states, is designed to reduce the high cost, long delays, and unnecessary formalities involved with probating an estate.

The Uniform Simultaneous Death Act, adopted by most states, establishes rules to be followed when the passage of property depends upon the time of death, and no sufficient evidence can establish which person died first.

Either the Uniform Gifts to Minors Act or the Uniform Transfers to Minors Act has been adopted by every state. The law provides an inexpensive, easy mechanism for transferring money and other property to minors. The *Gifts* to Minors Act provides for making gifts of securities and cash to a custodian for the benefit of a minor. The *Transfers* to Minors Act, which has been adopted by 38 states, allows the transfer of any kind of property, real or personal, to a custodian for the benefit of a minor. Gifts made to minors under either Act are irrevocable.

The Uniform Anatomical Gifts Act, which has been adopted in one form or another by every state, provides for a simplified manner of making a testamentary donation of vital organs for medical research or transplant. The Act was amended in 1987 in an attempt to close the gap between the need for organs and tissues and the supply of them.

QUESTIONS FOR REVIEW

1. Why do federal courts have no jurisdiction to probate a will or to administer an estate?

2. From what source do state courts obtain their jurisdiction to probate wills and to administer estates?
3. To what courts do states that have not established separate courts with probate jurisdiction give the authority to probate wills and to administer estates?
4. Why is the Registry of Probate housed in the same building as the Registry of Deeds in some states?
5. Must all states adopt uniform laws? Explain.
6. Why did the Uniform Probate Code come into existence?
7. When title to property depends upon priority of death, and there is insufficient evidence that the persons have died other than simultaneously:
   a. How will the property of each person be disposed?
   b. How will the property be disposed when the decedents are two beneficiaries who are designated to take successively?
   c. How will the property be disposed when the decedents are joint tenants?
   d. How will the property be disposed when the decedents are an insured and a beneficiary of a life insurance policy?
8. Why does the Uniform Transfers to Minors Act use the age of 21 rather than 18 as the age when custodianship terminates and the property is distributed to the former minor?
9. Under the Uniform Transfers to Minors Act, what language is used to open a bank account for a minor named Irene Buckley whose custodian is Joan M. Peabody?
10. For what two reasons was the Uniform Anatomical Gifts Act revised in 1987?

CASES TO DISCUSS

1. Mrs. Roig established three Shearson (investment) Accounts valued at $50,000, in which she was the custodian for each of her three children under the Uniform Gifts to Minors Act. Later, in a divorce proceeding, the trial court held that the three accounts were marital property belonging to Mrs. Roig and her husband. Was the trial court correct in its holding? Why or why not? *Roig v. Roig*, 364 S.E.2d 794 (W. Va. 1988).
2. At the time Kathy gave birth to Krystal, Kathy was living as a foster child in Edith's home. Edith petitioned the probate court to be appointed as guardian of Krystal. Under the law of that state, the probate court has equity jurisdiction in all matters relating to wills, trusts, and administration of decedents' estates. Another statute provides that only courts having full equity jurisidiction have power to adjudicate rights as to the custody of infants. Did the probate court have the power to

appoint Edith as guardian of Krystal? Why or why not? *In re Krystal S.*, 584 A.2d 672 (Me. 1991).

SHARPENING YOUR PROFESSIONAL SKILLS

1. Refer to the opening law office scenario and answer the following questions:
   a. Assuming that each child will inherit from his and her parent, what will the daughter inherit? What will the son inherit? Who will receive the proceeds from the life insurance policy?
   b. Under your state law, must an organ donor card be witnessed to be valid?
   c. Under your state law, may an estate transfer money to minors? Give statutory references to support your answers.
2. What is the name and location of the court in your county that has jurisdiction to probate wills and to administer estates? How near to the Registry of Deeds is the court located?
3. Examine your state statute and determine your state's version of the Uniform Gifts to Minors Act from among the following:
   a. the 1956 version,
   b. the 1966 version,
   c. its own version, or
   d. the 1983 version known as the Uniform Transfers to Minors Act.

   Give the reference number of that particular statute.
4. Examine Table 10-1 and make a list of the unifom laws that have been adopted by your state.
5. Make a survey of 10 friends and family members, asking the following questions:
   a. Are you aware of organ transplantation?
   b. Do you approve of the concept of organ donation?
   c. Is it very likely that you will donate your own organs?
   d. Have you completed an organ donor card?

   Compare the results with those of the Gallup poll taken in 1985 (discussed in § 10.3).

WILL
ESTATE
TRUST

CHAPTER 11
The Personal Representative

"Nobody has a more sacred obligation to obey the law than those who make the law."

Jean Anouilh

OUTLINE

LAW OFFICE SCENARIO

It was almost noon when Attorney Serena Hall stopped by the desk of her legal assistant, Ginamarie Orlando. "Ginamarie, I just received a call from Mrs. Greaves about her father's estate. It seems that her brother is the executor of the will, and he's been running their father's business for two years without authority."

"Oh really? What kind of a business is it?"

"It's a truck farm. They grow vegetables and take them into the market to sell. According to Mrs. Greaves, her brother went to a gambling casino in Nevada last year and lost all the money that belongs to the estate."

"Good grief!"

"Apparently, he tried to make up for it by growing a double crop of tomatoes and cucumbers this year, but now he's letting them rot on the vine. He told Mrs. Greaves that he's resigning as executor."

"Nice guy. I hope he was bonded," Ginamarie responded.

"Mrs. Greaves has an appointment with me tomorrow," Attorney Hall continued. "Before she comes, will you look up the state statute to see whether or not an executor can continue running a decedent's business? And, while you're at it, find out what an executor has to do to resign. You might as well draft a petition to have Mrs. Greaves appointed a special administrator. She'll need to be appointed right away to take care of the rotting vegetables."

"I'll begin right after lunch," Ginamarie answered.

"What are you having for lunch today?" queried Attorney Hall.

"A cucumber and tomato sandwich," Ginamarie replied with a smile.

At that moment, the office receptionist entered the room, interrupting the laughter. "Mrs. Greaves is on the phone, Ms. Hall. She said that her brother was rushed to the hospital with a perforated ulcer last night and passed away this morning."

11.1 APPOINTMENT OF PERSONAL REPRESENTATIVE

Paralegals may be asked to assist the individual assigned to manage the affairs and settle the estate of someone who dies and owns property. The one who performs that function is known as a **personal representative**. Because these duties involve good faith, trust, and special confidence, a personal representative is a type of **fiduciary** and acts in a **fiduciary capacity** (i.e., in a position of trust). The law imposes an unusually high standard of ethical and moral conduct on a fiduciary because he or she holds property interests for the benefit of others.

When someone dies testate, the person nominated in the will as personal representative, or some other interested person, petitions the court to have the will allowed and to be appointed personal representative. When someone dies intestate, one of the heirs, next of kin, or a creditor files a petition with the court requesting the appointment (see figure 11-1). With variations from state to state, notice of a hearing on the petition is given to all interested parties either by service of process, mail, or publication in a newspaper. A time period of about three to four weeks is established for interested parties to respond to the notice, after which a hearing is held on the petition. The hearing may be dispensed with if no one objects to the petition. If no contest arises, the court allows the will or grants the administration and

LEGAL TERMS

personal representative
Person who carries out the terms of a will or administers an estate; an executor or administrator.

fiduciary
Person who is appointed to serve in a position of trust, including an executor, administrator, guardian, or trustee.

fiduciary capacity
A position of trust.

(Form 98)

THE STATE OF NEW HAMPSHIRE

TO THE HONORABLE JUDGE OF PROBATE FOR THE COUNTY OF

Your petitioner ....

of ...., in said County of ....

respectfully represents that ...., late of ....

in said County died on the .... day of ....

A.D. 19...., testate, having at the time of h death estate in said County; that your petitioner was named in the will of said deceased as execut thereof and is willing to accept that trust; wehereupon h pray that said will be proved and allowed in common .... form; and that letters testamentary be granted to h , and that ....

.... all of ....

in said County, are suitable persons to be appointed to take inventory, and appraise the estate of said deceased.

Your petitioner declares that there is no child or issue of a deceased child of the deceased not named or referred to in said will, and the estate of the deceased, upon which he has petitioned for administration, consists, as nearly as can be ascertained, of property of the following value:

Real estate .... $..........

Personal estate ....

Whole amount of estate not exceeding .... $..........

Dated the .... day of .... A.D. 19....

....

....

, ss. COURT OF PROBATE.

At a Court of Probate holden at .... in said County, on the .... day of .... A.D. 19...., upon due consideration of the foregoing petition, it is decreed that the prayer thereof be granted, and that letters testamentary issue to the said petitioner accordingly.

....

Judge of Probate.

FIGURE 11-1 Petition for appointment of executor (New Hampshire)

LEGAL TERMS

letters testamentary
Certificate of appointment of a personal representative in a testate estate.

appoints the personal representative. When a contest does occur, a judge or jury decides the question in dispute.

In many states, the certificate of appointment of a personal representative is called **letters testamentary** in a testate estate and **letters of administration** in an intestate estate.

THE STATE OF NEW HAMPSHIRE

TO THE HONORABLE JUDGE OF PROBATE FOR THE COUNTY OF

Your petitioner ....

of ...., in said County of ....

respectfully represents that ...., late of ....

in said County, died on the .... day of .... A.D. 19....

testate, having at the time of h death estate in said County; that ....

was named in said Will execut thereof and ....

trust; whereupon h pray that said will be proved and allowed in common ....

form; and that letters of administration with will annexed be granted to ....

of ...., of said County and that ....

.... all of ....

in said County, are suitable persons to be appointed to take an inventory, and appraise the estate of said deceased.

Your petitioner declares that there is no child or issue of a deceased child of the deceased not named or referred to in said will, and that the estate of the deceased, upon which he has petitioned for administration, consists, as nearly as can be ascertained, of property of the following value:

Real estate .... $.............

Personal estate ....

Whole amount of estate not exceeding .... $.............

Dated the .... day of .... A.D. 19....

....

....

, ss. COURT OF PROBATE.

At a Court of Probate holden at .... in said County, on the .... day of.................................. A.D. 19...., upon due consideration of the foregoing petition, it is decreed that the prayer thereof be granted and that letters of administration with will annexed issue to the said accordingly.

....

Judge of Probate

FIGURE 11-1
(Continued)

11.2 PERSONAL REPRESENTATIVE'S BOND

letters of administration Certificate of appointment of a personal representative in an intestate estate, or a testate estate in which someone other than the person nominated as executor(-trix) in the will is appointed.

In some states, the appointment of a personal representative is not complete until the representative has given bond. A **bond** is a written promise by the personal representative and the sureties (if any) to pay the amount of the bond to the court if the representative does not faithfully perform his or her duties (see figure 11-2). **Sureties** are individuals or insurance companies that stand behind a fiduciary by agreeing to pay the amount of the bond

THE STATE OF NEW HAMPSHIRE

, ss. COURT OF PROBATE.

ESTATE OF .... LATE OF ....

RESIDENCE OF DECEASED ....
(Street Address)

DATE OF DEATH ....

Does the deceased own any real estate situated in New Hampshire? ....
(Answer "Yes" or "No")

Real Estate located at ....

Give names and residences of devisees of such real estate.

Name .... Street Address .... City or Town & State

Dated at .... this .... day of .... , 19 ... .

I certify that the foregoing statement is true to the best of my knowledge and belief.

....
(Executor or Administrator, c.t.a.)

....
(Address)

FIGURE 11-1
(Continued)

To be appointed executor, the person named as executor in the will must petition the probate court on a form such as this.

LEGAL TERMS

bond
A written promise by a fiduciary to pay a sum of money to the court if the fiduciary's duties are not faithfully performed.

to the court in the event the fiduciary fails to meet the obligations of the office. The bond requirement serves to enforce the obligations of the personal representative: suit can be brought on the bond for any losses caused by the personal representative's breach of duty.

In some states, no bond is required if the will includes a provision like the "No Surety on Bond" provision discussed in chapter 5, requesting that

Combined
(Form 12-22 inclusive)

THE STATE OF NEW HAMPSHIRE

ROCKINGHAM ......, ss. COURT OF PROBATE

KNOW ALL MEN BY THESE PRESENTS

That we, ... of ....
in the County of .... and State of ....
as principal, and ....
....
as surety, are holden and bounden unto the Judge of Probate for the above County in the sum of .... Dollars ($............) to be paid to said Judge, his successor or successors in office; to the true payment whereof we bind ourselves, our heirs, executors and administrators, or successors, jointly and severally by these presents.

Witness our hands and seals this .... day of .... 19 ...

The condition of this obligation is such that if the above bounden principal who is appointed to a certain trust and office pertaining to the estate of ....
as appears by a decree of said Court of Probate, shall well and faithfully discharge and perform said trust and office according to law and upon the conditions set forth in the applicable statutes of The State of New Hampshire relating thereto; then this obligation shall be void; otherwise it shall remain in full force and effect.

In the presence of .... (Seal)
Principal
.... (Seal)
.... (Seal)
Sureties

Approved

....
Judge of Probate

FIGURE 11-2
Fiduciary bond (New Hampshire)

the personal representative serve without bond. Under some circumstances, a bond is not required if all heirs agree to the appointment without sureties or waive the filing of a bond and the will does not require one. Under the Uniform Probate Code, a bond may be required when an interested person demands that a bond be given (see UPC §§ 3-603 through 3-606).

surety
One who stands behind a fiduciary by agreeing to pay the amount of the bond in the event the fiduciary becomes liable to pay it.

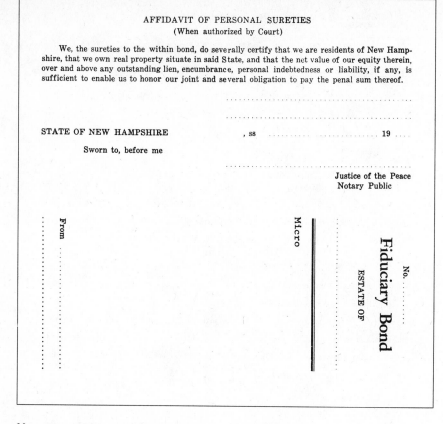

AFFIDAVIT OF PERSONAL SURETIES
(When authorized by Court)

We, the sureties to the within bond, do severally certify that we are residents of New Hampshire, that we own real property situate in said State, and that the net value of our equity therein, over and above any outstanding lien, encumbrance, personal indebtedness or liability, if any, is sufficient to enable us to honor our joint and several obligation to pay the penal sum thereof.

....

....

STATE OF NEW HAMPSHIRE , ss .... 19 ....

Sworn to, before me

....

Justice of the Peace
Notary Public

From ....

Micro

No. ....

Fiduciary Bond

ESTATE OF

FIGURE 11-2
(Continued)

Many states require personal representatives to file a fiduciary bond such as this, promising to pay the amount of the bond to the court if the representative does not faithfully perform his or her duties.

11.3 DUTIES OF PERSONAL REPRESENTATIVE

The duties of a personal representative are to collect and preserve the assets of the estate, pay the debts, taxes, and expenses of administration, and distribute the remainder according to the terms of the will, or the law of intestate succession if there is no will. Specific rules and regulations for carrying out the duties of a personal representative are set forth in the various state statutes. Under Uniform Probate Code §§ 3-705 through 3-709, the personal representatives must inform the heirs and devisees of the appointment within 30 days, file an inventory of the estate within 3 months, take possession and control of the decedent's property, and take all steps necessary for the management, protection, and preservation of the property.

Unless allowed by state statute or the decedent's will, a personal representative has no authority to continue a decedent's business.

Provision in Will Authorizing Executor to Continue Business [8 AM. JUR. *Legal Forms* 2d § 104:96]

I empower my executor, during the administration of my estate and pending the sale of the property thereof, to continue all business activities in which I may have been engaged at the time of my death. My executor may continue such activities either singly or in a copartnership or association with others until such time as the business or businesses may be sold to the best business advantage as my executor shall judge.

State Statute Authorizing Continuance of Decedent's Business [Mass. Gen. Laws ch. 195, § 17]

The probate court, upon such notice as it considers reasonable, may authorize an executor or administrator to continue the business of the deceased for the benefit of the estate for a period not exceeding one year from the date of his appointment. Such authority may be granted at the time of the appointment of an executor or administrator if the petition for such appointment contains a prayer therefor, and may be granted without special notice or with such special notice as the court may order to be given prior to or after the granting of such authority. The court, for cause shown, may extend such authority beyond one year.

Claims against the estate must be presented to the personal representative within a prescribed time period set by state statute. The personal representative must pay all taxes that are due and all legitimate claims against the estate that arose before the death of the decedent. If the assets of the estate are insufficient to pay all claims in full, state statutes provide the order of priority in which they must be paid (*see* UPC § 3-805).

Once the assets have been collected, the debts and taxes paid, and the time within which creditors may present claims expired, the personal representative may distribute the assets to the rightful heirs. The personal representative files periodic accounts with the court once a year (if the estate cannot be closed) and a final accounting when the estate is closed. The duties of the personal representative end when the final account is allowed by the court.

Authorized transactions of a personal representative are set forth in the following list.

Authorized Transactions of a Personal Representative
[31 AM. JUR. 2d § 379]
[UPC § 3-715]

With some exceptions, a personal representative may do the following:

1. Retain assets, including those in which the representative is personally interested or which are otherwise improper for trust investment;
2. Receive assets from fiduciaries or others;
3. Perform, compromise, or refuse to perform the decedent's contracts;
4. Satisfy written charitable pledges, even if not binding or not properly presented as claims, if in the representative's judgment the decedent would have wanted this done under the circumstances;

5. Deposit or invest liquid assets in prudent investments reasonable for trustees;
6. Acquire or dispose of assets for cash or on credit, at public or private sale; and manage, develop, improve, exchange, partition, change the character of, or abandon assets;
7. Make ordinary or extraordinary repairs or alterations in buildings and erect or demolish buildings;
8. Subdivide, develop, or dedicate land or easements to public use; vacate plats and adjust boundaries; or adjust differences in valuation on exchange or partition by giving or receiving consideration;
9. Lease (as lessor or lessee), with or without option to purchase or renew, for a term within or extending beyond administration;
10. Enter into a mineral lease or similar agreement;
11. Abandon property;
12. Vote securities in person or by proxy;
13. Pay calls, assessments, and other sums chargeable or accruing against or on account of securities, unless barred by the claims provisions;
14. Hold a security in the name of a nominee or other form without disclosing the estate's interest;
15. Insure assets against damage, loss, and liability, and himself or herself against liability to third persons;
16. Borrow money, with or without security, to be repaid from estate assets or otherwise; and advance money to protect the estate;
17. Compromise with any debtor or obligor; or extend, renew, or modify any obligation to the estate; or accept a transfer in lieu of foreclosure;
18. Pay taxes, assessments, the representative's own compensation, and other expenses;
19. Sell or exercise stock subscription or conversion rights and consent to the reorganization, consolidation, merger, dissolution, or liquidation of a business;
20. Allocate items of income or expense to income or principal, as permitted or provided by law;
21. Employ people;
22. Prosecute or defend claims or proceedings in any jurisdiction to protect the estate and himself or herself in performance of duties;
23. Sell, mortgage, or lease property or any interest in it for cash, credit, or both, with or without security;
24. Continue (with limitations) an unincorporated venture in which the decedent was engaged at death;
25. Incorporate any business or venture in which the decedent was engaged at death;
26. Provide for exoneration of the personal representative from personal liability in any contract made on behalf of the estate;
27. Satisfy and settle claims and distribute the estate.

The paralegal may be asked to assist the personal representative with the many procedures involved in settling the estate. The paralegal may compile the estate inventory; correspond with institutions (banks, insurance companies, etc.) for asset information; maintain records of creditors' claims, accumulated assets, and the like; file legal documents at the required times; draft legal documents and tax returns; and coordinate dates for filing. By providing such assistance, the paralegal insures that the complex probate process is manageable and completed correctly.

11.4 TITLES OF PERSONAL REPRESENTATIVE

Under the Uniform Probate Code, a personal representative is known simply as a "personal representative" (§ 1-201(30)). In states that have not adopted the Uniform Probate Code, personal representatives are given various titles, depending on how they are appointed and the extent of their duties. Some of the different titles are discussed here.

Executor(-trix)

A male who is nominated in a will by a testator to serve as personal representative and carry out the directions in the will is called an **executor**. A female who is nominated in a will by a testator to serve as personal representative and carry out the directions in the will is called an **executrix**. State statutes provide that the person named in a will to be the executor or executrix is entitled to be appointed to that position, provided he or she is legally competent and is generally a suitable person.

LEGAL TERMS

executor
Male nominated in the will of a decedent to carry out the terms of the will.

executrix
Female nominated in the will of a decedent to carry out the terms of the will.

IN RE ESTATE OF MILLER
568 So. 2d 487 (Fla. 1991)

FACTS: Pete Miller executed a will naming his nephew, Lloyd Smith, as personal representative of his estate. When Miller died, a relative filed a petition for appointment of a curator, alleging that Smith was improperly disposing of estate assets. [Under Florida law, a curator may be appointed to take charge of an estate before a personal representative is appointed.] Without holding a hearing to determine the validity of the relative's allegations, the trial court appointed the relative as curator rather than appointing Smith as personal representative of the estate.

LEGAL ISSUE: Unless he or she is disqualified, must the personal representative named in the will be appointed by the court?

COURT DECISION: Yes.

REASON: Although courts have a limited amount of discretion to refuse to appoint the personal representative named in the will, the general rule is that trial courts are without discretion to refuse to appoint the personal representative specified by the testator, unless the person is expressly disqualified under the statute or under the court's limited discretion. The Florida statute states that once a petition for administration is filed, "the court shall appoint the person entitled and qualified to be personal representative."

Administrator(-trix)

When someone dies intestate and leaves assets to be administered, the court must appoint a personal representative to perform that task (see figure 11-3). A male appointed to administer the estate of an intestate decedent is called an **administrator**. A female appointed to administer the estate of an intestate decedent is called an **administratrix**. State statutes set forth orders of priority for different people to be appointed administrators. The following is an example.

Administration, To Whom Granted
[Mass. Gen. Laws ch. 193, § 1]

Administration of the estate of a person deceased intestate shall be granted to one or more of the persons hereinafter mentioned and in the order named, if competent and suitable for the discharge of the trust and willing to undertake it, unless the court deems it proper to appoint some other person:

First, the widow or surviving husband of the deceased.

Second, the next of kin or their guardians or conservators as the court shall determine.

Third, if none of the above are competent or if they all renounce the administration or without sufficient cause neglect for thirty days after the death of the intestate to take administration of his estate, one or more of the principal creditors, after public notice upon the petition.

Fourth, if there is no widow, husband, or next of kin within the commonwealth, a public administrator.

Under the Uniform Probate Code, § 3-203, surviving spouses have first priority to be appointed personal representatives of intestate decedents. Other heirs of the decedent are second in line. Third in line are creditors, but only after 45 days have elapsed after the death of the decedent.

Administrator with the Will Annexed

Except in the case of an executor de son tort (discussed later), the only time that a personal representative can be called an "executor" or an

LEGAL TERMS

administrator
Male appointed to administer the estate of an intestate decedent.

administratrix
Female appointed to administer the estate of an intestate decedent.

administrator with the will annexed (also called administrator w.w.a or administrator cum testamento annexo [administrator c.t.a.])
Person appointed to administer a testate estate in which no executor is nominated or the named executor declines the nomination or is deceased or disqualified.

COMMONWEALTH OF MASSACHUSETTS
THE TRIAL COURT
THE PROBATE AND FAMILY COURT DEPARTMENT

__________ Division Docket No. __________

ADMINISTRATION - WITH - WITHOUT - SURETIES

Name of Decedent ______________________________

Domicile at Death ______________________________
(street and no.) (city or town) (county)

______________ Date of Death ______________

Name and address of Petitioner(s) ______________________________

______________________________ Status ______________

Heirs at law or next of kin of deceased:

Name Residence Relationship
(minors and incompetents must be so designated)

Petitioner(s) prays that ____h____ - or some other suitable person - ______________ ______________ of ______________ in the County of ______________ be appointed administrat______ of said estate with - without surety on______ bond and certifies under the penalties of perjury that the foregoing statements are true to the best of ______ knowledge and belief.

Dated______________ Signature(s) ______________

The undersigned hereby assent to the foregoing petition.

DECREE

All persons interested having been notified in accordance with the law or having assented and no objections being made thereto, it is decreed that ______________ ______________ of ______________ in the County of ______________ be appointed administrat______ of said estate first giving bond with______ sureties for the due performance of said trust.

Date______________ ______________
Justice of the Probate and Family Court

CJ-P1 (5/80)

FIGURE 11-3 Petition for administration (Massachusetts)

"executrix" is when that person is nominated in the will to serve in that capacity. Thus, when a testator dies and someone who is not nominated in the testator's will is appointed by the court to serve as personal representative, that person cannot be called an "executor," but is given another title. He or she is known as an **administrator with the will annexed** (also called an **administrator w.w.a.**) or an **administrator cum testamento annexo** (also called an **administrator c.t.a.**). Such a person is appointed to administer a testate estate in which no executor is nominated, or the named executor declines the nomination or dies or is

For Petitioner:	Docket No.
....	
....	________________________
Tel. No.	ADMINISTRATION
	With(out) Sureties
For Respondent:	Petition - Decree
....	Filed 198
....	Citation Issued 198
Tel. No.	Returnable 198
	Allowed 198
Publication in the	Recorded Vol. .... Page ....
....	

INSTRUCTIONS

Refer to Massachusetts General Laws Chapter 193, Section 1.

1. Assent of all persons required for filing Administrations Without Sureties.
2. Petitioner must be a party in interest or have assent of at least one interested person for filing with sureties.
3. Certified copy of appointment of a fiduciary is required if appointment is not in same Court.
4. Strike words "or some other suitable person" if this is a petition for Administration Without Sureties.

FIGURE 11-3
(Continued)

A petition such as this is used to seek appointment as administrator of an estate of someone who has died without a will. The appointment may or may not require sureties on the petitioner's bond.

disqualified before being appointed. In at least one state, as shown by the *Dismuke* case, an administrator with the will annexed may be appointed by a majority vote of the beneficiaries under the will.

DISMUKE V. DISMUKE
394 S.E.2d 371 (Ga. 1990)

FACTS: When R. T. Dismuke died, his widow, who was named executrix in the will, renounced the position and selected the decedent's son, Robert, to serve as administrator with the will annexed. A majority of the will's beneficiaries objected, proposing instead that the decedent's daughter, Diane, be appointed administratrix with the will annexed. A statute in that state (applied only to intestate cases) provided that a surviving spouse, upon declining to serve personally as administrator, is entitled to select the person to serve as replacement. A later-enacted statute provided: "in lieu of the foregoing rules, the beneficiaries under a will who are capable of expressing a choice shall be entitled to name an administrator with the will annexed."

LEGAL ISSUE: Under Georgia law, when an executrix named in a will renounces the position, is the person selected by the majority of beneficiaries, rather than the person selected by the executrix, entitled to be named administrator with the will annexed?

COURT DECISION: Yes.

REASON: Although the statute does not provide how the selection of an administrator must be made, clearly it does mandate that its language is to be applied "in lieu of" the remaining rules set forth in the statute—rules that historically have been applied solely in intestacy situations. Because the statute does not declare that *all* of the beneficiaries under the will must agree to the naming of the administrator, we hold that only a majority of the beneficiaries under the will are necessary to name an administrator with the will annexed.

Successor Personal Representative

Sometimes, when an administrator does not fully perform the task of settling an estate, a new administrator must be appointed to do so. The new person so appointed is called an **administrator of goods not administered** or an **administrator de bonis non** (also called an **administrator d.b.n.**). (See figure 11-4.)

When an executor or an administrator c.t.a. does not fully perform the task of settling an estate, the new person appointed to complete the task is called an **administrator of goods not administered with the will annexed** or an **administrator de bonis non cum testamento annexo** (also called an **administrator d.b.n.c.t.a.**).

The Uniform Probate Code eliminates these long titles and simply calls someone who takes over for another a "successor personal representative." Under UPC § 1-201(41), a **successor personal representative** is a personal representative (other than a special administrator, which will be discussed next) who is appointed to succeed a previously appointed personal representative.

LEGAL TERMS

administrator de bonis non (also called administrator d.b.n or administrator of goods not administered)
Person appointed to succeed to the office of an administrator who did not fully perform the task of settling the estate.

PETITION FOR LETTERS OF ADMINISTRATION DE BONIS NON (Illinois)

[*Heading—Caption—Docket Number*]

____________________, on oath states:

1. ____________________, whose place of residence at the time of death was [*address, city, county, state*] died ______________, 19___, at [*city, state*], leaving no will.

2. That Letters of Administration were issued by this Court to ________________, who acted as such administrator until ___________, 19___, when he ___________ without having fully administered said estate, so that it is now necessary to appoint an administrator de bonis non.

3. Petitioner asks that supervised administration of said estate be continued.

4. Approximate value of the estate in this state: [*Personal, real, annual income from real estate*].

5. The names and post office addresses of the decedent's heirs, indicating all persons entitled to nominate an administrator in preference to or equally with petitioner, are: [*Name, Relationship, Right to nominate, Preference—P, Equally—E, Minor—M, Disabled—D, Post office address (if unknown, so state)*].

6. Petitioner is a ___________ of decedent and is legally qualified to act as administrator or to nominate a resident of Illinois.

7. Petitioner asks that Letters of Administration issue to the following, qualified and willing to act: [*Name, post office address*]

[*Signature and address of Petitioner—Verification—Name, etc. of Attorney*]

FIGURE 11-4 Petition for letters of administration de bonis non (Illinois). Courtesy of *Estate Planning and Administration in Illinois* (2d ed., Lawyers Cooperative Publishing)

This petition is used in Illinois to seek appointment as administrator of a testate estate that someone else began to administrate but did not finish.

Special Administrator

Sometimes the need for someone to take immediate charge of an estate is so urgent that the somewhat slow appointment process must be bypassed. To allow for such a need, the court may at any time appoint a special administrator (*see* UPC §§ 3-614 through 3-618). A **special administrator** is appointed to handle the affairs of an estate for a limited time for a special purpose (see figure 11-5).

The chief duties of a special administrator are to collect and preserve the assets of the estate until the executor or administrator is appointed. The powers of a special administrator end when a regular executor or administrator is appointed; at that time, the special administrator must turn over the estate assets to the new appointee.

When there is a will contest (a lawsuit over the allowance or disallowance of a will), the court may appoint someone to serve as a personal representative during the suit. Such a person is called an **administrator**

LEGAL TERMS

administrator de bonis non cum testamento annexo (also called administrator d.b.n.c.t.a or administrator of goods not administered with the will annexed)
Person appointed to succeed to the office of an executor or an administrator c.t.a. who did not fully perform the task of settling the estate.

COMMONWEALTH OF MASSACHUSETTS
THE TRIAL COURT
THE PROBATE AND FAMILY COURT DEPARTMENT

______ Division Docket No. ______

SPECIAL ADMINISTRATION

Name of Decedent ______

Domicile at Death ______
(street and no.) (city or town) (county)

______ Date of Death ______

Name and address of Petitioner ______

______ Status ______

Respectfully represents that said deceased died possessed of goods and estate remaining to be administered, and that there is delay in securing the appointment of ______ of the estate of said deceased by reason of ______

Wherefore your petitioner___ pray___ that ___he ______ may be appointed special administrat______ of the estate of said deceased; and may be authorized to take charge of all the real estate of said deceased ______ and to collect rents and make necessary repairs; and may be authorized to continue the business of the deceased for the benefit of h___ estate, and certif___ under the penalties of perjury that the statements herein contained are true to the best of ___h___ knowledge and belief.

Date ______ Signature ______

The undersigned hereby assent to the foregoing petition.

DECREE

All persons interested having been notified in accordance with the law or having assented and no objections being made thereto, it is decreed that ______ of ______, in the County of ______ be appointed special administrat______ of said estate, first giving bond, with sureties for the performance of said trust.

Date ______ ______
Justice of the Probate and Family Court

CJ-P 8 (5/80)

FIGURE 11-5
Petition for special administrator (Massachusetts)

pendente lite and is a temporary administrator appointed before the adjudication of testacy or intestacy in order to preserve the assets of an estate.

Sometimes it is necessary to appoint an administrator solely for the purpose of a lawsuit other than a will contest. Such an administrator is called an **administrator ad litem**. He or she is appointed by the court to furnish a necessary party to a lawsuit in which a deceased has an interest. The *Traub* case illustrates this situation.

successor personal representative
Personal representative, other than a special administrator, who is appointed to succeed a previously appointed personal representative (UPC § 1-201(41)).

For Petitioner:	Docket No.
....	
....	______________________________
Tel No.	SPECIAL ADMINISTRATION
	Petition - Decree
For Respondent:	
....	
....	Filed 198
Tel. No.	Citation Issued 198
	Returnable 198
Publication in the	Allowed 198
....	Recorded Vol. .... Page...........

INSTRUCTIONS

Refer to Massachusetts General Laws Chapter 193, Section 10.

FIGURE 11-5
(Continued)

A special administrator may be appointed without delay when it is necessary for someone to take immediate action, such as to collect rents, make necessary repairs, or continue the operation of a business. The appointment is temporary, ending when the regular personal representative is appointed.

TRAUB V. ZLATKISS
559 So. 2d 443 (Fla. 1990)

FACTS: Not long before his death, Sheldon Traub transferred bank accounts and other property to his friend and business partner, Jerrod Zlatkiss. In his will, Traub named Zlatkiss as personal representative of his estate. Traub's estranged wife claimed that the transfers to Zlatkiss were done to deprive her of her elective share of his estate. Florida law permits only a personal representative (in this case, Zlatkiss) to bring an action to rescind (take back) a decedent's prior transfers; therefore, Mrs. Traub could not bring suit to protect her interests.

LEGAL ISSUE: May an administrator ad litem be appointed when the personal representative appears to have an interest that is adverse to the interest of the estate?

COURT DECISION: Yes.

REASON: When it is necessary that the estate of a decedent be represented in any probate proceedings and the personal representative is or may be interested adversely to the estate, the court may appoint an administrator ad litem, without bond or notice, for that particular proceeding.

Public Administrator

When an estate must be probated but no eligible person comes forward to serve as administrator, the court will appoint a public administrator to perform the task. A **public administrator** is an official appointed to administer the estate of an intestate decedent when no one appears who is entitled to act as administrator. (See figure 11-6.) State statutes provide for the appointment by the governor of a limited number of public administrators to serve in each county. The duties and obligations of public administrators are set forth in the statutes of the various states.

Voluntary Executor or Administrator

State statutes, including Uniform Probate Code § 3-1201, contain provisions for the informal administration of small estates. For an estate to qualify for informal administration, the value of the estate must not exceed an amount set by state statute; a prescribed period of time must have elapsed since the death of the decedent; and a petition for probate of the estate must not have been filed. A person who undertakes the informal administration of a small estate is referred to, in some states, as a **voluntary executor** if there is a will, and a **voluntary administrator** if there is no will. (See figure 11-7.)

Executor de Son Tort

A person who performs tasks of a personal representative and handles the property of the decedent without authority is called an **executor de son tort**. He or she acts like an executor or administrator, but without legal authority. Many states refuse to recognize such an intermeddler as an executor at all. Other states acknowledge such an individual as an executor de son tort, but only in order to sue or make him or her liable for the assets that were intermeddled. Some acts of intermeddling that have been considered sufficient to make someone an executor de son tort are: collecting money due a decedent, paying a decedent's debts, appropriating growing crops that belong to a decedent, and continuing the business of a decedent. When a lawful executor or administrator has been appointed, no executor de son tort can exist, because the assets of the estate can be reached only through the legally appointed or rightful executor or administrator.

LEGAL TERMS

special administrator(-trix)
Person appointed to handle the affairs of an estate for a limited time for a special purpose.

administrator pendente lite
Temporary administrator appointed before the adjudication of testacy or intestacy to preserve the assets of an estate.

administrator ad litem
Person appointed by a court to furnish a necessary party to a lawsuit in which a deceased has an interest.

public administrator(-trix)
Official appointed to administer the estate of an intestate decedent when no one appears who is entitled to act as administrator.

voluntary executor
Person who undertakes the informal administration of a small testate estate.

voluntary administrator
Person who undertakes the informal administration of a small intestate estate.

executor de son tort
Person who performs tasks of a personal representative and intermeddles with the property of a decedent without authority.

COMMONWEALTH OF MASSACHUSETTS
THE TRIAL COURT
THE PROBATE AND FAMILY COURT DEPARTMENT

_______Division Docket No._______

PUBLIC ADMINISTRATION WITH SURETIES

Name of Decedent _______________

Domicile at Death _______________
(street and no.) (city or town) (county)
_______________ Date of Death _______________
(county)
Name and address of Public Administrator _______________

Decedent left no known husband - widow - or heir in this Commonwealth; that said decedent left property in the County of_______________to be administered, _______________

Petitioner prays that ___he be appointed administrat___ of said estate with surety on h___ bond and certifies under the penalties of perjury that the foregoing statements are true to the best of h___ knowledge and belief.

Dated_______________ Signature _______________

DECREE

All persons interested having been notified in accordance with the law and no objections being made thereto, it is decreed that said public administrator be appointed administrator of said estate, first giving bond with sureties for the due performance of said trust.

Date _______________ _______________
Justice of the Probate and Family Court

CJ-P 9 (5/80)

FIGURE 11-6
Petition for public administration (Massachussetts)

11.5 REMOVAL OF PERSONAL REPRESENTATIVE

The death of a personal representative terminates the appointment. UPC § 3-609. The representative of the deceased personal representative must preserve the estate's assets and turn them over to the successor personal representative. (See figure 11-8.)

A personal representative cannot resign without the probate court's consent, and then only when a successor personal representative has been appointed. Under Uniform Probate Code § 3-610d, a personal representative may attempt to resign by filing a written statement to that effect

For Petitioner: ....

....

Tel No. ....

For Respondent:

....

....

Tel. No. ....

Publication in the ....

....

Docket No.

PUBLIC ADMINISTRATION

With Sureties

Petition - Decree

Filed 198

Citation Issued 198

Returnable 198

Allowed 198

Recorded Vol. .... Page..........

INSTRUCTIONS

Refer to Massachusetts General Laws Chapter 194, Section 1.

FIGURE 11-6
(Continued)

A public administrator is appointed by the court when no one appears who is entitled to act as administrator.

with the court and giving 15 days' notice to persons interested in the estate. If someone comes forward to succeed the personal representative, the resignation takes effect upon the appointment and qualification of the successor representative and delivery of assets to him or her. If no one applies to be successor representative, the attempted resignation is ineffective. The *Nelson* case addresses this distinction.

IN RE ESTATE OF NELSON
794 P.2d 677 (Mont. 1990)

FACTS: Ruth L. Nelson's will appointed Guy L. Robbins, her financial advisor, as personal representative. After Robbins submitted his final accounting to the court, one of the heirs objected to several claims against the estate made by Robbins, charged him with a number of counts of self-dealing, and petitioned for his removal. Robbins subsequently moved out of state, filed bankruptcy, and filed a letter of resignation as personal representative. The court thereafter removed Robbins for cause as personal representative.

Commonwealth of Massachusetts
The Trial Court
____________ **Division** **Probate and Family Court Department** **Docket No.** ____________

Voluntary Administration

Name of Decedent ________________________
Domicile at Death ________________________
(Street and No.) (City or Town) (County) (Zip)
Date of Death ________________________

Death Certificate shall be filed with application.

Name and address of applicant ________________________
________________________ Status of applicant ____________

Your applicant respectfully states that said estate consisting entirely of personal property the total value of which does not exceed five thousand dollars exclusive of the decedent's automobile as shown by the following schedule of all the assets of said deceased known to the applicant:

Name of Property	Estimated Value
	$
	$
	$
	$
	$
Total	$

That thirty days have expired since the date of death of said deceased and no petition for probate of will or appointment of administrat______ has been filed in said Court.

That your applicant has undertaken to act as voluntary administrator of the estate of said deceased and will administer the same according to law and apply the proceeds thereof in conformity with Section 16 of Chapter 195 of the General Laws.

That to the knowledge of the applicant the following are the names and addresses of all persons surviving who, with the deceased, were joint owners of property.

____
____
____

Date ____________ Signature(s) ____________

NOTARIZATION

____________, ss. Date ____________, 19____

Then personally appeared ________________________
to me known and made oath that the information contained in the foregoing statement is true to the best of his/her knowledge and belief.

Before me, ________________________
NOTARY PUBLIC/JUSTICE OF THE PEACE

My Commission expires ____________

CJ-P7 (8/88)

FIGURE 11-7
Petition for voluntary administration (Massachussetts)

LEGAL ISSUE: May a court remove a personal representative for cause after receiving the representative's letter of resignation?

COURT DECISION: Yes.

For Petitioner:

____

____

Docket No. ____________________

Voluntary Administration

Statement

Filed ____________________ 19____

Attested Copy Issued ______________ 19____

Recorded Vol. ________ Page ________

Instructions

Refer to Massachusetts General Laws Chapter 195, Section 16, as amended.

Death certificate must be filed with application.

Give motor vehicle identification number.

Status of applicant includes the following:

surviving spouse, child, grandchild, parent, brother, sister, niece, nephew, aunt or uncle if of full age and legal capacity and inhabitant of the Commonwealth of Massachusetts.

Notice Regarding Massachusetts Estate Taxes

You may need to file a Massachusetts Estate Tax Return and a Massachusetts Fiduciary Income Tax Return, especially if the decedent owned an interest in real estate, or if the decedent had more than $100 of income received after the date of death.

You may need to file a Massachusetts Estate Tax Return (Form M-706) in order to obtain a release of lien (Form M-792) on this real estate.

You may need to file a Massachusetts Fiduciary Income Tax Return (Form 2) to report income of more than $100 received after the date of death.

You should contact the Massachusetts Estate Tax Bureau for information and assistance regarding the estate tax law (617-727-4448) or the fiduciary income tax law (617-727-4305).

FIGURE 11-7
(Continued)

This form is used in Massachusetts to settle small estates that consist entirely of personal property. The procedure involves filing this form together with a death certificate and a filing fee.

REASON: A voluntary resignation by a personal representative is effective only upon the appointment and qualification of a successor representative and delivery of the assets to the successor. Robbins's resignation had no effect, because the court did not appoint a successor until it ordered his removal for cause.

Resignation by Administrator
[8 AM. JUR. *Legal Forms* § 104:45]

To: [Court]

County of ____________________

State of ______________________

I, of [address], City of ______________, County of ______________, State of ________________, heretofore appointed by this court on [date], as administrator of the estate of __________________, hereby resign, tendering my written resignation from office as administrator as aforesaid. I represent to this court that I stand ready to settle my accounts and deliver all of the estate which has come into my hands to the person whom this court shall appoint to receive the property.

Dated: [Signature]

FIGURE 11-8
Sample administrator's resignation

A personal representative may be removed by the court when it would be in the best interest of the estate to do so. UPC § 3-611. Grounds for removal include mismanagement of the estate, the disregarding of court orders, failure to perform required duties, breach of a fiduciary duty, and bad character. A personal representative who becomes insane, incapable of performing the required duties, or is unsuitable to perform the duties may be removed by the court. Any person with an interest in an estate may petition the court for removal of a personal representative for cause at any time. A hearing must be held to determine the cause before the personal representative can be discharged.

When a will is found after letters of administration have been granted as if there were no will, state laws generally provide that the letters of administration are revoked when the will is proved. Estate assets must be handed over to the executor or the administrator with the will annexed. Under Uniform Probate Code § 3-612, termination of a personal representative's appointment occurs only when a new person takes over; if no one does, the previously appointed personal representative may be appointed personal representative under the subsequently probated will.

THE RUBY ESTATE

One revolver
One Neiman-Marcus suit
One alligator belt
One Cavanagh hat
One ring
One watch
Two pairs of swim trunks
One shower cap
One athletic supporter

Despite the small size and meager items of this "estate," the gun alone sold for $200,000 in 1991: it is the .38 Colt Cobra revolver that Dallas strip-joint operator Jack Ruby used to kill President John F. Kennedy's accused assassin, Lee Harvey Oswald, on November 24, 1963. In November 1990, Ruby's former lawyer, Jules Mayer, was removed as executor of the estate. A six-member jury in Dallas, Texas, ruled that Mayer had grossly mismanaged the estate after Ruby's death in 1967. Mayer's removal marked the end of 23 years of legal wrangling between Mayer and the Ruby family. As the new executor, Ruby's brother was awarded possession, and promptly sold the gun. One major reason was to pay the $86,000 plus interest that Jack Ruby owed the IRS in back taxes when he died.

Dallas nightclub owner Jack Ruby was convicted of killing Lee Harvey Oswald, the accused assassin of President John F. Kennedy. Photo courtesy of AP/World Wide Photos.

SUMMARY

11.1 When someone dies, it is usually necessary for the court to appoint a fiduciary, called a personal representative, to settle the decedent's estate. In testate cases, a person nominated in the will, or some other interested person, petitions the court to have the will allowed and to be appointed as personal representative. In intestate cases, one of the heirs, next of kin, or a creditor files a petition with the court requesting the appointment.

11.2 In some states, the appointment of a personal representative is not complete until the representative has given bond. In other states, no bond is required if the will has a provision requesting that the personal representative serve without bond. Under some circumstances, a bond is not required if all heirs at law waive the filing of a bond and the will does not require one. Under the Uniform Probate Code, a bond may be required when an interested person demands that a bond be given.

11.3 The duties of a personal representative are to collect and preserve the assets of the estate, pay the debts, taxes, and expenses of administration, and distribute the remainder according to the terms of the will, or the law of intestate succession if there is no will. The paralegal may be asked to assist the personal representative with the many procedures involved in settling the estate. By providing such assistance, the paralegal helps ensure that the complex probate process is manageable and completed correctly.

Once the assets have been collected, the debts and taxes paid, and the time within which creditors may present claims expired, the personal representative may distribute the assets to the rightful heirs. The duties of the personal representative end when the final account is allowed by the court.

11.4 Under the Uniform Probate Code, a personal representative is known simply as a "personal representative." In states that have not adopted the UPC, personal representatives are given various titles, depending on how they are appointed and the extent of their duties.

A special administrator is appointed to handle the affairs of an estate for a limited time for a special purpose. The chief duties of a special administrator are to collect and preserve the assets of the estate for the executor or administrator when appointed. The powers of a special administrator end when a regular executor or administrator is appointed.

When it is necessary for an estate to be probated and no one who is eligible comes forward to serve as administrator, the court will appoint a public administrator to perform the task.

State statutes contain provisions for the informal administration of small estates. For an estate to qualify for informal administration, the value of the estate must not exceed an amount set by state statute; a prescribed period of time must have elapsed since the death of the decedent; and a petition for probate of the estate must not have been filed. A person who undertakes the informal administration of a small estate is referred to, in some states, as a voluntary executor if there is a will, and a voluntary administrator if there is no will.

A person who intrudes into the office of personal representative and intermeddles with the property of the decedent without authority is called an executor de son tort.

11.5 The death of a personal representative terminates the appointment. A personal representative cannot resign without the probate court's consent, and then only when a successor personal representative is appointed. A personal representative may be removed by the court when it would be in the best interest of the estate to do so. Grounds for removal include mismanagement of the estate, the disregarding of court orders, and failure to perform required duties.

QUESTIONS FOR REVIEW

1. Why is a personal representative known as a fiduciary?
2. Describe generally the procedure that occurs when a petition for appointment of personal representative is filed with the court.
3. What is the difference between letters testamentary and letters of administration?
4. Why must a personal representative give a bond under the laws of some states?
5. In general, what are the duties of a personal representative?
6. (a) When may a personal representative distribute assets to the rightful heirs? (b) When do the duties of a personal representative end?
7. When is a personal representative known as:
   a. An executrix?
   b. An administrator?
   c. An administrator with the will annexed?
   d. An administratrix de bonis non?
   e. An administrator de bonis non cum testamento annexo?
8. What are the chief duties of a special administrator and when do his or her powers end?
9. (a) What is the difference between an administrator pendente lite and an administrator ad litem? (b) Who is an executor de son tort?
10. (a) When may a personal representative resign? (b) When may he or she be removed?

CASES TO DISCUSS

1. The probate court admitted the will of Thomas R. McElhenney to probate and issued letters testamentary to Jeff E. Geeslin. Geeslin failed from the outset to assess the income of the estate and its taxes and other obligations, causing the estate to incur interest and penalties of over $150,000. Among other things, Geeslin failed to set aside funds when he became aware that there would be an additional estate-tax liability; he commingled estate funds with the decedent's pension funds; and he failed to make a timely request for an extension of time to pay the federal estate tax. Can Geeslin be removed by the court from his position as executor? Why or why not? *Geeslin v. McElhenney*, 788 S.W.2d 683 (Tex. 1990).

2. Although William Bearden's will named his wife, Katherine, as executrix, the court appointed someone else as a special administrator when he died, because Katherine was suffering the effects of alcoholism. Later, finding her to be competent, the court appointed Katherine as executrix. Bearden's children of a former marriage appealed the appointment, quoting the state statute: "No person is competent to serve as executor who at the time the will is admitted to probate is adjudged by the court incompetent to execute the duties of the trust by reason of drunkenness." Should Katherine be appointed executrix? Why or why not? *Matter of Estate of Bearden,* 800 P.2d 1086 (Okla. 1990).

SHARPENING YOUR PROFESSIONAL SKILLS

1. Refer to the law office scenario at the beginning of this chapter.
   a. Determine the title that would be given to the successor personal representative under the law of your state.
   b. Obtain the form used in your state and draft a petition for appointment of the successor personal representative.
2. In your state, what is the title given to the personal representative appointed by the court:
   a. When an executrix named in the will predeceases the testator?
   b. When an administrator dies before completing his duties?
   c. When an executrix dies before completing her duties?
3. Draft a $500,000 surety bond for an executor, using the form commonly used in your state.
4. Look up your state statute dealing with the powers of executors and administrators.
   a. Give the statutory reference where it is found.
   b. Determine whether a personal representative can continue running a decedent's business when that power is not provided for in a will.
5. Look up your state statute on special administrators.
   a. Give the statutory reference where it is found.
   b. Outline the administrators' duties and powers.

ituaries

Predich, 45; executive vice

ALLEY—James P. Predich, 45,
Avenue, died Thursday in
pital of coronary disease.

lude Mr. Predich's wife, Anna
wo sons, Gerald and Peter; and
ghters, Grace, Tanya, and Ellen,
s Valley. Also surviving are his
da Predich, of Enterston; two
Predich of Helteren and Kenneth
New York City; and a sister,
ington of Burnsville.

l be held at 11 a.m. Monday in
tar Funeral Home, 567 Newton
ders Valley, with burial in the
metery, Richmond.

quests that contributions be made
an Heart Association or the choir
enders Valley Alliance Church.

W. Brookes, 39, graphic

—Danny W. Brookes, 39, died
head injuries sustained in a
ccident late Thursday night.

graduated Magna Cum Laude
Francisco School of Graphic Arts
g two consecutive tours as a
lot in the Vietnam War. He opened
gn studio soon after returning to

is survived by his wife, Wendy
s) Brookes, and four daughters,
lene, Mariah and Melody, and
William and Helen Brookes, and
iam Brookes, Jr., of Chicago.

candlelight service will be held at
day in the chapel of the Whitfield
me, 368 Auburn Lane. Services
ld at 10 a.m. Tuesday at the
uneral Home, with burial in the
emetery, Richmond.

was a veteran of the Vietnam War
ily requests donations be sent to
an M.I.A./P.O.W. Agency, 9612
ulevard, Washington, D.C., in lieu

n announcement in the Obituary

9934 Oak Park Street, with burial in Lawnhome Cemetery immediately thereafter.

Consuela T. Martinez, 79; retired physician

MOUNTVIEW—Dr. Consuela "Connie" T. Martinez, age 79, died Monday of injuries sustained in an automobile accident. She retired from private practice only four years ago, and was a frequent volunteer at the Mountview Children's Shelter.

Dr. Martinez is survived by her daughter, Teresa Shillibaugh of Albany, and six grandchildren.

In addition to her service with the Children's Shelter, Dr. Martinez was active in Our Lady of Sorrows Church
Symphony Associatio
made to any of those o

Robert Thomas
assistant manager, Rob

MOUNTVIEW—Mr.
of the University of So

Survivors include hi
Barbara Joan (Beck
brothers, Andrew and

Visitation will be from 10 a.m. to noon Tuesday at Swan Lake Funeral Home, 1841 West Grace Street. Private family interment is planned.

Memorial contributions may be made to the M.A.D.D. (Mothers Against Drunk Drivers) organization in lieu of flowers.

Arlene Meghan Fullerton, 50, registered nurse

GEORGETOWN—Arlene Meghan (Gibson) Fullerton, 50, of Iroquois Avenue, died Sunday after a short illness. Mrs. Fullerton worked at General Hospital for 26 years and volunteered at the women's shelter.

Mrs. Fullerton is survived by her husband of 27 years, James Douglas, daughter Katherine Elizabeth Ryan, two sons, Alexander James and Michael Thomas, two sisters, Meghan Colleen Amble and Sarah Janette Hamilton, and a brother, Brian Michael Gibson.

No services are scheduled. The family requests that contributions be made to the American Lung Association or the American Cancer

Dinah Z. Norton, 67; Allied Gl
retiree

GREATER HILLTOWN—Dinah "Dinnie"
Norton, a resident of the Bellemar Apartme
died Friday in St. Mary's Hospital, Richmo
after a brief illness.

She was born in New York City and move
Hilltown as a teenager. She was graduate
Jefferson High School. She retired two y
ago from Allied Global, after 23 years
service.

She lived in Greater Hilltown for all of
working life, and was a resident of
Bellemar Apartments at the time of her de
She was active in the Bellemar Apartm
Tenants' Association and the First Un

Calling hours will be 3-5 and 7-9 p.m. Mo
in the Smith Funeral Home. Contributions
be made to the American Heart Associati
the Bellemar Tenants' Association.

Hallibert M. Nowell, 68; former
employee

TENSGROVE—Hallibert (Bert) M. Now
retired railroad worker, died Monday at th
of 68, after a long illness.

Mr. Nowell is survived by his wife
Roseanne (Marshall) Nowell, his two
John (Jack) Patrick and Kevin Norris
daughter, Rose Marie Patterson, and
grandchildren.

Mr. Nowell, who spent most of his wo
career in the Tensgrove Switching Station
a member of the Tensgrove United Churc
was certified as a master gardener.

A memorial service will be held at
Tensgrove United Church on Wednesd
11:00 a.m. Private inurnment will be a
Jackson Memorial Shrine.

Contributions may be made to the Tens

SECTION FOUR

Estate Administration

CHAPTER 12
Probating a Will and Administering an Estate

"The law's made to take care o' raskills."

George Eliot

OUTLINE

LAW OFFICE SCENARIO

Attorney Knutson asked her legal assistant, Lorna Garcia, to come into her office where she was meeting with a client.

"Mr. Notmeyer, this is my assistant, Lorna Garcia," Attorney Knutson said. "She'll be helping me with your father's estate."

"I'm pleased to meet you," Lorna said to Mr. Notmeyer with a smile.

"Mr. Notmeyer's father passed away about two years ago," Attorney Knutson explained, "and he's been handling the estate himself, until now."

"Yes, my brother, Oscar, is threatening to sue me, so I think I need some advice," Mr. Notmeyer volunteered. "I thought I did everything that I was supposed to do. I gave everything to my brothers and sisters equally just like my father wanted—except for my brother, Oscar. My father didn't like him, you know."

"Did your father leave a will?" Lorna asked.

"Yes, but my brother, Oscar, got hold of it first and won't let anyone see it. We think Oscar was left out of the will."

"Did you file any papers with the probate court?" Attorney Knutson asked.

"Oh, no!" Mr. Notmeyer responded. "I just divided by five and gave everyone their share. There are five of us, you know, not counting Oscar."

"Do you know the approximate value of the estate?" Attorney Knutson asked.

"Well, not exactly," Mr. Notmeyer replied. "There were five stock certificates, each worth about $100,000, so I gave each person, except Oscar, one of those. Then I divided the antique furniture five ways."

"Did you have it appraised?" Lorna inquired.

"No. I just gave everyone what they wanted—except for Oscar, of course. I didn't give him anything."

"Did your father own any real estate?" Attorney Knutson asked.

"Yes. He owned some vacant land on the ocean, somewhere out of state. It's supposed to be quite valuable—worth several hundred thousand dollars."

"What about debts?" queried Attorney Knutson. "Did your father owe any money to anyone before he died?"

"Well, yes," Mr. Notmeyer answered. "He had quite a few outstanding bills because all his money was tied up in stocks, antiques, and that out-of-state property. I figured that if I didn't let his creditors know he died, by the time they found out, it would be too late for them to collect."

"Mr. Notmeyer, I'm going to leave you with Lorna for a while. She will take down some basic information that we need. Then I'll talk to you about some of the things we'll do to settle your father's estate."

12.1 THE NEED FOR PROBATE

Paralegals may be asked to assist clients, such as Mr. Notmeyer, who have attempted unsuccessfully to undertake the details of settling an estate on their own, without legal assistance. More commonly, however, paralegals work with attorneys and clients from the very beginning, helping to perform the multitude of tasks that are involved when an estate is being settled. The average person lacks the legal knowledge necessary to correctly complete the steps required in settling an estate.

When someone dies owning property, the property must be protected; the decedent's debts must be paid; those individuals who should own the remainder of the property after the debts are paid must be identified; and the remainder must be distributed accordingly. The term **probate** (to test and to prove) is often used to describe this procedure. **Probating a will** is the process of proving or establishing before the probate court that the document being offered for official recognition as the will of the decedent is in fact genuine. **Administering an estate** means to settle and distribute the estate of a deceased person.

The probate process includes the appointment of a personal representative (described in chapter 11). This appointment gives him or her the legal authority to: (1) collect and preserve the assets owned by the decedent; (2) pay the decedent's debts and taxes; and (3) distribute the remainder of the assets according to the terms of the will or the law of intestate succession.

The probate process protects the decedent by seeing that his or her wishes are carried out. It protects the heirs by assuring that all of the decedent's property is collected and accounted for and by determining the lawful heirs. It also establishes title to property that has been inherited.

Protection of Decedent

When someone dies, it must first be determined whether there is a will. If a will is found, it must be turned over to the probate court in the county in which the decedent was domiciled, within a time period after death (often 30 days) that is set by state statute. Failure to give the will to the probate court may be a criminal offense. The following is an example of a state statute that allows anyone with an interest in an estate to file a complaint against another suspected of retaining or concealing a deceased person's will.

> A person having custody of a will, other than a register of probate, shall, within thirty days after notice of the death of the testator, deliver such will into the probate court having jurisdiction of the probate thereof, or to the executors named in the will, who shall themselves deliver it into such court within said time; and if a person neglects without reasonable cause so to deliver a will, after being duly cited for that purpose by such court, he may

> be committed to jail by warrant of the court until he delivers it as above provided, and shall be liable to a person who is aggrieved for the damage sustained by him by reason of such neglect.

Mass. Gen. Laws ch. 191, § 13.

Presentation of a will to the court, even if the person in possession of the will considers it to be invalid, is required by law. Normal probate procedure allows a will that is offered for probate to be challenged by evidence that it is not the last will of the decedent or that it was improperly executed, or defective in some way (see figure 12-1).

Protection of Heirs

Another important function of the probate procedure is the protection of heirs and next of kin. **Heirs**, in the term's broadest sense, are all person's who inherit property from a decedent's estate. In contrast, **next of kin** are those most nearly related by blood to the decedent. Heirs and next of kin are protected by the probate procedure in that their names must be listed on the petition for probate. They are notified of the probate proceeding and thereby allowed to present objections if the objections are legally sound.

The probate procedure also protects the decedent's property. As discussed later, one of the important duties of the personal representative after being appointed is to file an inventory of the estate with the probate court. The inventory lists all property owned by the decedent and is available for anyone to peruse in order to verify or challenge its contents. This requirement provides some assurance that all of the decedent's property will be listed. In addition, third parties such as banks will release funds from a decedent's bank account only to the personal representative, and then only upon receiving a certified copy of the representative's appointment. The same is true with stock certificates and bonds registered in the decedent's name. The personal representative is the only person who can legally enforce payment to the decedent's estate of money owed by others. Similarly, the personal representative of an estate is the only person who can be sued to collect money owed by the decedent's estate to others.

Establishing Title

The probate process also protects heirs by providing a system for establishing title to inherited property; this assures heirs, legatees, devisees, and future buyers that title is good. If the decedent left a will, legatees and devisees cannot prove their title to the property unless the will is probated. Similarly, in intestate estates, heirs must have the authority of the probate court to establish their title to property they inherit.

LEGAL TERMS

probate
To prove and allow by the court.

probating a will
Process of proving or establishing before the probate court that the document being offered for official recognition as the will of the decedent is in fact genuine.

administering an estate
Settling and distributing the estate of a deceased person.

heirs
Those persons, including the surviving spouse, who are entitled under the statutes of intestate succession to the property of a decedent. In its broadest sense, persons who inherit property from a decedent's estate.

next of kin
Those persons who are nearest of kindred to the decedent; that is, those who are most nearly related by blood.

State of New York—County of Albany

Surrogate's Court

Present: HON. RAYMOND E. MARINELLI, Surrogate

In the Matter of Proving the Last Will and Testament of

....

DECEASED

STATE OF NEW YORK }
COUNTY OF ALBANY } ss.:

....of the.................

of ....being duly sworn as a witness, doth depose and say that he was well acquainted with...

late of the..............................of..............................and with his manner and style of handwriting, having often seen him write, and that he verily believes that the signature "..."

purporting to be his, subscribed as a witness to the instrument in writing now produced and shown to this deponent, purporting to be the **Last Will and Testament** of .... deceased,

bearing date the..................day of..............................A. D., 19 , is the proper signature and handwriting of said...

And this deponent further says, that the said...

....

....

....

....

Subscribed and sworn, this.................. }
day of..............................19 , before me } ....

....

Surrogate.
Chief Clerk of the Surrogate's Court.
Notary Public

FIGURE 12-1
Deposition as to handwriting (New York)

This affidavit is used in New York to establish proof of a testator's handwriting.

12.2 FORMAL PROBATE PROCEEDINGS

Formal probate proceedings are followed when someone dies owning assets above a specific value set by state statute or when it is appropriate to have the court supervise all aspects of the estate's settlement. The Uniform Probate Code (UPC) defines **formal proceedings** as those conducted before a judge with notice to interested persons. UPC § 1-201(15). In some states, formal probate proceedings are known as **probate in solemn form.**

LEGAL TERMS

formal proceedings
Proceedings conducted before a judge with notice to interested persons (UPC § 1-201(15)).

Formal probate proceedings involve the following steps:

1. A petition is filed with the court
2. Notice is given to interested parties
3. In a testate estate, the will is proved
4. A bond is given by the personal representative, unless waived
5. Letters are issued by the court
6. An inventory is filed
7. Notice or a time period is given to creditors to make claims
8. Debts, taxes, and expenses of administration are paid
9. Distribution is made to the beneficiaries
10. An account is filed with the court

Under the UPC, formal probate proceedings can be either supervised or unsupervised. **Supervised administration** is a process whereby an estate is settled under the continued surveillance of the court from beginning to end. **Unsupervised administration** begins formally but becomes less supervised by the court once the personal representative is appointed.

Petition for Probate or Administration

In testate cases, probate proceedings begin when the executor named in the will files a **petition for probate** with the probate court (see figure 12-2). This is a formal, written application asking the court to prove and allow the will and to appoint the petitioner, who is nominated in the will, as executor(-trix). If someone other than the person nominated as personal representative in the will is the petitioner seeking the appointment, a different form, called a **petition for administration with the will annexed,** must be filed with the court. Each state has its own forms for these purposes, and the forms can be obtained from the particular court involved. In states that follow the Uniform Probate Code, the same form is used for both of these mentioned situations. A box on the form is checked to indicate the petitioner's status. (See figure 12-3.)

In intestate cases, probate proceedings begin when someone files a form called a **petition for administration** with the probate court. This is a written application by one or more heirs, next of kin, or creditors asking the court to appoint the petitioner or someone else as administrator(-trix) of the estate. Once again, states that follow the Uniform Probate Code, as well as some other states, use the same form for both testate and intestate estates. (See figure 12-4.)

Forms for petitions for probate and administration typically provide spaces to write: (1) the name of the decedent, (2) the decedent's domicile, (3) the date of death, (4) the name and address of the petitioner, (5) the names of the decedent's **heirs at law** (those people who would have inherited had the decedent died intestate) and (6) the petitioner's preference to serve with or without bond or, in some states, without giving a surety on the bond.

probate in solemn form
Formal probate proceedings.

supervised administration
Process in which an estate is settled under the continuing surveillance of the court from beginning to end.

unsupervised administration
Method of administering an estate, under the Uniform Probate Code, without court action unless it is requested by an interested person.

petition for probate
Formal, written application asking the court to prove and allow the will and to appoint the petitioner, who is nominated in the will, as executor(-trix) thereof.

petition for administration with the will annexed
Written application by someone other than the person nominated as personal representative in a will, asking the court to prove and allow the will and to appoint the petitioner as administrator(-trix).

petition for administration
Written application by one or more heirs, next of kin, or creditors asking the court to appoint the petitioner as administrator(-trix) of the estate.

heirs at law
Those people who would have inherited had the decedent died intestate.

Georgia Probate Court
Standard Form

PETITION TO PROBATE WILL IN SOLEMN FORM

GEORGIA, ______________ COUNTY

To the Honorable Judge of the Probate Court:

The petition of ______________________________,
whose mailing address is ______________________________,
respectfully shows to the Court:

1.

On______________, 19_____, ______________________________
First Middle Last
whose place of domicile was ______________________________
Street City County State
and whose legal residence was ______________________________
Street City County State
departed this life owning property in Georgia.

2.

While alive, decedent duly made and published a Last Will and Testament dated______________, which is herewith offered for probate in Solemn Form. Your petitioner is named as the Executor.

3.

Listed below are all of the deceased's heirs at law, with the age, address and relationship to deceased set opposite the name of each:

NAME	AGE	ADDRESS	RELATIONSHIP

Court Identification No.______

Effective 7/86 -1-

FIGURE 12-2
Petition to probate will in solemn form (Georgia)

Notice to Interested Parties

Upon receiving the will and the petition for probate or the petition for administration, the court issues an order, sometimes called a **citation** (see figure 12-5), requiring the petitioner to notify all heirs at law, devisees, and legatees, either by personal service, newspaper advertising, or both, that the petition has been filed. Personal service may be made either by delivering a copy in hand personally, or, with the consent of the court, by mail. In some states, the citation is prepared by the court; in others, it is prepared by the

4.

Additional Data: Where full particulars are lacking, state here the reasons for any such omission. Also, state here all pertinent facts which may govern the method of giving notice to any party and which may determine whether or not a guardian ad litem should be appointed for any party. If any heirs listed above are cousins, grandchildren, nephews or nieces of the deceased, please indicate the deceased ancestor through whom they are related to the deceased. If any executor nominated in the will has an equal or higher priority to the propounder, but will not qualify, indicate the name and reasons.

5.

To the knowledge of the petitioner, no other proceedings with respect to this estate are pending, or have been completed, in any other probate court in this state.

WHEREFORE, petitioner(s) pray(s) leave to prove said Will in solemn form, that due and legal notice be given as the law requires, that said Will be admitted to record on proper proof, that Letters Testamentary issue, and that this Court order such other relief as may be proper under the circumstances.

________________________	________________________
Signature of Attorney (or petitioner if pro se)	Signature of Attorney (or petitioner if pro se)
Address:	Address:
Telephone Number:	Telephone Number:

GEORGIA, ____________________ COUNTY

Personally appeared before me the undersigned petitioner(s) who on oath state(s) that the facts set forth in the foregoing application are true.

________________________	________________________
Petitioner	Petitioner
Residence Address:	Residence Address:
Telephone Number:	Telephone Number:

Sworn to and subscribed before me, this________day of____________________, 19______.

____
Clerk of Probate Court or Notary Public

-2-

FIGURE 12-2
(Continued)

law office and submitted to the court for issuance. Also in some states, the citation itself contains the notice that must be given to all interested parties. In other states, a separate form, called a Notice of Probate, is sent to interested parties. (See figure 12-6.)

Proof of Will

The procedure for proving a will varies from state to state. Even within a state, several different methods may be used. One method is to

LEGAL TERMS

citation
Written order of the court commanding the petitioner to appear on a day named and do something mentioned therein.

ORDER FOR CITATION

PROBATE COURT OF____________________COUNTY

The foregoing petition to probate Will in solemn form having been filed, and it appearing that:
(Initial any and all of the following which apply:)

_____Citation must issue and be served personally, together with a copy of the petition and this order, at least ten days before ____________________on the following heirs at law who reside in Georgia and have not acknowledged service:

_____Citation must issue, be published once a week for four weeks in the newspaper in which sheriff's advertisements are published in this county, before____________________, and be served by mailing copies of the first insertion of such published citation within three days after such first publication to the following heirs at law who reside out of Georgia and have not acknowledged service:____________________

_____Citation must issue and be published once a week for four weeks in the newspaper in which sheriff's advertisements are published in this county, before____________________, in order to serve by publication the following heirs at law whose addresses are unknown: ____________________

ORDERED that Citation be issued and served as indicated above.

____________________ DATE

____________________ JUDGE OF THE PROBATE COURT

-3-

FIGURE 12-2
(Continued)

have one or more of the attesting witnesses testify before the judge or the clerk of court as to how the will was executed and the testator's competence. A second method is to have one or more of the attesting witnesses sign a written affidavit before the register of probate stating facts about the execution of the will (figure 12-7). When witnesses have died or cannot be found, their handwriting may have to be proved. A third method is to obtain written approval of the surviving spouse and the heirs at law. If all interested parties agree to the allowance of a will, neither testimony of witnesses nor affidavits are necessary.

LEGAL TERMS

appearance
Formal, written entry submitting a person to the court's jurisdiction.

CITATION

PROBATE COURT OF____________________COUNTY

Re: PETITION OF____________________________________TO PROBATE IN SOLEMN FORM THE WILL OF ____________________, DECEASED, UPON WHICH AN ORDER FOR PERSONAL SERVICE AND/OR FOR PUBLICATION WAS GRANTED BY THIS COURT ON____________________, 19____.

TO: ____

____

and all and singular the heirs at law of said decedent, and to whom it may concern:

This is to notify you to appear before this Court on____________________, 19____, at____ ____.M., to show cause, if any there be, why said Will should not be probated in Solemn Form. You do not need to appear unless you wish to be heard concerning this matter. All objections to the petition must be in writing, setting forth the grounds of any such objections, and must be filed at or before the time stated in the citation.

(Strike the following paragraph if no heir is required to be personally served:)

This is further to notify ____________________________________

____,

who are required to be served personally, that you have until the later of (a) the time stated in the preceding paragraph or (b) 10 days after the date you are personally served, to respond to said petition in the manner indicated above.

WITNESS, the Hon.____________________, Judge

(SEAL) By:____________________
CLERK, PROBATE COURT OF____________________COUNTY

CERTIFICATE OF MAILING OF CITATION

This is to certify that I have this date forwarded by regular mail, in a stamped, addressed envelope supplied by the petitioner(s), a copy of the above Citation as it appeared in the newspaper, to each of the following heirs at law who reside out of state:

____

____

____

____

____________________ ____________________
DATE CLERK, PROBATE COURT

-4-

FIGURE 12-2
(Continued)

Under the laws of many states, a will containing a self-proof clause (see § 5.5) may be admitted to probate without the testimony or affidavits of witnesses.

The procedure for contesting a will varies from state to state. In some states, the contesting party files with the court an **appearance** (a formal written entry submitting that person to the court's jurisdiction). Following the appearance, the contesting party must file an affidavit of objection to the petition for probate, stating specific facts and grounds upon which the objection is based. In other states, a contesting party files a **caveat**, which is

caveat
Formal notice or warning to the court to prevent the proving of a will or the grant of administration of an estate.

RETURN OF SHERIFF

GEORGIA, ____________________ COUNTY

I have this day served ____

____

personally with a copy of the within and foregoing Petition, Order for Citation and Citation.

______________________ DATE

______________________ DEPUTY SHERIFF, ______________________ COUNTY, GEORGIA

APPOINTMENT OF GUARDIAN AD LITEM

PROBATE COURT OF ____________________ COUNTY

It appearing that the within named (minor____) (incompetent____), to wit:

____

____

ha____ been personally served with a copy of this proceeding, and that a guardian ad litem should be appointed for ______________________.

IT IS ORDERED that ____ be, and is hereby, appointed guardian ad litem to represent ____________ herein, and that said guardian ad litem be duly served with notice of this proceeding and appointment, and that following acceptance of the same, said guardian ad litem make answer hereto.

______________________ DATE

______________________ JUDGE OF THE PROBATE COURT

ANSWER OF GUARDIAN AD LITEM

I hereby accept the foregoing appointment, acknowledge service and notice of the proceedings as provided by law, and for answer say:

______________________ DATE

______________________ GUARDIAN AD LITEM

______________________ ADDRESS TELEPHONE

-5-

FIGURE 12-2
(Continued)

a formal notice or warning to the court to prevent the proving of the will or the granting of administration (see figure 12-8).

The grounds for contesting a will are:

1. The will was not properly executed.
2. The testator was not of sound mind at the time of the execution of the will.

ACKNOWLEDGMENT OF SERVICE
AND ASSENT TO PROBATE INSTANTER

GEORGIA, ______________ COUNTY

IN RE: PETITION OF ______________ TO PROBATE
THE WILL OF ______________, DECEASED,
IN SOLEMN FORM

We, the undersigned, being over 18 years of age, laboring under no legal disability and being heirs at law of the above-named deceased, hereby acknowledge service of the petition to probate said will in solemn form and notice, waive copies of same, waive issuance of citation and all further service and notice, and hereby assent to the probate of said will in solemn form without further delay.

ATTESTATION(S)	SIGNATURE(S) OF HEIRS
Sworn to and subscribed before me this ____ day of ______________, 19____. ______________ NOTARY/CLERK OF PROBATE COURT	______________
Sworn to and subscribed before me this ____ day of ______________, 19____. ______________ NOTARY/CLERK OF PROBATE COURT	______________
Sworn to and subscribed before me this ____ day of ______________, 19____. ______________ NOTARY/CLERK OF PROBATE COURT	______________
Sworn to and subscribed before me this ____ day of ______________, 19____. ______________ NOTARY/CLERK OF PROBATE COURT	______________
Sworn to and subscribed before me this ____ day of ______________, 19____. ______________ NOTARY/CLERK OF PROBATE COURT	______________
Sworn to and subscribed before me this ____ day of ______________, 19____. ______________ NOTARY/CLERK OF PROBATE COURT	______________
Sworn to and subscribed before me this ____ day of ______________, 19____. ______________ NOTARY/CLERK OF PROBATE COURT	______________

-6-

FIGURE 12-2
(Continued)

3. The execution of the will was obtained through fraud or undue influence.

The proponent of the will must show that the document was properly executed by the testator with knowledge of its contents, and that the testator was of sound mind. If undue influence or fraud is alleged, the burden of proof is on the person who claims that fraud or undue influence exists. Only those with an interest in opposing the will, such as a spouse or one of the heirs at law, or a legatee in an earlier-made will, can contest a will.

ORDER

PROBATE COURT OF______________________COUNTY

RE: ESTATE OF

____

DECEASED

PETITION FOR PROBATE IN SOLEMN FORM

It being shown to the Court in the matter of the alleged Last Will and Testament of the above-named deceased person, propounded by ____

____,

named as Executor(s), that the said deceased died a resident of said County; and that due notice of the intention of said propounder(s) to proceed with the proof in solemn form at this term of court has been served on all of the heirs at law of said deceased, all in accordance with the laws of this State, and all other requirements of law having been fulfilled, and the said Will having been proven by (one of) the witnesses thereto to be the Last Will and Testament of said deceased as alleged by the propounder(s);

IT IS ORDERED by this Court that said Will be established as the Last Will and Testament of said deceased; that the same be admitted to record, as proven in solemn form; and that said Executor(s) have leave to qualify as such, and upon so doing, that Letters Testamentary issue to said Executor(s).

(Initial and complete the following if applicable:)

______FURTHER ORDERED, that said Executor, being a non-resident of the State of Georgia, be relieved from posting bond, as provided in Item______of the Will and as provided by law.

________________________ DATE

________________________ JUDGE OF THE PROBATE COURT

OATH

I do solemnly swear (or affirm) that this writing contains the true last will of the within named____, deceased, so far as I know or believe, and that I will well and truly execute the same in accordance with the laws of the State. So help me God.

Sworn to and subscribed before me,
this______day of____________________19______.

________________________ Executor

________________________ Judge/Clerk of the Probate Court

________________________ Executor

-7-

FIGURE 12-2
(Continued)

This seven-page form is used in Georgia to begin the formal probate of a will.

Allowance of Bond and Issuance of Letters

Some states require all personal representatives to have a bond (see figure 12-9). In addition, they require a surety on the bond unless the will provides otherwise or unless all heirs agree to the appointment without sureties. In other states, a bond is not required when the will contains a clause to that effect. In those states, unless the will indicates that a bond is required, the bond can be waived if all beneficiaries named in the will assent

Approved, SCAO | JDC CODE: COP

STATE OF MICHIGAN PROBATE COURT COUNTY OF	PETITION FOR COMMENCEMENT OF PROCEEDINGS ☐ Supervised ☐ Independent ☐ Small estate	FILE NO.

Estate of ______________________________

1. I, ______________________________, am interested in the estate and make this petition as
Name
______________________________ of the deceased.
Relationship

2. Decedent information: __________ __________m. ______ ______________
Date of death | Time (if known) | Age | Social Security Number

3. Decedent ☐ did ☐ did not leave a will, dated __________. Subscribing witnesses are: __________
____

4. At date of death, decedent was an inhabitant and resident of ______________________________, in this County
City/Township/Village
and/or left an estate to be administered in this County with the estimated value: Real estate $ __________
Personal estate $ __________

5. The names, ages relationships and residences of the heirs-at-law, devisees and other interested persons are:
(Identify children of the deceased who are not issue of the surviving spouse)

NAME	AGE	RELATIONSHIP Also indicate if devisee	RESIDENCE

PLEASE SEE OTHER SIDE

Do not write below this line - For court use only

PC 04 (8/87) PETITION FOR COMMENCEMENT OF PROCEEDINGS

MCR 5.113, MCR 5.702
MCL 700.115-.145; MSA 27.5115-.5145

FIGURE 12-3
UPC petition to probate (Michigan)

to the waiver in writing. Before the probate petition is completed, the will must be reviewed to determine whether the personal representative is allowed to serve without a bond or without giving a surety on the bond.

The amount of the bond varies from state to state. In some states, it must equal the value of the personal property; in other states, it must equal twice the value of the personal property. Real property is not counted in determining the value of the bond unless the property is to be sold by the personal representative and the proceeds from the sale are to become assets of the estate.

5. (continued)

NAME	AGE	RELATIONSHIP Also indicate if devisee	RESIDENCE

6. Of the above interested persons, the following are under legal disability or otherwise represented and presently have or will require representations as follows:

NAME	LEGAL DISABILITY	REPRESENTED BY Name, address, and capacity

7. I further represent:

8. I request:
☐ the will be admitted to probate and administration be granted to ______________________ ,
Name
personal representative named in the will, who resides at ______________________
Complete address
☐ administration of the estate be granted to ______________________ ,
Name
who resides at ______________________
Complete address
or to some other suitable person.

9. I further request that this be a ☐ supervised ☐ independent ☐ small estate (MCL 700.101) administration.

10. I further request:

I declare that this petition has been examined by me and that its contents are true to the best of my information, knowledge, and belief.

Date

Attorney signature — Petitioner signature

Attorney name (type or print) — Bar no. — Petitioner name (type or print)

Attorney address — Petitioner address

City, state, zip — Telephone no. — City, state, zip — Telephone no.

FIGURE 12-3
(Continued)

This form is used in Michigan to begin the probate process.

Once the personal representative's bond is allowed, the court issues a certificate of appointment known as **letters testamentary**, for a testate estate, or **letters of administration**, for an intestate estate (see figure 12-10). This certificate is called *letters of authority* in Michigan (see figure 12-11). The letters serve as evidence of the right of the fiduciary to take possession of the property in the estate. In some states, the letters remain in full force and effect until completion of the estate or until resignation or

LEGAL TERMS

letters testamentary
Certificate of appointment of a personal representative in a testate estate.

ATTORNEY OR PARTY WITHOUT ATTORNEY *(Name and Address)*: TELEPHONE NO.: FOR COURT USE ONLY

ATTORNEY FOR *(Name)*:

SUPERIOR COURT OF CALIFORNIA, COUNTY OF

STREET ADDRESS:

MAILING ADDRESS:

CITY AND ZIP CODE:

BRANCH NAME:

ESTATE OF (NAME):

DECEDENT

CASE NUMBER:

HEARING DATE:

DEPT.: TIME:

PETITION FOR

(For deaths after December 31, 1984)

☐ Probate of Will and for Letters Testamentary
☐ Probate of Will and for Letters of Administration with Will Annexed
☐ Letters of Administration
☐ Letters of Special Administration
☐ Authorization to Administer Under the Independent Administration of Estates Act ☐ with limited authority

1. Publication will be in *(specify name of newspaper)*:
   a. ☐ Publication requested.
   b. ☐ Publication to be arranged.

(Signature of attorney or party without attorney)

2. **Petitioner** *(name of each)*:
   requests
   a. ☐ decedent's will and codicils, if any, be admitted to probate.
   b. ☐ *(name)*:
   be appointed (1) ☐ executor (2) ☐ administrator with will annexed (3) ☐ administrator (4) ☐ special administrator
   and Letters issue upon qualification.
   c. ☐ that ☐ full ☐ limited authority be granted to administer under the Independent Administration of Estates Act.
   d. ☐ bond not be required for the reasons stated in item 3d.
   ☐ $ bond be fixed. It will be furnished by an admitted surety insurer or as otherwise provided by law. *(Specify reasons in Attachment 2d if the amount is different from the maximum required by Probate Code, § 8482.)*
   ☐ $ in deposits in a blocked account be allowed. Receipts will be filed. *(Specify institution and location)*:

3. a. Decedent died on *(date)*: at *(place)*:
   ☐ a resident of the county named above.
   ☐ a nonresident of California and left an estate in the county named above located at *(specify location permitting publication in the newspaper named in item 1)*:
   b. Street address, city, and county of decedent's residence at time of death:
   c. Character and estimated value of the property of the estate
   (1) Personal property . . . . $
   (2) Annual gross income from
   (i) ☐ real property . . . . $
   (ii) ☐ personal property . . . . . . $
   Total . . . . . . $
   (3) Real property: $ *(If full authority under the Independent Administration of Estates Act is requested, state the fair market value of the real property less encumbrances.)*
   d. ☐ Will waives bond. ☐ Special administrator is the named executor and the will waives bond.
   ☐ All beneficiaries are adults and have waived bond, and the will does not require a bond. *(Affix waiver as Attachment 3d.)*
   ☐ All heirs at law are adults and have waived bond. *(Affix waiver as Attachment 3d.)*
   ☐ Sole personal representative is a corporate fiduciary.

(Continued on reverse)

Form Approved by the Judicial Council of California DE-111 [Rev. July 1, 1989]

PETITION FOR PROBATE

Probate Code, §§ 8002, 10450

FIGURE 12-4
Petition for probate (California)

removal of the personal representative. In other states, a time limit (such as 15 months) applies to the appointment, after which an extension must be obtained. An authenticated copy of the letters, issued by the court, may be used to establish their validity.

In California, when the petition for probate is allowed, the judge signs an *order for probate* ordering the appointment of the personal representative (see figure 12-12). The personal representative is given a form explaining the duties and liabilities of the position (figure 12-13), and letters are issued by the court (figure 12-14).

letters of administration
Certificate of appointment of a personal representative in an intestate estate, or a testate estate in which someone other than the person nominated as executor(-trix) in the will is appointed.

ESTATE OF (NAME): | CASE NUMBER:
DECEDENT

3. e. ☐ Decedent died intestate.
☐ Copy of decedent's will dated: ☐ codicils dated: are affixed as Attachment 3e.
☐ The will and all codicils are self-proving *(Probate Code, § 8220).*

Attach a typed copy of a holographic will and a translation of a foreign language will.

f. **Appointment of personal representative** *(check all applicable boxes)*
(1) Appointment of executor or administrator with will annexed
☐ Proposed executor is named as executor in the will and consents to act.
☐ No executor is named in the will.
☐ Proposed personal representative is a nominee of a person entitled to Letters. *(Affix nomination as Attachment 3f(1).)*
☐ Other named executors will not act because of ☐ death ☐ declination ☐ other reasons *(specify in Attachment 3f(1)).*
(2) Appointment of administrator
☐ Petitioner is a person entitled to Letters. *(If necessary, explain priority in Attachment 3f(2).)*
☐ Petitioner is a nominee of a person entitled to Letters. *(Affix nomination as Attachment 3f(2).)*
☐ Petitioner is related to the decedent as *(specify)*:
(3) ☐ Appointment of special administrator requested. *(Specify grounds and requested powers in Attachment 3f(3).)*
g. Proposed personal representative is a ☐ resident of California ☐ nonresident of California *(affix statement of permanent address as Attachment 3g)* ☐ resident of the United States ☐ nonresident of the United States.
4. ☐ Decedent's will does not preclude administration of this estate under the Independent Administration of Estates Act.
5. a. The decedent is survived by
(1) ☐ spouse ☐ no spouse as follows: ☐ divorced or never married ☐ spouse deceased
(2) ☐ child as follows: ☐ natural or adopted ☐ natural adopted by a third party ☐ step ☐ foster
☐ no child
(3) ☐ issue of a predeceased child ☐ no issue of a predeceased child
b. Petitioner ☐ has no actual knowledge of facts ☐ has actual knowledge of facts reasonably giving rise to a parent-child relationship under Probate Code section 6408(b).
c. ☐ All surviving children and issue of predeceased children have been listed in item 8.
6. *(Complete if decedent was survived by (1) a spouse but no issue (only a or b apply); or (2) no spouse or issue. Check the **first** box that applies):*
a. ☐ The decedent is survived by a parent or parents who are listed in item 8.
b. ☐ The decedent is survived by issue of deceased parents, all of whom are listed in item 8.
c. ☐ The decedent is survived by a grandparent or grandparents who are listed in item 8.
d. ☐ The decedent is survived by issue of grandparents, all of whom are listed in item 8.
e. ☐ The decedent is survived by issue of a predeceased spouse, all of whom are listed in item 8.
f. ☐ The decedent is survived by next of kin, all of whom are listed in item 8.
g. ☐ The decedent is survived by parents of a predeceased spouse or issue of those parents, if both are predeceased, all of whom are listed in item 8.
7. *(Complete only if no spouse or issue survived the decedent)* Decedent ☐ had no predeceased spouse ☐ had a predeceased spouse who (1) ☐ died not more than 15 years before decedent owning an interest in **real property** that passed to decedent,
(2) ☐ died not more than five years before decedent owning **personal property** valued at $10,000 or more that passed to decedent,
(3) ☐ neither (1) nor (2) apply. *(If you checked (1) or (2), check only the **first** box that applies)*:
a. ☐ The decedent is survived by issue of a predeceased spouse, all of whom are listed in item 8.
b. ☐ The decedent is survived by a parent or parents of the predeceased spouse who are listed in item 8.
c. ☐ The decedent is survived by issue of a parent of the predeceased spouse, all of whom are listed in item 8.
d. ☐ The decedent is survived by next of kin of the decedent, all of whom are listed in item 8.
e. ☐ The decedent is survived by next of kin of the predeceased spouse, all of whom are listed in item 8.
8. **Listed in Attachment 8** are the names, relationships, ages, and addresses of all persons named in decedent's will and codicils, whether living or deceased, and all persons checked in items 5, 6, and 7, so far as known to or reasonably ascertainable by petitioner, **including** stepchild and foster child heirs and devisees to whom notice is to be given under Probate Code section 1207.
9. ☐ Number of pages attached:

Date:

▶ (SIGNATURE OF PETITIONER*) ▶ (SIGNATURE OF PETITIONER*)

I declare under penalty of perjury under the laws of the State of California that the foregoing is true and correct.
Date:

(TYPE OR PRINT NAME) ▶ (SIGNATURE OF PETITIONER*)

* All petitioners must sign the petition. Only one need sign the declaration.

DE-111 (Rev. July 1, 1989) **PETITION FOR PROBATE** Page two

FIGURE 12-4
(Continued)

This two-page check-off form is used in California to begin the probate process for both testate and intestate estates. When the form is filed, the court clerk sets a date for a hearing.

In some states, only state residents may be appointed as personal representatives. Other states allow nonresidents to be appointed if they, in turn, appoint a state resident to act as their agent in the event a suit is brought against the estate. In this way, the court obtains personal jurisdiction over the fiduciary.

CITATION

THE PEOPLE OF THE STATE OF NEW YORK,
By the Grace of God Free and Independent

A petition having been duly filed by
who is domiciled at

YOU ARE HEREBY CITED TO SHOW CAUSE before the Surrogate's Court of the City and County of Albany, at the County Court House in the City of Albany on 19 , at 10 A.M. why a decree should not be made in the estate of
lately domiciled at

in the County of Albany, State of New York, admitting to probate a certain writing relating to real and personal property, and dated 19 , as the last Will and Testament of

, Deceased. (a copy of which is attached)

and ordering that letters testamentary issue to ....
and letters of trusteeship issue to ....
and [any further relief sought]

Dated, Attested and Sealed ______________________ 19 .

HON. RAYMOND E. MARINELLI, Surrogate

(L.S.) ______________________ Chief Clerk

Name of attorney ______________________ Tel. No
Address of attorney ______________________ Zip Code

This citation is served upon you as required by law. You are not obliged to appear in person. If you fail to appear it will be assumed that you do not object to the relief requested. You have a right to have an attorney-at-law appear for you.

Proof of service to be filed 72 hours in advance with the Chief Clerk (Rule 6).

FIGURE 12-5
Citation (New York)

LEGAL TERMS

preliminary letters testamentary
Certificate, used in some states, giving a preliminary executor the same powers that are given to an ordinary executor, with some limitations, when a delay in probate is anticipated.

In some states, when a delay in probate is anticipated, as in the case of a will contest or a missing heir, the court, upon petition, may issue **preliminary letters testamentary**. Such letters give a preliminary executor the same powers of an ordinary executor but with some limitations. A preliminary executor, for example, cannot make distributions to heirs or dispose of property that is specifically bequeathed or devised in the will. Other restrictions may be placed upon a preliminary executor by the court to protect the rights of all interested persons. By the use of a preliminary executor, an estate can be administered under normal time frames, without waiting for a

Note—If affidavit of service be made outside the state of New York, it must be authenticated in the manner prescribed by CPLR 2101, 2309.

AFFIDAVIT OF SERVICE OF CITATION

Specify clearly time and place of service of *each* party served.

State of New York
County of } ss.:

of , being duly sworn says that he is over the age of eighteen years; that he made personal service of the within citation and copy of will on the persons named below, whom deponent knew to be the persons mentioned and described in said citation, by delivering to and leaving with each of them personally a true copy of said citation, as follows:

On (Name): ______
Description: Sex: ____ Hgt.: ____ Wgt: ____ Age: ____ Hair Color: ____ Skin Color: ____
Date: ______ Location: ______

On (Name): ______
Description: Sex: ____ Hgt.: ____ Wgt: ____ Age: ____ Hair Color: ____ Skin Color: ____
Date: ______ Location: ______

On (Name): ______
Description: Sex: ____ Hgt.: ____ Wgt: ____ Age: ____ Hair Color: ____ Skin Color: ____
Date: ______ Location: ______

On (Name): ______
Description: Sex: ____ Hgt.: ____ Wgt: ____ Age: ____ Hair Color: ____ Skin Color: ____
Date: ______ Location: ______

On (Name): ______
Description: Sex: ____ Hgt.: ____ Wgt: ____ Age: ____ Hair Color: ____ Skin Color: ____
Date: ______ Location: ______

On (Name): ______
Description: Sex: ____ Hgt.: ____ Wgt: ____ Age: ____ Hair Color: ____ Skin Color: ____
Date: ______ Location: ______

On (Name): ______
Description: Sex: ____ Hgt.: ____ Wgt: ____ Age: ____ Hair Color: ____ Skin Color: ____
Date: ______ Location: ______

Sworn to before me the ______

day of 19

______
Notary Public, State of New York

FIGURE 12-5
(Continued)

When a probate petition is filed in New York, the court obtains jurisdiction over necessary parties by issuing this citation, which is prepared by the petitioner and served by the court on certain interested parties.

dispute to be settled or an heir to be located. Preliminary letters are revoked when letters testamentary are issued or when a will is denied probate.

The Inventory

One of the duties of a personal representative, after receiving letters of appointment, is to file an inventory with the probate court. This task is also

ATTORNEY OR PARTY WITHOUT ATTORNEY *(Name and Address)*: TELEPHONE NO.: FOR COURT USE ONLY

ATTORNEY FOR *(Name)*:

SUPERIOR COURT OF CALIFORNIA, COUNTY OF

STREET ADDRESS:
MAILING ADDRESS:
CITY AND ZIP CODE:
BRANCH NAME:

ESTATE OF (NAME):

DECEDENT

CASE NUMBER:

NOTICE OF PETITION TO ADMINISTER ESTATE

OF *(name)*:

1. To all heirs, beneficiaries, creditors, contingent creditors, and persons who may otherwise be interested in the will or estate, or both, of *(specify all names by which decedent was known)*:
2. A PETITION has been filed by *(name of petitioner)*:
in the Superior Court of California, County of *(specify)*:
3. THE PETITION requests that *(name)*:
be appointed as personal representative to administer the estate of the decedent.
4. ☐ THE PETITION requests the decedent's WILL and codicils, if any, be admitted to probate. The will and any codicils are available for examination in the file kept by the court.
5. ☐ THE PETITION requests authority to administer the estate under the Independent Administration of Estates Act. (This authority will allow the personal representative to take many actions without obtaining court approval. Before taking certain very important actions, however, the personal representative will be required to give notice to interested persons unless they have waived notice or consented to the proposed action.) The independent administration authority will be granted unless an interested person files an objection to the petition and shows good cause why the court should not grant the authority.
6. ☐ A PETITION for determination of or confirmation of property passing to or belonging to a surviving spouse under California Probate Code section 13650 IS JOINED with the petition to administer the estate.
7. A HEARING on the petition will be held
on *(date)*: at *(time)*: in Dept.: Room:
located at *(address of court)*:
8. IF YOU OBJECT to the granting of the petition, you should appear at the hearing and state your objections or file written objections with the court before the hearing. Your appearance may be in person or by your attorney.
9. IF YOU ARE A CREDITOR or a contingent creditor of the deceased, you must file your claim with the court and mail a copy to the personal representative appointed by the court within four months from the date of first issuance of letters as provided in section 9100 of the California Probate Code. The time for filing claims will not expire before four months from the hearing date noticed above.
10. YOU MAY EXAMINE the file kept by the court. If you are a person interested in the estate, you may file with the court a formal Request for Special Notice of the filing of an inventory and appraisal of estate assets or of any petition or account as provided in section 1250 of the California Probate Code. A Request for Special Notice form is available from the court clerk.
11. ☐ Petitioner ☐ Attorney for petitioner *(name)*:
(address):
▶ (SIGNATURE OF ☐ PETITIONER ☐ ATTORNEY FOR PETITIONER)
12. This notice was mailed on *(date)*: at *(place)*: California.

(Continued on reverse)

NOTE: If this notice is published, print the caption, beginning with the words NOTICE OF PETITION, and do not print the information from the form above the caption. The caption and decedent's name must be printed in at least 8-point type and the text in at least 7-point type. Print the case number as part of the caption. Print items preceded by a box only if the box is checked. Do not print the *italicized* instructions in parentheses, the paragraph numbers, the mailing information, or the material on the reverse.

Form Approved by the Judicial Council of California DE 121 (Rev. July 1, 1989)

NOTICE OF PETITION TO ADMINISTER ESTATE

Probate Code, § 8100

FIGURE 12-6 Notice of petition to administer estate (California)

one to which the paralegal may be assigned. An **inventory** is a detailed list of property owned by the decedent together with its estimated value as of the decedent's date of death. All property in the estate should be listed on the inventory in detail. The inventory should include serial numbers of automobiles, stock certificates, certificates of deposit, savings bond and savings account numbers, legal descriptions of real property, and the book and page where any deed is recorded at the registry of deeds. States have different time limits within which the inventory must be filed, ranging from one to six months from the date of the personal representative's appointment.

LEGAL TERMS

inventory
Detailed list of property owned by the decedent together with its estimated value as of the decedent's date of death.

ESTATE OF (NAME):	CASE NUMBER:
DECEDENT	

PROOF OF SERVICE BY MAIL

1. I am over the age of 18 and not a party to this cause. I am a resident of or employed in the county where the mailing occurred.
2. My residence or business address is *(specify)*:

3. I served the foregoing **Notice of Petition to Administer Estate** on each person named below by enclosing a copy in an envelope addressed as shown below AND
   a. ☐ **depositing** the sealed envelope with the United States Postal Service with the postage fully prepaid.
   b. ☐ **placing** the envelope for collection and mailing on the date and at the place shown in item 4 following our ordinary business practices. I am readily familiar with this business' practice for collecting and processing correspondence for mailing. On the same day that correspondence is placed for collection and mailing, it is deposited in the ordinary course of business with the United States Postal Service in a sealed envelope with postage fully prepaid.

4. a. Date of deposit: b. Place of deposit *(city and state)*:

5. ☐ I served with the Notice of Petition to Administer Estate a copy of the petition and other documents referred to in the notice.

I declare under penalty of perjury under the laws of the State of California that the foregoing is true and correct.
Date:

(TYPE OR PRINT NAME) (SIGNATURE OF DECLARANT)

NAME AND ADDRESS OF EACH PERSON TO WHOM NOTICE WAS MAILED

DE-121 (Rev. July 1, 1989) **NOTICE OF PETITION TO ADMINISTER ESTATE** **(Probate)** Page two

FIGURE 12-6
(Continued)

In California, after the petition for probate has been filed and a hearing date established, this notice must be mailed to all heirs, beneficiaries, and other persons named in Item 8 of the petition for probate (figure 12-4).

Sometimes it is necessary to have a disinterested appraiser assess the value of the estate's real and personal property. Appraisers may be particularly useful in situations in which the heirs disagree on the value, the market value is not easily determinable by a nonexpert, or a dispute about value is anticipated with the tax authorities.

State of New York—Surrogate's Court
ALBANY COUNTY

Present: HON. RAYMOND E. MARINELLI, Surrogate

In the Matter of Proving the Last Will and Testament of

....

DECEASED

County of Albany, ss.:

....of the

......................of......................................in the County of

....being duly sworn in open court,

deposes and says:

That he is a subscribing witness to the instrument now shown to h purporting to be the last will and testament of..

late of the......................................of......................................, County of Albany

deceased, and which bears date on the......................day of......................19........

That at the time aforesaid the said..

did, in my presence, and in the presence of..

the other subscribing witness thereto, sign h name at the end of said instrument and declare the same to be h last will and testament, and I thereupon at h request, and in h presence, and in the presence of..

the other subscribing witness, signed my name as an attesting witness thereto. That at the time when said testa signed said will, and declared the same to be h last will and testament as aforesaid, and at the time when I signed as a witness thereto, as aforesaid, the said......................

....

was of sound mind and memory, of full age to execute a will and was not under any restraint to the knowledge, information or belief of this deponent.

Subscribed and sworn this......................
day of......................, 19........, before me.

....

....
Chief Clerk of the Surrogate's Court
Notary Public

FIGURE 12-7
Affidavit of subscribing witness (New York)

In New York, the court may accept an affidavit such as this in place of a witness's testimony in court unless a party entitled to service of process objects or for some reason the court requires that the witness be examined.

Some assets, such as bank accounts, have a readily ascertainable value and need not be appraised. Requests may be made to financial institutions and brokerage houses for date-of-death values. Sometimes bankbooks must be updated and stock market quotations in newspapers must be reviewed to determine stock values as of the decedent's date of death. If the decedent died on a market day, the proper valuation of stock is the mean between high and low, or bid and asked for that day. If the decedent died on a day

AN ARTISTIC FORTUNE

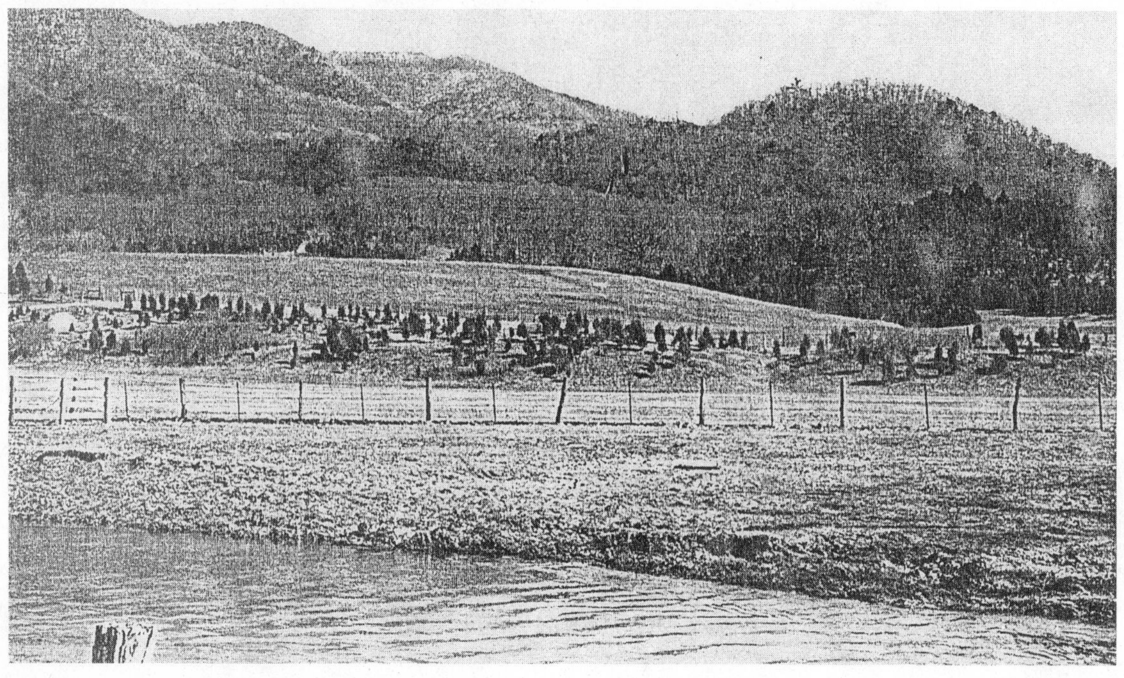

A ranch like this one was left to Juan Hamilton in Georgia O'Keeffe's will. Photo courtesy Camp, *Managing Our Natural Resources*, 2nd edition, copyright 1991 Delmar Publishers Inc.

Artist Georgia O'Keeffe died in 1986 at age 98 with an estate worth over $70 million. Excluded family members contested her will, claiming that Juan Hamilton, her male assistant for over 14 years and more than 50 years her junior, exerted "undue influence" over the aged artist. O'Keeffe had given Hamilton her power of attorney in 1978; as compensation, she left him her ranch and 21 paintings in her will of the following year. Over the years, she became even more liberal: in a second codicil of 1984, Hamilton's share of the estate jumped from 10 to 70 percent, or to an inheritance of over $40 million. What ultimately occurred, however, was a settlement agreement among Hamilton, O'Keeffe's sister, and O'Keeffe's niece. What remained unresolved was whether Hamilton's "influence" was a natural outgrowth of an enduring relationship or deliberate manipulation, and whether O'Keeffe would have favored the final compromise.

the market was closed, the proper valuation is a weighted average of the mean between high and low or bid and asked on the previous market day, and the mean of such quotes on the market day following the decedent's date of death. For variations of these rules, see IRS Reg. § 20.2031-2.

(Caveat to Petition to Probate Will in Solemn Form.)

IN THE PROBATE COURT OF _1.04_ COUNTY
STATE OF GEORGIA

IN RE: ESTATE OF ESTATE NO. ____

_1.01_,
Deceased
AND
PETITION TO PROBATE WILL IN SOLEMN FORM

CAVEAT TO PETITION TO PROBATE WILL IN SOLEMN FORM

COMES NOW the caveator in the above-referenced matter, ____, and files his caveat to the petition of _3.04_ to probate in solemn form the alleged will of _1.01_, deceased, and shows to this Court the following:

1.

The caveator is an heir at law of the decedent, as reflected in the Petition To Probate Will In Solemn Form filed by _3.04_.

2.

The caveator objects to the admission to record of said alleged will on the following grounds: (Here state specifically the grounds of the caveat)

WHEREFORE, caveator prays that this Court enter an Order refusing to admit the alleged will of _1.01_, deceased, to Probate In Solemn Form.

Respectfully Submitted,

____
Attorney For Caveator

VERIFICATION

STATE OF GEORGIA
COUNTY OF ____

Personally appeared before the undersigned attesting officer duly authorized to administer oaths, ____ who, after being sworn, on oath states that the facts contained in his/her Caveat To Petition To Probate Will In Solemn Form are true and correct to the best of his/her knowledge and belief.

____

Sworn to and Subscribed before me
this ____ day of ____, 19__

____
NOTARY PUBLIC

282

GEORGIA PROBATE
Copyright © 1986, LCP
11/86

FIGURE 12-8
Caveat to petition to probate will (Georgia)

This form is used in Georgia when an heir at law objects to the allowance of a will.

After values for all estate assets have been received and the inventory prepared, the inventory is filed with the court (see figures 12-15 and 12-16). A copy may be sent to interested persons who request it. In some states, a supplementary or amended inventory is necessary if additional property is discovered or if the value or description of any asset is found to be erroneous. In some states, an inventory is not required if the will or residuary beneficiaries waive the requirement.

Prob. 2

PROBATE COURT OF ______________ COUNTY, OHIO

ESTATE OF ______________________________, DECEASED

Case No. ______________ Docket ______________ Page ______________

FIDUCIARY'S BOND

[For Executors and all Administrators]

Amount of Bond $______________

The undersigned principal, and sureties if any, are obligated to the State of Ohio in the above amount, for payment of which we bind ourselves and our successors, heirs, executors and administrators, jointly and severally.

The principal has accepted in writing the duties of fiduciary in decedent's estate, including those imposed by law and such additional duties as may be required by the Court.

This obligation is void if the principal performs such duties as required.

This obligation remains in force if the principal fails to perform such duties, or performs them tardily, negligently, or improperly, or if the principal misuses or misappropriates estate assets or improperly converts them to his own use or the use of another.

[Check if personal sureties are involved] - ☐ The sureties certify that each of them owns real estate in this county, with a reasonable net value as stated below.

Date	Principal
Surety	Surety
by Attorney in Fact	by Attorney in Fact
Typed or Printed Name	Typed or Printed Name
Address	Address
Net value of real estate owned in this county $	Net value of real estate owned in this county $

FORM 4.2 - FIDUCIARY'S BOND

FIGURE 12-9 Fiduciary's bond (Ohio). Courtesy of Barrett Brothers, Publishers, Springfield, Ohio

A fiduciary bond such as this is used in Ohio. By signing the bond, an executor or administrator becomes obligated to the state of Ohio in the amount of the bond for failing to perform the duties of the office, or for performing them tardily, negligently, or improperly.

Payment of Debts, Taxes, and Expenses

After gathering the assets and preparing an inventory, the next task of the personal representative is to determine the extent of claims against the estate. Here again the paralegal may assist, particularly with preparing

GEORGIA PROBATE COURT
STANDARD FORM

STATE OF GEORGIA
COUNTY OF ____________________

LETTERS TESTAMENTARY
(Relieved of Filing Returns)

By ______________________________, Judge of the Probate Court of said County.

KNOW ALL WHOM IT MAY CONCERN:

That on the ______ day of ____________________, 19____, at a regular term of the Probate Court, the last Will and Testament dated ____________________, 19____, of ____________________ deceased, at the time of ______ death a resident of said County, was legally proven in ____________ form and was admitted to record by order, and it was further ordered that ______________________________, named as Executor(s) in said Will, be allowed to qualify, and that upon so doing, Letters Testamentary be issued to such Executor(s).

NOW, THEREFORE, the said ______________________________ having taken the oath of office and complied with all the necessary prerequisites of the law, is are legally authorized to discharge all the duties and exercise all the powers of Executor(s) under the Will of said deceased, according to the Will and the law.

Given under my hand and official seal, the ______ day of ____________________, 19____.

____
Judge of the Probate Court

NOTE: The following must be signed if the judge does not sign the original of this document:

Issued by: (Seal)

____
Clerk, Probate Court

GPCSF 24

FIGURE 12-10
Letters testamentary (Georgia)

Letters testamentary serve as evidence of the right of the fiduciary to take possession of the property in the estate.

correspondence and maintaining records of creditors' claims (see figure 12-17). Creditors are responsible for bringing claims to the personal representative's attention within a specific time period. Once the deadline has passed, creditors will not be able to collect the money due them. Time periods are established so that personal representatives will know by a specific

Approved, SCAO — JDC CODE: LET

STATE OF MICHIGAN PROBATE COURT COUNTY OF	LETTERS OF AUTHORITY	FILE NO.

Estate of ______________________________

____
Name

____
Address

has been appointed ______________________________

of the estate and has filed an acceptance of trust or a bond which has been approved as required by law, and by this instrument is granted full power and authority to take possession, collect, preserve, manage, and dispose of all the property of the estate according to law, and to perform all acts permitted or required by statute, court rule, and orders and decrees of this court, unless limited below.

RESTRICTIONS:

☐ None

☐ Conservator shall not sell or mortgage the real property without a prior court order of confirmation.

☐

Date ______________ Judge ______________ Bar no.

Attorney name (type or print) ______________ Bar no.

Address

City, state, zip ______________ Telephone no.

I certify that I have compared this copy with the original on file and that it is a correct copy of the whole of such original, and on this date, these letters are in full force and effect.

Date ______________ Deputy probate register

Do not write below this line - For court use only

PC 15 (9/88) LETTERS OF AUTHORITY — MCL 700.533, 700.534; MSA 27.5533, 27.5534, MCR 5.705

FIGURE 12-11
Letters of authority (Michigan)

In Michigan, the document giving the personal representative the power to act is known as letters of authority.

date the exact amount that is owed to creditors. This knowledge enables the personal representative to make decisions regarding the allocation of estate assets.

Notice to Creditors. Many states have statutes that require personal representatives to publish in a newspaper a notice to creditors, announcing their

ATTORNEY OR PARTY WITHOUT ATTORNEY (Name and Address): TELEPHONE NO. FOR COURT USE ONLY

ATTORNEY FOR (Name):

SUPERIOR COURT OF CALIFORNIA, COUNTY OF

STREET ADDRESS:
MAILING ADDRESS:
CITY AND ZIP CODE:
BRANCH NAME:

ESTATE OF (NAME):

DECEDENT

ORDER FOR PROBATE

CASE NUMBER:

ORDER APPOINTING ☐ Executor
☐ Administrator with Will Annexed
☐ Administrator ☐ Special Administrator

☐ Order Authorizing Independent Administration of Estate
☐ with full authority ☐ with limited authority

1. Date of hearing: Time: Dept/Rm: Judge:

THE COURT FINDS

2. a. All notices required by law have been given.
   b. Decedent died on *(date)*:
      (1) ☐ a resident of the California county named above
      (2) ☐ a nonresident of California and left an estate in the county named above
   c. Decedent died
      (1) ☐ intestate
      (2) ☐ testate and decedent's will dated:
      and each codicil dated:
      was admitted to probate by Minute Order on *(date)*:

THE COURT ORDERS

3. *(Name)*:
   is appointed **personal representative:**
   a. ☐ Executor of the decedent's will
   b. ☐ Administrator with will annexed
   c. ☐ Administrator
   d. ☐ Special Administrator
      (1) ☐ with general powers
      (2) ☐ with special powers as specified in Attachment 3d
      (3) ☐ without notice of hearing

   and letters shall issue on qualification.

4. a. ☐ **Full authority** is granted to administer the estate under the Independent Administration of Estates Act.
   b. ☐ **Limited authority** is granted to administer the estate under the Independent Administration of Estates Act (there is no authority, without court supervision, to (1) sell or exchange real property or (2) grant an option to purchase real property or (3) borrow money with the loan secured by an encumbrance upon real property).

5. a. ☐ Bond is not required.
   b. ☐ Bond is fixed at: $ to be furnished by an authorized surety company or as otherwise provided by law.
   c. ☐ Deposits of: $ are ordered to be placed in a blocked account at *(specify institution and location)*:
   and receipts shall be filed. No withdrawals shall be made without a court order.

6. ☐ *(Name)*: is appointed probate referee.

Date:

JUDGE OF THE SUPERIOR COURT

7. ☐ Number of pages attached: ☐ Signature follows last attachment

Form Approved by the Judicial Council of California DE-140 (Rev. July 1, 1988)

ORDER FOR PROBATE

Probate Code, § 329

FIGURE 12-12
Order for probate (California)

This order for probate is prepared by the petitioner, in California, and signed by the judge when the petition for probate is allowed and the will is admitted to probate.

appointment, giving their addresses, and asking creditors to present their claims within a specific time period. In the 1988 *Pope* case, the United States Supreme Court held that actual notice must be given to each creditor if the creditor can be readily identified. Since the Supreme Court decision, all states require that actual notice of the deadline to file a claim against an estate be delivered either by mail or some other means to each known or reasonably ascertainable creditor of the deceased.

TO COURT CLERK: This form is CONFIDENTIAL if local rule requires the Acknowledgment of Receipt to have a Social Security or driver's license number.

ATTORNEY OR PARTY WITHOUT ATTORNEY *(Name and Address)*: TELEPHONE NO.: ATTORNEY FOR *(Name)*:	*FOR COURT USE ONLY*
SUPERIOR COURT OF CALIFORNIA, COUNTY OF STREET ADDRESS: MAILING ADDRESS: CITY AND ZIP CODE: BRANCH NAME:	
ESTATE OF (NAME): DECEDENT	
DUTIES AND LIABILITIES OF PERSONAL REPRESENTATIVE **and Acknowledgment of Receipt**	CASE NUMBER:

DUTIES AND LIABILITIES OF PERSONAL REPRESENTATIVE

When you have been appointed by the court as personal representative of an estate, you become an officer of the court and assume certain duties and obligations. An attorney is best qualified to advise you about these matters. You should clearly understand the following:

1. MANAGING THE ESTATE'S ASSETS

a. **Prudent investments**
You must manage the estate assets with the care of a prudent person dealing with someone else's property. This means you must be cautious and you may not make any speculative investments.

b. **Keep estate assets separate**
You must keep the money and property in this estate separate from anyone else's, including your own. When you open a bank account for the estate, the account name must indicate that it is an estate account and not your personal account. Never deposit estate funds in your personal account or otherwise commingle them with anyone else's property. Securities in the estate must also be held in a name that shows they are estate property and not your personal property.

c. **Interest-bearing accounts and other investments**
Except for checking accounts intended for ordinary administration expenses, estate accounts must earn interest. You may deposit estate funds in insured accounts in financial institutions, but you should consult with an attorney before making other investments.

d. **Other restrictions**
There are many other restrictions on your authority to deal with estate property. You should not spend any of the estate's money unless you have received permission from the court or have been advised to do so by an attorney. You may reimburse yourself for official court costs paid by you to the county clerk and for the premium on your bond. Without prior order of the court, you may not pay fees to yourself or to your attorney, if you have one. If you do not obtain the court's permission when it is required, you may be removed as personal representative or you may be required to reimburse the estate from your own personal funds, or both. You should consult with an attorney concerning the legal requirements affecting sales, leases, mortgages, and investments of estate property.

2. INVENTORY OF ESTATE PROPERTY

a. **Locate the estate's property**
You must attempt to locate and take possession of all the decedent's property to be administered in the estate.

b. **Determine the value of the property**
You must arrange to have a court-appointed referee determine the value of the property unless the appointment is waived by the court. (You, rather than the referee, must determine the value of certain "cash items." An attorney can advise you about how to do this.)

c. **File an inventory and appraisal**
Within four months after your appointment as personal representative, you must file with the court an inventory and appraisal of all the assets in the estate.

(Continued on reverse)

Form Adopted by the Judicial Council of California DE-147 [New July 1, 1989] **DUTIES AND LIABILITIES OF PERSONAL REPRESENTATIVE (Probate)** Probate Code, § 8404

FIGURE 12-13
Duties and liabilities of personal representative (California)

Taxes and Expenses. Preparing and filing estate tax returns can be a major part of the work of a personal representative. The paralegal will often be asked to help complete various types of tax returns. State and federal individual income tax returns (Form 1040) often have to be prepared for the decedent's last year of life, up to the date of death. After that, if the estate has income, state and federal estate income tax returns (Form 1041) may have to be prepared from the date of death until the year's end. Finally, if the value of the estate exceeds certain limits, state and federal estate tax returns

ESTATE OF (NAME):	CASE NUMBER:
— DECEDENT	

d. **File a change of ownership**
At the time you file the inventory and appraisal, you must also file a change of ownership statement with the county recorder or assessor in each county where the decedent owned real property at the time of death, as provided in section 480 of the California Revenue and Taxation Code.

3. NOTICE TO CREDITORS

You must mail a notice of administration to each known creditor of the decedent within four months after your appointment as personal representative. If the decedent received Medi-Cal assistance you must notify the State Director of Health Services within 90 days after appointment.

4. INSURANCE

You should determine that there is appropriate and adequate insurance covering the assets and risks of the estate. Maintain the insurance in force during the entire period of the administration.

5. RECORD KEEPING

a. **Keep accounts**
You must keep complete and accurate records of each financial transaction affecting the estate. You will have to prepare an account of all money and property you have received, what you have spent, and the date of each transaction. You must describe in detail what you have left after the payment of expenses.

b. **Court review**
Your account will be reviewed by the court. Save your receipts because the court may ask to review them. If you do not file your accounts as required, the court will order you to do so. You may be removed as personal representative if you fail to comply.

6. CONSULTING AN ATTORNEY

If you have an attorney, you should cooperate with the attorney at all times. You and your attorney are responsible for completing the estate administration as promptly as possible. **When in doubt, contact your attorney.**

NOTICE: This statement of duties and liabilities is a summary and is not a complete statement of the law. Your conduct as a personal representative is governed by the law itself and not by this summary.

ACKNOWLEDGMENT OF RECEIPT

1. I have petitioned the court to be appointed as a personal representative of the estate of *(specify)*:
2. I acknowledge that I have received a copy of this statement of the duties and liabilities of the office of personal representative.

Date:

.... ▶ ______________________________
(TYPE OR PRINT NAME) (SIGNATURE OF PETITIONER)

*Social Security No.: ______________ *Driver's License No.: ______________

Date:

.... ▶ ______________________________
(TYPE OR PRINT NAME) (SIGNATURE OF PETITIONER)

*Social Security No.: ______________ *Driver's License No.: ______________

Date:

.... ▶ ______________________________
(TYPE OR PRINT NAME) (SIGNATURE OF PETITIONER)

*Social Security No.: ______________ *Driver's License No.: ______________

*Supply these numbers only if required to do so by local court rule. The law requires the court to keep this information CONFIDENTIAL. (Probate Code, § 8404(a).)

DE-147 (New July 1, 1989) **DUTIES AND LIABILITIES OF PERSONAL REPRESENTATIVE** **(Probate)** Page two

FIGURE 12-13
(Continued)

In California, to ensure that personal representatives are aware of their responsibilities, this form must be read and signed by the personal representative before letter will be issued by the clerk of court.

(Form 706) must be prepared. These are discussed in detail in chapter 13. Federal estate taxes must be paid within nine months after death.

Personal representatives may deduct from the assets of the estate all reasonable expenses incurred during the process of settling the estate.

ATTORNEY OR PARTY WITHOUT ATTORNEY *(Name and Address)*: TELEPHONE NO.: FOR COURT USE ONLY

ATTORNEY FOR *(Name)*:

SUPERIOR COURT OF CALIFORNIA, COUNTY OF

STREET ADDRESS:
MAILING ADDRESS:
CITY AND ZIP CODE:
BRANCH NAME:

ESTATE OF (NAME):

DECEDENT

LETTERS

☐ **TESTAMENTARY** ☐ **OF ADMINISTRATION**
☐ **OF ADMINISTRATION WITH WILL ANNEXED** ☐ **SPECIAL ADMINISTRATION**

CASE NUMBER:

LETTERS

1. ☐ The last will of the decedent named above having been proved, the court appoints *(name)*:
   a. ☐ Executor
   b. ☐ Administrator with will annexed
2. ☐ The court appoints *(name)*:
   a. ☐ Administrator of the decedent's estate
   b. ☐ Special administrator of decedent's estate
      (1) ☐ with the special powers specified in the Order for Probate
      (2) ☐ with the powers of a general administrator
3. ☐ The personal representative is authorized to administer the estate under the Independent Administration of Estates Act ☐ **with full authority** ☐ **with limited authority** (no authority, without court supervision, to (1) sell or exchange real property or (2) grant an option to purchase real property or (3) borrow money with the loan secured by an encumbrance upon real property).

WITNESS, clerk of the court, with seal of the court affixed.

Date:

Clerk, by ______________________, Deputy

(SEAL)

AFFIRMATION

1. ☐ PUBLIC ADMINISTRATOR: No affirmation required (Prob. Code, § 1140(b)).
2. ☐ INDIVIDUAL: **I solemnly affirm** that I will perform the duties of personal representative according to law.
3. ☐ INSTITUTIONAL FIDUCIARY *(name)*:

   I solemnly affirm that the institution will perform the duties of personal representative according to law.
   I make this affirmation for myself as an individual and on behalf of the institution as an officer.
   (Name and title):

4. Executed on *(date)*:
   at *(place)*: , California.

▶ ______________________
(SIGNATURE)

CERTIFICATION

I certify that this document is a correct copy of the original on file in my office and the letters issued the personal representative appointed above have not been revoked, annulled, or set aside, and are still in full force and effect.

(SEAL)

Date:
Clerk, by

____
(DEPUTY)

Form Approved by the Judicial Council of California DE-150 [Rev. July 1, 1988]

LETTERS (Probate)

Probate Code, §§ 463, 465, 501, 502, 540
Code of Civil Procedure, § 2015.6

FIGURE 12-14
Letters (California)

In California, letters such as this are prepared by the petitioner and certified by the clerk of court following the judge's signing of the order for probate. Court-certified letters are needed by the personal representative to obtain access to the decedent's bank accounts and other assets.

Administrative expenses may include attorney's and appraiser's fees, court costs, amounts paid to newspapers for publishing, and premiums on surety company bonds. In addition, personal representatives are allowed reasonable compensation for their services. The court determines the appropriate amount of compensation, as shown in the *Knight* case.

PROBATE COURT OF ______________ COUNTY, OHIO

ESTATE OF ______________________________, DECEASED

Case No. ______________ Docket ______________ Page ______

INVENTORY AND APPRAISAL

Revised Code Sec. 2115.01, 2115.02, 2115.06, 2117.20, 2117.24

The fiduciary says that to his knowledge the attached schedule of assets in decedent's estate is complete. The fiduciary further says that he determined the value of those assets whose values were readily ascertainable and which were not appraised by the appraiser, and that such values are correct.

The estate is recapitulated as follows:

Tangible personal property .... $ ______________

Intangible personal property .... $ ______________

Real Estate .... $ ______________

Total .... $ ______________

Automobile transferred to surviving spouse under Revised Code § 2113.532(A) .... $ ______________

Attached is a list of the surviving spouse, next of kin, legatees and devisees known to the fiduciary, which list includes those persons entitled to notice of the hearing on this inventory.

[Check if applicable] - ☐ The surviving spouse is the sole legatee and devisee under decedent's Will, and has not manifested an intention to take against it. It is therefore unnecessary to cite the surviving spouse to make an election.

____
Fiduciary

APPRAISER'S CERTIFICATE

The undersigned appraiser agreed to act as appraiser of decedent's estate, and to appraise the property exhibited to him honestly, impartially, and to the best of his knowledge and ability. The appraiser further says that he appraised those assets whose values were not readily ascertainable, indicated on the attached schedule by a check in the column "Appraiser" opposite each such item, and that such values are correct.

____
Appraiser

____
Appraisers Fee

☐ Check if paid by fiduciary

____
Appraiser's Address

FORM 6.0 - INVENTORY AND APPRAISAL

FIGURE 12-15 Inventory and appraisal (Ohio). Courtesy of Barrett Brothers, Publishers, Springfield, Ohio

Decedent's Debts. After the expiration of a time period set by state statute, the personal representative pays the claims against the estate. If the estate is **insolvent** (i.e., the assets of the estate are insufficient to pay all the debts), the personal representative pays claims according to a priority list that is established by state statute. Priority lists differ somewhat from state to state. The Uniform Probate Code, in § 3-805, sets forth the following order for the payment of claims:

LEGAL TERMS

insolvent
Unable to pay debts because of insufficient assets.

WAIVER OF NOTICE OF TAKING OF INVENTORY

The undersigned surviving spouse hereby waives notice of the time and place of taking the inventory of decedent's estate.

____
Surviving Spouse

WAIVER OF NOTICE OF HEARING ON INVENTORY

The undersigned, being persons entitled to notice of the hearing on the inventory of decedent's estate, hereby waive such notice.

______________________________ ______________________________

______________________________ ______________________________

______________________________ ______________________________

______________________________ ______________________________

______________________________ ______________________________

______________________________ ______________________________

______________________________ ______________________________

______________________________ ______________________________

______________________________ ______________________________

______________________________ ______________________________

ENTRY SETTING HEARING AND ORDERING NOTICE

The Court sets ______________________________ at __________ o'clock ______.M. as the date and time for hearing the inventory of decedent's estate. The Court orders notice of the hearing to be given, as provided by law and the Rules of Civil Procedure, to those persons entitled to notice, who have not waived notice.

______________________________ ______________________________
Date Probate Judge

FIGURE 12-15
(Continued)

One of the first duties of a personal representative is to make an inventory and to determine the value of the property belonging to the estate. This form is used in Ohio to summarize the assets; it breaks them into tangible personal property, intangible personal property, and real estate.

1. Costs and expenses of administration
2. Reasonable funeral expenses
3. Debts and taxes with preference under federal law

PROBATE COURT OF ______________ COUNTY, OHIO

ESTATE OF ______________________________________, DECEASED

Case No. ______________ Docket ______________ Page ______

SCHEDULE OF ASSETS

[Attach to inventory and appraisal]

Page ______ of ______ pages.

[Insert a check in the column "Appraiser" opposite an item if it was valued by the appraiser. Leave blank if the readily ascertainable value was determined by fiduciary]

Item	Appraiser	Value
		$

FORM 6.1 - SCHEDULE OF ASSETS

FIGURE 12-16 Schedule of assets (Ohio). Courtesy of Barrett Brothers, Publishers, Springfield, Ohio

4. Reasonable and necessary medical and hospital expenses of the last illness of the decedent, including compensation of persons attending the decedent
5. Debts and taxes with preference under state law
6. All other claims.

No payment is made to creditors of any class until all those of the preceding class or classes have been paid. If assets are inadequate to pay all the

Page ______ of ______ pages.

Item	Appraiser	Value
		$

Fiduciary

FIGURE 12-16
(Continued)

This Ohio form lists in detail the assets that are summarized on the inventory and appraisal form (figure 12-15).

debts of any class, the remaining assets are prorated to creditors of that class.

State laws set forth the order in which property is to be consumed for the payment of claims. A legal principle known as **marshaling of assets** ranks estate assets in a certain order for the payment of debts. In some states, unless a will directs otherwise, personal property and then real

Prob. 43

PROBATE COURT OF ______________ COUNTY, OHIO

ESTATE OF ____, DECEASED

Case No. ____________________ Docket ______________ Page __________

SCHEDULE OF CLAIMS

Revised Code, Sec. 2117.16 to 2117.17. 2117.25

[Use extra sheets if necessary]

The fiduciary says that to his knowledge this schedule lists all claims against decedent or his estate. Such claims are recapitulated as follows:

Claims allowed . . . . $ ____________

Claims rejected, contingent, or in suit . . . . $ ____________

Total . . . . $ ____________

[Check if applicable] - ☐ The surviving spouse is the sole legatee and devisee under decedent's Will, and has not manifested an intention to take against it. It is therefore unnecessary to cite the surviving spouse to make an election.

____
Fiduciary

[Under "Footnotes" opposite an item requiring explanation, place the number of the appropriate footnote. Such notes should be included on the reverse to explain: any security for claims; maturity dates of claims not due; contingent claims; claims in suit; and dates of rejection of rejected claims]

Name and Address of Claimant	Amount Claimed	Payment Class	Date Presented	Date Allowed	Foot-Notes
	$				

FORM 7.0 - SCHEDULE OF CLAIMS

FIGURE 12-17 Schedule of claims (Ohio). Courtesy of Barrett Brothers, Publishers, Springfield, Ohio

property is used to pay debts. In addition, property that is specifically bequeathed or devised will not be used to pay debts until after property that is not specifically bequeathed or devised has been exhausted. Then, as between specific legatees and devisees, the remaining debt is usually prorated.

Under UPC § 3-902, no distinction is made between real and personal property in the order that is used to satisfy claims. Property **abates** (is reduced) to pay claims, in the following order: (1) property not disposed of by will; (2) residuary devises; (3) general devises; and then (4) specific

LEGAL TERMS

marshaling of assets
Legal principle that ranks estate assets in a certain order for the payment of debts.

abate
To reduce, lessen, or diminish.

Name and Address of Claimant	Amount Claimed	Payment Class	Date Presented	Date Allowed	Foot-Notes
	$				

FOOTNOTES

FIGURE 12-17
(Continued)

This schedule, used in Ohio, summarizes and lists in detail all claims against the estate of which the personal representative is aware.

devises. In community property states, if the estate consists partly of separate property and partly of community property, community debts are charged against community property and separate debts are charged against separate property and then against the balance of community property.

TULSA PROFESSIONAL COLLECTION SERVICES, INC. V. POPE 108 S. Ct. 1340 (1988)

FACTS: H. Everett Pope, Jr., died at St. John Medical Center in Tulsa, Oklahoma, after being a patient there for five months. Following the directions of the court, the executrix of his estate published a notice in a newspaper for two consecutive weeks, advising creditors that they must file any claim they had against the estate within two months of the first publication of the notice. Tulsa Professional Collection Services, Inc., which had been assigned the claim from the St. John Medical Center for expenses connected with the decedent's stay at the hospital, did not file a claim within the two-month time period. The Oklahoma Supreme Court held that Collection Services was barred from collecting the money because it had failed to file a timely claim.

LEGAL ISSUE: Must actual notice be given to known and reasonably ascertainable creditors of the time limit within which creditors must file claims against an estate?

COURT DECISION: Yes.

REASON: Under the due process clause of the Fourteenth Amendment, actual notice is a minimum constitutional precondition to a proceeding that could adversely affect the property interests of any party. The executor must make reasonably diligent efforts to uncover the identity of creditors. Known or reasonably ascertainable creditors must be given notice by mail or other means that will ensure actual notice of the time limit for bringing claims. For creditors who are not reasonably ascertainable, publication notice can suffice. The Oklahoma Supreme Court's decision was reversed.

Sale of Real Property. In most states, title to real property owned by a decedent vests in the decedent's heirs immediately upon death. In contrast, title to personal property vests in the personal representative when he or she is appointed. Therefore, although real property is included in the inventory of the estate, it is not usually included in the final account, because the personal

ESTATE OF KNIGHT V. KNIGHT
559 N.E.2d 891 (Ill. 1990)

FACTS: Teresa Rai Knight requested the sum of $10,334.96 for 145 hours of work and expenses as administratrix of the estate of Arthur B. Knight. The trial judge awarded a fee of $4,000.

LEGAL ISSUE: Are personal representatives entitled to reasonable compensation for their services?

COURT DECISION: Yes.

REASON: Administrators are entitled to reasonable compensation for their services, and the determination of what is reasonable is a matter of discretion for the trial judge. Factors that may be considered include good faith, diligence, time expended, the size of the estate, and the benefits conferred upon the estate. The $4,000 fee in this case was not an abuse of the trial judge's discretion.

representative has no control over it. When the debts exceed the value of the personal property, however, the personal representative may sell the real property to obtain the money to pay the debts. Such a sale is done under the court's supervision (often by the issuance of a license to sell) unless the will gives the personal representative the power to sell real property without court supervision. The proceeds from the sale of real property are included in the personal representative's final account.

Distribution

After the time has expired for creditors to make claims and the debts and taxes have been paid, the remaining assets of the estate are distributed according to the terms of the will or the law of intestate succession. Some states have special rules allowing the distribution of property *in kind* (as it is), which avoids having to sell the property to distribute cash.

When there are not enough assets to pay the legacies and devises in a will, the rules of abatement, as previously explained, are applied. First, specific legacies and devises are paid in full. Next, general or pecuniary legacies and devises are paid: these abate pro rata if the assets are insufficient to pay them in full.

Final Account

The last task of the personal representative is to prepare and file a *final account* (called a *final return* in some states) with the court. Usually, only one account is filed; however, if an estate is open longer than a year, many states require an account to be filed annually, with a final account at the end.

The account is a listing of everything that the fiduciary has received and disbursed during the period covered in the account. With variations from state to state, a typical account lists receipts in one schedule, disbursements in another schedule, and the balance in a third schedule. If the account is final, no third schedule is necessary. (See figures 12-18 and 12-19.)

In some states, the allowance of the final account by the court formally closes the estate. In other states, the personal representative files a petition for discharge which, when allowed, formally closes the estate. Even after an account is allowed, however, the court may correct manifest error in a judgment or revoke a judgment altogether when the judgment was obtained through fraud.

12.3 INFORMAL PROBATE PROCEEDINGS

Informal probate proceedings may be followed in most states when someone dies owning assets below a specific value set by state statute, or when there is no reason to have the court supervise all aspects of the estate's settlement. The UPC defines **informal proceedings** as those conducted without notice to interested persons by an officer of the court acting as a registrar for probate of a will. UPC § 1-201(19). Informal proceedings, sometimes referred to as *unsupervised administration,* are relatively simple, with a minimum amount of paperwork and bureaucratic involvement.

In some states, informal probate proceedings are known as **independent probate**. Other states refer to it as **probate in common form**, as opposed to probate in solemn form. Still other states provide for the appointment of a **voluntary executor** or a **voluntary administrator** to settle small estates by the use of a very simple procedure. (See figure 12-20.)

LEGAL TERMS

informal proceedings
Proceedings conducted without notice to interested persons by an officer of the court acting as a registrar for probate of a will or appointment of a personal representative (UPC § 1-201(19)).

independent probate
Informal probate proceedings.

probate in common form
Informal probate proceedings.

voluntary executor
Person who undertakes the informal administration of a small testate estate.

voluntary administrator
Person who undertakes the informal administration of a small intestate estate.

PROBATE COURT OF ______________ COUNTY, OHIO

ESTATE OF ____, DECEASED

Case No. ______________________ Docket ______________________ Page ______________

FIDUCIARY'S ACCOUNT

[For Executors and all Administrators]

The fiduciary offers an account of his trust, given below and on the attached itemized statement of receipts and disbursements, and accompanying vouchers. The fiduciary says that to his knowledge the account is correct, and asks that it be approved and settled.

[Check one of the following four paragraphs]

☐ This is a partial account. A statement of the assets remaining in the fiduciary's hands is attached.

☐ This is a final account. A statement of the assets remaining in the fiduciary's hands for distribution to the beneficiaries is attached.

☐ This is a distributive account. and the fiduciary asks to be discharged from his trust upon its approval and settlement.

☐ This is a final and distributive account, and the fiduciary asks to be discharged from his trust upon its approval and settlement.

[Complete if this is a partial account, or if one or more accounts have previously been filed in the estate] The period of this account is from

______________________________ to ______________________________

[Complete if applicable] Accounts previously filed in the estate, the accounting periods, and the fiduciary and attorney fees paid for each period, are as follows:

Date Filed	Accounting Period	Fiduciary Fees Paid	Attorney Fees Paid
		$	$

13.0 - FIDUCIARY'S ACCOUNT

FIGURE 12-18 Fiduciary's account (Ohio). Courtesy of Barrett Brothers, Publishers, Springfield, Ohio

12.4 ANCILLARY ADMINISTRATION

A resident of one state often owns real and personal property in another state. After the decedent's death, the property in the other state must be recovered for the benefit of the decedent's estate and arrangements must be made for the payment of debts in that state. The term applied to this process is **ancillary administration**, which is the administration of an

This account is recapitulated as follows:

RECEIPTS

Personal property of decedent [not sold] .... $ ______

Proceeds from sale of personal property .... ______

Real estate of decedent [not sold] .... ______

Proceeds from sale of real estate .... ______

Income .... ______

Other receipts .... ______

Total receipts .... $ ______

DISBURSEMENTS

Fiduciary fees [this accounting period] .... $ ______

Attorney fees [this accounting period] .... ______

Other administration costs and expenses .... ______

Debts and claims against estate .... ______

Ohio and federal estate taxes .... ______

Personal property distributed in kind .... ______

Real property transferred .... ______

Other distributions to beneficiaries .... ______

Other disbursements .... ______

Total disbursements .... $ ______

BALANCE REMAINING IN FIDUCIARY'S HANDS .... $ ______

______
Fiduciary

ENTRY SETTING HEARING AND ORDERING NOTICE

The Court sets ______ at ______ o'clock ______ .M. as the date and time for hearing the above account, and orders notice of the hearing to be given as provided by law and the Rules of Civil Procedure.

______ Date

______ Probate Judge

FIGURE 12-18
(Continued)

The final account is a listing of everything that the fiduciary has received and disbursed during the period that is covered in the account.

estate in a state other than where the decedent was domiciled where the decedent owns property.

Most states have provisions for admitting to record in their probate courts an authenticated copy of a will that has been proved and allowed in another state, together with a certified copy of the personal representative's

LEGAL TERMS

ancillary administration
Administration of an estate in a state other than where the decedent was domiciled where the decedent owns property.

PROBATE COURT OF ______________ COUNTY, OHIO

ESTATE OF ____, DECEASED

Case No. ______________________ Docket ______________________ Page ____________

RECEIPTS AND DISBURSEMENTS

[Attach to fiduciary's account]

Page ______ of ______ pages

Following is an itemized statement of receipts and disbursements by the fiduciary in the administration of his trust.

Item	Voucher No.	Value or Amount	Value or Amount
		$	$

13.1 - RECEIPTS AND DISBURSEMENTS

FIGURE 12-19
Receipts and disbursements (Ohio). Courtesy of Barrett Brothers, Publishers, Springfield, Ohio

appointment. Similar provisions are available for intestate estates. This process allows the personal representative to exercise the powers of a local personal representative regarding all local assets. The various states have other methods, as well, for handling ancillary administration. (See figure 12-21.)

Page ______ of ______ pages

Item	Voucher No.	Value or Amount	Value or Amount
		$	$

____
Fiduciary

FIGURE 12-19
(Continued)

This form is attached to the fiduciary's account in Ohio (figure 12-18) to itemize the receipts and disbursements of the personal representative.

12.5 WILL ADMINISTRATION CHECKLIST

The following checklist sets forth in detail some of the preliminary steps that should be taken when a law office is given the task of settling a testate estate or administering a trust. This sample checklist is for use in

(Form 148)

The State of New Hampshire

ROCKINGHAM, SS.

COURT OF PROBATE

I, of in said County, on oath depose and say as follows:

1. That late of in said County, died on the day of 19

2. No petition under any section of RSA 553 has been filed or is about to be filed with the probate court for said County.

3. My relationship to said decedent is that of and I am of legal age and of legal capacity.

4. The estate of said decedent consists entirely of personal property of a gross value not exceeding (Five Hundred Dollars) (Two Thousand Dollars) consisting of the following assets:

5. I have undertaken to act as voluntary administrator of the estate of said decedent and will administer the same according to law.

6. I am filing herewith and with the division of inheritance taxes, State Tax commission, a report of gifts and transfers under RSA 86:22.

7. Out of the assets which I collect, I shall pay debts and expenses in accordance with RSA 554:19 and shall take no fee for my services.

8. If any balance remains, I shall distribute it according to the Will of the deceased, if any, or if there is no Will, to the surviving spouse, if any; otherwise in accordance with RSA 561.6.

9. If letters testamentary or of administration are later granted I acknowledge that my powers as voluntary administrator shall cease and I shall thereupon forthwith deliver to the rightful executor or administrator all assets and funds of said estate in my possession.

In Witness Whereof I have hereunto set my hand this day of A.D. 19

Voluntary Administrator

Post Office Address

THE STATE OF NEW HAMPSHIRE

ROCKINGHAM, SS. A.D.

Personally appeared the above named who took oath that the foregoing statements by subscribed are true and correct, according to the best of knowledge and belief.

Approved

Judge of Probate

Justice of the Peace — Notary Public

Date

NOTE: Approval of Judge not required in estates not exceeding $500.

FIGURE 12-20 Informal probate application (New Hampshire)

Small estates may be settled by the use of a simple procedure such as by filing this affidavit in New Hampshire.

Tennessee, but its guidelines can be adapted to the needs of the particular state and document in question. (Adapted from *Tennessee Post Mortem Estate Planning Checklist* (Lawyers Cooperative Publishing). Annotations refer to *American Law Reports.*)

Application/Ancillary Probate of Will (PC-201)

APPLICATION/ANCILLARY PROBATE OF WILL
PC-201 REV. 7/85
(PRC-15)

STATE OF CONNECTICUT

COURT OF PROBATE
[*Type or print. File in duplicate.*]
[*Use Second Sheet PC-180 (PRC-17) for additional data.*]

Recorded:

TO: COURT OF PROBATE, DISTRICT OF | DISTRICT NO.

ESTATE OF [*Include all names and initials under which any asset was held.*] | SOCIAL SECURITY # | DATE OF DEATH

DECEDENT'S RESIDENCE AT TIME OF DEATH [*Include full address.*]

PETITIONER [*Name, address and zip code*] | SURVIVING SPOUSE [*Name, address and zip code. If no surviving spouse, so state.*]

JURISDICTION APPERTAINS TO THIS COURT BASED ON THE FOLLOWING: [*Gen. Stat. §45-171*]

- ☐ The decedent last resided in this district.
- ☐ The decedent has real or tangible personal property located in this district.
- ☐ The decedent has maintained bank accounts or evidence of other tangible property in this district.
- ☐ An executor or trustee named in the will resides, or in the case of a bank or trust company, has an office, in this district.
- ☐ A cause of action in favor of the decedent arose in this district or a debtor of the decedent resides or has an office in this district.

HEIRS, NEXT OF KIN, BENEFICIARIES and TRUSTEES, if any. [*Give names, addresses, zip codes and relationships. If heir, indicate ancestor through whom heir takes. If beneficiary, indicate paragraph of will where interest is stated or may arise. For all minors listed, give date of birth. Indicate any person who is under legal disability or in the military service.*] Gen. Stat. §§45-274, 276; 45-273a.

THE PETITIONER REPRESENTS that:

No other application for ancillary probate has been filed in the State of Connecticut.

Decedent, or spouse or children of the decedent ☐ *did* ☐ *did not* receive aid or care from the State of Connecticut.

[*If affirmative, check appropriate box(es).*] ☐ State of Connecticut ☐ Veterans Home & Hospital. Gen. Stat. §45-204e.

THE PETITIONER HEREWITH PRESENTS to the Court the duly authenticated and exemplified copy of the Last Will and Testament and codicils, if any, of the decedent dated .... and the record of the proceedings proving and establishing the same by a court of competent jurisdiction and REPRESENTS that the time for taking an appeal therefrom ☐ *has* ☐ *has not* expired, and no appeals are presently pending. Attached hereto is a complete statement of the property and estate of the decedent in Connecticut. Gen. Stat. §45-171.

WHEREFORE THE PETITIONER REQUESTS this Court to order said copies to be filed and recorded and that letters ancillary testamentary be issued below named fiduciary.

....
Petitioner's Signature

SUBSCRIBED AND SWORN TO BEFORE ME this.................. day of .... 19......

....
Judge, Ass't Clerk, Notary Public, Comm. Sup. Ct.

PROPOSED FIDUCIARY

IF APPOINTED, I WILL ACCEPT SAID POSITION OF TRUST.

Signature ....
[*Type or print name*]
Address and zip code ....
Telephone number ....

ATTORNEY FOR PROPOSED FIDUCIARY [*Name, address, zip code, telephone number, Conn. Bar Juris #*]

The undersigned waive notice of hearing on the foregoing application. [*If space insufficient, use General Waiver, PC-181 (PRC-19).*]

APPLICATION/ANCILLARY PROBATE OF WILL

FIGURE 12-21
Application for ancillary administration (Connecticut). Courtesy of *The Connecticut Probate Deskbook* (Lawyers Cooperative Publishing)

Ancillary administration is used to clear title to property located in one state that was owned by a decedent whose estate was settled in a different state.

For another excellent discussion of practical probate administration, *see* Kirk, "Strategies for Efficient Probate Administration," 9 *Legal Assistant Today* 95-101 (Sept./Oct. 1992).

Checklist of Preliminary Steps when Probating a Will or Administering a Trust

	N/A	To be Done	Done	By Whom
Preliminary Steps				
1. Obtain custody of the will and all codicils, revocable trust agreement and all amendments, as well as any signed copies and all prior documents.	( )	( )	( )	____
Annotations: 31 ALR4th 306, 42 ALR4th 176, 7 ALR3d 1143, 12 ALR3d 56, 17 ALR2d 805, 21 ALR2d 821, 33 ALR2d 922, 59 ALR2d 11, 89 ALR2d 177				
2. Apply for preliminary letters testamentary pursuant to TCA § 32-2-101, or letters of temporary administration pursuant to TCA § 32-1-101, particularly if a probate delay or will contest is anticipated, or if the decedent had a cause of action that will soon be barred by the statute of limitations.	( )	( )	( )	____
3. Examine the will and all codicils for physical evidence of possible irregularities including: removal of staples, different kinds of paper, different type styles, and interlineations; attempt to obtain explanations for these.	( )	( )	( )	____
Annotations: 17 ALR3d 705, 28 ALR3d 994, 24 ALR2d 514, 34 ALR2d 619				
4. Ascertain whether interlineations or deletions made by the decedent after the execution of the will manifested an intent to revoke it or merely to change it.	( )	( )	( )	____
5. Investigate the circumstances surrounding the execution of the will or revocable trust agreement, and verify the genuineness of the decedent's signature on those documents.	( )	( )	( )	____

	N/A	To be Done	Done	By Whom

Annotations: 7 ALR3d 317, 37 ALR3d 889, 44 ALR3d 701, 71 ALR3d 877, 40 ALR2d 1223, 45 ALR2d 1365, 60 ALR2d 124, 45 ALR2d 1365, 69 ALR2d 662, 75 ALR2d 318, 91 ALR2d 737, 98 ALR2d 824, 98 ALR2d 841

	N/A	To be Done	Done	By Whom
6. Examine all facts concerning the decedent's emotional condition to refute any contention that the decedent was suffering from an insane delusion.	( )	( )	( )	____

Annotations: 89 ALR2d 1120

	N/A	To be Done	Done	By Whom
7. Ascertain the decedent's physical and emotional condition when the will or revocable trust agreement was executed; determine whether the decedent may have then been under the influence of alcohol, medication or other drugs.	( )	( )	( )	____

Annotations: 9 ALR3d 15, 17 ALR3d 503

	N/A	To be Done	Done	By Whom
8. Assemble factual data to refute the exercise of undue influence, if anyone benefiting from the will or revocable trust agreement drafted it, procured its execution, or had a confidential relationship with the decedent.	( )	( )	( )	____

Annotations: 13 ALR3d 381, 19 ALR3d 575, 48 ALR3d 961, 76 ALR3d 743, 25 ALR2d 657, 98 ALR2d 1234

	N/A	To be Done	Done	By Whom
9. Inquire whether anyone exerted any influence on the decedent to change or not to change the will or revocable trust agreement.	( )	( )	( )	____

Annotations: 22 ALR4th 1229, 11 ALR2d 808

	N/A	To be Done	Done	By Whom
10. Ascertain whether it is necessary to interview the witnesses to the will, to assure compliance with all formalities of execution prescribed by TCA § 32-1-109.	( )	( )	( )	____

	N/A	To be Done	Done	By Whom
11. Determine whether any interested person may have grounds to object to any provision of the will or revocable trust agreement without objecting to all of its provisions.	( )	( )	( )	_____
Annotations: 64 ALR3d 261				
12. Review all facts concerning the decedent's domicile, to determine if the decedent may have had more than one domicile.	( )	( )	( )	_____
Annotations: 31 ALR2d 775, 96 ALR2d 1236				
13. Consider which jurisdiction's law would uphold the validity of the will or revocable trust agreement, if a multiple domicile problem exists.	( )	( )	( )	_____
14. Ascertain the existence of any document in the decedent's handwriting that may constitute an unattested holographic will in the state where signed.	( )	( )	( )	_____
Annotations: 37 ALR4th 528, 46 ALR3d 938, 49 ALR3d 1223				
15. Consider the effect of any letters from the decedent regarding the disposition of personal effects, small cash bequests, and charitable gifts to be made by the family members.	( )	( )	( )	_____
Annotations: 22 ALR3d 1346, 3 ALR2d 682, 40 ALR2d 698				
16. Determine whether the decedent's former spouse may have acquired the rights of a surviving spouse after a divorce or annulment, by subsequently living with the decedent.	( )	( )	( )	_____

SUMMARY

12.1 The probate process protects the decedent by seeing that his or her wishes are carried out. It protects the heirs by assuring that all of the decedent's property is collected and accounted for and by determining the lawful heirs. It also establishes title to property that has been inherited.

12.2 Formal probate proceedings involve the following steps: (1) a petition is filed with the court; (2) interested parties are given notice; (3) in a testate estate, the will must be proved; (4) unless waived, a bond is given by the personal representative; (5) letters are issued by the court; (6) an inventory is filed; (7) notice or a time period is given to creditors; (8) debts, taxes, and expenses of administration are paid; (9) distribution is made to the beneficiaries; (10) an account is filed with the court.

12.3 Informal probate proceedings may be followed in most states when someone dies owning assets below a specific value or when there is no reason to have the court supervise all aspects of the estate's settlement. Informal proceedings are relatively simple, with a minimum amount of paperwork and bureaucratic involvement.

12.4 As part of their ancillary administration provisions, most probate courts admit to record authenticated copies of wills that have been proved and allowed in other states, together with certified copies of the appointment of out-of-state personal representatives.

12.5 A checklist of steps for administering a will can be an invaluable guide to the estate's representative or legal assistant, as it helps to ensure that nothing is forgotten and all actions are timely.

QUESTIONS FOR REVIEW

1. What is the consequence of failing to turn over to the probate court a will of a deceased person?
2. How are heirs and next of kin protected by the probate procedure?
3. What steps are followed in formal probate proceedings?
4. How do probate proceedings begin in testate cases? In intestate cases?
5. How do the decedent's heirs learn that a will is being probated?
6. What are three methods that are used to prove a will? Why is a self-proof clause in a will helpful?
7. Describe one of the first duties of a personal representative after receiving letters of appointment.
8. What did the United States Supreme Court hold in 1988 regarding notice to creditors?
9. How do legacies and devises abate when there are not enough assets to pay them?

10. What is one method states use to provide for ancillary administration?

CASES TO DISCUSS

1. Jeremy Mindlin executed a will naming his father, Leo Mindlin, as personal representative. When Jeremy died, the court appointed Jeremy's wife, Karen, rather than Leo as personal representative. Leo appealed. How would you decide? *Estate of Mindlin v. Mindlin,* 571 So. 2d 90 (Fla. 1990).
2. Agnes Minkus-Whalen was appointed administratrix of the estate of Stephen J. Minkus. The petition for administration listed three first cousins as the only heirs. Before filing the account, however, the administratrix was notified of the discovery in Lithuania of 11 additional first cousins of the decedent. Without disclosing the discovery, the administratrix filed an account, obtained allowance from the court, and distributed the estate to the three first cousins. Can the allowance of the account be revoked by the court? Explain. *Altshuler v. Minkus-Whalen,* 579 N.E.2d 1369 (Mass. 1991).

SHARPENING YOUR PROFESSIONAL SKILLS

1. Refer to the law office scenario at the beginning of this chapter.
   a. Determine the penalty, under your state law, for failing to turn a decedent's will over to the probate court.
   b. Decide the most appropriate method that would be used in your state to settle Mr. Notmeyer's estate.
   c. Prepare a notice of claim that creditors use in your state to notify the court of a claim against an estate.
   d. Determine whether Mr. Notmeyer's estate would be required to file a federal estate tax return.
2. Using your state form, prepare a petition for the formal probate of a will. Use a fictitious name, domicile, and date of death of a decedent who is survived by two adult children, and one grandchild who is the adopted daughter of a deceased child.
3. From the business section of a newspaper, determine the values to be used in the inventory for each of the following stocks that were owned by a decedent who died on the day before you are doing this assignment:
   a. 55 shares of AT&T
   b. 15 shares of NYNX
   c. 15 shares of Bell South
   d. 24 shares of IBM
   e. 116 shares of Exxon.

Show the calculations you used to determine the values.

4. Using your state form, prepare an inventory for the hypothetical estate used in question 2. Include in the inventory:
   a. A dwelling house
   b. Household furniture
   c. Personal effects
   d. An automobile
   e. A checking account
   f. A savings account in a different bank
   g. A certificate of deposit in a different bank
   h. 15 Series E U.S. Savings bonds
   i. The stocks listed in question 3.

   Provide details including values, fictitious account numbers, and fictitious serial numbers for the automobile and the securities.
5. Using your state form, prepare a final account for the hypothetical estate used in questions 2, 3, and 4. Include the following:
   a. Interest income from the checking account, savings account, certificate of deposit, and Series E bonds
   b. Dividend income from the stocks
   c. Gains (or losses) on the sale of the stock certificates
   d. Funeral expenses
   e. An outstanding credit card bill
   f. Real estate taxes
   g. Utility bills
   h. Loss on the sale of the automobile
   i. Legal fees
   j. Expenses incurred in settling the estate
   k. An executor's fee
   l. Distribution of the balance to the heirs.

WILL
ESTATE
TRUST

CHAPTER 13
Estate Taxes

"Everything appears to promise that it will last, but in this world nothing is certain but death and taxes."

Benjamin Franklin,
in a letter to M. Leroy on the U.S. Constitution

OUTLINE

LAW OFFICE SCENARIO

It was 9:00 a.m. on December 5. Attorney Knight was discussing the day's activities with Tiffany Casey, the office paralegal.

"My first appointment this morning is at ten o'clock with Ms. Shulman. Her father passed away a few days ago, and we're going to be settling his estate."

"I remember when we did Mr. Shulman's will," Tiffany offered. "I was one of the witnesses. He was a jovial man with a nice sense of humor. He used to joke about our Macintosh computer."

"You have a good memory, Tiffany," Attorney Knight replied. "Can you join us at ten o'clock? I'd like you to help with the estate right from the beginning."

"Sure. I'll be glad to," Tiffany replied. "Let me know when you want me to come in."

Later that morning, Tiffany and Attorney Knight met with Ms. Shulman in Attorney Knight's office.

"I always did my father's income taxes, you know," Ms. Shulman was saying, "but I don't know how to do this year's return."

"We'll help you with that," Attorney Knight responded. "That's part of our work in settling your father's estate. Tiffany, as soon as Ms. Shulman is appointed executrix, we'll need to notify the IRS that a fiduciary relationship exists."

"Right. I'll see that they are notified."

"Also, you'll need to send for an '04' number from the IRS."

"Yes. I'll do that, too. Ms. Shulman, I'll have some forms for you to sign before you leave today."

"Okay, but one thing is bothering me," Ms. Shulman responded. "My father owned an apple orchard, and the day before he died, he sold $3,000 worth of MacIntosh apples to the cannery. When the money comes in, do I declare that as income on his tax return?"

"Don't worry about it," Attorney Knight countered. "We'll do the taxes when the time comes. You've got enough things to worry about for now."

13.1 FIDUCIARY'S TAX OBLIGATIONS

As mentioned in chapter 12, the paralegal often plays a key role in assisting the attorney and the personal representative with the many procedures involved in settling an estate. Because a major responsibility of the personal representative is to prepare and file tax returns when they are due, the paralegal often becomes involved with this task as well. Federal and state returns that sometimes must be filed include: (1) a final income tax return for the decedent, (2) an income tax return for the decedent's estate, and (3) an estate tax return. The federal tax returns are discussed in this chapter. (State tax returns differ so much from state to state that discussion of each state's return is beyond the scope of this text.)

Notifying the Internal Revenue Service

The first step in the taxation procedure is to notify the Internal Revenue Service (IRS) that the taxpayer has died and that a fiduciary relationship now exists. *Form 56* (Notice Concerning Fiduciary Relationship) is available as a convenience from the IRS for this purpose (see figure 13-1). It is not mandatory that Form 56 be filed. However, by filing the form, any subsequent correspondence from the IRS will be sent to the fiduciary's address rather than to the decedent's last-known address. This will ensure that the fiduciary is informed of all tax liabilities and other tax matters.

Obtaining Identification Number

The next step is to obtain an **employer identification number** for the estate. This is an "04" number assigned by the IRS to identify an estate, and is used in place of a Social Security number. The number is required if any estate tax returns are to be filed or if a bank account is to be opened for estate funds. The number is referred to as an "04 number" because all employer identification numbers begin with the figures 04. To obtain the number, it is merely necessary to fill out *Form SS-4* (Application for Employer Identification Number) and file it with the IRS (see figure 13-2). The number will be mailed by the IRS to the person requesting it without delay.

13.2 DECEDENT'S FINAL INCOME TAX RETURN

The personal representative must file the final income tax return of the decedent for the year of death, as well as any returns not filed for preceding years. In the case of a joint return, the surviving spouse may file the return alone if no personal representative has been appointed before the due date.

If an individual died after the close of the tax year, but before the return for that year was filed, the return for the year just closed may not be the final return. The return for that year will be a regular return. The

Notice Concerning Fiduciary Relationship (IRS Form 56)

Form **56** (Rev. February 1989) Department of the Treasury Internal Revenue Service

Notice Concerning Fiduciary Relationship

(Internal Revenue Code sections 6036 and 6903)

OMB No. 1545-0013 Expires 1-31-92

Part I Identification

Name of person for whom you are acting (as shown on the tax return) | Identifying number

Address of person for whom you are acting (number and street, including apartment number)

City, town, or post office, state, and ZIP code

Fiduciary's name

Fiduciary's address (number and street, including apartment number, or P.O. Box)

City, town, or post office, state, and ZIP code | Telephone number (optional)

Part II Authority

1 Evidence of fiduciary authority (check applicable boxes):

a ☐ Certified copy of will and codicils attached . . . . Date of death ....

b ☐ Certified copy of court order appointing the fiduciary attached . . . . Date (see instructions) ....

c ☐ Copy of valid trust instrument and amendments attached

d ☐ Other evidence of creation of fiduciary relationship (describe) ▶ ....

Part III Tax Notices

Send all notices and other written communications addressed to the fiduciary(ies) (listed in Part I) involving the following tax matters:

2 Type of tax (estate, gift, generation-skipping transfer, income, excise, etc.) ....

3 Federal tax form number (706, 1040, 1041, 1120, etc.) ....

4 Year(s) or period(s) (If estate tax, date of death)

Part IV Revocation or Termination of Notice

Section A.—Total Revocation or Termination

5 Check this box if you are revoking or terminating all prior notices concerning fiduciary relationships on file with the Internal Revenue Service for the same tax matters and years or periods covered by this notice concerning fiduciary relationship . . . . ▶ ☐

Evidence of termination of fiduciary authority (check applicable boxes):

a ☐ Certified copy of court order revoking fiduciary authority attached

b ☐ Copy of certificate of dissolution or termination of a business entity attached

c ☐ Other evidence of termination of fiduciary relationship (describe) ▶

Section B.—Partial Revocation

6a Check this box if you are revoking earlier notices concerning fiduciary relationships on file with the Internal Revenue Service for the same tax matters and years or periods covered by this notice concerning fiduciary relationship . . . . ▶ ☐

b Specify to whom granted, date, and address, including ZIP code, or refer to attached copies of earlier notices and authorizations.

....

Section C.—Substitute Fiduciary

7 Check this box if a new fiduciary or fiduciaries have been or will be substituted for the revoking or terminating fiduciary(ies) and specify the name(s) and address(es), including ZIP code(s), of the new fiduciary(ies) . . . . ▶ ☐

Part V Court and Administrative Proceedings

Name of court (if other than a court proceeding, identify the type of proceeding and name of agency) | Date proceeding initiated

Address of court or other proceeding | Docket number of proceeding

City, town, or post office, state and ZIP code | Date | Time | a.m. p.m. | Place of other proceedings

Please Sign Here

I certify that I have the authority to execute this notice concerning fiduciary relationship on behalf of the taxpayer.

▶ Fiduciary's signature | (Title, if applicable) | Date

▶ Fiduciary's signature | (Title, if applicable) | Date

For Paperwork Reduction Act and Privacy Act Notices, see back page. Form **56** (Rev. 2-89)

FIGURE 13-1 Internal Revenue Service Form 56

personal representative must file that return for the year before death and the final return for the year in which death occurred.

Income

The decedent's income that is includable on the final return is generally determined in the same way as if the person were still alive, except that the taxable period is usually shorter because it ends on the date of death.

LEGAL TERMS

employer identification number
Number beginning with "04" that is assigned by the IRS to identify an estate; used in place of a Social Security number.

Form 56 (Rev 2-89) Page 2

General Instructions

Paperwork Reduction Act Notice

We ask for this information to carry out the Internal Revenue laws of the United States. We need it to ensure that taxpayers are complying with these laws and to allow us to figure and collect the right amount of tax. You are required to give us this information.

The time needed to complete and file this form will vary depending on individual circumstances. The estimated average time is:

Recordkeeping . . . . 8 min.
Learning about the law or the form . . . . . . 32 min.
Preparing the form . . . . . . 46 min.
Copying, assembling, and sending the form to IRS . . . .15 mins.

If you have comments concerning the accuracy of these time estimates or suggestions for making this form more simple, we would be happy to hear from you. You can write to the **Internal Revenue Service,** Washington, DC 20224, Attention: IRS Reports Clearance Officer, TR:FP; or the **Office of Management and Budget,** Paperwork Reduction Project (1545-0013), Washington DC, 20503.

Privacy Act Notice

Sections 6903 of the Internal Revenue Code and 26 CFR 301.6903-1 state that a fiduciary who wants to receive notices of tax liability for someone else must file a written notice. Sections 6036 of the Code and 26 CFR 301.6036-1 state that a notice is required of a receiver in proceedings other than bankruptcy, and other like fiduciaries.

Purpose of Form

Use Form 56 to notify IRS of a fiduciary relationship.

Form 56 is available as a convenience and its use is therefore not mandatory. The principal purpose of the notice is to inform the IRS that you are a fiduciary. Until you notify the IRS, notices of tax liability sent to the last known address of the taxpayer, transferee, or other person subject to liability are considered sufficient compliance by the IRS with the requirements of the Internal Revenue Code.

A bankruptcy trustee, debtor in possession, or other like fiduciary in a bankruptcy proceeding is not required under the Internal Revenue Code to give notice of appointment, qualification, or authorization. See, however, the notice requirements of Title 11 of the United States Code.

Identifying Number.—Under Code section 6109, the taxpayer's identifying number must be disclosed. The principal purpose is to properly identify the person for whom you are acting. If the identifying number is not disclosed, the IRS may suspend processing the notice concerning fiduciary relationship until the number is provided.

Who Should File

Form 56 should be filed by the fiduciary to notify the IRS of the creation or termination of a fiduciary relationship for each of the following:

- **an individual**
- **a decedent's estate**
- **a receiver in a receivership proceeding**
- **a trust**
- **a bankruptcy estate**
- **an assignee for the benefit of creditors and**
- **terminating entities .**—A terminating entity, such as a corporation, partnership, trust, etc., only has the legal capacity to establish a fiduciary relationship while it is in existence. Establishing a fiduciary relationship prior to termination of the entity allows the fiduciary to represent the entity on all tax matters after it is terminated.

Definitions

Fiduciary.—Fiduciary means any person acting in a fiduciary capacity for any other person, such as an administrator, conservator, designee, executor, guardian, receiver, trustee of a trust, trustee in bankruptcy, personal representative, person in possession of property of a decedent's estate or debtor in possession of assets in any bankruptcy proceeding by order of the court.

Person.—A person means any individual, trust, estate, partnership, association, company or corporation.

Decedent's estate.—An estate of a deceased person is a taxable entity separate from the decedent. It generally continues to exist until the final distribution of the assets of the estate is made to the heirs and other beneficiaries.

Bankruptcy estate.—A bankruptcy estate is a separate and distinct taxable entity from the individual debtor. It is created when an individual debtor files for bankruptcy under chapter 7 or 11 of the Bankruptcy Code. This creates a separate "estate" consisting of property that belonged to the debtor before the filing date. See **Publication 908,** Bankruptcy, for more information.

When and Where to File

1. Taxable Persons.—Generally, Form 56 should be filed when you first create a fiduciary relationship or when you decide to terminate it for an individual, a decedent's estate, a trust, or a terminating entity. However, when a fiduciary relationship is first created, a fiduciary who is required to file a return can file Form 56 with the first tax return filed.

Form 56 must be filed with the IRS service center where the person for whom you are acting is required to file tax returns.

2. Proceedings and Assignments for the Benefit of Creditors.—Generally, Form 56 must be filed within 10 days from the date the fiduciary is appointed or authorized to act as:

- a receiver in a receivership proceeding or similar fiduciary (including a fiduciary in aid of foreclosure),
- an assignee for the benefit of creditors.

In the case of bankruptcy proceedings, with an appointment date on or after January 29, 1988, written notice must comply with the requirements of Title 11 of the United States Code.

File Form 56 with the Chief, Special Procedures Staff, of the District office of the IRS where the fiduciary is or was required to file returns.

Specific Instructions

Part I.—Identification

Provide all the information called for in this part.

Identifying number.—If you are acting for an individual, an individual debtor, or other person whose assets are controlled, the identifying number is the social security number. If you are acting for a person other than an individual, including an estate or trust, the identifying number is the employer identification number.

Part II.—Authority

Line 1a.—Testate decedent.—Check this box if the decedent died testate and enter the date of the decedent's death.

Line 1b.—

- **Intestate decedent.**—Enter the decedent's date of death and write "Date of Death" next to the date.
- **Bankruptcy estates or similar cases.**—Enter the date you were appointed trustee of a bankruptcy estate or the date you took possession of the assets of the debtor or other person whose assets are controlled.
- **Assignment for the benefit of creditors.**—Enter the date the assets were assigned to you and write "Assignment date" after the date.
- **Proceedings Other Than Bankruptcy .**—Enter the date you were appointed or took possession of the assets of the debtor or other person whose assets are controlled.

Part III.—Tax Notices

Complete Part III if you want the IRS to send you tax notices regarding the person for whom you are acting.

Specify the type of tax involved. This line should also identify a transferee tax liability under section 6901 of the Code or fiduciary tax liability under 31 U.S.C. 192 when either exists.

Part IV.—Revocation or Termination of Notice

Complete this part only if you are revoking or terminating a prior notice concerning a fiduciary relationship. Completing this part will relieve you of any further duty or liability if used as a notice of termination.

Part V.—Court and Administrative Proceedings

Complete this part only if you have been appointed a receiver, trustee, or a fiduciary by a court or other governmental unit in a proceeding other than a bankruptcy proceeding.

If proceedings are scheduled for more than one date, time or place, attach a separate schedule of the proceedings.

Assignment for the Benefit of Creditors.—You must attach:

1) Your name and address and the date the assets were assigned to you,

2) The name, address, and taxpayer identification number of the debtor whose assets were assigned,

3) A brief description of the assets that were assigned, and

4) An explanation of the action to be taken regarding such assets, including any hearings, meetings of creditors, sale or other scheduled action.

Signature

Sign Form 56 and enter a title describing your role as a fiduciary (for example: assignee; guardian; trustee; personal representative; receiver; or conservator).

*U.S. Government Printing Office: 1988-242-473/80078

FIGURE 13-1
(Continued)

This form may be used to notify the IRS that a taxpayer has died and that a fiduciary relationship now exists.

Only income that was received up to the date of death is included in the decedent's final income tax return. Income that is received after the date of death (such as bank account interest and stock dividends) is taxable either to the decedent's estate or to a joint owner. For this reason, it is necessary to provide the payor of interest or dividends with the new identification number so that the correct number will be reported to the IRS on the payor's

Form **SS-4** (Rev. August 1989) Department of the Treasury Internal Revenue Service

Application for Employer Identification Number

(For use by employers and others. Please read the attached instructions before completing this form.) Please type or print clearly.

EIN

OMB No. 1545-0003 Expires 7-31-91

1 Name of applicant (True legal name) (See instructions.)

2 Trade name of business, if different from name in line 1 | 3 Executor, trustee, "care of name"

4a Mailing address (street address) (room, apt., or suite no.) | 5a Address of business. (See instructions.)

4b City, state, and ZIP code | 5b City, state, and ZIP code

6 County and state where principal business is located

7 Name of principal officer, grantor, or general partner. (See instructions.) ▶

8a Type of entity (Check only one box.) (See instructions.)
- ☐ Individual SSN ______
- ☐ REMIC
- ☐ Personal service corp.
- ☐ State/local government
- ☐ National guard
- ☐ Other nonprofit organization (specify) ______
- ☐ Other (specify) ▶
- ☐ Estate
- ☐ Plan administrator SSN ______
- ☐ Other corporation (specify) ______
- ☐ Federal government/military
- ☐ Church or church controlled organization
- If nonprofit organization enter GEN (if applicable) ______
- ☐ Trust
- ☐ Partnership
- ☐ Farmers' cooperative

8b If a corporation, give name of foreign country (if applicable) or state in the U.S. where incorporated ▶ | Foreign country | State

9 Reason for applying (Check only one box)
- ☐ Started new business
- ☐ Hired employees
- ☐ Created a pension plan (specify type) ▶
- ☐ Banking purpose (specify) ▶
- ☐ Changed type of organization (specify) ▶
- ☐ Purchased going business
- ☐ Created a trust (specify) ▶
- ☐ Other (specify) ▶

10 Date business started or acquired (Mo., day, year) (See instructions.) | 11 Enter closing month of accounting year. (See instructions.)

12 First date wages or annuities were paid or will be paid (Mo., day, year). **Note:** *If applicant is a withholding agent, enter date income will first be paid to nonresident alien. (Mo., day, year).* ▶

13 Enter highest number of employees expected in the next 12 months. **Note:** *If the applicant does not expect to have any employees during the period, enter "0."* ▶ | Nonagricultural | Agricultural | Household

14 Does the applicant operate more than one place of business? ☐ **Yes** ☐ **No**
If "Yes," enter name of business. ▶

15 Principal activity or service (See instructions.) ▶

16 Is the principal business activity manufacturing? ☐ **Yes** ☐ **No**
If "Yes," principal product and raw material used ▶

17 To whom are most of the products or services sold? Please check the appropriate box. ☐ Business (wholesale)
☐ Public (retail) ☐ Other (specify) ▶ ☐ N/A

18a Has the applicant ever applied for an identification number for this or any other business? ☐ **Yes** ☐ **No**
Note: *If "Yes," please complete lines 18b and 18c.*

18b If you checked the "Yes" box in line 18a, give applicant's true name and trade name, if different than name shown on prior application.
True name ▶ Trade name ▶

18c Enter approximate date, city, and state where the application was filed and the previous employer identification number if known.
Approximate date when filed (Mo., day, year) | City and state where filed | Previous EIN

Under penalties of perjury, I declare that I have examined this application, and to the best of my knowledge and belief, it is true, correct, and complete. | Telephone number (include area code)

Name and title (Please type or print clearly.) ▶

Signature ▶ Date ▶

Note: *Do not write below this line. For official use only.*

Please leave blank ▶	Geo.	Ind.	Class	Size	Reason for applying

For Paperwork Reduction Act Notice, see attached instructions. Form **SS-4** (Rev. 8-89)

FIGURE 13-2
Internal Revenue Service Form SS-4

This form is used to obtain an employer identification number for an estate. The number is required if any estate tax returns are to be filed or if a bank account is to be opened for estate funds.

Form 1099. The correct identification number will be either the estate "04" number or the Social Security number of the joint owner.

The amounts reported to the IRS on *Forms 1099* (Statement for Recipients of Income) by payors may not be the correct amount that should be reported on the decedent's final tax return. This is because the amount that should be reported is the amount received up to the date of death; amounts received after death are reported either on the estate income tax return or a joint owner's return. If you are preparing a decedent's final return and have received Forms 1099 for the decedent that include amounts paid after the decedent's death, report the total interest and dividends shown on the Forms 1099; then show any interest and dividends belonging to another recipient separately, subtract it, and report the net result.

If an income tax refund is due the decedent, *Form 1310* (Statement of Person Claiming Refund Due a Deceased Taxpayer) must be filed together with the decedent's tax return. (See figure 13-3.)

Exemptions and Deductions

Generally, the rules for exemptions and deductions allowed to an individual also apply to the decedent's final income tax return. The return should show any deductible items the decedent paid before death.

Medical expenses paid before death by the decedent are deductible on the final income tax return if deductions are itemized. Medical expenses that

Form **1310** (Rev. October 1988) Department of the Treasury Internal Revenue Service

Statement of Person Claiming Refund Due a Deceased Taxpayer

OMB No. 1545-0073 Expires 3-31-90

Attachment Sequence No. **87**

Tax year decedent was due a refund:

Calendar year , or other tax year beginning , 19 , and ending , 19

Please type or print

Name of decedent	Date of death	Social security number of decedent

Name of person claiming refund

Address (number and street)

City or town, state, and ZIP code

Part I Check the box that applies to you (check only one box) (sign and date in Part III below)

A ☐ Surviving spouse, requesting reissuance of a refund check. (See instructions on back of form.)

B ☐ Personal representative appointed or certified by a court. You may have to attach a court certificate showing your appointment. (See instructions on back of form.)

C ☐ Person, **other** than **A** or **B**, claiming refund for the decedent's estate. Complete Part II and attach a copy of the death certificate or proof of death. (See instructions on back of form.)

Part II (Complete this part only if you checked Box C above)

	Yes	No
1 Did the decedent leave a will?		
2a Has a personal representative been appointed by a court for the estate of the decedent?		
b If "No," will one be appointed?		
If 2a or 2b is answered "Yes," the personal representative must file for the refund.		
3 As the person claiming the refund for the decedent's estate, will you pay out the refund according to the laws of the state where the decedent was a legal resident?		

If "No," a refund cannot be made until you submit a court certificate showing your appointment as personal representative or other evidence that you are entitled, under state law, to receive the refund.

Part III Signature and Verification

I request a refund of taxes overpaid by or on behalf of the decedent. Under penalties of perjury, I declare that I have examined this claim, and to the best of my knowledge and belief, it is true, correct, and complete.

Signature of person claiming refund ▶ **Date ▶**

For Paperwork Reduction Act Notice, see instructions on back of form. Form **1310** (Rev. 10-88)

FIGURE 13-3
Internal Revenue Service Form 1310

This form may have to be filed with the IRS to obtain a tax refund that is due a deceased taxpayer.

are not paid before the decedent's death are liabilities of the decedent's estate and are shown on the estate tax return. However, if medical expenses for the decedent are paid out of the estate during the one-year period beginning with the day after death, an election may be made to treat all or part of the expenses as paid by the decedent at the time they were incurred. If the election is made, all or part of the medical expenses can be claimed on the decedent's income tax return rather than on the federal estate tax return (the Form 706 described later).

13.3 FIDUCIARY INCOME TAX RETURN

An estate is a taxable entity that is separate from the decedent. It originates with the death of the individual and exists until the final distribution of its assets to the heirs and other beneficiaries. An estate's income of $600 or more must be reported annually on either a calendar or fiscal year basis. The income is reported on IRS *Form 1041* (U.S. Fiduciary Income Tax Return). (See figure 13-4.)

Income

Generally, an estate's income is the same as the individual's income, with certain exceptions. Gross income of an estate consists of all income received or accrued during the tax year. It includes interest, dividends, rents, royalties, gain from the sale of property, and income from businesses, partnerships, trusts, and any other sources.

Income in Respect of the Decedent

All gross income that the decedent would have received in a future year had death not occurred is **income in respect of the decedent**. Such income must be included in the gross income of (1) the decedent's estate, if the estate receives it; or (2) the beneficiary, if the right to income is passed directly to the beneficiary and the beneficiary receives it; or (3) any person to whom the estate properly distributes the right to receive it.

For example, suppose that Valerie Miller owned and operated a tomato farm. She used the cash method of accounting and therefore recorded income only when it was received. She sold and delivered $5,000 worth of tomatoes to a canning factory, but did not receive payment before her death. When the estate was settled, payment had not yet been made, and the estate transferred the right to receive the payment to her surviving spouse. When Miller's surviving spouse collects the $5,000, he must include the amount in his income tax return. It should not be reported on the final return of the decedent or on the return of Miller's estate.

Suppose, instead, that Valerie Miller was an author who received royalties (promised future payments against work already performed). Upon

LEGAL TERMS

income in respect of the decedent
All gross income that a decedent would have received, had death not occurred, that was not properly includable on the decedent's final income tax return.

Form **1041** Department of the Treasury—Internal Revenue Service
U.S. Fiduciary Income Tax Return 1991

For the calendar year 1991 or fiscal year beginning , 1991, and ending , 19 OMB No. 1545-0092

A Type of Entity
- ☐ Decedent's estate
- ☐ Simple trust
- ☐ Complex trust
- ☐ Grantor type trust
- ☐ Bankruptcy estate
- ☐ Family estate trust
- ☐ Pooled income fund

Name of estate or trust (grantor type trust, see instructions)

Name and title of fiduciary

Number, street, and room or suite no. (If a P.O. box, see page 4 of instructions.)

City, state, and ZIP code

C Employer identification number

D Date entity created

E Nonexempt charitable and split-interest trusts, check applicable boxes (see instructions):
- ☐ Described in section 4947(a)(1)
- ☐ Not a private foundation
- ☐ Described in section 4947(a)(2)

B Number of Schedules K-1 attached (see instructions) ▶

Check applicable boxes: ☐ Initial return ☐ Final return ☐ Amended return Change in Fiduciary's ▶ ☐ Name or ☐ Address

Income

1	Interest income	1	
2	Dividends	2	
3	Business income or (loss) (attach Schedule C (Form 1040))	3	
4	Capital gain or (loss) (attach Schedule D (Form 1041))	4	
5	Rents, royalties, partnerships, other estates and trusts, etc. (attach Schedule E (Form 1040))	5	
6	Farm income or (loss) (attach Schedule F (Form 1040))	6	
7	Ordinary gain or (loss) (attach Form 4797)	7	
8	Other income (state nature of income)	8	
9	**Total** income (combine lines 1 through 8) ▶	9	

Deductions

10	Interest	10	
11	Taxes	11	
12	Fiduciary fees	12	
13	Charitable deduction (from Schedule A, line 6)	13	
14	Attorney, accountant, and return preparer fees	14	
15a	Other deductions NOT subject to the 2% floor (attach schedule)	15a	
b	Allowable miscellaneous itemized deductions subject to the 2% floor	15b	
c	Add lines 15a and 15b	15c	
16	**Total** (add lines 10 through 14, and 15c)	16	
17	Adjusted total income or (loss) (subtract line 16 from line 9). Enter here and on Schedule B, line 1 ▶	17	
18	Income distribution deduction (from Schedule B, line 17) (see instructions) (attach Schedules K-1 (Form 1041))	18	
19	Estate tax deduction (including certain generation-skipping transfer taxes) (attach computation)	19	
20	Exemption	20	
21	**Total** deductions (add lines 18 through 20) ▶	21	

Tax and Payments (Please attach check or money order here)

22	Taxable income of fiduciary (subtract line 21 from line 17)	22	
23	**Total** tax (from Schedule G, line 7)	23	
24	Payments: **a** 1991 estimated tax payments and amount applied from 1990 return	24a	
b	Treated as credited to beneficiaries (from Form 1041-T)	24b	
c	Subtract line 24b from line 24a	24c	
d	Tax paid with extension of time to file: ☐ Form 2758 ☐ Form 8736 ☐ Form 8800	24d	
e	Federal income tax withheld	24e	
	Credits: **f** Form 2439 ....; **g** Form 4136 ....; **h** Other ....; Total ▶	24i	
25	**Total** payments (add lines 24c through 24e, and 24i) ▶	25	
26	**Penalty** for underpayment of estimated tax (see instructions)	26	
27	If the total of lines 23 and 26 is larger than line 25, enter **TAX DUE**	27	
28	If line 25 is larger than the total of lines 23 and 26, enter **OVERPAYMENT**	28	
29	Amount of line 28 to be: **a Credited to 1992 estimated tax ▶** ; **b Refunded ▶**	29	

Please Sign Here

Under penalties of perjury, I declare that I have examined this return, including accompanying schedules and statements, and to the best of my knowledge and belief, it is true, correct, and complete. Declaration of preparer (other than fiduciary) is based on all information of which preparer has any knowledge.

▶ Signature of fiduciary or officer representing fiduciary | Date | ▶ EIN of fiduciary (see instructions)

Paid Preparer's Use Only

Preparer's signature ▶ | Date | Check if self-employed ▶ ☐ | **Preparer's social security no.**

Firm's name (or yours if self-employed) and address ▶ | E.I. No. ▶ | ZIP code ▶

For Paperwork Reduction Act Notice, see page 1 of the separate instructions. Cat. No. 11370H Form **1041** (1991)

13

FIGURE 13-4
Internal Revenue Service Form 1041

This form must be filed with the IRS when an estate's annual income amounts to $600 or more.

Valerie's death, the IRS will estimate the royalties that heirs can expect to receive in the future. This amount must be reported on Line 8 of the estate income tax return (Form 1041), and the full tax must be paid when the return is filed, even though the actual royalty income will not be received by the heirs until years later.

Exemptions and Deductions

An estate is allowed an exemption of $600 in computing its taxable income. No exemption for dependents is allowed to an estate. Deductions for gifts to charity are allowed only if a specific provision for such gifts is contained in the decedent's will. Generally, an estate can claim a deduction for a loss that it sustains from the sale of property. Losses incurred for casualty and theft during the administration of the estate can be deducted only if they have not been claimed on the federal estate tax return (Form 706).

Expenses of administering an estate can be deducted either from the gross estate in figuring the federal estate tax (Form 706) (see figure 13-5) or from the estate's gross income in figuring the estate's income tax (Form 1041). However, to prevent a double deduction, these expenses cannot be claimed for both estate tax and income tax purposes.

13.4 ESTATE TAX RETURN

The federal estate tax applies to the transfer of property at death. The estate of a person who died is liable for the tax on the entire taxable estate. However, the beneficiaries of the estate may have to pay the tax if the estate does not pay it when it is due. Each beneficiary's liability is limited to the value of the part of the estate that he or she received.

A federal estate tax return must be filed if the gross estate is more than $600,000. If a return must be filed, IRS *Form 706* (United States Estate Tax Return) is used. The return is due, and the tax must be paid, within nine months after the date of death, unless an extension of time for filing has been granted. A reasonable extension may be granted if it is impossible or impractical for the return to be completed within nine months after the date of death; however, the extension is usually not for more than six months.

THE COMING ESTATE TAX BOOM

The largest transfer of wealth in American history will occur over the next 20 years, when "baby boomers"—people born between 1946 and 1964—inherit the assets of their parents. The estimated $8 trillion in cash and other assets that will change hands results from the meteoric rise in the stock market, in the value of real estate bought during the 1950s and 1960s, and in the number of family-owned enterprises. Among the largest recipients in this exchange of wealth will be federal and state governments, which will likely receive half of that $8 trillion in estate taxes.

Form **706** (Rev. October 1991) Department of the Treasury Internal Revenue Service

United States Estate (and Generation-Skipping Transfer) Tax Return

Estate of a citizen or resident of the United States (see separate instructions). To be filed for decedents dying after October 8, 1990, and before January 1, 1993. For Paperwork Reduction Act Notice, see page 1 of the instructions.

OMB No. 1545-0015 Expires 6-30-93

Part 1.—Decedent and Executor

1a Decedent's first name and middle initial (and maiden name, if any) | 1b Decedent's last name | 2 Decedent's social security no.

3a Domicile at time of death (county and state, or foreign country) | 3b Year domicile established | 4 Date of birth | 5 Date of death

6a Name of executor (see instructions) | 6b Executor's address (number and street including apartment or suite no. or rural route; city, town, or post office; state; and ZIP code)

6c Executor's social security number (see instructions)

7a Name and location of court where will was probated or estate administered | 7b Case number

8 If decedent died testate, check here ▶ ☐ and attach a certified copy of the will. | 9 If Form 4768 is attached, check here ▶ ☐

10 If Schedule R-1 is attached, check here ▶ ☐

Part 2.—Tax Computation

1	Total gross estate (from Part 5, Recapitulation, page 3, item 10)	1	
2	Total allowable deductions (from Part 5, Recapitulation, page 3, item 20)	2	
3	Taxable estate (subtract line 2 from line 1)	3	
4	Adjusted taxable gifts (total taxable gifts (within the meaning of section 2503) made by the decedent after December 31, 1976, other than gifts that are includible in decedent's gross estate (section 2001(b))	4	
5	Add lines 3 and 4	5	
6	Tentative tax on the amount on line 5 from Table A in the instructions	6	
7a	If line 5 exceeds $10,000,000, enter the lesser of line 5 or $21,040,000. If line 5 is $10,000,000 or less, skip lines 7a and 7b and enter -0- on line 7c	7a	
b	Subtract $10,000,000 from line 7a	7b	
c	Enter 5% (.05) of line 7b	7c	
8	Total tentative tax (add lines 6 and 7c)	8	
9	Total gift tax payable with respect to gifts made by the decedent after December 31, 1976. Include gift taxes by the decedent's spouse for such spouse's share of split gifts (section 2513) only if the decedent was the donor of these gifts and they are includible in the decedent's gross estate (see instructions)	9	
10	Gross estate tax (subtract line 9 from line 8)	10	
11	Maximum unified credit against estate tax	11	192,800 00
12	Adjustment to unified credit. (This adjustment may not exceed $6,000. See instructions.)	12	
13	Allowable unified credit (subtract line 12 from line 11)	13	
14	Subtract line 13 from line 10 (but do not enter less than zero)	14	
15	Credit for state death taxes. Do not enter more than line 14. Compute the credit by using the amount on line 3 less $60,000. See Table B in the instructions and **attach credit evidence** (see instructions)	15	
16	Subtract line 15 from line 14	16	
17	Credit for Federal gift taxes on pre-1977 gifts (section 2012) (attach computation)	17	
18	Credit for foreign death taxes (from Schedule(s) P). (Attach Form(s) 706CE)	18	
19	Credit for tax on prior transfers (from Schedule Q)	19	
20	Total (add lines 17, 18, and 19)	20	
21	Net estate tax (subtract line 20 from line 16)	21	
22	Generation-skipping transfer taxes (from Schedule R, Part 2, line 10)	22	
23	Section 4980A increased estate tax (from Schedule S, Part I, line 17) (see instructions)	23	
24	Total transfer taxes (add lines 21, 22, and 23)	24	
25	Prior payments. Explain in an attached statement	25	
26	United States Treasury bonds redeemed in payment of estate tax	26	
27	Total (add lines 25 and 26)	27	
28	Balance due (or overpayment) (subtract line 27 from line 24)	28	

Under penalties of perjury, I declare that I have examined this return, including accompanying schedules and statements, and to the best of my knowledge and belief, it is true, correct, and complete. Declaration of preparer other than the executor is based on all information of which preparer has any knowledge.

Signature(s) of executor(s) — Date

Signature of preparer other than executor — Address (and ZIP code) — Date

Cat. No. 20548R

FIGURE 13-5
Internal Revenue Service Form 706

This form must be filed with the IRS when the gross estate is more than $600,000. See appendix E of this text for the complete Form 706.

The Gross Estate

One of the first steps required in preparing an estate tax return is to determine the decedent's gross estate. The **gross estate** is all of the property owned by a decedent that is subject to the federal estate tax. It includes individually owned property, jointly owned property, property held in trust, life insurance, pensions and annuities, and certain gifts made over the decedent's lifetime. As a general rule, all property that the decedent had the right to use and enjoy or over which the decedent had control will be part of the decedent's gross estate. Form 706 has a separate schedule to list each type of property that is included in the gross estate. (See appendix E.)

Valuation. Generally, the value of the decedent's property interest for estate tax purposes is its fair market value at the date of death. The **fair market value** is the price that a willing buyer would pay a willing seller when neither is under pressure to buy or sell and both have knowledge of the relevant facts. The personal representative may elect to use the **alternate valuation method**, which allows property to be valued as of six months after the date of death. The purpose of the alternate valuation method is to permit a reduction of the tax liability if the total value of the estate's property has decreased since the date of death. The election applies to all of the property in the estate and cannot be used for only part of the property.

Real Estate. All real estate owned solely by the decedent is reported on Schedule A. The decedent's community property interest in real estate and any real estate the decedent contracted to buy should be reported. Each parcel of real estate must be described on the return in sufficient detail so that the IRS can inspect the property to determine its value. An appraisal by a competent appraiser is often necessary to determine the fair market value of the property.

If any interest in real property is subject to a mortgage for which the estate is liable, the full value of the property must still be listed. The mortgage indebtedness will be listed on Schedule K (described later) and subtracted from the gross estate.

Stocks and Bonds. All of the decedent's individually owned stocks and bonds are reported on Schedule B. Stocks must be listed in detail, including the number of shares, whether common or preferred, the issue, the par value, the price per share, the exact name of the corporation, the principal exchange upon which the stock is sold, and the CUSIP number if available. The **CUSIP** (*Committee on Uniform Security Identification Procedure*) **number** is a nine-digit number that is assigned to all stocks and bonds traded on major exchanges and many unlisted securities. Usually, the number is printed on the face of the stock certificate. Bonds must indicate the quantity and denomination, name of obligor, date of maturity, interest rate, interest due date, principal exchange, and CUSIP number.

The fair market value of the stocks and bonds must be listed. The fair market value is the mean between the highest and lowest selling prices quoted on the valuation date. For example, suppose a person dies owning 100 shares of American Telephone & Telegraph stock, and the executor of the estate decides to use the date-of-death valuation. Suppose further that

LEGAL TERMS

gross estate
All property owned by a decedent that is subject to the federal estate tax. It includes individually owned property, jointly owned property, property held in trust, life insurance, pensions and annuities, and certain gifts made over the decedent's lifetime.

fair market value
Price at which property would change hands between a willing buyer and a willing seller if neither one is under any compulsion to buy or sell and if both have reasonable knowledge of all relevant facts.

alternate valuation method
Method that allows property to be valued as of a date other than the date of death for estate tax purposes.

CUSIP number (Committee on Uniform Security Identification Procedure)
Nine-digit number assigned to all stocks and bonds traded on major exchanges and many unlisted securities.

the highest selling price of AT&T for the date of death was 38⅞ and the lowest selling price for that day was 37⅛. The fair market value would be 38 (38⅞ + 37⅛ = 76 ÷ 2 = 38). Selling prices for most stocks can be obtained from the stock quotations listed in the newspaper.

Mortgages, Notes, and Cash. All of the decedent's individually owned interests in mortgages, notes, bank accounts, and cash are reported on Schedule C. This includes cash on hand and in safe deposit boxes, cash in banks, mortgages and notes owed to the decedent, and contracts made by the decedent to sell (but not to buy) real estate.

Bank accounts must be listed in detail, including the name and address of the bank, the account number, the amount, and the nature of the account, such as checking, savings, or time deposit.

Insurance on Decedent's Life. Insurance on the decedent's life is reported on Schedule D. Insurance must be listed if the proceeds are receivable by or for the benefit of the decedent's estate or the decedent possessed any incident of ownership in the policy. **Incidents of ownership** include the power to change the beneficiary, to surrender or cancel the policy, to assign the policy, to revoke an assignment, to pledge the policy for a loan, or to obtain a loan against the policy's cash surrender value. The *Perry* case illustrates this definition.

ESTATE OF PERRY V. COMMISSIONER
927 F.2d 209 (5th Cir. 1991)

FACTS: Less than a year before he died of gunshot wounds sustained in a hunting accident, Frank Perry filled out applications for two life insurance policies with face amounts totaling $600,000. Perry paid the premiums that were due on the policies before his death. Perry's sons were designated as the owners and beneficiaries of both policies. Following Perry's death, the proceeds of both policies were paid in lump sums to Perry's sons. The proceeds were not included in the gross estate on the decedent's federal estate tax return.

LEGAL ISSUE: Must the proceeds of life insurance policies in which the decedent had no incidents of ownership, but for which the decedent paid the premiums, be included in the decedent's gross estate for federal estate tax purposes?

COURT DECISION: No.

REASON: The proceeds were not includable in the decedent's gross estate because the decedent possessed no incidents of ownership in the insurance policies. The policies and all incidents of ownership were owned from their inception by the decedent's sons.

For every policy of life insurance listed on the schedule, a statement on *Form 712* (Life Insurance Statement) must be obtained from the insurance company that issued the policy. The forms must be attached to Schedule D of the return.

Jointly Owned Property. All property, of whatever kind or character, in which the decedent held an interest, either as a joint tenant with the right of survivorship or as a tenant by the entirety, must be entered on Schedule E. Although all joint property must be reported, only one-half of property held jointly with the surviving spouse is includable in the decedent's gross estate— the other half is excludable as belonging to the surviving spouse. The entire value of property the decedent held jointly with anyone except the surviving spouse is presumed to be includable in the gross estate. However, this presumption can be rebutted by an affidavit showing that the other joint owner furnished some of the purchase price, or that the property was acquired by the decedent and the other joint owner by gift, bequest, devise or inheritance from a third person.

Other Miscellaneous Property. All items that must be included in the gross estate that are not reported on any other schedule are reported on Schedule F. Items to be reported include household effects, clothing, automobiles, boats, aircraft, jewelry, antiques, objects of art, collections, accrued salary, vacation pay and bonuses due the decedent, individual proprietorships and business ventures, professional practices, farm machinery, livestock and growing crops, partnership interests, patents and copyrights, insurance on the life of another, remainders and reversionary interests, interests in other estates and trusts, unsecured debts due the decedent, claims due the decedent, royalties, judgments, and uncashed checks payable to the decedent.

LEGAL TERMS

incidents of ownership
Indications of ownership of life insurance, such as the power to change the beneficiary, surrender or cancel the policy, assign the policy, revoke an assignment, pledge the policy for a loan, or obtain a loan against the policy's cash surrender value.

Transfers During Decedent's Life. Transfers made during the decedent's life are reported on Schedule G. These include transfers in which the decedent reserved a life estate to the property itself or to its income. These also include transfers over which the decedent reserved the right to designate who shall possess or enjoy the property or its income.

The types of transfers reportable on this schedule include transfers of an interest in a life insurance policy made within three years before death, gift taxes paid within three years before death, assets contained in a revocable trust, assets contained in a Totten trust, assets held by the decedent under the Uniform Gifts to Minors Act if the decedent was also the donor, and transfers made by the decedent in which the decedent had the power to determine who will receive the property transferred.

Powers of Appointment. The value of property over which the decedent possessed, exercised, or released certain powers of appointment must be reported on Schedule H. A **power of appointment** is a right created in a will, trust, or other instrument which allows the holder to direct the disposition of property. The term **general power of appointment**, with some limitations, means a power that can be exercised in favor of the decedent, the decedent's estate, the decedent's creditors, or the creditors of the decedent's estate.

Annuities. The value of any annuity receivable by a beneficiary because of the decedent's death, under which the decedent had certain rights, must be reported on Schedule I. An **annuity** is a right to receive fixed, periodic payments either for life or for a term of years. For tax purposes, the term includes one or more payments extending over any period of time. Typical annuities are those under employer-sponsored plans. Also included are payments to a beneficiary under an individual retirement account (IRA).

The Taxable Estate

After the gross estate is computed, certain items are deducted to reach the amount of the estate that is taxable. The **taxable estate** is the gross estate minus administration and funeral expenses, claims against the estate, outstanding obligations, casualty and theft losses, the marital deduction, and the charitable deduction.

Administration and Funeral Expenses. The estate is entitled to deduct administration and funeral expenses on Schedule J. Administration expenses include personal representative's commissions, attorney's fees, court filing fees, appraisal fees, accountant's fees, and expenses for collecting, protecting, maintaining, and selling assets. Funeral expenses include funeral director's charges; monument, mausoleum, and burial charges; perpetual care payments;

LEGAL TERMS

power of appointment
Right created in a will, trust, or other instrument that allows the holder to direct the disposition of property.

general power of appointment
Power of appointment that gives the donee the right to appoint the property to any appointee he or she desires, including the donee or the donee's estate.

cost of transporting the body to the place of burial; and payments to clergy officiating at the funeral.

Claims Against the Estate. All enforceable personal obligations of the decedent at the time of death may be deducted as claims against the estate on Schedule K. These claims include such things as medical expenses, outstanding tax bills, unpaid mortgages, utility bills, credit card bills, and other obligations that were due at the time of death.

Casualty and Theft Losses. Losses from thefts, fires, storms, shipwrecks, or other casualties that occurred during the settlement of the estate are deductible on Schedule L. They are deductible only to the extent that the losses are not compensated for by insurance or by someone who caused the loss.

Marital Deduction. The **marital deduction** is a deduction from the gross estate of the value of property that passes to a surviving spouse. All property passing to a surviving spouse qualifies for the marital deduction and is reported on Schedule M. Included in this category are such things as outright bequests and devises to the surviving spouse, life insurance proceeds in

annuity
Right to receive fixed, periodic payments either for life or for a term of years.

taxable estate
Under federal estate tax law, the gross estate minus administration and funeral expenses, claims against the estate, outstanding obligations, casualty and theft losses, the marital deduction, and the charitable deduction.

marital deduction
Under federal estate tax law, property passing from a decedent to a surviving spouse. It is not taxable.

A BROADWAY LEGACY

Books and Lyrics by
ALAN JAY LERNER

"What's Up"—1943
"The Day Before Spring"—1945
"Brigadoon"—1947
"Love Life"—1948
"Paint Your Wagon"—1951
"My Fair Lady"—1956
"Gigi"—1958
"Camelot"—1960
"On a Clear Day You Can See Forever"—1965
"Coco"—1969
"1600 Pennsylvania Avenue"—1976
"Carmelina"—1979

Alan Jay Lerner, prolific lyricist and playwright, collaborated with the composer Frederick Loewe to make musical theater history. Both men quickly amassed fortunes from the proceeds of the shows as well as film and recording rights. Despite his prosperity, however, Lerner experienced financial difficulties as a result of seven divorce settlements and his extravagant lifestyle. When Lerner died in June 1986, the IRS was still trying to recover $1.4 million in back taxes and penalties.

which the spouse was the beneficiary, and property owned jointly with the surviving spouse. Marital deduction trusts, including credit-shelter trusts and QTIP trusts (discussed in chapter 7), are commonly used devices to reduce estate taxes.

Charitable Deduction. A deduction is allowed on Schedule O for the value of property in the gross estate that the decedent transfers to a public or charitable organization. To qualify, charitable organizations must be organized and operated exclusively for religious, charitable, scientific, literary, or educational purposes. In addition to legacies given to charitable organizations, charitable remainder annuity trusts and unitrusts (discussed in chapter 7) are popular estate planning devices to reduce estate taxes. However, "split-interest" bequests (i.e., bequests of the same property to both charitable and noncharitable beneficiaries, without distinguishing the amount to each) cannot be deducted as a gift to charity.

Estate Tax Computation

The estate tax computation begins by subtracting the various deductions from the gross estate to yield the taxable estate previously discussed. Then the value of all taxable gifts that were made while the decedent was alive after 1976 are added to the taxable estate.

Taxable Gifts. A federal gift tax is imposed on the gratuitous transfer of property. Usually, the **donor** (the person making the gift) must pay the tax; however, if he or she does not pay it, the **donee** (the person receiving the gift) may have to pay the gift tax. In 1976, the federal government unified—that is, combined—the estate tax with the gift tax, making them one tax. With the exception of a $10,000 ($20,000 for a husband and wife) per donee per year exclusion, the federal government taxes all gifts made during one's lifetime as part of the estate tax. The *Dillingham* case addresses the issue of gifts.

LEGAL TERMS

donor
Person who makes a gift; person who establishes a trust (also called settlor, trustor, and grantor); person who creates a power of appointment.

DILLINGHAM V. COMMISSIONER
Nos. 89-9003, 89-9004 (10th Cir. May 14, 1990)

FACTS: On December 24, 1980, Elizabeth Dillingham delivered six checks to various people, each in the amount of $3,000. [In that year, the annual exclusion for gift-tax purposes was $3,000 per donee. Since then, the annual exclusion per donee has increased to $10,000.] The checks were presented to the bank for payment on January 28, 1981, and paid. That same day, January 28, 1981, Dillingham delivered six additional $3,000 checks to the same donees. These checks were paid by the bank on the day they were drawn. Dillingham died on June 7, 1981.

LEGAL ISSUE: For gift-tax purposes, do checks drawn in one year and paid the next year constitute a gift made during the year in which they are drawn?

COURT DECISION: No.

REASON: Checks drawn in one year and paid the next year constitute a gift made during the year in which they are paid by the bank. Under U.S. Treasury regulations, a gift is complete when the donor has so parted with dominion and control over the property as to leave in the donor no power to change its disposition. "A gift is incomplete when a donor reserves the power to revest the beneficial title to the property in himself." Under Oklahoma law [where this case occurred], absent consideration from the payee to the drawer of a check, a stop-payment order by the drawer operates to extinguish liability of the drawer to the payee. Thus, under Oklahoma law, the decedent retained the power to stop payment and thereby defeat the claims of the donees from the time the checks were delivered in 1980 until they were cashed in 1981. Accordingly, the decedent retained dominion and control over the checks during 1980.

Each year, the total of all gifts over and above the exclusion must be reported to the IRS on *Form 709* (United States Gift Tax Return) (see figure 13-6). This return is used mainly to provide information to the IRS; however, if a tax is shown to be due, it must be paid when the gift tax return is filed.

donee
Person who receives a gift; one who has the right to exercise a power of appointment.

gross estate tax
Tentative estate tax computed by applying the unified rate schedule to the sum of the taxable estate and all taxable gifts.

Credits Against the Tax. A tentative tax, called the **gross estate tax**, is computed by applying the unified rate schedule (see table 13-1) to the sum of the taxable estate and all taxable gifts. The following credits are then deducted from the gross estate tax:

United States Gift (and Generation-Skipping Transfer) Tax Return (IRS Form 709)

Form **709** (Rev. December 1988) Department of the Treasury Internal Revenue Service

United States Gift (and Generation-Skipping Transfer) Tax Return

(Section 6019 of the Internal Revenue Code) (For gifts made after December 31, 1986, and before January 1, 1990)

Calendar year 19 ____

▶ **For Privacy Act Notice, see the Instructions for Form 1040.**

OMB No. 1545-0020 Expires 10-31-91

Part 1.—General Information

1 Donor's first name and middle initial	2 Donor's last name	3 Social security number
4 Address (number and street)		5 Domicile
6 City, state, and ZIP code		7 Citizenship

	Yes	No
8 If the donor died during the year, check here ▶ ☐ and enter date of death ______________, 19 ____		
9 If you received an extension of time to file this Form 709, check here ▶☐ and attach the Form 4868, 2688, 2350, or extension letter.		
10 If you (the donor) filed a previous Form 709 (or 709-A), has your address changed since the last Form 709 (or 709-A) was filed?		
11 Gifts by husband or wife to third parties.—Do you consent to have the gifts (including generation-skipping transfers) made by you and by your spouse to third parties during the calendar year considered as made one-half by each of you? (See instructions.) (If the answer is "Yes," the following information must be furnished and your spouse is to sign the consent shown below. If the answer is "No," skip lines 12–17 and go to Schedule A.)		
12 Name of consenting spouse — 13 SSN		
14 Were you married to one another during the entire calendar year? (See instructions.)		
15 If the answer to 14 is "No," check whether ☐ married ☐ divorced or ☐ widowed, and give date (see instructions) ▶		
16 Will a gift tax return for this calendar year be filed by your spouse?		

17 **Consent of Spouse**—I consent to have the gifts (and generation-skipping transfers) made by me and by my spouse to third parties during the calendar year considered as made one-half by each of us. We are both aware of the joint and several liability for tax created by the execution of this consent.

Consenting spouse's signature ▶ **Date** ▶

Part 2.—Tax Computation

1 Enter the amount from Schedule A, Part 3, line 15	1	
2 Enter the amount from Schedule B, line 3	2	
3 Total taxable gifts (add lines 1 and 2)	3	
4 Tax computed on amount on line 3 (see Table for Computing Tax in separate instructions)	4	
Note: *If you are reporting gifts made before January 1, 1988, see instructions.*		
5a Enter the lesser of line 3 or $21,040,000 — 5a		
b Subtract $10,000,000 from line 5a (do not enter less than zero) — 5b		
c Enter 5% (.05) of line 5b	5c	
6 Total tentative tax on the amount on line 3 (add lines 4 and 5c)	6	
7 Tax computed on amount on line 2 (see Table for Computing Tax in separate instructions)	7	
8a Enter the lesser of line 2 or $21,040,000 — 8a		
b Subtract $10,000,000 from line 8a (do not enter less than zero) — 8b		
c Enter 5% (.05) of line 8b	8c	
9 Total tentative tax on the amount on line 2 (add lines 7 and 8c)	9	
10 Balance (subtract line 9 from line 6)	10	
11 Maximum unified credit (nonresident aliens, see instructions)	11	192,800 00
12 Enter the unified credit against tax allowable for all prior periods (from Sch. B, line 1, col. C)	12	
13 Balance (subtract line 12 from line 11)	13	
14 Enter 20% (.20) of the amount allowed as a specific exemption for gifts made after September 8, 1976, and before January 1, 1977 (see instructions)	14	
15 Balance (subtract line 14 from line 13)	15	
16 Unified credit (enter the smaller of line 10 or line 15)	16	
17 Credit for foreign gift taxes (see instructions)	17	
18 Total credits (add lines 16 and 17)	18	
19 Balance (subtract line 18 from line 10) (do not enter less than zero)	19	
20 Generation-skipping transfer taxes (from Schedule C, Part 4, col. H, total)	20	
21 Total tax (add lines 19 and 20)	21	
22 Gift and generation-skipping transfer taxes prepaid with extension of time to file	22	
23 If line 22 is less than line 21, enter BALANCE DUE (see instructions)	23	
24 If line 22 is greater than line 21, enter AMOUNT TO BE REFUNDED	24	

Please attach check or money order here

Under penalties of perjury, I declare that I have examined this return, including any accompanying schedules and statements, and to the best of my knowledge and belief it is true, correct, and complete. Declaration of preparer (other than donor) is based on all information of which preparer has any knowledge.

Donor's signature ▶ Date ▶

Preparer's signature (other than donor) ▶ Date ▶

Preparer's address (other than donor) ▶

FIGURE 13-6 Internal Revenue Service Form 709

1. A unified credit in the amount of $192,800
2. State death taxes, up to a certain limit, paid by the estate
3. Any gift taxes paid before 1976 on gifts that are included in the gross estate
4. Taxes paid on certain prior transfers
5. Foreign death taxes paid by the estate.

Form 709 (Rev. 12-88) Page 2

SCHEDULE A Computation of Taxable Gifts

Part 1.—Gifts Subject Only to Gift Tax. *Gifts less political organization, medical, and educational exclusions—see instructions*

A Item number	B Donee's name and address and description of gift. If the gift was made by means of a trust, enter trust's identifying number below and attach a copy of the trust instrument. If the gift was securities, enter the CUSIP number(s), if available.	C Donor's adjusted basis of gift	D Date of gift	E Value at date of gift
1				

Part 2.—Gifts Subject to Both Gift Tax and Generation-Skipping Transfer Tax. You must list the gifts in chronological order. *Gifts less political organization, medical, and educational exclusions—see instructions*

A Item number	B Donee's name and address and description of gift. If the gift was made by means of a trust, enter trust's identifying number below and attach a copy of the trust instrument. If the gift was securities, enter the CUSIP number(s), if available.	C Donor's adjusted basis of gift	D Date of gift	E Value at date of gift
1				

Part 3.—Gift Tax Reconciliation

1 Total value of gifts of donor (add column E of Parts 1 and 2) . . . 1
2 One-half of items ________ attributable to spouse (see instructions) 2
3 Balance (subtract line 2 from line 1) . . . 3
4 Gifts of spouse to be included (from Schedule A, Part 3, line 2 of spouse's return—see instructions) . 4
If any of the gifts included on this line are also subject to the generation-skipping transfer tax, check here ▶ ☐ and enter those gifts also on Schedule C, Part 1.
5 Total gifts (add lines 3 and 4) . . . 5
6 Total annual exclusions for gifts listed on Schedule A (including line 4, above) (see instructions) . . 6
7 Total included amount of gifts (subtract line 6 from line 5) . . . 7

Deductions (see instructions)

8 Gifts of interests to spouse for which a marital deduction will be claimed, based on items ________ of Schedule A . . . 8
9 Exclusions attributable to gifts on line 8 . . . 9
10 Marital deduction—subtract line 9 from line 8 . . . 10
11 Charitable deduction, based on items ________ to ________ less exclusions . 11
12 Total deductions—add lines 10 and 11 . . . 12
13 Subtract line 12 from line 7 . . . 13
14 Generation-skipping transfer taxes payable with this Form 709 (from Schedule C, Part 4, col. H, Total) 14
15 Taxable gifts (add lines 13 and 14). Enter here and on line 1 of the Tax Computation on page 1 . . . 15

(If more space is needed, attach additional sheets of same size.)

FIGURE 13-6
(Continued)

The **net estate tax** is the amount of tax that must be paid to the government. This amount is determined by deducting the credits mentioned here from the gross estate tax.

LEGAL TERMS

net estate tax
Amount of estate tax that must be paid to the government; determined by deducting certain allowable credits, including a unified credit of $192,000, from the gross estate tax.

Example of Estate Tax Computation. Agnes Outreach, a widow, died in 1991, leaving the following individually owned property: real estate valued at $180,000, tangible personal property valued at $35,000, and bank accounts

Form 709 (Rev. 12-88) Page 3

SCHEDULE A **Computation of Taxable Gifts** (continued)

16 Terminable Interest (QTIP) Marital Deduction. (See instructions.)

☐ ◄ Check here if you elected, under the rules of section 2523(f), to include gifts of qualified terminable interest property on line 8, on page 2. Enter the item numbers (from Schedule A) of the gifts for which you made this election ► ....

SCHEDULE B **Gifts From Prior Periods**

Did you (the donor) file gift tax returns for prior periods? (If "Yes," see instructions for completing Schedule B below.) ☐ Yes ☐ No

A Calendar year or calendar quarter (see instructions)	B Internal Revenue office where prior return was filed	C Amount of unified credit against gift tax for periods after December 31, 1976	D Amount of specific exemption for prior periods ending before January 1, 1977	E Amount of taxable gifts

1 Totals for prior periods (without adjustment for reduced specific exemption) 1

2 Amount, if any, by which total specific exemption, line 1, column D, is more than $30,000 2

3 Total amount of taxable gifts for prior periods (add amount, column E, line 1, and amount, if any, on line 2). (Enter here and on line 2 of the Tax Computation on page 1.) 3

SCHEDULE C **Computation of Generation-Skipping Transfer Tax**

Note: *Inter vivos direct skips which are completely excluded by the grandchild exclusion and/or the GST exemption must still be fully reported (including value and exclusions and exemptions claimed) on Schedule C.*

Part 1.—Generation-Skipping Transfers

A Item No. (from Schedule A, Part 2, col. A)	B Value (from Schedule A, Part 2, col. E)	C Split Gifts (enter ½ of col. B) (see instructions)	D Subtract col. C from col. B	E Annual Exclusion Claimed	F Subtract col. E from col. D	G Grandchild Exclusion Claimed	H Net Transfer (subtract col. G from col. F)
1							
2							
3							
4							
5							
6							
7							
8							
If you elected gift splitting and your spouse was required to file a separate Form 709 (see the instructions for "Split Gifts"), you must enter all of the gifts shown on Schedule A, Part 2, of your spouse's Form 709 here. In column C, enter the item number of each gift in the order it appears in column A of your spouse's Schedule A, Part 2. We have preprinted the prefix "S-" to distinguish your spouse's item numbers from your own when you complete column A of Schedule C, Part 4. In column D, for each gift, enter the amount reported in column C, Schedule C, Part 1, of your spouse's Form 709.		Split gifts from spouse's Form 709 (enter item number)	Value included from spouse's Form 709				
		S-					
		S-					
		S-					
		S-					
		S-					
		S-					
		S-					
		S-					
		Total grandchild exclusions claimed on this return. Must equal total of column D, Schedule C, Part 2					

(If more space is needed, attach additional sheets of same size)

FIGURE 13-6
(Continued)

totaling $75,000. She owned several bank accounts and stock certificates (to which Agnes had contributed the entire amount, totaling $800,000) jointly with her daughter, Bertha. She owned a life insurance policy with a face value of $5,000 on which her daughter, Bertha, was named beneficiary. Claims against Agnes's estate for medical bills not covered by insurance and other outstanding bills when she died totaled $65,000. Administration expenses in settling her estate came to $85,000. Her funeral expenses were $6,000. Agnes had made taxable gifts before 1976 while she was alive

Form 709 (Rev. 12-88) Page 4

SCHEDULE C Computation of Generation-Skipping Transfer Tax (continued)

Part 2.—Grandchild Exclusion Reconciliation

Name of Grandchild	A Maximum Allowable Exclusion	B Total of Exclusions Claimed on Previous Returns	C Exclusion Available for This Return (subtract col. B from col. A)	D Exclusion Claimed on this Return	E Exclusion Available for Future Returns (subtract col. D from col. C)
	$2,000,000				
	$2,000,000				
	$2,000,000				
	$2,000,000				
	$2,000,000				
	$2,000,000				
	$2,000,000				
	$2,000,000				
Total grandchild exclusions claimed on this return. Must equal total of column G, Part 1					

Part 3.—GST Exemption Reconciliation (Code section 2631)

1	Maximum allowable exemption	1	$1,000,000
2	Total exemption used for periods before filing this return	2	
3	Exemption available for this return (subtract line 2 from line 1)	3	
4	Exemption claimed on this return (from Part 4, col. C total, below)	4	
5	Exemption allocated to transfers not shown on Part 4, below. You must attach a Notice of Allocation. (See instructions.)	5	
6	Add lines 4 and 5	6	
7	Exemption available for future transfers (subtract line 6 from line 3)	7	

Part 4.—Tax Computation

A Item No. (from Schedule C, Part 1)	B Net transfer (from Schedule C, Part 1, col. H)	C GST Exemption Allocated	D Divide col. C by col. B	E Inclusion Ratio (subtract col. D from 1.000)	F Maximum Gift Tax Rate	G Applicable Rate (multiply col. E by col. F)	H Generation-Skipping Transfer Tax (multiply col. B by col. G)
1					55% (.55)		
2					55% (.55)		
3					55% (.55)		
4					55% (.55)		
5					55% (.55)		
6					55% (.55)		
7					55% (.55)		
8					55% (.55)		
					55% (.55)		
					55% (.55)		
					55% (.55)		
					55% (.55)		
					55% (.55)		
					55% (.55)		
					55% (.55)		
					55% (.55)		
Total exemption claimed. Enter here and on line 4, Part 3, above. May not exceed line 3, Part 3, above			**Total generation-skipping transfer tax.** Enter here, on line 14 of Schedule A, Part 3, and on line 20 of the Tax Computation on page 1				

(If more space is needed, attach additional sheets of same size.)

☆U.S. Government Printing Office: 1989-242-473/80041

FIGURE 13-6
(Continued)

totaling $150,000; however, she had paid no gift taxes on them. Her will left all of her real estate to a church that abutted her property. The executor of her estate paid a state estate tax in the amount of $18,600, which did not exceed the limit that could be deducted from the gross estate tax.

The federal net estate tax on Agnes Outreach's estate would be computed as follows:

Column A Taxable amount over	Column B Taxable amount not over	Column C Tax on amount in column A	Column D Rate of tax on excess over amount in column A
			(Percent)
0	$10,000	0	18
$10,000	20,000	$1,800	20
20,000	40,000	3,800	22
40,000	60,000	8,200	24
60,000	80,000	13,000	26
80,000	100,000	18,200	28
100,000	150,000	23,800	30
150,000	250,000	38,800	32
250,000	500,000	70,800	34
500,000	750,000	155,800	37
750,000	1,000,000	248,300	39
1,000,000	1,250,000	345,800	41
1,250,000	1,500,000	448,300	43
1,500,000	2,000,000	555,800	45
2,000,000	2,500,000	780,800	49
2,500,000	3,000,000	1,025,800	53
3,000,000	- - - - - - - -	1,290,800	55

TABLE 13-1
Unified Rate Schedule

This table is used to compute the gross estate tax, from which is deducted the unified credit of $192,800, state death taxes up to a certain limit, and certain other taxes.

Gross Estate:

Real estate	$180,000
Tangible personal property	35,000
Cash in bank accounts	75,000
Jointly owned property	800,000
Life insurance	5,000
Total Gross Estate	$1,095,000

Taxable Estate:

Gross Estate		$1,095,000
Less: Administrative expenses	$85,000	
Funeral expenses	6,000	
Claims against the estate	65,000	
Charitable deduction	180,000	(336,000)
Taxable Estate		$759,000

Gross Estate Tax:

Taxable Estate	$759,000
Plus: Taxable gifts	150,000
Taxable amount	$909,000

Applying the unified rate schedule (Table 13-1), the gross estate tax on $909,000 = $310,310 [$248,300 + (39% × 159,000)].

Net Estate Tax:

Gross Estate Tax		$310,310
Less: Unified credit	$192,800	
State death taxes	18,600	211,400
Net Estate Tax		$ 98,910

Generation-Skipping Transfer Tax

A **generation-skipping transfer tax** is a tax imposed when property exceeding $1 million is transferred to a person who is two or more generations below the donor or decedent, thereby skipping the generation directly below the transferor. For example, a trust established for the benefit of a grandchild, with the trust property passing to the grandchild's estate on the grandchild's death, would be a direct skip and would be subject to this tax. The person receiving the property in a generation-skipping transfer is called a **skip person**. When a generation-skipping transfer occurs, a tax is imposed based on the value of the property transferred. However, there is a $1 million exemption ($2 million for a husband and wife) before the tax applies. The generation-skipping transfer tax is reported on Schedule R of Form 706.

SUMMARY

13.1 State and federal tax returns must sometimes be filed by the personal representative of an estate; among these is an estate tax return. The IRS may be notified of a fiduciary relationship by filing Form 56. An estate "04" number (which replaces the Social Security number) may be obtained by filing Form SS-4.

13.2 The final income tax return must be filed by the personal representative. Only income that was received up to the date of death is included on the final return. Medical expenses paid before death by the decedent are deductible on the final income tax return if deductions are itemized. Form 1310 must be filed with the decedent's final return if a refund is due the decedent.

13.3 An estate's income of $600 or more must be reported to the IRS on Form 1041. Gross income consists of all items of income received or accrued during the tax year. An estate is allowed an exemption deduction of $600. In

LEGAL TERMS

generation-skipping transfer tax
Federal tax imposed when property exceeding $1 million is transferred to a person who is two or more generations below the donor or decedent, thereby skipping the generation directly below the transferor.

skip person
Person receiving the property in a generation-skipping transfer.

addition, an estate can deduct losses from the sale of property, losses incurred for casualty and theft, and expenses of administration.

13.4 A federal estate tax return must be filed within nine months after the date of death if the gross estate is more than $600,000. The gross estate includes individually owned property, jointly owned property, property held in trust, life insurance, pensions and annuities, and certain gifts made over the decedent's lifetime. The taxable estate is the gross estate minus administration and funeral expenses, claims against the estate, outstanding obligations, casualty and theft losses, the marital deduction, and the charitable deduction. The gross estate tax is computed by applying the unified rate schedule to the sum of the taxable estate and all taxable gifts. The net estate tax is computed by deducted the following from the gross estate tax: a unified credit of $192,000, state death taxes up to a certain limit, gift taxes paid before 1976, taxes paid on certain prior transfers, and foreign death taxes.

QUESTIONS FOR REVIEW

1. What three tax returns must often be filed by the personal representative of an estate?
2. For what purpose is an employer identification number used for an estate, and how is one obtained?
3. What income is included in the decedent's final income tax return?
4. How is "income in respect of the decedent" reported to the IRS?
5. How much income must an estate earn before it must be reported to the IRS? On what form is the income reported?
6. On what tax returns may expenses of administering an estate be deducted?
7. On what occasion must a federal estate tax return be filed? What form is used? On what date must the return be filed and the tax paid?
8. What property does the gross estate include?
9. What is the difference between the gross estate and the taxable estate?
10. How is the gross estate tax computed? How is the net estate tax computed?

CASES TO DISCUSS

1. Forrest J. Johnson's will established one trust with three purposes: to support his three sisters; to maintain the Johnson family gravesite; and to create a charitable trust to pay for religious education in certain Catholic parishes. After Johnson's death, money from the trust was set aside for the support of his sisters and $235,398.30 was used to fund a charitable trust, as he had requested. Can the amount in the charitable

trust be used as a deduction on Johnson's estate tax return? Explain. *Estate of Johnson v. United States,* 941 F.2d 1318 (5th Cir. 1991).

2. Before she died, Jennie Owen transferred 251 shares of stock as gifts to 29 different people. The recipients did not know that they were receiving gifts of stock and believed they were merely participating in stock transfers. Each recipient's share was less than $10,000. Upon receiving the stock certificates, the recipients endorsed them over to members of the decedent's family, whose shares exceeded $10,000. Can the gifts of stock be excluded from the decedent's gift tax return? Why or why not? *Heyen v. United States,* 945 F.2d 359 (10th Cir. 1991).

SHARPENING YOUR PROFESSIONAL SKILLS

1. Refer to the law office scenario at the beginning of this chapter and answer the following questions:
   a. What income would be included on Mr. Shulman's final income tax return, assuming that Mr. Shulman died on December 1?
   b. What form will Tiffany use to notify the IRS of the fiduciary relationship?
   c. What form will Tiffany use to obtain an "04" number?
   d. What is the money from the sale of the apples called, and on what return will it be reported?
2. Assume that Mr. Shulman owned 100 shares of Exxon stock and 250 shares of General Electric stock when he died on December 1. The highest selling price for Exxon on that day was 60; the lowest selling price was 57¼. The highest selling price for G.E. on that day was 70⅜; the lowest selling price was 67¼. Calculate the fair market value of all of the stock as of December 1.
3. Assume that Mr. Shulman's gross estate was $950,000. Administration and funeral expenses amounted to $34,000; claims against the estate totaled $9,000; and there was a gift to charity in Mr. Shulman's will for $5,000. Mr. Shulman made taxable gifts while he was alive after 1976 totaling $50,000. He paid no gift taxes while he was alive. His executor paid a state estate tax of $25,000 which did not exceed the limit that could be deducted from the gross estate tax.
   a. What is the amount of the federal taxable estate?
   b. What is the amount of the federal gross estate tax?
   c. What is the amount of the federal net estate tax?

CHAPTER 14
Final Choices

"The most terrible thing is your own judgment."

Robert Frost

OUTLINE

LAW OFFICE SCENARIO

"Good morning, Marie," Attorney Pierce said to Marie Perez, the office paralegal. "I've got a little research project for you to start off the day."

"Fine, I could use something besides coffee to wake me up," Marie replied with a smile.

Attorney Pierce handed Marie a document. "This is an ordinary power of attorney that was on our computer. Will you look up our state statute to see what language we need to add to it to make it a durable power of attorney?"

"Sure," Marie said eagerly. "I think our state has adopted the Uniform Durable Power of Attorney Act, and the language is right in the statute."

"Good. After you've found it, draw up a durable power of attorney for Mr. LaBella. He's mentally sound now, but he's getting along in years and needs to be protected. Here's his file."

"Okay. Who does he want to name as his agent in the durable power of attorney?" Marie asked.

"His daughter," replied Attorney Pierce. "You'll find her name and address in my notes in the file—if you can read them. Oh, and while you're at it, you had better draw up a living will for Mr. LaBella. He mentioned to me that if he ever went into the hospital, he wouldn't want to be kept alive by artificial means."

"That's a good idea."

"We may have trouble with his daughter, though. She told Mr. LaBella that he has a constitutional right to die and doesn't need a living will."

"I hope he believes you instead of his daughter," Marie responded.

"She also told him he shouldn't sign an anatomical gift card because his body would be disfigured at his funeral and it wouldn't be very pleasant."

"She is certainly uninformed about the details of dying!"

14.1 THE RIGHT TO DIE

Paralegals may have to educate clients about the details of death when discussing the various legal options concerning organ donations and the decision to extend or terminate their lives.

The question of whether a person should have the right to choose a swift, natural death instead of involuntary prolongation has been debated for some time. The dilemma arose when medical technology developed faster than the ethical guidelines for dealing with the effects of that technology. Doctors, health care professionals, judges, lawyers, politicians, clergy, ethicists, and others have grappled with the conflicting issues for many years. In a case decided as long ago as 1976, the New Jersey Supreme Court wrote:

> Medicine, with its combination of advanced technology and professional ethics, is both able and inclined to prolong biological life. Law, with its felt obligation to protect the life and freedom of the individual, seeks to assure each person's right to live out his human life until its natural and inevitable conclusion. Theology, with its acknowledgment of man's dissatisfaction with biological life as the ultimate source of joy . . . , defends the sacredness of human life and defends it from all direct attack.

In re Quinlan, 70 N.J. 10, 355 A.2d 647 (1976).

A body of law has begun to develop which deals with the right of a dying person to refuse extraordinary treatment to prolong life. The cases and statutes emerging from this relatively new body of law are often referred to as **right-to-die laws**.

The United States Supreme Court discussed the question for the first time in 1990 in *Cruzan v. Director, Missouri Department of Health.* Although the case decided a very narrow question of law, it was significant in that the Court answered some important questions about the right to die. The Court recognized the common law right of a competent individual to refuse medical treatment. In addition, the Court stated that the right to refuse medical treatment is found in, and protected by, the "liberty interest" created by the Fourteenth Amendment. The Court also said that the individual's interest must be balanced against the state's interest in protecting and preserving the lives of its citizens. It further stated that incompetent individuals have the same rights as competent ones, but their rights must be exercised by some sort of surrogate decision maker.

LEGAL TERMS

right-to-die laws
Cases and statutes that deal with the right of a dying person to refuse extraordinary treatment to prolong life.

CRUZAN V. DIRECTOR, MISSOURI DEPARTMENT OF HEALTH 110 S. Ct. 2841, 111 L. Ed. 2d 224 (1990)

FACTS: At the age of 25, Nancy Cruzan sustained severe injuries in an automobile accident which left her in a persistent vegetative state. She remained unconscious for nearly five years, nourished by a feeding and hydration tube. Nancy's parents asked the Missouri court for permission to remove their daughter's feeding tube so that she could die as they believed she would want. The lower court approved the request, but on appeal, the Supreme Court of Missouri reversed the lower court's decision. The appeals court said that no person can assume the choice of terminating medical treatment for an incompetent person in the absence of either the formalities required under the living will statute or "clear and convincing, inherently reliable evidence" of the patient's wishes. [See figure 14-1.]

LEGAL ISSUE: Is it constitutional for a state to require that an incompetent's wishes as to the withdrawal of life-sustaining treatment be proven by clear and convincing evidence?

COURT DECISION: Yes.

REASON: A state can assert an unqualified interest in the preservation of human life. It can legitimately seek to safeguard the personal element of the choice between life and death of an incompetent individual through the imposition of heightened evidentiary requirements. A state can also guard against potential abuses in situations in which family members either are unavailable to serve as surrogate decision makers or would not act to protect a patient.

Cruzan case chronology

Here is a chronology of major events in the Nancy Cruzan right-to-die case:

- **Jan. 11, 1983:** Nancy Cruzan, then 25, has a wreck on a country road southeast of Carthage, in the Ozarks of southwest Missouri, and is thrown from the car. Paramedics restart her breathing, but her brain is without oxygen for so long she never regains consciousness.
- **Feb. 5:** Doctors implant a feeding tube in Cruzan's stomach. She is not put on any life support system, such as a respirator.
- **Oct. 23, 1987:** Joe and Joyce Cruzan ask Jasper County Probate Judge Charles Teel for permission to remove their daughter's feeding tube so she can die as they believe she would want.
- **July 27, 1988:** Teel approves the request.
- **Aug. 3:** Missouri Attorney General William Webster files notice that the state will appeal to the state Supreme Court.
- **Nov. 16:** The state Supreme Court votes 4-3 to overturn the lower court. The family appeals to the US Supreme Court.
- **Dec. 6:** The US Supreme Court hears arguments, the first time it has considered a right-to-die case.
- **June 25, 1990:** In a 5-4 decision, the court blocks removal of the tube. It says the state could keep a patient on life support in the absence of "clear and convincing" evidence the person would want to die.
- **Aug. 30:** Cruzan's parents ask Teel for a second hearing, saying they have new evidence their daughter once indicated to three people she would rather die than live in a vegetative state.
- **Nov. 1:** Three former co-workers tell Teel they recalled conversations with Cruzan in which she said she would never want to live "like a vegetable" on medical machines. Cruzan's physician, who previously opposed removing the feeding tube, terms her life "a living hell" and testifies she should be allowed to die.
- **Dec. 5:** Cruzan's court-appointed guardian recommends the tube be removed.
- **Dec. 14:** Teel approves.
- **Dec. 18-24:** State and federal courts reject injunction requests by antieuthanasia groups.
- **Dec. 26:** Nancy Cruzan dies in the Missouri Rehabilitation Center.

FIGURE 14-1
Cruzan case chronology. Reprinted courtesy of the *Boston Globe*

The *Cruzan* case pointed out the need for **advance directives** in which individuals specify, in writing, whether they want life-sustaining medical treatment if they become desperately ill. Following the *Cruzan* case, people nationwide flocked to lawyers and other professionals to prepare living wills, durable powers of attorney, and health care proxies. Such advance directives are important tools for making medical decisions for incompetent patients. These instructions enable a competent person to make certain decisions now regarding future medical treatment when he or she may be incompetent.

The Living Will

A **living will** is a written expression of one's wishes to be allowed to die a natural death and not be kept alive by heroic measures or artificial means. At least 80 percent of the states in the United States have enacted living will laws. (See figure 14-2.) Even in states that have not enacted living will laws, lawyers are sometimes asked to draft living wills for people who wish to have their desires known.

Checklist for Living Will
[22A AM. JUR. 2d § 686]

The following facts and statements are among those that may be set forth in a request that a person not be kept alive by artificial means or heroic measures:

1. The names, addresses, and telephone numbers of the declarant and, if applicable, his or her treating physician, and medical facility where he or she is being cared for.
2. Statement that the declarant is of sound mind.
3. Statement that the declarant willfully and voluntarily desires that his or her life shall not be artificially prolonged at any time should the declarant have an incurable injury, disease, or illness certified to be a terminal condition, where the use or application of artificial, extraordinary, extreme, or radical medical or surgical means or procedures calculated to prolong life could serve only to artificially prolong the moment of death, and where the declarant's physician has determined that death is imminent.
4. Direction by the declarant that, under the circumstances mentioned above, life-sustaining medical procedures be withheld or withdrawn, and that the declarant be permitted to die naturally and with dignity.
5. Statement that, in the absence of the ability of the declarant to give directions regarding the use of life-sustaining procedures, it is the declarant's intention that the directive shall be honored by his or her family and physicians as the final expression of the legal right to refuse medical or surgical treatment and accept the consequences of such refusal.

LEGAL TERMS

advance directives
Written statements in which individuals specify whether they want life-sustaining medical treatment if they become desperately ill.

living will
Written expression of one's wishes to be allowed to die a natural death and not be kept alive by heroic measures or artificial means.

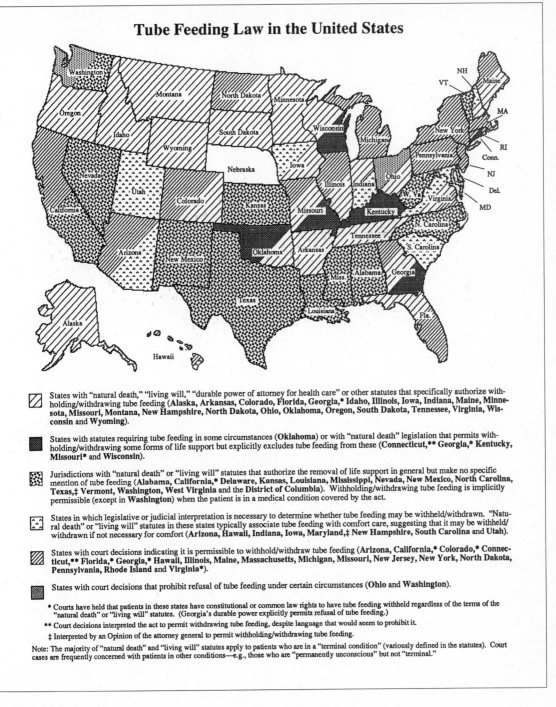

Tube Feeding Law in the United States

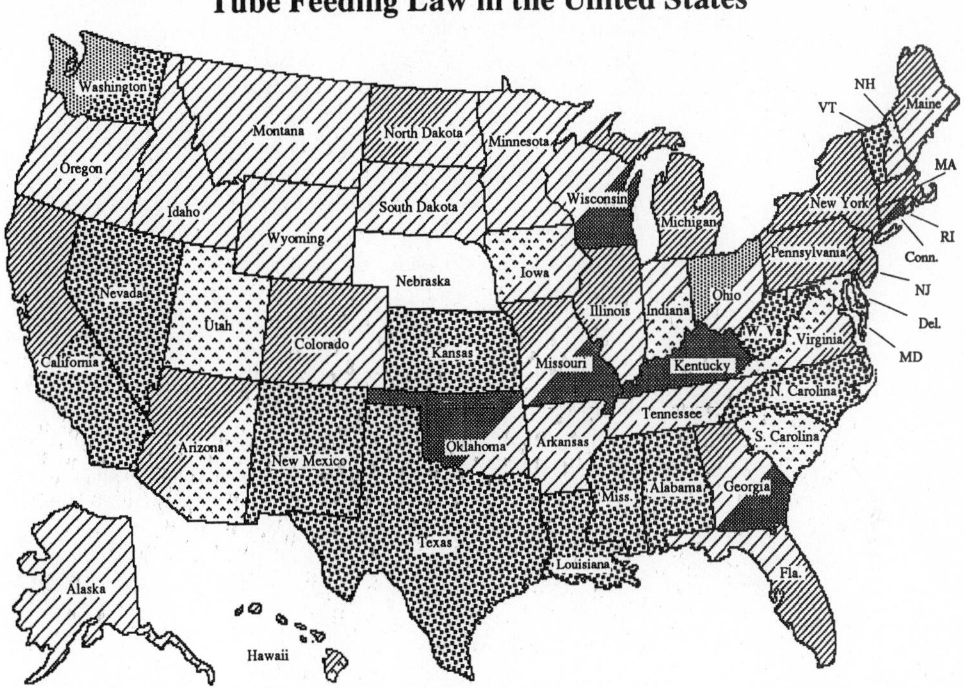

States with "natural death," "living will," "durable power of attorney for health care" or other statutes that specifically authorize withholding/withdrawing tube feeding (**Alaska, Arkansas, Colorado, Florida, Georgia,* Idaho, Illinois, Iowa, Indiana, Maine, Minnesota, Missouri, Montana, New Hampshire, North Dakota, Ohio, Oklahoma, Oregon, South Dakota, Tennessee, Virginia, Wisconsin** and **Wyoming**).

States with statutes requiring tube feeding in some circumstances (**Oklahoma**) or with "natural death" legislation that permits withholding/withdrawing some forms of life support but explicitly excludes tube feeding from these (**Connecticut,** Georgia,* Kentucky, Missouri*** and **Wisconsin**).

Jurisdictions with "natural death" or "living will" statutes that authorize the removal of life support in general but make no specific mention of tube feeding (**Alabama, California,* Delaware, Kansas, Louisiana, Mississippi, Nevada, New Mexico, North Carolina, Texas,‡ Vermont, Washington, West Virginia** and the **District of Columbia**). Withholding/withdrawing tube feeding is implicitly permissible (except in **Washington**) when the patient is in a medical condition covered by the act.

States in which legislative or judicial interpretation is necessary to determine whether tube feeding may be withheld/withdrawn. "Natural death" or "living will" statutes in these states typically associate tube feeding with comfort care, suggesting that it may be withheld/withdrawn if not necessary for comfort (**Arizona, Hawaii, Indiana, Iowa, Maryland,‡ New Hampshire, South Carolina** and **Utah**).

States with court decisions indicating it is permissible to withhold/withdraw tube feeding (**Arizona, California,* Colorado,* Connecticut,** Florida,* Georgia,* Hawaii, Illinois, Maine, Massachusetts, Michigan, Missouri, New Jersey, New York, North Dakota, Pennsylvania, Rhode Island** and **Virginia***).

States with court decisions that prohibit refusal of tube feeding under certain circumstances (**Ohio** and **Washington**).

* Courts have held that patients in these states have constitutional or common law rights to have tube feeding withheld regardless of the terms of the "natural death" or "living will" statutes. (Georgia's durable power explicitly permits refusal of tube feeding.)

** Court decisions interpreted the act to permit withdrawing tube feeding, despite language that would seem to prohibit it.

‡ Interpreted by an Opinion of the attorney general to permit withholding/withdrawing tube feeding.

Note: The majority of "natural death" and "living will" statutes apply to patients who are in a "terminal condition" (variously defined in the statutes). Court cases are frequently concerned with patients in other conditions—e.g., those who are "permanently unconscious" but not "terminal."

FIGURE 14-2

Tube feeding laws in the United States. Reprinted by permission of Choice In Dying, Inc. (formerly Concern for Dying/Society for the Right to Die), 200 Varick Street, New York, NY 10014

6. The date and notification given by the treating physician of the diagnosis of the patient's terminal condition and nature of that diagnosis, if applicable.
7. Statement that, if the declarant has been diagnosed as pregnant, the directive shall have no force or effect during the course of the declarant's pregnancy.
8. Statement reflecting the declarant's understanding that any person, hospital, or medical institution who executes or carries out the directive shall be immune from liability otherwise arising out of such failure to use or apply artificial, extraordinary, extreme, or radical medical or surgical means calculated to prolong the declarant's life.
9. Signatures by witnesses and declarant and date.

Living will laws vary from state to state. Generally, they provide a procedure for people to leave instructions which permit them to die a natural death. If properly executed, the instructions are binding on health care providers. Some states require that living wills be witnessed; others do not. Some states require them to be acknowledged before a notary public; others do not. Some states require the use of a particular form; others have no particular form. Figure 14-3 shows a sample living will.

Health Care Proxy Laws

Some state legislatures have been reluctant to pass laws allowing people to make living wills (see figure 14-4). New York and Massachusetts, for example, have passed laws allowing people to execute health care proxies rather than living wills. A **health care proxy** authorizes an **agent** or **surrogate** (one appointed to act in place of another) to make medical treatment decisions for the principal in the event of the principal's incapacity. Agents are to receive full medical information from their principal's doctor before making decisions. Doctors may rely on an agent's decision without fear of liability when the agent is acting under a health care proxy. A health care proxy can be completed by any competent adult and must be signed in the presence of two witnesses (see figure 14-5).

Durable Power of Attorney

Prior to the 1960s, when someone became incapacitated, the only option was to have a guardian or conservator appointed by a court to handle the person's affairs. A **guardian** is a person appointed to care for and manage the person, property, or both of a minor or incompetent. A **conservator** is appointed to care for the property of persons who, by reason of their advanced age, mental weakness, or physical incapacity, are unable to do so themselves, but who are not mentally ill. Obtaining such an appointment from the court can be time-consuming and expensive, requiring affidavits by attending physicians and court appearances by attorneys. To make it easier

LEGAL TERMS

health care proxy
Written statement authorizing an agent or surrogate to make medical treatment decisions for a principal in the event of the principal's incapacity.

agent
One appointed to act in place of another.

surrogate
An agent; one appointed to act in place of another.

guardian
Person appointed to care for and manage the person, property, or both of a minor or incompetent.

conservator
Person appointed to care for the property of another person who, by reason of advanced age, mental weakness, or physical incapacity, is unable to do so himself or herself, but who is not mentally ill.

TO MY FAMILY, MY PHYSICIAN, MY LAWYER AND ALL OTHERS WHOM IT MAY CONCERN

Death is as much a reality as birth, growth, maturity, and old age—it is the one certainty of life. If the time comes when I can no longer take part in decisions for my own future, let this statement stand as an expression of my wishes and directions, while I am still of sound mind.

If at such a time the situation should arise in which there is no reasonable expectation of my recovery from physical or mental disability, I, JOHN P. DOE, of N. Main Avenue, Mytown, Wisconsin, direct that I be allowed to die and not be kept alive by medications, artificial means, or heroic measures. I do, however, ask that medication be mercifully administered to me to alleviate suffering even though this may shorten my remaining life. I do not fear death as much as I fear the indignity of deterioration, dependence, and hopeless pain.

This statement is made after careful consideration and is in accordance with my strong convictions and beliefs. I want the wishes and directions here expressed carried out to the extent permitted by law. Insofar as they are not legally enforceable, I hope that you will regard yourselves as morally bound by these provisions. I recognize that it places a heavy burden of responsibility upon you, and it is with the intention of sharing that responsibility and of mitigating any feelings of guilt that this statement is made this ___________ day of ___________, 199___.

___________________________ ___________________________
Witness John P. Doe

____
Witness

SUBSCRIBED AND SWORN to before me this ____________ day of ____________, 199___.

____
Notary Public

FIGURE 14-3
Example of a living will

and less expensive for someone to act on behalf of an incompetent, all states in the United States have enacted legislation authorizing the durable power of attorney.

June 23, 1992

State Law Governing Durable Power of Attorney • Health Care Agents • Proxy Appointments •

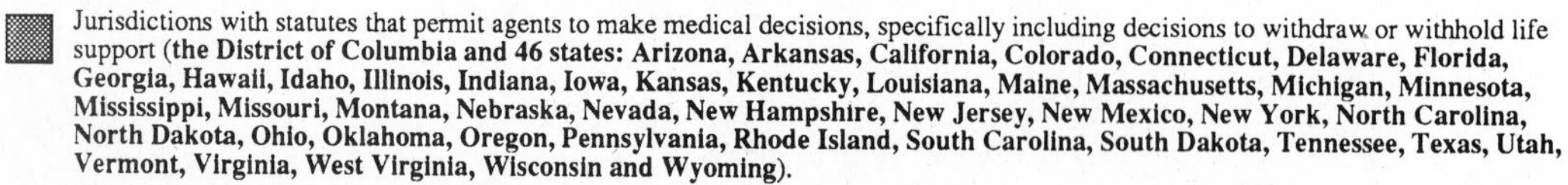

Jurisdictions with statutes that permit agents to make medical decisions, specifically including decisions to withdraw or withhold life support (**the District of Columbia and 46 states: Arizona, Arkansas, California, Colorado, Connecticut, Delaware, Florida, Georgia, Hawaii, Idaho, Illinois, Indiana, Iowa, Kansas, Kentucky, Louisiana, Maine, Massachusetts, Michigan, Minnesota, Mississippi, Missouri, Montana, Nebraska, Nevada, New Hampshire, New Jersey, New Mexico, New York, North Carolina, North Dakota, Ohio, Oklahoma, Oregon, Pennsylvania, Rhode Island, South Carolina, South Dakota, Tennessee, Texas, Utah, Vermont, Virginia, West Virginia, Wisconsin and Wyoming**).

States with statutes interpreted by court decisions, Attorney General Opinions or other statutes to permit agents to make medical decisions, including decisions to withhold or withdraw life support (**2 states: Maryland and Washington**).

State with a statute that authorizes consent to medical treatment, but specifically bars agents from consenting to the withholding/withdrawal of life support (**Alaska**).

State with no statutory means of appointing an agent to make medical decisions (**Alabama**).

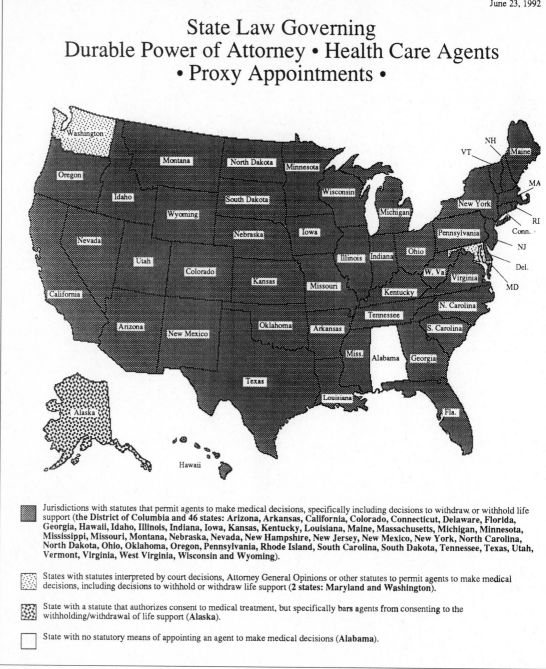

FIGURE 14-4

State law governing proxy appointments. Reprinted by permission of Choice In Dying, Inc. (formerly Concern for Dying/Society for the Right to Die), 200 Varick Street, New York, NY 10014

HEALTH CARE PROXY

TO MY FAMILY, DOCTORS, AND ALL THOSE CONCERNED WITH MY CARE:

1. *Appointment*

I, [the principal], residing at [address], being a competent adult at least eighteen years of age or older, of sound mind and under no constraint or undue influence, hereby appoint the following person to be my HEALTH CARE AGENT under the terms of this document:

Name:

Address:

Telephone:

In so doing, I intend to create a Health Care Proxy according to Chapter 201D of the General Laws of Massachusetts. In making this appointment, I am giving my Health Care Agent the authority to make any and all health care decisions on my behalf, subject to any limitations I state in this document, in the event that I should at some future time become incapable of making health care decisions for myself.

2. *Powers Given to Health Care Agent*

A. I give my Health Care Agent full authority to make any and all health care decisions for me, including decisions about life-sustaining treatment, subject only to the limitations I state below.

B. My Health Care Agent shall have authority to act on my behalf only if, when, and for so long as a determination has been made that I lack the capacity to make or to communicate health care decisions for myself. This determination shall be made in writing by my attending physician according to accepted standards of medical judgment and the requirements of Chapter 201D of the General Laws of Massachusetts.

C. The authority of my Health Care Agent shall cease if my attending physician determines that I have regained capacity. The authority of my Health Care Agent shall recommence if I subsequently lose capacity and consent for treatment is required.

D. I shall be notified of any determination that I lack capacity to make or communicate health care decisions where there is any indication that I am able to comprehend this notice.

E. My Health Care Agent shall make health care decisions for me only after consultation with my health care providers and after full consideration of acceptable medical alternatives regarding diagnosis, prognosis, treatments, and their side effects.

F. My Health Care Agent shall make health care decisions for me only in accordance with my Health Care Agent's assessment of my wishes, including my religious and moral beliefs, or, if my wishes are unknown, in accordance with my Health Care Agent's assessment of my best interests.

G. My Health Care Agent shall have the right to receive any and all medical information necessary to make informed decisions regarding my health care, including any and all confidential medical information that I would be entitled to receive.

FIGURE 14-5
Sample health care proxy (Massachusetts)

H. The decisions made by my Health Care Agent on my behalf shall have the same priority as my decisions would have if I were competent over decisions by any other person, including a person acting pursuant to a durable power of attorney, except for any limitation I state below or a specific Court Order overriding this Health Care Proxy.

I. If I object to a health care decision made by my Health Care Agent, my decision shall prevail unless it is determined by Court Order that I lack capacity to make health care decisions.

J. Nothing in this proxy shall preclude any medical procedure deemed necessary by my attending physician to provide comfort care or pain alleviation, including but not limited to treatment with sedatives and painkilling drugs, non-artificial oral feeding, suction, and hygienic care.

K. [Optional] I specifically limit my Health Care Agent's authority as follows:

3. *Revocation*

This Health Care Proxy shall be revoked upon any of the following events:

A. My execution of a subsequent Health Care Proxy.

B. My divorce or legal separation from my spouse where my spouse is named as my Health Care Agent.

C. My notification to my Health Care Agent or a health care provider orally or in writing or by any other act evidencing a specific intent to revoke the Health Care Proxy.

4. *Signature of Health Care Agent* [optional]

I have read this document carefully and accept the appointment.

____
[Agent]

5. *Signature of Principal*

I hereby sign my name on this date, ____________________, to this Health Care Proxy in the presence of two witnesses.

____
[Principal]

Complete here if the principal is physically incapable of signing:

I hereby sign the name of the principal at the principal's direction and in the presence of the principal and two witnesses.

Name of Principal:

Name of Signatory:

Date:

Address of Signatory:

FIGURE 14-5
(Continued)

6. *Witnesses*

Witness 1:

I, the undersigned, have witnessed the signing of this document by the principal or at the direction of the principal and state that the principal appears to be at least eighteen years of age, of sound mind, and under no constraint or undue influence. I have not been named as Health Care Agent in this document.

Signature:

Name [print]:

Address:

Date:

Witness 2:

I, the undersigned, have witnessed the signing of this document by the principal or at the direction of the principal and state that the principal appears to be at least eighteen years of age, of sound mind, and under no constraint or undue influence. I have not been named as Health Care Agent in this document.

Signature:

Name [print]:

Address:

Date:

FIGURE 14-5
(Continued)

An ordinary **power of attorney** is a written instrument authorizing another person to perform certain specified acts on one's behalf. One who authorizes another to act on one's behalf is called a **principal**. One who is authorized to act on another's behalf is called either an *agent* or an **attorney-in-fact**. A **durable power of attorney** is a power of attorney with language indicating that the power is to survive incapacity or become effective when the principal becomes incapacitated. *See* UPC § 5-501. The durable power of attorney must be executed by the principal at a time when he or she is in good mental health and is still capable of handling his or her own affairs.

In some states, a power of attorney is made durable by such language as: "This power of attorney shall not be affected by subsequent disability or incapacity of the principal." With this provision, the power becomes effective when the document is executed and continues to be effective even though the principal becomes incapacitated. See figure 14-6. In other states, the following words are used to make a power of attorney durable: "This power of attorney shall become effective upon the disability or incapacity of the principal." This is known as a **springing power** because the document does not become effective unless and until the principal becomes incapacitated.

LEGAL TERMS

power of attorney
Written instrument authorizing another person to perform certain specified acts on one's behalf.

principal
One who authorizes another to act on one's behalf.

attorney-in-fact
An agent; one who is authorized to act on another's behalf.

durable power of attorney
Power of attorney with language indicating that the power is to survive incapacity or become effective when the principal becomes incapacitated.

DURABLE POWER OF ATTORNEY
OF JANE P. DOE

I, JANE P. DOE, of Mytown, Smith County, Massachusetts, appoint my son, DAVID J. DOE, my attorney to conduct all my affairs, with full power and authority to act in my name and on my behalf as fully as I could do if personally present. Without limiting the generality of his powers, I specifically authorize him to do the following:

1. To manage and have the general control and supervision of all my property and interests in property, real or personal, tangible or intangible, including power to buy, sell, lease, and mortgage.
2. To maintain bank accounts for me in my name, or in the name of my said attorney, and to make deposits or withdrawals of money belonging to me in such accounts, and to disburse any money from such accounts on the signature of my said attorney.
3. To pay all my bills and to expend funds for any purposes which my said attorney deems for my benefit.
4. To collect, demand and receive any income, interest, dividends, rents, profits, or other property due or payable to me.
5. To borrow money on my behalf, to execute contracts on my behalf, and to execute on my behalf any other deed or instrument in my name or in the name of my said attorney, which in the discretion of my said attorney, appears to be necessary or advisable in the management of my affairs.
6. To have access to all safe deposit boxes in my name and the right to remove their contents.
7. To prepare or have prepared and to sign tax returns of any sort on my behalf.
8. To prosecute or defend or submit to arbitration any claim by or against me or my property and to receive and give full or partial releases of any kind.
9. To consent to surgery or any other medical procedures or assistance to me.
10. To transfer funds or property of mine to any trust established by me, whether before or after the date of this instrument.
11. To substitute another to act under this power of attorney and to revoke the substitution at any time.
12. To do any of the foregoing in the Commonwealth or elsewhere in the U.S.A.

No person dealing with my said attorney shall be required to see to the application of any funds or property paid or transferred to him. Any person may rely on this power of attorney or a copy of it certified by a notary public until notified in writing of its revocation.

I intend that this power of attorney shall not be affected by my subsequent disability or incapacity.

IN WITNESS WHEREOF, I hereunto set my hand and seal this ____ day of ___________, 199____.

____
Jane P. Doe

FIGURE 14-6
Sample durable power of attorney

COMMONWEALTH OF MASSACHUSETTS

_________ County, ss. _________, 199___

Then personally appeared the above-named JANE P. DOE and acknowledged the foregoing instrument to be her free act and deed, before me,

____
Notary public

FIGURE 14-6
(Continued)

Under the Uniform Probate Code, all acts done by an attorney-in-fact under a durable power of attorney during any period of disability or incapacity of the principal have the same effect as if the principal were competent and not disabled. UPC § 5-502 If a guardian or conservator is appointed to handle the affairs of the principal, the attorney-in-fact is accountable to the guardian or conservator, and the latter may revoke or amend the power of attorney. UPC § 5-503(a)

In some states, a *durable power of attorney for health care* is used instead of a living will. In these states, the statutes set forth the exact form to be used, along with rules for the form's execution. The statutes also grant immunity to health care providers. In addition to other powers, they authorize:

1. Access to medical records and other personal information.
2. The employment and discharge of health care personnel.
3. The giving and withholding of consent to medical treatment.
4. The granting of releases to medical personnel.

State laws governing the decision-making process for patients without advance directives are not uniform. Figure 14-7 summarizes the various state laws that existed in 1992. Even paralegals who are familiar with a state's law should be wary, as statutes on these subjects are changing constantly.

Patient Self-Determination Act

To encourage the use of advance directives, Congress passed the Patient Self-Determination Act in 1991. Under that Act, health care facilities that participate in Medicare and Medicaid are required to advise patients of their right to sign advance directives for health care decisions. Health facilities must provide written information to each patient about the individual's rights under state law to make medical care decisions, including advance directives. In addition, health care facilities must disclose their internal policies governing patient's rights. They must also note in patients' medical records whether or not patients have executed an advance directive.

LEGAL TERMS

springing power
Power in a durable power of attorney that does not become effective unless and until the principal becomes incapacitated.

June 23, 1992

State Law Governing Surrogate or Family Decisionmaking For Patients Without Advance Directives

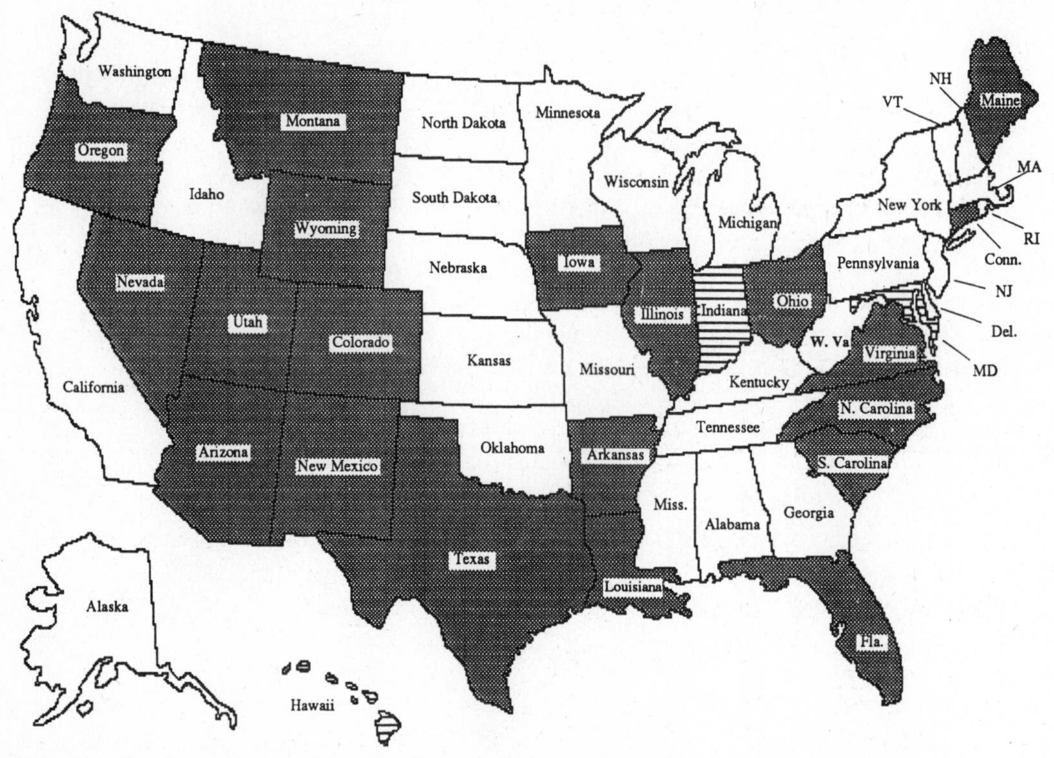

Jurisdictions with statutes that authorize surrogate decisionmaking on behalf of incapacitated patients who do not have advance directives (**the District of Columbia and 20 states: Arizona, Arkansas**, Colorado, Connecticut, Florida, Illinois**, Iowa, Louisiana**, Maine, Montana, Nevada, New Mexico**, North Carolina, Ohio, Oregon, South Carolina, Texas**, Utah, Virginia and Wyoming**).

States with statutes interpreted by Attorney General Opinions or court decisions to authorize surrogate decisionmaking (**3 states: Hawaii, Indiana* and Maryland***).

States with no statutes governing surrogate decisionmaking (**27 states: Alabama, Alaska, California, Delaware, Georgia, Idaho, Kansas, Kentucky, Massachusetts, Michigan, Minnesota, Mississippi, Missouri, Nebraska, New Hampshire, New Jersey, New York, North Dakota, Oklahoma, Pennsylvania, Rhode Island, South Dakota, Tennessee, Vermont, Washington, West Virginia and Wisconsin**).

* The surrogacy laws in these states may not allow for the withdrawal of artificial nutrition and hydration.

** The surrogacy laws in these states allow for medical decisions to be made on behalf of a minor.

FIGURE 14-7

State law governing surrogate decision making. Reprinted by permission of Choice In Dying, Inc. (formerly Concern for Dying/Society for the Right to Die), 200 Varick Street, New York, NY 10014

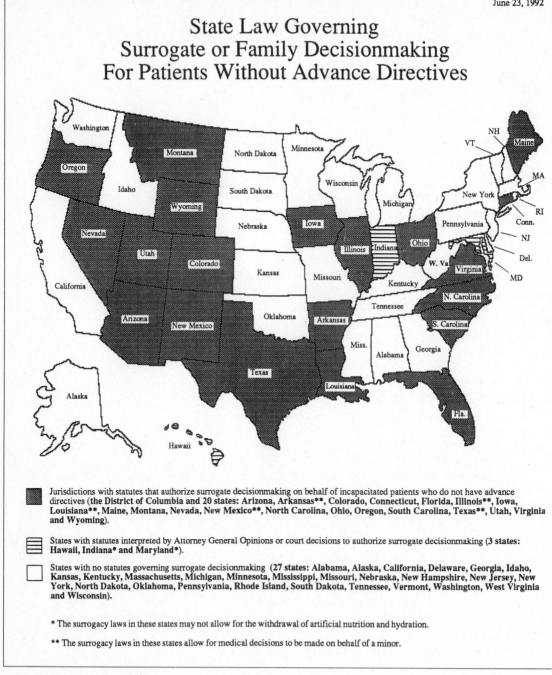

14.2 ANATOMICAL GIFTS

Each year, organ and tissue donations save the lives of thousands of grateful recipients and give sight and mobility to many more. Surgeons can recover the heart, lungs, pancreas, liver, and kidneys from brain-dead donors and transplant them successfully 80 to 95 percent of the time. Doctors can also transplant tissues, including skin grafts to burn victims, heart valves to patients with congenital heart disease, corneas to the sightless, and ligaments to persons crippled by sports injuries. Because of organ donors, many people are able to walk again, to hear, to survive severe burns, and to live a better quality of life. See table 14-1.

Every state in the United States has enacted the Uniform Anatomical Gifts Act (UAGA). An **anatomical gift** is a donation of all or part of a human body, which donation takes effect upon or after death. Under the UAGA, any individual who is at least 18 years of age may give all or any part of his or her body upon death to a donee. The donee may be a hospital, physician, surgeon, medical or dental school, college or university, organ bank or storage facility, or any specified individual for therapy or transplantation.

Donation by Will

Under the Uniform Anatomical Gift Act, a gift of all or part of a decedent's body may be made by will. The gift becomes effective upon the death of the testator, without waiting for probate. If the will is not probated or if it is declared invalid for testamentary purposes, the gift is nevertheless valid to the extent that it has been acted upon in good faith. UAGA § 4(a).

LEGAL TERMS

anatomical gift
Donation of all or part of a human body, to take effect upon or after death.

Organ	Transplants in 1987	Transplants in 1990	People Waiting for transplants in 1991	Waiting Time for Transplants in 1991
Kidney	8,967	9,455	19,029	427 days
Heart	1,512	2,012	2,228	141 days
Liver	1,182	2,547	1,577	53 days

TABLE 14-1

Demand for organs

Clause in Will for Gift of Body Organs
[7 Am. Jur. *Legal Forms* 2d § 84:67]

I direct that on my death, the executor of my estate immediately contact [hospital], at [address] and offer any of the organs of my body to whomever [hospital] deems might benefit therefrom, regardless of such person's race, creed, or color. Because of my utmost confidence in the staff of [hospital], it is my desire that the appropriate staff member have sole and exclusive authority to decide if such organ or organs might benefit another human, and should he or she decide that such organ or organs can and should be used, I direct he or she be permitted to remove same from my body and utilize them as he or she sees fit, and further direct that my estate indemnify him or her against any and all liability resulting from such act.

Donation by Signed Document

A gift of all or part of a decedent's body may also be made by a document other than a will. The document, often called an **organ-tissue donor's card**, must be signed by the donor in the presence of two witnesses, who must also sign the document in the donor's presence. If the donor cannot sign, the document may be signed by someone else at the donor's request, in his or her presence, and in the presence of two witnesses (see figure 14-8).

In addition to keeping a card on their persons, organ-tissue donors may register with the Living Bank, P.O. Box 6725, Houston, TX 77265, or call toll free 1-800-528-2971 (24 hours a day). To register, a donor fills out a simple form (see figure 14-9) and mails it to the Living Bank. The information is kept in a networked computer system, and a donor card is sent to all registered members. There is no charge for the service.

AN ANATOMICAL GIFT REFLECTION

Katherine Saunders, a Norwood, Massachusetts, poet known for her whimsical poems, wrote this poem which was included in her obituary when she died in 1992 at the age of 86:

Spare Parts

They're waiting around for my kidneys;
they're eager to get at my eyes.
They covet my liver and look on the giver
as taking her time when she dies.

They grin in anticipation:
Do you s'pose her kidneys will "take"?
Her arm or her heart or some other part?
What lovely skin grafts she'll make.

UNIFORM DONOR CARD

☐ Any needed organs or tissues

☐ Only the following organs or tissues:

(Specify)____________________

Signed by the donor in the presence of two witnesses who also sign.

Donor signature — Date of birth

City/State — Date signed

Witness — Witness

This is a legal document under the UNIFORM ANATOMICAL GIFT ACT or similar laws. For further information, call: Kidney Foundation 1-800-542-4001 or New England Organ Bank 1-800-446-NEOB.

FIGURE 14-8
Uniform donor card

Signing a donor card such as this is important to signify a person's commitment legally, but organs and tissue are rarely removed simply on the basis of a signed donor card. Family permission is sought as well. Thus, it is important for donors to discuss their commitment with their families. This way, each family member can make his or her wishes known. By expressing how one feels and knowing the feelings of loved ones, the decision about donation is easier when the time comes.

The Living Bank is the only national multi-organ donor registry in the United States. It is not a medical or storage facility. If the Living Bank is notified of a registrant's imminent death, the case is referred to the regional organ procurement agency to comply with the donor's wishes. Medical professionals will make decisions as to what is medically acceptable for transplant. Once organs and tissues are removed, the family has the responsibility of arranging for burial or cremation. Organ and tissue donation does not delay or increase costs of the funeral arrangements, and the decedent's body is not disfigured.

The Registry of Motor Vehicles in many states has programs that allow people to make anatomical gifts as a part of the process of issuing and renewing licenses. A person's driver's license, under this method, identifies the individual as a donor of an anatomical gift.

Besides a written document, the decedent may use a telegraphic, recorded telephonic, or other recorded message to authorize an anatomical donation. The gift may be made to a specified donee or without specifying a donee. In the latter case, the gift may be accepted by the attending physician as donee upon or following the donor's death.

If a gift is made to a specified donee who is not available at the time and place of the donor's death, the attending physician may accept the gift

LEGAL TERMS

organ-tissue donor's card
Document, signed by a donor in the presence of two witnesses, donating all or part of the donor's body; the donation takes effect upon or after death.

Uniform Anatomical Gift Act Donor Form

Please type or print. Complete lines 1 through 18.

1. Social Security #________________

2. Date of Birth ________________

3. Donor's full name

4. Mailing Address

5. City | 6. State | 7. Zip Code

8. Donor's next of kin (name) | 9. Relationship to donor

10. Street Address of next of kin | 11. City | 12. State | 13. Zip Code

In the hope that I may help others, I hereby make this anatomical gift, if medically acceptable, to take effect upon my death. The words and marks below indicate my desires.

14. I give

a. ☐ any needed organs and tissue.

b. ☐ only the following organs or tissue:

____

Limitations or special wishes ________

15. Donor Signature

16. First Witness'

17. Second Witness'

18. Date Signed

The Living Bank was founded in 1968 as the national organ and tissue donor registry to educate the public on organ donation and to maintain a registry of informed, identified donors.

The Living Bank is not a medical or storage facility. It has remained the only multi-organ and tissue donor registry in the United States. When The Living Bank is notified of a member's impending death, the case is referred to the nearest organ procurement agency to comply with the donor's wishes.

The Living Bank is a non-profit organization, it charges no fee for its services and receives no government funds. It is supported entirely by voluntary tax deductible contributions.

THE LIVING BANK
P. O. Box 6725
Houston, Texas 77265-6725
National 24-Hour Number
1-800-528-2971

Wear The Living Bank medallions so that you may be immediately identified to medical professionals as a registered organ donor.

Medallions:

Sterling Silver ________ @ $35 each

Gold Filled ________ @ $30 each

Bronze ________ @ $15 each

Donor Card & Driver License Case ________ @ $2 each

Keychain ________ @ $10 each

Decals ________ @ $1 each

Identification Kit ________ @ $20 each
Includes bronze medallion, keychain and two decals.

Name | Address | City | State | Zip

☐ I wish to make a **VOLUNTARY TAX DEDUCTIBLE CONTRIBUTION OF $**________.

☐ Enclosed is my check payable to The Living Bank. Credit Card Expiration Date ________

☐ Charge my Mastercard Number ________ Signature ________

Visa Card Number ________ Social Security Number ________

DETACH AND RETURN IN THE ATTACHED ENVELOPE

FIGURE 14-9 Uniform Anatomical Gift Act donor form. Courtesy of the Living Bank, Houston, Texas

as donee, unless instructed otherwise by the donor. However, in this situation, the physician who becomes a donee may not participate in the medical procedures for removing or transplanting a part.

Donors may amend or revoke their gifts either orally or in writing. If an amendment or revocation is made orally, the oral statement must be made either in the presence of two persons and communicated to the donee, or by a statement to a physician during a terminal illness which is known to the donee. If it is done in writing, the writing must be signed by the donor and delivered to a specified donee or retrieved after death. An anatomical

Thanks To People Like You

You can be proud of your life-giving decision to become an organ donor. You will have joined the thousands of people who recognize the tremendous need for organ and tissue donors and who understand the reliability and effectiveness of the surgery. Because of what you can do with the stroke of a pen in completing the attached donor form, others may live longer, healthier lives as a living legacy to your wisdom, foresight and generosity.

Questions On Organ Donation

Is there any cost to the family?

There is no cost to the donor family or estate. Your family is responsible for the cost of saving your life. They are not responsible for any charges after you are declared brain dead and the decision is made to donate organs. The cost for removing any organs or tissue is taken care of by the transplant team removing the organs.

Can I be certain the organs will be used?

Acceptance of organ and tissue donations for transplant is a medical decision. Surgeons remove no organ or tissue unless it is needed and acceptable. The need is so great they make every effort to use all medically acceptable organs and tissue. The condition of the organ or tissue itself is more a factor in determining utilization at the time of death than age. Each transplant facility has its own age criteria for donation of vital organs. The age requirement is less restrictive in cases of tissue such as eyes and skin. Corneas, for example, may be utilized despite advanced age or diminished vision.

If I am a registered organ donor, will every effort still be made to save my life?

A doctor's first responsibility is preserving and prolonging life. Organs and tissue are removed for transplant only after the donor's own medical team declares him legally dead. A transplant surgeon is not allowed to make that declaration. One patient is never 'sacrificed' for the benefit of another.

Who will receive the donated organs?

The United Network for Organ Sharing's computer system determines recipients, finding the person in the greatest need for that particular organ or tissue. Organs and tissue are procured and matched on the basis of medical compatibility, blood type, tissue matching and body size.

Should my wishes as a donor be made a part of my will?

This is a personal decision. Your attorney can draw up a document stating your wishes upon death. Your will in combination with your donor card can help insure that your wishes are honored. Please remember that a will is usually read long after the deadline for organ donation. Family dicussion is the most important factor influencing organ donation.

How important is time?

Time is critical in organ and tissue transplantation. Quick notification if death is imminent or has occurred increases the chances of a successful transplant. Always carry your Living Bank donor card which gives information on your next of kin. Living Bank decals and medallions or key chains identify you to medical professionals as a registered organ donor.

Should I tell my doctor?

It is important that doctors be told when patients wish to become organ and tissue donors. There is greater assurance your final wishes will be fulfilled when more people know of your decision to become a donor.

Can I still have a funeral?

There is no disfigurement of the body or delay in funeral services. You can have an open casket funeral, if desired.

What do religious groups think?

All major denominations approve of organ and tissue donation.

THE LIVING BANK

P.O. Box 6725
Houston, Texas 77265-6725
National 24-Hour Number
1-800-528-2971

Can I register with The Living Bank if I have already registered elsewhere?

Yes. We all work together to carry out your wishes as an organ and tissue donor. Transplant centers, medical schools, hospitals and driver license bureaus all share our goals. But please remember that The Living Bank is the only multi-organ and tissue donor registry in the United States.

What do I do if I change my name and address?

When a name change occurs or there are several changes to be made, we recommend that you fill out new forms and have them witnessed. If you move, please notify our office of your new address. It is very important to keep your records with us up to date. A current address also enables us to keep you informed on the latest developments in organ donation and transplantation.

Why do you need my Social Security number?

We ask members to use their Social Security numbers when contacting us because it helps identify you in our computer files. Please include your Social Security number when changing addresses, making other changes or inquiries as it enables us to make the changes more efficiently.

How do I donate my body to medical science?

People wishing to donate their bodies for anatomical study must contact the nearest medical school for preregistration. The Living Bank can provide addresses of medical schools near you. Living Bank members registered with medical schools should have us include this information in your files. Please include a long self-addressed, stamped envelope to obtain a medical school listing or any other information needed.

FIGURE 14-9
(Continued)

gift that is not revoked by the donor before death is irrevocable and does not require the consent or concurrence of any person, including next of kin, after the donor's death.

Donation by Others

Unless the decedent has indicated otherwise, the following persons, listed in order of priority, may also make a gift of all or any part of a decedent's body: a surviving spouse, adult son or daughter, parent, brother or sister, or guardian. A gift may not be made in this manner, however, if an objection is made by someone of the same or higher priority on the list.

14.3 THE DECEDENT'S BODY

When someone dies, a decision must be made as to what to do with the decedent's body. Occasionally family members will disagree about arrangements, such as the type of funeral service, the place of burial, or cremation of the remains. Sometimes these questions must be decided by a court.

Under early English common law, no one had any rights in a dead body, and a decedent's wishes made in a will or otherwise prior to death did not have to be carried out. Even today, some courts hold that a dead body is not an "effect" within the meaning of the "persons, houses, papers, and effects" clause of the Fourth Amendment to the U.S. Constitution, because it is neither real nor personal property. In recognizing family members' rights to possession of a deceased's body for purposes of preparation, mourning, and burial, courts hold that it is merely a possessory right, not a property right. No one can own a dead body.

State laws differ as to whether directions in a will for the disposal of a body must be carried out. Some courts take the position that every person has the right to determine the disposition of his or her body after death. Others declare that the wishes of the decedent will be carried out as far as possible, but that such wishes are not absolute and will be governed by rules of propriety and reasonableness. Oral statements as to funeral and burial arrangements made by a person before death will sometimes take precedence over contradictory directions found in an earlier-made will.

A clause that is commonly used in wills to give directions for one's funeral and burial appears in chapter 5. The following clause may be used in a will when funeral directions have been given to a funeral director.

GRAVE DIGGING . . . FOR A PRESIDENT!

In 1991, the crypt of Zachary Taylor, 12th President of the United States, was opened to determine if his death in 1850 resulted from arsenic poisoning. Questions about the cause of his death were raised by an author who was preparing a Taylor biography and who suspected that political enemies had poisoned and, therefore, murdered Taylor. Tests of the remains revealed, however, that Taylor had *not* been poisoned. If he had been, history would have changed dramatically: Abraham Lincoln, the nation's 16th president, would no longer have been the first president to have been assassinated.

Clause in Will Providing for Funeral and Burial [20 AM. JUR. *Legal Forms* 2d § 266:322].

I direct that my funeral and burial is to be conducted in accordance with my written instructions therefor which are on file at [name of funeral director or mortician] at [address], City of _________, County of _________, State of ___________. The said written instructions are hereby incorporated into and made a part of this will.

Usually, the decedent's surviving spouse has the right to the possession of the decedent's body, along with the duty of burial or other disposal. If there is no surviving spouse, this right and duty is given to the decedent's **next of kin**, that is, those persons who are most nearly related by blood (see chapter 6). The executor or administrator of the decedent's estate has no right or duty relating to the decedent's body unless the will provides otherwise or unless there is no surviving spouse and no next of kin.

Ordinarily, the person who has the right of burial is entitled to select the place of burial, giving due consideration to any expressed wishes of the decedent. A court will not order or permit a body to be **disinterred** (unearthed) unless there is a strong showing that it is necessary and that the interests of justice require it. However, there is no universal rule, and each case depends on its own facts and circumstances. As the *Estes* case illustrates, a decedent's spouse who has consented to the burial of the decedent's body in a certain place cannot afterward remove the remains against the will of the decedent's next of kin.

LEGAL TERMS

next of kin
Persons nearest of kindred to the decedent; those most nearly related by blood.

disinterred
Unearthed.

ESTES V. WOODLAWN MEMORIAL PARK, INC.
780 S.W.2d 759 (Tenn. 1989)

FACTS: When his wife died, A. M. Estes signed a paper authorizing his wife's niece to make the funeral arrangements. He had lost his daughter six months earlier. Estes attended his wife's funeral and burial and made no objections to having her buried in a family plot near their daughter. Two years later, Estes wanted his wife and daughter buried in another place, but his wife's niece objected.

LEGAL ISSUE: Can the paramount right of a surviving husband and parent to select the final burial place for his deceased wife and daughter be overridden by the wishes of the wife's relatives?

COURT DECISION: Yes.

REASON: Disinterment of a body is not favored in the law. Except in cases of necessity and for laudable purposes, it is the policy of the law that the sanctity of the grave should be maintained and that a body, once suitably buried, should remain undisturbed.

In a Pennsylvania case, the court refused to follow the directions in a decedent's will that he be buried next to his ex-wife, saying that it would be a great injustice to the surviving spouse. The decedent, it seems, had led a double life: he had been secretly married to two women and had separate families in separate locations. The court held that the decedent, by his own deceitfulness and activities, had forfeited any right to have consideration given to his desires as to a final resting place.

SUMMARY

14.1 In the *Cruzan* case, the United States Supreme Court recognized the right to refuse medical treatment. The Court held that the rights of incompetent individuals must be exercised by some sort of surrogate decision maker and that a state can require clear and convincing evidence of an incompetent's wishes.

At least 80 percent of the states have enacted living will laws that set forth procedures for people to leave instructions allowing them to die a natural death. Some states have passed laws allowing people to execute a written health care proxy, which appoints an agent to make health care decisions in the event of incapacity. Still other states have authorized the use of a durable power of attorney for health care, which empowers another person to make health care decisions when one is incapacitated. The federal Patient Self-Determination Act requires health facilities to advise patients of state law, as well as of their own policies, regarding advance directives. Facilities must also note in patients' medical records whether patients have executed an advance directive.

14.2 Because of organ donors, many people are able to walk again, to hear, to survive severe burns, and to live a better quality of life. Every state in the United States has enacted the Uniform Anatomical Gifts Act, under which any individual who is at least 18 years of age may give all or any part of his or her body upon death to a donee.

14.3 Some states take the position that every person has the right to determine the disposition of his or her body after death. Others hold that the wishes of the decedent will be carried out so far as possible, but that such wishes are not absolute and will be governed by rules of propriety and reasonableness.

Usually the decedent's surviving spouse has the right to possession of the decedent's body, along with the duty of burial. If there is no surviving spouse, this right and duty are given to the decedent's next of kin. The person who has the right of burial is entitled, in most situations, to select the place of burial, giving due consideration to any expressed wishes of the decedent.

QUESTIONS FOR REVIEW

1. What did the United States Supreme Court say about the right to refuse medical treatment in *Cruzan v. Director?*
2. For what reason have all states enacted legislation authorizing the durable power of attorney?
3. a. What sentence creates a durable power of attorney in some states? When does the power become effective?
   b. What sentence is used in other states? When does the power become effective?
4. Who may be a donor under the Uniform Anatomical Gifts Act? Who may be a donee?
5. When a gift of all or part of a person's body is made by will, when does the gift become effective? What happens to the gift if the will is declared to be invalid for testamentary purposes?
6. How many people are required to witness the signature of the donor on an organ-tissue donor statement or card?
7. How may organ-tissue donors revoke their gifts orally? How may they revoke their gifts in writing?
8. Under what circumstances and by whom may someone other than the decedent make a gift of all or any part of a decedent's body?
9. In what way do the states differ as to whether directions in a will for the disposal of a body must be carried out?
10. Who usually has the right to possession of the decedent's body, along with the duty of burial?

CASES TO DISCUSS

1. Sidney Greenspan, age 76, suffered a stroke that left him permanently and irreversibly unconscious. He was placed in a nursing home where he lay in a fetal position and received nasogastric tube feeding for some five years. Earlier, Greenspan had told his wife many times that he would "rather be shot than reside in a nursing home." He had discussed the *Quinlan* case with his daughter and said that he would not want to live under such conditions. On the very day of his stroke,

he discussed the disability of a mutual friend with a former co-worker and said that he would never wish to be either on life support or in a nursing home. May a state require that an incompetent's wishes as to the withdrawal of life-sustaining treatment be proven by clear and convincing evidence? Explain. *In re Greenspan,* 558 N.E.2d 1194 (Ill. 1990).

2. Steven Brotherton was found "pulseless" in an automobile and taken to a hospital where he was pronounced dead. When asked if she would consider an anatomical gift, the decedent's wife refused because of her husband's strong feelings against such a gift. An autopsy was performed and, without asking the family or looking at hospital records, the coroner's office permitted the decedent's corneas to be removed and utilized as anatomical gifts. In a suit that followed, the question arose as to whether family members have property rights in a deceased's body. What is your opinion? Explain. *Brotherton v. Cleveland,* 733 F. Supp. 56 (S.D. Ohio 1989).
3. John Hough, an alcoholic, died from injuries suffered during a fall down the basement stairs. Because of questions about the cause of his death, an inquest was held. The jury found that his death was accidental. Later, over the objections of Hough's widow, his daughter sought to have Hough's body disinterred for further medical tests. When and for what reason will a court permit a body to be disinterred? *Hough v. Weber,* 560 N.E.2d 5 (Ill. 1990).

SHARPENING YOUR PROFESSIONAL SKILLS

1. Refer to the law office scenario at the beginning of this chapter and answer the following questions:
   a. Why might Mr. LaBella need a living will?
   b. Was Mr. LaBella's daughter correct when she said that his body would be disfigured if he made an anatomical gift?
2. Look up the Uniform Durable Power of Attorney Act in your state, make a note of its statutory reference, and write down the sentence that is used to create a durable power of attorney. Does this create an immediate power or a springing power?
3. Draft either a living will, a durable power of attorney for health care, or a health care proxy, whichever is preferred under your state law. Write down the statutory reference where this law is found.
4. Under your state statute, who has the right to make decisions as to the disposition of a dead body? Give the statutory reference where the provision is found.
5. Telephone (toll-free) the Living Bank at 1-800-528-2971 for information about organ-tissue donor registration.

APPENDIX A

Uniform Simultaneous Death Act

An Act providing for the disposition of property where there is no sufficient evidence that persons have died otherwise than simultaneously, and to make uniform the law with reference thereto.

Be it enacted. . . . . . .

§ 1. No Sufficient Evidence of Survivorship

Where the title to property or the devolution thereof depends upon priority of death and there is no sufficient evidence that the persons concerned have died otherwise than simultaneously, the property of each person shall be disposed of as if he had survived, except as otherwise provided in this act.

§ 2. Survival of Beneficiaries

If property is so disposed of that the right of a beneficiary to succeed to any interest therein is conditional upon his surviving another person, and both persons die, and there is no sufficient evidence that the two have died otherwise than simultaneously, the beneficiary shall be deemed not to have survived. If there is no sufficient evidence that two or more beneficiaries have died otherwise than simultaneously and property has been disposed of in such a way that at the time of their death each of such beneficiaries would have been entitled to the property if he had survived the others, the property shall be divided into as many equal portions as there were such beneficiaries and these portions shall be distributed respectively to those who would have taken in the event that each of such beneficiaries had survived.

§ 3. Joint Tenants or Tenants by the Entirety

Where there is no sufficient evidence that two joint tenants or tenants by the entirety have died otherwise than simultaneously the property so held shall be distributed one-half as if one had survived and one-half as if the other had survived. If there are more than two joint tenants and all of them have so died the property thus distributed shall be in the proportion that one bears to the whole number of joint tenants.

The term "joint tenants" includes owners of property held under circumstances which entitled one or more to the whole of the property on the death of the other or others.

§ 4. Community Property

Where a husband and wife have died, leaving community property, and there is no sufficient evidence that they have died otherwise than simultaneously, one-half of all the community property shall pass as if the husband had survived [and as if said one-half were his separate property,] and the other one-half thereof shall pass as if the wife had survived [and as if said other one-half were her separate property.]

§ 5. Insurance Policies

Where the insured and the beneficiary in a policy of life or accident insurance have died and there is no sufficient evidence that they have died otherwise than simultaneously the proceeds of the policy shall be distributed as if the insured had survived the beneficiary, [except if the policy is community property of the insured and his spouse, and there is no alternative beneficiary except the estate or personal representatives of the insured, the proceeds shall be distributed as community property under Section 4.]

§ 6. Act Does Not Apply If Decedent Provides Otherwise

This act shall not apply in the case of wills, living trusts, deeds, or contracts of insurance, or any other situation where provision is made for distribution of property different from the provisions of this act, or where provision is made for a presumption as to survivorship which results in a distribution of property different from that here provided.

§ 7. Uniformity of Interpretation

This act shall be so construed and interpreted as to effectuate its general purpose to make uniform the law in those states which enact it.

§ 8. Short Title

This act may be cited as the Uniform Simultaneous Death Act.

§ 9. Repeal

All laws or parts of laws inconsistent with the provisions of this act are hereby repealed.

§ 10. Severability

If any of the provisions of this act or the application thereof to any persons or circumstances is held invalid such invalidity shall not affect other provisions or applications of the act which can be given effect without the invalid provisions or application, and to this end the provisions of this act are declared to be severable.

§ 11. Time of Taking Effect

This act shall take effect ____________________.

APPENDIX B

Uniform Anatomical Gift Act (1987)

§ 1. Definitions.

As used in this [Act]:

(1) "Anatomical gift" means a donation of all or part of a human body to take effect upon or after death.

(2) "Decedent" means a deceased individual and includes a stillborn infant or fetus.

(3) "Document of gift" means a card, a statement attached to or imprinted on a motor vehicle operator's or chauffeur's license, a will, or other writing used to make an anatomical gift.

(4) "Donor" means an individual who makes an anatomical gift of all or part of the individual's body.

(5) "Enucleator" means an individual who is [licensed] [certified] by the [State Board of Medical Examiners] to remove or process eyes or parts of eyes.

(6) "Hospital" means a facility licensed, accredited, or approved as a hospital under the law of any state or a facility operated as a hospital by the United States government, a state, or a subdivision of a state.

(7) "Part" means an organ, tissue, eye, bone, artery, blood, fluid, or other portion of a human body.

(8) "Person" means an individual, corporation, business trust, estate, trust, partnership, joint venture, association, government, governmental subdivision or agency, or any other legal or commercial entity.

(9) "Physician" or "surgeon" means an individual licensed or otherwise authorized to practice medicine and surgery or osteopathy and surgery under the laws of any state.

(10) "Procurement organization" means a person licensed, accredited, or approved under the laws of any state for procurement, distribution, or storage of human bodies or parts.

(11) "State" means a state, territory, or possession of the United States, the District of Columbia, or the Commonwealth of Puerto Rico.

(12) "Technician" means an individual who is [licensed] [certified] by the [State Board of Medical Examiners] to remove or process a part.

§ 2. Making, Amending, Revoking, and Refusing to Make Anatomical Gifts by Individual.

(a) An individual who is at least [18] years of age may (i) make an anatomical gift for any of the purposes stated in Section 6(a), (ii) limit an anatomical gift to one or more of those purposes, or (iii) refuse to make an anatomical gift.

(b) An anatomical gift may be made only by a document of gift signed by the donor. If the donor cannot sign, the document of gift must be signed by another individual and by two witnesses, all of whom have signed at the direction and in the presence of the donor and of each other, and state that it has been so signed.

(c) If a document of gift is attached to or imprinted on a donor's motor vehicle operator's or chauffeur's license, the document of gift must comply with subsection (b). Revocation, suspension, expiration, or cancellation of the license does not invalidate the anatomical gift.

(d) A document of gift may designate a particular physician or surgeon to carry out the appropriate procedures. In the absence of a designation or if the designee is not available, the donee or other person authorized to accept the anatomical gift may employ or authorize any physician, surgeon, technician, or enucleator to carry out the appropriate procedures.

(e) An anatomical gift by will takes effect upon death of the testator, whether or not the will is probated. If, after death, the will is declared invalid for testamentary purposes, the validity of the anatomical gift is unaffected.

(f) A donor may amend or revoke an anatomical gift, not made by will, only by:

(1) a signed statement;

(2) an oral statement made in the presence of two individuals;

(3) any form of communication during a terminal illness or injury addressed to a physician or surgeon; or

(4) the delivery of a signed statement to a specified donee to whom a document of gift had been delivered.

(g) The donor of an anatomical gift made by will may amend or revoke the gift in the manner provided for amendment or revocation of wills, or as provided in subsection (f).

(h) An anatomical gift that is not revoked by the donor before death is irrevocable and does not require the consent or concurrence of any person after the donor's death.

(i) An individual may refuse to make an anatomical gift of the individual's body or part by (i) a writing signed in the same manner as a document of gift, (ii) a statement attached to or imprinted on a donor's motor vehicle operator's or chauffeur's license, or (iii) any other writing used to identify the individual as refusing to make an anatomical gift. During a terminal illness or injury, the refusal may be an oral statement or other form of communication.

(j) In the absence of contrary indications by the donor, an anatomical gift of a part is neither a refusal to give other parts nor a limitation on an anatomical gift under Section 3 or on a removal or release of other parts under Section 4.

(k) In the absence of contrary indications by the donor, a revocation or amendment of an anatomical gift is not a refusal to make another anatomical gift. If the donor intends a revocation to be a refusal to make an anatomical gift, the donor shall make the refusal pursuant to subsection (i).

§ 3. Making, Revoking, and Objecting to Anatomical Gifts, by Others.

(a) Any member of the following classes of persons, in the order of priority listed, may make an anatomical gift of all or a part of the decedent's body for an authorized purpose, unless the decedent, at the time of death, has made an unrevoked refusal to make that anatomical gift:

(1) the spouse of the decedent;

(2) an adult son or daughter of the decedent;

(3) either parent of the decedent;

(4) an adult brother or sister of the decedent;

(5) a grandparent of the decedent; and

(6) a guardian of the person of the decedent at the time of death.

(b) An anatomical gift may not be made by a person listed in subsection (a) if:

(1) a person in a prior class is available at the time of death to make an anatomical gift;

(2) the person proposing to made an anatomical gift knows of a refusal or contrary indications by the decedent; or

(3) the person proposing to make an anatomical gift knows of an objection to making an anatomical gift by a member of the person's class or a prior class.

(c) An anatomical gift by a person authorized under subsection (a) must be made by (i) a document of gift signed by the person or (ii) the person's telegraphic, recorded telephonic, or other recorded message, or other form of communication from the person that is contemporaneously reduced to writing and signed by the recipient.

(d) An anatomical gift by a person authorized under subsection (a) may be revoked by any of the same or a prior class if, before procedures have begun for the removal of a part from the body of the decedent, the physician, surgeon, technician, or enucleator removing the part knows of the revocation.

(e) A failure to make an anatomical gift under subsection (a) is not an objection to the making of an anatomical gift.

§ 4. Authorization by [Coroner] [Medical Examiner] or [Local Public Health Official].

(a) The [coroner] [medical examiner] may release and permit the removal of a part from a body within that official's custody, for transplantation or therapy, if:

(1) the official has received a request for the part from a hospital, physician, surgeon, or procurement organization;

(2) the official has made a reasonable effort, taking into account the useful life of the part, to locate and examine the decedent's medical

records and inform persons listed in Section 3(a) of their option to make, or object to making, an anatomical gift;

(3) the official does not know of a refusal or contrary indication by the decedent or objection by a person having priority to act as listed in Section 3(a);

(4) the removal will be by a physician, surgeon, or technician; but in the case of eyes, by one of them or by an enucleator;

(5) the removal will not interfere with any autopsy or investigation;

(6) the removal will be in accordance with accepted medical standards; and

(7) cosmetic restoration will be done, if appropriate.

(b) If the body is not within the custody of the [coroner] [medical examiner], the [local public health officer] may release and permit the removal of any part from a body in the [local public health officer's] custody for transplantation or therapy if the requirements of subsection (a) are met.

(c) An official releasing and permitting the removal of a part shall maintain a permanent record of the name of the decedent, the person making the request, the date and purpose of the request, the part requested, and the person to whom it was released.

§ 5. Routine Inquiry and Required Request; Search and Notification.

(a) On or before admission to a hospital, or as soon as possible thereafter, a person designated by the hospital shall ask each patient who is at least [18] years of age: "Are you an organ or tissue donor?" If the answer is affirmative the person shall request a copy of the document of gift. If the answer is negative or there is no answer and the attending physician consents, the person designated shall discuss with the patient the option to make or refuse to make an anatomical gift. The answer to the question, an available copy of any document of gift or refusal to make an anatomical gift, and any other relevant information, must be placed in the patient's medical record.

(b) If, at or near the time of death of a patient, there is no medical record that the patient has made or refused to make an anatomical gift, the hospital [administrator] or a representative designed by the [administrator] shall discuss the option to make or refuse to make an anatomical gift and request the making of an anatomical gift pursuant to Section 3(a). The request must be made with reasonable discretion and sensitivity to the circumstances of the family. A request is not required if the gift is not suitable, based upon accepted medical standards, for a purpose specified in Section 6. An entry must be made in the medical record of the patient, stating the name and affiliation of the individual making the request, and of the name, response, and relationship to the patient of the person to whom the request was made. The [Commissioner of Health] shall [establish guidelines] [adopt regulations] to implement this subsection.

(c) The following persons shall make a reasonable search for a document of gift or other information identifying the bearer as a donor or as an individual who has refused to make an anatomical gift:

(1) a law enforcement officer, fireman, paramedic, or other emergency rescuer finding an individual who the searcher believes is dead or near death; and

(2) a hospital, upon the admission of an individual at or near the time of death, if there is not immediately available any other source of that information.

(d) If a document of gift or evidence of refusal to make an anatomical gift is located by the search required by subsection (c)(1), and the individual or body to whom it relates is taken to a hospital, the hospital must be notified of the contents and the document or other evidence must be sent to the hospital.

(e) If, at or near the time of death of a patient, a hospital knows that an anatomical gift has been made pursuant to Section 3(a) or a release and removal of a part has been permitted pursuant to Section 4, or that a patient or an individual identified as in transit to the hospital is a donor, the hospital shall notify the donee if one is named and known to the hospital; if not, it shall notify an appropriate procurement organization. The hospital shall cooperate in the implementation of the anatomical gift or release and removal of a part.

(f) A person who fails to discharge the duties imposed by this section is not subject to criminal or civil liability but is subject to appropriate administrative sanctions.

§ 6. Persons Who May Become Donees; Purposes for Which Anatomical Gifts may be Made.

(a) The following persons may become donees of anatomical gifts for the purposes stated:

(1) a hospital, physician, surgeon, or procurement organization, for transplantation, therapy, medical or dental education, research, or advancement of medical or dental science;

(2) an accredited medical or dental school, college, or university for education, research, advancement of medical or dental science; or

(3) a designated individual for transplantation or therapy needed by that individual.

(b) An anatomical gift may be made to a designated donee or without designating a donee. If a donee is not designated or if the donee is not available or rejects the anatomical gift, the anatomical gift may be accepted by any hospital.

(c) If the donee knows of the decedent's refusal or contrary indications to make an anatomical gift or that an anatomical gift by a member of a class having priority to act is opposed by a member of the same class or a prior class under Section 3(a), the donee may not accept the anatomical gift.

§ 7. Delivery of Document of Gift.

(a) Delivery of a document of gift during the donor's lifetime is not required for the validity of an anatomical gift.

(b) If an anatomical gift is made to a designated donee, the document of gift, or a copy, may be delivered to the donee to expedite the appropriate procedures after death. The document of gift, or a copy, may be deposited in any hospital, procurement organization, or registry office that accepts it for safekeeping or for facilitation of procedures after death. On request of an interested person, upon or after the donor's death, the person in possession shall allow the interested person to examine or copy the document of gift.

§ 8. Rights and Duties at Death.

(a) Rights of a donee created by an anatomical gift are superior to rights of others except with respect to autopsies under Section 11(b). A donee may accept or reject an anatomical gift. If a donee accepts an anatomical gift of an entire body, the donee, subject to the terms of the gift, may allow embalming and use of the body in funeral services. If the gift is of a part of a body, the donee, upon the death of the donor and before embalming, shall cause the part to be removed without unnecessary mutilation. After removal of the part, custody of the remainder of the body vests in the person under obligation to dispose of the body.

(b) The time of death must be determined by a physician or surgeon who attends the donor at death or, if none, the physician or surgeon who certifies the death. Neither the physician or surgeon who attends the donor at death nor the physician or surgeon who determines the time of death may participate in the procedures for removing or transplanting a part unless the document of gift designates a particular physician or surgeon pursuant to Section 2(d).

(c) If there has been an anatomical gift, a technician may remove any donated parts and an enucleator may remove any donated eyes or parts of eyes, after determination of death by a physician or surgeon.

§ 9. Coordination of Procurement and Use.

Each hospital in this State, after consultation with other hospitals and procurement organizations, shall establish agreements or affiliations for coordination of procurement and use of human bodies and parts.

§ 10. Sale or Purchase of Parts Prohibited.

(a) A person may not knowingly, for valuable consideration, purchase or sell a part for transplantation or therapy, if removal of the part is intended to occur after the death of the decedent.

(b) Valuable consideration does not include reasonable payment for the removal, processing, disposal, preservation, quality control, storage, transportation, or implantation of a part.

(c) A person who violates this section is guilty of a [felony] and upon conviction is subject to a fine not exceeding [$50,000] or imprisonment not exceeding [five] years, or both.

§ 11. Examination, Autopsy, Liability.

(a) An anatomical gift authorizes any reasonable examination necessary to assure medical acceptability of the gift for the purposes intended.

(b) The provisions of this [Act] are subject to the laws of this State governing autopsies.

(c) A hospital physician, surgeon, [coroner], [medical examiner], [local public health officer], enucleator, technician, or other person, who acts in accordance with this [Act] or with the applicable anatomical gift law of another state [or a foreign country] or attempts in good faith to do so is not liable for that act in a civil action or criminal proceeding.

(d) An individual who makes an anatomical gift pursuant to Section 2 or 3 and the individual's estate are not liable for any injury or damage that may result from the making or the use of the anatomical gift.

§ 12. Transitional Provisions.

This [Act] applies to a document of gift, revocation, or refusal to make an anatomical gift signed by the donor or a person authorized to make or object to making an anatomical gift before, on, or after the effective date of this [Act].

§ 13. Uniformity of Application and Construction.

This [Act] shall be applied and construed to effectuate its general purpose to make uniform the law with respect to the subject of this [Act] among states enacting it.

§ 14. Severability.

If any provision of this [Act] or its application thereof to any person or circumstance is held invalid, the invalidity does not affect other provisions or applications of this [Act] which can be given effect without the invalid provision or application, and to this end the provisions of this [Act] are severable.

§ 15. Short Title.

This [Act] may be cited as the "Uniform Anatomical Gift Act (1987)."

§ 16. Repeals.

The following acts and parts of acts are repealed:

(1)

(2)

(3)

§ 17. Effective Date.

This [Act] takes effect ____________________.

APPENDIX C

Uniform Transfers to Minors Act

§ 1. Definitions.

In this [Act]:

(1) "Adult" means an individual who has attained the age of 21 years.

(2) "Benefit plan" means an employer's plan for the benefit of an employee or partner.

(3) "Broker" means a person lawfully engaged in the business of effecting transactions in securities or commodities for the person's own account or for the account of others.

(4) "Conservator" means a person appointed or qualified by a court to act as general, limited, or temporary guardian of a minor's property or a person legally authorized to perform substantially the same functions.

(5) "Court" means [________ court].

(6) "Custodial property" means (i) any interest in property transferred to a custodian under this [Act] and (ii) the income from and proceeds of that interest in property.

(7) "Custodian" means a person so designated under Section 9 or a successor or substitute custodian designated under Section 18.

(8) "Financial institution" means a bank, trust company, savings institution, or credit union, chartered and supervised under state or federal law.

(9) "Legal representative" means an individual's personal representative or conservator.

(10) "Member of the minor's family" means the minor's parent, stepparent, spouse, grandparent, brother, sister, uncle, or aunt, whether of the whole or half blood or by adoption.

(11) "Minor" means an individual who has not attained the age of 21 years.

(12) "Person" means an individual, corporation, organization, or other legal entity.

(13) "Personal representative" means an executor, administrator, successor personal representative, or special administrator of a decedent's estate or a person legally authorized to perform substantially the same functions.

(14) "State" includes any state of the United States, the District of Columbia, the Commonwealth

of Puerto Rico, and any territory or possession subject to the legislative authority of the United States.

(15) "Transfer" means a transaction that creates custodial property under Section 9.

(16) "Transferor" means a person who makes a transfer under this [Act].

(17) "Trust company" means a financial institution, corporation, or other legal entity, authorized to exercise general trust powers.

§ 2. Scope and Jurisdiction.

(a) This [Act] applies to a transfer that refers to this [Act] in the designation under Section 9(a) by which the transfer is made if at the time of the transfer, the transferor, the minor, or the custodian is a resident of this State or the custodial property is located in this State. The custodianship so created remains subject to this [Act] despite a subsequent change in residence of a transferor, the minor, or the custodian, or the removal of custodial property from this State.

(b) A person designated as custodian under this [Act] is subject to personal jurisdiction in this State with respect to any matter relating to the custodianship.

(c) A transfer that purports to be made and which is valid under the Uniform Transfers to Minors Act, the Uniform Gifts to Minors Act, or a substantially similar act, of another state is governed by the law of the designated state and may be executed and is enforceable in this State if at the time of the transfer, the transferor, the minor, or the custodian is a resident of the designated state or the custodial property is located in the designated state.

§ 3. Nomination of Custodian.

(a) A person having the right to designate the recipient of property transferable upon the occurrence of a future event may revocably nominate a custodian to receive the property for a minor beneficiary upon the occurrence of the event by naming the custodian followed in substance by the words: "as custodian for __________ (name of minor) under the [name of Enacting State] Uniform Transfers to Minors Act." The nomination may name one or more persons as substitute custodians to whom the property must be transferred, in the order named, if the first nominated custodian dies before the transfer or is unable, declines, or is ineligible to serve. The nomination may be made in a will, a trust, a deed, an instrument exercising a power of appointment, or in a writing designating a beneficiary of contractual rights which is registered with or delivered to the payor, issuer, or other obligor of the contractual rights.

(b) A custodian nominated under this section must be a person to whom a transfer of property of that kind may be made under Section 9(a).

(c) The nomination of a custodian under this section does not create custodial property until the nominating instrument becomes irrevocable or a transfer to the nominated custodian is completed under Section 9. Unless the nomination of a custodian has been revoked, upon the occurrence of the future event the custodianship becomes effective and the custodian shall enforce a transfer of the custodial property pursuant to Section 9.

§ 4. Transfer by Gift or Exercise of Power of Appointment.

A person may make a transfer by irrevocable gift to, or the irrevocable exercise of a power of appointment in favor of, a custodian for the benefit of a minor pursuant to Section 9.

§ 5. Transfer Authorized by Will or Trust.

(a) A personal representative or trustee may make an irrevocable transfer pursuant to Section 9 to a custodian for the benefit of a minor as authorized in the governing will or trust.

(b) If the testator or settlor has nominated a custodian under Section 3 to receive the custodial property, the transfer must be made to that person.

(c) If the testator or settlor has not nominated a custodian under Section 3, or all persons so nominated as custodian die before the transfer or are unable, decline, or are ineligible to serve, the personal representative or the trustee, as the case may be, shall designate the custodian from among those eligible to serve as custodian for property of that kind under Section 9(a).

§ 6. Other Transfer by Fiduciary.

(a) Subject to subsection (c) a personal representative or trustee may make an irrevocable transfer to another adult or another trust company as custodian for the benefit of a minor pursuant to Section 9, in the absence of a will or under a will or trust that does not contain an authorization to do so.

(b) Subject to subsection (c), a conservator may make an irrevocable transfer to another adult or trust company as custodian for the benefit of the minor pursuant to Section 9.

(c) A transfer under subsection (a) or (b) may be made only if (i) the personal representative, trustee, or conservator considers the transfer to be in the best interest of the minor, (ii) the transfer is not prohibited by or inconsistent with provisions of the applicable will, trust agreement, or other governing instrument, and (iii) the transfer is authorized by the court if it exceeds [$10,000] in value.

§ 7. Transfer by Obligor.

(a) Subject to subsections (b) and (c), a person not subject to Section 5 or 6 who holds property of or owes a liquidated debt to a minor not having a conservator may make an irrevocable transfer to a custodian for the benefit of the minor pursuant to Section 9.

(b) If a person having the right to do so under Section 3 has nominated a custodian under that section to receive the custodial property, the transfer must be made to that person.

(c) If no custodian has been nominated under Section 3, or all persons so nominated as custodian die before the transfer or are unable, decline, or are ineligible to serve, a transfer under this section may be made to an adult member of the minor's family or to a trust company unless the property exceeds [$10,000] in value.

§ 8. Receipt for Custodial Property.

A written acknowledgment of delivery by a custodian constitutes a sufficient receipt and discharge for custodial property transferred to the custodian pursuant to this [Act].

§ 9. Manner of Creating Custodial Property and Effecting Transfer; Designation of Initial Custodian; Control.

(a) Custodial property is created and a transfer is made whenever:

(1) an uncertificated security or a certificated security in registered form is either:

(i) registered in the name of the transferor, an adult other than the transferor, or a trust company, followed in substance by the words: "as custodian for ____________ (name of minor) under the [Name of Enacting State] Uniform Transfers to Minors Act"; or

(ii) delivered if in certificated form, or any document necessary for the transfer of an uncertificated security is delivered, together with any necessary endorsement to an adult other than the transferor or to a trust company as custodian, accompanied by an instrument in substantially the form set forth in subsection (b);

(2) money is paid or delivered to a broker or financial institution for credit to an account in the name of the transferor, an adult other than the transferor, or a trust company, followed in substance by the words: "as custodian for _______ (name of minor) under the [Name of Enacting State] Uniform Transfers to Minors Act";

(3) the ownership of a life or endowment insurance policy or annuity contract is either:

(i) registered with the issuer in the name of the transferor, an adult other than the transferor, or a trust company, followed in substance by the words: "as custodian for _________ (name of minor) under the [Name of Enacting State] Uniform Transfers to Minors Act"; or

(ii) assigned in a writing delivered to an adult other than the transferor or to a trust company whose name in the assignment is followed in substance by the words: "as custodian for ______ (name of minor) under the [Name of Enacting State] Uniform Transfers to Minors Act";

(4) an irrevocable exercise of a power of appointment or an irrevocable present right to future payment under a contract is the subject of a written notification delivered to the payor, issuer, or other obligor that the right is transferred to the transferor, an adult other than the transferor, or a trust company, whose name in the notification is followed in substance by the words: "as custodian for _________ (name of minor) under the [Name of Enacting State] Uniform Transfers to Minors Act";

(5) an interest in real property is recorded in the name of the transferor, an adult other than the transferor, or a trust company, followed in substance by the words: "as custodian for (name of minor) under the [Name of Enacting State] Uniform Transfers to Minors Act";

(6) a certificate of title issued by a department or agency of a state or of the United States which evidences title to tangible personal property is either:

(i) issued in the name of the transferor, an adult other than the transferor, or a trust company, followed in substance by the words: "as custodian for _________ (name of minor) under the [Name of Enacting State] Uniform Transfers to Minors Act"; or

(ii) delivered to an adult other than the transferor or to a trust company, endorsed to that person followed in substance by the words: "as custodian for _________ (name of minor) under the [Name of Enacting State] Uniform Transfers to Minors Act"; or

(7) an interest in any property not described in paragraphs (1) through (6) is transferred to an adult other than the transferor or to a trust company by a written instrument in substantially the form set forth in subsection (b).

(b) An instrument in the following form satisfies the requirements of paragraphs (1)(ii) and (7) of subsection (a):

"TRANSFER UNDER THE [NAME OF ENACTING STATE] UNIFORM TRANSFERS TO MINORS ACT

I, _________ (name of transferor or name and representative capacity if a fiduciary) hereby transfer to _________ (name of custodian), as custodian for _______ (name of minor) under the [Name of Enacting State] Uniform Transfers to Minors Act, the following: (insert a description of the custodial property sufficient to identify it).

Dated:_____________________

____

(Signature)

_________ (name of custodian) acknowledges receipt of the property described above as custodian for the minor named above under the [Name of Enacting State] Uniform Transfers to Minors Act.

Dated:____________________

____________________________"

(Signature of Custodian)

(c) A transferor shall place the custodian in control of the custodial property as soon as practicable.

§ 10. Single Custodianship.

A transfer may be made only for one minor, and only one person may be the custodian. All custodial property held under this [Act] by the same custodian for the benefit of the same minor constitutes a single custodianship.

§ 11. Validity and Effect of Transfer.

(a) The validity of a transfer made in a manner prescribed in this [Act] is not affected by:

(1) failure of the transferor to comply with Section 9(c) concerning possession and control;

(2) designation of an ineligible custodian, except designation of the transferor in the case of property for which the transferor is ineligible to serve as custodian under Section 9(a); or

(3) death or incapacity of a person nominated under Section 3 or designated under Section 9 as custodian or the disclaimer of the office by that person.

(b) A transfer made pursuant to Section 9 is irrevocable, and the custodial property is indefeasibly vested in the minor, but the custodian has all the rights, powers, duties, and authority provided in this [Act], and neither the minor nor the minor's legal representative has any right, power, duty, or authority with respect to the custodial property except as provided in this [Act].

(c) By making a transfer, the transferor incorporates in the disposition all the provisions of this [Act] and grants to the custodian, and to any third person dealing with a person designated as custodian, the respective powers, rights, and immunities provided in this [Act].

§ 12. Care of Custodial Property.

(a) A custodian shall:

(1) take control of custodial property;

(2) register or record title to custodial property if appropriate; and

(3) collect, hold, manage, invest, and reinvest custodial property.

(b) In dealing with custodial property, a custodian shall observe the standard of care that would be observed by a prudent person dealing with property of another and is not limited by any other statute restricting investments by fiduciaries. If a custodian has a special skill or expertise or is named custodian on the basis of representations of a special skill or expertise, the custodian shall use that skill or expertise. However, a custodian, in the custodian's discretion and without liability to the minor or the minor's estate, may retain any custodial property received from a transferor.

(c) A custodian may invest in or pay premiums on life insurance or endowment policies on (i) the life of the minor only if the minor or the minor's estate is the sole beneficiary, or (ii) the life of another person in whom the minor has an insurable interest only to the extent that the minor, the minor's estate, or the custodian in the capacity of custodian, is the irrevocable beneficiary.

(d) A custodian at all times shall keep custodial property separate and distinct from all other property in a manner sufficient to identify it clearly as custodial property of the minor. Custodial property consisting of an undivided interest is so identified if the minor's interest is held as a tenant in common and is fixed. Custodial property subject to recordation is so identified if it is recorded, and custodial property subject to registration is so identified if it is either registered, or held in an account designated, in the name of the custodian, followed in substance by the words: "as a custodian for _________ (name of minor) under the [Name of Enacting State] Uniform Transfers to Minors Act."

(e) A custodian shall keep records of all transactions with respect to custodial property, including information necessary for the preparation of the minor's tax returns, and shall make them available for inspection at reasonable intervals by a parent or legal representative of the minor or by the minor if the minor has attained the age of 14 years.

§ 13. Powers of Custodian.

(a) A custodian, acting in a custodial capacity, has all the rights, powers, and authority over custodial property that unmarried adult owners have over their own property, but a custodian may exercise those rights, powers, and authority in that capacity only.

(b) This section does not relieve a custodian from liability for breach of Section 12.

§ 14. Use of Custodial Property.

(a) A custodian may deliver or pay to the minor or expend for the minor's benefit so much of the custodial property as the custodian considers advisable for the use and benefit of the minor, without court order and without regard to (i) the duty or ability of the custodian personally or of any other person to support the minor, or (ii) any other income or property of the minor which may be applicable or available for that purpose.

(b) On petition of an interested person or the minor if the minor has attained the age of 14 years, the court may order the custodian to deliver or pay to the minor or expend for the minor's benefit so much of the custodial property as the court considers advisable for the use and benefit of the minor.

(c) A delivery, payment, or expenditure under this section is in addition to, not in substitution for, and does not affect any obligation of a person to support the minor.

§ 15. Custodian's Expenses, Compensation, and Bond.

(a) A custodian is entitled to reimbursement from custodial property for reasonable expenses incurred in the performance of the custodian's duties.

(b) Except for one who is a transferor under Section 4, a custodian has a noncumulative election during each calendar year to charge reasonable compensation for services performed during that year.

(c) Except as provided in Section 18(f), a custodian need not give a bond.

§ 16. Exemption of Third Person from Liability.

A third person in good faith and without court order may act on the instructions of or otherwise deal with any person purporting to make a transfer or purporting to act in the capacity of a custodian and, in the absence of knowledge, is not responsible for determining:

(1) the validity of the purported custodian's designation;

(2) the property of, or the authority under this [Act] for, any act of the purported custodian;

(3) the validity or propriety under this [Act] of any instrument or instructions executed or given either by the person purporting to make a transfer or by the purported custodian; or

(4) the propriety of the application of any property of the minor delivered to the purported custodian.

§ 17. Liability to Third Persons.

(a) A claim based on (i) a contract entered into by a custodian acting in a custodial capacity, (ii) an obligation arising from the ownership or control of custodial property, or (iii) a tort committed during the custodianship, may be asserted against the custodial property by proceeding against the custodian in the custodial capacity, whether or not the custodian or the minor is personally liable therefor.

(b) A custodian is not personally liable:

(1) on a contract properly entered into in the custodial capacity unless the custodian fails to reveal that capacity and to identify the custodianship in the contract; or

(2) for an obligation arising from control of custodial property or for a tort committed during the custodianship unless the custodian is personally at fault.

(c) A minor is not personally liable for an obligation arising from ownership of custodial property or for a tort committed during the custodianship unless the minor is personally at fault.

§ 18. Renunciation, Resignation, Death, or Removal of Custodian; Designation of Successor Custodian.

(a) A person nominated under Section 3 or designated under Section 9 as custodian may decline to serve by delivering a valid disclaimer [under the Uniform Disclaimer of Property Interests Act of the Enacting State] to the person who made the nomination or to the transferor or the transferor's legal representative. If the event giving rise to a transfer has not occurred and no substitute custodian able, willing, and eligible to serve was nominated under Section 3, the person who made the nomination may nominate a substitute custodian under said Section 3; otherwise the transferor or the transferor's legal representative shall designate a substitute custodian at the time of the transfer, in either case from among the persons eligible to serve as custodian for that kind of property under Section 9(a). The custodian so designated has the rights of a successor custodian.

(b) A custodian at any time may designate a trust company or an adult other than a transferor under Section 4 as successor custodian by executing and dating an instrument of designation before a subscribing witness other than the successor. If the instrument of designation does not contain or is not accompanied by the resignation of the custodian, the designation of the successor does not take effect until the custodian resigns, dies, becomes incapacitated, or is removed.

(c) A custodian may resign at any time by delivering written notice to the minor if the minor has attained the age of 14 years and to the successor custodian and by delivering the custodial property to the successor custodian.

(d) If a custodian is ineligible, dies, or becomes incapacitated without having effectively designated a successor and the minor has attained the age of 14 years, the minor may designate as successor custodian, in the manner prescribed in subsection (b), an adult member of the minor's family, a conservator of the minor, or a trust company. If the minor has not attained the age of 14 years or fails to act within 60 days after the ineligibility, death, or incapacity, the conservator of the minor becomes successor custodian. If the minor has no conservator or the conservator declines to act, the transferor, the legal representative of the transferor or of the custodian, an adult member of the minor's family, or any other interested person may petition the court to designate a successor custodian.

(e) A custodian who declines to serve under subsection (a) or resigns under subsection (c), or the legal representative of a deceased or incapacitated custodian, as soon as practicable, shall put the custodian property and records in the possession and control of the successor custodian. The successor custodian by action may enforce the obligation to deliver custodial property and records and becomes responsible for each item as received.

(f) A transferor, the legal representative of a transferor, an adult member of the minor's family, a guardian of the person of the minor, the conservator of the minor, or the minor if the minor has attained the age of 14 years may petition the court to remove the custodian for cause and to designate a successor custodian other than a transferor under Section 4 or to require the custodian to give appropriate bond.

§ 19. Accounting by and Determination of Liability of Custodian.

(a) A minor who has attained the age of 14 years, the minor's guardian of the person or legal representative, an adult member of the minor's family, a transferor, or a transferor's legal representative may petition the court (i) for an accounting by the custodian or the custodian's legal representative; or (ii) for a determination of responsibility, as between the custodial property and the custodian personally, for claims against the custodial property unless the responsibility has been adjudicated in an action under Section 17 to which the minor or the minor's legal representative was a party.

(b) A successor custodian may petition the court for an accounting by the predecessor custodian.

(c) The court, in a proceeding under this [Act] or in any other proceeding, may require or permit the custodian or the custodian's legal representative to account.

(d) If a custodian is removed under Section 18(f), the court shall require an accounting and order delivery of the custodial property and records to the successor custodian and the execution of all instruments required for transfer of the custodial property.

§ 20. Termination of Custodianship.

The custodian shall transfer in an appropriate manner the custodial property to the minor or to the minor's estate upon the earlier of:

(1) the minor's attainment of 21 years of age with respect to custodial property transferred under Section 4 or 5;

(2) the minor's attainment of [majority under the laws of this State other than this [Act]] [age 18 or other statutory age of majority of Enacting State] with respect to custodial property transferred under Section 6 or 7; or

(3) the minor's death.

§ 21. Applicability.

This [Act] applies to a transfer within the scope of Section 2 made after its effective date if:

(1) the transfer purports to have been made under [the Uniform Gifts to Minors Act of the Enacting State]; or

(2) the instrument by which the transfer purports to have been made uses in substance the designation "as custodian under the Uniform Gifts to Minors Act" or "as custodian under the Uniform Transfers to Minors Act" of any other state, and the application of this [Act] is necessary to validate the transfer.

§ 22. Effect on Existing Custodianships.

(a) Any transfer of custodial property as now defined in this [Act] made before [the effective date of this Act] is validated notwithstanding that there was no specific authority in [the Uniform Gifts to Minors Act of the Enacting State] for the coverage of custodial property of that kind or for a transfer from that source at the time the transfer was made.

(b) This [Act] applies to all transfers made before the effective date of this [Act] in a manner and form prescribed in [the Uniform Gifts to Minors Act of the Enacting State], except insofar as the application impairs constitutionally vested rights or extends the duration of custodianships in existence on the effective date of this [Act].

(c) Sections 1 and 20 with respect to the age of a minor for whom custodial property is held under this [Act] do not apply to custodial property held in a custodianship that terminated because of the minor's attainment of the age of [18] after [date prior Act was amended to specify [18] as age of majority] and before [the effective date of this Act].

§ 23. Uniformity of Application and Construction.

This [Act] shall be applied and construed to effectuate its general purpose to make uniform the law with respect to the subject of this [Act] among states enacting it.

§ 24. Short Title.

This [Act] may be cited as the "[Name of Enacting State] Uniform Transfers to Minors Act."

§ 25. Severability.

If any provisions of this [Act] or its application to any person or circumstance is held invalid, the invalidity does not affect other provisions or applications of this [Act] which can be given effect without the invalid provision or application, and to this end provisions of this [Act] are severable.

§ 26. Effective Date.

This [Act] takes effect ____________________.

§ 27. Repeals.

[Insert appropriate reference to the existing Gifts to Minors Act of the Enacting State or other jurisdiction] is hereby repealed. To the extent that this [Act], by virtue of Section 22(b), does not apply to transfers made in a manner prescribed in [the Gifts to Minors Act of the Enacting State] or to the powers, duties, and immunities conferred by transfers in that manner upon custodians and persons dealing with custodians, the repeal of [the Gifts to Minors Act of the Enacting State] does not affect those transfers or those powers, duties, and immunities.

APPENDIX D

Uniform Probate Code (1990 Revision)

Official Text Approved by the National Conference of Commissioners on Uniform State Laws

ARTICLE I
GENERAL PROVISIONS, DEFINITIONS AND PROBATE JURISDICTION OF COURT

PART I
SHORT TITLE, CONSTRUCTION, GENERAL PROVISIONS

§ 1-101 [Short Title.]
§ 1-102 [Purposes; Rule of Construction.]
§ 1-103 [Supplementary General Principles of Law Applicable.]
§ 1-104 [Severability.]
§ 1-105 [Construction Against Implied Repeal.]
§ 1-106 [Effect of Fraud and Evasion.]
§ 1-107 [Evidence as to Death or Status.]
§ 1-108 [Acts by Holder of General Power.]

PART 2
DEFINITIONS

§ 1-201 [General Definitions.]

PART 3
SCOPE, JURISDICTION AND COURTS

§ 1-301 [Territorial Application.]
§ 1-302 [Subject Matter Jurisdiction.]
§ 1-303 [Venue; Multiple Proceedings; Transfer.]
§ 1-304 [Practice in Court.]
§ 1-305 [Records and Certified Copies.]
§ 1-306 [Jury Trial.]
§ 1-307 [Registrar; Powers.]
§ 1-308 [Appeals.]
§ 1-309 [Qualifications of Judge.]
§ 1-310 [Oath or Affirmation on Filed Documents.]

PART 4
NOTICE, PARTIES AND REPRESENTATION IN ESTATE LITIGATION AND OTHER MATTERS

§ 1-401 [Notice; Method and Time of Giving]
§ 1-402 [Notice; Waiver.]
§ 1-403 [Pleadings; When Parties Bound by Others; Notice.]

ARTICLE II
INTESTACY, WILLS, AND DONATIVE TRANSFERS

Revised Table of Sections (1990)

PART I
INTESTATE SUCCESSION

§ 2-101 [Intestate Estate.]
§ 2-102 [Share of Spouse.]
§ 2-102A [Share of Spouse.]
§ 2-103 [Share of Heirs Other Than Surviving Spouse.]
§ 2-104 [Requirement That Heir Survive Decedent For 120 Hours.]
§ 2-105 [No Taker.]
§ 2-106 [Representation.]
§ 2-107 [Kindred of Half Blood.]
§ 2-108 [Afterborn Heirs.]
§ 2-109 [Advancements.]
§ 2-110 [Debts to Decedent.]
§ 2-111 [Alienage.]
§ 2-112 [Dower and Curtesy Abolished.]
§ 2-113 [Individuals Related to Decedent Through Two Lines.]
§ 2-114 [Parent and Child Relationship.]

PART 2
ELECTIVE SHARE OF SURVIVING SPOUSE

§ 2-201 [Elective Share.]
§ 2-202 [Augmented Estate.]
§ 2-203 [Right of Election Personal to Surviving Spouse.]
§ 2-204 [Waiver of Right to Elect and of Other Rights.]
§ 2-205 [Proceeding for Elective Share; Time Limit.]
§ 2-206 [Effect of Election on Statutory Benefits.]
§ 2-207 [Charging Spouse with Owned Assets and Gifts Received; Liability of Others for Balance of Elective Share.]

PART 3
SPOUSE AND CHILDREN UNPROVIDED FOR IN WILLS

§ 2-301 [Entitlement of Spouse; Premarital Will.]
§ 2-302 [Omitted Children.]

PART 4
EXEMPT PROPERTY AND ALLOWANCES

§ 2-401 [Applicable Law.]
§ 2-402 [Homestead Allowance.]
§ 2-402A [Constitutional Homestead.]
§ 2-403 [Exempt Property.]
§ 2-404 [Family Allowance.]
§ 2-405 [Source, Determination, and Documentation.]

PART 5
WILLS, WILL CONTRACTS, AND CUSTODY AND DEPOSIT OF WILLS

§ 2-501 [Who May Make Will.]
§ 2-502 [Execution; Witnessed Wills; Holographic Wills.]
§ 2-503 [Writings Intended as Wills, etc.]
§ 2-504 [Self-proved Will.]
§ 2-505 [Who May Witness.]
§ 2-506 [Choice of Law as to Execution.]
§ 2-507 [Revocation by Writing or by Act.]
§ 2-508 [Revocation by Change of Circumstances.]
§ 2-509 [Revival of Revoked Will.]
§ 2-510 [Incorporation by Reference.]
§ 2-511 [Testamentary Additions to Trusts.]
§ 2-512 [Events of Independent Significance.]
§ 2-513 [Separate Writing Identifying Devise of Certain Types of Tangible Personal Property.]
§ 2-514 [Contracts Concerning Succession.]
§ 2-515 [Deposit of Will With Court in Testator's Lifetime.]
§ 2-516 [Duty of Custodian of Will; Liability.]
§ 2-517 [Penalty Clause for Contest.]

PART 6
RULES OF CONSTRUCTION APPLICABLE ONLY TO WILLS.

§ 2-601 [Scope.]
§ 2-602 [Will May Pass All Property and After-Acquired Property.]
§ 2-603 [Antilapse; Deceased Devisee; Class Gifts.]
§ 2-604 [Failure of Testamentary Provision.]
§ 2-605 [Increase in Securities; Accessions.]
§ 2-606 [Nonademption of Specific Devises; Unpaid Proceeds of Sale, Condemnation, or Insurance; Sale by Conservator or Agent.]
§ 2-607 [Nonexoneration.]
§ 2-608 [Exercise of Power of Appointment.]
§ 2-609 [Ademption by Satisfaction.]

PART 7
RULES OF CONSTRUCTION APPLICABLE TO DONATIVE DISPOSITIONS IN WILLS AND OTHER GOVERNING INSTRUMENTS

§ 2-701 [Scope.]
§ 2-702 [Requirement of Survival by 120 Hours.]
§ 2-703 [Choice of Law as to Meaning and Effect of Donative Dispositions.]
§ 2-704 [Power of Appointment; Meaning of Specific Reference Requirement.]
§ 2-705 [Class Gifts Construed to Accord with Intestate Succession.]
§ 2-706 [Life Insurance; Retirement Plan; Account With POD Designation; Transfer-on-Death Registration; Deceased Beneficiary.]
§ 2-707 [Survivorship with Respect to Future Interests Under Terms of Trust; Substitute Takers.]
§ 2-708 [Class Gifts to "Descendants," "Issue," or "Heirs of the Body"; Form of Distribution If None Specified.]
§ 2-709 [Representation; Per Capita at Each Generation; Per Stirpes.]
§ 2-710 [Worthier-Title Doctrine Abolished.]
§ 2-711 [Future Interest in "Heirs" and Like.]

PART 8
GENERAL PROVISIONS CONCERNING PROBATE AND NONPROBATE TRANSFERS

§ 2-801 [Disclaimer of Property Interests.]
§ 2-802 [Effect of Divorce, Annulment, and Decree of Separation.]
§ 2-803 [Effect of Homicide on Intestate Succession, Wills, Trusts, Joint Assets, Life Insurance, and Beneficiary Designations.]
§ 2-804 [Revocation of Probate and Nonprobate Transfers by Divorce; No Revocation by Other Changes of Circumstances.]

PART 9
STATUTORY RULE AGAINST PERPETUITIES; HONORARY TRUSTS

Subpart 1.
Statutory Rule Against Perpetuities

§ 2-901 [Statutory Rule Against Perpetuities.]
§ 2-902 [When Nonvested Property Interest or Power of Appointment Created.]
§ 2-903 [Reformation.]
§ 2-904 [Exclusions from Statutory Rule Against Perpetuities.]
§ 2-905 [Prospective Application.]
§ 2-906 [Supersession] [Repeal.]

Subpart 2.
Honorary Trusts

§ 2-907 [Honorary Trusts; Trusts for Pets.]

ARTICLE III
PROBATE OF WILLS AND ADMINISTRATION

PART 1
GENERAL PROVISIONS

§ 3-101 [Devolution of Estate at Death; Restrictions.]
§ 3-101A [Devolution of Estate at Death; Restrictions.]
§ 3-102 [Necessity of Order of Probate For Will.]
§ 3-103 [Necessity of Appointment For Administration.]
§ 3-104 [Claims Against Decedent; Necessity of Administration.]
§ 3-105 [Proceedings Affecting Devolution and Administration; Jurisdiction of Subject Matter.]
§ 3-106 [Proceedings Within the Exclusive Jurisdiction of Court; Service; Jurisdiction Over Persons.]
§ 3-107 [Scope of Proceedings; Proceedings Independent; Exception.]
§ 3-108 [Probate, Testacy and Appointment Proceedings; Ultimate Time Limit.]
§ 3-109 [Statutes of Limitation on Decedent's Cause of Action.]

PART 2
VENUE FOR PROBATE AND ADMINISTRATION; PRIORITY TO ADMINISTER; DEMAND FOR NOTICE

§ 3-201 [Venue for First and Subsequent Estate Proceedings; Location of Property.]
§ 3-202 [Appointment or Testacy Proceedings; Conflicting Claim of Domicile in Another State.]
§ 3-203 Priority Among Persons Seeking Appointment as Personal Representative.]
§ 3-204 [Demand for Notice of Order or Filing Concerning Decedent's Estate.]

PART 3
INFORMAL PROBATE AND APPOINTMENT PROCEEDINGS; SUCCESSION WITHOUT ADMINISTRATION

§ 3-301 [Informal Probate or Appointment Proceedings; Application; Contents.]
§ 3-302 [Informal Probate; Duty of Registrar; Effect of Informal Probate.]
§ 3-303 [Informal Probate; Proof and Findings Required.]
§ 3-304 [Informal Probate; Unavailable in Certain Cases.]
§ 3-305 [Informal Probate; Registrar Not Satisfied.]
§ 3-306 [Informal Probate; Notice Requirements.]
§ 3-307 [Informal Appointment Proceedings; Delay in Order; Duty of Registrar; Effect of Appointment.]
§ 3-308 [Informal Appointment Proceedings; Proof and Findings Required.]
§ 3-309 [Informal Appointment Proceedings; Registrar Not Satisfied.]
§ 3-310 [Informal Appointment Proceedings; Notice Requirements.]
§ 3-311 [Informal Appointment Unavailable in Certain Cases.]
§ 3-312 [Universal Succession; In General.]
§ 3-313 [Universal Succession; Application; Contents.]
§ 3-314 [Universal Succession; Proof and Findings Required.]
§ 3-315 [Universal Succession; Duty of Registrar; Effect of Statement of Universal Succession.]
§ 3-316 [Universal Succession; Universal Successors' Powers.]
§ 3-317 [Universal Succession; Universal Successors' Liability to Creditors, Other Heirs, Devisees and Persons Entitled to Decedent's Property; Liability of Other Persons Entitled to Property.]
§ 3-318 [Universal Succession; Universal Successors' Submission to Jurisdiction; When Heirs or Devisees May Not Seek Administration.]
§ 3-319 [Universal Succession; Duty of Universal Successors; Information to Heirs and Devisees.]
§ 3-320 [Universal Succession; Universal Successors' Liability For Restitution to Estate.]
§ 3-321 [Universal Succession; Liability of Universal Successors For Claims, Expenses, Intestate Shares and Devises.]

PART 3
JURISDICTION OVER FOREIGN REPRESENTATIVES

PART 4
JUDGMENTS AND PERSONAL REPRESENTATIVE

ARTICLE V
PROTECTION OF PERSONS UNDER DISABILITY AND THEIR PROPERTY

PART 1
GENERAL PROVISIONS AND DEFINITIONS

PART 2
GUARDIANS OF MINORS

PART 3
GUARDIANS OF INCAPACITATED PERSONS

PART 4
PROTECTION OF PROPERTY OF PERSONS UNDER DISABILITY AND MINORS

PART 3

DUTIES AND LIABILITIES OF TRUSTEES

ARTICLE VIII
EFFECTIVE DATE AND REPEALER

ARTICLE I
GENERAL PROVISIONS, DEFINITIONS AND PROBATE JURISDICTION OF COURT

Part I
Short Title, Construction, General Provisions

§ 1-101. [Short Title.]

This Act shall be known and may be cited as the Uniform Probate Code.

§ 1-102. [Purposes; Rule of Construction.]

(a) This Code shall be liberally construed and applied to promote its underlying purposes and policies.

(b) The underlying purposes and policies of this Code are:

(1) to simplify and clarify the law concerning the affairs of decedents, missing persons, protected persons, minors and incapacitated persons;

(2) to discover and make effective the intent of a decedent in distribution of his property;

(3) to promote a speedy and efficient system for liquidating the estate of the decedent and making distribution to his successors;

(4) to facilitate use and enforcement of certain trusts;

(5) to make uniform the law among the various jurisdictions.

§ 1-103. [Supplementary General Principles of Law Applicable.]

Unless displaced by the particular provisions of this Code, the principles of law and equity supplement its provisions.

§ 1-104. [Severability.]

If any provision of this Code or the application thereof to any person or circumstances is held invalid, the invalidity shall not affect other provisions or applications of the Code which can be given effect without the invalid provision or application, and to this end the provisions of this Code are declared to be severable.

§ 1-105. [Construction Against Implied Repeal.]

This Code is a general act intended as a unified coverage of its subject matter and no part of it shall be deemed impliedly repealed by subsequent legislation if it can reasonably be avoided.

§ 1-106. [Effect of Fraud and Evasion.]

Whenever fraud has been perpetrated in connection with any proceeding or in any statement filed under this Code or if fraud is used to avoid or circumvent the provisions or purposes of this Code, any person injured thereby may obtain appropriate relief against the perpetrator of the fraud or restitution from any person (other than a bona fide purchaser) benefitting from the fraud, whether innocent or not. Any proceeding must be commenced within 2 years after the discovery of the fraud, but no proceeding may be brought against one not a perpetrator of the fraud later than 5 years after the time of commission of the fraud. This section has no bearing on remedies relating to fraud practiced on a decedent during his lifetime which affects the succession of his estate.

§ 1-107. [Evidence as to Death or Status.]

In proceedings under this Code the rules of evidence in courts of general jurisdiction including any relating to simultaneous deaths, are applicable unless specifically displaced by the Code. In addition, the following rules relating to determination of death and status are applicable.

(1) a certified or authenticated copy of a death certificate purporting to be issued by an official or agency of the place where the death purportedly occurred is prima facie proof of the fact, place, date and time of death and the identity of the decedent;

(2) a certified or authenticated copy of any record or report of a governmental agency, domestic or foreign, that a person is missing, detained, dead, or alive is prima facie evidence of the status and of the dates, circumstances and places disclosed by the record or report;

(3) in the absence of prima facie evidence of death under (1) or (2) above, the fact of death may be established by clear and convincing evidence, including circumstantial evidence;

(4) a person whose death is not established under the preceding subparagraphs who is absent for a continuous period of 5 years, during which he has not been heard from, and whose absence is not

satisfactorily explained after diligent search or inquiry is presumed to be dead. His death is presumed to have occurred at the end of the period unless there is sufficient evidence for determining that death occurred earlier.

As amended in 1987.

§ 1-108. [Acts by Holder of General Power.]

For the purpose of granting consent or approval with regard to the acts or accounts of a personal representative or trustee, including relief from liability or penalty for failure to post bond, to register a trust, or to perform other duties, and for purposes of consenting to modification or termination of a trust or to deviation from its terms, the sole holder or all co-holders of a presently exercisable general power of appointment, including one in the form of a power of amendment or revocation, are deemed to act for beneficiaries to the extent their interests (as objects, takers in default, or otherwise) are subject to the power.

Part 2
Definitions

§ 1-201. [General Definitions.]

Subject to additional definitions contained in the specific subsequent Articles which are applicable to specific Articles or parts, and unless the context otherwise requires, in this Code:

(1) "Application" means a written request to the Registrar for an order of informal probate or appointment under Part 3 of Article III.

(2) "Beneficiary", as it relates to trust. beneficiaries, includes a person who has any present or future interest, vested or contingent, and also includes the owner of an interest by assignment or other transfer and as it relates to a charitable trust, includes any person entitled to enforce the trust.

(3) "Child" includes any individual entitled to take as a child under this Code by intestate succession from the parent whose relationship is involved and excludes any person who is only a stepchild, a foster child, a grandchild or any more remote descendant.

(4) "Claims", in respect to estates of decedents and protected persons, includes liabilities of the decedent or protected person whether arising in contract, in tort or otherwise, and liabilities of the estate which arise at or after the death of the decedent or after the appointment of a conservator, including funeral expenses and expenses of administration. The term does not include estate or inheritance taxes, or demands or disputes regarding title of a decedent or protected person to specific assets alleged to be included in the estate.

(5) "Court" means the Court or branch having jurisdiction in matters relating to the affairs of decedents. This Court in this state is known as [_______].

(6) "Conservator" means a person who is appointed by a Court to manage the estate of a protected person.

(7) "Devise", when used as a noun, means a testamentary disposition of real or personal property and when used as a verb, means to dispose of real or personal property by will.

(8) "Devisee" means any person designated in a will to receive a devise. In the case of a devise to an existing trust or trustee, or to a trustee on trust described by will, the trust or trustee is the devisee and the beneficiaries are not devisees.

(9) "Disability" means cause for a protective order as described by Section 5-401.

(10) "Distributee" means any person who has received property of a decedent from his personal representative other than as a creditor or purchaser. A testamentary trustee is a distributee only to the extent of distributed assets or increment thereto remaining in his hands. A beneficiary of a testamentary trust to whom the trustee has distributed property received from a personal representative is a distributee of the personal representative. for purposes of this provision, "testamentary trustee" includes a trustee to whom assets are transferred by will, to the extent of the devised assets.

(11) "Estate" includes the property of the decedent, trust, or other person whose affairs are subject to this Code as originally constituted and as it exists from time to time during administration.

(12) "Exempt property" means that property of a decedent's estate which is described in Section 2-402.

(13) "Fiduciary" includes personal representative, guardian, conservator and trustee.

(14) "Foreign personal representative" means a personal representative of another jurisdiction.

(15) "Formal proceedings" means those conducted before a judge with notice to interested persons.

(16) "Guardian" means a person who has qualified as a guardian of a minor or incapacitated person pursuant to testamentary or court appointment, but excludes one who is merely a guardian ad litem.

(17) "Heirs" means those persons, including the surviving spouse who are entitled under the statutes of intestate succession to the property of a decedent.

(18) "Incapacitated person" is as defined in Section 5-103.

(19) "Informal proceedings" mean those conducted without notice to interested persons by an officer of the Court acting as a registrar for probate of a will or appointment of a personal representative.

(20) "Interested person" includes heirs, devisees, children, spouses, creditors, beneficiaries and any others having a property right in or claim against a trust estate or the estate of a decedent, ward or protected person which may be affected by the proceeding. It also includes persons having priority for

appointment as personal representative, and other fiduciaries representing interested persons. The meaning as it relates to particular persons may vary from time to time and must be determined according to the particular purposes of, and matter involved in, any proceeding.

(21) "Issue" of a person means all his lineal descendants of all generations, with the relationship of parent and child at each generation being determined by the definitions of child and parent contained in this Code.

(22) "Lease" includes an oil, gas, or other mineral lease.

(23) "Letters" includes letters testamentary, letters of guardianship, letters of administration, and letters of conservatorship.

(24) "Minor" means a person who is under [21] years of age.

(25) "Mortgage" means any conveyance, agreement or arrangement in which property is used as security.

(26) "Nonresident decedent" means a decedent who was domiciled in another jurisdiction at the time of his death.

(27) "Organization" includes a corporation, government or governmental subdivision or agency, business trust, estate, trust, partnership or association, 2 or more persons having a joint or common interest, or any other legal entity.

(28) "Parent" includes any person entitled to take, or who would be entitled to take if the child died without a will, as a parent under this Code by intestate succession from the child whose relationship is in question and excludes any person who is only a stepparent, foster parent, or grandparent.

(29) "Person" means an individual, a corporation, an organization or other legal entity.

(30) "Personal representative" includes executor, administrator, successor personal representative, special administrator, and persons who perform substantially the same function under the law governing their status. "General personal representative" excludes special administrator.

(31) "Petition" means a written request to the Court for an order after notice.

(32) "Proceeding" includes action at law and suit in equity.

(33) "Property" includes both real and personal property or any interest therein and means anything that may be the subject of ownership.

(34) "Protected person" is as defined in Section 5-103.

(35) "Protective proceeding" is as defined in Section 5-103.

(36) "Registrar" refers to the official of the Court designated to perform the functions of Registrar as provided in Section 1-307.

(37) "Security" includes any note, stock, treasury stock, bond, debenture, evidence of indebtedness, certificate of interest or participation in an oil, gas or mining title or lease or in payments out of production under such a title or lease, collateral trust certificate, transferable share, voting trust certificate or, in general, any interest or instrument commonly known as a security, or any certificate of interest or participation, any temporary or interim certificate, receipt or certificate of deposit for, or any warrant or right to subscribe to or purchase, any of the foregoing.

(38) "Settlement," in reference to a decedent's estate, includes the full process of administration, distribution and closing.

(39) "Special administrator" means a personal representative as described by Sections 3-614 through 3-618.

(40) "State" includes any state of the United States, the District of Columbia, the Commonwealth of Puerto Rico, and any territory or possession subject to the legislative authority of the United States.

(41) "Successor personal representative" means a personal representative, other than a special administrator, who is appointed to succeed a previously appointed personal representative.

(42) "Successors" means those persons, other than creditors, who are entitled to property of a decedent under his will or this Code.

(43) "Supervised administration" refers to the proceedings described in Article III, Part 5.

(44) "Testacy proceeding" means a proceeding to establish a will or determine intestacy.

(45) "Trust" includes any express trust, private or charitable, with additions thereto, wherever and however created. It also includes a trust created or determined by judgment or decree under which the trust is to be administered in the manner of an express trust. "Trust" excludes other constructive trusts, and it excludes resulting trusts, conservatorships, personal representatives, trust accounts as defined in Article VI, custodial arrangements pursuant to [each state should list its legislation, including that relating to gifts to minors, dealing with special custodial situations], business trusts providing for certificates to be issued to beneficiaries, common trust funds, voting trusts, security arrangements liquidation trusts, and trusts for the primary purpose of paying debts dividends, interest, salaries, wages, profits, pensions, or employee benefits of any kind, and any arrangement under which a person is nominee or escrowee for another.

(46) "Trustee" includes an original, additional, or successor trustee, whether or not appointed or confirmed by court.

(47) "Ward" is as defined in Section 5-103.

(48) "Will" includes codicil and any testamentary instrument which merely appoints an executor or revokes or revises another will.

[FOR ADOPTION IN COMMUNITY PROPERTY STATES]

[(49) "Separate property" (if necessary, to be defined locally in accordance with existing concept in adopting state).

(50) "Community property" (if necessary, to be defined locally in accordance with existing concept in adopting state).]

Part 3
Scope, Jurisdiction and Courts

§ 1-301. [Territorial Application.]

Except as otherwise provided in this Code, this Code applies to (1) the affairs and estates of decedents, missing persons, and persons to be protected, domiciled in this state, (2) the property of nonresidents located in this state or property coming into the control of a fiduciary who is subject to the laws of this state, (3) incapacitated persons and minors in this state, (4) survivorship and related accounts in this state, and (5) trusts subject to administration in this state.

§ 1-302. [Subject Matter Jurisdiction.]

(a) To the full extent permitted by the constitution, the Court has jurisdiction over all subject matter relating to (1) estates of decedents, including construction of wills and determination of heirs and successors of decedents, and estates of protected persons; (2) protection of minors and incapacitated persons; and (3) trusts.

(b) The Court has full power to make orders, judgments and decrees and take all other action necessary and proper to administer justice in the matters which come before it.

(c) The Court has jurisdiction over protective proceedings and guardianship proceedings.

(d) If both guardianship and protective proceedings as to the same person are commenced or pending in the same court, the proceedings may be consolidated.

§ 1-303. [Venue; Multiple Proceedings; Transfer.]

(a) Where a proceeding under this Code could be maintained in more than one place in this state, the Court in which the proceeding is first commenced has the exclusive right to proceed.

(b) If proceedings concerning the same estate, protected person, ward, or trust are commenced in more than one Court of this state, the Court in which the proceeding was first commenced shall continue to hear the matter, and the other courts shall hold the matter in abeyance until the question of venue is decided, and if the ruling Court determines that venue is properly in another Court, it shall transfer the proceeding to the other Court.

(c) If a Court finds that in the interest of justice a proceeding or a file should be located in another Court of this state, the Court making the finding may transfer the proceeding or file to the other Court.

§ 1-304. [Practice in Court.]

Unless specifically provided to the contrary in this Code or unless inconsistent with its provisions, the rules of civil procedure including the rules concerning vacation of orders and appellate review govern formal proceedings under this Code.

§ 1-305. [Records and Certified Copies.]

The [Clerk of Court] shall keep a record for each decedent, ward, protected person or trust involved in any document which may be filed with the Court under this Code, including petitions and applications, demands for notices or bonds, trust registrations, and of any orders or responses relating thereto by the Registrar or Court, and establish and maintain a system for indexing, filing or recording which is sufficient to enable users of the records to obtain adequate information. Upon payment of the fees required by law the clerk must issue certified copies of any probated wills, letters issued to personal representatives, or any other record or paper filed or recorded. Certificates related to probated wills must indicate whether the decedent was domiciled in this state and whether the probate was formal or informal. Certificates relating to letters must show the date of appointment.

§ 1-306. [Jury Trial.]

(a) If duly demanded, a party is entitled to trial by jury in [a formal testacy proceeding and] any proceeding in which any controverted question of fact arises as to which any party has a constitutional right to trial by jury.

(b) If there is no right to trial by jury under subsection (a) or the right is waived, the Court in its discretion may call a jury to decide any issue of fact, in which case the verdict is advisory only.

§ 1-307. [Registrar; Powers.]

The acts and orders which this Code specifies as performable by the Registrar may be performed either by a judge of the Court or by a person, including the clerk, designated by the Court by a written order filed and recorded in the office of the Court.

§ 1-308. [Appeals.]

Appellate review, including the right to appellate review, interlocutory appeal, provisions as to time, manner, notice, appeal bond, stays, scope of review, record on appeal, briefs, arguments and power of the appellate court, is governed by the rules applicable to the appeals to the [Supreme Court] in equity cases from the [court of general jurisdiction], except that in proceedings where jury trial has been had as a matter of right, the rules applicable to the scope of review in jury cases apply.

§ 1-309. [Qualifications of Judge.]

A judge of the Court must have the same qualifications as a judge of the [court of general jurisdiction].

§ 1-310. [Oath or Affirmation on Filed Documents.]

Except as otherwise specifically provided in this Code or by rule, every document filed with the Court under this Code including applications, petitions, and demands for notice, shall be deemed to include an oath, affirmation, or statement to the effect that its representations are true as far as the person executing or filing it knows or is informed, and penalties for perjury may follow deliberate falsification therein.

Part 4
Notice, Parties and Representation in Estate Litigation and Other Matters

§ 1-401. [Notice; Method and Time of Giving.]

(a) If notice of a hearing on any petition is required and except for specific notice requirements as otherwise provided, the petitioner shall cause notice of the time and place of hearing of any petition to be given to any interested person or his attorney if he has appeared by attorney or requested that notice be sent to his attorney. Notice shall be given:

(1) by mailing a copy thereof at least 14 days before the time set for the hearing by certified, registered or ordinary first class mail addressed to the person being notified at the post office address given in his demand for notice, if any, or at his office or place of residence, if known;

(2) by delivering a copy thereof to the person being notified personally at least 14 days before the time set for the hearing; or

(3) if the address or identity of any person is not known and cannot be ascertained with reasonable diligence, by publishing at least once a week for 3 consecutive weeks, a copy thereof in a newspaper having general circulation in the county where the hearing is to be held, the last publication of which is to be at least 10 days before the time set for the hearing.

(b) The Court for good cause shown may provide for a different method or time of giving notice for any hearing.

(c) Proof of the giving of notice shall be made on or before the hearing and filed in the proceeding.

§ 1-402. [Notice; Waiver.]

A person, including a guardian ad litem, conservator, or other fiduciary, may waive notice by a writing signed by him or his attorney and filed in the proceeding. A person for whom a guardianship or other protective order is sought, a ward, or a protected person may not waive notice.

§ 1-403. [Pleadings; When Parties Bound by Others; Notice.]

In formal proceedings involving trusts or estates of decedents, minors, protected persons, or incapacitated persons, and in judicially supervised settlements, the following apply:

(1) Interests to be affected shall be described in pleadings which give reasonable information to owners by name or class, by reference to the instrument creating the interests, or in other appropriate manner.

(2) Persons are bound by orders binding others in the following cases:

(i) Orders binding the sole holder or all coholders of a power of revocation or a presently exercisable general power of appointment, including one in the form of a power of amendment, bind other persons to the extent their interests (as objects, takers in default, or otherwise) are subject to the power.

(ii) To the extent there is no conflict of interest between them or among persons represented, orders binding a conservator bind the person whose estate he controls; orders binding a guardian bind the ward if no conservator of his estate has been appointed; orders binding a trustee bind beneficiaries of the trust in proceedings to probate a will establishing or adding to a trust, to review the acts or accounts of a prior fiduciary and in proceedings involving creditors or other third parties; and orders binding a personal representative bind persons interested in the undistributed assets of a decedent's estate in actions or proceedings by or against the estate. If there is no conflict of interest and no conservator or guardian has been appointed, a parent may represent his minor child.

(iii) An unborn or unascertained person who is not otherwise represented is bound by an order to the extent his interest is adequately represented by another party having a substantially identical interest in the proceeding.

(3) Notice is required as follows:

(i) Notice as prescribed by Section 1-401 shall be given to every interested person or to one who can bind an interested person as described in (2) (i) or (2) (ii) above. Notice may be given both to a person and to another who may bind him.

(ii) Notice is given to unborn or unascertained persons, who are not represented under (2) (i) or (2) (ii) above, by giving notice to all known persons whose interests in the proceedings are substantially identical to those of the unborn or unascertained persons.

(4) At any point in a proceeding, a court may appoint a guardian ad litem to represent the interest of a minor an incapacitated, unborn, or unascertained person, or a person whose identity or address is unknown, if the Court determines that representation of the interest otherwise would be inadequate. If not precluded by conflict of interests, a guardian ad litem may be appointed to represent several persons or interests. The Court shall set out its reasons for appointing a guardian ad litem as a part of the record of the proceeding.

ARTICLE II
INTESTACY, WILLS, AND DONATIVE TRANSFERS
(1990)

(See page 427 for the earlier version of this article.)

Part 1
Intestate Succession

§ 2-101. [Intestate Estate.]

(a) Any part of a decedent's estate not effectively disposed of by will passes by intestate succession to the decedent's heirs as prescribed in this Code, except as modified by the decedent's will.

(b) A decedent by will may expressly exclude or limit the right of an individual or class to succeed to property of the decedent passing by intestate succession. If that individual or a member of that class survives the decedent, the share of the decedent's intestate estate to which that individual or class would have succeeded passes as if that individual or each member of that class had disclaimed his [or her] intestate share.

§ 2-102. [Share of Spouse.]

The intestate share of a decedent's surviving spouse is:

(1) the entire intestate estate if:

(i) no descendant or parent of the decedent survives the decedent; or

(ii) all of the decedent's surviving descendants are also descendants of the surviving spouse and there is no other descendant of the surviving spouse who survives the decedent;

(2) the first [$200,000], plus three-fourths of any balance of the intestate estate, if no descendant of the decedent survives the decedent, but a parent of the decedent survives the decedent;

(3) the first [$150,000], plus one-half of any balance of the intestate estate, if all of the decedent's surviving descendants are also descendants of the surviving spouse and the surviving spouse has one or more surviving descendants who are not descendants of the decedent;

(4) the first [$100,000], plus one-half of any balance of the intestate estate, if one or more of the decedent's surviving descendants are not descendants of the surviving spouse.

[ALTERNATIVE PROVISION FOR COMMUNITY PROPERTY STATES]

[§ 2-102A. [Share of Spouse.]

(a) The intestate share of the surviving spouse in separate property is:

(1) the entire intestate estate if:

(i) no surviving issue or parent of the decedent, the entire intestate estate;

(ii) if there is no surviving issue but the decedent is survived by a parent or parents, the first [$50,000], plus one-half of the balance of the intestate estate;

(2) the first [$200,000], plus three-fourths of any balance of the intestate estate, if no descendant of the decedent survives the decedent, but a parent of the decedent survives the decedent;

(3) the first [$150,000], plus one-half of any balance of the intestate estate, if all of the decedent's surviving descendants are also descendants of the surviving spouse and the surviving spouse has one or more surviving descendants who are not descendants of the decedent;

(4) the first [$100,000], plus one-half of any balance of the intestate estate, if one or more of the decedent's surviving descendants are not descendants of the surviving spouse.

(b) The one-half of community property belonging to the decedent passes to the [surviving spouse] as the intestate share.]

§ 2-103. [Share of Heirs Other Than Surviving Spouse.]

Any part of the intestate estate not passing to the decedent's surviving spouse under Section 2-102, or the entire intestate estate if there is no surviving spouse, passes in the following order to the individuals designated below who survive the decedent:

(1) to the decedent's descendants by representation;

(2) if there is no surviving descendant, to the decedent's parents equally if both survive, or to the surviving parent;

(3) if there is no surviving descendant or parent, to the descendants of the decedent's parents or either of them by representation;

(4) if there is no surviving issue, parent or descendant of a parent, but the decedent is survived by one or more grandparents or descendants of grandparents, half of the estate passes

to the decedent's paternal grandparents equally if both survive, or to the surviving paternal grandparent, or to the descendants of the decedent's paternal grandparents or either of them if both are deceased, the descendants taking by representation; and the other half passes to the decedent's maternal relatives in the same manner; but if there is no surviving grandparent or descendant of a grandparent on either the paternal or the maternal side, the entire estate passes to the decedent's relatives on the other side in the same manner as the half.

§ 2-104. [Requirement That Heir Survive Decedent For 120 Hours.]

An individual who fails to survive the decedent by 120 hours is deemed to have predeceased the decedent for purposes of homestead allowance, exempt property and intestate succession, and the decedent's heirs are determined accordingly. If it is not established by clear and convincing evidence that an individual who would otherwise be an heir survived the decedent by 120 hours, it is deemed that the individual failed to survive for the required period. This section is not to be applied if its application would result in a taking of intestate estate by the state under Section 2-105.

§ 2-105. [No Taker.]

If there is no taker under the provisions of this Article, the intestate estate passes to the [state].

§ 2-106. [Representation.]

(a) [Definitions.] In this section:

(1) "Deceased descendant," "deceased parent," or "deceased grandparent" means a descendant, parent or grandparent who either predeceased the decedent or is deemed to have predeceased the decedent under Section 2-104.

(2) "Surviving descendant" means a descendant who neither predeceased the decedent nor is deemed to have predeceased the decedent under Section 2-104.

(b) [Decedent's Descendants.] If, under Section 2-103(1), a decedent's intestate estate or a part thereof passed "by representation" to the decedent's descendants, the estate or part thereof is divided into as many equal shares as there are (i) surviving descendants in the generation nearest to the decedent which contains one or more surviving descendants and (ii) deceased descendants in the same generation who left surviving descendants, if any. Each surviving descendant in the nearest generation is allocated one share. The remaining shares, if any, are combined and then divided in the same manner among the surviving descendants of the deceased descendants as if the surviving descendants who were allocated a share and their surviving descendants had predeceased the decedent.

(c) [Descendants of Parents or Grandparents.] If, under Section 2-103(3) or (4), a decedent's intestate estate or a part thereof passed "by representation" to the descendants of the decedent's deceased parents or either of them or to the descendants of the decedent's deceased paternal or maternal grandparents or either of them, the estate or part thereof is divided into as many equal shares as there are (i) surviving descendants in the generation nearest the deceased parents or either of them, or the deceased grandparents or either of them, that contains one or more surviving descendants and (ii) deceased descendants in the same generation who left surviving descendants, if any. Each surviving descendant in the nearest generation is allocated one share. The remaining shares, if any are combined and then divided in the same manner among the surviving descendants of the deceased descendants as if the surviving descendants who were allocated a share and their surviving descendants had predeceased the decedent.

§ 2-107. [Kindred of Half Blood.]

Relatives of the half blood inherit the same share they would inherit if they were of the whole blood.

§ 2-108. [Afterborn Heirs.]

An individual in gestation at a particular time is treated as living at that time if the individual lives 120 hours or more after birth.

§ 2-109. [Advancements.]

(a) If an individual person dies intestate as to all or a portion of his [or her] estate, property the decedent gave during the decedent's lifetime to an individual who, at the decedent's death, is an heir is treated as an advancement against the heir's intestate share only if (i) the decedent declared in a contemporaneous writing or the heir acknowledged in writing that the gift is an advancement or (ii) the decedent's contemporaneous writing or the heir's written acknowledgment otherwise indicates that the gift is to be taken into account in computing the division and distribution of the decedent's intestate estate.

(b) For purposes of subsection (a), property advanced is valued as of the time the heir came into possession or enjoyment of the property or as of the time of the decedent's death, whichever first occurs.

(c) If the recipient of the property fails to survive the decedent, the property is not taken into account in computing the division and distribution of the decedent's intestate estate, unless the decedent's contemporaneous writing provides otherwise.

§ 2-110. [Debts to Decedent.]

A debt owed to a decedent is not charged against the intestate share of any individual except the debtor. If the debtor fails to survive the decedent, the debt is not taken into account in computing the intestate share of the debtor's descendant.

§ 2-111. [Alienage.]

No individual is disqualified to take as an heir because the individual or an individual through whom he [or she] claims is or has been an alien.

[§ 2-112. [Dower and Curtesy Abolished.]

The estates of dower and curtesy are abolished.]

§ 2-113. [Persons Related to Decedent Through Two Lines.]

An individual who is related to the decedent through two lines of relationship is entitled to only a single share based on the relationship that would entitle the individual to the larger share.

§ 2-114. [Parent and Child Relationship.]

(a) Except as provided in subsections (b) and (c), for purposes of intestate succession by, through, or from a person, an individual is the child of his [or her] natural parents, regardless of their marital status. The parent and child relationship may be established under [the Uniform Parentage Act] [applicable state law] [insert appropriate statutory reference].

(b) An adopted individual is the child of his [or her] adopting parent or parents and not of his [or her] natural parents, but adoption of a child by the spouse of either natural parent has no effect on (i) the relationship between the child and that natural parent or (ii) the right of the child or a descendant of the child to inherit from or through the other natural parent.

(c) Inheritance from or through a child by either natural parent or his [of her] kindred is precluded unless that natural parent has openly treated the child as his [or hers], and has not refused to support the child.

Part 2
Elective Share of Surviving Spouse

§ 2-201. [Elective Share.]

(a) Elective-Share Amount. The surviving spouse of a decedent who dies domiciled in this State has a right of election, under the limitations and condition stated in this Part, to take an elective-share amount equal to the value of the elective-share percentage of the augmented estate, determined by the length of time the spouse and the decedent were married to each other, in accordance with the following schedule:

If the decedent and the spouse were married to each other:	The elective-share percentage is:
Less than 1 year	Supplemental Amount Only.
1 year but less than 2 years	3% of the augmented estate.
2 years but less than 3 years	6% of the augmented estate.
3 years but less than 4 years	9% of the augmented estate.
4 years but less than 5 years	12% of the augmented estate.
5 years but less than 6 years	15% of the augmented estate.
6 years but less than 7 years	18% of the augmented estate.
7 years but less than 8 years	21% of the augmented estate.
8 years but less than 9 years	24% of the augmented estate.
9 years but less than 10 years	27% of the augmented estate.
10 years but less than 11 years	30% of the augmented estate.
11 years but less than 12 years	34% of the augmented estate.
12 years but less than 13 years	38% of the augmented estate.
13 years but less than 14 years	42% of the augmented estate.
14 years but less than 15 years	46% of the augmented estate.
15 years or more	50% of the augmented estate.

(b) Supplemental Elective-Share Amount. If the sum of the amounts described in Sections 2-202(b)(3) and (4), 2-207(a)(1) and (3), and that part of the elective-share amount payable from the decedent's probate and reclaimable estates under Sections 2-207(b) and (c) is less than [$50,000], the surviving spouse is entitled to a supplemental elective-share amount equal to [$50,000], minus the sum of the amounts described in those sections. The supplemental elective-share amount is payable from the decedent's probate estate and from recipients of the decedent's reclaimable estate in the order of priority set forth in Sections 2-207(b) and (c).

(c) Non-Domiciliary. The right, if any, of the surviving spouse of a decedent who dies domiciled outside this State to take an elective share in property in this State is governed by the law of the decedent's domicile at death.

§ 2-202. [Augmented Estate.]

(a) Definitions.

(1) In this section:

(i) "Bona fide purchaser" means a purchaser for value in good faith and without notice of an adverse claim. The notation of a state documentary fee on a recorded instrument pursuant to [insert appropriate reference] is prima facie evidence that the transfer described therein was made to a bona fide purchaser.

(ii) "Nonadverse party" means a person who does not have a substantial beneficial interest in the trust or other property arrangement that would be adversely affected by the exercise or nonexercise of the power that he [or she] possesses respecting the trust or other property arrangement. A person having a general power of appointment over property is deemed to have a beneficial interest in the property.

(iii) "Presently exercisable general power of appointment" means a power of appointment under which, at the time in question, the decedent by an exercise of the power could have created an interest, present or future, in himself [or herself] or his [or her] creditors.

(iv) "Probate estate" means property, whether real or personal, movable or immovable, wherever situated, that would pass by intestate succession if the decedent died without a valid will.

(v) "Right to income" includes a right to payments under an annuity or similar contractual arrangement.

(vi) "Value of property owned by the surviving spouse at the decedent's death" and "value of property to which the surviving spouse succeeds by reason of the decedent's death" include the commuted value of any present or future interest then held by the surviving spouse and the commuted value of amounts payable to the surviving spouse after the decedent's death under any trust, life insurance settlement option, annuity contract, public or private pension, disability compensation, death benefit or retirement plan, or any similar arrangement, exclusive of the federal Social Security system.

(2) In subsections (b)(2)(iii) and (iv), "transfer" includes an exercise or release of a power of appointment, but does not include a lapse of a power of appointment.

(b) Property Included in Augmented Estate. The augmented estate consists of the sum of:

(1) the value of the decedent's probate estate, reduced by funeral and administration expenses, homestead allowance, family allowances and exemptions, and enforceable claims;

(2) the value of the decedent's reclaimable estate. The decedent's reclaimable estate is composed of all property, whether real or personal, movable or immovable, wherever situated, not included in the decedent's probate estate, of any of the following types:

(i) property to the extent the passing of the principal thereof to or for the benefit of any person, other than the decedent's surviving spouse, was subject to a presently exercisable general power of appointment held by the decedent alone, if the decedent held that power immediately before his [or her] death or if and to the extent the decedent, while married to his [or her] surviving spouse and during the two-year period next preceding the decedent's death, released that power or exercised that power in favor of any person other than the decedent or the decedent's estate, spouse, or surviving spouse;

(ii) property, to the extent of the decedent's unilaterally severable interest therein, held by the decedent and any other person, except the decedent's surviving spouse, with right of survivorship, if the decedent held that interest immediately before his [or her] death or if and to the extent the decedent, while married to his [or her] surviving spouse and during the two-year period preceding the decedent's death, transferred that interest to any person other than the decedent's surviving spouse;

(iii) proceeds of insurance, including accidental death benefits, on the life of the decedent payable to any person other than the decedent's surviving spouse, if the decedent owned the insurance policy, had the power to change the beneficiary of the insurance policy, or the insurance policy was subject to a presently exercisable general power of appointment held by the decedent alone immediately before his [or her] death if and to the extent the decedent, while married to his [or her] surviving spouse and during the two-year period next preceding the decedent's death, transferred that policy to any person other than the decedent's surviving spouse; and

(iv) property transferred by the decedent to any person other than a bona fide purchaser at any time during the decedent's marriage to the surviving spouse, to or for the benefit of any person, other than the decedent's surviving spouse, if the transfer is of any of the following types:

(A) any transfer to the extent that the decedent retained at the time of his [or her] death the possession or enjoyment of, or right to income from, the property;

(B) any transfer to the extent that, at the time of or during the two-year period next preceding the decedent's death, the income or principal was subject to a power, exercisable by the decedent alone or in conjunction with any other person or exercisable by a nonadverse party, for the benefit of the decedent or the decedent's estate;

(C) any transfer of property, to the extent the decedent's contribution to it, as a percentage of the whole, was made within two years before the decedent's death, by which the property is held, at the time of or during the two-year period next preceding the decedent's death, by the decedent and another, other than the decedent's surviving spouse, with right of survivorship; or

(D) any transfer made to a donee within two years before the decedent's death to the extent that the aggregate transfers to any one donee in either of the years exceed $10,000.00;

(3) the value of property to which the surviving spouse succeeds by reason of the decedent's death, other than by homestead allowance,

exempt property, family allowance, testate succession, or intestate succession, including the proceeds of insurance, including accidental death benefits, on the life of the decedent and benefits payable under a retirement plan in which the decedent was a participant, exclusive of the federal Social Security system; and

(4) the value of property owned by the surviving spouse at the decedent's death, reduced by enforceable claims against that property or that spouse, plus the value of amounts that would have been includible in the surviving spouse's reclaimable estate had the spouse predeceased the decedent. But amounts that would have been includible in the surviving spouse's reclaimable estate under subsection (b)(2)(iii) are not valued as if he [or she] were deceased.

(c) [Exclusions.] Any transfer or exercise or release of a power of appointment is excluded from the decedent's reclaimable estate (i) to the extent the decedent received adequate and full consideration in money or money's worth for the transfer, exercise, or release or (ii) if irrevocably made with the written consent or joinder of the surviving spouse.

(d) [Valuation.] Property is valued as of the decedent's death, but property irrevocably transferred during the two-year period next preceding the decedent's death which is included in the decedent's reclaimable estate under subsection (b)(2)(i), (ii), and (iv) is valued as of the time of the transfer. If the terms of more than one of the subparagraphs or sub-subparagraphs of subsection (b)(2) apply, the property is included in the augmented estate under the subparagraph or sub-subparagraph that yields the highest value. For the purposes of this subsection, an "irrevocable transfer of property" includes an irrevocable exercise or release of a power of appointment.

(e) [Protection of Payors and Other Third Parties.]

(1) Although under this section a payment, item of property, or other benefit is included in the decedent's reclaimable estate, a payor or other third party is not liable for having made a payment or transferred an item of property or other benefit to a beneficiary designated in a governing instrument, or for having taken any other action in good faith reliance on the validity of a governing instrument, upon request and satisfactory proof of the decedent's death, before the payor or other third party received written notice from the surviving spouse or spouse's representative of an intention to file a petition for the elective share or that a petition for the elective share has been filed. A payor or other third party is liable for payments made or other actions taken after the payor or other third party received written notice of an intention to file a petition for the elective share or that a petition for the elective share has been filed.

(2) The written notice of intention to file a petition for the elective share or that a petition for the elective share has been filed must be mailed to the payor's or other third party's main office or home by registered or certified mail, return receipt requested, or served upon the payor or other third party in the same manner as a summons in a civil action. Upon receipt of written notice of intention to file a petition for the elective share or that a petition for the elective share has been filed, a payor or other third party may pay any amount owed or transfer or deposit any item of property held by it to or with the court having jurisdiction of the probate proceedings relating to the decedent's estate, or if no proceedings have been commenced, to or with the court having jurisdiction of probate proceedings relating to decedents' estates located in the county of the decedent's residence. The court shall hold the funds or item of property and, upon its determination under Section 2-205 (d), shall order disbursement in accordance with the determination. If no petition is filed in the court within the specified time under Section 2-205(a) or, if filed, the demand for an elective share is withdrawn under Section 2-205(c), the court shall file disbursement to the designated beneficiary. Payments, transfers, or deposits made to or with the court discharge the payor or other third party from all claims for the value of amounts paid to or items of property transferred to or deposited with the Court.

(3) Upon petition to the probate court by the beneficiary designated in a governing instrument, the court may order that all or part of the property be paid to the beneficiary in an amount and subject to conditions consistent with this section.

(f) [Protection of Bona Fide Purchasers; Personal Liability of Recipient.]

(1) A person who purchases property from a recipient for value and without notice, or who receives a payment or other item of property in partial or full satisfaction of a legally enforceable obligation, is neither obligated under this Part to return the payment, item of property, or benefit nor is liable under this Part for the amount of the payment or the value of the item of property or benefit. But a person who, not for value, receives a payment, item of property, or any other benefit included in the decedent's reclaimable estate is obligated to return the payment, item of property, or benefit, or is personally liable for the amount of the payment or the value of the item of property or benefit, as provided in Section 2-207.

(2) If any section or part of any section of this Part is preempted by federal law with respect to a payment, an item of property or any other benefit included in the decedent's reclaimable estate, a person who, not for value, receives the

payment, item of property, or any other benefit is obligated to return that payment, item of property, or benefit, or is personally liable for the amount of that payment or the value of that item of property or benefit, as provided in Section 2-207, to the person who would have been entitled to it were that section or part of that section not preempted.

§ 2-203. [Right of Election Personal to Surviving Spouse.]

(a) [Surviving Spouse Must Be Living at Time of Election.] The right of election may be exercised only by a surviving spouse who is living when the petition for the elective share is filed in the court under Section 2-205(a). If the election is not exercised by the surviving spouse personally, it may be exercised on the surviving spouse's behalf by his [or her] conservator, guardian, or agent under the authority of a power of attorney.

(b) [Incapacitated Surviving Spouse.] If the election is exercised on behalf of a surviving spouse who is an incapacitated person, that portion of the elective-share and supplemental elective-share amounts due from the decedent's probate estate and recipients of the decedent's reclaimable estate under Sections 2-207(b) and (c) must be placed in a custodial trust for the benefit of the surviving spouse under the provisions of the [Enacting state] Uniform Custodial Trust Act, except as modified below. For the purposes of this subsection, an election on behalf of a surviving spouse by an agent under a durable power of attorney is presumed to be on behalf of a surviving spouse who is an incapacitated person. For purposes of the custodial trust established by this subsection, (i) the electing guardian, conservator, or agent is the custodial trustee, (ii) the surviving spouse is the beneficiary, (iii) the custodial trust is deemed to have been created by the decedent spouse by written transfer that takes effect at the decedent spouse's death and that directs the custodial trustee to administer the custodial trust as for an incapacitated beneficiary.

(c) [Custodial Trust.] For the purposes of subsection (b), the [Enacting state] Uniform Custodial Trust Act must be applied as if Section 6(b) thereof were repealed and Sections 2(e), 9(b), and 17(a) were amended to read as follows:

(1) Neither an incapacitated beneficiary nor anyone acting on behalf of an incapacitated beneficiary has a power to terminate the custodial trust; but if the beneficiary regains capacity, the beneficiary then acquires the power to terminate the custodial trust by delivering to the custodial trustee a writing signed by the beneficiary declaring the termination. If not previously terminated, the custodial trust terminates on the death of the beneficiary.

(2) If the beneficiary is incapacitated, the custodial trustee shall expend so much or all of the custodial trust property as the custodial trustee considers advisable for the use and benefit of the beneficiary and individuals who were supported by the beneficiary when the beneficiary became incapacitated, or who are legally entitled to support the beneficiary. Expenditures may be made in the manner, when, and to the extent that the custodial trustee determines suitable and proper, without court order but with regard to other support, income, and property of the beneficiary [exclusive of] [and] benefits of medical or other forms of assistance from any state or federal government or governmental agency for which the beneficiary must qualify on the basis of need.

(3) Upon the beneficiary's death, the remaining custodial trust property, in the following order: (i) under the residuary clause, if any, of the will of the beneficiary's predeceased spouse against whom the elective share was taken, as if that predeceased spouse died immediately after the beneficiary; or (ii) to that predeceased spouse's heirs under Section 2-711 of [this State's] Uniform Probate Code.

[STATES THAT HAVE HAVE NOT ADOPTED THE UNIFORM CUSTODIAL TRUST ACT SHOULD ADOPT THE FOLLOWING ALTERNATIVE SUBSECTION (B) AND NOT ADOPT SUBSECTION (B) OR (C) ABOVE]

[(b) [Incapacitated Surviving Spouse.] If the election is exercised on behalf of a surviving spouse who is an incapacitated person, the court must set aside that portion of the elective-share and supplemental elective-share amounts due from the decedent's probate estate and recipients of the decedent's reclaimable estate under Section 2-207(b) and (c) and must appoint a trustee to administer that property for the support of the surviving spouse. For the purposes of this subsection, an election on behalf of a surviving spouse by an agent under a durable power of attorney is presumed to be on behalf of a surviving spouse who is an incapacitated person. The trustee must administer the trust in accordance with the following terms and such additional terms as the court determines appropriate:

(1) Expenditures of income and principal may be made in the manner, when, and to the extent that the trustee determines suitable and proper for the surviving spouse's support, without court order but with regard to other support, income, and property of the surviving spouse [exclusive of] [and] benefits of medical or other forms of assistance from any state or federal government or governmental agency

for which the surviving spouse must qualify on the basis of need.

(2) During the surviving spouse's incapacity, neither the surviving spouse nor anyone acting on behalf of the surviving spouse has a power to terminate the trust; but if the surviving spouse regains capacity, the surviving spouse then acquires the power to terminate the trust and acquire full ownership of the trust property free of trust, by delivering to the trustee a writing signed by the surviving spouse declaring the termination.

(3) Upon the surviving spouse's death, the trustee shall transfer the unexpended trust property in the following order: (i) under the residuary clause, if any, of the will of the predeceased spouse against whom the elective share was taken, as if that predeceased spouse died immediately after the surviving spouse; or (ii) to that predeceased spouse's heirs under Section 2-711.]

§ 2-204. [Waiver of Right to Elect and of Other Rights.]

(a) The right of election of a surviving spouse and the rights of the surviving spouse to homestead allowance, exempt property, and family allowance, or any of them, may be waived, wholly or partially, before or after marriage, by a written contract, agreement, or waiver signed by the surviving spouse.

(b) A surviving spouse's waiver is not enforceable if the surviving spouse proves that:

(1) he [or she] did not execute the waiver voluntarily; or

(2) the waiver was unconscionable when it was executed and, before execution of the waiver, he [or she]:

(i) was not provided a fair and reasonable disclosure of the property or financial obligations of the decedent;

(ii) did not voluntarily and expressly waive, in writing, any right to disclosure of the property or financial obligations of the decedent beyond the disclosure provided; and

(iii) did not have, or reasonably could not have had, an adequate knowledge of the property or financial obligations of the decedent.

(c) An issue of unconscionability of a waiver is for decision by the court as a matter of law.

(d) Unless it provides to the contrary, a waiver of "all rights" or equivalent language, in the property or estate of a present or prospective spouse or a complete property settlement entered into after or in anticipation of separation or divorce is a waiver of all rights to elective share, homestead allowance, exempt property, and family allowance by each spouse in the property of the other and a renunciation by each of all benefits that would otherwise pass to him [or her] from the other by intestate succession or by virtue of the provisions of any will executed before the waiver or property settlement.

§ 2-205. [Proceeding for Elective Share; Time Limit.]

(a) Except as provided in subsection (b), the election must be made by filing in the court and mailing or delivering to the personal representative, if any, a petition for the elective share within nine months after the decedent's death, or within six months after the probate of the decedent's will, whichever limitation later expires. The surviving spouse must give notice of the time and place set for hearing to persons interested in the estate and to the distributees and recipients of portions of the augmented estate whose interests will be adversely affected by the taking of the elective share. Except as provided in subsection (b), the decedent's reclaimable estate, described in Section 2-202(b)(2), is not included within the augmented estate for the purpose of computing the elective share, if the petition is filed later than nine months after the decedent's death.

(b) Within nine months after the decedent's death, the surviving spouse may petition the court for an extension of time for making an election. If, within nine months after the decedent's death, the spouse gives notice of the petition to all persons interested in the decedent's reclaimable estate, the court for cause shown by the surviving spouse may extend the time for election. If the court grants the spouse's petition for an extension, the decedent's reclaimable estate, described in Section 2-202(b)(2), is not excluded from the augmented estate for the purpose of computing the elective-share and supplemental elective-share amounts, if the spouse makes an election by filing in the court and mailing or delivering to the personal representative, if any, a petition for the elective share within the time allowed by the extension.

(c) The surviving spouse may withdraw his [or her] demand for an elective share at any time before entry of a final determination by the court.

(d) After notice and hearing, the Court shall determine the elective-share amounts, and supplemental elective-share amounts, and shall order its payment from the assets of the augmented estate or by contribution as appears appropriate under Section 2-207. If it appears that a fund or property included in the augmented estate has not come into the possession of the personal representative, or has been distributed by the personal representative, the court nevertheless shall fix the liability of any person who has any interest in the fund or property or who has possession thereof, whether as trustee or otherwise. The proceeding may be maintained against fewer than all persons against whom relief could be sought, but no person is subject to contribution in any greater amount than he [or she] would have been under Section 2-207 had relief been secured against all persons subject to contribution.

(e) An order or judgment of the court may be enforced as necessary in suit for contribution or payment in other courts of this State or other jurisdictions.

§ 2-206. [Effect of Election on Statutory Benefits.]

If the right of election is exercised by or on behalf of the surviving spouse, the surviving spouse's homestead allowance, exempt property, and family allowance, if any, are not charged against but are in addition to the elective-share and supplemental elective-share amounts.

§ 2-207. [Charging Spouse with Owned Assets and Gifts Received; Liability of Others for Balance of Elective Share.]

(a) [Elective-Share Amount Only.] In a proceeding for an elective share, the following are applied first to satisfy the elective-share amount and to reduce or eliminate any contributions due from the decedent's probate estate and recipients of the decedent's reclaimable estate:

(1) amounts included in the augmented estate which pass or have passed to the surviving spouse by testate or intestate succession;

(2) amounts included in the augmented estate under Section 2-202(b)(3);

(3) amounts included in the augmented estate which would have passed to the spouse but were disclaimed; and

(4) amounts included in the augmented estate under Section 2-202(b)(4) up to the applicable percentage thereof. For the purposes of this subsection, the "applicable percentage" is twice the elective-share percentage set forth in the schedule in Section 2-201(a) appropriate to the length of time the spouse and the decedent were married to each other.

(b) [Unsatisfied Balance of Elective Share-amount; Supplemental Elective-Share Amount.] If, after the application of subsection (a), the elective share is not fully satisfied or the surviving spouse is entitled to a supplemental elective-share amount, amounts included in the decedent's probate estate and that portion of the decedent's reclaimable estate other than amounts irrevocably transferred within two years before the decedent's death are applied first to satisfy the unsatisfied balance of the elective-share amount or the supplemental elective-share amount. The decedent's probate estate and that portion of the decedent's reclaimable estate are so applied that liability for the unsatisfied balance of the elective-share amount or for the supplemental elective-share amount is equitably apportioned among the recipients of the decedent's probate estate and that portion of the decedent's reclaimable estate in proportion to the value of their interests therein.

(c) [Unsatisfied Balance of Elective-Share and Supplemental Elective-Share Amounts.] If, after the application of subsections (a) and (b), the elective-share or supplemental elective-share amount is not fully satisfied, the remaining portion of the decedent's reclaimable estate is so applied that liability for the unsatisfied balance of the elective-share or supplemental elective-share amount is equitably apportioned among the recipients of that portion of the decedent's reclaimable estate in proportion to the value of their interests therein.

(d) [Liability of Recipients of Reclaimable Estate and Their Donees.] Only original recipients of the reclaimable estate described in Section 2-202(b)(2), and the donees of the recipients of the reclaimable estate to the extent the donees have the property or its proceeds, are liable to make a proportional contribution toward satisfaction of the surviving spouse's elective-share or supplemental elective-share amount. A person liable to make contribution may choose to give up the proportional part of the reclaimable estate or to pay the value of the amount for which he [or she] is liable.

Part 3
Spouse and Children Unprovided for in Wills

§ 2-301. [Entitlement of Spouse; Premarital Will.]

(a) If a testator's surviving spouse married the testator after the testator executed his [or her] will, the surviving spouse is entitled to receive, as an intestate share, no less than the value of the share of the estate he [or she] would have received if the testator had died intestate as to that portion of the testator's estate, if any, that neither is devised to a child of the testator who was born before the testator married the surviving spouse and who is not a child of the surviving spouse nor is devised or passes under Sections 2-603 or 2-604 to a descendant of such a child, unless:

(1) it appears from the will or other evidence that the will was made in contemplation of the testator's marriage to the surviving spouse;

(2) the will expresses the intention that it is to be effective notwithstanding any subsequent marriage; or

(3) the testator provided for the spouse by transfer outside the will and the intent that the transfer be in lieu of a testamentary provision is shown by the testator's statements or is reasonably inferred from the amount of the transfer or other evidence.

(b) In satisfying the share provided by this section, devises made by the will to the testator's surviving spouse, if any, are applied first, and other devises, other than a devise to a child of the testator who was born before the testator married the surviving spouse and who is not a child of the surviving spouse or a devise or substitute gift under Sections 2-603 or 2-604 to a descendant of such a child, abate as provided in Section 3-902.

§ 2-302. [Omitted Children.]

(a) Except as provided in subsection (b), if a testator fails to provide in his [or her] will for any of his [or her] children born or adopted after the execution of the will, the omitted after-born or after-adopted child receives a share in the estate as follows:

(1) If the testator had no child living when [or she] executes the will, an omitted after-born or after-adopted child receives a share in the estate equal in value to that which the child would have received had the testator died intestate, unless the will devised all or substantially all the estate to the other parent of the omitted child and that other parent survives the testator and is entitled to take under the will.

(2) If the testator had one or more children living when he [or she] executed the will, and the will devised property or an interest in property to one or more of the the-living children, an omitted after-born or after-adopted child is entitled to share in the testator's estate as follows:

(i) The portion of the testator's estate in which the omitted after-born or after-adopted child is entitled to share is limited to devises made to the testator's then-living children under the will.

(ii) The omitted after-born or after-adopted child is entitled to receive the share of the testator's estate, as limited in subparagraph (i), that the child would have received had the testator included all omitted after-born or after-adopted children with the children to whom devises were made under the will and had given an equal share of the estate to each child.

(iii) To the extent feasible, the interest granted and omitted after-born or after-adopted child under this section must be of the same character, whether equitable or legal, present or future, as that devised to the testator's then-living children under the will.

(iv) In satisfying a share provided by this paragraph, devises to the testator's children who were living when the will was executed abate ratably. In abating the devises of the then-living children, the court shall preserve to the maximum extent possible the character of the testamentary plan adopted by the testator.

(b) Neither subsection (a)(1) nor subsection (a)(2) applies if:

(1) it appears from the will that the omission was intentional; or

(2) the testator provided for the omitted after-born or after-adopted child by transfer outside the will and the intent that the transfer be in lieu of a testamentary provision is shown by testator's statements or is reasonably inferred from the amount of the transfer or other evidence.

(c) If at the time of execution of the will the testator fails to provide in his [or her] will for a living child solely because he believes the child to be dead, the child receives a share in the estate equal in value to that which the child would have received had the testator died intestate.

(d) In satisfying a share provided by subsection (a)(1) or (c), devises made by the will abate as provided in Section 3-902.

Part 4
Exempt Property and Allowances

§ 2-401. [Applicable Law.]

This Part applies to the estate of a decedent who dies domiciled in this State. Rights to homestead allowance, exempt property, and family allowance for a decedent who dies not domiciled in this State are governed by the law of the decedent's domicile at death.

§ 2-402. [Homestead Allowance.]

A decedent's surviving spouse is entitled to a homestead allowance of [$15,000]. If there is no surviving spouse, each minor child and each dependent child of the decedent is entitled to a homestead allowance amounting to [$15,000] divided by the number of minor and dependent children of the decedent. The homestead allowance is exempt from and has priority over all claims against the estate. Homestead allowance is in addition to any share passing to the surviving spouse or minor or dependent child by the will of the decedent, unless otherwise provided, by intestate succession, or by way of elective share.

[§ 2-402A. [Constitutional Homestead.]

The value of any constitutional right of homestead in the family home received by a surviving spouse or child must be charged against that spouse or child's homestead allowance to the extent that the family home is part of the decedent's estate or would have been but for the homestead provision of the constitution.]

§ 2-403. [Exempt Property.]

In addition to the homestead allowance, the decedent's surviving spouse is entitled from the estate to a value, not exceeding $10,000 in excess of any security interests therein, in household furniture, automobiles, furnishings, appliances and personal effects. If there is no surviving spouse, the decedent's children are entitled jointly to the same value. If encumbered chattels are selected and the value in excess of security interests, plus that of other exempt property in the estate, is less than $10,000, or if there is not $10,000 worth of exempt property in the estate, the spouse or children are entitled to other assets of the estate, if any, to the extent necessary to make up the $10,000 value. Rights to exempt property and assets needed to make up a deficiency of exempt property have priority over all claims against the estate, but the right to any assets to make up a deficiency of exempt property abates as necessary to permit earlier payment of homestead allowance and family allowance. These rights are in addition to any benefit or share passing to the surviving spouse or children by the decedent's will, unless otherwise provided, by intestate succession, or by way of elective share.

§ 2-404. [Family Allowance.]

(a) In addition to the right to homestead allowance and exempt property, the decedent's surviving spouse and minor children whom the decedent was obligated to support and children who were in fact being supported by the decedent are entitled to a reasonable allowance in money out of the estate for their maintenance during the period of administration, which allowance may not continue for longer than one year if the estate is inadequate to discharge allowed claims. The allowance may be paid as a lump sum or in periodic installments. It is payable to the surviving spouse, if living, for the use of the surviving spouse and minor and dependent children; otherwise to the children, or persons having their care and custody. If a minor child or dependent child is not living with the surviving spouse, the allowance may be made partially to the child or his [or her] guardian or other person having the child's care and custody, and partially to the spouse, as their needs may appear. The family allowance is exempt from and has priority over all claims except the homestead allowance.

(b) The family allowance is not chargeable against any benefit or share passing to the surviving spouse or children by the will of the decedent, unless otherwise provided, by intestate succession, or by way of elective share. The death of any person entitled to family allowance terminates his right to allowances not yet paid.

§ 2-405. [Source, Determination, and Documentation.]

(a) If the estate is otherwise sufficient, property specifically devised may not be used to satisfy rights to homestead allowance or exempt property. Subject to this restriction, the surviving spouse, the guardians of minor children, or children who are adults may select property of the estate as homestead allowance and exempt property. The personal representative may make those selections if the surviving spouse, the children, or the guardians of the minor children are unable or fail to do so within a reasonable time or if there is no guardian of the minor child. The personal representative may execute an instrument or deed of distribution to establish the ownership of property taken as homestead allowance or exempt property. The personal representative may determine the family allowance in a lump sum not exceeding $18,000 or periodic installments not exceeding $1,500 per month for one year, and may disburse funds of the estate in payment of the family allowance and any part of the homestead allowance payable in cash. The personal representative or any interested person aggrieved by any selection, determination, payment, proposed payment, or failure to act under this section may petition the court for appropriate relief, which relief may include a family allowance other than that which the personal representative determined or could have determined.

(b) If the right to an elective share is exercised on behalf of a surviving spouse who is an incapacitated person, the personal representative may add any unexpended portions payable under the homestead allowance, exempt property, and family allowance to the trust established under Section 2-203(b).

Part 5
Wills, Will Contracts, and Custody and Deposit of Wills

§ 2-501. [Who May Make Will.]

An individual 18 or more years of age who is of sound mind may make a will.

§ 2-502. [Execution; Witnessed Wills; Holographic Wills.]

(a) Except as provided in subsection (b) and in Sections 2-503, 2-506, and 2-513, a will must be:

(1) in writing;

(2) signed by the testator or in the testator's name by some other individual in the testator's conscious presence and by the testator's direction; and

(3) signed by at least two individuals, each of whom signed within a reasonable time after he [or she] witnessed either the signing of the will as described in paragraph (2) or the testator's acknowledgment of that signature or acknowledgment of the will.

(b) A will that does not comply with subsection (a) is valid as a holographic will, whether or not witnessed, if the signature and material portions of the document are in the testator's handwriting.

(c) Intent that the document constitute the testator's will can be established by extrinsic evidence, including, for holographic wills, portions of the document that are not in the testator's handwriting.

§ 2-503. [Writings Intended as Wills, etc.]

Although a document or writing added upon a document was not executed in compliance with Section 2-502, the document or writing is treated as if it had been executed in compliance with that section if the proponent of the document or writing establishes by clear and convincing evidence that the decedent intended the document or writing to constitute (i) the decedent's will, (ii) a partial or complete revocation of the will, (iii) an addition to or an alteration of the will, or (iv) a partial or complete revival of his [or her] formerly revoked will or of a formerly revoked portion of the will.

§ 2-504. [Self-proved Will.]

(a) A will may be simultaneously executed, attested, and made self-proved, by acknowledgment thereof by the testator and affidavits of the witnesses, each made before an officer authorized to administer oaths under the laws of the state in which execution occurs and evidenced by the officer's certificate, under official seal, in substantially the following form:

I, _________, the testator, sign my name to this instrument this ____ day of _________, 19____, and being first duly sworn, do hereby declare to the undersigned authority that I sign if willingly (or willingly direct another to sign for me), that I execute it as my free and voluntary act for the purposes therein expressed, and that I am eighteen years of age or older, of sound mind, and under no constraint or undue influence.

____
Testator

We, __________, __________, the witnesses, sign our names to this instrument, being first duly sworn, and do hereby declare to the undersigned authority that the testator signs and executes this instrument as his [her] last will and that [he] [she] signs it willingly (or willingly directs another to sign for [him] [her]), and that each of us, in the presence and hearing of the testator, hereby signs this will as witness to the testator's signing, and that to the best of our knowledge the testator is eighteen years of age or older, of sound mind, and under no constraint or undue influence.

____
Witness

____
Witness

The State of__________
County of ___________

Subscribed, sworn to and acknowledged before me by __________, the testator and subscribed and sworn to before me by _________, and _________, witness, this ____ day of ____.

(Seal)

(Signed) _____________________
(Official capacity of officer)

(b) An attested will may be made self-proved at any time after its execution by the acknowledgment thereof by the testator and the affidavits of the witnesses, each made before an officer authorized to administer oaths under the laws of the state in which the acknowledgment occurs and evidenced by the officer's certificate, under the official seal, attached or annexed to the will in substantially the following form:

The State of ______________
County of ________________

We, _________, _________, and _________, the testator and the witnesses, respectively, whose names are signed to the attached or foregoing instrument, being first duly sworn, do hereby declare to the undersigned authority that the testator signed and executed the instrument as his last will and that [he] [she] had signed willingly (or willingly directed another to sign for [him] [her]), and that [he] [she] executed it as [his] [her] free and voluntary act for the purposes therein expressed, and that each of the witnesses, in the presence and hearing of the testator, signed the will as witness and that to the best of [his] [her] knowledge the testator was at that time eighteen years of age or older, of sound mind and under no constraint or undue influence.

____
Testator

____
Witness

____
Witness

Subscribed, sworn to and acknowledged before me by _________, the testator, and subscribed and sworn to before me by _________, and witnesses, this ____ day of ____

(Seal)

(Signed) _____________________
(Official capacity of officer)

(c) A signature affixed to a self-proving affidavit attached to a will is considered a signature affixed to the will, if necessary to prove the will's due execution.

§ 2-505. [Who May Witness.]

(a) An individual generally competent to be a witness may act as a witness to a will.

(b) The signing of a will by an interested witness does not invalidate the will or any provision of it.

§ 2-506. [Choice of Law as to Execution.]

A written will is valid if executed in compliance with Section 2-502 or 2-503 or if its execution complies with the law at the time of execution of the place where the will is executed, or of the law of the place where at the time of execution or at the time of death the testator is domiciled, has a place of abode, or is a national.

§ 2-507. [Revocation by Writing or by Act.]

(a) A will or any part thereof is revoked:

(1) by executing a subsequent will that revokes the previous will or part expressly or by inconsistency; or

(2) by performing a revocatory act on the will, if the testator performed the act with the intent and for the purpose of revoking the will or part or if another individual performed the act in the testator's conscious presence and by the testator's direction. For purposes of this paragraph, "revocatory act on the will" includes burning, tearing, canceling, obliterating, or destroying the will or any part of it. A burning, tearing, or canceling is a "revocatory act on the will," whether or not the burn, tear, or cancellation touched any of the words on the will.

(b) If a subsequent will does not expressly revoke a previous will, the execution of the subsequent will wholly revokes the previous will by inconsistency if the testator intended the subsequent will to replace rather than supplement the previous will.

(c) The testator is presumed to have intended a subsequent will to replace rather than supplement a previous will if the subsequent will makes a complete disposition of the testator's estate. If this presumption arises and is not rebutted by clear and convincing evidence, the previous will is revoked; only the subsequent will is operative on the testator's death.

(d) The testator is presumed to have intended a subsequent will to supplement rather than replace a previous will if the subsequent will does not make a complete disposition of the testator's estate. If this presumption arises and is not rebutted by clear and convincing evidence, the subsequent will revokes the previous will only to the extent the subsequent will is inconsistent with the previous will; each will is fully operative on the testator's death to the extent they are not inconsistent.

§ 2-508. [Revocation by Change of Circumstances.]

Except as provided in Sections 2-803 and 2-804, a change of circumstances does not revoke a will or any part of it.

§ 2-509. [Revival of Revoked Will.]

(a) If a subsequent will that wholly revoked a previous will is thereafter revoked by a revocatory act under Section 2-507(a)(2), the previous will remains revoked unless it is revived. The previous will is revived if it is evident from the circumstances of the revocation of the subsequent will or from the testator's contemporary or subsequent declarations that the testator intended the previous will to take effect as executed.

(b) If a subsequent will that partly revoked a previous will is thereafter revoked by a revocatory act under Section 2-507(a)(2), a revoked part of the previous will is revived unless it is evident from circumstances of the revocation of the subsequent will or from the testator's contemporary or subsequent declarations that the testator did not intend the revoked part to to take effect as executed.

(c) If a subsequent will that revoked a previous will in whole or in part is thereafter revoked by another, later, will, the previous will remains revoked in whole or in part, unless it or its revoked part is revived. The previous will or its revoked part is revived to the extent it appears from the terms of the later will that the testator intended the previous will to take effect.

§ 2-510. [Incorporation by Reference.]

A writing in existence when a will is executed may be incorporated by reference if the language of the will manifests this intent and describes the writing sufficiently to permit its identification.

§ 2-511. [Testamentary Additions to Trusts.]

(a) A will may validly devise property to the trustee of a trust established or to be established (i) during the testator's lifetime by the testator, or by the testator and some other person, or by some other person, including a funded or unfunded life insurance trust, although the settlor has reserved any or all rights of ownership of the insurance contracts, or (ii) at the testator's death by the testator's devise to the trustee, if the trust is identified in the testator's will and its terms are set forth in a written instrument, other than a will, executed before, concurrently with, or after the execution of the testator's will or in another individual's will if that other individual has predeceased the testator, regardless of the existence, size, or character of the corpus of the trust. The devise is not invalid because the trust is amendable or revocable, or because the trust was amended after the execution of the will or the death of the testator.

(b) Unless the testator's will provides otherwise, property devised to a trust described in subsection (a) is not held under a testamentary trust of the testator, but it becomes a part of the trust to which it is devised, and must be administered and disposed of in accordance with the provisions of the governing instrument setting forth the terms of the trust, including any amendments thereto made before or after the testator's death.

(c) Unless the testator's will provides otherwise, a revocation or termination of the trust before the testator's death causes the devise to lapse.

§ 2-512. [Events of Independent Significance.]

A will may dispose of property by reference to acts and events that have significance apart from their effect upon the dispositions made by the will, whether they occur before or after the execution of the will or before or after the testator's death. The execution or revocation of another individual's will is such an event.

§ 2-513. [Separate Writing Identifying Devise of Certain Types of Tangible Personal Property.]

Whether or not the provisions relating to holographic wills apply, a will may refer to a written statement or list to dispose of items of tangible personal property not otherwise specifically disposed of by the will, other than money. To be admissible under this section as evidence of the intended disposition, the writing must be signed by the testator and must describe the items and the devisees with reasonable certainty. The writing may be referred to as one to be in existence at the time of the testator's death; it may be prepared before or after the execution of the will; it may be altered by the testator after its preparation; and it may be a writing which has no significance apart from its effect on the dispositions made by the will.

§ 2-514. [Contracts Concerning Succession.]

A contract to make a will or devise, or not to revoke a will or devise, or to die intestate, if executed after the effective date of this Article, may be established only by (i) provisions of a will stating material provisions of the contract, (ii) an express reference in a will to a contract and extrinsic evidence proving the terms of the contract, or (iii) a writing signed by the decedent evidencing the contract. The execution of a joint will or mutual wills does not create a presumption of a contract not to revoke the will or wills.

§ 2-515. [Deposit of Will with Court in Testator's Lifetime.]

A will may be deposited by the testator or the testator's agent with any court for safekeeping under rules of the court. The will must be sealed and kept confidential. During the testator's lifetime, a deposited will must be delivered only to the testator or to a person authorized in writing signed by the testator to receive the will. A conservator may be allowed to examine a deposited will of a protected testator under procedures designed to maintain the confidential character of the document to the extent possible, and to ensure that it will be resealed and kept on deposit after the examination. Upon being informed of the testator's death, the court shall notify any person designated to receive the will and deliver it to that person on request; or the court may deliver the will to the appropriate court.

§ 2-516. [Duty of Custodian of Will; Liability.]

After death of a testator and on request of an interested person, a person having custody of a will of the testator shall deliver it with reasonable promptness to a person able to secure its probate and if none is known, to an appropriate court. A person who wilfully fails to deliver a will is liable to any person aggrieved for any damages that may be sustained by the failure. A person who wilfully refuses or fails to deliver a will after being ordered by the court in a proceeding brought for the purpose of compelling delivery is subject to penalty for contempt of court.

§ 2-517. [Penalty Clause for Contest.]

A provision in a will purporting to penalize an interested person for contesting the will or institution other proceedings relating to the estate is unenforceable if probable cause exists for instituting proceedings.

Part 6
Rules of Construction Applicable Only to Wills

§ 2-601. [Scope.]

In the absence of a finding of a contrary intention, the rules of construction in this Part control the construction of a will.

§ 2-602. [Will May Pass All Property and After-Acquired Property.]

A will may provide for the passage of all property the testator owns at death and all property acquired by the estate after the testator's death.

§ 2-603. [Antilapse; Deceased Devisee; Class Gifts.]

(a) [Definitions.] In this section:

(1) "Alternative devise" means a devise that is expressly created by the will and, under the terms of the will, can take effect instead of another devise on the happening of one or more events, including survival of the testator or failure to survive the testator, whether an event is expressed in condition-precedent, condition-subsequent, or any other form. A residuary clause

constitutes an alternative devise with respect to a nonresiduary devise only if the will specifically proves that, upon lapse or failure, the nonresiduary devise, or nonresiduary devises in general, pass under the residuary clause.

(2) "Class member" includes an individual who fails to survive the testator but who would have taken under a devise in the form of a class gift had he [or she] survived the testator.

(3) "Devise" includes an alternative devise, a devise in the form of a class gift, and an exercise of a power of appointment.

(4) "Devisee" includes (i) a class member if the devise is in the form of a class gift, (ii) the beneficiary of a trust but not the trustee, (iii) an individual or class member who was deceased at the time the testator executed his [or her] will as well as an individual or class member who was then living but who failed to survive the testator, and (iv) an appointee under a power of appointment exercised by the testator's will.

(5) "Stepchild" means a child of the surviving, deceased, or former spouse of the testator or of the donor of a power of appointment, and not of the testator or donor.

(6) "Surviving devisee" or "surviving descendant" means a devisee or a descendant who neither predeceased the testator nor is deemed to have predeceased the testator under Section 2-702.

(7) "Testator" includes the donee of a power of appointment if the power is exercised in the testator's will.

(b) [Substitute Gift.] If a devisee fails to survive the testator and is a grandparent, a descendant of a grandparent, or a stepchild of either the testator or the donor of a power of appointment exercised by the testator's will, the following apply:

(1) Except as provided in paragraph (4), if the devise is not in the form of a class gift and the deceased devisee leaves surviving descendants, a substitute gift is created in the devisee's surviving descendants. They take by representation the property to which the devisee would have been entitled had the devisee survived the testator.

(2) Except as provided in paragraph (4), if the devise is in the form of a class gift, other than a devise to "issue," "descendants," "heirs of the body," "heirs," "next to kin," "relatives," or "family," or a class described by language of similar import, a substitute gift is created in the deceased devisee or devisee's surviving descendants. The property to which the devisees would have been entitled had all of them survived the testator passes to the surviving devisees and the surviving descendants of the deceased devisees. Each surviving devisee takes the share to which he [or she] would have been entitled had the deceased devisees survived the testator. Each deceased devisee's surviving descendants who are substituted for the deceased devisee take by representation the share to which the deceased devisee would have been entitled had the deceased devisee survived the testator. For the purposes of this paragraph, "deceased devisee" means a class member who failed to survive the testator and left one or more surviving descendants.

(3) For the purposes of Section 2-601, words of survivorship, such as in a devise to an individual "if he survives me," or in a devise to "my surviving children," are not, in the absence of additional evidence, a sufficient indication of an intent contrary to the application of this section.

(4) If the will creates an alternative devise with respect to a devise for which a substitute gift is created by paragraph (1) or (2), the substitute gift is superseded by the alternative devise only if an expressly designated devisee of the alternative devise is entitled to take under the will.

(5) Unless the language creating a power of appointment expressly excludes the substitution of the descendants of an appointee for the appointee, a surviving descendant of a deceased appointee of a power of appointment can be substituted for the appointee under this section, whether or not the descendant is an object of the power.

(c) [More Than One Substitute Gift; Which One Takes.] If, under subsection (b), substitute gifts are created and not superseded with respect to more than one devise and the devises are alternative devises, one to the other, the determination of which of the substitute gifts takes effect is resolved as follows:

(1) Except as provided in paragraph (2), the devised property passes under the primary substitute gift.

(2) If there is a younger-generation devise, the devised property passes under the younger-generation substitute gift and not under the primary substitute gift.

(3) In this subsection:

(i) "Primary devise" means the devise that would have taken effect had all the deceased devisees of the alternative devises who left surviving descendants survived the testator.

(ii) "Primary substitute gift" means the substitute gift created with respect to the primary devise.

(iii) "Younger-generation devise" means a devise that (A) is to a descendant of a devisee of the primary devise, (B) is an alternative devise with respect to the primary devise, (C) is a devise for which a substitute gift is created, and (D) would have taken effect had all the deceased devisees who left surviving descendants survived the testator except the deceased devisee or devisees of the primary devise.

(iv) "Younger-generation substitute gift" means the substitute gift created with respect to the younger-generation devise.

§ 2-604. [Failure of Testamentary Provision.]

(a) Except as provided in Section 2-603, a devise, other than a residuary devise, that fails for any reason becomes a part of the residue.

(b) Except as provided in Section 2-603, if the residue is devised to two or more persons, the share of a residuary devisee that fails for any reason, his share passes to the other residuary devisee, or to other residuary devisees in proportion to the interest of each in the remaining part of the residue.

§ 2-605. [Increase in Securities; Accessions.]

(a) If a testator executes a will that devises securities and the testator then owned securities that meet the description in the will, the devise includes additional securities owned by the testator at death to the extent the additional securities were acquired by the testator after the will was executed as a result of the testator's ownership of the described securities and are securities of any of the following types:

(1) securities of the same organization acquired by reason of action initiated by the organization or any successor, related, or acquiring organization, excluding any acquired by exercise of purchase options;

(2) securities of another organization acquired as a result of a merger, consolidation, reorganization, or other distribution by the organization or any successor, related, or acquiring organization; or

(3) securities of the same organization acquired as a result of a plan of reinvestment.

(b) Distributions in cash before death with respect to a described security are not part of the devise.

§ 2-606. [Nonademption of Specific Devises; Unpaid Proceeds of Sale, Condemnation, or Insurance; Sale by Conservator or Agent.]

(a) A specific devisee has a right to the remaining specifically devised property in the testator's estate at death and:

(1) any balance of the purchase price, together with any security agreement, owing from a purchaser to the testator at death by reason of sale of the property;

(2) any amount of a condemnation award for the taking of the property unpaid at death;

(3) any proceeds unpaid at death on fire or casualty insurance on or other recovering for injury to the property;

(4) property owned by the testator at death and acquired as a result of foreclosure, or obtained in lieu of foreclosure, of the security interest for a specifically devised obligation;

(5) real or tangible personal property owned by the testator at death which the testator acquired as a replacement for specifically devised real or tangible personal property; and

(6) unless the facts and circumstances indicate that ademption of the devise was intended by the testator or ademption of the devise is consistent with the testator's manifested plan of distribution, the value of the specifically devised property to the extent the specifically devised property is not in the testator's estate at death and its value or its replacement is not covered by paragraphs (1) through (5).

(b) If specifically devised property is sold or mortgaged by a conservator or an agent acting within the authority of a durable power of attorney for an incapacitated principal, or if a condemnation award, insurance proceeds, or recovery for injury to the property are paid to a conservator or to an agent acting within the authority of a durable power of attorney for an incapacitated principal, the specific devisee has the right to a general pecuniary devise equal to the net sale price, the amount of the unpaid loan, the condemnation award, the insurance proceeds, or the recovery.

(c) The right of a specific devisee under subsection (b) is reduced by any right the devisee has under subsection (a).

(d) For the purposes of the references in subsection (b) to a conservator, subsection (b) does not apply if after the sale, mortgage, condemnation, casualty, or recovery, it was adjudicated that the testator's incapacity ceased and the testator survived the adjudication by one year.

(e) For the purposes of the reference in subsection (b) to an agent acting within the authority of a durable power of attorney for an incapacitated principal, (i) "incapacitated principal" means a principal who is an incapacitated person, (ii) no adjudication of incapacity before death is necessary, and (iii) the acts of an agent within the authority of a durable power of attorney are presumed to be for an incapacitated principal.

§ 2-607. [Nonexoneration.]

A specific devise passes subject to any mortgage interest existing at the date of death, without right of exoneration, regardless of a general directive in the will to pay debts.

§ 2-608. [Exercise of Power of Appointment.]

In the absence of a requirement that a power of appointment be exercised by a reference, or by an express of specific reference, to the power, a general residuary clause in a will, or a will making general disposition of all of the testator's property, expresses an intention to exercise a power of appointment held by the testator only if (i) the power is a general power and the creating instrument does not contain a gift if the power is not exercised or (ii) the testator's will manifests an intention to include the property subject to the power.

§ 2-609. [Ademption by Satisfaction.]

(a) Property which a testator gave in his [or her] lifetime to a person is treated as a satisfaction of a devise in whole or in part, only if (i) the will provides for deduction of the lifetime gift, (ii) the testator declared in a contemporaneous writing that the gift is in satisfaction of the devise or that its value is to be deducted from the devise, or (iii) the devisee acknowledges in writing that the gift is in satisfaction of the devise or that its value is to be deducted from the value of the devise.

(b) For purposes of partial satisfaction, property given during lifetime is valued as of the time the devisee came into possession or enjoyment of the property or at the testator's death, whichever occurs first.

(c) If the devisee fails to survive the testator, the gift is treated as a full or partial satisfaction of the devise, as appropriate, in applying Sections 2-603 and 2-604, unless the testator's contemporaneous writing provides otherwise.

Part 7
Rules of Construction Applicable to Donative Dispositions in Wills and Other Governing Instruments

§ 2-701. [Scope.]

In the absence of a finding of a contrary intention, the rules of construction in this Part control the construction of a governing instrument. The rules of construction in this Part apply to a governing instrument of any type, except as the application of a particular section is limited by its terms to a specific type or types of donative disposition or governing instrument.

§ 2-702. [Requirement of Survival by 120 Hours.]

(a) [Requirement of Survival by 120 Hours Under Probate Code.] For the purposes of this Code, except for purposes of Part 3 of Article VI [Uniform TOD Security Registration Act] and except as provided in subsection (d), an individual who is not established by clear and convincing evidence to have survived an event, including the death of another individual, by 120 hours is deemed to have predeceased the event.

(b) [Requirement of Survival by 120 Hours under Donative Provision of Governing Instrument.] Except as provided in subsection (d) and except for a security registered in beneficiary form (TOD) under Part 3 of Article VI [Uniform TOD Security Registration Act], for purposes of a donative provision of a governing instrument, an individual who is not established by clear and convincing evidence to have survived an event, including the death of another individual, by 120 hours is deemed to have predeceased the event.

(c) [Co-owners with Right of Survivorship; Requirement of Survival by 120 Hours.] Except as provided in subsection (d), if (i) it is not established by clear and convincing evidence that one of two co-owners with right of survivorship survived the other co-owner by 120 hours, one-half of the property passes as if one had survived by 120 hours and one-half as if the other had survived by 120 hours and (ii) there are more than two co-owners and it is not established by clear and convincing evidence that at least one of them survived the others by 120 hours, the property passes in the proportion that one bears to the whole number of co-owners. For the purposes of this subsection, "co-owners with right of survivorship" includes joint tenants, tenants by the entireties, and other co-owners of property or accounts held under circumstances that entitles one or more to the whole of the property or account on the death of the other or others.

(d) [Exceptions.] This section does not apply if:

(1) the governing instrument contains language dealing explicitly with simultaneous deaths or deaths in a common disaster and that language is operable under the facts of the case;

(2) the governing instrument expressly indicates that an individual is not required to survive an event, including the death of another individual, by any specified period or expressly requires the individual to survive the event by a specified period;

(3) the imposition of a 120-hour requirement of survival would cause a nonvested property interest or a power of appointment to fail to qualify for validity under Section 2-901(a)(1), (b)(1), or (c)(1) or to become invalid under Section 2-901(a)(2), (b)(2), or (c)(2); or

(4) the application of this section to multiple governing instruments would result in an unintended failure or duplication of a disposition.

(e) [Protection of Payors and Other Third Parties.]

(1) A payor or other third party is not liable for having made a payment or transferred an item of property or any other benefit to a beneficiary designated in a governing instrument who, under this section, is not entitled to the payment or item of property, or for having taken any other action in good faith reliance on the beneficiary's apparent entitlement under the terms of the governing instrument, before the payor or other third party received written notice of a claimed lack of entitlement under this section. A payor or other third party is liable for a payment made or other action taken after the payor or other third party received written notice of a claimed lack of entitlement under this section.

(2) Written notice of a claimed lack of entitlement under paragraph (1) must be mailed to the payor's or other third party's main office or home by registered or certified mail, return receipt requested, or served upon the payor or other third party in the same manner as a summons in a civil action. Upon receipt of written notice of a claimed lack of entitlement under this section, a payor or other third party may pay any amount owed or transfer or deposit any item of property held by it to or with the court having jurisdiction of the probate proceedings relating to the decedent's estate, or if no proceedings have been commenced, to or with the court having jurisdiction of probate proceedings relating to decedents' estates located in the county of the decedent's residence. The court shall hold the funds or item of property and, upon its determination under this section, shall order disbursement in accordance with the determination. Payments, transfers, or deposits made to or with the court discharge the payor or other third party from all claims for the value of amounts paid to or items of property transferred to or deposited with the court.

(f) [Protection of Bona Fide Purchaser; Personal Liability of Recipient.]

(1) A person who purchases property for value and without notice, or who receives a payment or other item of property in partial or full satisfaction of a legally enforceable obligation, is neither obligated under this section to return the payment, item of property, or benefit nor is liable under this section for the amount of the payment or the value of the item of property or benefit. But a person who, not for value, receives a payment, item of property or any other benefit to which the person is not entitled under this section is obligated to return the payment, item of property, or benefit, or is personally liable for the amount of the payment or the value of the item of property or benefit, to the person who is entitled to it under this section.

(2) If this section or any part of this section is preempted by federal law with respect to a payment, an item of property, or any other benefit covered by this section, a person who, not for value, receives the payment, item of property, or any other benefit to which the person is not entitled under this section is obligated to return the payment, item of property, or benefit or is personally liable for the amount of the payment or the value of the item of property or benefit, to the person who would have been entitled to it were this section or part of this section not preempted.

§ 2-703. [Choice of Law as to Meaning and Effect of Donative Dispositions.]

The meaning and legal effect of a donative disposition is determined by the local law of the state selected by the transferor in the governing instrument, unless the application of that law is contrary to the provisions relating to the elective share described in Part 2, the provisions relating to exempt property and allowances described in Part 4, or any other public policy of this State otherwise applicable to the disposition.

§ 2-704. [Power of Appointment; Meaning of Specific Reference Requirement.]

If a governing instrument creating a power of appointment expressly requires that the power be exercised by a reference, an express reference, or a specific reference, to the power or its source, it is presumed that the donor's intention, in requiring that the donee exercise the power by making reference to the particular power or to the creating instrument, was to prevent an inadvertent exercise of the power.

§ 2-705. [Class Gifts Construed to Accord With Intestate Succession.]

(a) Adopted individuals and individuals born out of wedlock, and their respective descendants if appropriate to the class, are included in class gifts and other terms of relationship in accordance with the rules for intestate succession. Terms of relationship that do not differentiate relationships by blood from those by affinity, such as "uncles," "aunts," "nieces," or "nephews," are construed to exclude relatives by affinity. Terms of relationship that do not differentiate relationships by the half blood from those by the whole blood, such as "brothers," "sisters," "nieces," or "nephews," are construed to include both types of relationships.

(b) In addition to the requirements of subsection (a), in construing a donative disposition by a transferor who is not the natural parent, an individual born to the natural parent is not considered the child of that parent unless the individual lived while a minor as a regular member of the household of that natural parent or of that parent's parent, brother, sister, spouse, or surviving spouse.

(c) In addition to the requirements of subsection (a), in construing a donative disposition by a transferor who is not the adopting parent, an adopted individual is not considered the child of the adopting parent unless the adopted individual lived while a minor, either before or after the adoption, as a regular member of the household of the adopting parent.

§ 2-706. [Life Insurance; Retirement Plan; Account With POD Designation; Transfer-on-Death Registration; Deceased Beneficiary.]

(a) [Definitions.] In this section:

(1) "Alternative beneficiary designation" means a beneficiary designation that is expressly created by the governing instrument and, under the terms of the governing instrument, can take effect instead of another beneficiary designation

on the happening of one or more events, including survival of the decedent or failure to survive the decedent, whether an event is expressed in condition-precedent, condition-subsequent, or any other form.

(2) "Beneficiary" means the beneficiary of a beneficiary designation and includes (i) a class member if the beneficiary designation is in the form of a class gift and (ii) an individual or class member who was deceased at the time the beneficiary designation was executed as well as an individual or class member who was then living but who failed to survive the decedent.

(3) "Beneficiary designation" includes an alternative beneficiary designation and a beneficiary designation in the form of a class gift.

(4) "Class member" includes an individual who fails to survive the decedent but who would have taken under a beneficiary designation in the form of a class gift had he [or she] survived the decedent.

(5) "Stepchild" means a child of the decedent's surviving, deceased, or former spouse, and not of the decedent.

(6) "Surviving beneficiary" or "surviving descendant" means a beneficiary or a descendant who neither predeceased the decedent nor is deemed to have predeceased the decedent under Section 2-702.

(b) [Substitute Gift.] If a beneficiary fails to survive the decedent and is a grandparent, a descendent of a grandparent, or a stepchild of the decedent, the following apply:

(1) Except as provided in paragraph (4), if the beneficiary designation is not in the form of a class gift and the deceased beneficiary leaves surviving descendants, a substitute gift is created in the beneficiary's surviving descendants. They take by representation the property to which the beneficiary would have been entitled had the beneficiary survived the decedent.

(2) Except as provided in paragraph (4), if the beneficiary designation is in the form of a class gift, other than a beneficiary designation to "issue," "descendants," "heirs of the body," "heirs," "next of kin," "relatives," or "family," or a class described by language of similar import, a substitute gift is created in the deceased beneficiary or beneficiaries' surviving descendants. The property to which the beneficiaries would have been entitled had all of them survived the decedent passes to the surviving beneficiaries and the surviving descendants of the deceased beneficiaries. Each deceased beneficiary's surviving descendants takes the share to which he [or she] would have been entitled had the deceased beneficiaries survived the decedent. Each deceased beneficiary's surviving descendants who are substituted for the deceased beneficiary take by representation the share to which the deceased beneficiary would have been entitled had the deceased beneficiary survived the decedent. For the purposes of this paragraph, "deceased beneficiary" means a class member who failed to survive the decedent and left one or more surviving descendants.

(3) For the purposes of Section 2-701, words of survivorship, such as in a beneficiary designation to an individual "if he survives me," or in a beneficiary designation to "my surviving children," are not, in the absence of additional evidence, a sufficient indication of an intent contrary to the application of this section.

(4) If a governing instrument creates an alternative beneficiary designation with respect to a beneficiary designation for which a substitute gift is created by paragraph (1) or (2), the substitute gift is superseded by the alternative beneficiary designation only if an expressly designated beneficiary of the alternative beneficiary designation is entitled to take.

(c) [More Than One Substitute Gift; Which One Takes.] If, under subsection (b), substitute gifts are created and not superseded with respect to more than one beneficiary designation and the beneficiary designations are alternative beneficiary designations, one to the other, the determination of which of the substitute gifts takes effect is resolved as follows:

(1) Except as provided in paragraph (2), the devised property passes under the primary substitute gift.

(2) If there is a younger-generation beneficiary designation, the devised property passes under the younger-generation substitute gift and not under the primary substitute gift.

(3) In this subsection:

(i) "Primary beneficiary designation" means the beneficiary designation that would have taken effect had all the deceased beneficiaries of the alternative beneficiary designations who left surviving descendants survived the decedent.

(ii) "Primary substitute gift" means the substitute gift created with respect to the primary beneficiary designation.

(iii) "Younger-generation beneficiary designation" means a beneficiary designation that (A) is to a descendant of a beneficiary of the primary beneficiary designation, (B) is an alternative beneficiary designation with respect to the primary beneficiary designation, (C) is a beneficiary designation for which a substitute gift is created, and (D) would have taken effect had all the deceased beneficiaries who left surviving descendants survived the testator except the deceased beneficiary or beneficiaries of the primary beneficiary designation.

(iv) "Younger-generation substitute gift" means the substitute gift created with respect to the younger-generation beneficiary designation.

(d) [Protection of Payors.]

(1) A payor is protected from liability in making payments under the terms of the beneficiary designation until the payor has received written notice of a claim to a substitute gift under this section. Payment made before the receipt of written notice of a claim to a substitute gift under this section discharges the payor, but not the recipient, from all claims for the amounts paid. A payor is liable for a payment made after the payor has received written notice of the claim. A recipient is liable for a payment received, whether or not written notice of the claim is given.

(2) The written notice of the claim must be mailed to the payor's main office or home by registered or certified mail, return receipt requested, or served upon the payor in the same manner as a summons in a civil action. Upon receipt of written notice of the claim, a payor may pay any amount owed by it to the court having jurisdiction of the probate proceedings relating to the decedent's estate, or if no proceedings have been commenced, to the court having jurisdiction of probate proceedings relating to decedents' estates located in the county of the decedent's residence. The court shall hold the funds and, upon its determination under this section, shall order disbursement in accordance with the determination. Payment made to the court discharges the payor from all claims for the amounts paid.

(e) [Protection of Bona Fide Purchasers; Personal Liability of Recipient.]

(1) A person who purchases property for value and without notice, or who receives a payment or other item of property in partial or full satisfaction of a legally enforceable obligation, is neither obligated under this section to return the payment, item of property, or benefit nor is liable under this section for the amount of the payment or the value of the item of property or benefit. But a person who, not for value, receives a payment, item of property, or any other benefit to which the person is not entitled under this section is obligated to return the payment, item of property, or benefit, or is personally liable for the amount of the payment or the value of the item of property or benefit, to the person who is entitled to it under this section.

(2) If this section or any part of this section is preempted by federal law with respect to a payment, an item of property or any other benefit covered by this section, a person who, not for value, receives the payment, item of property, or any other benefit to which the person is not entitled under this section is obligated to return the payment, item of property, or benefit, or is personally liable for the amount of that payment or the value of that item of property or benefit, to the person who would have been entitled to it were this section or part of this section not preempted.

§ 2-707. [Survivorship with Respect to Future Interests Under Terms of Trust; Substitute Takers.]

(a) Definitions. In this section:

(1) "Alternative future interest" means an expressly created future interest that can take effect in possession or enjoyment instead of another future interest on the happening of one or more events, including survival of an event or failure to survive an event, whether an event is expressed in condition-precedent, condition-subsequent, or any other form. A residuary clause in a will does not create an alternative future interest with respect to a future interest created in a nonresiduary devise in the will, whether or not the will specifically provides that lapsed or failed devises are to pass under the residuary clause.

(2) "Beneficiary" means the beneficiary of a future interest and includes a class member if the future interest is in the form of a class gift.

(3) "Class member" includes an individual who fails to survive the distribution date but who would have taken under a future interest in the form of a class gift had he [or she] survived the distribution date.

(4) "Distribution date," with respect to a future interest means the time when the future interest is to take effect in possession or enjoyment. The distribution date need not occur at the beginning or end of a calendar day, but can occur at a time during the course of a day.

(5) "Future interest" includes an alternative future interest and a future interest in the form of a class gift.

(6) "Future interest under the terms of a trust" means a future interest that was created by a trust or to an existing trust or by an exercise of a power of appointment to an existing trust, directing the continuance of an existing trust, designating a beneficiary of an existing trust, or creating a trust.

(7) "Surviving beneficiary" or "surviving descendant" means a beneficiary or a descendant who neither predeceased the distribution date nor is deemed to have predeceased the distribution date under Section 2-702.

(b) [Survivorship Required: Substitute Gift.] A future interest under the terms of a trust is contingent on the beneficiary's surviving the distribution date. If a beneficiary a future interest under the terms of a trust fails to survive the distribution date, the following apply:

(1) Except as provided in paragraph (4), if the future interest is not in the form of a class gift and the deceased beneficiary leaves surviving descendants, a substitute gift is created in the

beneficiary's surviving descendants. They take by representation the property to which the beneficiary would have been entitled had the beneficiary survived the decedent.

(2) Except as provided in paragraph (4), if the future interest is in the form of a class gift, other than a future interest to "issue," "descendants," "heirs of the body," "heirs," "next of kin," "relatives," or "family," or a class described by language of similar import, a substitute gift is created in the deceased beneficiary or beneficiaries' surviving descendants. The property to which the beneficiaries would have been entitled had all of them survived the distribution date passes to the surviving beneficiaries and the surviving descendants of the deceased beneficiaries. Each surviving beneficiary takes the share to which he [or she] would have been entitled had the deceased beneficiaries survived the distribution date. Each deceased beneficiary's surviving descendants who are substituted for the deceased beneficiary take by representation the share to which the deceased beneficiary would have been entitled had the deceased beneficiary survived the distribution date. For the purposes of this paragraph, "deceased beneficiary" means a class member who failed to survive the distribution date and left one or more surviving descendants.

(3) For the purposes of Section 2-701, words of survivorship, attached to a future interest are not, in the absence of additional evidence, a sufficient indication of an intent contrary to the application of this section. Words of survivorship include words of survivorship that relate to the distribution date or to an earlier or an unspecified time, whether those words of survivorship are expressed in condition-precedent, condition-subsequent, or any other form.

(4) If a governing instrument creates an alternative future interest with respect to a future interest for which a substitute gift is created by paragraph (1) or (2), the substitute gift is superseded by the alternative future interest only if an expressly designated beneficiary of the alternative future interest is entitled to take in possession or enjoyment.

(c) [More Than One Substitute Gift; Which One Takes.] If, under subsection (b), substitute gifts are created and not superseded with respect to more than one future interest and the future interests are alternative future interests, one to the other, the determination of which of the substitute gifts takes effect is resolved as follows:

(1) Except as provided in paragraph (2), the property passes under the primary substitute gift.

(2) If there is a younger-generation future interest, the property passes under the younger-generation substitute gift and not under the primary substitute gift.

(3) In this subsection:

(i) "Primary future interest" means the future interest that would have taken effect had all the deceased beneficiaries of the alternative future interests who left surviving descendants survived the distribution date.

(ii) "Primary substitute gift" means the substitute gift created with respect to the primary future interest.

(iii) "Younger-generation future interest" means a future interest that (A) is to a descendant of a beneficiary of the primary future interest, (B) is an alternative future interest with respect to the primary future interest, (C) is a future interest for which a substitute gift is created, and (D) would have taken effect had all the deceased beneficiaries who left surviving descendants survived the distribution date except the deceased beneficiary or beneficiaries of the primary future interest.

(iv) "Younger-generation substitute gift" means the substitute gift created with respect to the younger-generation future interest.

(d) [If No Other Takers, Property Passes Under Residuary Clause or to Transferor's Heirs.] If after the application of subsections (b) and (c), there is no surviving taker, the property passes in the following order:

(1) if the trust was created in a nonresiduary devise in the transferor's will or in a codicil to the transferor's will, the property passes under the residuary clause in the transferor's will; for purposes of this section, the residuary clause is treated as creating a future interest under the terms of a trust.

(2) if no taker is produced by the application of paragraph (1), the property passes to the transferor's heirs under Section 2-711.

§ 2-708. [Class Gifts to "Descendants," "Issue," or "Heirs of the Body"; Form of Distribution if None Specified.]

If a class gift in favor of "descendants," "issue," or "heirs of the body" does not specify the manner in which the property is to be distributed among the class members, the property is distributed among the class members who are living when the interest is to take effect in possession or enjoyment, in such shares as they would receive, under the applicable law of intestate succession, if the designated ancestor had then died intestate owning the subject matter of the class gift.

§ 2-709. [Representation; Per Capita at Each Generation; Per Stirpes.]

(a) [Definitions.] In this section:

(1) "Deceased child" or "deceased descendant" means a child or a descendant who either predeceased the distribution date or is deemed to have predeceased the distribution date under Section 2-702.

(2) "Distribution date," with respect to an interest means the time when the interest is to take effect in possession or enjoyment. The distribution date need not occur at the beginning or end of a calendar day, but can occur at a time during the course of a day.

(3) "Surviving ancestor," "surviving child," or "surviving descendant" means an ancestor, a child, or a descendant who neither predeceased the distribution date nor is deemed to have predeceased the distribution date under Section 2-702.

(b) [Representation; Per Capita at Each Generation.] If an applicable statute or a governing instrument calls for property to be distributed "by representation" or "per capita at each generation," the property is divided into as many equal shares as there are (i) surviving descendants in the generation nearest to the designated ancestor which contains one or more surviving descendants (ii) and deceased descendants in the same generation who left surviving descendants, if any. Each surviving descendant in the nearest generation is allocated one share. The remaining shares, if any, are combined and then divided in the same manner among the surviving descendants of the deceased descendants as if the surviving descendants who were allocated a share and their surviving descendants had predeceased the distribution date.

(c) [Per Stirpes.] If a governing instrument calls for property to be distributed "per stirpes," the property is divided into as many equal shares as there are (i) surviving children of the designated ancestor and (ii) deceased children who left surviving descendants. Each surviving child is allocated one share. The share of each deceased child with surviving descendants is divided in the same manner, with subdivision repeating at each succeeding generation until the property is fully allocated among surviving descendants.

(d) [Deceased Descendant With No Surviving Descendant Disregarded.] For the purposes of subsection (b) and (c), an individual who is deceased and left no surviving descendant is disregarded, and an individual who leaves a surviving ancestor who is a descendant of the designated ancestor is not entitled to a share.

§ 2-710. [Worthier-Title Doctrine Abolished.]

The doctrine of worthier title is abolished as a rule of law and a rule of construction. Language in a governing instrument describing the beneficiaries of a donative disposition as the transferor's "heirs," "heirs at law," "next of kin," "distributees," "relatives," or "family," or language of similar import, does not create or presumptively create a reversionary interest in the transferor.

§ 2-711. [Future Interests in "Heirs" and Like.]

If an applicable statue or a governing instrument calls for a future distribution to or creates a future interest in a designated individual's "heirs," "heirs at law," "next of kin," "relatives," or "family," or language of similar import, the property passes to those persons, including the state under Section 2-105, and in such shares as would succeed to the designated individual's intestate estate under the intestate succession law of the designated individual's domicile if the designated individual died when the donative disposition is to take effect in possession or enjoyment. If the designated individual's surviving spouse is living but is remarried at the time the interest is to take effect in possession or enjoyment, the surviving spouse is not an heir of the designated individual.

Part 8
General Provisions Concerning Probate and Nonprobate Transfers

§ 2-801. [Disclaimer of Property Interests.]

(a) [Right to Disclaim Interest in Property.] A person or the representative to whom an interest in or with respect to property or an interest therein devolves by whatever means may disclaim it in whole or in part by delivering or filing a written disclaimer under this section. The right to disclaim exists notwithstanding (i) any limitation on the interest of the disclaimant in the nature of a spendthrift provision or similar restriction or (ii) any restriction or limitation on the right to disclaim contained in the governing instrument. For purposes of this subsection, the "representative of a person" includes a personal representative of a decedent, a conservator of a disabled person, a guardian of a minor or incapacitated person and an agent acting on behalf of the person within the authority of a power of attorney.

(b) [Time of Disclaimer.] The following rules govern the time when a disclaimer must be filed or delivered:

(1) If the property or interest has devolved to the disclaimant under a testamentary instrument or by the laws of intestacy, the disclaimer must be filed, if of a present interest not later than [nine] months after the death of the deceased owner or deceased donee of a power of appointment and, if of a future interest, not later than [nine] months after the event determining that the taker of the property or interest is finally ascertained and his [or her] interest is indefeasibly vested. The disclaimer must be filed in the [probate] court of the county in which proceedings for the administration of the estate of the deceased owner or deceased donee of the power have been commenced. A copy of the disclaimer must be delivered in person or mailed by registered or certified mail, return receipt requested, to any personal

representative or other fiduciary of the decedent or donee of the power.

(2) If a property or interest has devolved to the disclaimant under a nontestamentary instrument or contract, the disclaimer must be delivered or filed, if of a present interest, not later than [nine] months after the effective date of the nontestamentary instrument or contract and, if of a future interest, not later than [nine] months after the event determining that the taker of the property or interest is finally ascertained and his [or her] interest is indefeasibly vested. If the person entitled to disclaim does not know of the existence of the interest, the disclaimer must be delivered or filed not later than [nine] months after the person learns of the existence of the interest. The effective date of a revocable instrument or contract is the date on which the maker no longer has power to revoke it or to transfer to himself [or herself] or another the entire legal and equitable ownership of the interest. The disclaimer of a copy thereof must be delivered in person or mailed by registered or certified mail, return receipt requested, to the person who has legal title to or possession of the interest disclaimed.

(3) A surviving joint tenant [or tenant by the entireties] may disclaim as a separate interest any property or interest therein devolving to him [or her] by right of entire interest in any property or interest therein that is the subject of a joint tenancy [or tenancy by the entireties] devolving to him [or her], if the joint tenancy [or tenancy by the entireties] was created by act of a deceased joint tenant [or tenancy by the entireties], the survivor did not join in creating the join tenancy [or tenancy by the entireties], and has not accepted a benefit under it.

(4) If real property or an interest therein is disclaimed, a copy of the disclaimer may be recorded in the office of the [Recorder of Deeds] of the county in which the property or interest disclaimed is located.

(c) [Form of Disclaimer.] The disclaimer must (i) describe the property or interest disclaimed, (ii) declare the disclaimer and extent thereof, and (iii) be signed by the disclaimant.

(d) [Effect of Disclaimer.] The effects of a disclaimer are:

(1) If property or an interest therein devolves to a disclaimant under a testamentary instrument, under a power of appointment exercised by a testamentary instrument, or under the laws of intestacy, and the decedent has not provided for another disposition of that interest, should it be disclaimed, or of disclaimed or failed interests in general, the disclaimed interest devolves as if the disclaimant had predeceased the decedent, but if by law or under the testamentary instrument the descendants of the disclaimant would take the disclaimant's share by representation were the disclaimant to predecease the decedent, then the disclaimed interest passes by representation to the descendants of the disclaimant who survive the decedent. A future interest that takes effect in possession or enjoyment after the termination of the estate or interest disclaimed takes effect as if the disclaimant had predeceased the decedent. A disclaimer relates back for all purposes to the date of death of the decedent.

(2) If property or an interest therein devolves to a disclaimant under a nontestamentary instrument, and the instrument or contract does not provide for another disposition of that interest, should it be disclaimed, or of disclaimed or failed interests in general, the disclaimed interest devolves as if the disclaimant had predeceased the effective date of the instrument or contract, but if by law or under the nontestamentary instrument or contract the descendants of the disclaimant would take the disclaimant's share by representation were the disclaimant to predecease the effective date of the instrument, then the disclaimed interest passes by representation to the descendants of the disclaimant who survive the effective date of the instrument. A disclaimer relates back for all purposes to that date. A future interest that takes effect in possession or enjoyment at or after the termination of the disclaimed interest takes effect as if the disclaimant had died before the effective date of the instrument or contract that transferred the disclaimed interest.

(3) The disclaimer or the written waiver of the right to disclaim is binding upon the disclaimant or person waiving and all persons claiming through or under either of them.

(e) [Waiver and Bar.] The right to disclaim property or an interest therein is barred by (i) an assignment, conveyance, encumbrance, pledge, or transfer of the property or interest, or a contract therefor, (ii) a written waiver of the right to disclaim, (iii) an acceptance of the property or interest or benefit under it, or (iv) a sale of the property or interest under judicial sale made before the disclaimer is made.

(f) [Remedy Not Exclusive.] This section does not abridge the right of a person to waive, release, disclaim, or renounce property or an interest therein under any other statute.

(g) [Application.] An interest in property existing on the effective date of this section as to which, if a present interest, the time for filing a disclaimer under this section has not expired or, if a future interest, the interest has not become indefeasibly vested or the taker finally ascertained, may be disclaimed within [nine] months after the effective date of this section.

§ 2-802. [Effect of Divorce, Annulment, and Decree of Separation.]

(a) An individual who is divorced from the decedent or whose marriage to the decedent has been annulled is not a surviving spouse unless, by virtue of a subsequent marriage, he [or she] is married to the decedent at the time of death. A decree of separation that does not terminate the status of husband and wife is not a divorce for purposes of this section.

(b) For purposes of Parts 1, 2, 3 & 4 of this Article, and of Section 3-203, a surviving spouse does not include:

(1) an individual who obtains or consents to a final decree or judgment of divorce from the decedent or an annulment of their marriage, which decree or judgment is not recognized as valid in this State, unless subsequently they participate in a marriage ceremony purporting to marry each to the other or live together as man and wife;

(2) an individual who, following an invalid decree or judgment of divorce or annulment obtained by the decedent, participates in a marriage ceremony with a third individual; or

(3) an individual who was a party to a valid proceeding concluded by an order purporting to terminate all marital property rights.

§ 2-803. [Effect of Homicide on Intestate Succession, Wills, Trusts, Joint Assets, Life Insurance, and Beneficiary Designations.]

(a) [Definitions.] In this section:

(1) "Disposition or appointment of property" includes a transfer of an item of property or any other benefit to a beneficiary designated in a governing instrument.

(2) "Governing instrument" means a governing instrument executed by the decedent.

(3) "Revocable," with respect to a disposition, appointment, provision, or nomination, means one under which the decedent, at the time of or immediately before death, was alone empowered, by law or under the governing instrument, to cancel the designation in favor of the killer, whether or not the decedent was then empowered to designate himself [or herself] in place of his [or her] killer and or the decedent then had capacity to exercise the power.

(b) [Forfeiture of Statutory Benefits.] An individual who feloniously and intentionally kills the decedent forfeits all benefits under this Article with respect to the decedent's estate, including an intestate share, an elective share, an omitted spouse's or child's share, a homestead allowance, exempt property, and a family allowance. If the decedent died intestate, the decedent's intestate estate passes as if the killer disclaimed his [or her] intestate share.

(c) [Revocation of Benefits Under Governing Instrument.] The felonious and intentional killing of the decedent:

(1) revokes any revocable (i) disposition or appointment of property made by the decedent to the killer in a governing instrument, (ii) provision in a governing instrument conferring a general or nongeneral power of appointment on the killer, and (iii) nomination of the killer in a governing instrument, nominating or appointing the killer to serve in any fiduciary or representative capacity, including a personal representative, executor, trustee, or agent; and

(2) severs the interests of the decedent and killer in property held by them at the time of the killing as joint tenants with the right of survivorship [or as community property with the right of survivorship], transforming the interests of the decedent and killer into tenancies in common.

(d) [Effect of Severance.] A severance under subsection (c)(2) does not affect any third-party interest in property acquired for value and in good faith reliance on an apparent title by survivorship in the killer unless a writing declaring the severance has been noted, registered, filed, or recorded in records appropriate to the kind and location of the property which are relied upon, in the ordinary course of transactions involving such property, as evidence of ownership.

(e) [Effect of Revocation.] Provisions of a governing instrument that are not revoked by this section are given effect as if the killer disclaimed all revoked provisions or, in the case of a revoked nomination in a fiduciary or representative capacity, as if the killer predeceased the decedent.

(f) [Wrongful Acquisition of Property.] A wrongful acquisition of property or interest by a killer not covered by this section must be treated in accordance with the principle that a killer cannot profit from his [or her] wrong.

(g) [Felonious and Intentional Killing; How Determined.] After all right to appeal has been exhausted, a judgment of conviction establishing criminal accountability for the felonious and intentional killing of the decedent conclusively establishes the convicted individual as the decedent's killer for purposes of this section. In the absence of a conviction, the court, upon the petition of an interested person must determine whether, under the preponderance of evidence standard, the individual would be found criminally accountable for the felonious and intentional killing of the decedent. If the court determines that, under that standard, the individual would be found criminally accountable for the felonious and intentional killing of the decedent, the determination conclusively establishes that individual as the decedent's killer for purposes of this section.

(h) [Protection of Payors and Other Third Parties.]

(1) A payor or other third party is not liable for having made a payment or transferred an item of property or any other benefit to a beneficiary designated in a governing instrument affected by an intentional and felonious killing, or for having taken any other action in good faith reliance on the validity of the governing instrument, upon request and satisfactory proof of the decedent's death, before the payor or other third party received written notice of a claimed forfeiture or revocation under this section. A payor or other third party is liable for a payment made or other action taken after the payor or other third party received written notice of a claimed forfeiture or revocation under this section.

(2) Written notice of a claimed forfeiture or revocation under paragraph (1) must be mailed to the payor's or other third party's main office or home by registered or certified mail, return receipt requested, or served upon the payor or other third party in the same manner as a summons in a civil action. Upon receipt of written notice of a claimed forfeiture or revocation under this section, a payor or other third party may pay any amount owed or transfer or deposit any item of property held by it to or with the court having jurisdiction of the probate proceedings relating to the decedent's estate, or if no proceedings have been commenced, to or with the court having jurisdiction of probate proceedings relating to decedents' estates located in the county of the decedent's residence. The court shall hold the funds or item of property and, upon its determination under this section, shall order disbursement in accordance with the determination. Payments, transfers, or deposits made to or with the court discharge the payor or other third party from all claims for the value of amounts paid to or items of property transferred to or deposited with the court.

(i) [Protection of Bona Fide Purchasers; Personal Liability of Recipient.]

(1) A person who purchases property for value and without notice, or who receives a payment or other item of property in partial or full satisfaction of a legally enforceable obligation, is neither obligated under this section to return the payment, item of property, or benefit nor is liable under this section for the amount of the payment or the value of the item of property or benefit. But a person who, not for value, receives a payment, item of property, or any other benefit to which the person is not entitled under this section is obligated to return the payment, item of property, or benefit, or is personally liable for the amount of the payment or the value of the item of property or benefit, to the person who is entitled to it under this section.

(2) If this section or any part of this section is preempted by federal law with respect to a payment, an item of property or any other benefit covered by this section, a person who, not for value, receives the payment, item of property, or any other benefit is obligated to return that payment, item of property, or benefit, or is personally liable for the amount of that payment or the value of that item of property or benefit, to the person who would have been entitled to it were that section or part of that section not preempted.

§ 2-804. [Revocation of Probate and Nonprobate Transfers by Divorce; No Revocation by Other Changes of Circumstances.]

(a) [Definitions.] In this section:

(1) "Disposition or appointment of property" includes a transfer of an item of property or any other benefit to a beneficiary designated in a governing instrument.

(2) "Divorce or annulment" means any divorce or annulment, or any dissolution or declaration of invalidity of a marriage, that would exclude the spouse as a surviving spouse within the meaning of Section 2-802. A decree of separation that does not terminate the status of husband and wife is not a divorce for purposes of this section.

(3) "Divorced individual" includes an individual whose marriage has been annulled.

(4) "Governing instrument" means a governing instrument executed by the decedent.

(5) "Relative of the divorced individual's former spouse" means an individual who is related to the divorced individual's former spouse by blood, adoption, or affinity and who, after the divorce or annulment, is not related to the divorced individual by blood, adoption, or affinity.

(6) "Revocable," with respect to a disposition, appointment, provision, or nomination, means one under which the divorced individual, at the time of the divorce or annulment, was alone empowered, by law or under the governing instrument, to cancel the designation of his [or her] former spouse or former spouse's relative, whether or not the divorced individual was then empowered to designate himself [or herself] in place of his [or her] former spouse or in place of his [or her] former spouse's relative and whether or not the divorced individual then had capacity to exercise the power.

(b) [Revocation Upon Divorce.] Except as provided by the express terms of a governing instrument, a court order, or a contract relating to the division of the marital estate made between the divorced individuals before or after the marriage, divorce, or annulment, the divorce or annulment of a marriage:

(1) revokes any revocable (i) disposition or appointment of property made by a divorced individual to his [or her] former spouse in a governing instrument and any disposition or appointment created by law or in a governing instrument to a relative of the divorced individual's former spouse, (ii) provision in a governing instrument conferring a general or nongeneral power of appointment on the divorced individual's former spouse or on a relative of the divorced individual's former spouse, and (iii) nomination in a governing instrument, nominating a divorced individual's former spouse or a relative of the divorced individual's former spouse to serve in any fiduciary or representative capacity, including a personal representative, executor, trustee, conservator, agent, or guardian; and

(2) severs the interests of the former spouses in property held by them at the time of the divorce as joint tenants with the right of survivorship [or as community property with the right of survivorship], transforming the interests of the former spouses into tenancies in common.

(c) [Effect of Severance.] A severance under subsection (b)(2) does not affect any third-party interest in property acquired for value and in good faith reliance on an apparent title by survivorship in the former spouses unless a writing declaring the severance has been noted, registered, filed, or recorded in records appropriate to the kind and location of the property which are relied upon, in the ordinary course of transactions involving such property, as evidence of ownership.

(d) [Effect of Revocation.] Provisions of a governing instrument that are not revoked by this section are given effect as if the former spouse and relatives of the former spouse disclaimed the revoked provisions or, in the case of a revoked nomination in a fiduciary or representative capacity, as if the former spouse and relatives of the former spouse died immediately before the divorce or annulment.

(e) [Revival if Divorce Nullified.] Provisions revoked solely by this section are revived by the divorced individual's remarriage to the former spouse or by a nullification of the divorce or annulment.

(f) [No Revocation for Other Change of Circumstances.] No change of circumstances other than as described in this section and in Section 2-803 effects a revocation.

(g) [Protection of Payors and Other Third Parties.]

(1) A payor or other third party is not liable for having made a payment or transferred an item of property or any other benefit to a beneficiary designated in a governing instrument affected by a divorce, annulment, or remarriage, or for having taken any other action in good faith reliance on the validity of the governing instrument, before the payor or other third party received written notice of the divorce, annulment, or remarriage. A payor or other third party is liable for a payment made or other action taken after the payor or other third party received written notice of a claimed forfeiture or revocation under this section.

(2) Written notice of the divorce, annulment, or remarriage under subsection (g)(2) must be mailed to the payor's or other third party's main office or home by registered or certified mail, return receipt requested, or served upon the payor or other third party in the same manner as a summons in a civil action. Upon receipt of written notice the divorce, annulment, or remarriage, a payor or other third party may pay any amount owed or transfer or deposit any item of property held by it to or with the court having jurisdiction of the probate proceedings relating to the decedent's estate, or if no proceedings have been commenced, to or with the court having jurisdiction of probate proceedings relating to decedents' estates located in the county of the decedent's residence. The court shall hold the funds or item of property and, upon its determination under this section, shall order disbursement in accordance with the determination. Payments, transfers, or deposits made to or with the court discharge the payor or other third party from all claims for the value of amounts paid to or items of property transferred to or deposited with the court.

(h) [Protection of Bona Fide Purchasers; Personal Liability of Recipient.]

(1) A person who purchases property from a former spouse, relative of a former spouse, or any other person for value and without notice, or who receives from a former spouse, relative of a former spouse, or any other person a payment or other item of property in partial or full satisfaction of a legally enforceable obligation, is neither obligated under this section to return the payment, item of property, or benefit nor is liable under this section for the amount of the payment or the value of the item of property or benefit. But a former spouse, relative of a former spouse, or any other person who, not for value, receives a payment, item of property, or any other benefit to which that person is not entitled under this section is obligated to return the payment, item of property, or benefit, or is personally liable for the amount of the payment or the value of the item of property or benefit, to the person who is entitled to it under this section.

(2) If this section or any part of this section is preempted by federal law with respect to a payment, an item of property or any other benefit covered by this section, a former spouse, relative of a former spouse, or any other person who, not

for value, received a payment, item of property, or any other benefit to which that person is not entitled under this section is obligated to return that payment, item of property, or benefit, or is personally liable for the amount of that payment or the value of that item of property or benefit, to the person who would have been entitled to it were this section or part of this section not preempted.

Part 9
Statutory Rule Against Perpetuities; Honorary Trusts

SUBPART 1. STATUTORY RULE AGAINST PERPETUITIES

§ 2-901. [Statutory Rule Against Perpetuities.]

(a) [Validity of Nonvested Property Interest.] A nonvested property interest is invalid unless:

(1) when the interest is created, it is certain to vest or terminate no later than 21 years after the death of an individual then alive; or

(2) the interest either vests or terminates within 90 years after its creation.

(b) [Validity of General Power of Appointment Subject to a Condition Precedent.] A general power of appointment not presently exercisable because of a condition precedent is invalid unless:

(1) when the power is created, the condition precedent is certain to be satisfied or become impossible to satisfy no later than 21 years after the death of an individual then alive; or

(2) the condition precedent either is satisfied or becomes impossible to satisfy within 90 years after its creation.

(c) [Validity of Nongeneral or Testamentary Power of Appointment.] A nongeneral power of appointment or a general testamentary power of appointment is invalid unless:

(1) when the power is created, it is certain to be irrevocably exercised or otherwise to terminate no later than 21 years after the death of an individual then alive; or

(2) the power is irrevocably exercised or otherwise terminates within 90 years after its creation.

(d) [Possibility of Post-death Child Disregarded.] In determining whether a nonvested property interest or a power of appointment is valid under subsection (a)(1), (b)(1), or (c)(1), the possibility that a child will be born to an individual after the individual's death is disregarded.

(e) [Effect of Certain "Later-of" Type Language.] If, in measuring a period from the creation of a trust or other property arrangement, language in a governing instrument (i) seeks to disallow the vesting or termination of any interest or trust beyond, (ii) seeks to postpone the vesting or termination of any interest or trust until, or (iii) seeks to operate in effect in any similar fashion upon, the later of (A) the expiration of a period of time not exceeding 21 years after the death of the survivor of specified lives in being at the creation of the trust or other property arrangement or (B) the expiration of a period of time that exceeds or might exceed 21 years after the death of the survivor of lives in being at the creation of the trust or other property arrangement, that language is inoperative to the extent it produces a period of time that exceeds 21 years after the death of the survivor of the specified lives.

§ 2-902. [When Nonvested Property Interest or Power of Appointment Created.]

(a) Except as provided in subsections (b) and (c) and in Section 2-905(a), the time of creation of a nonvested property interest or a power of appointment is determined under general principles of property law.

(b) For purposes of Subpart 1 of this Part, if there is a person who alone can exercise a power created by a governing instrument to become the unqualified beneficial owner of (i) a nonvested property interest or (ii) a property interest subject to a power of appointment described in Section 2-901(b) or (c), the nonvested property interest or power of appointment is created when the power to become the unqualified beneficial owner terminates. [For purposes of Subpart 1 of this Part, a joint power with respect to community property or to marital property under the Uniform Marital Property Act held by individuals married to each other is a power exercisable by one person alone.]

(c) For purposes of Subpart 1 of this Part, a nonvested property interest or a power of appointment arising from a transfer of property to a previously funded trust or other existing property arrangement is created when the nonvested property interest or power of appointment in the original contribution was created.

§ 2-903. [Reformation.]

Upon the petition of an interested person, a court shall reform a disposition in the manner that most closely approximates the transferor's manifested plan of distribution and is within the 90 years allowed by Section 2-901(a)(2), 2-901(b)(2), or 2-901(c)(2) if:

(1) a nonvested property interest or a power of appointment becomes invalid under Section 2-901 (statutory rule against perpetuities);

(2) a class gift is not but might become invalid under Section 2-901 (statutory rule against perpetuities) and the time has arrived when the share of any class member is to take effect in possession or enjoyment; or

(3) a nonvested property interest that is not validated by Section 2-901(a)(1) can vest but not within 90 year after its creation.

§ 2-904. [Exclusions from Statutory Rule Against Perpetuities.]

Section 2-901 (statutory rule against perpetuities) does not apply to:

(1) a nonvested property interest or a power of appointment arising out of a nondonative transfer except a nonvested property interest or a power of appointment arising out of (i) a premarital or post-marital agreement, (ii) a separation or divorce settlement, (iii) a spouse's election, (iv) a similar arrangement arising out of a prospective, existing, or previous marital relationship between the parties, (v) a contract to make or not to revoke a will or trust, (vi) a contract to exercise or not to exercise a power of appointment, (vii) a transfer in satisfaction of a duty of support, or (viii) a reciprocal transfer;

(2) a fiduciary's power relating to the administration or management of assets, including the power of a fiduciary to sell, lease, or mortgage property, and the power of a fiduciary to determine principal and income;

(3) a power to appoint a fiduciary;

(4) a discretionary power of a trustee to distribute principal before termination of a trust to a beneficiary having an indefeasibly vested interest in the income and principal;

(5) a nonvested property interest held by a charity, government, or governmental agency or subdivision, if the nonvested property interest is preceded by an interest held by another charity, government or governmental agency or subdivision;

(6) a nonvested property interest in or a power of appointment with respect to a trust or other property arrangement forming part of a pension, profit-sharing, stock bonus, health, disability, death benefit, income deferral, or other current or deferred benefit plan for one or more employees, independent contractors, or their beneficiaries or spouses, to which contributions are made for the purpose of distributing to or for the benefit of the participants or their beneficiaries or spouses the property, income, or principal in the trust or other property arrangement, except a nonvested property interest or a power of appointment that is created by an election of a participant or a beneficiary or spouse; or

(7) a property interest, power of appointment, or arrangement that was not subject to the common-law rule against perpetuities or is excluded by another statute of this State.

§ 2-905. [Prospective Application.]

(a) Except as extended by subsection (b), Subpart 1 of this Part applies to a nonvested property interest or a power of appointment that is created on or after the effective date of Subpart 1 of this Part. For purposes of this section, a nonvested property interest or a power of appointment is created when the power is irrevocably exercised or when a revocable exercise becomes irrevocable.

(b) If a nonvested property interest or a power of appointment was created before the effective date of Subpart 1 of this Part and is determined in a judicial proceeding, commenced on or after the effective date of Subpart 1 of this Part, to violate this State's rule against perpetuities as that rule existed before the effective date of Subpart 1 of this Part, a court upon the petition of an interest person may reform the disposition in the manner that most closely approximates the transferor's manifested plan of distribution and is within the limits of the rule against perpetuities applicable when the nonvested property interest or power of appointment was created.

§ 2-906. [Supersession] [Repeal.]

Subpart 1 of this Part [supersedes the rule of the common law known as the rule against perpetuities] [repeals (list statutes to be repealed)].

SUBPART 2. HONORARY TRUSTS

[Optional provision for validating and limiting the duration of so-called honorary trusts and trusts for pets.]

§ 2-907. [Honorary Trusts; Trusts for Pets.]

(a) [Honorary Trust.] A trust for a noncharitable corporation or unincorporated society or for a lawful noncharitable purpose may be performed by the trustee for [21] years but no longer, whether or not there is a beneficiary who can seek the trust's enforcement or termination and whether or not the terms of the trust contemplate a longer duration.

(b) [Trust for Pets.] Subject to this subsection, a trust for the care of a designated domestic or pet animal and the animal's offspring is valid. Except as expressly provided otherwise in the trust instrument:

(1) No portion of the principal or income may be converted to the use of the trustee or to any other use than for the benefit of a covered animal.

(2) The trust terminates at the earlier of [21] years after the trust was created or when no living animal is covered by the trust.

(3) Upon termination, the trustee shall transfer the unexpended trust property in the following order:

(i) as directed in the trust instrument;

(ii) if the trust was created in a nonresiduary clause in the transferor's will or in a codicil to the transferor's will; and

(iii) if no taker is produced by the application of subparagraph (i) or (ii), to the transferor's heirs under Section 2-711.

(4) For the purposes of Section 2-707, the residuary clause is treated as creating a future interest under the terms of the trust.

(5) The intended use of the principal or income can be enforced by an individual designated for that purpose in the trust instrument or, if none, by an individual appointed by a court upon application to it by an individual.

(6) Except as ordered by the court or required by the trust instrument, no filing, report, registration, periodic accounting, separate maintenance of funds, appointment, or fee is required by reason of the existence of the fiduciary relationship of the trustee.

(7) A governing instrument must be liberally construed to bring the transfer within this section, to presume against the merely precatory or honorary nature of the disposition, and to carry out the general intent of the transferor. Extrinsic evidence is admissible in determining the transferor's intent.

(8) A court may reduce the amount of the property transferred, if it determines that that amount substantially exceeds the amount required for the intended use. The amount of the reduction, if any passes as unexpended trust property under subsection (b)(3).

(9) If no trustee is designated or no designated trustee is willing or able to serve, a court shall name a trustee. A court may order the transfer of the property to another trustee, if required to assure that the intended use is carried out and if no successor trustee is designated in the trust instrument or if no designated successor trustee agrees to serve or is able to serve. A court may also make such other orders and determinations as shall be advisable to carry out the intent of the transferor and the purpose of this section.

The following version of UPC Article II is the earlier one, which precedes the 1990 amendment. It is reproduced here for reference in states that have not adopted the newer version.

ARTICLE II
INTESTATE SUCCESSION AND WILLS (1969)

Part 1
Intestate Succession

§ 2-101 [Intestate Estate.]
§ 2-102 [Share of the Spouse.]
[§ 2-102A [Share of the Spouse.]]
§ 2-103 [Share of Heirs Other Than Surviving Spouse.]
§ 2-104 [Requirement That Heir Survive Decedent For 120 Hours.]
§ 2-105 [No Taker.]
§ 2-106 [Representation.]
§ 2-107 [Kindred of Half Blood.]
§ 2-108 [Afterborn Heirs.]
§ 2-109 [Meaning of Child and Related Terms.]
§ 2-110 [Advancements.]
§ 2-111 [Debts to Decedent.]
§ 2-112 [Alienage.]
[§ 2-113 [Dower and Curtesy Abolished.]]
§ 2-114 [Persons Related to Decedent Through Two Lines.]

Part 2
Elective Share of Surviving Spouse

§ 2-201 [Right to Elective Share.]
§ 2-202 [Augmented Estate.]
§ 2-203 [Right of Election Personal to Surviving Spouse.]
§ 2-204 [Waiver of Right to Elect and of Other Rights.]
§ 2-205 [Proceeding for Elective Share; Time Limit.]
§ 2-206 [Effect of Election on Benefits by Will or Statute.]
§ 2-207 [Charging Spouse With Gifts Received; Liability of Others For Balance of Elective Share.]

Part 3
Spouse and Children Unprovided For in Wills

§ 2-301 [Omitted Spouse.]
§ 2-302 [Pretermitted Children.]

Part 4
Exempt Property and Allowances

§ 2-401 [Homestead Allowance.]
[§ 2-401A [Constitutional Homestead.]]
§ 2-402 [Exempt Property.]
§ 2-403 [Family Allowance.]
§ 2-404 [Source, Determination and Documentation.]

Part 5
Wills

§ 2-501 [Who May Make a Will.]
§ 2-502 [Execution.]
§ 2-503 [Holographic Will.]
§ 2-504 [Self-proved Will.]
§ 2-505 [Who May Witness.]
§ 2-506 [Choice of Law as to Execution.]
§ 2-507 [Revocation by Writing or by Act.]
§ 2-508 [Revocation by Divorce; No Revocation by Other Changes of Circumstances.]
§ 2-509 [Revival of Revoked Will.]
§ 2-510 [Incorporation by Reference.]
§ 2-511 [Testamentary Additions to Trusts.]
§ 2-512 [Events of Independent Significance.]

Part 1
Intestate Succession

§ 2-101. [Intestate Estate.]

Any part of the estate of a decedent not effectively disposed of by his will passes to his heirs as prescribed in the following sections of this Code.

§ 2-102. [Share of the Spouse.]

The intestate share of the surviving spouse is:

(1) if there is no surviving issue or parent of the decedent, the entire intestate estate;

(2) if there is no surviving issue but the decedent is survived by a parent or parents, the first [$50,000], plus one-half of the balance of the intestate estate;

(3) if there are no surviving issue all of whom are issue of the surviving spouse also, the first [$50,000], plus one-half of the balance of the intestate estate;

(4) if there are surviving issue one or more of whom are not issue of the surviving spouse, one-half of the intestate estate.

ALTERNATIVE PROVISION FOR COMMUNITY PROPERTY STATES

[§ 2-102A. [Share of the Spouse.]

The intestate share of the surviving spouse is as follows:

(1) as to separate property

(i) if there is no surviving issue or parent of the decedent, the entire intestate estate;

(ii) if there is no surviving issue but the decedent is survived by a parent or parents, the first [$50,000], plus one-half of the balance of the intestate estate;

(iii) if there are surviving issue all of whom are issue of the surviving spouse also, the first [$50,000], plus one-half of the balance of the intestate estate;

(iv) if there are surviving issue one or more of whom are not issue of the surviving spouse, one-half of the intestate estate.

(2) as to community property

(i) The one-half of community property which belongs to the decedent passes to the [surviving spouse].]

§ 2-103. [Share of Heirs Other Than Surviving Spouse.]

The part of the intestate estate not passing to the surviving spouse under Section 2-102, or the entire intestate estate if there is no surviving spouse, passes as follows:

(1) to the issue of the decedent; if they are all of the same degree of kinship to the decedent they take equally, but if of unequal degree, then those of more remote degree take by representation;

(2) if there is no surviving issue, to his parent or parents equally;

(3) if there is no surviving issue or parent, to the issue of the parents or either of them by representation;

(4) if there is no surviving issue, parent or issue of a parent, but the decedent is survived by one or more grandparents or issue of grandparents, half of the estate passes to the paternal grandparents if both survive, or to the surviving paternal grandparent, or to the issue of the paternal grandparents if both are deceased, the issue taking equally if they are all of the same degree of kinship to the decedent, but if of unequal degree those of more remote degree take by representation; and the other half passes to the maternal relatives in the same manner; but if there be no surviving grandparent or issue of grandparent on either the paternal or the maternal side, the entire estate passes to the relatives on the other side in the same manner as the half.

§ 2-104. [Requirement That Heir Survive Decedent For 120 Hours.]

Any person who fails to survive the decedent by 120 hours is deemed to have predeceased the decedent for purposes of homestead allowance, exempt property and intestate succession, and the decedent's heirs are determined accordingly. If the time of death of the decedent or of the person who would otherwise be an heir, or the times of death of both, cannot be determined, and it cannot be established that the person who would otherwise be an heir has survived the decedent by 120 hours, it is deemed that the person failed to survive for the required period. This section is not to be applied where its application would result in a taking of intestate estate by the state under Section 2-105.

§ 2-105. [No Taker.]

If there is no taker under the provisions of this Article, the intestate estate passes to the [state].

§ 2-106. [Representation.]

If representation is called for by this Code, the estate is divided into as many shares as there are surviving heirs in the nearest degree of kinship and deceased persons in the same degree who left issue who survive the decedent, each surviving heir in the nearest degree receiving one share and the share of each deceased person in the same degree being divided among his issue in the same manner.

§ 2-107. [Kindred of Half Blood.]

Relatives of the half blood inherit the same share they would inherit if they were of the whole blood.

§ 2-108. [Afterborn Heirs.]

Relatives of the decedent conceived before his death but born thereafter inherit as if they had been born in the lifetime of the decedent.

§ 2-109. [Meaning of Child and Related Terms.]

If, for purposes of intestate succession, a relationship of parent and child must be established to determine succession by, through, or from a person,

(1) an adopted person is the child of an adopting parent and not of the natural parents except that adoption of a child by the spouse of a natural parent has no effect on the relationship between the child and either natural parent.

(2) In cases not covered by Paragraph (1), a person is the child of its parents regardless of the marital status of its partners and the parent and child relationship may be established under the [Uniform Parentage Act].

Alternative subsection (2) for states that have not adopted the Uniform Parentage Act.

[(2) In cases not covered by Paragraph (1), a person born out of wedlock is a child of the mother. That person is also a child of the father, if:

(i) the natural parents participated in a marriage ceremony before or after the birth of the child, even though the attempted marriage is void; or

(ii) the paternity is established by an adjudication before the death of the father or is established thereafter by clear and convincing proof, but the paternity established under this subparagraph is ineffective to qualify the father or his kindred to inherit from or through the child unless the father has openly treated the child as his, and has not refused to support the child.]

§ 2-110. [Advancements.]

If a person dies intestate as to all his estate, property which he gave in his lifetime to an heir is treated as an advancement against the latter's share of the estate only if declared in a contemporaneous writing by the decedent or acknowledged in writing by the heir to be an advancement. For this purpose the property advanced is valued as of the time the heir came into possession or enjoyment of the property or as of the time of death of the decedent, whichever first occurs. If the recipient of the property fails to survive the decedent, the property is not taken into account in computing the intestate share to be received by the recipient's issue, unless the declaration or acknowledgment provides otherwise.

§ 2-111. [Debts to Decedent.]

A debt owed to the decedent is not charged against the intestate share of any person except the debtor. If the debtor fails to survive the decedent, the debt is not taken into account in computing the intestate share of the debtor's issue.

§ 2-112. [Alienage.]

No person is disqualified to take as an heir because he or a person through whom he claims is or has been an alien.

[§ 2-113. [Dower and Curtesy Abolished.]

The estates of dower and curtesy are abolished.]

§ 2-114. [Persons Related to Decedent Through Two Lines.]

A person who is related to the decedent through 2 lines of relationship is entitled to only a single share based on the relationship which would entitle him to the larger share.

Part 2
Elective Share of Surviving Spouse

§ 2-201. [Right to Elective Share.]

(a) If a married person domiciled in this state dies, the surviving spouse has a right of election to take an elective share of one-third of the augmented estate under the limitations and conditions hereinafter stated.

(b) If a married person not domiciled in this state dies, the right, if any, of the surviving spouse to take an elective share in property in this state is governed by the law of the decedent's domicile at death.

§ 2-202. [Augmented Estate.]

The augmented estate means the estate reduced by funeral and administration expenses, homestead allowance, family allowances and exemptions, and enforceable claims, to which is added the sum of the following amounts:

(1) The value of property transferred to anyone other than a bona fide purchaser by the decedent at any time during marriage, to or for the benefit of any person other than the surviving spouse, to the extent that the decedent did not receive adequate and full consideration in money or money's worth for the transfer, if the transfer is of any of the following types:

(i) any transfer under which the decedent retained at the time of his death the possession or enjoyment of, or right to income from, the property;

(ii) any transfer to the extent that the decedent retained at the time of his death a power, either alone or in conjunction with any other person, to revoke or to consume, invade or dispose of the principal for his own benefit;

(iii) any transfer whereby property is held at the time of decedent's death by decedent and another with right of survivorship;

(iv) any transfer made to a donee within two years of death of the decedent to the extent that the aggregate transfers to any one donee in either of the years exceed $3,000.00.

Any transfer is excluded if made with the written consent or joinder of the surviving spouse. Property is valued as of the decedent's death except that property given irrevocably to a donee during lifetime of the decedent is valued as of the date the donee came into possession or enjoyment if that occurs first. Nothing herein shall cause to be included in the augmented estate any life insurance, accident insurance, joint annuity, or pension payable to a person other than the surviving spouse.

(2) The value of property owned by the surviving spouse at the decedent's death, plus the value of property transferred by the spouse at any time during marriage to any person other than the decedent which would have been includible in the spouse's augmented estate if the surviving spouse had predeceased the decedent to the extent the owned or transferred property is derived from the decedent by any means other than testate or intestate succession without a full consideration in money or money's worth. For purposes of this paragraph:

(i) Property derived from the decedent includes, but is not limited to, any beneficial interest of the surviving spouse in a trust created by the decedent during his lifetime, any property appointed to the spouse by the decedent's exercise of a general or special power of appointment also exercisable in favor of others than the spouse, any proceeds of insurance (including accidental death benefits) on the life of the decedent attributable to premiums paid by him, any lump sum immediately payable and the commuted value of the proceeds of annuity contracts under which the decedent was the primary annuitant attributable to premiums paid by him, the commuted value of amounts payable after the decedent's death under any public or private pension, disability compensation, death benefit or retirement plan, exclusive of the Federal Social Security system, by reason of service performed or disabilities incurred by the decedent, any property held at the time of decedent's death by decedent and the surviving spouse with right of survivorship, any property held by decedent and transferred by contract to the surviving spouse by reason of the decedent's death and the value of the share of the surviving spouse resulting from rights in community property in this or any other state formerly owned with the decedent. Premiums paid by the decedent's employer, his partner, a partnership of which he was a member, or his creditors, are deemed to have been paid by the decedent.

(ii) Property owned by the spouse at the decedent's death is valued as of the date of death. Property transferred by the spouse is valued at the time the transfer became irrevocable, or at the decedent's death, whichever occurred first. Income earned by included property prior to the decedent's death is not treated as property derived from the decedent.

(iii) Property owned by the surviving spouse as of the decedent's death, or previously transferred by the surviving spouse, is presumed to have been derived from the decedent except to the extent that the surviving spouse establishes that it was derived from another source.

(3) For purposes of this section a bona fide purchaser is a purchaser for value in good faith and without notice of any adverse claim. Any recorded instrument on which a state documentary fee is noted pursuant to [insert appropriate reference] is prima facie evidence that the transfer described therein was made to a bona fide purchaser.

§ 2-203. [Right of Election Personal to Surviving Spouse.]

The right of election of the surviving spouse may be exercised only during his lifetime by him. In the case of a protected person, the right of election may be exercised only by order of the court in which protective proceedings as to his property are pending, after finding that exercise is necessary to provide adequate support for the protected person during his probable life expectancy.

§ 2-204. [Waiver of Right to Elect and of Other Rights.]

The right of election of a surviving spouse and the rights of the surviving spouse to homestead allowance, except property and family allowance, or any of them, may be waived, wholly or partially, before or after marriage, by a written contract, agreement or waiver signed by the party waiving after fair disclosure. Unless it provides to the contrary, a waiver of "all rights" (or equivalent language) in the property or estate of a present or prospective spouse or a complete property settlement entered into after or in anticipation of separation or divorce is a waiver of all rights to elective share, homestead allowance, exempt property and family allowance by each spouse in the property of the other and a renunciation by each of all benefits which would otherwise pass to him from the other by intestate succession or by virtue of the provisions of any will executed before the waiver or property settlement.

§ 2-205. [Proceeding for Elective Share; Time Limit.]

(a) The surviving spouse may elect to take his elective share in the augmented estate by filing in the Court and mailing or delivering to the personal representative, if any, a petition for the elective share within 9 months after the date of death, or within 6 months after the probate of the decedent's will, whichever limitation last expires. However, non-probate transfers, described in Section 2-202(1), shall not be included within the augmented estate for the purpose of computing the elective share, if the petition is filed later than 9 months after death.

The Court may extend the time for election as it sees fit for cause shown by the surviving spouse before the time for election has expired.

(b) The surviving spouse shall give notice of the time and place set for hearing to persons interested in the estate and to the distributees and recipients of portions of the augmented net estate whose interests will be adversely affected by the taking of the elective share.

(c) the surviving spouse may withdraw his demand for an elective share at any time before entry of a final determination by the Court.

(d) After notice and hearing, the Court shall determine the amount of the elective share and shall order its payment from the assets of the augmented net estate or by contribution as appears appropriate under Section 2-207. If it appears that a fund or property included in the augmented net estate has not come into the possession of the personal representative, or has been distributed by the personal representative, the court nevertheless shall fix the liability of any person who has any interest in the fund or property or who has possession thereof, whether as trustee or otherwise. The proceeding may be maintained against fewer than all persons against whom relief could be sought, but no person is subject to contribution in any greater amount than he would have been if relief had been secured against all persons subject to contribution.

(e) The order or judgment of the court may be enforced as necessary in suit for contribution or payment in other courts of this state or other jurisdictions.

§ 2-206. [Effect of Election on Benefits by Will or Statute.]

A surviving spouse is entitled to homestead allowance, exempt property, and family allowance, whether or not he elects to take an elective share.

§ 2-207. [Charging Spouse With Gifts Received; Liability of Others For Balance of Elective Share.]

(a) In the proceeding for an elective share, values included in the augmented estate which pass or have passed to the surviving spouse, or which would have passed to the spouse but were renounced, are applied first to satisfy the elective share and to reduce any contributions due from other recipients of transfers included in the augmented estate. For purposes of this subsection, the electing spouse's beneficial interest in any life estate or in any trust shall be computed as if worth one half of the total value of the property subject to the life estate, or of the trust estate, unless higher or lower values for these interests are established by proof.

(b) Remaining property of the augmented estate is so applied that liability for the balance of the elective share of the surviving spouse is equitably apportioned among the recipients of the augmented estate in proportion to the value of their interests therein.

(c) Only original transferrees from, or appointees of, the decedent and their donees, to the extent the donees have the property or its proceeds, are subject to the contribution to make up the elective share of the surviving spouse. A person liable to contribution may choose to give up the property transferred to him or to pay its value as of the time it is considered in computing the augmented estate.

Part 3
Spouse and Children Unprovided For in Wills

§ 2-301. [Omitted Spouse.]

(a) If a testator fails to provide by will for his surviving spouse who married the testator after the execution of the will, the omitted spouse shall receive the same share of the estate he would have received if the decedent left no will unless it appears from the will that the omission was intentional or the testator provided for the spouse by transfer outside the will and the intent that the transfer be in lieu of a testamentary provision is shown by statements of the testator or from the amount of the transfer or other evidence.

(b) In satisfying a share provided by this section, the devises made by the will abate as provided in Section 3-902.

§ 2-302. [Pretermitted Children.]

(a) If a testator fails to provide in his will for any of his children born or adopted after the execution of his will, the omitted child receives a share in the estate equal in value to that which he would have received if the testator had died intestate unless:

(1) it appears from the will that the omission was intentional;

(2) when the will was executed the testator had one or more children and devised substantially all his estate to the other parent of the omitted child; or

(3) the testator provided for the child by transfer outside the will and the intent that the transfer be in lieu of a testamentary provision is shown by statements of the testator or from the amount of the transfer or other evidence.

(b) If at the time of execution of the will the testator fails to provide in his will for a living child solely because he believes the child to be dead, the child receives a share in the estate equal in value to that which he would have received if the testator had died intestate.

(c) In satisfying a share provided by this section, the devises made by the will abate as provided in Section 3-902.

Part 4
Exempt Property and Allowances

§ 2-401. [Homestead Allowance.]

A surviving spouse of a decedent who was domiciled in this state is entitled to a homestead allowance of [$5,000]. If there is no surviving spouse, each minor child and each dependent child of the decedent is entitled to a homestead allowance amounting to [$5,000] divided by the number of minor and dependent children of the decedent. The homestead allowance is exempt from and has priority over all claims against the estate. Homestead allowance is in addition to any share passing to the surviving spouse or minor or dependent child by the will of the decedent unless otherwise provided, by intestate succession or by way of elective share.

[§ 2-401A. [Constitutional Homestead.]

The value of any constitutional right of homestead in the family home received by a surviving spouse or child shall be charged against that spouse or child's homestead allowance to the extent that the family home is part of the decedent's estate or would have been but for the homestead provision of the constitution.]

§ 2-402. [Exempt Property.]

In addition to the homestead allowance, the surviving spouse of a decedent who was domiciled in this state is entitled from the estate to value not exceeding $3,500 in excess of any security interests therein in household furniture, automobiles, furnishings, appliances and personal effects. If there is no surviving spouse, children of the decedent are entitled jointly to the same value. If encumbered chattels are selected and if the value in excess of security interests, plus that of other exempt property, is less than $3,500, or if there is not $3,500 worth of exempt property in the estate, the spouse or children are entitled to other assets of the estate, if any, to the extent necessary to make up the $3,500 value. Rights to exempt property and assets needed to make up a deficiency of exempt property have priority over all claims against the estate, except that the right to any assets to make up a deficiency of exempt property shall abate as necessary to permit prior payment of homestead allowance and family allowance. These rights are in addition to any benefit or share passing to the surviving spouse or children by the will of the decedent unless otherwise provided, by intestate succession, or by way of elective share.

§ 2-403. [Family Allowance.]

In addition to the right to homestead allowance and exempt property, if the decedent was domiciled in this state, the surviving spouse and minor children whom the decedent was obligated to support and children who were in fact being supported by him are entitled to a reasonable allowance in money out of the estate for their maintenance during the period of administration, which allowance may not continue for longer than one year if the estate is inadequate to discharge allowed claims. The allowance may be paid as a lump sum or in periodic installments. It is payable to the surviving spouse, if living, for the use of the surviving spouse and minor and dependent children; otherwise to the children, or persons having their care and custody; but in case any minor child or dependent child is not living with the surviving spouse, the allowance may be made partially to the child or his guardian or other person having his care and custody, and partially to the spouse, as their needs may appear. The family allowance is exempt from and has priority over all claims but not over the homestead allowance.

The family allowance is not chargeable against any benefit or share passing to the surviving spouse or children by the will of the decedent unless otherwise provided, by intestate succession, or by way of elective share. The death of any person entitled to family allowance terminates his right to allowances not yet paid.

§ 2-404. [Source, Determination and Documentation.]

If the estate is otherwise sufficient, property specifically devised is not used to satisfy rights to homestead and exempt property. Subject to this restriction, the surviving spouse, the guardians of the minor children, or children who are adults may select property of the estate as homestead allowance and exempt property. The personal representative may make these selection if the surviving spouse, the children or the guardians of the minor children are unable or fail to do so within a reasonable time or if there are no guardians of the minor children. The personal representative may execute an instrument or deed of distribution to establish the ownership of property taken as homestead allowance or exempt property. He may determine the family allowance in a lump sum not exceeding $6,000 or periodic installments not exceeding $500 per month for one year, and may disburse funds of the estate in payment of the family allowance and any part of the homestead allowance payable in cash. The personal representative or any interested person aggrieved by any selection, determination, payment, proposed payment, or failure to act under this section may petition the Court for appropriate relief, which relief may provide a family allowance larger or smaller than that which the personal representative determined or could have determined.

Part 5
Wills

§ 2-501. [Who May Make a Will.]

Any person 18 or more years of age who is of sound mind may make a will.

§ 2-502. [Execution.]

Except as provided for holographic wills, writings within Section 2-513, and wills within Section 2-506, every will shall be in writing signed by the testator or in the testator's name by some other person in the testator's presence and by his direction, and shall be signed by at least 2 persons each of whom witnessed either the signing or the testator's acknowledgment of the signature or of the will.

§ 2-503. [Holographic Will.]

A will which does not comply with Section 2-502 is valid as a holographic will, whether or not witnessed, if the signature and the material provisions are in the handwriting of the testator.

§ 2-504. [Self-proved Will.]

(a) Any will may be simultaneously executed, attested, and made self-proved, by acknowledgment thereof by the testator and affidavits of the witnesses, each made before an officer authorized to administer oaths under the laws of the state where execution occurs and evidenced by the officer's certificate, under official seal, in substantially the following form:

I, ____________, the testator, sign my name to this instrument this __________ day of __________, 19____, and being first duly sworn, do hereby declare to the undersigned authority that I sign and execute this instrument as my last will and that I sign it willingly (or willingly direct another to sign for me), that I execute it as my free and voluntary act for the purposes therein expressed, and that I am eighteen years of age or older, of sound mind, and under no constraint or undue influence.

____
Testator

We, ____________, ____________, the witnesses, sign our names to this instrument, being first duly sworn, and do hereby declare to the undersigned authority that the testator signs and executes this instrument as his last will and that he signs it willingly (or willingly directs another to sign for him), and that each of us, in the presence and hearing of the testator, hereby signs this will as witness to the testator's signing, and that to the best of our knowledge the testator is eighteen years of age or older, of sound mind, and under no constraint or undue influence.

____
Witness

____
Witness

The State of _________
County of __________

Subscribed, sworn to and acknowledged before me by __________, the testator and subscribed and sworn to before me by ________, and __________, witnesses, this ____ day of ____.

(Seal) (Signed) ____________________

____
(Official capacity of officer)

(b) An attested will may at any time subsequent to its execution be made self-proved by the acknowledgment thereof by the testator and the affidavits of the witnesses, each made before an officer authorized to administer oaths under the laws of the state where the acknowledgment occurs and evidenced by the officer's certificate, under the official seal, attached or annexed to the will in substantially the following form:

The State of _________
County of __________

We, __________, __________, and __________, the testator and the witnesses, respectively, whose names are signed to the attached or foregoing instrument, being first duly sworn, do hereby declare to the undersigned authority that the testator signed and executed the instrument as his last will and that he had signed willingly (or willingly directed another to sign for him), and that he executed it as his free and voluntary act for the purposes therein expressed, and that each of the witnesses, in the presence and hearing of the testator, signed the will as witness and that to the best of his knowledge the testator was at that time eighteen years of age or older, of sound mind and under no constraint or undue influence.

____
Testator

____
Witness

____
Witness

Subscribed, sworn to and acknowledged before me by __________, the testator, and subscribed and sworn to before me by ________, and __________, witnesses, this ____ day of ____.

(Seal) (Signed) ____________________

____
(Official capacity of officer)

§ 2-505. [Who May Witness.]

(a) Any person generally competent to be a witness may act as a witness to a will.

(b) A will or any provision thereof is not invalid because the will is signed by an interested witness.

§ 2-506. [Choice of Law as to Execution.]

A written will is valid if executed in compliance with Section 2-502 or 2-503 or if its execution complies with the law at the time of execution of the place where the will is executed, or of the law of the place where at the time of execution or at the time of death the testator is domiciled, has a place of abode or is a national.

§ 2-507. [Revocation by Writing or by Act.]

A will or any part thereof is revoked

(1) by a subsequent will which revokes the prior will or part expressly or by inconsistency; or

(2) by being burned, torn, canceled, obliterated, or destroyed, with the intent and for the purpose of revoking it by the testator or by another person in his presence and by his direction.

§ 2-508. [Revocation by Divorce; No Revocation by Other Changes of Circumstances.]

If after executing a will the testator is divorced or his marriage annulled, the divorce or annulment revokes any disposition or appointment of property made by the will to the former spouse, any provision conferring a general or special power of appointment on the former spouse, and any nomination of the former spouse as executor, trustee, conservator, or guardian, unless the will expressly provides otherwise. Property prevented from passing to a former spouse because of revocation by divorce or annulment passes as if the former spouse failed to survive the decedent, and other provisions conferring some power or office on the former spouse are interpreted as if the spouse failed to survive the decedent. If provisions are revoked solely by this section, they are revived by testator's remarriage to the former spouse. For purposes of this section, divorce or annulment means any divorce or annulment which would exclude the spouse as a surviving spouse within the meaning of Section 2-802(b). A decree of separation which does not terminate the status of husband and wife is not a divorce for purposes of this section. No change of circumstances other than as described in this section revokes a will.

§ 2-509. [Revival of Revoked Will.]

(a) If a second will which, had it remained effective at death, would have revoked the first will in whole or in part, is thereafter revoked by acts under Section 2-507, the first will is revoked in whole or in part unless it is evident from the circumstances of the revocation of the second will or from testator's contemporary or subsequent declarations that he intended the first will to take effect as executed.

(b) If a second will which, had it remained effective at death, would have revoked the first will in whole or in part, is thereafter revoked by a third will, the first will is revoked in whole or in part, except to the extent it appears from the terms of the third will that the testator intended the first will to take effect.

§ 2-510. [Incorporation by Reference.]

Any writing in existence when a will is executed may be incorporated by reference if the language of the will manifests this intent and describes the writing sufficiently to permit its identification.

§ 2-511. [Testamentary Additions to Trusts.]

A devise or bequest, the validity of which is determinable by the law of this state, may be made by a will to the trustee of a trust established or to be established by the testator or by the testator and some other person or by some other person (including a funded or unfunded life insurance trust, although the trustor has reserved any or all rights of ownership of the insurance contracts) if the trust is identified in the testator's will and its terms are set forth in a written instrument (other than a will) executed before or concurrently with the execution of the testator's will or in the valid last will of a person who has predeceased the testator (regardless of the existence, size, or character of the corpus of the trust). The devise is not invalid because the trust is amendable or revocable, or because the trust was amended after the execution of the will or after the death of the testator. Unless the testator's will provides otherwise, the property so devised (1) is not deemed to be held under a testamentary trust of the testator but becomes a part of the trust to which it is given and (2) shall be administered and disposed of in accordance with the provisions of the instrument or will setting forth the terms of the trust, including any amendments thereto made before the death of the testator (regardless of whether made before or after the execution of the testator's will), and, if the testator's will so provides, including any amendments to the trust made after the death of the testator. A revocation or termination of the trust before the death of the testator causes the devise to lapse.

§ 2-512. [Events of Independent Significance.]

A will may dispose of property by reference to acts and events which have significance apart from their effect upon the dispositions made by the will, whether they occur before or after the execution of the will or before or after the testator's death. The execution or revocation of a will of another person is such an event.

§ 2-513. [Separate Writing Identifying Bequest of Tangible Property.]

Whether or not the provisions relating to holographic wills apply, a will may refer to a written statement or list to dispose of items of tangible personal property not otherwise specifically disposed of by the will, other than money, evidences of indebtedness, documents of title, and securities, and property used in trade or business. To be admissible under this section as evidence of the intended disposition, the writing must either be in the handwriting of the testator or be signed by him and must describe the items and the devisees with reasonable certainty. The writing may be referred to as one to be in existence at the time of the testator's death; it may be prepared before or after the execution of the will; it may be altered by the testator after its preparation; and it may be a writing which has no significance apart from its effect upon the dispositions made by the will.

Part 6
Rules of Construction

§ 2-601. [Requirement That Devisee Survive Testator by 120 Hours.]

A devisee who does not survive the testator by 120 hours is treated as if he predeceased the testator, unless the will of decedent contains some language dealing explicitly with simultaneous deaths or deaths in a common disaster, or requiring that the devisee survive the testator or survive the testator for a stated period in order to take under the will.

§ 2-602. [Choice of Law as to Meaning and Effect of Wills.]

The meaning and legal effect of a disposition in a will shall be determined by the local law of a particular state selected by the testator in his instrument unless the application of that law is contrary to the provisions relating to the elective share described in Part 2 of this Article, the provisions relating to exempt property and allowances described in Part 4 of this Article, or any other public policy of this State otherwise applicable to the disposition.

§ 2-603. [Rules of Construction and Intention.]

The intention of a testator as expressed in his will controls the legal effect of his dispositions. The rules of construction expressed in the succeeding sections of this Part apply unless a contrary intention is indicated by the will.

§ 2-604. [Construction That Will Passes All Property; After-Acquired Property.]

A will is construed to pass all property which the testator owns at his death including property acquired after the execution of the will.

§ 2-605. [Anti-lapse; Deceased Devisee; Class Gifts.]

If a devisee who is a grandparent or a lineal descendant of a grandparent of the testator is dead at the time of execution of the will, fails to survive the testator, or is treated as if he predeceased the testator, the issue of the deceased devisee who survive the testator by 120 hours take in place of the deceased devisee and if they are all of the same degree of kinship to the devisee they take equally, but if of unequal degree than those of more remote degree take by representation. One who would have been a devisee under a class gift if he had survived the testator is treated as a devisee for purposes of this section whether his death occurred before or after the execution of the will.

§ 2-606. [Failure of Testamentary Provision.]

(a) Except as provided in Section 2-605 if a devise other than a residuary devise fails for any reason, it becomes a part of the residue.

(b) Except as provided in Section 2-605 if the residue is devised to two or more persons and the share of one of the residuary devisees fails for any reason, his share passes to the other residuary devisee, or to other residuary devisees in proportion to their interests in the residue.

§ 2-607. [Change in Securities; Accessions; Nonademption.]

(a) If the testator intended a specific devise of certain securities rather than the equivalent value thereof, the specific devisee is entitled only to:

(1) as much of the devised securities as is a part of the estate at time of the testator's death;

(2) any additional or other securities of the same entity owned by the testator by reason of action initiated by the entity excluding any acquired by exercise of purchase options;

(3) securities of another entity owned by the testator as a result of a merger, consolidation, reorganization or other similar action initiated by the entity; and

(4) any additional securities of the entity owned by the testator as a result of a plan of reinvestment.

(b) Distributions prior to death with respect to a specifically devised security not provided for in subsection (a) are not part of the specific devise.

As amended in 1987.

§ 2-608. [Nonademption of Specific Devises in Certain Cases; Unpaid Proceeds of Sale, Condemnation or Insurance; Sale by Conservator.]

(a) A specific devisee has the right to the remaining specifically devised property and:

(1) any balance of the purchase price (together with any security interest) owing from a purchaser to the testator at death by reason of sale of the property;

(2) any amount of a condemnation award for the taking of the property unpaid at death;

(3) any proceeds unpaid at death on fire or casualty insurance on the property; and

(4) property owned by testator at his death as a result of foreclosure, or obtained in lieu of foreclosure, of the security for a specifically devised obligation.

(b) If specifically devised property is sold by a conservator or an agent acting within the authority of a durable power of attorney for a principal who is under a disability, or if a condemnation award or insurance proceeds are paid to a conservator or an agent acting within the authority of a durable power of attorney for a principal who is under a disability as a result of condemnation, fire, or casualty, the specific devisee has the right to a general pecuniary devise equal to the net sale price, the condemnation award, or the insurance proceeds. This subsection does not apply if after the sale, condemnation or casualty, it is adjudicated that the disability of the testator has ceased and the testator survives the adjudication by one year. The right of the specific devisee under this subsection is reduced by any right he has under subsection (a).

As amended in 1987.

§ 2-609. [Non-Exoneration.]

A specific devise passes subject to any mortgage interest existing at the date of death, without right of exoneration, regardless of a general directive in the will to pay debts.

§ 2-610. [Exercise of Power of Appointment.]

A general residuary clause in a will, or a will making general disposition of all of the testator's property, does not exercise a power of appointment held by the testator unless specific reference is made to the power or there is some other indication of intention to include the property subject to the power.

§ 2-611. [Construction of Generic Terms to Accord with Relationships as Defined for Intestate Succession.]

Halfbloods, adopted persons, and persons born out of wedlock are included in class gift terminology and terms of relationship in accordance with rules for determining relationships for purposes of intestate succession. [However, a person born out of wedlock is not treated as the child of the father unless the person is openly and notoriously so treated by the father.]

§ 2-612. [Ademption by Satisfaction.]

Property which a testator gave in his lifetime to a person is treated as a satisfaction of a devise to that person in whole or in part, only if the will provides for deduction of the lifetime gift, or the testator declares in a contemporaneous writing that the gift is to be deducted from the devise or is in satisfaction of the devise, or the devisee acknowledges in writing that the gift is in satisfaction. For purpose of partial satisfaction, property given during lifetime is valued as of the time the devisee came into possession or enjoyment of the property or as of the time of death of the testator, whichever occurs first.

Part 7
Contractual Arrangements Relating to Death

(See also Article VI, Non-Probate Transfers)

§ 2-701. [Contracts Concerning Succession.]

A contract to make a will or devise, or not to revoke a will or devise, or to die intestate, if executed after the effective date of this Act, can be established only by (1) provisions of a will stating material provisions of the contract; (2) an express reference in a will to a contract and extrinsic evidence proving the terms of the contract; or (3) a writing signed by the decedent evidencing the contract. The execution of a joint will or mutual wills does not create a presumption of a contract not to revoke the will or wills.

Part 8
General Provisions

§ 2-801. [Renunciation of Succession.]

(a) A person or the representative of an incapacitated or protected person, who is an heir, devisee, person succeeding to a renounced interest, beneficiary under a testamentary instrument, or appointee under a power of appointment exercised by a testamentary instrument, may renounce in whole or in part the right of succession to any property or interest therein, including a future interest, by filing a written renunciation under this Section. The right to renounce does not survive the death of the person having it. The instrument shall (1) describe the property or interest renounced, (2) declare the renunciation and extent thereof, and (3) be signed by the person renouncing.

(b)(1) An instrument renouncing a present interest shall be filed not later than [9] months after the death of the decedent or the donee of the power.

(2) An instrument renouncing a future interest may be filed not later than [9] months after the event determining that the taker of the property or interest is finally ascertained and his interest is indefeasibly vested.

(3) The renunciation shall be filed in the [probate] court of the county in which proceedings have been commenced for the administration of the estate of the deceased owner or deceased donee of the power or, if they have not been commenced, in which they could be commenced. A copy of the renunciation shall be delivered in person or mailed by registered or certified mail to any personal representative, or other fiduciary of the decedent or donee of the power. If real property or an interest therein is renounced, a copy of the renunciation may be recorded in the office of the [Recorder of Deeds] of the county in which the real estate is situated.

(c) Unless the decedent or donee of the power has otherwise provided, the property or interest renounced devolves as though the person renouncing had predeceased the decedent or, if the person renouncing is designated to take under a power of appointment exercised by a testamentary instrument, as though the person renouncing had predeceased the donee of the power. A future interest that takes effect in possession or enjoyment after the termination of the estate or interest renounced takes effect as though the person renouncing had predeceased the decedent or the donee of the power. A renunciation relates back for all purposes to the date of the death of the decedent or the donee of the power.

(d)(1) The right to renounce property or an interest therein is barred by (i) an assignment, conveyance, encumbrance, pledge, or transfer of the property or interest, or a contract therefor, (ii) a written waiver of the right to renounce, (iii) an acceptance of the property or interest or benefit thereunder, or (iv) a sale of the property or interest under judicial sale made before the renunciation is effected.

(2) The right to renounce exists notwithstanding any limitation on the interest of the person renouncing in the nature of a spendthrift provision or similar restriction.

(3) A renunciation or a written waiver of the right to renounce is binding upon the person renouncing or person waiving and all persons claiming through or under him.

(e) This Section does not abridge the right of a person to waive, release, disclaim, or renounce property or an interest therein under any other statute.

(f) An interest in property existing on the effective date of this Section as to which the time for filing a renunciation under this Section would have begun to run were this Section in effect when the interest was created, may be renounced within [9] months after the effective date of this Section.

§ 2-802. [Effect of Divorce, Annulment, and Decree of Separation.]

(a) A person who is divorced from the decedent or whose marriage to the decedent has been annulled is not a surviving spouse unless, by virtue of a subsequent marriage, he is married to the decedent at the time of death. A decree of separation which does not terminate the status of husband and wife is not a divorce for purposes of this section.

(b) For purposes of Parts 1, 2, 3 & 4 of this Article, and of Section 3-203, a surviving spouse does not include:

(1) a person who obtains or consents to a final decree or judgment of divorce fro the decedent or an annulment of their marriage, which decree or judgment is not recognized as valid in this state, unless they subsequently participate in a marriage ceremony purporting to marry each to the other, or subsequently live together as man and wife;

(2) a person who, following a decree or judgment of divorce or annulment obtained by the decedent, participates in a marriage ceremony with a third person; or

(3) a person who was a party to a valid proceeding concluded by an order purporting to terminate all marital property rights.

[§ 2-803. [Effect of Homicide on Intestate Succession, Wills, Joint Assets, Life Insurance and Beneficiary Designations.]

(a) A surviving spouse, heir or devisee who feloniously and intentionally kills the decedent is not entitled to any benefits under the will or under this Article, and the estate of decedent passes as if the killer had predeceased the decedent. Property appointed by the will of the decedent to or for the benefit of the killer passes as if the killer had predeceased the decedent.

(b) Any joint tenant who feloniously and intentionally kills another joint tenant thereby effects a severance of the interest of the decedent so that the share of the decedent passes as his property and the killer has no rights by survivorship. This provision applies to joint tenancies [and tenancies by the entirety] in real and personal property, joint and multiple-party accounts in banks, savings and loan associations, credit unions and other institutions, and any other form of co-ownership with survivorship incidents.

(c) A named beneficiary of a bond, life insurance policy, or other contractual arrangement who feloniously and intentionally kills the principal obligee or the person upon whose life the policy is issued is not entitled to any benefit under the bond, policy or other contractual arrangement, and it becomes payable as though the killer had predeceased the decedent.

(d) Any other acquisition of property or interest by the killer shall be treated in accordance with the principles of this section.

(e) A final judgment of conviction of felonious and intentional killing is conclusive for purposes of this section. In the absence of a conviction of felonious and intentional killing the Court may determine by a preponderance of evidence whether the killing was felonious and intentional for purposes of this section.

(f) This section does not affect the rights of any person who, before rights under this section have been adjudicated, purchases from the killer for value and without notice property which the killer would have acquired except for this section, but the killer is liable for the amount of the proceeds or the value of the property. Any insurance company, bank, or other obligor making payment according to the terms of its policy or obligation is not liable by reason of this section unless prior to payment it has received at its home office or principal address written notice of a claim under this section.]

Part 9
Custody and Deposit of Wills

§ 2-901. [Deposit of Will With Court in Testator's Lifetime.]

A will may be deposited by the testator or his agent with any Court for safekeeping, under rules of the Court. The will shall be kept confidential. During the testator's lifetime a deposited will shall be delivered only to him or to a person authorized in writing signed by him to receive the will. A conservator may be allowed to examine a deposited will of a protected testator under procedures designed to maintain the confidential character of the document to the extent possible, and to assure that it will be resealed and left on deposit after the examination. Upon being informed of the testator's death, the Court shall notify any person designated to receive the will and deliver it to him on request; or the Court may deliver the will to the appropriate Court.

§ 2-902. [Duty of Custodian of Will; Liability.]

After the death of a testator and on request of an interested person, any person having custody of a will of the testator shall deliver it with reasonable promptness to a person able to secure its probate and if none is known, to an appropriate Court. Any person who wilfully fails to deliver a will is liable to any person aggrieved for the damages which may be sustained by the failure. Any person who wilfully refuses or fails to deliver a will after being ordered by the Court in a proceeding brought for the purpose of compelling delivery is subject to penalty for contempt of Court.

Part 10
Uniform International Wills Act
[International Will; Information Registration]

§ 1. [2-1001.] [Definitions.]

In this Act: [Part:]

(1) "International will" means a will executed in conformity with Sections 2 [2-1002] through 5 [2-1005].

(2) "Authorized person" and "person authorized to act in connection with international wills" mean a person who by Section 9 [2-1009], or by the laws of the United States including members of the diplomatic and consular service of the United States designated by Foreign Service Regulations, is empowered to supervise the execution of international wills.

§ 2. [2-1002.] [International Will; Validity.]

(a) A will is valid as regards form, irrespective particularly of the place where it is made, of the location of the assets and of the nationality, domicile, or residence of the testator, if it is made in the form of an international will complying with the requirements of this Act. [Part.]

(b) The invalidity of the will as an international will shall not affect its formal validity as a will of another kind.

(c) This Act [Part] shall not apply to the form of testamentary dispositions made by two or more persons in one instrument.

§ 3. [2-1003.] [International Will; Requirements.]

(a) The will must be made in writing. It need not be written by the testator himself. It may be written in any language, by hand or by any other means.

(b) The testator shall declare in the presence of two witnesses and of a person authorized to act in connection with international wills that the document is his will and that he knows the contents thereof. The testator need not inform the witnesses, or the authorized person, of the contents of the will.

(c) In the presence of the witnesses, and of the authorized person, the testator shall sign the will or, if he has previously signed it, shall acknowledge his signature.

(d) If the testator is unable to sign, the absence of his signature does not affect the validity of the international will if the testator indicates the reason for his inability to sign and the authorized person makes note thereof on the will. In that case, it is permissible for any other person present, including the authorized person or one of the witnesses, at the direction of the testator to sign the testator's name for him, if the authorized person makes note of this on the will, but it is not required that any person sign the testator's name for him.

(e) The witnesses and the authorized person shall there and then attest the will by signing in the presence of the testator.

§ 4. [2-1004.] [International Will; Other Points of Form.]

(a) The signatures must be placed at the end of the will. If the will consists of several sheets, each sheet must be signed by the testator or, if he is unable to sign, by the person signing on his behalf or, if there is no such person, by the authorized person. In addition, each sheet shall be numbered.

(b) The date of the will shall be the date of its signature by the authorized person. That date must be noted at the end of the will by the authorized person.

(c) The authorized person shall ask the testator whether he wishes to make a declaration concerning the safekeeping of his will. If so and at the express request of the testator, the place where he intends to have his will kept shall be mentioned in the certificate provided for in Section 5.

(d) A will executed in compliance with Section 3 shall not be invalid merely because it does not comply with this section.

§ 5. [2-1005.] [International Will; Certificate.]

The authorized person shall attach to the will a certificate to be signed by him establishing that the requirements of this Act [Part] for valid execution of an international will have been complied with. The authorized person shall keep a copy of the certificate and deliver another to the testator. The certificate must be substantially in the following form:

CERTIFICATE

(Convention of October 26, 1973)

1. I, __________ (name, address and capacity), a person authorized to act in connection with international wills

2. Certify that on __________ (date) at __________ (place)

3. (testator) ______________ (name, address, date and place of birth) in my presence and that of the witnesses

4. (a) ______________ (name, address, date and place of birth)

(b) ______________ (name, address, date and place of birth) has declared that the attached document is his will and that he knows the contents thereof.

5. I furthermore certify that:

6. (a) in my presence and in that of the witnesses

(1) the testator has signed the will or has acknowledged his signature previously affixed.

*(2) following a declaration of the testator stating that he was unable to sign his will for the following reason __________, I have mentioned this declaration on the will *and the signature has been affixed by __________ (name and address)

7. (b) the witnesses and I have signed the will;

8. *(c) each page of the will has been signed by ____________ and numbered;

9. (d) I have satisfied myself as to the identity of the testator and of the witnesses as designated above;

10. (e) the witnesses met the conditions requisite to act as such according to the law under which I am acting;

11. *(f) the testator has requested me to include the following statement concerning the safekeeping of his will: ____________

12. PLACE OF EXECUTION

13. DATE

14. SIGNATURE and, if necessary, SEAL

*To be completed if appropriate

§ 6. [2-1006.] [International Will; Effect of Certificate.]

In the absence of evidence to the contrary, the certificate of the authorized person shall be conclusive of the formal validity of the instrument as a will under this Act. [Part. The absence or irregularity of a certificate does not affect the formal validity of a will under this Act. [Part.]

§ 7. [2-1007.] [International Will; Revocation.]

The international will shall be subject to the ordinary rules of revocation of wills.

§ 8. [2-1008.] [Source and Construction.]

Sections 1 [2-1001] through 7 [2-1007] derive from Annex to Convention of October 26, 1973, Providing a Uniform Law on the Form of an International Will. In interpreting and applying this Act [Part], regard shall be had to its international origin and to the need for uniformity in its interpretation.

§ 9. [2-1009.] [Persons Authorized to Act in Relation to International Will; Eligibility; Recognition by Authorizing Agency.]

Individuals who have been admitted to practice law before the courts of this state and who are in good standing as active law practitioners in this state, are hereby declared to be authorized persons in relation to international wills.

[§ 10. [2-1010.] [International Will Information Registration.]

The [Secretary of State] shall establish a registry system by which authorized persons may register in a central information center, information regarding the execution of international wills, keeping that information in strictest confidence until the death of the maker and then making it available to any person desiring information about any will who presents a death certificate or other satisfactory evidence of the testator's death to the center. Information that may be received, preserved in confidence until death, and reported as indicated is limited to the name, social security or any other individual-identifying number established by law, address, and date and place of birth of the testator, and the intended place of deposit or safekeeping of the instrument pending the death of the maker. The [Secretary of State], at the request of the authorized person, may cause the information it receives about execution of any international will to be transmitted to the registry system of another jurisdiction as identified by the testator, if that other system adheres to rules protecting the confidentiality of the information similar to those established in this State.]

ARTICLE III
PROBATE OF WILLS AND ADMINISTRATION

Part 1
General Provisions

§ 3-101. [Devolution of Estate at Death; Restrictions.]

The power of a person to leave property by will, and the rights of creditors, devisees, and heirs to his property are subject to the restrictions and limitations contained in this Code to facilitate the prompt settlement of estates. Upon the death of a person, his real and personal property devolves to the person to whom it is devised by his last will or to those indicated as substitutes for them in cases involving lapse, renunciation or other circumstances affecting the devolution of testate estate, or in the absence of testamentary disposition, to his heirs, or to those indicated as substitutes for them in cases involving renunciation or other circumstances affecting devolution of intestate estates, subject to homestead allowance, exempt property and family allowance, to rights of creditors elective share of the surviving spouse, and to administration.

ALTERNATIVE SECTION FOR COMMUNITY PROPERTY STATES

[§ 3-101A. [Devolution of Estate at Death; Restrictions.]

The power of a person to leave property by will, and the rights of creditors, devisees, and heirs to his property are subject to the restrictions and limitations contained in this Code to facilitate the prompt settlement of estates. Upon the death of a person, his separate property devolves to the persons to whom it is devised by his last will, or to those indicated as substitutes for them in cases involving lapse, renunciation or other circumstances affecting the devolution of estate estates, or in the absence of testamentary disposition to his heirs, or to those indicated as substitutes for them in cases involving renunciation or other circumstances affecting the devolution of intestate estates, and upon the death of a husband or wife, the decedent's share of their community property devolves to the persons to whom it is devised by his last will, or in the absence of testamentary disposition, to his heirs, but all of their community property which is under the management and control of the decedent is subject to his debts and administration, and that portion of their community property which is not under the management and control of the decedent but which is necessary to carry out the provisions of his will is subject to administration; but the devolution of all the above described property is subject to rights to homestead allowance, exempt property and family allowances, to renunciation, to rights of creditors, [elective share of the surviving spouse] and to administration.]

§ 3-102. [Necessity of Order of Probate For Will.]

Except as provided in Section 3-1201, to be effective to prove the transfer of any property or to nominate an executor, a will must be declared to be valid by an order of informal probate by the Registrar, or an adjudication of probate by the Court, except that a duly executed and unrevoked will which has not been probated may be admitted as evidence of a devise if (1) no Court proceeding concerning the succession of administration of the estate has occurred, and (2) either the devisee or his successors and assigns possessed the property devised in accordance with the provisions of the will, or the property devised was not possessed or claimed by anyone by virtue of the decedent's title during the time period tor testacy proceedings.

§ 3-103. [Necessity of Appointment For Administration.]

Except as otherwise provided in Article IV, to acquire the powers and undertake the duties and liabilities of a personal representative of a decedent, a person must be appointed by order of the Court or Registrar, qualify and be issued letters. Administration of an estate is commenced by the issuance of letters.

§ 3-104. [Claims Against Decedent; Necessity of Administration.]

No proceeding to enforce a claim against the estate of a decedent or his successors may be revived or commenced before the appointment of a personal representative. After the appointment and until distribution, all proceedings and actions to enforce a claim against the estate are governed by the procedure prescribed by this Article. After distribution a creditor whose claim has not been barred may recover from the distributees as provided in Section 3-1004 or from a former personal representative individually liable as provided in Section 3-1005. This section has no application to a proceeding by a secured creditor of the decedent to enforce his right to his security except as to any deficiency judgment which might be sought therein.

§ 3-105. [Proceedings Affecting Devolution and Administration; Jurisdiction of Subject Matter.]

Persons interested in decedents' estates may apply to the Registrar for determination in the informal proceedings provided in this Article, and may petition the Court for orders in formal proceedings within the Court's jurisdiction including but not limited to those described in this Article. The Court has exclusive jurisdiction of formal proceedings to determine how decedents' estates subject to the laws of this state are to be administered, expended and distributed. The Court has concurrent jurisdiction of any other action or proceeding concerning a succession or to which an estate, through a personal representative, may be a party, including actions to determine title to property alleged to belong to the estate, and of any action or proceeding in which property distributed by a personal representative or its value is sought to be subjected to rights of creditors or successors of the decedent.

§ 3-106. [Proceedings Within the Exclusive Jurisdiction of Court; Service; Jurisdiction Over Persons.]

In proceedings within the exclusive jurisdiction of the Court where notice is required by this Code or by rule, and in proceedings to construe probated wills or determine heirs which concern estates that have not been and cannot now be open for administration, interested persons may be bound by the orders of the Court in respect to property in or subject to the laws of this state by notice in conformity with Section 1-401 An order is binding as to all who are given notice of the proceeding though less than all interested persons are notified.

§ 3-107. [Scope of Proceedings; Proceedings Independent; Exception.]

Unless supervised administration as described in Part 5 is involved, (1) each proceeding before the Court or Registrar is independent of any other proceeding involving the same estate; (2) petitions for formal orders of the Court may combine various requests for relief in a single proceeding if the orders sought may be finally granted without delay. Except as required for proceedings which are particularly described by other sections of this Article, no petition is defective because it fails to embrace all matters which might then be the subject of a final order; (3) proceedings for probate of wills or adjudications of no will may be combined with proceedings for appointment of personal representatives; and (4) a proceeding for appointment of a personal representative is concluded by an order making or declining the appointment.

§ 3-108. [Probate, Testacy and Appointment Proceedings; Ultimate Time Limit.]

No informal probate or appointment proceeding or formal testacy or appointment proceeding, other than a proceeding to probate a will previously probated at the testator's domicile and appointment proceedings relating to an estate in which there has been a prior appointment, may be commenced more than 3 years after the decedent's death, except (1) if a previous proceeding was dismissed because of doubt about the fact of the decedent's death, appropriate probate, appointment or testacy proceedings may be maintained at any time thereafter upon a finding that the decedent's death occurred prior to the initiation of the previous proceeding and the applicant or petitioner has not delayed unduly in initiating the subsequent proceeding; (2) appropriate probate, appointment or testacy proceedings may be maintained in relation to the estate of an absent, disappeared or missing person for whose estate a conservator has been appointed, at any time within three years after the conservator becomes able to establish the death of the protected person; and (3) a proceeding to contest an informally probated will and to secure appointment of the person with legal priority for appointment in the event the contest is successful, may be commenced within the later of twelve months from the informal probate or three years from the decedent's death; and (4) if no proceeding concerning the succession or administration of the estate has occurred within 3 years after decedent's death, a formal testacy proceeding may be commenced at any time thereafter for the sole purpose of establishing a devise of property which the devisee or his successors and assigns possessed in accordance with the will or property which was not possessed or claimed by anyone by virtue of the decedent's title during the 3-year period, and the order of the Court shall be limited to that property. These limitations do not apply to proceedings to construe probated wills or determine heirs of an intestate. In cases under (1) or (2) above, the date on which a testacy or appointment proceeding is properly commenced shall be deemed to be the date of the decedent's death for purposes of other limitations provisions of this Code which relate to the date of death.

As amended in 1987.

§ 3-109. [Statutes of Limitation on Decedent's Cause of Action.]

No statute of limitation running on a cause of action belonging to a decedent which had not been barred as of the date of his death, shall apply to bar a cause of action surviving the decedent's death sooner than four months after death. A cause of action which, but for this section, would have been barred less than four months after death, is barred after four months unless tolled.

Part 2
Venue for Probate and Administration; Priority to Administer; Demand for Notice

§ 3-201. [Venue for First and Subsequent Estate Proceedings; Location of Property.]

(a) Venue for the first informal or formal testacy or appointment proceedings after a decedent's death is:

(1) in the [county] where the decedent had his domicile at the time of his death; or

(2) if the decedent was not domiciled in this state, in any [county] where property of the decedent was located at the time of his death.

(b) Venue for all subsequent proceedings within the exclusive jurisdiction of the Court is in the place where the initial proceeding occurred, unless the initial proceeding has been transferred as provided in Section 1-303 or (c) of this section.

(c) If the first proceeding was informal, on application of an interested person and after notice to the proponent in the first proceeding, the Court, upon finding that venue is elsewhere, may transfer the proceeding and the file to the other court.

(d) For the purpose of aiding determinations concerning location of assets which may be relevant in cases involving non-domiciliaries, a debt other than one evidenced by investment or commercial paper or other instrument in favor of a non-domiciliary is located where the debtor resides or, if the debtor is a person other than an individual, at the place where it has its principal office. Commercial paper, investment paper and other instruments are located where the instrument is. An interest in property held in trust is located where the trustee may be sued.

§ 3-202. [Appointment or Testacy Proceedings; Conflicting Claim of Domicile in Another State.]

If conflicting claims as to the domicile of a decedent are made in a formal testacy or appointment proceeding commenced in this state, and in a testacy or appointment proceeding after notice pending at the same time in another state, the Court of this state must stay, dismiss, or permit suitable amendment in, the proceeding here unless it is determined that the local proceeding was commenced before the proceeding elsewhere. The determination of domicile in the proceeding first commenced must be accepted as determinative in the proceeding in this state.

§ 3-203. [Priority Among Persons Seeking Appointment as Personal Representative.]

(a) Whether the proceedings are formal or informal, persons who are not disqualified have priority for appointment in the following order:

(1) the person with priority as determined by a probated will including a person nominated by a power conferred in a will;

(2) the surviving spouse of the decedent who is a devisee of the decedent;

(3) other devisees of the decedent;

(4) the surviving spouse of the decedent;

(5) other heirs of the decedent;

(6) 45 days after the death of the decedent, any creditor.

(b) An objection to an appointment can be made only in formal proceedings. In case of objection the priorities stated in (a) apply except that

(1) if the estate appears to be more than adequate to meet exemptions and costs of administration but inadequate to discharge anticipated unsecured claims, the Court, on petition of creditors, may appoint any qualified person;

(2) in case of objection to appointment of a person other than one whose priority is determined by will by an heir or devisee appearing to have a substantial interest in the estate, the Court may appoint a person who is acceptable to heirs and devisees whose interests in the estate appear to be worth in total more than half of the probable distributable value, or, in default of this accord any suitable person.

(c) A person entitled to letters under (2) through (5) of (a) above, and a person aged [18] and over who would be entitled to letters but for his age, may nominate a qualified person to act as personal representative. Any person aged [18] and over may renounce his right to nominate or to an appointment by appropriate writing filed with the Court. When two or more persons share a priority, those of them who do not renounce must concur in nominating another to act for them, or in applying for appointment.

(d) Conservators of the estates of protected persons, or if there is no conservator, any guardian except a guardian ad litem of a minor or incapacitated person, may exercise the same right to nominate, to object to another's appointment, or to participate in determining the preference of a majority in interest of the heirs and devisees that the protected person or ward would have if qualified for appointment.

(e) Appointment of one who does not have priority, including priority resulting from renunciation or nomination determined pursuant to this section, may be made only in formal proceedings. Before appointing one without priority, the Court must determine that those having priority, although given notice of the proceedings, have failed to request appointment or to nominate another for appointment, and that administration is necessary.

(f) No person is qualified to serve as a personal representative who is:

(1) under the age of [21];

(2) a person whom the Court finds unsuitable in formal proceedings

(g) A personal representative appointed by a court of the decedent's domicile has priority over all other persons except where the decedent's will nominates different persons to be personal representative in this state and in the state of domicile. The domiciliary personal representative may nominate another, who shall have the same priority as the domiciliary personal representative.

(h) This section governs priority for appointment of a successor personal representative but does not apply to the selection of a special administrator.

§ 3-204. [Demand for Notice of Order or Filing Concerning Decedent's Estate.]

Any person desiring notice of any order or filing pertaining to a decedent's estate in which he has a financial or property interest, may file a demand for notice with the Court at any time after the death of the decedent stating the name of the decedent, the nature of his interest in the estate, and the demandant's address or that of his attorney. The clerk shall mail a copy of the demand to the personal representative if one has been appointed. After filing of a demand, no order or filing to which the demand relates shall be made or accepted without notice as prescribed in Section 1-101 to the demandant or his attorney. The validity of an order which is issued or filing which is accepted without compliance with this requirement shall not be affected by the error, but the petitioner receiving the order or the person making the filing may be liable for any damage caused by the absence of notice. The requirement of notice arising from a demand under this provision may be waived in writing by the demandant and shall cease upon the termination of his interest in the estate.

Part 3
Informal Probate and Appointment Proceedings; Succession Without Administration

§ 3-301. [Informal Probate or Appointment Proceedings; Application; Contents.]

(a) Applications for informal probate or informal appointment shall be directed to the Registrar, and verified by the applicant to be accurate and complete to the best of his knowledge and belief as to the following information:

(1) Every application for informal probate of a will or for informal appointment of a personal representative, other than a special or successor representative, shall contain the following:

(i) a statement of the interest of the applicant;

(ii) the name, and date of death of the decedent, his age, and the county and state of his domicile at the time of death, and the names and addresses of the spouse, children, heirs and devisees and the ages of any who are minors so far as known or ascertainable with reasonable diligence by the applicant;

(iii) if the decedent was not domiciled in the state at the time of his death, a statement showing venue;

(iv) a statement identifying and indicating the address of any personal representative of the decedent appointed in this state or elsewhere whose appointment has not been terminated;

(v) a statement indicating whether the applicant has received a demand for notice, or is aware of any demand for notice of any probate or appointment proceeding concerning the decedent that may have been filed in this state or elsewhere; and

(vi) that the time limit for informal probate or appointment as provided in this Article has not expired either because 3 years or less have passed since the decedent's death, or, if more than 3 years from death have passed, circumstances as described by Section 3-108 authorizing tardy probate or appointment have occurred.

(2) An application for informal probate of a will shall state the following in addition to the statements required by (1):

(i) that the original of the decedent's last will is in the possession of the court, or accompanies the application, or that an authenticated copy of a will probated in another jurisdiction accompanies the application;

(ii) that the applicant, to the best of his knowledge, believes the will to have been validly executed;

(iii) that after the exercise of reasonable diligence, the applicant is unaware of any instrument revoking the will, and that the applicant believes that the instrument which is the subject of the application is the decedent's last will.

(3) An application for informal appointment of a personal representative to administer an estate under a will shall describe the will by date of execution and state the time and place of probate or the pending application or petition for probate. The application for appointment shall adopt the statements in the application or petition for probate and state the name, address and priority for appointment of the person whose appointment is sought.

(4) An application for informal appointment of an administrator in intestacy shall state in addition to the statements required by (1):

(i) that after the exercise of reasonable diligence, the applicant is unaware of any unrevoked testamentary instrument relating to property having a situs in this state under Section 1-301, or, a statement why any such instrument of which he may be aware is not being probated;

(ii) the priority of the person whose appointment is sought and the names of any other persons having a prior or equal right to the appointment under Section 3-203.

(5) An application for appointment of a personal representative to succeed a personal representative appointed under a different testacy status shall refer to the order in the most recent testacy proceeding, state the name and address of the person whose appointment is sought and of the person whose appointment will be terminated if the application is granted, and describe the priority of the applicant.

(6) An application for appointment of a personal representative to succeed a personal representative who has tendered a resignation as provided in Section 3-610(c), or whose appointment has been terminated by death or removal, shall adopt the statements in the application or petition which led to the appointment of the person being succeeded except as specifically changed or corrected, state the name and address of the person who seeks appointment as successor, and describe the priority of the applicant.

(b) By verifying an application for informal probate, or informal appointment, the applicant submits personally to the jurisdiction of the court in any proceeding for relief from fraud relating to the application, or for perjury, that may be instituted against him.

§ 3-302. [Informal Probate; Duty of Registrar; Effect of Informal Probate.]

Upon receipt of an application requesting informal probate of a will, the Registrar, upon making the findings required by Section 3-303 shall issue a written statement of informal probate if at least 120 hours have elapsed since the decedent's death. Informal probate is conclusive as to all persons until superseded by an order in a formal testacy proceeding. No defect in the application or procedure relating thereto which leads to informal probate of a will renders the probate void.

§ 3-303. [Informal Probate; Proof and Findings Required.]

(a) In an informal proceeding for original probate of a will, the Registrar shall determine whether:

(1) the application is complete;

(2) the applicant has made oath or affirmation that the statements contained in the application are true to the best of his knowledge and belief;

(3) the applicant appears from the application to be an interested person as defined in Section 1-201(20);

(4) on the basis of the statements in the application, venue is

(5) an original, duly executed and apparently unrevoked will is in the Registrar's possession;

(6) any notice required by Section 3-204 has been given and that the application is not within Section 3-304; and

(7) it appears from the application that the time limit for original probate has not expired.

(b) The application shall be denied if it indicates that a personal representative has been appointed in another [county] of this state or except as provided in subsection (d) below, if it appears that this or another will of the decedent has been the subject of a previous probate order.

(c) A will which appears to have the required signatures and which contains an attestation clause showing that requirements of execution under Section 2-502, 2-503 or 2-506 have been met shall be probated without further proof. In other cases, the Registrar may assume execution if the will appears to have been properly executed, or he may accept a sworn statement or affidavit of any person having knowledge of the circumstances of execution, whether or not the person was a witness to the will.

(d) Informal probate of a will which has been previously probated elsewhere may be granted at any time upon written application by any interested person, together with deposit of an authenticated copy of the will and of the statement probating it from the office or court where it was first probated.

(e) A will from a place which does not provide for probate of a will after death and which is not eligible for probate under subsection (a) above, may be probated in this state upon receipt by the Registrar of a duly authenticated copy of the will and a duly authenticated certificate of its legal custodian that the copy filed is a true copy and that the will has become operative under the law of the other place.

§ 3-304. [Informal Probate; Unavailable in Certain Cases.]

Applications for informal probate which relate to one or more of a known series of testamentary instruments (other than a will and one or more codicils thereto), the latest of which does not expressly revoke the earlier, shall be declined.

As amended in 1987.

§ 3-305. [Informal Probate; Registrar Not Satisfied.]

If the Registrar is not satisfied that a will is entitled to be probated in informal proceedings because of failure to meet the requirements of Sections 3-303 and 3-304 or any other reason, he may decline the application. A declination of informal probate is not an adjudication and does not preclude formal probate proceedings.

§ 3-306. [Informal Probate; Notice Requirements.]

(*) The moving party must give notice as described by Section 1-401 of his application for informal probate to any person demanding it pursuant to Section 3-204, and to any personal representative of the decedent whose appointment has not been terminated. No other notice of informal probate is required.

[(b) If an informal probate is granted, within 30 days thereafter the applicant shall give written information of the probate to the heirs and devisees. The information shall include the name and address of the applicant, the name and location of the court granting the informal probate, and the date of the probate. The information shall be delivered or sent by ordinary mail to each of the heirs and devisees whose address is reasonably available to the applicant. No duty to give information is incurred if a personal representative is appointed who is required to give the written information required by Section 3-705. An applicant's failure to give information as required by this section is a breach of his duty to the heirs and devisees but does not affect the validity of the probate.]

* This paragraph becomes (a) if optional subsection (b) accepted.

§ 3-307. [Informal Appointment Proceedings; Delay in Order; Duty of Registrar; Effect of Appointment.]

(a) Upon receipt of an application for informal appointment of a personal representative other than a special administrator as provided in Section 3-614, if at least 120 hours have elapsed since the decedent's death, the Registrar, after making the findings required by Section 3-308, shall appoint the applicant subject to qualification and acceptance; provided, that if the decedent was a non-resident, the Registrar shall delay the order of appointment until 30 days have elapsed since death unless the personal representative appointed at the decedent's domicile is the applicant, or unless the decedent's will directs that his estate be subject to the laws of this state.

(b) The status of personal representative and the powers and duties pertaining to the office are fully established by informal appointment. An appointment, and the office of personal representative created thereby, is subject to termination as provided in

Sections 3-608 through 3-612, but is not subject to retroactive vacation.

§ 3-308. [Informal Appointment Proceedings; Proof and Findings Required.]

(a) In informal appointment proceedings, the Registrar must determine whether:

(1) the application for informal appointment of a personal representative is complete;

(2) the applicant has made oath or affirmation that the statements contained in the application are true to the best of his knowledge and belief;

(3) the applicant appears from the application to be an interested person as defined in Section 1-201(20);

(4) on the basis of the statements in the application, venue is proper;

(5) any will to which the requested appointment relates has been formally or informally probated; but this requirement does not apply to the appointment of a special administrator;

(6) any notice required by Section 3-204 has been given;

(7) from the statements in the application, the person whose appointment is sought has priority entitling him to the appointment.

(b) Unless Section 3-612 controls, the application must be denied if it indicates that a personal representative who has not filed a written statement of resignation as provided in Section 3-610(c) has been appointed in this or another [county] of this state, that (unless the applicant is the domiciliary personal representative or his nominee) the decedent was not domiciled in this state and that a personal representative whose appointment has not been terminated has been appointed by a Court in the state of domicile, or that other requirements of this section have not been met.

§ 3-309. [Informal Appointment Proceedings; Registrar Not Satisfied.]

If the Registrar is not satisfied that a requested informal appointment of a personal representative should be made because of failure to meet the requirements of Sections 3-307 and 3-308, or for any other reason, he may decline the application. A declination of informal appointment is not an adjudication and does not preclude appointment in formal proceedings.

§ 3-310. [Informal Appointment Proceedings; Notice Requirements.]

The moving party must give notice as described by Section 1-401 of his intention to seek an appointment informally: (1) to any person demanding it pursuant to Section 3-204; and (2) to any person having a prior or equal right to appointment not waived in writing and filed with the Court. No other notice of an informal appointment proceeding is required.

§ 3-311. [Informal Appointment Unavailable in Certain Cases.]

If an application for informal appointment indicates the existence of a possible unrevoked testamentary instrument which may relate to property subject to the laws of this state, and which is not filed for probate in this court, the Registrar shall decline the application.

§ 3-312. [Universal Succession; In General.]

The heirs of an intestate or the residuary devisees under a will, excluding minors and incapacitated, protected, or unascertained persons, may become universal successors to the decedent's estate by assuming personal liability for (1) taxes, (2) debts of the decedent, (3) claims against the decedent or the estate, and (4) distributions due other heirs, devisees, and persons entitled to property of the decedent as provided in Sections 3-313 through 3-322.

§ 3-313. [Universal Succession; Application; Contents.]

(a) An application to become universal successors by the heirs of an intestate or the residuary devisees under a will must be directed to the [Registrar], signed by each applicant, and verified to be accurate and complete to the best of the applicant's knowledge and belief as follows:

(1) An application by heirs of an intestate must contain the statements required by Section 3-301(a)(1) and (4)(i) and state that the applicants constitute all the heirs other than minors and incapacitated, protected, or unascertained persons.

(2) An application by residuary devisees under a will must be combined with a petition for informal probate if the will has not been admitted to probate in this State and must contain the statements required by Section 3-301(a)(1) and (2). If the will has been probated in this State, an application by residuary devisees must contain the statements required by Section 3-301(a)(2)(iii). An application by residuary devisees must state that the applicants constitute the residuary devisees of the decedent other than any minors and incapacitated, protected, or unascertained persons. If the estate is partially intestate, all of the heirs other than minors and incapacitated, protected, or unascertained persons must join as applicants.

(b) The application must state whether letters of administration are outstanding, whether a petition for appointment of a personal representative of the decedent is pending in any court of this State, and that the applicants waive their right to seek appointment of a personal representative.

(c) The application may describe in general terms the assets of the estate and must state that the applicants accept responsibility for the estate and assume personal liability for (1) taxes, (2) debts of the decedent, (3) claims against the decedent or the estate, and (4) distributions due other heirs, devisees, and persons entitled to property of the decedent as provided in Sections 3-316 through 3-322.

§ 3-314. [Universal Succession; Proof and Findings Required.]

(a) The [Registrar] shall grant the application if:

(1) the application is complete in accordance with Section 3-313;

(2) all necessary persons have joined and have verified that the statements contained therein are true, to the best knowledge and belief of each;

(3) venue is proper;

(4) any notice required by Section 3-204 has been given or waived;

(5) the time limit for original probate or appointment proceedings has not expired and the applicants claim under a will;

(6) the application requests informal probate of a will, the application and findings conform with Sections 3-301(a)(2) and 3-303(a) (c)(d) and (e) so the will is admitted to probate; and

(7) none of the applicants is a minor or an incapacitated or protected person.

(b) The [Registrar] shall deny the application if letters of administration are outstanding.

(c) Except as provided in Section 3-322, the [Registrar] shall deny the application if any creditor, heir, or devisee who is qualified by Section 3-605 to demand bond files an objection.

§ 3-315. [Universal Succession; Duty of Registrar; Effect of Statement of Universal Succession.]

Upon receipt of an application under Section 3-313, if at least 120 hours have elapsed since the decedent's death, the [Registrar], upon granting the application, shall issue a written statement of universal succession describing the estate as set forth in the application and stating that the applicants (i) are the universal successors to the assets of the estate as provided in Section 3-312, (ii) have assumed liability for the obligations of the decedent, and (iii) have acquired the powers and liabilities of universal successors. The statement of universal succession is evidence of the universal successors' title to the assets of the estate. Upon its issuance, the powers and liabilities of universal successors provided in Sections 3-316 through 3-322 attach and are assumed by the applicants.

§ 3-316. [Universal Succession; Universal Successors' Powers.]

Upon the [Registrar's] issuance of a statement of universal succession:

(1) Universal successors have full power of ownership to deal with the assets of the estate subject to the limitations and liabilities in this [Act]. The universal successors shall proceed expeditiously to settle and distribute the estate without adjudication but if necessary may invoke the jurisdiction of the court to resolve questions concerning the estate.

(2) Universal successors have the same powers as distributees from a personal representative under Sections 3-908 and 3-909 and third persons with whom they deal are protected as provided in Section 3-910.

(3) For purposes of collecting assets in another state whose law does not provide for universal succession, universal successors have the same standing and power as personal representatives or distributees in this State.

§ 3-317. [Universal Succession; Universal Successors' Liability to Creditors, Other Heirs, Devisees and Persons Entitled to Decedent's Property; Liability of Other Persons Entitled to Property.]

(a) In the proportions and subject to limits expressed in Section 3-321, universal successors assume all liabilities of the decedent that were not discharged by reason of death and liability for all taxes, claims against the decedent or the estate, and charges properly incurred after death for the preservation of the estate, to the extent those items, if duly presented, would be valid claims against the decedent's estate.

(b) In the proportions and subject to the limits expressed in Section 3-321, universal successors are personally liable to other heirs, devisees, and persons entitled to property of the decedent for the assets or amounts that would be due those heirs, were the estate administered, but no allowance having priority over devisees may be claimed for attorney's fees or charges for preservation of the estate in excess of reasonable amounts properly incurred.

(c) Universal successors are entitled to their interests in the estate as heirs or devisees subject to priority and abatement pursuant to Section 3-902 and to agreement pursuant to Section 3-912.

(d) Other heirs, devisees, and persons to whom assets have been distributed have the same powers and liabilities as distributees under Sections 3-908, 3-909, and 3-910.

(e) Absent breach of fiduciary obligations or express undertaking, a fiduciary's liability is limited to the assets received by the fiduciary.

§ 3-318. [Universal Succession; Universal Successors' Submission to Jurisdiction; When Heirs or Devisees May Not Seek Administration.]

(a) Upon issuance of the statement of universal succession, the universal successors become subject to the personal jurisdiction of the courts of this state in any proceeding that may be instituted relating to the estate or to any liability assumed by them.

(b) Any heir or devisee who voluntarily joins in an application under Section 3-313 may not subsequently seek appointment of a personal representative.

§ 3-319. [Universal Succession; Duty of Universal Successors; Information to Heirs and Devisees.]

Not later than thirty days after issuance of the statement of universal succession, each universal successor shall inform the heirs and devisees who did not join in the application of the succession without administration. The information must be delivered or be sent by ordinary mail to each of the heirs and devisees whose address is reasonably available to the universal successors. The information must include the names and addresses of the universal successors, indicate that it is being sent to persons who have or may have some interest in the estate, and describe the court where the application and statement of universal succession has been filed. The failure of a universal successor to give this information is a breach of duty to the persons concerned but does not affect the validity of the approval of succession without administration or the powers or liabilities of the universal successors. A universal successor may inform other persons of the succession without administration by delivery or by ordinary first class mail.

§ 3-320. [Universal Succession; Universal Successors' Liability For Restitution to Estate.]

If a personal representative is subsequently appointed, universal successors are personally liable for restitution of any property of the estate to which they are not entitled as heirs or devisees of the decedent and their liability is the same as a distributee under Section 3-909, subject to the provisions of Sections 3-317 and 3-321 and the limitations of Section 3-1006.

§ 3-321. [Universal Succession; Liability of Universal Successors For Claims, Expenses, Intestate Shares and Devises.]

The liability of universal successors is subject to any defenses that would have been available to the decedent. Other than liability arising from fraud, conversion, or other wrongful conduct of a universal successor, the personal liability of each universal successor to any creditor, claimant, other heir, devisee, or person entitled to decedent's property may not exceed the proportion of the claim that the universal successor's share bears to the share of all heirs and residuary devisees.

§ 3-322. [Universal Succession; Remedies of Creditors, Other Heirs, Devisees or Persons Entitled to Decedent's Property.]

In addition to remedies otherwise provided by law, any creditor, heir, devisee, or person entitled to decedent's property qualified under Section 3-605, may demand bond of universal successors. If the demand for bond precedes the granting of an application for universal succession, it must be treated as an objection under Section 3-314(c) unless it is withdrawn, the claim satisfied, or the applicants post bond in an amount sufficient to protect the demandant. If the demand for bond follows the granting of an application for universal succession, the universal successors, within 10 days after notice of the demand, upon satisfying the claim or posting bond sufficient to protect the demandant, may disqualify the demandant from seeking administration of the estate.

Part 4
Formal Testacy and Appointment Proceedings

§ 3-401. [Formal Testacy Proceedings; Nature; When Commenced.]

A formal testacy proceeding is litigation to determine whether a decedent left a valid will. A formal testacy proceeding may be commenced by an interested person filing a petition as described in Section 3-402(a) in which he requests that the Court, after notice and hearing, enter an order probating a will, or a petition to set aside an informal probate of a will or to prevent informal probate of a will which is the subject of a pending application, or a petition in accordance with Section 3-402(b) for an order that the decedent died intestate.

A petition may seek formal probate of a will without regard to whether the same or a conflicting will has been informally probated. A formal testacy proceeding may, but need not, involve a request for appointment of a personal representative.

During the pendency of a formal testacy proceeding, the Registrar shall not act upon any application for informal probate of any will of the decedent or any application for informal appointment of a personal representative of the decedent.

Unless a petition in a formal testacy proceeding also requests confirmation of the previous informal appointment, a previously appointed personal representative, after receipt of notice of the commencement of a formal probate proceeding, must refrain from exercising his power to make any further distribution of the estate during the pendency of the formal proceeding. A petitioner who seeks the appointment of a different personal representative in a formal proceeding also may request an order restraining the acting personal representative from exercising any of the powers of his office and requesting the appointment of a special administrator. In the absence of a request, or if the request is denied, the commencement of a formal proceeding has no effect on the powers and duties of a previously appointed personal representative other than those relating to distribution.

§ 3-402. [Formal Testacy or Appointment Proceedings; Petition; Contents.]

(a) Petitions for formal probate of a will, or for adjudication of intestacy with or without request for appointment of a personal representative, must be directed to the Court, request a judicial order after notice and hearing and contain further statements as indicated in this section. A petition for formal probate of a will

(1) requests an order as to the testacy of the decedent in relation to a particular instrument which may or may not have been informally probated and determining the heirs,

(2) contains the statements required for informal applications as stated in the six subparagraphs under Section 3-301(a)(1), the statements required by subparagraphs (ii) and (iii) of Section 3-301(a)(2), and

(3) states whether the original of the last will of the decedent is in the possession of the Court or accompanies the petition.

If the original will is neither in the possession of the Court nor accompanies the petition and no authenticated copy of a will probated in another jurisdiction accompanies the petition, the petition also must state the contents of the will, and indicate that it is lost, destroyed, or otherwise unavailable.

(b) A petition for adjudication of intestacy and appointment of an administrator in intestacy must request a judicial finding and order that the decedent left no will and determining the heirs, contain the statements required by (1) and (4) of Section 3-301(a) and indicate whether supervised administration is sought. A petition may request an order determining intestacy and heirs without requesting the appointment of an administrator, in which case, the statements required by subparagraph (ii) of Section 3-301(a)(4) above may be omitted.

§ 3-403. [Formal Testacy Proceedings; Notice of Hearing on Petition.]

(a) Upon commencement of a formal testacy proceeding, the Court shall fix a time and place of hearing. Notice shall be given in the manner prescribed by Section 1-401 by the petitioner to the persons herein enumerated and to any additional person who has filed a demand for notice under Section 3-204 of this Code.

Notice shall be given to the following persons: the surviving spouse, children, and other heirs of the decedent, the devisees and executors named in any will that is being, or has been, probated, or offered for informal or formal probate in the [county,] or that is known by the petitioner to have been probated, or offered for informal or formal probate elsewhere, and any personal representative of the decedent whose appointment has not been terminated. Notice may be given to other persons. In addition, the petitioner shall give notice by publication to all unknown persons and to all known persons whose addresses are unknown who have any interest in the matters being litigated.

(b) If it appears by the petition or otherwise that the fact of the death of the alleged decedent may be in doubt, or on the written demand of any interested person, a copy of the notice of the hearing on said petition shall be sent by registered mail to the alleged decedent at his last known address. The Court shall direct the petitioner to report the results of, or make and report back concerning, a reasonably diligent search for the alleged decedent in any manner that may seem advisable, including any or all of the following methods:

(1) by inserting in one or more suitable periodicals a notice requesting information from any person having knowledge of the whereabouts of the alleged decedent;

(2) by notifying law enforcement officials and public welfare agencies in appropriate locations of the disappearance of the alleged decedent;

(3) by engaging the services of an investigator. The costs of any search so directed shall be paid by the petitioner if there is no administration or by the estate of the decedent in case there is administration.

§ 3-404. [Formal Testacy Proceedings; Written Objections to Probate.]

Any party to a formal proceeding who opposes the probate of a will for any reason shall state in his pleadings his objections to probate of the will.

§ 3-405. [Formal Testacy Proceedings; Uncontested Cases; Hearings and Proof.]

If a petition in a testacy proceeding is unopposed, the Court may order probate or intestacy on the strength of the pleadings if satisfied that the conditions of Section 3-309 have been met, or conduct a hearing in Open court and require proof of the matters necessary to support the order sought. If evidence concerning execution of the will is necessary, the affidavit or testimony of one of any attesting witnesses to the instrument is sufficient. If the affidavit or testimony of an attesting witness is not available, execution of the will may be proved by other evidence or affidavit.

§ 3-406. [Formal Testacy Proceedings; Contested Cases; Testimony of Attesting Witnesses.]

(a) If evidence concerning execution of an attested will which is not selfproved is necessary in contested cases, the testimony of at least one of the attesting witnesses, if within the state, competent and able to testify, is required. Due execution of an attested or unattested will may be proved by other evidence.

(b) If the will is self-proved, compliance with signature requirements for execution is conclusively presumed and other requirements of execution are presumed subject to rebuttal without the testimony of any witness upon filing the will and the acknowledgment and affidavits annexed or attached thereto, unless there is proof of fraud or forgery affecting the acknowledgment or affidavit.

§ 3-407. [Formal Testacy Proceedings; Burdens in Contested Cases.]

In contested cases, petitioners who seek to establish intestacy have the burden of establishing prima facie proof of death, venue, and heirship. Proponents of a will have the burden of establishing prima facie proof of due execution in all cases, and, if they are also petitioners, prima facie proof of death and venue. Contestants of a will have the burden of establishing lack of testamentary intent or capacity, undue influence, fraud, duress, mistake or revocation. Parties have the ultimate burden of persuasion as to matters with respect to which they have the initial burden of proof. If a will is opposed by the petition for probate of a later will revoking the former, it shall be determined first whether the later will is entitled to probate, and if a will is opposed by a petition for a declaration of intestacy, it shall be determined first whether the will is entitled to probate.

§ 3-408. [Formal Testacy Proceedings; Will Construction; Effect of Final Order in Another Jurisdiction.]

A final order of a court of another state determining testacy, the validity or construction of a will, made in a proceeding involving notice to and an opportunity for contest by all interested persons must be accepted as determinative by the courts of this state if it includes, or is based upon, a finding that the decedent was domiciled at his death in the state where the order was made.

§ 3-409. [Formal Testacy Proceedings; Order; Foreign Will.]

After the time required for any notice has expired, upon proof of notice, and after any hearing that may be necessary, if the Court finds that the testator is dead, venue is proper and that the proceeding was commenced within the limitation prescribed by Section 3-108, it shall determine the decedent's domicile at death, his heirs and his state of testacy. Any will found to be valid and unrevoked shall be formally probated. Termination of any previous informal appointment of a personal representative, which may be appropriate in view of the relief requested and findings, is governed by Section 3-612. The petition shall be dismissed or appropriate amendment allowed if the court is not satisfied that the alleged decedent is dead. A will from a place which does not provide for probate of a will after death, may be proved for probate in this state by a duly authenticated certificate of its legal custodian that the copy introduced is a true copy and that the will has become effective under the law of the other place.

§ 3-410. [Formal Testacy Proceedings; Probate of More Than One Instrument.]

If two or more instruments are offered for probate before a final order is entered in a formal testacy proceeding, more than one instrument may be probated if neither expressly revokes the other or contains provisions which work a total revocation by implication. If more than one instrument is probated, the order shall indicate what provisions control in respect to the nomination of an executor, if any. The order may, but need not, indicate how any provisions of a particular instrument are affected by the other instrument. After a final order in a testacy proceeding has been entered, no petition for probate of any other instrument of the decedent may be entertained, except incident to a petition to vacate or modify a previous probate order and subject to the time limits of Section 3-412.

§ 3-411. [Formal Testacy Proceedings; Partial Intestacy.]

If it becomes evident in the course of a formal testacy proceeding that, though one or more instruments are entitled to be probated, the decedent's estate is or may be partially intestate, the Court shall enter an order to that effect.

§ 3-412. [Formal Testacy Proceedings; Effect of Order; Vacation.]

Subject to appeal and subject to vacation as provided herein and in Section 3-413, a formal testacy order under Sections 3-409 to 3-411, including an order that the decedent left no valid will and determining heirs, is final as to all persons with respect to all issues concerning the decedent's estate that the court considered or might have considered incident to its rendition relevant to the question of whether the decedent left a valid will, and to the determination of heirs, except that:

(1) The court shall entertain a petition for modification or vacation of its order and probate of another will of the decedent if it is shown that the proponents of the later-offered will were unaware of its existence at the time of the earlier proceeding or were unaware of the earlier proceeding and were given no notice thereof, except by publication.

(2) If intestacy of all or part of the estate has been ordered, the determination of heirs of the decedent may be reconsidered if it is shown that one or more persons were omitted from the determination and it is also shown that the persons were unaware of their relationship to the decedent, were unaware of his death or were given no notice of

any proceeding concerning his estate, except by publication.

(3) A petition for vacation under either (1) or (2) above must be filed prior to the earlier of the following time limits:

(i) If a personal representative has been appointed for the estate, the time of entry of any order approving final distribution of the estate, or, if the estate is closed by statement, 6 months after the filing of the closing statement.

(ii) Whether or not a personal representative has been appointed for the estate of the decedent, the time prescribed by Section 3-108 when it is no longer possible to initiate an original proceeding to probate a will of the decedent.

(iii) 12 months after the entry of the order sought to be vacated.

(4) The order originally rendered in the testacy proceeding may be modified or vacated, if appropriate under the circumstances, by the order of probate of the later-offered will or the order redetermining heirs.

(5) The finding of the fact of death is conclusive as to the alleged decedent only if notice of the hearing on the petition in the formal testacy proceeding was sent by registered or certified mail addressed to the alleged decedent at his last known address and the court finds that a search under Section 3-403(b) was made.

If the alleged decedent is not dead, even if notice was sent and search was made, he may recover estate assets in the hands of the personal representative. In addition to any remedies available to the alleged decedent by reason of any fraud or intentional wrongdoing, the alleged decedent may recover any estate or its proceeds from distributees that is in their hands, or the value of distributions received by them, to the extent that any recovery from distributees is equitable in view of all of the circumstances.

§ 3-413. [Formal Testacy Proceedings; Vacation of Order For Other Cause.]

For good cause shown, an order in a formal testacy proceeding may be modified or vacated within the time allowed for appeal.

§ 3-414. [Formal Proceedings Concerning Appointment of Personal Representative.]

(a) A formal proceeding for adjudication regarding the priority or qualification of one who is an applicant for appointment as personal representative, or of one who previously has been appointed personal representative in informal proceedings, if an issue concerning the testacy of the decedent is or may be involved, is governed by Section 3-302, as well as by this section. In other cases, the petition shall contain or adopt the statements required by Section 3-301(1) and describe the question relating to priority or qualification of the personal representative which is to be resolved. If the proceeding precedes any appointment of a personal representative, it shall stay any pending informal appointment proceedings as well as any commenced thereafter. If the proceeding is commenced after appointment, the previously appointed personal representative, after receipt of notice thereof, shall refrain from exercising any power of administration except as necessary to preserve the estate or unless the Court orders otherwise.

(b) After notice to interested persons, including all persons interested in the administration of the estate as successors under the applicable assumption concerning testacy, any previously appointed personal representative and any person having or claiming priority for appointment as personal representative, the Court shall determine who is entitled to appointment under Section 3-203, make a proper appointment and, if appropriate, terminate any prior appointment found to have been inproper as provided in cases of removal under Section 3-611.

Part 5
Supervised Administration

§ 3-501. [Supervised Administration; Nature of Proceeding.]

Supervised administration is a single in rem proceeding to secure complete administration and settlement of a decedent's estate under the continuing authority of the Court which extends until entry of an order approving distribution of the estate and discharging the personal representative or other order terminating the proceeding. A supervised personal representative is responsible to the Court, as well as to the interested parties, and is subject to directions concerning the estate made by the Court on its own motion or on the motion of any interested party. Except as otherwise provided in this Part, or as otherwise ordered by the Court, a supervised personal representative has the same duties and powers as a personal representative who is not supervised.

§ 3-502. [Supervised Administration; Petition; Order.]

A petition for supervised administration may be filed by any interested person or by a personal representative at any time or the prayer for supervised administration may be joined with a petition in a testacy or appointment proceeding. If the testacy of the decedent and the priority and qualification of any personal representative have not been adjudicated previously, the petition for supervised administration shall include the matters required of a petition in a formal testacy proceeding and the notice requirements and procedures applicable to a formal testacy proceeding apply. If not previously adjudicated, the Court shall adjudicate the testacy of the decedent and questions relating to the priority and qualifications of the personal representative in any case involving a request for supervised administration, even though the request for supervised administration may be denied. After notice to interested persons, the Court shall order supervised administration of a decedent's estate: (1) if the decedent's will directs supervised administration, it shall be ordered unless the Court finds that circumstances bearing on the need for supervised administration have changed since the execution of the will and that there is no necessity for supervised administration; (2) if the decedent's will directs unsupervised administration, supervised administration shall be ordered only upon a finding that it is necessary for protection of persons interested in the estate; or (3) in other cases if the Court finds that supervised administration is necessary under the circumstances.

§ 3-503. [Supervised Administration; Effect on Other Proceedings.]

(a) The pendency of a proceeding for supervised administration of a decedent's estate stays action on any informal application then pending or thereafter filed.

(b) If a will has been previously probated in informal proceedings, the effect of the filing of a petition for supervised administration is as provided for formal testacy proceedings by Section 3-401.

(c) After he has received notice of the filing of a petition for supervised administration, a personal representative who has been appointed previously shall not exercise his power to distribute any estate. The filing of the petition does not affect his other powers and duties unless the Court restricts the exercise of any of them pending full hearing on the petition.

§ 3-504. [Supervised Administration; Powers of Personal Representative.]

Unless restricted by the Court, a supervised personal representative has, without interim orders approving exercise of a power, all powers of personal representatives under this Code, but he shall not exercise his power to make any distribution of the estate without prior order of the Court. Any other restriction on the power of a personal representative which may be ordered by the Court must be endorsed on his letters of appointment and, unless so endorsed, is ineffective as to persons dealing in good faith with the personal representative.

§ 3-505. [Supervised Administration; Interim Orders; Distribution and Closing Orders.]

Unless otherwise ordered by the Court, supervised administration is terminated by order in accordance with time restrictions, notices and contents of orders prescribed for proceedings under Section 3-1001. Interim orders approving or directing partial distributions or granting other relief may be issued by the Court at any time during the pendency of a supervised administration on the application of the personal representative or any interested person.

Part 6
Personal Representative; Appointment, Control and Termination of Authority

§ 3-601. [Qualification.]

Prior to receiving letters, a personal representative shall qualify by filing with the appointing Court any required bond and a statement of acceptance of the duties of the office.

§ 3-602. [Acceptance of Appointment; Consent to Jurisdiction.]

By accepting appointment, a personal representative submits personally to the jurisdiction of the Court in any proceeding relating to the estate that may be instituted by any interested person. Notice of any proceeding shall be delivered to the personal representative, or mailed to him by ordinary first class mail at his address as listed in the application or petition for appointment or as thereafter reported to the Court and to his address as then known to the petitioner.

§ 3-603. [Bond Not Required Without Court Order, Exceptions.]

No bond is required of a personal representative appointed in informal proceedings, except (1) upon the appointment of a special administrator; (2) when an executor or other personal representative is appointed to administer an estate under a will containing an express requirement of bond or (3) when bond is required under Section 3-605. Bond may be required by court order at the time of appointment of a personal representative appointed in any formal proceeding except that bond is not required of a personal representative appointed in formal proceedings if the will relieves the personal representative of bond, unless bond has been requested by an interested party and the Court is satisfied that it is desirable. Bond required by any will may be dispensed with in formal proceedings upon determination by the Court that it is not necessary. No bond is required of any personal representative who, pursuant to statute, has deposited cash or collateral with an agency of this state to secure performance of his duties.

§ 3-604. [Bond Amount; Security; Procedure; Reduction.]

If bond is required and the provisions of the will or order do not specify the amount, unless stated in his application or petition, the person qualifying shall file a statement under oath with the Registrar indicating his best estimate of the value of the personal estate of the decedent and of the income expected from the personal and real estate during the next year, and he shall execute and file a bond with the Registrar, or give other suitable security, in an amount not less than the estimate. The Registrar shall determine that the bond is duly executed by a corporate surety, or one or more individual sureties whose performance is secured by pledge of personal property, mortgage on real property or other adequate security. The Registrar may permit the amount of the bond to be reduced by the value of assets of the estate deposited with a domestic financial institution (as defined in Section 6-101) in a manner that prevents their unauthorized disposition. On petition of the personal representative or another interested person the Court may excuse a requirement of bond, increase or reduce the amount of the bond, release sureties, or permit the substitution of another bond with the same or different sureties.

§ 3-605. [Demand For Bond by Interested Person.]

Any person apparently having an interest in the estate worth in excess of [$1,000], or any creditor having a claim in excess of [$1,000], may make a written demand that a personal representative give bond. The demand must be filed with the Registrar and a copy mailed to the personal representative, if appointment and qualification have occurred. Thereupon, bond is required, but the requirement ceases if the person demanding bond ceases to be interested in the estate, or if bond is excused as provided in Section 3-603 or 3-604. After he has received notice and until the filing of the bond or cessation of the requirement of bond, the personal representative shall refrain from exercising any powers of his office except as necessary to preserve the estate. Failure of the personal representative to meet a requirement of bond by giving suitable bond within 30 days after receipt of notice is cause for his removal and appointment of a successor personal representative.

§ 3-606. [Terms and Conditions of Bonds.]

(a) The following requirements and provisions apply to any bond required by this Part:

(1) Bonds shall name the [state] as obligee for the benefit of the persons interested in the estate and shall be conditioned upon the faithful discharge by the fiduciary of all duties according to law.

(2) Unless otherwise provided by the terms of the approved bond, sureties are jointly and severally liable with the personal representative and with each other. The address of sureties shall be stated in the bond.

(3) By executing an approved bond of a personal representative, the surety consents to the jurisdiction of the probate court which issued letters to the primary obligor in any proceedings pertaining to the fiduciary duties of the personal representative and naming the surety as a party. Notice of any proceeding shall be delivered to the surety or mailed to him by registered or certified mail at his address as listed with the court where the bond is filed and to his address as then known to the petitioner.

(4) On petition of a successor personal representative, any other personal representative of the same decedent, or any interested person, a proceeding in the Court may be initiated against a surety for breach of the obligation of the bond of the personal representative.

(5) The bond of the personal representative is not void after the first recovery but may be proceeded against from time to time until the whole penalty is exhausted.

(b) No action or proceeding may be commenced against the surety on any matter as to which an action or proceeding against the primary obligor is barred by adjudication or limitation.

§ 3-607. [Order Restraining Personal Representative.]

(a) On petition of any person who appears to have an interest in the estate, the Court by temporary order may restrain a personal representative from performing specified acts of administration, disbursement, or distribution, or exercise of any powers or discharge of any duties of his office, or make any other order to secure proper performance of his duty, if it appears to the Court that the personal representative otherwise may take some action which would jeopardize unreasonably the interest of the applicant or of some other interested person. Persons with whom the personal representative may transact business may be made parties.

(b) The matter shall be set for hearing within 10 days unless the parties otherwise agree. Notice as the Court directs shall be given to the personal representative and his attorney of record, if any, and to another parties named defendant in the petition.

§ 3-608. [Termination of Appointment; General.]

Termination of appointment of a personal representative occurs as indicated in Sections 3-609 to 3-612, inclusive. Termination ends the right and power pertaining to the office of personal representative as conferred by this Code or any will, except that a personal representative, at any time prior to distribution or until restrained or enjoined by court order, may perform acts necessary to protect the estate and may deliver the assets to a successor representative. Termination does not discharge a personal representative from liability for transactions or omissions occurring before termination, or relieve him of the duty to preserve assets subject to his control, to account therefor and to deliver the assets. Termination does not affect the jurisdiction of the Court over the personal representative, but terminates his authority to represent the estate in any pending or future proceeding.

§ 3-609. [Termination of Appointment; Death or Disability.]

The death of a personal representative or the appointment of a conservator for the estate of a personal representative, terminates his appointment. Until appointment and qualification of a successor or special representative to replace the deceased or protected representative, the representative of the estate of the deceased or protected personal representative, if any, has the duty to protect the estate possessed and being administered by his decedent or ward at the time his appointment terminates, has the power to perform acts necessary for protection and shall account for and deliver the estate assets to a successor or special personal representative upon his appointment and qualification.

§ 3-610. [Termination of Appointment; Voluntary.]

(a) An appointment of a personal representative terminates as provided in Section 3-1003, one year after the filing of a closing statement.

(b) An order closing an estate as provided in Section 3-1001 or 3-1002 terminates an appointment of a personal representative.

(c) A personal representative may resign his position by filing a written statement of resignation with the Registrar after he has given at least 15 days written notice to the persons known to be interested in the estate. If no one applies or petitions for appointment of a successor representative within the time indicated in the notice, the filed statement of resignation is ineffective as a termination of appointment and in any event is effective only upon the appointment and qualification of a successor representative and delivery of the assets to him.

§ 3-611. [Termination of Appointment by Removal; Cause; Procedure.]

(a) A person interested in the estate may petition for removal of a personal representative for cause at any time. Upon filing of the petition, the Court shall fix a time and place for hearing. Notice shall be given by the petitioner to the personal representative, and to other persons as the Court may order. Except as otherwise ordered as provided in Section 3-607, after receipt of notice of removal proceedings, the personal representative shall not act except to account, to correct maladministration or preserve the estate. If removal is ordered, the Court also shall direct by order the disposition of the assets remaining in the name of, or under the control of, the personal representative being removed.

(b) Cause for removal exists when removal would be in the best interests of the estate, or if it is shown that a personal representative or the person seeking his appointment intentionally misrepresented material facts in the proceedings leading to his appointment, or that the personal representative has disregarded an order of the Court, has become incapable of discharging the duties of his office, or has mismanaged the estate or failed to perform any duty pertaining to the office. Unless the decedent's will directs otherwise, a personal representative appointed at the decedent's domicile, incident to securing appointment of himself or his nominee as ancillary personal representative, may obtain removal of another who was appointed personal representative in this state to administer local assets.

§ 3-612. [Termination of Appointment; Change of Testacy Status.]

Except as otherwise ordered in formal proceedings, the probate of a will subsequent to the appointment of a personal representative in intestacy or under a will which is superseded by formal probate of another will, or the vacation of an informal probate of a will subsequent to the appointment of the personal representative thereunder, does not terminate the appointment of the personal representative although his powers may be reduced as provided in Section 3-401. Termination occurs upon appointment in informal or formal appointment proceedings of a person entitled to appointment under the later assumption concerning testacy. If no request for new appointment is made within 30 days after expiration of time for appeal from the order in formal testacy proceedings, or from the informal probate, changing the assumption concerning testacy, the previously appointed personal representative upon request may be appointed personal representative under the subsequently probated will, or as in intestacy as the case may be.

§ 3-613. [Successor Personal Representative.]

Parts 3 and 4 of this Article govern proceedings for appointment of a personal representative to succeed one whose appointment has been terminated. After appointment and qualification, a successor personal representative may be substituted in all actions and proceedings to which the former personal representative was a party, and no notice, process or claim which was given or served upon the former personal representative need be given to or served upon the successor in order to preserve any position or right the person giving the notice or filing the claim may thereby have obtained or preserved with reference to the former personal representative. Except as otherwise ordered by the Court, the successor personal representative has the powers and duties in respect to the continued administration which the former personal representative would have had if his appointment had not been terminated.

§ 3-614. [Special Administrator; Appointment.]

A special administrator may be appointed:

(1) informally by the Registrar on the application of any interested person when necessary to protect the estate of a decedent prior to the appointment of a general personal representative or if a prior appointment has been terminated as provided in Section 3-609;

(2) in a formal proceeding by order of the Court on the petition of any interested person and finding, after notice and hearing, that appointment is necessary to preserve the estate or to secure its proper administration including its administration in circumstances where a general personal representative cannot or should not act. If it appears to the Court that an emergency exists, appointment may be ordered without notice.

§ 3-615. [Special Administrator; Who May Be Appointed.]

(a) If a special administrator is to be appointed pending the probate of a will which is the subject of a pending application or petition for probate, the person named executor in the will shall be appointed if available, and qualified.

(b) In other cases, any proper person may be appointed special administrator.

§ 3-616. [Special Administrator; Appointed Informally; Powers and Duties.]

A special administrator appointed by the Registrar in informal proceedings pursuant to Section 3-614(1) has the duty to collect and manage the assets of the estate, to preserve them, to account therefor and to deliver them to the general personal representative upon his qualification. The special administrator has the power of a personal representative under the Code necessary to perform his duties.

§ 3-617. [Special Administrator; Formal Proceedings; Power and Duties.]

A special administrator appointed by order of the Court in any formal proceeding has the power of a general personal representative except as limited in the appointment and duties as prescribed in the order. The appointment may be for a specified time, to perform particular acts or on other terms as the Court may direct.

§ 3-618. [Termination of Appointment; Special Administrator.]

The appointment of a special administrator terminates in accordance with the provisions of the order of appointment or on the appointment of a general personal representative. In other cases, the appointment of a special administrator is subject to termination as provided in Sections 3-608 through 3-611.

Part 7
Duties and Powers of Personal Representatives

§ 3-701. [Time of Accrual of Duties and Powers.]

The duties and powers of a personal representative commence upon his appointment. The powers of a personal representative relate back in time to give acts by the person appointed which are beneficial to the estate occurring prior to appointment the same effect as those occurring thereafter. Prior to appointment, a person named executor in a will may carry out written instructions of the decedent relating to his body, funeral and burial arrangements. A personal representative may ratify and accept acts on behalf of the estate done by others where the acts would have been proper for a personal representative.

§ 3-702. [Priority Among Different Letters.]

A person to whom general letters are issued first has exclusive authority under the letters until his appointment is terminated or modified. If, through error, general letters are afterwards issued to another, the first appointed representative may recover any property of the estate in the hands of the representative subsequently appointed, but the acts of the latter done in good faith before notice of the first letters are not void for want of validity of appointment.

§ 3-703. [General Duties; Relation and Liability to Persons Interested in Estate; Standing to Sue.]

(a) A personal representative is a fiduciary who shall observe the standards of care applicable to trustees as described by Section 7-302. A personal representative is under a duty to settle and distribute the estate of the decedent in accordance with the terms of any probated and effective will and this Code, and as expeditiously and efficiently as is consistent with the best interests of the estate. He shall use the authority conferred upon him by this Code, the terms of the will, if any, and any order in proceedings to which he is party for the best interests of successors to the estate.

(b) A personal representative shall not be surcharged for acts of administration or distribution if the conduct in question was authorized at the time. Subject to other obligations of administration, an informally probated will is authority to administer and distribute the estate according to its terms. An order of appointment of a personal representative, whether issued in informal or formal proceedings, is authority to distribute apparently intestate assets to the heirs of the decedent if, at the time of distribution, the personal representative is not aware of a pending testacy proceeding, a proceeding to vacate an order entered in an earlier testacy proceeding, a formal proceeding questioning his appointment or fitness to continue, or a supervised administration proceeding. Nothing in this section affects the duty of the personal representative to administer and distribute the estate in accordance with the rights of claimants, the surviving spouse, any minor and dependent children and any pretermitted child of the decedent as described elsewhere in this Code.

(c) Except as to proceedings which do not survive the death of the decedent, a personal representative of a decedent domiciled in this state at his death has the same standing to sue and be sued in the courts of this state and the courts of any other jurisdiction as his decedent had immediately prior to death.

§ 3-704. [Personal Representative to Proceed Without Court Order; Exception.]

A personal representative shall proceed expeditiously with the settlement and distribution of a decedent's estate and, except as otherwise specified or ordered in regard to a supervised personal representative, do so without adjudication, order, or direction of the Court, but he may invoke the jurisdiction of the Court, in proceedings authorized by this Code, to resolve questions concerning the estate or its administration.

§ 3-705. [Duty of Personal Representative; Information to Heirs and Devisees.]

Not later than 30 days after his appointment every personal representative, except any special administrator, shall give information of his appointment to the heirs and devisees, including, if there has been no formal testacy proceeding and if the personal representative was appointed on the assumption that the decedent died intestate, the devisees in any will mentioned in the application for appointment of a personal representative. The information shall be delivered or sent by ordinary mail to each of the heirs and devisees whose address is reasonably available to the personal representative. The duty does not extend to require information to persons who have been adjudicated in a prior formal testacy proceeding to have no interest in the estate. The information shall include the name and address of the personal representative, indicate that it is being sent to persons who have or may have some interest in the estate being administered, indicate whether bond has been filed, and describe the court where papers relating to the estate are on file. The information shall state that the estate is being administered by the personal representative under the [State] Probate Code without supervision by the Court but that recipients are entitled to information regarding the administration from the personal representative and can petition the Court in any matter relating to the estate, including distribution of assets and expenses of administration. The personal representative's failure to give this information is a breach of his duty to the persons concerned but does not affect the validity of his appointment, his powers or other duties. A personal representative may inform other persons of his appointment by delivery or ordinary first class mail.

As amended in 1987.

§ 3-706. [Duty of Personal Representative; Inventory and Appraisement.]

Within 3 months after his appointment, a personal representative, who is not a special administrator or a successor to another representative who has previously discharged this duty, shall prepare and file or mail an inventory of property owned by the decedent at the time of his death, listing it with reasonable detail, and indicating as to each listed item, its fair market value as of the date of the decedent's death, and the type and amount of any encumbrance that may exist with reference to any item.

The personal representative shall send a copy of the inventory to interested persons who request it. He may also file the original of the inventory with the court.

§ 3-707. [Employment of Appraisers.]

The personal representative may employ a qualified and disinterested appraiser to assist him in ascertaining the fair market value as of the date of the decedent's death of any asset the value of which may be subject to reasonable doubt. Different persons may be employed to appraise different kinds of assets included in the estate. The names and addresses of any appraiser shall be indicated on the inventory with the item or items he appraised.

§ 3-708. [Duty of Personal Representative; Supplementary Inventory.]

If any property not included in the original inventory comes to the knowledge of a personal representative or if the personal representative learns that the value or description indicated in the original inventory for any item is erroneous or misleading, he shall make a supplementary inventory or appraisement showing the market value as of the date of the decedent's death of the new item or the revised market value or descriptions, and the appraisers or other data relied upon, if any, and file it with the Court if the original inventory was filed, or furnish copies thereof or information thereof to persons interested in the new information.

§ 3-709. [Duty of Personal Representative; Possession of Estate.]

Except as otherwise provided by a decedent's will, every personal representative has a right to, and shall take possession or control of, the decedent's property, except that any real property or tangible personal property may be left with or surrendered to the person presumptively entitled thereto unless or until, in the judgment of the personal representative, possession of the property by him will be necessary for purposes of administration. The request by a personal representative for delivery of any property possessed by an heir or devisee is conclusive evidence, in any action against the heir or devisee for possession thereof, that the possession of the property by the personal representative is necessary for purposes of administration. The personal representative shall pay taxes on, and take all steps reasonably necessary for the management, protection and preservation of, the estate in his possession. He may maintain an action to recover possession of property or to determine the title thereto.

§ 3-710. [Power to Avoid Transfers.]

The property liable for the payment of unsecured debts of a decedent includes all property transferred by him by any means which is in law void or voidable as against his creditors, and subject to prior liens, the right to recover this property, so far as necessary for the payment of unsecured debts of the decedent, is exclusively in the personal representative.

§ 3-711. [Powers of Personal Representatives; In General.]

Until termination of his appointment a personal representative has the same power over the title to property of the estate that an absolute owner would have, in trust however, for the benefit of the creditors and others interested in the estate. This power may be exercised without notice, hearing, or order of court.

§ 3-712. [Improper Exercise of Power; Breach of Fiduciary Duty.]

If the exercise of power concerning the estate is improper, the personal representative is liable to interested persons for damage or loss resulting from breach of his fiduciary duty to the same extent as a trustee of an express trust. The rights of purchasers and others dealing with a personal representative shall be determined as provided in Sections 3-713 and 3-714.

§ 3-713. [Sale, Encumbrance or Transaction Involving Conflict of Interest; Voidable; Exceptions.]

Any sale or encumbrance to the personal representative, his spouse, agent or attorney, or any corporation or trust in which he has a substantial beneficial interest, or any transaction which is affected by a substantial conflict of interest on the part of the personal representative, is voidable by any person interested in the estate except one who has consented after fair disclosure, unless (1) the will or a contract entered into by the decedent expressly authorized the transaction; or (2) the transaction is approved by the Court after notice to interested persons.

§ 3-714. [Persons Dealing with Personal Representative; Protection.]

A person who in good faith either assists a personal representative or deals with him for value is protected as if the personal representative properly exercised his power. The fact that a person knowingly deals with a personal representative does not alone require the person to inquire into the existence of a power or the propriety of its exercise. Except for restrictions on powers of supervised personal representatives which are endorsed on letters as provided in Section 3-504, no provision in any will or order of court purporting to limit the power of a personal representative is effective except as to persons with actual knowledge thereof. A person is not bound to see to the proper application of estate assets paid or delivered to a personal representative. The protection here expressed extends to instances in which some procedural irregularity or jurisdictional defect occurred in proceedings leading to the issuance of letters, including a case in which the alleged decedent is found to be alive. The protection here expressed is not by substitution for that provided by comparable provisions of the laws relating to commercial transactions and laws simplifying transfers of securities by fiduciaries.

§ 3-715. [Transactions Authorized for Personal Representatives; Exceptions.]

Except as restricted or otherwise provided by the will or by an order in a formal proceeding and subject to the priorities stated in Section 3-902, a personal representative, acting reasonably for the benefit of the interested persons, may properly:

(1) retain assets owned by the decedent pending distribution or liquidation including those in which the representative is personally interested or which are otherwise improper for trust investment;

(2) receive assets from fiduciaries, or other sources;

(3) perform, compromise or refuse performance of the decedent's contracts that continue as obligations of the estate, as he may determine under the circumstances. in performing enforceable contracts by the decedent to convey or lease land, the personal representative, among other possible courses of action, may:

(i) execute and deliver a deed of conveyance for cash payment of all sums remaining due or the purchaser's note for the sum remaining due secured by a mortgage or deed of trust on the land; or

(ii) deliver a deed in escrow with directions that the proceeds, when paid in accordance with the escrow agreement, be paid to the successors of the decedent, as designated in the escrow agreement;

(4) satisfy written charitable pledges of the decedent irrespective of whether the pledges constituted binding obligations of the decedent or were properly presented as claims, if in the judgment of the personal representative the decedent would have wanted the pledges completed under the circumstances;

(5) if funds are not needed to meet debts and expenses currently payable and are not immediately distributable, deposit or invest liquid assets of the estate, including moneys received From the sale of other assets, in federally insured interest-bearing accounts, readily marketable secured loan arrangements or other prudent investments which would be reasonable for use by trustees generally;

(6) acquire or dispose of an asset, including land in this or another state, for cash or on credit, at public or private sale; and manage, develop, improve, exchange, partition, change the character of, or abandon an estate asset;

(7) make ordinary or extraordinary repairs or alterations in buildings or other structures, demolish any improvements, raze existing or erect new party walls or buildings;

(8) subdivide, develop or dedicate land to public use; make or obtain the vacation of plats and adjust boundaries; or adjust differences in valuation on exchange or partition by giving or receiving considerations; or dedicate easements to public use without consideration;

(9) enter for any purpose into a lease as lessor or lessee, with or without option to purchase or renew, for a term within or extending beyond the period of administration;

(10) enter into a lease or arrangement for exploration and removal of minerals or other natural resources or enter into a pooling or unitization agreement;

(11) abandon property when, in the opinion of the personal representative, it is valueless, or is so encumbered, or is in condition that it is of no benefit to the state;

(12) vote stocks or other securities in person or by general or limited proxy;

(13) pay calls, assessments, and other sums chargeable or accruing against or on account of securities, unless barred by the provisions relating to claims;

(14) hold a security in the name of a nominee or in other form without disclosure of the interest of the estate but the personal representative is liable for any act of the nominee in connection with the security so held;

(15) insure the assets of the estate against damage, loss and liability and himself against liability as to third persons;

(16) borrow money with or without security to be repaid from the estate assets or otherwise; and advance money for the protection of the estate;

(17) effect a fair and reasonable compromise with any debtor or obligor, or extend, renew or in any manner modify the terms of any obligation owing to the estate. If the personal representative holds a mortgage, pledge or other lien upon property of another person, he may, in lieu of foreclosure, accept a conveyance or transfer of encumbered assets from the owner thereof in satisfaction of the indebtedness secured by lien;

(18) pay taxes, assessments, compensation of the personal representative, and other expenses incident to the administration of the estate;

(19) sell or exercise stock subscription or conversion rights; consent, directly or through a committee or other agent, to the reorganization, consolidation, merger, dissolution, or liquidation of a corporation or other business enterprise;

(20) allocate items of income or expense to either estate income or principal, as permitted or provided by law;

(21) employ persons, including attorneys, auditors, investment advisors, or agents, even if they are associated with the personal representative, to advise or assist the personal representative in the performance of his administrative duties; act without independent investigation upon their recommendations; and instead of acting personally, employ one or more agents to perform any act of administration, whether or not discretionary;

(22) prosecute or defend claims, or proceedings in any jurisdiction for the protection of the estate and of the personal representative in the performance of his duties;

(23) sell, mortgage, or lease any real or personal property of the estate or any interest therein for cash, credit, or for part cash and part credit, and with or without security for unpaid balances;

(24) continue any unincorporated business or venture in which the decedent was engaged at the time of his death (i) in the same business form for a period of not more than 4 months from the date of appointment of a general personal representative if continuation is a reasonable means of preserving the value of the business including good will, (ii) in the same business form for any additional period of time that may be approved by order of the Court in a formal proceeding to which the persons interested in the estate are parties; or (iii) throughout the period of administration if the business is incorporated by the personal representative and if none of the probable distributees of the business who are competent adults object to its incorporation and retention in the estate;

(25) incorporate any business or venture in which the decedent was engaged at the time of his death;

(26) provide for exoneration of the personal representative from personal liability in any contract entered into on behalf of the estate;

(27) satisfy and settle claims and distribute the estate as provided in this Code.

§ 3-716. [Powers and Duties of Successor Personal Representative]

A successor personal representative has the same power and duty as the original personal representative to complete the administration and distribution of the estate, as expeditiously as possible, but he shall not exercise any power expressly made personal to the executor named in the will.

§ 3-717. [Co-representatives; When Joint Action Required.]

If two or more persons are appointed co-representatives and unless the will provides otherwise, the concurrence of all is required on all acts connected with the administration and distribution of the estate. This restriction does not apply when any co-representative receives any receipts for property due the estate, when the concurrence of all cannot readily be obtained in the time reasonably available for emergency action necessary to preserve the estate, or when a co-representative has been delegated to act for the others. Persons dealing with a co-representative if actually unaware that another has been appointed to serve with him or if advised by the personal representative with whom they deal that he has authority to act alone for any of the reasons mentioned herein, are as fully protected as if the person with whom they dealt had been the sole personal representative.

§ 3-718. [Powers of Surviving Personal Representative.]

Unless the terms of the will otherwise provide, every power exercisable by personal co-representatives may be exercised by the one or more remaining after the appointment of one or more is terminated, and if one of 2 or more nominated as co-executors is not appointed, those appointed may exercise all the powers incident to the office.

§ 3-719. [Compensation of Personal Representative.]

A personal representative is entitled to reasonable compensation for his services. If a will provides for compensation of the personal representative and there is no contract with the decedent regarding compensation, he may renounce the provision before qualifying and be entitled to reasonable compensation. A personal representative also may renounce his right to all or any part of the compensation. A written renunciation of fee may be filled with the Court.

§ 3-720. [Expenses in Estate Litigation.]

If any personal representative or person nominated as personal representative defends or prosecutes any proceeding in good faith, whether successful or not he is entitled to receive from the estate his necessary expenses and disbursements including reasonable attorneys' fees incurred.

§ 3-721. [Proceedings for Review of Employment of Agents and Compensation of Personal Representatives and Employees of Estate.]

After notice to all interested persons or on petition of an interested person or on appropriate motion if administration is supervised, the propriety of employment of any person by a personal representative including any attorney, auditor, investment advisor or other specialized agent or assistant, the reasonableness of the compensation of any person so employed, or the reasonableness of the compensation determined by the personal representative for his own services, may be reviewed by the Court. Any person who has received excessive compensation from an estate for services rendered may be ordered to make appropriate refunds.

Part 8
Creditors' Claims

§ 3-801. [Notice to Creditors.]

(a) Unless notice has already been given under this section, a personal representative upon appointment [may] [shall] publish a notice to creditors once a week for three successive weeks in a newspaper of general circulation in the [county] announcing the appointment and the personal representative's address and notifying creditors of the estate to present their claims within four months after the date of the first publication of the notice or be forever barred.

(b) A personal representative may give written notice by mail or other delivery to a creditor, notifying the creditor to present his [or her] claim within four months after the published notice, if given as provided in subsection (a), or within 60 days after the mailing or other delivery of the notice, whichever is later, or be forever barred. Written notice must be the notice described in subsection (a) above or a similar notice.

(c) The personal representative is not liable to a creditor or to a successor of the decedent for giving or failing to give notice under this section.

As amended in 1989.

§ 3-802. [Statutes of Limitations.]

(a) Unless an estate is insolvent, the personal representative, with the consent of all successors whose interests would be affected, may waive any defense of limitations available to the estate. If the defense is not waived, no claim barred by a statute of limitations at the time of the decedent's death may be allowed or paid.

(b) The running of a statute of limitations measured from an event other than death or the giving of notice to creditors is suspended for four months after the decedent's death, but resumes thereafter as to claims not barred by other sections.

(c) For purposes of a statute of limitations, the presentation of a claim pursuant to Section 3-804 is equivalent to commencement of a proceeding on the claim.

As amended in 1989.

§ 3-803. [Limitations on Presentation of Claims.]

(a) All claims against a decedent's estate which arose before the death of the decedent, including claims of the state and any subdivision thereof whether due or to become due, absolute or contingent, liquidated or unliquidated, founded on contract, tort, or other legal basis, if not barred earlier by another statute of limitations or non-claim statute, are barred against the estate, the personal representative, and the heirs and devisees of the decedent, unless presented within the earlier of the following:

(1) one year after the decedent's death; or

(2) the time provided by Section 3-801(b) for creditors who are given actual notice, and within the time provided in 3-801 (a) for all creditors barred by publication.

(b) A claim described in subsection (a) which is barred by the non-claim statute of the decedent's domicile before the giving of notice to creditors in this State is barred in this State.

(c) All claims against a decedent's estate which arise at or after the death of the decedent, including claims of the state and any subdivision thereof, whether due or to become due, absolute or contingent, liquidated or unliquidated, founded on contract, tort, or other legal basis, are barred against the estate, the personal representative, and the heirs and devisees of the decedent, unless presented as follows:

(1) a claim based on a contract with the personal representative, within four months after performance by the personal representative is due; or

(2) any other claim, within the later of four months after it arises, or the time specified in subsection (a)(1).

(d) Nothing in this section affects or prevents:

(1) any proceeding to enforce any mortgage, pledge, or other lien upon property of the estate;

(2) to the limits of the insurance protection only, any proceeding to establish liability of the decedent or the personal representative for which he is protected by liability insurance; or

(3) collection of compensation for services rendered and reimbursement for expenses advanced by the personal representative or by the attorney or accountant for the personal representative of the estate.

As amended in 1989.

§ 3-804. [Manner of Presentation of Claims.]

Claims against a decedent's estate may be presented as follows:

(1) The claimant may deliver or mail to the personal representative a written statement of the claim indicating its basis, the name and address of the claimant, and the amount claimed, or may file a written statement of the claim, in the form prescribed by rule, with the clerk of the Court. The claim is deemed presented on the first to occur of receipt of the written statement of claim by the personal representative, or the filing of the claim with the Court. If a claim is not yet due, the date when it will become due shall be stated. If the claim is contingent or unliquidated, the nature of the uncertainty shall be stated. If the claim is secured, the security shall be described. Failure to describe correctly the security, the nature of any uncertainty, and the due date of a claim not yet due does not invalidate the presentation made.

(2) The claimant may commence a proceeding against the personal representative in any Court where the personal representative may be subjected to jurisdiction, to obtain payment of his claim against the estate, but the commencement of the proceeding must occur within the time limited for presenting the claim. No presentation of claim is required in regard to matters claimed in proceedings against the decedent which were pending at the time of his death.

(3) If a claim is presented under subsection (1), no proceeding thereon may be commenced more than 60 days after the personal representative has mailed a notice of disallowance; but, in the case of a claim which is not presently due or which is contingent or unliquidated, the personal representative may consent to an extension of the 60-day period, or to avoid injustice the Court, on petition, may order an extension of the 60-day period, but in no event shall the extension run beyond the applicable statute of limitations.

§ 3-805. [Classification of Claims.]

(a) If the applicable assets of the estate are insufficient to pay all claims in full, the personal representative shall make payment in the following order:

(1) costs and expenses of administration;

(2) reasonable funeral expenses;

(3) debts and taxes with preference under federal law;

(4) reasonable and necessary medical and hospital expenses of the last illness of the

decedent, including compensation of persons attending him;

(5) debts and taxes with preference under other laws of this state;

(6) all other claims.

(b) No preference shall be given in the payment of any claim over any other claim of the same class, and a claim due and payable shall not be entitled to a preference over claims not due.

§ 3-806. [Allowance of Claims.]

(a) As to claims presented in the manner described in Section 3-804 within the time limit prescribed in 3-803, the personal representative may mail a notice to any claimant stating that the claim has been disallowed. If, after allowing or disallowing a claim, the personal representative changes his decision concerning the claim, he shall notify the claimant. The personal representative may not change a disallowance of a claim after the time for the claimant to file a petition for allowance or to commence a proceeding on the claim has run and the claim has been barred. Every claim which is disallowed in whole or in part by the personal representative is barred so far as not allowed unless the claimant files a petition for allowance in the Court or commences a proceeding against the personal representative not later than 60 days after the mailing of the notice of disallowance or partial allowance if the notice warns the claimant of the impending bar. Failure of the personal representative to mail notice to a claimant of action on his claim for 60 days after the time for original presentation of the claim has expired has the effect of a notice of allowance.

(b) After allowing or disallowing a claim the personal representative may change the allowance or disallowance as hereafter provided. The personal representative may prior to payment change the allowance to a disallowance in whole or in part, but not after allowance by a court order or judgment or an order directing payment of the claim. He shall notify the claimant of the change to disallowance, and the disallowed claim is then subject to bar as provided in subsection (a). The personal representative may change a disallowance to an allowance, in whole or in part, until it is barred under subsection (a); after it is barred, it may be allowed and paid only if the estate is solvent and all successors whose interests would be affected consent.

(c) Upon the petition of the personal representative or a claimant in a proceeding for the purpose, the Court may allow in whole or in part any claim or claims presented to the personal representative or filed with the clerk of the Court in due time and not barred by subsection (a) of this section. Notice in this proceeding shall be given to the claimant, the personal representative and those other persons interested in the estate as the Court may direct by order entered at the time the proceeding is commenced.

(d) A judgment in a proceeding in another court against a personal representative to enforce a claim against a decedent's estate is an allowance of the claim.

(e) Unless otherwise provided in any judgment in another court entered against the personal representative, allowed claims bear interest at the legal rate for the period commencing 60 days after the time for original presentation of the claim has expired unless based on a contract making a provision for interest, in which case they bear interest in accordance with that provision.

As amended in 1987.

§ 3-807. [Payment of Claims.]

(a) Upon the expiration of the earlier of the time limitations provided in Section 3-803 for the presentation of claims, the representative shall proceed to pay the claims allowed against the estate in the order of priority prescribed, after making provision for homestead, family and support allowances, for claims already presented that have not yet been allowed or whose allowance has been appealed, and for unbarred claims that may yet be presented, including costs and expenses of administration. By petition to the Court in a proceeding for the purpose, or by appropriate motion if the administration is supervised, a claimant whose claim has been allowed but not paid may secure an order directing the personal representative to pay the claim to the extent funds of the estate are available to pay it.

(b) The personal representative at any time may pay any just claim that has not been barred, with or without formal presentation, but is personally liable to any other claimant whose claim is allowed and who is injured by its payment if

(1) payment was made before the expiration of the time limit stated in subsection (a) and the personal representative failed to require the payee to give adequate security for the refund of any of the payment necessary to pay other claimants; or

(2) payment was made, due to negligence or willful fault of the personal representative, in such manner as to deprive the injured claimant of priority.

As amended in 1989.

§ 3-808. [Individual Liability of Personal Representative.]

(a) Unless otherwise provided in the contract, a personal representative is not individually liable on a contract properly entered into in his fiduciary capacity in the court of administration of the estate unless he fails to reveal his representative capacity and identify the estate in the contract.

(b) A personal representative is individually liable for obligations arising from ownership or control of the estate or for torts committed in the course of administration of the estate only if he is personally at fault.

(c) Claims based on contracts entered into by a personal representative in his fiduciary capacity, on obligations arising from ownership or control of the estate or on torts committed in the course of estate administration may be asserted against the estate by proceeding against the personal representative in his fiduciary capacity, whether or not the personal representative is individually liable therefor.

(d) Issues of liability as between the estate and the personal representative individually may be determined in a proceeding for accounting, surcharge or indemnification or other appropriate proceeding.

§ 3-809. [Secured Claims.]

Payment of a secured claim is upon the basis of the amount allowed if the creditor surrenders his security; otherwise payment is upon the basis of one of the following:

(1) if the creditor exhausts his security before receiving payment [unless precluded by other law] upon the amount of the claim allowed less the fair value of the security; or

(2) if the creditor does not have the right to exhaust his security or has not done so, upon the amount of the claim allowed less the value of the security determined by converting it into money according to the terms of the agreement pursuant to which the security was delivered to the creditor, or by the creditor and personal representative by agreement, arbitration, compromise or litigation.

§ 3-810. [Claims Not Due and Contingent or Unliquidated Claims.]

(a) If a claim which will become due at a future time or a contingent or unliquidated claim becomes due or certain before the distribution of the estate, and if the claim has been allowed or established by a proceeding, it is paid in the same manner as presently due and absolute claims of the same class.

(b) In other cases the personal representative or, on petition of the personal representative or the claimant in a special proceeding for the purpose, the Court may provide for payment as follows:

(1) if the claimant consents, he may be paid the present or agreed value of the claim, taking any uncertainty into account;

(2) arrangement for future payment, or possible payment, on the happening of the contingency or on liquidation may be made by creating a trust, giving a mortgage, obtaining a bond or security from a distributee, or otherwise.

§ 3-811. [Counterclaims.]

In allowing a claim the personal representative may deduct any counterclaim which the estate has against the claimant. In determining a claim against an estate a Court shall reduce the amount allowed by the amount of any counterclaims and, if the counterclaims exceed the claim, render a judgment against the claimant in the amount of the excess. A counterclaim, liquidated or unliquidated, may arise from a transaction other than that upon which the claim is based. A counter-claim may give rise to relief exceeding in amount or different in kind from that sought in the claim.

§ 3-812. [Execution and Levies Prohibited.]

No execution may issue upon nor may any levy be made against any property of the estate under any judgment against a decedent or a personal representative, but this section shall not be construed to prevent the enforcement of mortgages, pledges or liens upon real or personal property in an appropriate proceeding.

§ 3-813. [Compromise of Claims.]

When a claim against the estate has been presented in any manner, the personal representative may, if it appears for the best interest of the estate, compromise the claim, whether due or not due, absolute or contingent, liquidated or unliquidated.

§ 3-814. [Encumbered Assets.]

If any assets of the estate are encumbered by mortgage, pledge, lien, or other security interest, the personal representative may pay the encumbrance or any part thereof, renew or extend any obligation secured by the encumbrance or convey or transfer the assets to the creditor in satisfaction of his lien, in whole or in part, whether or not the holder of the encumbrance has presented a claim, if it appears to be for the best interest of the estate. Payment of an encumbrance does not increase the share of the distributee entitled to the encumbered assets unless the distributee is entitled to exoneration.

§ 3-815. [Administration in More Than One State; Duty of Personal Representative.]

(a) All assets of estates being administered in this state are subject to all claims, allowances and charges existing or established against the personal representative wherever appointed.

(b) If the estate either in this state or as a whole is insufficient to cover all family exemptions and allowances determined by the law of the decedent's domicile, prior charges and claims, after satisfaction of the exemptions, allowances and charges, each claimant whose claim has been allowed either in this state or elsewhere in administrations of which the personal representative is aware, is entitled to receive payment of an equal proportion of his claim. If a preference or security in regard to a claim is allowed in another jurisdiction but not in this state, the creditor so benefited is to receive dividends from local assets only upon the balance of his claim after deducting the amount of the benefit.

(c) In case the family exemptions and allowances, prior charges and claims of the entire estate exceed the total value of the portions of the estate being administered separately and this state is not the state of the decedent's last domicile, the claims allowed in this state shall be paid their proportion if local assets are adequate for the purpose, and the balance of local assets shall be transferred to the domiciliary personal representative. if local assets are not sufficient to pay all claims allowed in this state the amount to which they are entitled, local assets shall be marshalled so that each claim allowed in this state is paid its proportion as far as possible, after taking into account all dividends on claims allowed in this state from assets in other jurisdictions.

§ 3-816. [Final Distribution to Domiciliary Representative.]

The estate of a non-resident decedent being administered by a personal representative appointed in this state shall, if there is a personal representative of the decedent's domicile willing to receive it, be distributed to the domiciling personal representative for the benefit of the successors of the decedent unless (1) by virtue of the decedent's will, if any, and applicable choice of law rules, the successors are identified pursuant to the local law of this state without reference to the local law of the decedent's domicile; (2) the personal representative of this state, after reasonable inquiry, is unaware of the existence or identity of a domiciliary personal representative; or (3) the Court orders otherwise in a proceeding for a closing order under Section 3-1001 or incident to the closing of a supervised administration. In other cases, distribution of the estate of a decedent shall be made in accordance with the other Parts of this Article.

Part 9
Special Provisions Relating to Distribution

§ 3-901. [Successors' Rights if No Administration.]

In the absence of administration, (the heirs and devisees are entitled to the estate in accordance with the terms of a probated will or the laws of intestate succession. Devisees may establish title by the probated will to devised property. Persons entitled to property by homestead allowance, exemption or intestacy may establish title thereto by proof of the decedent's ownership, his death, and their relationship to the decedent. Successors take subject to all charges incident to administration, including the claims of creditors and allowances of surviving spouse and dependent children, and subject to the rights of others resulting from abatement, retainer, advancement, and adoption.

§ 3-902. [Distribution; Order in Which Assets Appropriated; Abatement.]

(a) except as provided in subsection (b) and except as provided in connection with the share of the surviving spouse who elects to take an elective share, shares of distributees abate, without any preference or priority as between real and personal property, in the following order: (1) property not disposed of by the will; (2) residuary devises; (3) general devises; (4) specific devises. For purposes of abatement, a general devise charged on any specific property or fund is a specific devise to the extent of the value of the property on which it is charged, and upon the failure or insufficiency of the property on which it is charged, a general devise to the extent of the failure or insufficiency. Abatement within each classification is in proportion to the amounts of property each of the beneficiaries would have received if full distribution of the property had been made in accordance with the terms of the will.

(b) If the will expresses an order of abatement, or if the testamentary plan or the express or implied purpose of the devise would be defeated by the order of abatement stated in subsection (a), the shares of the distributees abate as may be found necessary to give effect to the intention of the testator.

(c) If the subject of a preferred devise is sold or used incident to administration, abatement shall be achieved by appropriate adjustments in, or contribution from, other interests in the remaining assets.

[§ 3-902A. [Distribution; Order in Which Assets Appropriated; Abatement.]

(addendum for adoption in community property states)

[(a) and (b) as above.]

(c) If an estate of a decedent consists partly of separate property and partly of community property, the debts and expenses of administration shall be apportioned and charged against the different kinds of property in proportion to the relative value thereof.

[(d) same as (c) in common law state.]]

§ 3-903. [Right of Retainer.]

The amount of a non-contingent indebtedness of a successor to the estate if due, or its present value if not due, shall be offset against the successor's interest; but the successor has the benefit of any defense which would be available to him in a direct proceeding for recovery of the debt.

§ 3-904. [Interest on General Pecuniary Devise.]

General pecuniary devises bear interest at the legal rate beginning one year after the first appointment of a personal representative until payment, unless a contrary intent is indicated by the will.

§ 3-905. [Penalty Clause for Contest.]

A provision in a will purporting to penalize any interested person for contesting the will or instituting other proceedings relating to the estate is unenforceable if probable cause exists for instituting proceedings.

§ 3-906. [Distribution in Kind; Valuation; Method.]

(a) Unless a contrary intention is indicated by the will, the distributable assets of a decedent's estate shall be distributed in kind to the extent possible through application of the following provisions:

(1) A specific devisee is entitled to distribution of the thing devised to him, and a spouse or child who has selected particular assets of an estate as provided in Section 2-402 shall receive the items selected.

(2) Any homestead or family allowance or devise of a stated sum of money may be satisfied in kind provided (i) the person entitled to the payment has not demanded payment in cash; (ii) the property distributed in kind is valued at fair market value as of the date of its distribution, and (iii) no residuary devisee has requested that the asset in question remain a part of the residue of the estate.

(3) For the purpose of valuation under paragraph (2) securities regularly traded on recognized exchanges, if distributed in kind, are valued at the price for the last sale of like securities traded on the business day prior to distribution, or if there was no sale on that day, at the median between amounts bid and offered at the close of that day. Assets consisting of sums owed the decedent or the estate by solvent debtors as to which there is no known dispute or defense are valued at the sum due with accrued interest or discounted to the date of distribution For assets which do not have readily ascertainable values, a valuation as of a date not more than 30 days prior to the date of distribution, if otherwise reasonable, controls. For purposes of facilitating distribution, the personal representative may ascertain the value of the assets as of the time of the proposed distribution in any reasonable way, including the employment of qualified appraisers, even if the assets may have been previously appraised.

(4) The residuary estate shall be distributed in any equitable manner.

(b) After the probable charges against the estate are known, the personal representative may mail or deliver a proposal for distribution to all persons who have a right to object to the proposed distribution. The right of any distributee to object to the proposed distribution on the basis of the kind or value of asset he is to receive, if not waived earlier in writing, terminates if he fails to object in writing received by the personal representative within 30 days after mailing or delivery of the proposal.

As amended in 1987.

§ 3-907. [Distribution in Kind; Evidence.]

If distribution in kind is made, the personal representative shall execute an instrument or deed of distribution assigning, transferring or releasing the assets to the distributee as evidence of the distributee's title to the property.

§ 3-908. [Distribution; Right or Title of Distributee.]

Proof that a distributee has received an instrument or deed of distribution of assets in kind, or payment in distribution, from a personal representative, is conclusive evidence that the distributee has succeeded to the interest of the estate in the distributed assets, as against all persons interested in the estate, except that the personal representative may recover the assets or their value if the distribution was improper.

§ 3-909. [Improper Distribution; Liability of Distributee.]

Unless the distribution or payment no longer can be questioned because of adjudication, estoppel, or limitation, a distributee of property improperly distributed or paid, or a claimant who was improperly paid, is liable to return the property improperly received and its income since distribution if he has the property. If he does not have the property, then he is liable to return the value as of the date of disposition of the property improperly received and its income and gain received by him.

§ 3-910. [Purchasers from Distributees Protected.]

If property distributed in kind or a security interest therein is acquired for value by a purchaser from or lender to a distributee who has received an instrument or deed of distribution from the personal representative, or is so acquired by a purchaser from or lender to a transferee from such distributee, the purchaser or lender takes title free of rights of any interested person in the estate and incurs no personal liability to the estate, or to any interested person, whether or not the distribution was proper or supported by court order or the authority of the personal representative was terminated before execution of the instrument or deed. This section protects a purchaser from or lender to a distributee who, as personal representative, has executed a deed of distribution to himself, as well as a purchaser from or lender to any other distributee or his transferee. To be protected under this provision, a purchaser or lender need not inquire whether a personal representative acted properly in making the distribution in kind, even if the personal representative and the distributee are the same person, or whether the authority of the personal representative had terminated before the distribution. Any recorded instrument described in this section on which a state documentary fee is noted pursuant to [insert appropriate reference] shall be prima facie evidence that such transfer was made for value.

§ 3-911. [Partition for Purpose of Distribution.]

When two or more heirs or devisees are entitled to distribution of undivided interests in any real or personal property of the estate, the personal representative or one or more of the heirs or devisees may petition the Court prior to the formal or informal closing of the estate, to make partition. After notice to the interested heirs or devisees, the Court shall partition the property in the same manner as provided by the law for civil actions of partition. The Court may direct the personal representative to sell any property which cannot be partitioned without prejudice to the owners and which cannot conveniently be allotted to any one party.

§ 3-912. [Private Agreements Among Successors to Decedent Binding on Personal Representative.]

Subject to the rights of creditors and taxing authorities, competent successors may agree among themselves to alter the interests, shares or amounts to which they are entitled under the will of the decedent or under the laws of intestacy, in any way that they provide in a written contract executed by all who are affected by its provisions. The personal representative shall abide by the terms of the agreement subject to his obligation to administer the estate for the benefit of creditors, to pay all taxes and costs of administration, and to carry out the responsibilities of his office for the benefit of any successors of the decedent who are not parties. Personal representatives of decedents' estates are not required to see to the performance of trusts if the trustee thereof is another person who is willing to accept the trust. Accordingly, trustees of a testamentary trust are successors for the purposes of this section. Nothing herein relieves trustees of any duties owed to beneficiaries of trusts.

§ 3-913. [Distributions to Trustee.]

(a) Before distributing to a trustee, the personal representative may require that the trust be registered if the state in which it is to be administered provides for registration and that the trustee inform the beneficiaries as provided in Section 7-303.

(b) If the trust instrument does not excuse the trustee from giving bond, the personal representative may petition the appropriate Court to require that the trustee post bond if he apprehends that distribution might jeopardize the interests of persons who are not able to protect themselves, and he may withhold distribution until the Court has acted.

(c) No inference of negligence on the part of the personal representative shall be drawn from his failure to exercise the authority conferred by subsections (a) and (b).

§ 3-914. [Disposition of Unclaimed Assets.]

(a) If an heir, devisee or claimant cannot be found, the personal representative shall distribute the share of the missing person to his conservator, if any, otherwise to the state treasurer to become a part of the state escheat fund.

(b) The money received by [state treasurer] shall be paid to the person entitled on proof of his right thereto or, if the [state treasurer] refuses or fails to pay, the person may petition the Court which appointed the personal representative, whereupon the Court upon notice to the [state treasurer] may determine the person entitled to the money and order the [treasurer] to pay it to him. No interest is allowed thereon and the heir, devisee or claimant shall pay all costs and expenses incident to the proceeding. If no petition is made to the [court] within 8 years after payment to the [state treasurer], the right of recovery is barred.]

§ 3-915. [Distribution to Person Under Disability.]

(a) A personal representative may discharge his obligation to distribute to any person under legal disability by distributing in a manner expressly provided in the will.

(b) Unless contrary to an express provision in the will, the personal representative may discharge his obligation to distribute to a minor or person under other disability as authorized by Section 5-501 or any other statute. If the personal representative knows that a conservator has been appointed or that a proceeding for appointment of a conservator is pending, the personal representative is authorized to distribute only to the conservator.

(c) If the heir or devisee is under disability other than minority, the personal representative is authorized to distribute to:

(1) an attorney in fact who has authority under a power of attorney to receive property for that person; or

(2) the spouse, parent or other close relative with whom the person under disability resides if the distribution is of amounts not exceeding [$10,000] a year, or property not exceeding [$10,000] in value, unless the court authorizes a larger amount or greater value.

Persons receiving money or property for the disabled person are obligated to apply the money or property to the support of that person, but may not pay themselves except by way of reimbursement for out of pocket expenses for goods and services necessary for the support of the disabled person. Excess sums must be preserved for future support of the disabled person. The personal representative is not responsible for the proper application of money or property distributed pursuant to this subsection.

As amended in 1987.

§ 3-916. [Apportionment of Estate Taxes.]

(a) For purposes of this section:

(1) "estate" means the gross estate of a decedent as determined for the purpose of federal estate tax and the estate tax payable to this state;

(2) "person" means any individual, partnership, association, joint stock company, corporation, government, political subdivision, governmental agency, or local governmental agency;

(3) "person interested in the estate" means any person entitled to receive, or who has received, from a decedent or by reason of the death of a decedent any property or interest therein included in the decedent's estate. It includes a personal representative, conservator, and trustee;

(4) "state" means any state, territory, or possession of the United States, the District of Columbia, and the Commonwealth of Puerto Rico;

(5) "tax" means the federal estate tax and the additional inheritance tax imposed by and interest and penalties imposed in addition to the tax;

(6) "fiduciary" means personal representative or trustee.

(b) Except as provided in subsection (i) and, unless the will otherwise provides, the tax shall be apportioned among all persons interested in the estate. The apportionment is to be made in the proportion that the value of the interest of each person interested in the estate bears to the total value of the interests of all persons interested in the estate. The values used in determining the tax are to be used for that purpose. If the decedent's will directs a method of apportionment of tax different from the method described in this Code, the method described in the will controls.

(c)(1) The Court in which venue lies for the administration of the estate of a decedent, on petition for the purpose may determine the apportionment of the tax.

(2) If the Court finds that it is inequitable to apportion interest and penalties in the manner provided in subsection (b), because of special circumstances, it may direct apportionment thereof in the manner it finds equitable.

(3) If the Court finds that the assessment of penalties and interest assessed in relation to the tax is due to delay caused by the negligence of the fiduciary, the Court may charge him with the amount of the assessed penalties and interest.

(4) In any action to recover from any person interested in the estate the amount of the tax apportioned to the person in accordance with this Code the determination of the Court in respect thereto shall be prima facie correct.

(d)(1) The personal representative or other person in possession of the property of the decedent required to pay the tax may withhold from any property distributable to any person interested in the estate, upon its distribution to him, the amount of tax attributable to his interest. If the property in possession of the personal representative or other person required to pay the tax and distributable to any person interested in the estate is insufficient to satisfy the proportionate amount of the tax determined to be due from the person, the personal representative or other person required to pay the tax may recover the deficiency from the person interested in the estate. If the property is not in the possession of the personal representative or the other person required to pay the tax, the personal representative or the other person required to pay the tax may recover from any person interested in the estate the amount of the tax apportioned to the person in accordance with this Act.

(2) If property held by the personal representative is distributed prior to final apportionment of the tax, the distributee shall provide a bond or other security for the apportionment liability in the form and amount prescribed by the personal representative.

(e)(1) In making an apportionment, allowances shall be made for any exemptions granted, any classification made of persons interested in the estate and for any deductions and credits allowed by the law imposing the tax.

(2) Any exemption or deduction allowed by reason of the relationship of any person to the decedent or by reason of the purposes of the gift inures to the benefit of the person bearing such relationship or receiving the gift; but if an interest is subject to a prior present interest which is not allowable as a deduction, the tax apportionable against the present interest shall be paid from principal.

(3) Any deduction for property previously taxed and any credit for gift taxes or death taxes of a foreign country paid by the decedent or his estate inures to the proportionate benefit of all persons liable to apportionment.

(4) Any credit for inheritance, succession or estate taxes or taxes in the nature thereof applicable to property or interests includable in the estate, inures to the benefit of the persons or interests chargeable with the payment thereof to the extent proportionately that the credit reduces the tax.

(5) To the extent that property passing to or in trust for a surviving spouse or any charitable, public or similar purpose is not an allowable deduction for purposes of the tax solely by reason of an inheritance tax or other death tax imposed

upon and deductible from the property, the property is not included in the computation provided for in subsection (b) hereof, and to that extent no apportionment is made against the property. The sentence immediately preceding does not apply to any case if the result would be to deprive the estate of a deduction otherwise allowable under Section 2053(d) of the Internal Revenue Code of 1954, as amended, of the United States, relating to deduction for state death taxes on transfers for public, charitable, or religious uses.

(f) No interest in income and no estate for years or for life or other temporary interest in any property or fund is subject to apportionment as between the temporary interest and the remainder. The tax on the temporary interest and the tax, if any, on the remainder is chargeable against the corpus of the property or funds subject to the temporary interest and remainder.

(g) Neither the personal representative nor other person required to pay the tax is under any duty to institute any action to recover from any person interested in the estate the amount of the tax apportioned to the person until the expiration of the 3 months next following final determination of the tax. A personal representative or other person required to pay the tax who institutes the action within a reasonable time after the 3 months' period is not subject to any liability or surcharge because any portion of the tax apportioned to any person interested in the estate was collectible at a time following the death of the decedent but thereafter became uncollectible. If the personal representative or other person required to pay the tax cannot collect from any person interested in the estate the amount of the tax apportioned to the person, the amount not recoverable shall be equitably apportioned among the other persons interested in the estate who are subject to apportionment.

(h) A personal representative acting in another state or a person required to pay the tax domiciled in another state may institute an action in the courts of this state and may recover a proportionate amount of the federal estate tax, of an estate tax payable to another state or of a death duty due by a decedent's estate to another state, from a person interested in the estate who is either domiciled in this state or who owns property in this state subject to attachment or execution. For the purposes of the action the determination of apportionment by the Court having jurisdiction of the administration of the decedent's estate in the other state is prima facie correct.

(i) If the liabilities of persons interested in the estate as prescribed by this act differ from those which result under the federal estate tax law, the liabilities imposed by the federal law will control and the balance of this Section shall apply as if the resulting liabilities had been prescribed herein.

Part 10
Closing Estates

§ 3-1001. [Formal Proceedings Terminating Administration; Testate or Intestate; Order of General Protection.]

(a) A personal representative or any interested person may petition for an order of complete settlement of the estate. The personal representative may petition at any time, and any other interested person may petition after one year from the appointment of the original personal representative except that no petition under this section may be entertained until the time for presenting claims which arose prior to the death of the decedent has expired. The petition may request the Court to determine testacy, if not previously determined, to consider the final account or compel or approve an accounting and distribution, to construe any will or determine heirs and adjudicate the final settlement and distribution of the estate. After notice to all interested persons and hearing the Court may enter an order or orders, on appropriate conditions, determining the persons entitled to distribution of the estate, and, as circumstances require, approving settlement and directing or approving distribution of the estate and discharging the personal representative from further claim or demand of any interested person.

(b) If one or more heirs or devisees were omitted as parties in, or were not given notice of, a previous formal testacy proceeding, the Court, on proper petition for an order of complete settlement of the estate under this section, and after notice to the omitted or unnotified persons and other interested parties determined to be interested on the assumption that the previous order concerning testacy is conclusive as to those given notice of the earlier proceeding, may determine testacy as it affects the omitted persons and confirm or alter the previous order of testacy as it affects all interested persons as appropriate in the light of the new proofs. In the absence of objection by an omitted or unnotified person, evidence received in the original testacy proceeding shall constitute prima facie proof of due execution of any will previously admitted to probate, or of the fact that the decedent left no valid will if the prior proceedings determined this fact.

§ 3-1002. [Formal Proceedings Terminating Testate Administration; Order Construing Will Without Adjudicating Testacy.]

A personal representative administering an estate under an informally probated will or any devisee under an informally probated will may petition for an order of settlement of the estate which will not adjudicate the testacy status of the decedent. The personal representative may petition at any time, and a devisee may petition after one year, from the appointment of the original personal representative, except that no petition under this section may be entertained until the time for presenting claims which arose prior to the death of the decedent has expired. The petition may request the Court to consider the final account or compel or approve an accounting and distribution, to construe the will and adjudicate final settlement and distribution of the estate. After notice to all devisees and the personal representative and hearing, the Court may enter an order or orders, on appropriate conditions, determining the persons entitled to distribution of the estate under the will, and, as circumstances require, approving settlement and directing or approving distribution of the estate and discharging the personal representative from further claim or demand of any devisee who is a party to the proceeding and those he represents. If it appears that a part of the estate is intestate, the proceedings shall be dismissed or amendments made to meet the provisions of Section 3-1001.

§ 3-1003. [Closing Estates; By Sworn Statement of Personal Representative.]

(a) Unless prohibited by order of the Court and except for estates being administered in supervised administration proceedings, a personal representative may close an estate by filing with the court no earlier than six months after the date of original appointment of a general personal representative for the estate, a verified statement stating that the personal representatives or a previous personal representative, has:

(1) determined that the time limited for presentation of creditors' claims has expired.

(2) fully administered the estate of the decedent by making payment, settlement or other disposition of all claims which were presented, expenses of administration and estate, inheritance and other death taxes, except as specified in the statement, and that the assets of the estate have been distributed to the persons entitled. If any claims remain undischarged, the statement must state whether the personal representative has distributed the estate subject to possible liability with the agreement of the distributees or state in detail other arrangements that have been made to accommodate outstanding liabilities; and

(3) sent a copy of the statement to all distributees of the estate and to all creditors or other claimants of whom the personal representative is aware whose claims are neither paid nor barred and has furnished a full account in writing of the personal representative's administration to the distributees whose interests are affected thereby.

(b) If no proceedings involving the personal representative are pending in the Court one year after the closing statement is filed, the appointment of the personal representative terminates.

As amended in 1989.

§ 3-1004. [Liability of Distributees to Claimants.]

After assets of an estate have been distributed and subject to Section 3-1006, an undischarged claim not barred may be prosecuted in a proceeding against one or more distributees. No distributee shall be liable to claimants for amounts received as exempt property, homestead or family allowances, or for amounts in excess of the value of his distribution as of the time of distribution. As between distributees, each shall bear the cost of satisfaction of unbarred claims as if the claim had been satisfied in the course of administration. Any distributee who shall have failed to notify other distributees of the demand made upon him by the claimant in sufficient time to permit them to join in any proceeding in which the claim was asserted against him loses his right of contribution against other distributees.

§ 3-1005. [Limitations on Proceedings Against Personal Representative.]

Unless previously barred by adjudication and except as provided in the closing statement, the rights of successors and of creditors whose claims have not otherwise been barred against the personal representatives for breach of fiduciary duty are barred unless a proceeding to assert the same is commenced within 6 months after the filing of the closing statement. The rights thus barred do not include rights to recover from a personal representative for fraud, misrepresentation, or inadequate disclosure related to the settlement of the decedent's estate.

§ 3-1006. [Limitations on Actions and Proceedings Against Distributees.]

Unless previously adjudicated in a formal testacy proceeding or in a proceeding settling the accounts of a personal representative or otherwise barred, the claim of a claimant to recover from a distributee who is liable to pay the claim, and the right of an heir or devisee, or of a successor personal representative acting in their behalf, to recover property improperly distributed or its value from any distributee is forever barred at the later of three years after the decedent's death or one year after the time of its distribution thereof, but all claims of creditors of the decedent, are barred one year after the decedent's death. This section does not bar an action to recover property or value received as the result of fraud.

Amended in 1989.

§ 3-1007. [Certificate Discharging Liens Securing Fiduciary Performance.]

After his appointment has terminated, the personal representative, his sureties, or any successor of either, upon the filing of a verified application showing, so far as is known by the applicant, that no action concerning the estate is pending in any court, is entitled to receive a certificate from the Registrar that the personal representative appears to have fully administered the estate in question. The certificate evidences discharge of any lien on any property given to secure the obligation of the personal representative in lieu of bond or any surety, but does not preclude action against the personal representative or the surety.

§ 3-1008. [Subsequent Administration.]

If other property of the estate is discovered after an estate has been settled and the personal representative discharged or after one year after a closing statement has been filed, the Court upon petition of any interested person and upon notice as it directs may appoint the same or a successor personal representative to administer the subsequently discovered estate. If a new appointment is made, unless the Court orders otherwise, the provisions of this Code apply as appropriate; but no claim previously barred may be asserted in the subsequent administration.

Part 11
Compromise of Controversies

§ 3-1101. [Effect of Approval of Agreements Involving Trusts, Inalienable Interests, or Interests of Third Persons.]

A compromise of any controversy as to admission to probate of any instrument offered for formal probate as the will of a decedent, the construction, validity, or effect of any probated will, the rights or interests in the estate of the decedent, of any successor, or the administration of the estate, if approved in a formal proceeding in the Court for that purpose, is binding on all the parties thereto including those unborn, unascertained or who could not be located. An approved compromise is binding even though it may affect a trust or an inalienable interest. A compromise does not impair the rights of creditors or of taxing authorities who are not parties to it.

§ 3-1102. [Procedure for Securing Court Approval of Compromise.]

The procedure for securing court approval of a compromise is as follows:

(1) The terms of the compromise shall be set forth in an agreement in writing which shall be executed by all competent persons and parents acting for any minor child having beneficial interests or having claims which will or may be affected by the compromise. Execution is not required by any person whose identity cannot be ascertained or whose whereabouts is unknown and cannot reasonably be ascertained.

(2) Any interested person, including the personal representative or a trustee, then may submit the agreement to the Court for its approval and for execution by the personal representative, the trustee of every affected testamentary trust, and other fiduciaries and representatives.

(3) After notice to all interested persons or their representatives, including the personal representative of the estate and all affected trustees of trusts, the Court, if it finds that the contest or controversy is in good faith and that the effect of the agreement upon the interests of persons represented by fiduciaries or other representatives is just and reasonable, shall make an order approving the agreement and directing all fiduciaries subject to Its jurisdiction to execute the agreement. Minor children represented only by their parents may be bound only if their parents join with other competent persons in execution of the compromise. Upon the making of the order and the execution of the agreement, all further disposition of the estate is in accordance with the terms of the agreement.

Part 12
Collection of Personal Property by Affidavit and Summary Administration Procedure for Small Estates

§ 3-1201. [Collection of Personal Property by Affidavit.]

(a) Thirty days after the death of a decedent, any person indebted to the decedent or having possession of tangible personal property or an instrument evidencing a debt, obligation, stock or chose in action belonging to the decedent shall make payment of the indebtedness or deliver the tangible personal property or an instrument evidencing a debt, obligation, stock or chose in action to a person claiming to be the successor of the decedent upon being presented an affidavit made by or on behalf of the successor stating that:

(1) the value of the entire estate, wherever located, less liens and encumbrances, does not exceed $5,000;

(2) 30 days have elapsed since the death of the decedent;

(3) no application or petition for the appointment of a personal representative is pending or has been granted in any jurisdiction; and

(4) the claiming successor is entitled to payment or delivery of the property.

(b) A transfer agent of any security shall change the registered ownership on the books of a corporation from the decedent to the successor or successors upon the presentation of an affidavit as provided in subsection (a).

§ 3-1202. [Effect of Affidavit.]

The person paying, delivering, transferring, or issuing personal property or the evidence thereof pursuant to affidavit is discharged and released to the same extent as if he dealt with a personal representative of the decedent. He is not required to see to the application of the personal property or evidence thereof or to inquire into the truth of any statement in the affidavit. If any person to whom an affidavit is delivered refuses to pay, deliver, transfer, or issue any personal property or evidence thereof, it may be recovered or its payment, delivery, transfer, or issuance compelled upon proof of their right in a proceeding brought for the purpose by or on behalf of the persons entitled thereto. Any person to whom payment, delivery, transfer or issuance is made is answerable and accountable therefor to any personal representative of the estate or to any other person having a superior right.

§ 3-1203. [Small Estates; Summary Administrative Procedure.]

If it appears from the inventory and appraisal that the value of the entire estate, less liens and encumbrances, does not exceed homestead allowance, exempt property, family allowance, costs and expenses of administration, reasonable funeral expenses, and reasonable and necessary medical and hospital expenses of the last illness of the decedent, the personal representative, without giving notice to creditors, may immediately disburse and distribute the estate to the persons entitled thereto and file a closing statement as provided in Section 3-1204.

§ 3-1204. [Small Estates; Closing by Sworn Statement of Personal Representative.]

(a) Unless prohibited by order of the Court and except for estates being administered by supervised personal representatives, a personal representative may close an estate administered under the summary procedures of Section 3-1203 by filing with the Court, at any time after disbursement and distribution of the estate, a verified statement stating that:

(1) to the best knowledge of the personal representative, the value of the entire estate, less liens and encumbrances, did not exceed homestead allowance, exempt property, family allowance, costs and expenses of administration, reasonable funeral expenses, and reasonable, necessary medical and hospital expenses of the last illness of the decedent;

(2) the personal representative has fully administered the estate by disbursing and distributing it to the persons entitled thereto; and

(3) the personal representative has sent a copy of the closing statement to all distributees of the estate and to all creditors or other claimants of whom he is aware whose claims are neither paid nor barred and has furnished a full account in writing of his administration to the distributees whose interests are affected.

(b) If no actions or proceedings involving the personal representative are pending in the Court one year after the closing statement is filed, the appointment of the personal representative terminates.

(c) A closing statement filed under this section has the same effect as one filed under Section 3-1003.

ARTICLE IV
FOREIGN PERSONAL REPRESENTATIVES; ANCILLARY ADMINISTRATION

Part 1
Definitions

§ 4-101. [Definitions.]

In this Article

(1) "local administration" means administration by a personal representative appointed in this state pursuant to appointment proceedings described in Article III.

(2) "local personal representative" includes any personal representative appointed in this state pursuant to appointment proceedings described in Article III and excludes foreign personal representatives who acquire the power of a local personal representative pursuant to Section 4-205.

(3) "resident creditor" means a person domiciled in, or doing business in this state, who is, or could be, a claimant against an estate of a nonresident decedent.

Part 2
Powers of Foreign Personal Representatives

§ 4-201. [Payment of Debt and Delivery of Property to Domiciliary Foreign Personal Representative Without Local Administration.]

At any time after the expiration of sixty days from the death of a nonresident decedent, any person indebted to the estate of the nonresident decedent or having possession or control of personal property, or of an instrument evidencing a debt, obligation, stock or chose in action belonging to the estate of the nonresident decedent may pay the debt, deliver the personal property, or the instrument evidencing the debt, obligation, stock or chose in action, to the domiciliary foreign personal representative of the nonresident decedent upon being presented with proof of his appointment and an affidavit made by or on behalf of the representative stating:

(1) the date of the death of the nonresident decedent,

(2) that no local administration, or application or petition therefor, is pending in this state,

(3) that the domiciliary foreign personal representative is entitled to payment or delivery.

§ 4-202. [Payment or Delivery Discharges.]

Payment or delivery made in good faith on the basis of the proof of authority and affidavit releases the debtor or person having possession of the personal property to the same extent as if payment or delivery had been made to a local personal representative.

§ 4-203. [Resident Creditor Notice.]

Payment or delivery under Section 4-201 may not be made if a resident creditor of the nonresident decedent has notified the debtor of the nonresident decedent or the person having possession of the personal property belonging to the nonresident decedent that the debt should not be paid nor the property delivered to the domiciliary foreign personal representative.

§ 4-204. [Proof of Authority-Bond.]

If no local administration or application or petition therefor is pending in this state, a domiciliary foreign personal representative may file with a Court in this State in a [county] in which property belonging to the decedent is located, authenticated copies of his appointment and of any official bond he has given.

§ 4-205. [Powers.]

A domiciliary foreign personal representative who has complied with Section 4-204 may exercise as to assets in this state all powers of a local personal representative and may maintain actions and proceedings in this state subject to any conditions imposed upon nonresident parties generally.

§ 4-206. [Power of Representatives in Transition.]

The power of a domiciliary foreign personal representative under Section 4-201 or 4-205 shall be exercised only if there is no administration or application therefor pending in this state. An application or petition for local administration of the estate terminates the power of the foreign personal representative to act under Section 4-205, but the local Court may allow the foreign personal representative to exercise limited powers only to preserve the estate. No person who, before receiving actual notice of a pending local administration, has changed his position in reliance upon the powers of a foreign personal representative shall be prejudiced by reason of the application or petition for, or grant of, local administration. The local personal representative is subject to all duties and obligations which have accrued by virtue of the exercise of the powers by the foreign personal representative and may be substituted for him in any action or proceedings in this state.

§ 4-207. [Ancillary and Other Local Administrations; Provisions Governing.]

In respect to a non-resident decedent, the provisions of Article III of this Code govern (1) proceedings, if any, in a Court of this state for probate of the will, appointment, removal, supervision, and discharge of the local personal representative, and any other order concerning the estate; and (2) the status, powers, duties and liabilities of any local personal representative and the rights of claimants, purchasers, distributees and others in regard to a local administration.

Part 3
Jurisdiction Over Foreign Representatives

§ 4-301. [Jurisdiction by Act of Foreign Personal Representative.]

A foreign personal representative submits personally to the jurisdiction of the Courts of this state in any proceeding relating to the estate by (1) filing authenticated copies of his appointment as provided in Section 4-204, (2) receiving payment of money or taking delivery of personal property under Section 4-201, or (3) doing any act as a personal representative in this state which would have given the state jurisdiction over him as an individual. Jurisdiction under (2) is limited to the money or value of personal property collected.

§ 4-302. [Jurisdiction by Act of Decedent.]

In addition to jurisdiction conferred by Section 4-301, a foreign personal representative is subject to the jurisdiction of the courts of this state to the same extent that his decedent was subject to jurisdiction immediately prior to death.

§ 4-303. [Service on Foreign Personal Representative.]

(a) Service of process may be made upon the foreign personal representative by registered or certified mail, addressed lo his last reasonably ascertainable address, requesting a return receipt signed by addressee only. Notice by ordinary first class mail is sufficient if registered or certified mail service to the addressee is unavailable. Service may be made upon a foreign personal representative in the manner in which service could have been made under other laws of this state on either the foreign personal representative or his decedent immediately prior to death.

(b) If service is made upon a foreign personal representative as provided in subsection (a), he shall be allowed at least [30] days within which to appear or respond.

Part 4
Judgments and Personal Representative

§ 4-401. [Effect of Adjudication For or Against Personal Representative.]

An adjudication rendered in any jurisdiction in favor of or against any personal representative of the estate is as binding on the local personal representative as if he were a party to the adjudication.

ARTICLE V
PROTECTION OF PERSONS UNDER DISABILITY AND THEIR PROPERTY

Part 1
General Provisions and Definitions

§ 5-101. [Facility of Payment or Delivery.]

(a) Any person under a duty to pay or deliver money or personal property to a minor may perform the duty, in amounts not exceeding $5,000 a year, by paying or delivering the money or property to:

(1) the minor if 18 or more years of age or married;

(2) any person having the care and custody of the minor with whom the minor resides;

(3) a guardian of the minor; or

(4) a financial institution incident to a deposit in a state or federally insured savings account or certificate in the sole name of the minor with notice of the deposit to the minor.

(b) This section does not apply if the person making payment or delivery knows that a conservator has been appointed or proceedings for appointment of a conservator of the estate of the minor are pending.

(c) Persons, other than the minor or any financial institution, receiving money or property for a minor, are obligated to apply the money to the support and education of the minor, but may not pay themselves except by way of reimbursement for out-of-pocket expenses for goods and services necessary for the minor's support. Any excess sums must be preserved for future support and education of the minor and any balance not so used and any property received for the minor must be turned over to the minor when majority is attained. A person who pays or delivers money or property in accordance with provisions of this section is not responsible for the proper application thereof.

§ 5-102. [Delegation of Powers by Parent or Guardian.]

A parent or guardian of a minor or incapacitated person, by a properly executed power of attorney, may delegate to another person, for a period not exceeding 6 months, any power regarding care, custody or property of the minor child or ward, except the power to consent to marriage or adoption of a minor ward.

§ 5-103. [General Definitions.]

As used in Parts 1, 2, 3 and 4 of this Article:

(1) "Claims," in respect to a protected person, includes liabilities of the protected person, whether arising in contract, tort, or otherwise, and liabilities of the estate which arise at or after the appointment of a conservator, including expenses of administration.

(2) "Court" means the [__________] court.

(3) "Conservator" means a person who is appointed by a Court to manage the estate of a protected person and includes a limited conservator described in Section 5-419(a).

(4) "Disability" means cause for a protective order as described in Section 5-401.

(5) "Estate" includes the property of the person whose affairs are subject to this Article.

(6) "Guardian" means a person who has qualified as a guardian of a minor or incapacitated person pursuant to parental or spousal nomination or court appointment and includes a limited guardian as described in Sections 5-209(e) and 5-306(c), but excludes one who is merely a guardian ad litem.

(7) "Incapacitated person" means any person who is impaired by reason of mental illness, mental deficiency, physical illness or disability, advanced age, chronic use of drugs, chronic intoxication, or other cause (except minority) to the extent of lacking sufficient understanding or capacity to make or communicate responsible decisions.

(8) "Lease" includes an oil, gas, or other mineral lease.

(9) "Letters" includes letters of guardianship and letters of conservatorship.

(10) "Minor" means a person who is under [21] years of age.

(11) "Mortgage" means any conveyance, agreement, or arrangement in which property is used as collateral.

(12) "Organization" includes a corporation, business trust, estate, trust, partnership, association, 2 or more persons having a joint or common interest, government, governmental subdivision or agency, or any other legal entity

(13) "Parent" includes any person entitled to take, or who would be entitled to take if the child

died without a will, as a parent by intestate succession from the child whose relationship is in question and excludes any person who is only a stepparent, foster parent, or grandparent.

(14) "Person" means an individual or an organization.

(15) "Petition" means a written request to the Court for an order after notice.

(16) "Proceeding" includes action at law and suit in equity.

(17) "Property" includes both real and personal property or any interest therein and means anything that may be the subject of ownership.

(18) "Protected person" means a minor or other person for whom a conservator has been appointed or other protective order has been made as provided in Sections 5-407 and 5-408.

(19) "Protective proceeding" means a proceeding under the provisions of Part 4 of this Article.

(20) "Security" includes any note, stock, treasury stock, bond, debenture, evidence of indebtedness, certificate of interest or participation in an oil, gas, or mining title or lease or in payments out of production under such a title or lease, collateral trust certificate, transferable share, pivoting trust certificate or, in general, any interest or instrument commonly known as a security, or any certificate of interest or participation, any temporary or interim certificate, receipt or certificate of deposit for, or any warrant or right to subscribe to or purchase any of the foregoing.

(21) "Visitor" means a person appointed in a guardianship or protective proceeding who is trained in law, nursing, or social work, is an officer, employee, or special appointee of the Court, and has no personal interest in the proceeding.

(22) "Ward" means a person for whom a guardian has been appointed. A "minor ward" is a minor for whom a guardian has been appointed.

§ 5-104. [Request for Notice; Interested Person.]

Upon payment of any required fee, an interested person who desires to be notified before any order is made in a guardianship proceeding, including any proceeding subsequent to the appointment of a guardian under Section 5-312, or in a protective proceeding under Section 5-401, may file a request for notice with the clerk of the court in which the proceeding is pending. The clerk shall mail a copy of the request to the guardian and to the conservator if one has been appointed. A request is not effective unless it contains a statement showing the interest of the person making it and the address of that person or an attorney to whom notice is to be given. The request is effective only as to proceedings occurring after the filing. Any governmental agency paying or planning to pay benefits to the person to be protected is an interested person in protective proceedings.

Part 2
Guardians of Minors

§ 5-201. [Appointment and Status of Guardian of Minor.]

A person may become a guardian of a minor by parental appointment or upon appointment by the Court. The guardianship status continues until terminated, without regard to the location from time to time of the guardian or minor ward.

§ 5-202. [Parental Appointment of Guardian for Minor.]

(a) The parent of an unmarried minor may appoint a guardian for the minor by will, or other writing signed by the parent and attested by at least 2 witnesses.

(b) Subject to the right of the minor under Section 5-203, if both parents are dead or incapacitated or the surviving parent has no parental rights or has been adjudged to be incapacitated, a parental appointment becomes effective when the guardian's acceptance is filed in the Court in which a nominating instrument is probated, or, in the case of a nontestamentary nominating instrument, in the Court at the place where the minor resides or is present. If both parents are dead, an effective appointment by the parent who died later has priority.

(c) A parental appointment effected by filing the guardian's acceptance under a will probated in the state of the testator's domicile is effective in this State.

(d) Upon acceptance of appointment, the guardian shall give written notice of acceptance to the minor and to the person having the minor's care or the minor's nearest adult relative.

§ 5-203. [Objection by Minor of Fourteen or Older to Parental Appointment.]

A minor 14 or more years of age who is the subject of a parental appointment may prevent the appointment or cause it to terminate by filing in the Court in which the nominating instrument is filed a written objection to the appointment before it is accepted or within 30 days after receiving notice of its acceptance. An objection may be withdrawn. An objection does not preclude appointment by the Court in a proper proceeding of the parental nominee or any other suitable person.

§ 5-204. [Court Appointment of Guardian of Minor; Conditions for Appointment.]

(a) The Court may appoint a guardian for an unmarried minor if all parental rights have been terminated or suspended by circumstances or prior Court order. A guardian appointed pursuant to

Section 5-202 whose appointment has not been prevented or nullified under Section 5-203 has priority over any guardian who may be appointed by the Court, but the Court may proceed with another appointment upon a finding that the parental nominee has failed to accept the appointment within 30 days after notice of the guardianship proceeding.

(b) If necessary, and on appropriate petition or application, the Court may appoint a temporary guardian who shall have the full authority of a general guardian of a minor, but the authority of a temporary guardian may not last longer than 6 months. The appointment of a temporary guardian for a minor may occur even though the conditions described in subsection (a) have not been established.

§ 5-205. [Venue.]

The venue for guardianship proceedings for a minor is in the court at the place where the minor resides or is present at the time the proceedings are commenced.

§ 5-206. [Procedure for Court-appointment of Guardian of Minor.]

(a) A minor or any person interested in the welfare of the minor may petition for appointment of a guardian.

(b) After the filing of a petition, the Court shall set a date for hearing, and the petitioner shall give notice of the time and place of hearing the petition in the manner prescribed by Section 1-401 to:

(1) the minor, if 14 or more years of age and not the petitioner;

(2) any person alleged to have had the principal care and custody of the minor during the 60 days preceding the filing of the petition; and

(3) any living parent of the minor.

(c) Upon hearing, if the Court finds that a qualified person seeks appointment, venue is proper, the required notices have been given, the conditions of Section 5-204 (a) have been met, and the welfare and best interest of the minor will be served by the requested appointment, it shall make the appointment and issue letters. In other cases, the Court may dismiss the proceedings or make any other disposition of the matter that will serve the best interest of the minor.

(d) If the Court determines at any time in the proceeding that the interests of the minor are or may be inadequately represented, it may appoint an attorney to represent the minor, giving consideration to the preference of the minor if the minor is 14 or more years of age.

§ 5-207. [Court Appointment of Guardian of Minor; Qualifications; Priority of Minor's Nominee.]

The Court may appoint as guardian any person whose appointment would be in the best interest of the minor. The Court shall appoint a person nominated by the minor, if the minor is 14 or more years of age, unless the Court finds the appointment contrary to the best interest of the minor.

§ 5-208. [Consent to Service by Acceptance of Appointment; Notice.]

By accepting a parental or court appointment as guardian, a guardian submits personally to the jurisdiction of the Court in any proceeding relating to the guardianship that may be instituted by any interested person. The petitioner shall cause notice of any proceeding to be delivered or mailed to the guardian at the guardian's address listed in the Court records and to the address then known to the petitioner. Letters of guardianship must indicate whether the guardian was appointed by court order or parental nomination.

§ 5-209. [Powers and Duties of Guardian of Minor.]

(a) A guardian of a minor ward has the powers and responsibilities of a parent regarding the ward's support, care, and education, but a guardian is not personally liable for the ward's expenses and is not liable to third persons by reason of the relationship for acts of the ward.

(b) In particular and without qualifying the foregoing, a guardian shall:

(1) become or remain personally acquainted with the ward and maintain sufficient contact with the ward to know of the ward's capacities, limitations, needs, opportunities, and physical and mental health;

(2) take reasonable care of the ward's personal effects and commence protective proceedings if necessary to protect other property of the ward;

(3) apply any available money of the ward to the ward's current needs for support, care, and education;

(4) conserve any excess money of the ward for the ward's future needs, but if a conservator has been appointed for the estate of the ward, the guardian, at least quarterly, shall pay to the conservator money of the ward to be conserved for the ward's future needs; and

(5) report the condition of the ward and of the ward's estate that has been subject to the guardian's possession or control, as ordered by the Court on petition of any person interested in the ward's welfare or as required by Court rule.

(c) A guardian may:

(1) receive money payable for the support of the ward to the ward's parent. Guardian, or custodian under the terms of any statutory benefit or insurance system or any private contract, devise, trust, conservatorship, or custodianship, and

money or property of the ward paid or delivered pursuant to Section 5-101;

(2) if consistent with the terms of any order by a court of competent jurisdiction relating to detention or commitment of the ward, take custody of the person of the ward and establish the ward's place of abode within or without this State;

(3) if no conservator for the estate of the ward has been appointed, institute proceedings, including administrative proceedings, or take other appropriate action to compel the performance by any person of a duty to support the ward or to pay sums for the welfare of the ward;

(4) consent to medical or other professional care, treatment, or advice for the ward without liability by reason of the consent for injury to the ward resulting from the negligence or acts of third persons unless a parent would have been liable in the circumstances;

(5) consent to the marriage or adoption of the ward; and

(6) if reasonable under all of the circumstances, delegate to the ward certain responsibilities for decisions affecting the ward's well-being.

(d) A guardian is entitled to reasonable compensation for services as guardian and to reimbursement for room, board and clothing personally provided to the ward, but only as approved by order of the Court. If a conservator, other than the guardian or one who is affiliated with the guardian has been appointed for the estate of the ward, reasonable compensation and reimbursement to the guardian may be approved and paid by the conservator without order of the Court controlling the guardian.

(e) In the interest of developing self-reliance on the part of a ward or for other good cause, the Court, at the time of appointment or later, on its own motion or on appropriate petition or motion of the minor or other interested person, may limit the powers of a guardian otherwise conferred by this section and thereby create a limited guardianship. Any limitation on the statutory power of a guardian of a minor must be endorsed on the guardian's letters or, in the case of a guardian by parental appointment, must be reflected in letters that are issued at the time any limitation is imposed. Following the same procedure, a limitation may be removed and appropriate letters issued.

§ 5-210. [Termination of Appointment of Guardian; General.]

A guardian's authority and responsibility terminates upon the death, resignation or removal of the guardian or upon the minor's death, adoption, marriage or attainment of majority, but termination does not affect the guardian's liability for prior acts or the obligation to account for funds and assets of the ward. Resignation of a guardian does not terminate the guardianship until it has been approved by the Court. A parental appointment under an informally probated will terminates if the will is later denied probate in a formal proceeding.

§ 5-211. [Proceedings Subsequent to Appointment; Venue.]

(a) The Court at the place where the ward resides has concurrent jurisdiction with the Court that appointed the guardian or in which acceptance of a parental appointment was filed over resignation, removal, accounting and other proceedings relating to the guardianship.

(b) If the Court at the place where the ward resides is neither the appointing court nor the court in which acceptance of appointment is filed, the court in which proceedings subsequent to appointment are commenced in all appropriate cases shall notify the other court, in this or another state, and after consultation with that court determine whether to retain jurisdiction or transfer the proceedings to the other court, whichever is in the best interest of the ward. A copy of any order accepting a resignation or removing a guardian must be sent to the appointing court or the court in which acceptance of appointment is filed.

§ 5-212. [Resignation, Removal, and Other Post-appointment Proceedings.]

(a) Any person interested in the welfare of a ward or the ward, if 14 or more years of age, may petition for removal of a guardian on the ground that removal would be in the best interest of the ward or for any other order that is in the best interest of the ward. A guardian may petition for permission to resign. A petition for removal or for permission to resign may, but need not, include a request for appointment of a successor guardian.

(b) Notice of hearing on a petition for an order subsequent to appointment of a guardian must be given to the ward, the guardian, and any other person as ordered by the court.

(c) After notice and hearing on a petition for removal or for permission to resign, the Court may terminate the guardianship and make any further order that may be appropriate.

(d) If the Court determines at any time in the proceeding that the interest of the ward is or may be inadequately represented, it may appoint an attorney to represent the minor, giving consideration to the preference of the minor if the minor is 14 or more years of age.

Part 3
Guardians of Incapacitated Persons

§ 5-301. [Appointment of Guardian for Incapacitated Person by Will or Other Writing.]

(a) The parent of an unmarried incapacitated person may appoint by will, or other writing signed by the parent and attested by at least 2 witnesses, a guardian of the incapacitated person. If both parents are dead or the surviving parent is adjudged incapacitated, a parental appointment becomes effective when, after having given 7 days prior written notice of intention to do so to the incapacitated person and to the person having the care of the person or to the nearest adult relative, the guardian files acceptance of appointment in the court in which the will is [informally or formally] probated, or in the case of a non-testamentary nominating instrument, in the Court at the place where the incapacitated person resides or is present. The notice shall state that the appointment may be terminated by filing a written objection in the Court, as provided by subsection (d). If both parents are dead, an effective appointment by the parent who died later has priority.

(b) The spouse of a married incapacitated person may appoint by will, or other writing signed by the spouse and attested by at least 2 witnesses, a guardian of the incapacitated person. The appointment becomes effective when, after having given 7 days prior written notice of intention to do so to the incapacitated person and to the person having care of the incapacitated person or to the nearest adult relative, the guardian files acceptance of appointment in the Court in which the will is informally or formally probated or, in the case of non-testamentary nominating instrument, in the Court at the place where the incapacitated person resides or is present. The notice shall state that the appointment may be terminated by filing a written objection in the Court, as provided by subsection (d). An effective appointment by a spouse has priority over an appointment by a parent.

(c) An appointment effected by filing the guardian's acceptance under a will probated in the state of the decedent's domicile is effective in this State.

(d) Upon the filing in the Court in which the will was probated or, in the case of a non-testamentary nominating instrument, in the Court at the place where the incapacitated person resides or is present, of written objection to the appointment by the incapacitated person for whom a parental or spousal appointment of guardian has been made, the appointment is terminated. An objection does not prevent appointment by the Court in a proper proceeding of the parental or spousal nominee or any other suitable person upon an adjudication of incapacity in proceedings under the succeeding sections of this Part.

As amended in 1987.

§ 5-302. [Venue.]

The venue for guardianship proceedings for an incapacitated person is in the place where the incapacitated person resides or is present at the time the proceedings are commenced. If the incapacitated person is admitted to an institution pursuant to order of a court of competent jurisdiction, venue is also in the [county] in which that Court is located.

§ 5-303. [Procedure for Court Appointment of a Guardian of an Incapacitated Person.]

(a) The incapacitated person or any person interested in the welfare of the incapacitated person may petition for appointment of a guardian, limited or general.

(b) After the filing of a petition, the Court shall set a date for hearing on the issue of incapacity so that notices may be given as required by Section 5-304, and, unless the allegedly incapacitated person is represented by counsel, appoint an attorney to represent the person in the proceeding. The person so appointed may be granted the powers and duties of a guardian ad litem. The person alleged to be incapacitated must be examined by a physician or other qualified person appointed by the Court who shall submit a report in writing to the Court. The person alleged to be incapacitated also must be interviewed by a visitor sent by the Court. The visitor also shall interview the person who appears to have caused the petition to be filed and any person who is nominated to serve as guardian and visit the present place of abode of the person alleged to be incapacitated and the place it is proposed that the person will be detained or reside if the appointment is made and submit a report in writing to the Court. The Court may utilize the service of any public or charitable agency as an additional visitor to evaluate the condition of the allegedly incapacitated person and to make appropriate recommendations to the Court.

(c) A person alleged to be incapacitated is entitled to be present at the hearing in person. The person is entitled to be represented by counsel, to present evidence, to cross examine witnesses, including the Court-appointed physician or other qualified person and any visitor [, and to trial by jury]. The issue may be determined at a closed hearing [or without a jury] if the person alleged to be incapacitated or counsel for the person so requests.

(d) Any person may apply for permission to participate in the proceeding, and the Court may grant the request, with or without hearing, upon determining that the best interest of the alleged incapacitated person will be served thereby. The Court may attach appropriate conditions to the permission.

§ 5-304. [Notice in Guardianship Proceeding.]

(a) In a proceeding for the appointment of a guardian of an incapacitated person, and, if notice is required in a proceeding for appointment of a temporary guardian, notice of hearing must be given to each of the following:

(1) the person alleged to be incapacitated and spouse, or, if none, adult children, or if none, parents;

(2) any person who is serving as guardian, conservator, or who has the care and custody of the person alleged to be incapacitated;

(3) in case no other person is notified under paragraph (1), at least one of the nearest adult relatives, if any can be found; and

(4) any other person as directed by the Court.

(b) Notice of hearing on a petition for an order subsequent to appointment of a guardian must be given to the ward, the guardian and any other person as ordered by the Court.

(c) Notice must be served personally on the alleged incapacitated person. Notices to other persons as required by subsection (a)(1) must be served personally if the person to be notified can be found within the state. In all other cases, required notices must be given as provided in Section 1-401.

(d) The person alleged to be incapacitated may not waive notice.

§ 5-305. [Who May Be Guardian; Priorities.]

(a) Any qualified person may be appointed guardian of an incapacitated person.

(b) Unless lack of qualification or other good cause dictates the contrary, the Court shall appoint a guardian in accordance with the incapacitated person's most recent nomination in a durable power of attorney.

(c) Except as provided in subsection (b), the following are entitled to consideration for appointment in the order listed:

(1) the spouse of the incapacitated person or a person nominated by will of a deceased spouse or by other writing signed by the spouse and attested by at least 2 witnesses;

(2) an adult child of the incapacitated person;

(3) a parent of the incapacitated person, or a person nominated by will of a deceased parent or by other writing signed by a parent and attested by at least two witnesses;

(4) any relative of the incapacitated person with whom the person has resided for more than 6 months prior to the filing of the petition; and

(5) a person nominated by the person who is caring for or paying for the care of the incapacitated person.

(d) With respect to persons having equal priority, the Court shall select the one it deems best qualified to serve. The Court, acting in the best interest of the incapacitated person, may pass over a person having priority and appoint a person having a lower priority or no priority.

§ 5-306. [Findings; Order of Appointment.]

(a) The Court shall exercise the authority conferred in this Part so as to encourage the development of maximum self-reliance and independence of the incapacitated person and make appointive and other orders only to the extent necessitated by the incapacitated person's mental and adaptive limitations or other conditions warranting the procedure.

(b) The Court may appoint a guardian as requested if it is satisfied that the person for whom a guardian is sought is incapacitated and that the appointment is necessary or desirable as a means of providing continuing care and supervision of the person of the incapacitated person. The Court, on appropriate findings, may (i) treat the petition as one for a protective order under Section 5-401 and proceed accordingly, (ii) enter any other appropriate order, or (iii) dismiss the proceedings.

(c) The Court, at the time of appointment or later, on its own motion or on appropriate petition or motion of the incapacitated person or other interested person, may limit the powers of a guardian otherwise conferred by Parts 1, 2, 3 and 4 of this Article and thereby create a limited guardianship. Any limitation on the statutory power of a guardian of an incapacitated person must be endorsed on the guardian's letters or, in the case of a guardian by parental or spousal appointment, must be reflected in letters issued at the time any limitation is imposed. Following the same procedure, a limitation may be removed or modified and appropriate letters issued.

§ 5-307. [Acceptance of Appointment; Consent to Jurisdiction.]

By accepting appointment, a guardian submits personally to the jurisdiction of the Court in any proceeding relating to the guardianship that may be instituted by any interested person. Notice of any proceeding must be delivered or mailed to the guardian at the address listed in the Court records and at the address as then known to the petitioner.

§ 5-308. [Emergency Orders; Temporary Guardians.]

(a) If an incapacitated person has no guardian, an emergency exists, and no other person appears to have authority to act in the circumstances, on appropriate petition the Court may appoint a temporary guardian whose authority may not extend beyond [15 days] [the period of effectiveness of ex parte restraining orders], and who may exercise those powers granted in the order.

(b) If an appointed guardian is not effectively performing duties and the Court further finds that the welfare of the incapacitated person requires immediate action, it may appoint, with or without notice, a temporary guardian for the incapacitated person having the powers of a general guardian for a specified period not to exceed 6 months. The authority of any permanent guardian previously appointed by the Court is suspended as long as a temporary guardian has authority.

(c) The Court may remove a temporary guardian at any time. A temporary guardian shall make any report the Court requires. In other respects the provisions of Parts 1, 2, 3 and 4 of this Article concerning guardians apply to temporary guardians.

§ 5-309. [General Powers and Duties of Guardian.]

Except as limited pursuant to Section 5-306(c), a guardian of an incapacitated person is responsible for care, custody, and control of the ward, but is not liable to third persons by reason of that responsibility for acts of the ward. In particular and without qualifying the foregoing, a guardian has the same duties, powers and responsibilities as a guardian for a minor as described in Section 5-209(b), (c) and (d).

§ 5-310. [Termination of Guardianship for Incapacitated Person.]

The authority and responsibility of a guardian of an incapacitated person terminates upon the death of the guardian or ward, the determination of incapacity of the guardian, or upon removal or resignation as provided in Section 5-311. Testamentary appointment under an informally probated will terminates if the will is later denied probate in a formal proceeding. Termination does not affect a guardian's liability for prior acts or the obligation to account for funds and assets of the ward.

§ 5-311. [Removal or Resignation of Guardian; Termination of Incapacity.]

(a) On petition of the ward or any person interested in the ward's welfare, the Court, after hearing, may remove a guardian if in the best interest of the ward. On petition of the guardian, the Court, after hearing, may accept a resignation.

(b) An order adjudicating incapacity may specify a minimum period, not exceeding six months, during which a petition for an adjudication that the ward is no longer incapacitated may not be filed without special leave. Subject to that restriction, the ward or any person interested in the welfare of the ward may petition for an order that the ward is no longer incapacitated and for termination of the guardianship. A request for an order may also be made informally to the Court and any person who knowingly interferes with transmission of the request may be adjudged guilty of contempt of court.

(c) Upon removal, resignation, or death of the guardian, or if the guardian is determined to be incapacitated, the Court may appoint a successor guardian and make any other appropriate order. Before appointing a successor guardian, or ordering that a ward's incapacity has terminated, the Court shall follow the same procedures to safeguard the rights of the ward that apply to a petition for appointment of a guardian. As amended in 1987.

§ 5-312. [Proceedings Subsequent to Appointment; Venue.]

(a) The Court at the place where the ward resides has concurrent jurisdiction with the Court that appointed the guardian or in which acceptance of a parental or spousal appointment was filed over resignation, removal, accounting, and other proceedings relating to the guardianship, including proceedings to limit the authority previously conferred on a guardian or to remove limitations previously imposed.

(b) If the Court at the place where the ward resides is not the Court in which acceptance of appointment is filed, the Court in which proceedings subsequent to appointment are commenced, in all appropriate cases, shall notify the other Court, in this or another state, and after consultation with that Court determine whether to retain jurisdiction or transfer the proceedings to the other Court, whichever may be in the best interest of the ward. A copy of any order accepting a resignation, removing a guardian, or altering authority must be sent to the Court in which acceptance of appointment is filed.

Part 4
Protection of Property of Persons Under Disability and Minors

§ 5-401. [Protective Proceedings.]

(a) Upon petition and after notice and hearing in accordance with the provisions of this Part, the Court may appoint a conservator or make any other protective order for cause as provided in this section.

(b) Appointment of a conservator or other protective order may be made in relation to the estate and affairs of a minor if the Court determines that a minor owns money or property requiring management or protection that cannot otherwise be provided or has or may have business affairs that may be jeopardized or prevented by minority, or that funds are needed for support and education and that protection is necessary or desirable to obtain or provide funds.

(c) Appointment of a conservator or other protective order may be made in relation to the estate and affairs of a person if the Court determines that (i) the person is unable to manage property and business affairs effectively for such reasons as mental illness, mental deficiency, physical illness or disability, chronic use of drugs, chronic intoxication, confinement, detention by a foreign power, or disappearance; and (ii) the person has property that will be wasted or dissipated unless property management is provided or money is needed for the support, care, and welfare of the person or those entitled to the person's support and that protection is necessary or desirable to obtain or provide money.

As amended in 1988.

§ 5-402. [Protective Proceedings; Jurisdiction of Business Affairs of Protected Persons.]

After the service of notice in a proceeding seeking the appointment of a conservator or other protective order and until termination of the proceeding, the Court in which the petition is filed has:

(1) exclusive jurisdiction to determine the need for a conservator or other protective order until the proceedings are terminated;

(2) exclusive jurisdiction to determine how the estate of the protected person which is subject to the laws of this State must be managed, expended, or distributed to or for the use of the protected person, the protected person's dependents, or other claimants; and

(3) concurrent jurisdiction to determine the validity of claims against the person or estate of the protected person and questions of title concerning any estate asset.

§ 5-403. [Venue.]

Venue for proceedings under this Part is:

(1) in the court at the place in this State where the person to be protected resides whether or not a guardian has been appointed in another place; or

(2) if the person to be protected does not reside in this State, in the Court at any place where property of the person is located.

§ 5-404. [Original Petition for Appointment or Protective Order.]

(a) The person to be protected or any person who is interested in the estate, affairs, or welfare of the person, including a parent, guardian, custodian, or any person who would be adversely affected by lack of effective management of the person's property and business affairs may petition for the appointment of a conservator or for other appropriate protective order.

(b) The petition must set forth to the extent known the interest of the petitioner; the name, age, residence, and address of the person to be protected; the name and address of the guardian, if any; the name and address of the nearest relative known to the petitioner; a general statement of the person's property with an estimate of the value thereof, including any compensation, insurance, pension, or allowance to which the person is entitled; and the reason why appointment of a conservator or other protective order is necessary. If the appointment of a conservator is requested, the petition must also set forth the name and address of the person whose appointment is sought and the basis of the claim to priority for appointment.

§ 5-405. [Notice.]

(a) On a petition for appointment of a conservator or other protective order, the requirements for notice described in Section 5-304 apply, but

(i) if the person to be protected has disappeared or is otherwise situated so as to make personal service of notice impracticable, notice to the person must be given by publication as provided in Section 1-401, and

(ii) if the person to be protected is a minor, the provisions of Section 5-206 also apply.

(b) Notice of hearing on a petition for an order subsequent to appointment of a conservator or other protective order must be given to the protected person, any conservator of the protected person's estate, and any other person as ordered by the Court.

§ 5-406. [Procedure Concerning Hearing and Order on Original Petition.]

(a) Upon receipt of a petition for appointment of a conservator or other protective order because of minority, the Court shall set a date for hearing. If the Court determines at any time in the proceeding that the interests of the minor are or may be inadequately represented, it may appoint an attorney to represent the minor, giving consideration to the choice of the minor if 14 or more years of age. An attorney appointed by the Court to represent a minor may be granted the powers and duties of a guardian ad litem.

(b) Upon receipt of a petition for appointment of a conservator or he other protective order for reasons other than minority, the Court shall set a date for hearing. Unless the person to be protected has chosen counsel, the Court shall appoint an attorney to represent the person who may be granted the powers and duties of a guardian ad litem. If the alleged disability is mental illness, mental deficiency, physical illness or disability, chronic use of drugs, or chronic intoxication, the Court may direct that the person to be protected be examined by a physician designated by the Court, preferably a physician who is not connected with any institution in which the person is a patient or is detained. The Court may send a visitor to interview the person to be protected. The visitor may be a guardian ad litem or an officer or employee of the Court.

(c) The Court may utilize, as an additional visitor, the service of any public or charitable agency to evaluate the condition of the person to be protected and make appropriate recommendations to the Court.

(d) The person to be protected is entitled to be present at the hearing in person. The person is entitled to be represented by counsel, to present evidence, to cross-examine witnesses, including any Court-appointed physician or other qualified person and any visitor [, and to trial by jury]. The issue may be determined at a closed hearing [or without a jury] if the person to be protected or counsel for the person so requests.

(e) Any person may apply for permission to participate in the proceeding and the Court may grant the request, with or without hearing, upon determining that the best interest of the person to be protected will be served thereby. The Court may attach appropriate conditions to the permission.

(f) After hearing, upon finding that a basis for the appointment of a conservator or other protective order has been established, the Court shall make an appointment or other appropriate protective order.

§ 5-407. [Permissible Court Orders.]

(a) The Court shall exercise the authority conferred in this Part to encourage the development of maximum self-reliance and independence of a protected person and make protective orders only to the extent necessitated by the protected person's mental and adaptive limitations and other conditions warranting the procedure.

(b) The Court has the following powers that may be exercised or through a conservator in respect to the estate and business affairs of a protected person:

(1) While a petition for appointment of a conservator or other protective order is pending and after preliminary hearing and without notice to others, the Court may preserve and apply the property of the person to be protected as may be required for the support of the person or dependents of the person.

(2) After hearing and upon determining that a basis for an appointment or other protective order exists with respect to a minor without other disability, the Court has all those powers over the estate and business affairs of the minor which are or may be necessary for the best interest of the minor and members of the minor's immediate family.

(3) After hearing and upon determining that a basis for an appointment or other protective order exists with respect to a person for reasons other than minority, the Court, for the benefit of the person and members of the person's immediate family, has all the powers over the estate and business affairs which the person could exercise if present and not under disability, except the power to make a will. Those powers include, but are not limited to, power to make gifts; to convey or release contingent and expectant interests in property, including marital property rights and any right of survivorship incident to joint tenancy or tenancy by the entirety; to exercise or release powers held by the protected person as trustee, personal representative, custodian for minors, conservator, or donee of a power of appointment; to enter into contracts; to create revocable or irrevocable trusts of property of the estate which may extend beyond the disability or life of the protected person; to exercise options of the protected person to purchase securities or other property; to exercise rights to elect options and change beneficiaries under insurance and annuity policies and to surrender the policies for their cash value; to exercise any right to an elective share in the estate of the person's deceased spouse and to renounce or disclaim any interest by testate or intestate succession or by transfer.

(c) The Court may exercise or direct the exercise of the following powers only if satisfied, after notice and hearing, that it is in the best interest of the protected person, and that the person either is incapable of consenting or has consented to the proposed exercise of power:

(1) to exercise or release powers of appointment of which the protected person is donee;

(2) to renounce or disclaim interests;

(3) to make gifts in trust or otherwise exceeding 20 percent of any year's income of the estate; and

(4) to change beneficiaries under insurance and annuity policies.

(d) A determination that a basis for appointment of a conservator or other protective order exists has no effect on the capacity of the protected person.

§ 5-408. [Protective Arrangements and Single Transactions Authorized.]

(a) If it is established in a proper proceeding that a basis exists as described in Section 5-401 for affecting the property and business affairs of a person, the Court, without appointing a conservator, may authorize, direct or ratify any transaction necessary or desirable to achieve any security, service, or care arrangement meeting the foreseeable needs of the protected person. Protective arrangements include payment, delivery, deposit, or retention of funds or property; sale, mortgage, lease, or other transfer of property; entry into an annuity contract, a contract for life care, a deposit contract or a contract for training and education; or addition to or establishment of a suitable trust.

(b) If it is established in a proper proceeding that a basis exists as described in Section 5-401 for affecting the property and business affairs of a person, the Court, without appointing a conservator, may authorize, direct, or ratify any contract, trust, or other transaction relating to the protected person's property and business affairs if the Court determines that the transaction is in the best interest of the protected person.

(c) Before approving a protective arrangement or other transaction under this section, the Court shall consider the interests of creditors and dependents of the protected person and, in view of the disability, whether the protected person needs the continuing protection of a conservator. The Court may appoint a special conservator to assist in the accomplishment of any protective arrangement or other transaction authorized under this section who shall have the authority conferred by the order and serve until discharged by order after report to the Court of all matters done pursuant to the order of appointment.

§ 5-409. [Who May Be Appointed Conservator; Priorities.]

(a) The Court may appoint an individual or a corporation with general power to serve as trustee or conservator of the estate of a protected person. The following are entitled to consideration for appointment in the order listed:

(1) a conservator, guardian of property, or like other fiduciary appointed or recognized by an appropriate court of any other jurisdiction in which the protected person resides;

(2) an individual or corporation nominated by the protected person 14 or more years of age and of sufficient mental capacity to make an intelligent choice;

(3) the spouse of the protected person;

(4) an adult child of the protected person;

(5) a parent of the protected person, or a person nominated by the will of a deceased parent;

(6) any relative of the protected person who has resided with the protected person for more than 6 months before the filing of the petition; and

(7) a person nominated by one who is caring for or paying benefits to the protected person.

(b) A person in priorities (1), (3), (4), (5), or (6) may designate in writing a substitute to serve instead and thereby transfer the priority to the substitute. With respect to persons having equal priority, the Court shall select the one it deems best qualified to serve. The Court, acting in the best interest of the protected person, may pass over a person having priority and appoint a person having a lower priority or no priority.

§ 5-410. [Bond.]

The Court may require a conservator to furnish a bond conditioned upon faithful discharge of all duties of the trust according to law, with sureties it shall specify. Unless otherwise directed, the bond must be in the amount of the aggregate capital value of the property of the estate in the conservator's control, plus one year's estimated income, and minus the value of securities deposited under arrangements requiring an order of Court for their removal and the value of any land which the fiduciary, by express limitation of power, lacks power to sell or convey without Court authorization. The Court, in lieu of sureties on a bond, may accept other collateral for the performance of the bond, including a pledge of securities or a mortgage of land.

§ 5-411. [Terms and Requirements of Bonds.]

(a) The following requirements and provisions apply to any bond required under Section 5-410.

(1) Unless otherwise provided by the terms of the approved bond, sureties are jointly and severally liable with the conservator and with each other.

(2) By executing an approved bond of a conservator, the surety consents to the jurisdiction of the Court that issued letters to the primary obligor in any proceeding pertaining to the fiduciary duties of the conservator and naming the surety as a party respondent. Notice of any proceeding must be delivered to the surety or mailed by registered or certified mail to the address listed with the Court at the place where the bond is filed and to the address as then known to the petitioner.

(3) On petition of a successor conservator or any interested person, a proceeding may be initiated against a surety for breach of the obligation of the bond of the conservator.

(4) The bond of the conservator is not void after the first recovery but may be proceeded against from time to time until the whole penalty is exhausted.

(b) No proceeding may be commenced against the surety on any matter as to which an action or proceeding against the primary obligor is barred by adjudication or limitation.

§ 5-412. [Effect of Acceptance of Appointment.]

By accepting appointment, a conservator submits personally to the jurisdiction of the Court in any proceeding relating to the estate which may be instituted by any interested person. Notice of any proceeding must be delivered to the conservator or mailed by registered or certified mail to the address as listed in the petition for appointment or as thereafter reported to the Court and to the address as then known to the petitioner.

§ 5-413. [Compensation and Expenses.]

If not otherwise compensated for services rendered, any visitor, attorney, physician, conservator, or special conservator appointed in a protective proceeding and any attorney whose services resulted in a protective order or in an order that was beneficial to a protected person's estate is entitled to reasonable compensation from the estate.

§ 5-414. [Death, Resignation, or Removal of Conservator.]

The Court may remove a conservator for good cause, upon notice and hearing, or accept the resignation of a conservator. Upon the conservator's death, resignation, or removal, the Court may appoint another conservator. A conservator so appointed succeeds to the title and powers of the predecessor.

§ 5-415. [Petitions for Orders Subsequent to Appointment.]

(a) Any person interested in the welfare of a person for whom a conservator has been appointed may file a petition in the appointing court for an order:

(1) requiring bond or collateral or additional bond or collateral, or reducing bond;

(2) requiring an accounting for the administration of the trust;

(3) directing distribution;

(4) removing the conservator and appointing a temporary or successor conservator; or

(5) granting other appropriate relief:

(b) A conservator may petition the appointing court for instructions concerning fiduciary responsibility.

(c) Upon notice and hearing, the Court may give appropriate instructions or make any appropriate order.

§ 5-416. [General Duty of Conservator.]

A conservator, in relation to powers conferred by this Part, or implicit in the title acquired by virtue of the proceeding, shall act as a fiduciary and observe the standards of care applicable to trustees.

§ 5-417. [Inventory and Records.]

(a) Within 90 days after appointment, each conservator shall prepare and file with the appointing Court a complete inventory of the estate subject to the conservatorship together with an oath or affirmation that the inventory is believed to be complete and accurate as far as information permits. The conservator shall provide a copy thereof to the protected person if practicable and the person has attained the age of 14 years and has sufficient mental capacity to understand the arrangement A copy also shall be provided to any guardian or parent with whom the protected person resides.

(b) The conservator shall keep suitable records of the administration and exhibit the same on request of any interested person.

§ 5-418. [Accounts.]

Each conservator shall account to the Court for administration of the trust not less than annually unless the Court directs otherwise, upon resignation or removal and at other times as the Court may direct. On termination of the protected person's minority or disability, a conservator shall account to the Court or to the formerly protected person or the successors of that person. Subject to appeal or vacation within the time permitted, an order after notice and hearing allowing an intermediate account of a conservator adjudicates as to liabilities concerning the matters considered in connection therewith; and an order, following notice and hearing, allowing a final account adjudicates as to all previously unsettled liabilities of the conservator to the protected person or the protected person's successors relating to the conservatorship. In connection with any account, the Court may require a conservator to submit to a physical check of the estate, to be made in any manner the Court specifies.

As amended in 1987.

§ 5-419. [Conservators; Title by Appointment.]

(a) The appointment of a conservator vests in the conservator title as trustee to all property, or to the part thereof specified in the order, of the protected person, presently held or thereafter acquired, including title to any property theretofore held for the protected person by custodians or attorneys-in-fact. An order specifying that only a part of the property of the protected person vests in the conservator creates a limited conservatorship.

(b) Except as otherwise provided herein, the interest of the protected person in property vested in a conservator by this section is not transferable or assignable by the protected person. An attempted transfer or assignment by the protected person, though ineffective to affect property rights, may generate a claim for restitution or damages which, subject to presentation and allowance, may be satisfied as provided in Section 5-427.

(c) Neither property vested in a conservator by this section nor the interest of the protected person in that property is subject to levy, garnishment, or similar process other than an order issued in the protective proceeding made as provided in Section 5-427.

§ 5-420. [Recording of Conservator's Letters.]

(a) Letters of conservatorship are evidence of transfer of all assets, or the part thereof specified in the letters, of a protected person to the conservator. An order terminating a conservatorship is evidence of transfer of all assets subjected to the conservatorship from the conservator to the protected person, or to successors of the person.

(b) Subject to the requirements of general statutes governing the filing or recordation of documents of title to land or other property, letters of conservatorship and orders terminating conservatorships, may be filed or recorded to give record notice of title as between the conservator and the protected person.

§ 5-421. [Sale, Encumbrance, or Transaction Involving Conflict of Interest; Voidable; Exceptions.]

Any sale or encumbrance to a conservator, the spouse, agent, attorney of a conservator, or any corporation, trust, or other organization in which the conservator has a substantial beneficial interest, or any other transaction involving the estate being administered by the conservator which is affected by a substantial conflict between fiduciary and personal interests is voidable unless the transaction is approved by the Court after notice as directed by the Court.

§ 5-422. [Persons Dealing with Conservators; Protection.]

(a) A person who in good faith either assists or deals with a conservator for value in any transaction other than those requiring a Court order as provided in Section 5-407 is protected as if the conservator properly exercised the power. The fact that a person knowingly deals with a conservator does not alone require the person to inquire into the existence of a power or the propriety of its exercise, but restrictions on powers of conservators which are endorsed on letters as provided in Section 5-425 are effective as to third persons. A person is not bound to see the proper application of estate assets paid or delivered to a conservator.

(b) The protection expressed in this section extends to any procedural irregularity or jurisdictional defect occurred in proceedings leading to the issuance of letters and is not a substitution for protection provided by comparable provisions of the law relating to commercial transactions or to simplifying transfers of securities by fiduciaries.

§ 5-423. [Powers of Conservator in Administration.]

(a) Subject to limitation provided in Section 5-425, a conservator has all of the powers conferred in this section and any additional powers conferred by law on trustees in this State. In addition, a conservator of the estate of an unmarried minor [under the age of 18 years], as to whom no one has parental rights, has the duties and powers of a guardian of a minor described in Section 5-209 until the minor attains [the age of 18 years] or marries, but the parental rights so conferred on a conservator do not preclude appointment of a guardian as provided in Part 2.

(b) A conservator without Court authorization or confirmation, may invest and reinvest funds of the estate as would a trustee.

(c) A conservator, acting reasonably in efforts to accomplish the purpose of the appointment, may act without Court authorization or confirmation, to

(1) collect, hold, and retain assets of the estate including land in another state, until judging that disposition of the assets should be made, and the assets may be retained even though they include an asset in which the conservator is personally interested;

(2) receive additions to the estate;

(3) continue or participate in the operation of any business or other enterprise;

(4) acquire an undivided interest in an estate asset in which the conservator, in any fiduciary capacity, holds an undivided interest;

(5) invest and reinvest estate assets in accordance with subsection (b);

(6) deposit estate funds in a state or federally insured financial institution, including one operated by the conservator;

(7) acquire or dispose of an estate asset, including land in another state, for cash or on credit, at public or private sale, and manage, develop, improve, exchange, partition, change the character of, or abandon an estate asset;

(8) make ordinary or extraordinary repairs or alterations in buildings or other structures; demolish any improvements; and raze existing or erect new party walls or buildings;

(9) subdivide, develop, or dedicate land to public use; make or obtain the vacation of plats and adjust boundaries; adjust differences in valuation or exchange or partition by giving or receiving considerations; and dedicate easements to public use without consideration;

(10) enter for any purpose into a lease as lessor or lessee with or without option to purchase or renew for a term within or extending beyond the term of the conservatorship;

(11) enter into a lease or arrangement for exploration and removal of minerals or other natural resources or enter into a pooling or unitization agreement;

(12) grant an option involving disposition of an estate asset and take an option for the acquisition of any asset;

(13) vote a security, in person or by general or limited proxy;

(14) pay calls, assessments, and any other sums chargeable or accruing against or on account of securities;

(15) sell or exercise stock-subscription or conversion rights;

(16) consent, directly or through a committee or other agent, to the reorganization, consolidation, merger, dissolution, or liquidation of a corporation or other business enterprise;

(17) hold a security in the name of a nominee or in other form without disclosure of the conservatorship so that title to the security may pass by delivery, but the conservator is liable for any act of the nominee in connection with the stock so held;

(18) insure the assets of the estate against damage or loss and the conservator against liability with respect to third persons;

(19) borrow money to be repaid from estate assets or otherwise; advance money for the protection of the estate or the protected person and for all expenses, losses, and liability sustained

in the administration of the estate or because of the holding or ownership of any estate assets, for which the conservator has a lien on the estate as against the protected person for advances so made;

(20) pay or contest any claim; settle a claim by or against the estate or the protected person by compromise, arbitration, or otherwise; and release, in whole or in part, any claim belonging to the estate to the extent the claim is uncollectible;

(21) pay taxes, assessments, compensation of the conservator, and other expenses incurred in the collection, care, administration, and protection of the estate;

(22) allocate items of income or expense to either state income or principal, as provided by law, including creation of reserves out of income for depreciation, obsolescence, or amortization, or for depletion in mineral or timber properties;

(23) pay any sum distributable to a protected person or dependent of the protected person by paying the sum to the distributee or by paying the sum for the use of the distributee to the guardian of the distributee, or, if none, to a relative or other person having custody of the distributee;

(24) employ persons, including attorneys, auditors, investment advisors, or agents, even though they are associated with the conservator, to advise or assist in the performance of administrative duties; act upon their recommendation without independent investigation; and instead of acting personally, employ one or more agents to perform any act of administration, whether or not discretionary;

(25) prosecute or defend actions, claims, or proceedings in any jurisdiction for the protection of estate assets and of the conservator in the performance of fiduciary duties; and

(26) execute and deliver all instruments that will accomplish or facilitate the exercise of the powers vested in the conservator.

§ 5-424. [Distributive Duties and Powers of Conservator.]

(a) A conservator may expend or distribute income or principal of the estate without Court authorization or confirmation for the support, education, care, or benefit of the protected person and dependents in accordance with the following principles:

(1) The conservator shall consider recommendations relating to the appropriate standard of support, education, and benefit for the protected person or dependent made by a parent or guardian, if any. The conservator may not be surcharged for sums paid to persons or organizations furnishing support, education, or care to the protected person or a dependent pursuant to the recommendations of a parent or guardian of the protected person unless the conservator knows that the parent or guardian derives personal financial benefit therefrom, including relief from any personal duty of support or the recommendations are clearly not in the best interest of the protected person.

(2) The conservator shall expend or distribute sums reasonably necessary for the support, education, care, or benefit of the protected person and dependents with due regard to (i) the size of the estate, the probable duration of the conservatorship), and the likelihood that the protected person, at some future time, may be fully able to be wholly self-sufficient and able to manage business affairs and the estate; (ii) the accustomed standard of living of the protected person and dependents; and (iii) other funds or sources used for the support of the protected person.

(3) The conservator may expend funds of the estate for the support of persons legally dependent on the protected person and others who are members of the protected person's household who are unable to support themselves, and who are in need of support.

(4) Funds expended under this subsection may be paid by the conservator to any person, including the protected person, to reimburse for expenditures that the conservator might have made, or in advance for services to be rendered to the protected person if it is reasonable to expect the services will be performed and advance payments are customary or reasonably necessary under the circumstances.

(5) A conservator, in discharging the responsibilities conferred by Court order and this Part, shall implement the principles described in Section 5-407(a), to the extent possible.

(b) If the estate is ample to provide for the purposes implicit in the distributions authorized by the preceding subsections, a conservator for a protected person other than a minor has power to make gifts to charity and other objects as the protected person might have been expected to make, in amounts that do not exceed in total for any year 20 percent of the income from the estate.

(c) When a minor who has not been adjudged disabled under Section 5-401(c) attains majority, the conservator, after meeting all claims and expenses of administration, shall pay over and distribute all funds and properties to the formerly protected person as soon as possible.

(d) If satisfied that a protected person's disability, other than minority, has ceased, the conservator, after meeting all claims and expenses of administration, shall pay over and distribute all funds and properties to the formerly protected person as soon as possible.

(e) If a protected person dies, the conservator shall deliver to the Court for safekeeping any will of the deceased protected person which may have come into the conservator's possession, inform the executor or beneficiary named therein of the delivery, and retain the estate for delivery to a duly appointed personal representative of the decedent or other persons entitled thereto. If, 40 days after the death of the protected person, no other person has been appointed personal representative and no application or petition for appointment is before the Court, the conservator may apply to exercise the powers and duties of a personal representative in order to be able to proceed to administer and distribute the decedent's estate. Upon application for an order granting the powers of a personal representative to a conservator, after notice to any person nominated personal representative by any will of which the applicant is aware, the Court may grant the application upon determining that there is no objection and endorse the letters of the conservator to note that the formerly protected person is deceased and that the conservator has acquired all of the powers and duties of a personal representative. The making and entry of an order under this section has the effect of an order of appointment of a personal representative [as provided in Section 3-308 and Parts 6 through 10 of Article III], but the estate in the name of the conservator, after administration, may be distributed to the decedent's successors without prior re-transfer to the conservator as personal representative.

§ 5-425. [Enlargement or Limitation of Powers of Conservator.]

Subject the restrictions in Section 5-407(c), the Court may confer on a conservator at the lime of appointment or later, in addition to the powers conferred by Sections 5-423 and 5-424, any power that the Court itself could exercise under Sections 5-407(b)(2) and 5-407(b)(3). The Court, at the time of appointment or later, may limit the powers of a conservator otherwise conferred by Sections 5-423 and 5-424 or previously conferred by the Court and may at any time remove or modify any limitation. If the Court limits any power conferred on the conservator by Section 5-423 or Section 5-424, or specifies, as provided in Section 5-419(a), that title to some but not all assets of the protected person vest in the conservator, the limitation or specification of assets subject to the conservatorship must be endorsed upon the letters of appointment.

§ 5-426. [Preservation of Estate Plan; Right to Examine.]

In (i) investing the estate, (ii) selecting assets of the estate for distribution under subsections (a) and (b) of Section 5-424, and (iii) utilizing powers of revocation or withdrawal available for the support of the protected person and exercisable by the conservator or the Court, the conservator and the Court shall take into account any estate plan of the protected person known to them, including a will, any revocable trust of which the person is settlor, and any contract, transfer, or joint ownership arrangement originated by the protected person with provisions for payment or transfer of benefits or interests at the person's death to another or others. The conservator may examine the will of the protected person.

§ 5-427. [Claims Against Protected Person; Enforcement.]

(a) A conservator may pay or secure from the estate claims against the estate or against the protected person arising before or after the conservatorship upon their presentation and allowance in accordance with the priorities stated in subsection (c). A claim may be presented by either of the following methods:

(1) The claimant may deliver or mail to the conservator a written statement of the claim indicating its basis, the name and mailing address of the claimant, and the amount claimed; or

(2) The claimant may file a written statement of the claim, in the form prescribed by rule, with the clerk of Court and deliver or mail a copy of the statement to the conservator.

(b) A claim is deemed presented on the first to occur of receipt of the written statement of claim by the conservator or the filing of the claim with the Court. A presented claim is allowed if it is not disallowed by written statement mailed by the conservator to the claimant within 60 days after its presentation. The presentation of a claim tolls any statute of limitation relating to the claim until 30 days after its disallowance.

(c) A claimant whose claim has not been paid may petition the [appropriate] Court for determination of the claim at any time before it is barred by the applicable statute of limitation and, upon due proof, procure an order for its allowance, payment, or security from the estate. If a proceeding is pending against a protected person at the time of appointment of a conservator or is initiated against the protected person thereafter, the moving party shall give notice of the proceeding to the conservator if the proceeding could result in creating a claim against the estate.

(d) If it appears that the estate in conservatorship is likely to be exhausted before all existing claims are paid, the conservator shall distribute the estate in money or in kind in payment of claims in the following order:

(1) costs and expenses of administration;

(2) claims of the federal or state government having priority under other laws;

(3) claims incurred by the conservator for care, maintenance, and education, previously

provided to the protected person or the protected person's dependents;

(4) claims arising prior to the conservatorship;

(5) all other claims.

(e) No preference may be given in the payment of any claim over any other claim of the same class, and a claim due and payable is not entitled to a preference over claims not due; but if it appears that the assets of the conservatorship are adequate to meet all existing claims, the Court, acting in the best interest of the protected person, may order the conservator to give a mortgage or other security on the conservatorship estate to secure payment at some future date of any or all claims in class 5.

§ 5-428. [Personal Liability of Conservator.]

(a) Unless otherwise provided in the contract, a conservator is not personally liable on a contract properly entered into in fiduciary capacity in the course of administration of the estate unless the conservator fails to reveal the representative capacity and identify the estate in the contract.

(b) The conservator is personally liable for obligations arising from ownership or control of property of the estate or for torts committed in the course of administration of the estate only if personally at fault.

(c) Claims based on (i) contracts entered into by a conservator in fiduciary capacity, (ii) obligations arising from ownership or control of the estate, or (iii) torts committed in the course of administration of the estate, may be asserted against the estate by proceeding against the conservator in fiduciary capacity, whether or not the conservator is personally liable therefor.

(d) Any question of liability between the estate and the conservator personally may be determined in a proceeding for accounting, surcharge, or indemnification, or other appropriate proceeding or action.

§ 5-429. [Termination of Proceedings.]

The protected person, conservator, or any other interested person, may petition the Court to terminate the conservatorship. A protected person seeking termination is entitled to the same rights and procedures as in an original proceeding for a protective order. The Court, upon determining after notice and hearing that the minority or disability of the protected person has ceased, shall terminate the conservatorship. Upon termination, title to assets of the estate passes to the formerly protected person or to successors. The order of termination must provide for expenses of administration and direct the conservator to execute appropriate instruments to evidence the transfer.

§ 5-430. [Payment of Debt and Delivery of Property to Foreign Conservator without Local Proceedings.]

(a) Any person indebted to a protected person or having possession of property or of an instrument evidencing a debt, stock, or chose in action belonging to a protected person may pay or deliver it to a conservator, guardian of the estate, or other like fiduciary appointed by a court of the state of residence of the protected person upon being presented with proof of appointment and an affidavit made by or on behalf of the fiduciary stating:

(1) that no protective proceeding relating to the protected person is pending in this State; and

(2) that the foreign fiduciary is entitled to payment or to receive delivery.

(b) If the person to whom the affidavit is presented is not aware of any protective proceeding pending in this State, payment or delivery in response to the demand and affidavit discharges the debtor or possessor.

§ 5-431. [Foreign Conservator; Proof of Authority; Bond; Powers.]

If a conservator has not been appointed in this State and no petition in a protective proceeding is pending in this State, a conservator appointed in the state in which the protected person resides may file in a Court of this State in a [county] in which property belonging to the protected person is located, authenticated copies of letters of appointment and of any bond. Thereafter, the domiciliary foreign conservator may exercise as to assets in this State all powers of a conservator appointed in this State and may maintain actions and proceedings in this State subject to any conditions imposed upon non-resident parties generally.

Part 5
Durable Power of Attorney

§ 5-501. [Definition.]

A durable power of attorney is a power of attorney by which a principal designates another his attorney in fact in writing and the writing contains the words "This power of attorney shall not be affected by subsequent disability or incapacity of the principal, or lapse of time," or "This power of attorney shall become effective upon the disability or incapacity of the principal," or similar words showing the intent of the principal that the authority conferred shall be exercisable notwithstanding the principal's subsequent disability or incapacity, and, unless it states a time of termination, notwithstanding the lapse of time since the execution of the instrument.

As amended in 1984.

§ 5-502. [Durable Power of Attorney Not Affected by Lapse of Time, Disability or Incapacity.]

All acts done by an attorney in fact pursuant to a durable power of attorney during any period of disability or incapacity of the principal have the same effect and inure to the benefit of and bind the principal and his successors in interest as if the principal were competent and not disabled. Unless the instrument states a time of termination, the power is exercisable notwithstanding the lapse of time since the execution of the instrument.

As amended in 1987.

§ 5-503. [Relation of Attorney in Fact to Court-appointed Fiduciary.]

(a) If, following execution of a durable power of attorney, a court of the principal's domicile appoints a conservator, guardian of the estate, or other fiduciary charged with the management of all of the principal's property or all of his property except specified exclusions, the attorney in fact is accountable to the fiduciary as well as to the principal. The fiduciary has the same power to revoke or amend the power of attorney that the principal would have had if he were not disabled or incapacitated.

(b) A principal may nominate, by a durable power of attorney, the conservator, guardian of his estate, or guardian of his person for consideration by the court if protective proceedings for the principal's person or estate are thereafter commenced. The court shall make its appointment in accordance with the principal's most recent nomination in a durable power of attorney except for good cause or disqualification.

§ 5-504. [Power of Attorney Not Revoked Until Notice.]

(a) The death of a principal who has executed a written power of attorney, durable or otherwise, does not revoke or terminate the agency as to the attorney in fact or other person, who, without actual knowledge of the death of the principal, acts in good faith under the power. Any action so taken, unless otherwise invalid or unenforceable, binds successors in interest of the principal.

(b) The disability or incapacity of a principal who has previously executed a written power of attorney that is not a durable power does not revoke or terminate the agency as to the attorney in fact or other person, who, without actual knowledge of the disability or incapacity of the principal, acts in good faith under the power. Any action so taken, unless otherwise invalid or unenforceable, binds the principal and his successors in interest.

§ 5-505. [Proof of Continuance of Durable and Other Powers of Attorney by Affidavit.]

As to acts undertaken in good faith reliance thereon, an affidavit executed by the attorney in fact under a power of attorney, durable or otherwise, stating that he did not have at the time of exercise of the power actual knowledge of the termination of the power by revocation or of the principal's death, disability, or incapacity is conclusive proof of the nonrevocation or nontermination of the power at that time. If the exercise of the power of attorney requires execution and delivery of any instrument that is recordable, the affidavit when authenticated for record is likewise recordable. This section does not affect any provision in a power of attorney for its termination by expiration of time or occurrence of an event other than express revocation or a change in the principal's capacity.

ARTICLE VI
NONPROBATE TRANSFERS ON DEATH

Part 1
Provisions Relating to Effect of Death

§ 6-101. [Nonprobate Transfers on Death.]

(a) A provision for a nonprobate transfer on death in an insurance policy, contract of employment, bond, mortgage, promissory note, certificated or uncertificated security, account agreement, custodial agreement, deposit agreement, compensation plan, pension plan, individual retirement plan, employee benefit plan, trust, conveyance, deed of gift, marital property agreement, or other written instrument of a similar nature is nontestamentary. This subsection includes a written provision that:

(1) money or other benefits due to, controlled by, or owned by a decedent before death must be paid after the decedent's death to a person whom the decedent designates either in the instrument or in a separate writing, including a will, executed either before or at the same time as the instrument, or later;

(2) money due or to become due under the instrument ceases to be payable in the event of death of the promisee or the promisor before payment or demand; or

(3) any property controlled by or owned by the decedent before death which is the subject of the instrument passes to a person the decedent designates either in the instrument or in a separate writing, including a will, executed either before or at the same time as the instrument, or later.

(b) This section does not limit rights of creditors under other laws of this State.

Part 2
Multiple-Person Accounts

SUBPART 1
DEFINITIONS AND GENERAL PROVISIONS

§ 6-201. [Definitions.]

In this part:

(1) "Account" means a contract of deposit between a depositor and a financial institution, and includes a checking account, savings account, certificate of deposit, and share account.

(2) "Agent" means a person authorized to make account transactions for a party.

(3) "Beneficiary" means a person named as one to whom sums on deposit in an account are payable on request after death of all parties or for whom a party is named as trustee.

(4) "Financial institution" means an organization authorized to do business under state or federal laws relating to financial institutions, and includes a bank, trust company, savings bank, building and loan association, savings and loan company or association, and credit union.

(5) "Multiple-party account" means an account payable on request to one or more of two or more parties, whether or not a right of survivorship is mentioned.

(6) "Party" means a person who, by the terms of an account, has a present right, subject to request, to payment from the account rather than as a beneficiary or agent.

(7) "Payment" of sums on deposit includes withdrawal, payment to a party or third person pursuant to check or other request, and a pledge of sums on deposit by a party, or a set-off, reduction, or other disposition of all or part of all account pursuant to a pledge.

(8) "POD designation" means the designation of (i) a beneficiary in an account payable on request to one party during the party's lifetime and on the party's death to one or more beneficiaries, or to one or more parties during their lifetimes and on death of all of them to one or more beneficiaries, or (ii) a beneficiary in an account in the name of one or more parties as trustee for one or more beneficiaries if the relationship is established by the terms of the account and there is no subject of the trust other than the sums on deposit in the account, whether or not payment to the beneficiary is mentioned.

(9) "Receive," as it relates to notice to a financial institution, means receipt in the office or branch office of the financial institution in which the account is established, but if the terms of the account require notice at a particular place, in the place required.

(10) "Request" means a request for payment complying with all terms of the account, including special requirements concerning necessary signatures and regulations of the financial institution; but, for purposes of this part, if terms of the account condition payment on advance notice, a request for payment is treated as immediately effective and a notice of intent to withdraw is treated as a request for payment.

(11) "Sums on deposit" means the balance payable on on account, including interest and dividends earned, whether or not included in the current balance, and any deposit life insurance proceeds added to the account by reason of death of a party.

(12) "Terms of the account" includes the deposit agreement and other terms and conditions, including the form, of the contract of deposit.

§ 6-202. [Limitation on Scope of Part.]

This part does not apply to (i) an account established for a partnership, joint venture, or other organization for a business purpose, (ii) an account controlled by one or more persons as an agent or trustee for a corporation, unincorporated association, or charitable or civic organization, or (iii) a fiduciary or trust account in which the relationship is established other than by the terms of the account.

§ 6-203. [Types of Account; Existing Accounts.]

(a) An account may be for a single party or multiple parties. A multiple-party account may be with or without a right of survivorship between the parties. Subject to Section 6-212(c), either a single-party account or a multiple-party account may have a POD designation, an agency designation, or both.

(b) An account established before, on, or after the effective date of this part, whether in the form prescribed in Section 6-204 or in any other form, is either a single-party account or a multiple-party account, with or without right of survivorship, and with or without a POD designation or an agency designation, within the meaning of this part, and is governed by this part.

§ 6-204. [Forms.]

(a) A contract of deposit that contains provisions in substantially the following form establishes the type of account provided, and the account is governed by the provisions of this part applicable to an account of that type:

UNIFORM SINGLE- OR MULTIPLE-PARTY ACCOUNT FORM

PARTIES [Name One or More Parties]:

_______________ _______________

OWNERSHIP [Select One and Initial]:

___ SINGLE-PARTY ACCOUNT
___ MULTIPLE-PARTY ACCOUNT

Parties own account in proportion to net contributions unless there is clear and convincing evidence of a different intent.

RIGHTS AT DEATH [Select One and Initial]:

___ SINGLE-PARTY ACCOUNT

At death of party, ownership passes as part of party's estate.

___ SINGLE-PARTY ACCOUNT WITH POD (PAY ON DEATH) DESIGNATION

[Name one Or More Beneficiaries]:

_______________ _______________

At death of party, ownership passes to POD beneficiaries and is not part of party's estate.

___ MULTIPLE-PARTY ACCOUNT WITH RIGHT OF SURVIVORSHIP

At death of party, ownership passes to surviving parties.

___ MULTIPLE-PARTY ACCOUNT WITH RIGHT OF SURVIVORSHIP AND POD (PAY ON DEATH) DESIGNATION

[Name One or More Beneficiaries]:

_______________ _______________

At death of last surviving party, ownership passes to POD beneficiaries and is not part of last surviving party's estate.

___ MULTIPLE-PARTY ACCOUNT WITHOUT RIGHT OF SURVIVORSHIP

At death of party, deceased party's ownership passes as part of deceased party's estate.

AGENCY (POWER OF ATTORNEY) DESIGNATION [Optional]

Agents may make account transactions for parties but have no ownership or rights at death unless named as POD beneficiaries.

[To Add Agency Designation To Account, Name One or More Agents]:

_______________ _______________

[Select One And Initial]:

___ AGENCY DESIGNATION SURVIVES DISABILITY OR INCAPACITY OF PARTIES

___ AGENCY DESIGNATION TERMINATES ON DISABILITY OR INCAPACITY OF PARTIES

(b) A contract of deposit that does not contain provisions in substantially the form provided in subsection (a) is governed by the provisions of this part applicable to the type of account that most nearly conforms to the depositor's intent.

§ 6-205. [Designation of Agent.]

(a) By a writing signed by all parties, the parties may designate as agent of all parties on an account a person other than a party.

(b) Unless the terms of an agency designation provide that the authority of the agent terminates on disability or incapacity of a party, the agent's authority survives disability and incapacity. The agent may act for a disabled or incapacitated party until the authority of the agent is terminated.

(c) Death of the sole party or last surviving party terminates the authority of an agent.

§ 6-206. [Applicability of Part.]

The provisions of Subpart 2 concerning beneficial ownership as between parties or as between parties and beneficiaries apply only to controversies between those persons and their creditors and other successors, and do not apply to the right of those persons to payment as determined by the terms of the account. Subpart 3 governs the liability and set-off rights of financial institutions that make payments pursuant to it.

SUBPART 2
OWNERSHIP AS BETWEEN PARTIES AND OTHERS

§ 6-211. [Ownership During Lifetime.]

(a) In this section, "net contribution" of a party means the sum of all deposits to an account made by or for the party, less all payments from the account made to or for the party which have not been paid to or applied to the use of another party and a proportionate share of any charges deducted from the account, plus a proportionate share of any interest or dividends earned, whether or not included in the current balance. The term includes deposit life insurance proceeds added to the account by reason of death of the party whose net contribution is in question.

(b) During the lifetime of all parties, an account belongs to the parties in proportion to the net contribution of each to the sums on deposit, unless there is clear and convincing evidence of a different intent. As between parties married to each other, in the absence of proof otherwise, the net contribution of each is presumed to be an equal amount.

(c) A beneficiary in an account having a POD designation has no right to sums on deposit during the lifetime of any party.

(d) An agent in an account with an agency designation has no beneficial right to sums on deposit.

§ 6-212. [Rights at Death.]

(a) Except as otherwise provided in this section, on death of a party sums on deposit in a multiple-party account belong to the surviving party or parties. If two or more parties survive and one is the surviving spouse of the decedent, the amount to which the decedent, immediately before death, was beneficially entitled under Section 6-211 belongs to the surviving spouse. If two or more parties survive and none is the surviving spouse of the decedent, the amount to which the decedent, immediately before death, was beneficially entitled under Section 6-211 belongs to the surviving parties in equal shares, and augments the proportion to which each survivor, immediately before the decedent's death, was beneficially entitled under Section 6-211, and the right of survivorship continues between the surviving parties.

(b) In an account with a POD designation:

(1) On death of one of two or more parties, the rights in sums on deposit are governed by subsection (a).

(2) On death of the sole party or the last survivor of two or more parties, sums on deposit belong to the surviving beneficiary or beneficiaries. If two or more beneficiaries survive, sums on deposit belong to them in equal and undivided shares, and there is no right of survivorship in the event of death of a beneficiary thereafter. If no beneficiary survives, sums on deposit belong to the estate of the last surviving party.

(c) Sums on deposit in a single-party account without a POD designation, or in a multiple-party account that, by the terms of the account, is without right of survivorship, are not affected by death of a party, but the amount to which the decedent, immediately before death, was beneficially entitled under Section 6-211 is transferred as part of the decedent's estate. A POD designation in a multiple-party account without right of survivorship is ineffective. For purposes of this section, designation of an account as a tenancy in common establishes that the account is without right of survivorship.

(d) The ownership right of a surviving party or beneficiary, or of the decedent's estate, in sums on deposit is subject to requests for payment made by a party before the party's death, whether paid by the financial institution before or after death, or unpaid. The surviving party or beneficiary, or the decedent's estate, is liable to the payee of an unpaid request for payment. The liability is limited to a proportionate share of the amount transferred under this section, to the extent necessary to discharge the request for payment.

§ 6-213. [Alteration of Rights.]

(a) Rights at death under Section 6-212 are determined by the type of account at the death of a party. The type of account may be altered by written notice given by a party to the financial institution to change the type of account or to stop or vary payment under the terms of the account. The notice must be signed by a party and received by the financial institution during the party's lifetime.

(b) A right of survivorship arising from the express terms of the account, Section 6-212, or a POD designation, may not be altered by will.

§ 6-214. [Accounts and Transfers Nontestamentary.]

Except as provided in Part 2 of Article II (elective share of surviving spouse) or as a consequence of, and to the extent directed by, Section 6-215, a transfer resulting from the application of Section 6-212 is effective by reason of the terms of the account involved and this part and is not testamentary or subject to Articles I through IV (estate administration).

§ 6-215. [Rights of Creditors and Others.]

(a) If other assets of the estate are insufficient, a transfer resulting from a right of survivorship or POD designation under this part is not effective against the estate of a deceased party to the extent needed to pay claims against the estate and statutory allowances to the surviving spouse and children.

(b) A surviving party or beneficiary who receives payment from an account after death of a party is liable to account to the personal representative of the decedent for a proportionate share of the amount received to the extent necessary to discharge the claims and allowances described in subsection (a) remaining unpaid after application of the decedent's estate. A proceeding to assert the liability may not be commenced unless the personal representative has received a written demand by the surviving spouse, a creditor, a child, or a person acting for a child of the decedent. The proceeding must be commenced within one year after death of the decedent.

(c) A surviving party or beneficiary against whom a proceeding to account is brought may join as a party to the proceeding a surviving party or beneficiary of any other account of the decedent.

(d) Sums recovered by the personal representative must be administered as part of the decedent's estate. This section does not affect the protection from claims of the personal representative or estate of a deceased party provided in Section 6-226 for a financial institution that makes payment in accordance with the terms of the account.

§ 6-216. [Community Property and Tenancy by the Entireties.]

(a) A deposit of community properly in an account does not alter the community character of the property or community rights in the property, but a right of survivorship between parties married to each other arising from the express terms of the account or Section 6-212 may not be altered by will.

(b) This part does not affect the law governing tenancy by the entireties.

SUBPART 3
PROTECTION OF FINANCIAL INSTITUTIONS

§ 6-221. [Authority of Financial Institution.]

A financial institution may enter into a contract of deposit for a multiple-party account to the same extent it may enter into a contract of deposit for a single-party account, and may provide for a POD designation and an agency designation in either a single-party account or a multiple-party account. A financial institution need not inquire as to the source of a deposit to an account or as to the proposed application of a payment from an account.

§ 6-222. [Payment on Multiple-Party Account.]

A financial institution, on request, may pay sums on deposit in a multiple-party account to:

(1) one or more of the parties, whether or not another party is disabled, incapacitated, or deceased when payment is requested and whether or not the party making the request survives another party; or

(2) the personal representative, if any, or, if there is none, the heirs or devisees of a deceased party if proof of death is presented to the financial institution showing that the deceased party was the survivor of all other persons named on the account either as a party or beneficiary, unless the account is without right of survivorship under Section 6-212.

§ 6-223. [Payment on POD Designation.]

A financial institution, on request, may pay sums on deposit in an account with a POD designation to:

(1) one or more of the parties, whether or not another party is disabled, incapacitated, or deceased when the payment is requested and whether or not a party survives another party;

(2) the beneficiary or beneficiaries, if proof of death is presented to the financial institution showing that the beneficiary or beneficiaries survived all persons named as parties; or

(3) the personal representative, if any, or, if there is none, the heirs or devisees of a deceased party, if proof of death is presented to the financial institution showing that the deceased party was the survivor of all other persons named on the account either as a party or beneficiary.

§ 6-224. [Payment to Designated Agent.]

A financial institution, on request of an agent under an agency designation for an account, may pay to the agent sums on deposit in the account, whether or not a party is disabled. incapacitated, or deceased when the request is made or received, and whether or not the authority of the agent terminates on the disability or incapacity of a party.

§ 6-225. [Payment to Minor.]

If a financial institution is required or permitted to make payment pursuant to this part to a minor designated as a beneficiary, payment may be made pursuant to the Uniform Transfers to Minors Act.

§ 6-226. [Discharge.]

(a) Payment made pursuant to this part in accordance with the type of account discharges the financial institution from all claims for amounts so paid, whether or not the payment is consistent with the beneficial ownership of the account as between parties, beneficiaries, or their successors. Payment may be made whether or not a party, beneficiary, or agent is disabled, incapacitated, or deceased when payment is requested, received, or made.

(b) Protection under this section does not extend to payments made after a financial institution has received written notice from a party, or from the personal representative, surviving spouse, or heir or devisee of a deceased party, to the effect that payments in accordance with the terms of the account, including one having an agency designation, should not be permitted, and the financial institution has had a reasonable opportunity to act on it when the payment is made. Unless the notice is withdrawn by the person giving it, the successor of any deceased party must concur in a request for payment if the financial institution is to be protected under this section. Unless a financial institution has been served with process in an action or proceeding, no other notice or other information shown to have been available to the financial institution affects its right to protection under this section.

(c) A financial institution that receives written notice pursuant to this section or otherwise has reason to believe that a dispute exists as to the rights of the parties may refuse, without liability, to make payments in accordance with the terms of the account.

(d) Protection of a financial institution under this section does not affect the rights of parties in disputes between themselves or their successors concerning the beneficial ownership of sums on deposit in accounts or payments made from accounts.

§ 6-227. [Set-off.]

Without qualifying any other statutory right to set-off or lien and subject to any contractual provision, if a party is indebted to a financial institution, the financial institution has a right to set-off against the account. The amount of the account subject to set-off is the proportion to which the party is, or immediately before death was, beneficially entitled under Section 6-211 or, in the absence of proof of that proportion, an equal share with all parties request is made or received, and whether or not the authority of the agent terminates on the disability or incapacity of a party.

Part 3
Uniform TOD Security Registration Act

§ 6-301. [Definitions.]

In this part:

(1) "Beneficiary form" means a registration of a security which indicates the present owner of the security and the intention of the owner regarding the person who will become the owner of the security upon the death of the owner

(2) "Register," including its derivatives, means to issue a certificate showing the ownership of a certificated security or, in the case of an uncertificated security, to initiate or transfer an account showing ownership of securities.

(3) "Registering entity" means a person who originates or transfers a security title by registration, and includes a broker maintaining security accounts for customers and a transfer agent or other person acting for or as an issuer of securities.

(4) "Security" means a share, participation, or other interest in property, in a business, or in an obligation of an enterprise or other issuer, and includes a certificated security, an uncertificated security, and a security account.

(5) "Security account" means (i) a reinvestment account associated with a security, a securities account with a broker, a cash balance in a brokerage account, cash, interest, earnings, or dividends earned or declared on a security in an account, a reinvestment account, or a brokerage account, whether or not credited to the account before the owner's death, or (ii) a cash balance or other property held for or due to the owner of a security as a replacement for or product of an account security, whether or not credited to the account before the owner's death.

§ 6-302. [Registration in Beneficiary Form; Sole or Joint Tenancy Ownership.]

Only individuals whose registration of a security shows sole ownership by one individual or multiple ownership by two or more with right of survivorship, rather than as tenants in common, may obtain registration in beneficiary form. Multiple owners of a security registered in beneficiary form hold as joint tenants with right of survivorship, as tenants by the entireties, or as owners of community property held in survivorship form, and not as tenants in common.

§ 6-303. [Registration in Beneficiary Form; Applicable Law.]

A security may be registered in beneficiary form if the form is authorized by this or a similar statute of the state of organization of the issuer or registering entity, the location of the registering entity's principal office, the office of its transfer agent or its office making the registration, or by this or a similar statute of the law of the state listed as the owner's address at the time of registration. A registration governed by the law of a jurisdiction in which this or similar legislation is not in force or was not in force when a registration in beneficiary form was made is nevertheless presumed to be valid and authorized as a matter of contract law.

§ 6-304. [Origination of Registration in Beneficiary Form.]

A security, whether evidenced by certificate or account, is registered in beneficiary form when the registration includes a designation of a beneficiary to take the ownership at the death of the owner or the deaths of all multiple owners.

§ 6-305. [Form of Registration in Beneficiary Form.]

Registration in beneficiary form may be shown by the words "transfer on death" or the abbreviation "TOD," or by the words "pay on death" or the abbreviation "POD," after the name of the registered owner and before the name of a beneficiary.

§ 6-306. [Effect of Registration in Beneficiary Form.]

The designation of a TOD beneficiary on a registration in beneficiary form has no effect on ownership until the owner's death. A registration of a security in beneficiary form may be canceled or changed at any time by the sole owner or all then surviving owners without the consent of the beneficiary.

§ 6-307. [Ownership on Death of Owner.]

On death of a sole owner or the last to die of all multiple owners, ownership of securities registered in beneficiary form passes to the beneficiary or beneficiaries who survive all owners. On proof of death of all owners and compliance with any applicable requirements of the registering entity, a security registered in beneficiary form may be registered in the name of the beneficiary or beneficiaries who survive the death of all owners. Until division of the security after the death of all owners, multiple beneficiaries surviving the death of all owners hold their interests as tenants in common. If no beneficiary survives the death of all owners, the security belongs to the estate of the deceased sole owner or the estate of the last to die of all multiple owners.

§ 6-308. [Protection of Registering Entity.]

(a) A registering entity is not required to offer or to accept a request for security registration in beneficiary form. If a registration in beneficiary form is offered by a registering entity, the owner requesting registration in beneficiary form assents to the protections given to the registering entity by this part.

(b) By accepting a request for registration of a security in beneficiary form, the registering entity agrees that the registration will be implemented on death of the deceased owner as provided in this part.

(c) A registering entity is discharged from all claims to a security by the estate, creditors, heirs, or devisees of a deceased owner if it registers a transfer of the security in accordance with Section 6-307 and does so in good faith reliance (i) on the registration, (ii) on this part, and (iii) on information provided to it by affidavit of the personal representative of the deceased owner, or by the surviving beneficiary or by the surviving beneficiary's representatives, or other information available to the registering entity. The protections of this part do not extend to a reregistration or payment made after a registering entity has received written notice from any claimant to any interest in the security objecting to implementation of a registration in beneficiary form. No other notice or other information available to the registering entity affects its right to protection under this part.

(d) The protection provided by this part to the registering entity of a security does not affect the rights of beneficiaries in disputes between themselves and other claimants to ownership of the security transferred or its value or proceeds.

§ 6-309. [Nontestamentary Transfer on Death.]

(a) A transfer on death resulting from a registration in beneficiary form is effective by reason of the contract regarding the registration between the owner and the registering entity and this part and is not testamentary.

(b) This part does not limit the rights of creditors of security owners against beneficiaries and other transferees under other laws of this State.

§ 6-310. [Terms, Conditions, and Forms for Registration.]

(a) A registering entity offering to accept registrations in beneficiary form may establish the terms and conditions under which it will receive requests (i) for registrations in beneficiary form, and (ii) for implementation of registrations in beneficiary form, including requests for cancellation of previously registered POD beneficiary designations and requests for reregistration to effect a change of beneficiary. The terms and conditions so established may provide for proving death, avoiding or resolving any problems concerning fractional shares, designating primary and contingent beneficiaries, and substituting a named beneficiary's descendants to take in the place of the named beneficiary in the event of the beneficiary's death. Substitution may be indicated by appending to the name of the primary beneficiary the letters LDPS, standing for "lineal descendants per stirpes." This designation substitutes a deceased beneficiary's descendants who survive the owner for a beneficiary who fails to so survive, the descendants to be identified and to share in accordance with the law of the beneficiary's domicile at the owner's death governing inheritance by descendants of an intestate. Other forms of identifying beneficiaries who are to take on one or more contingencies, and rules for providing proofs and assurances needed to satisfy reasonable concerns by registering entities regarding conditions and identities relevant to accurate implementation of registrations in beneficiary form, may be contained in a registering entity's terms and conditions.

(b) The following are illustrations of registrations in beneficiary form which a registering entity may authorize:

(1) Sole owner-sole beneficiary: John S. Brown TOD (or POD) John S. Brown Jr.

(2) Multiple owners-sole beneficiary: John S. Brown Mary B. Brown JT TEN TOD John S. Brown Jr.

(3) Multiple owners-primary and secondary (substituted) beneficiaries: John S. Brown Mary B. Brown JT TEN TOD John S. Brown Jr SUB BENE Peter Q. Brown or John S. Brown Mary B. Brown JT TEN TOD John S. Brown Jr LDPS.

§ 6-311. [Application of Part.]

This part applies to registrations of securities in beneficiary form made before or after [effective date], by decedents dying on or after [effective date].

ARTICLE VII
TRUST ADMINISTRATION

Part 1
Trust Registration

§ 7-101. [Duty to Register Trusts.]

The trustee of a trust having its principal place of administration in this state shall register the trust in the Court of this state at the principal place of administration. Unless otherwise designated in the trust instrument, the principal place of administration of a trust is the trustee's usual place of business where the records pertaining to the trust are kept, or at the trustee's residence if he has no such place of business. In the case of co-trustees, the principal place of administration, if not otherwise designated in the trust instrument, is (1) the usual place of business of the corporate trustee if there is but one corporate co-trustee, or (2) the usual place of business or residence of the individual trustee who is a professional fiduciary if there is but one such person and no corporate co-trustee, and otherwise (3) the usual place of business or residence of any of the co-trustees as agreed upon by them. The duty to register under this Part does not apply to the trustee of a trust if registration would be inconsistent with the retained jurisdiction of a foreign court from which the trustee cannot obtain release.

§ 7-102. [Registration Procedures.]

Registration shall be accomplished by filing a statement indicating the name and address of the trustee in which it acknowledges the trusteeship. The statement shall indicate whether the trust has been registered elsewhere. The statement shall identify the trust:

(1) in the case of a testamentary trust, by the name of the testator and the date and place of domiciliary probate;

(2) in the case of a written inter vivos trust, by the name of each settlor and the original trustee and the date of the trust instrument; or

(3) in the case of an oral trust, by information identifying the settlor or other source of funds and describing the time and manner of the trust's creation and the terms of the trust, including the subject matter, beneficiaries and time of performance. If a trust has been registered elsewhere, registration in this state is ineffective until the earlier registration is released by order of the Court where prior registration occurred, or an instrument executed by the trustee and all beneficiaries, filed with the registration in this state.

§ 7-103. [Effect of Registration.]

(a) By registering a trust, or accepting the trusteeship of a registered trust, the trustee submits personally to the jurisdiction of the Court in any proceeding under 7-201 of this Code relating to the trust that may be initiated by any interested person while the trust remains registered. Notice of any proceeding shall be delivered to the trustee, or mailed to him by ordinary first class mail at his address as listed in the registration or as thereafter reported to the Court and to his address as then known to the petitioner.

(b) To the extent of their interests in the trust, all beneficiaries of a trust properly registered in this state are subject to the jurisdiction of the court of registration for the purposes of proceedings under Section 7-201, provided notice is given pursuant to Section 1-401.

§ 7-104. [Effect of Failure to Register.]

A trustee who fails to register a trust in a proper place as required by this Part, for purposes of any proceedings initiated by a beneficiary of the trust prior to registration, is subject to the personal jurisdiction of any Court in which the trust could have been registered. In addition, any trustee who, within 30 days after receipt of a written demand by a settlor or beneficiary of the trust, fails to register a trust as required by this Part is subject to removal and denial of compensation or to surcharge as the Court may direct. A provision in the terms of the trust purporting to excuse the trustee from the duty to register, or directing that the trust or trustee shall not be subject to the jurisdiction of the Court, is ineffective.

§ 7-105. [Registration, Qualification of Foreign Trustee.]

A foreign corporate trustee is required to qualify as a foreign corporation doing business in this state if it maintains the principal place of administration of any trust within the state. A foreign co-trustee is not required to qualify in this state solely because its co-trustee maintains the principal place of administration in this state. Unless otherwise doing business in this state, local qualification by a foreign trustee, corporate or individual, is not required in order for the trustee to receive distribution from a local estate or to hold, invest in, manage or acquire property located in this state, or maintain litigation. Nothing in this section affects a determination of what other acts require qualification as doing business in this state.

Part 2
Jurisdiction of Court Concerning Trusts

§ 7-201. [Court; Exclusive Jurisdiction of Trusts.]

(a) The Court has exclusive jurisdiction of proceedings initiated by interested parties concerning the internal affairs of trusts. Proceedings which may be maintained under this section are those concerning the administration and distribution of trusts, the declaration of rights and the determination of other matters involving trustees and beneficiaries of trusts. These include, but are not limited to, proceedings to:

(1) appoint or remove a trustee;

(2) review trustees' fees and to review and settle interim or final accounts;

(3) ascertain beneficiaries, determine any question arising in the administration or distribution of any trust including questions of construction of trust instruments, to instruct trustees, and determine the existence or nonexistence of any immunity, power, privilege, duty or right; and

(4) release registration of a trust.

(b) Neither registration of a trust nor a proceeding under this section result in continuing supervisory proceedings. The management and distribution of a trust estate, submission of accounts and reports to beneficiaries, payment of trustee's fees and other obligations of a trust, acceptance and change of trusteeship, and other aspects of the administration of a trust shall proceed expeditiously consistent with the terms of the trust, free of judicial intervention and without order, approval or other action of any court, subject to the jurisdiction of the Court as invoked by interested parties or as otherwise exercised as provided by law.

§ 7-202. [Trust Proceedings; Venue.]

Venue for proceedings under Section 7-102 involving registered trusts is in the place of registration. Venue for proceedings under Section 7-201 involving trusts not registered in this state is in any place where the trust properly could have been registered, and otherwise by the rules of civil procedure.

§ 7-203. [Trust Proceedings; Dismissal of Matters Relating to Foreign Trusts.]

The Court will not, over the objection of a party, entertain proceedings under Section 7-201 involving a trust registered or having its principal place of administration in another state, unless (1) when all appropriate parties could not be bound by litigation in the courts of the state where the trust is registered or has its principal place of administration or (2) when the interests of justice otherwise would seriously be impaired. The Court may condition a stay or dismissal of a proceeding under this section on the consent of any party to jurisdiction of the state in which the trust is registered or has its principal place of business, or the Court may grant a continuance or enter any other appropriate order.

§ 7-204. [Court; Concurrent Jurisdiction of Litigation Involving Trusts and Third Parties.]

The Court of the place in which the trust is registered has concurrent jurisdiction with other courts of this state of actions and proceedings to determine the existence or nonexistence of trusts created other than by will, of actions by or against creditors or debtors of trusts, and of other actions and proceedings involving trustees and third parties. Venue is determined by the rules generally applicable to civil actions.

§ 7-205. [Proceedings for Review of Employment of Agents and Review of Compensation of Trustee and Employees of Trust.]

On petition of an interested person, after notice to all interested persons, the Court may review the propriety of employment of any person by a trustee including any attorney, auditor, investment advisor or other specialized agent or assistant, and the reasonableness of the compensation of any person so employed, and the reasonableness of the compensation determined by the trustee for his own services. Any person who has received excessive compensation from a trust may be ordered to make appropriate refunds.

§ 7-206. [Trust Proceedings; Initiation by Notice; Necessary Parties.]

Proceedings under Section 7-201 are initiated by filing a petition in the Court and giving notice pursuant to Section 1-401 to interested parties. The Court may order notification of additional persons. A decree is valid as to all who are given notice of the proceeding though fewer than all interested parties are notified.

Part 3
Duties and Liabilities of Trustees

§ 7-301. [General Duties Not Limited.]

Except as specifically provided, the general duty of the trustee to administer a trust expeditiously for the benefit of the beneficiaries is not altered by this Code.

§ 7-302. [Trustee's Standard of Care and Performance.]

Except as otherwise provided by the terms of the trust, the trustee shall observe the standards in dealing with the trust assets that would be observed by a prudent man dealing with the property of another, and if the trustee has special skills or is named trustee on the basis of representations of special skills or expertise, he is under a duty to use those skills.

§ 7-303. [Duty to Inform and Account to Beneficiaries.]

The trustee shall keep the beneficiaries of the trust reasonably informed of the trust and its administration. In addition:

(a) Within 30 days after his acceptance of the trust, the trustee shall inform in writing the current beneficiaries and if possible, one or more persons who under Section 1-403 may represent beneficiaries with future interests, of the Court in which the trust is registered and of his name and address.

(b) Upon reasonable request, the trustee shall provide the beneficiary with a copy of the terms of the trust which describe or affect his interest and with relevant information about the assets of the trust and the particulars relating to the administration.

(c) Upon reasonable request, a beneficiary is entitled to a statement of the accounts of the trust annually and on termination of the trust or change of the trustee.

§ 7-304. [Duty to Provide Bond.]

A trustee need not provide bond to secure performance of his duties unless required by the terms of the trust, reasonably requested by a beneficiary or found by the Court to be necessary to protect the interests of the beneficiaries who are not able to protect themselves and whose interests otherwise are not adequately represented. On petition of the trustee or other interested person the Court may excuse a requirement of bond, reduce the amount of the bond, release the surety, or permit the substitution of another bond with the same or difficult sureties If bond is required, it shall be filed in the Court of registration or other appropriate Court in amounts and with sureties and liabilities as provided in Sections 3-604 and 3-606 relating to bonds or personal representatives.

§ 7-305. [Trustee's Duties; Appropriate Place of Administration; Deviation.]

A trustee is under a continuing duty to administer the trust at a place appropriate to the purposes of the trust and to its sound, efficient management. If the principal place of administration becomes inappropriate for any reason, the Court may enter any order furthering efficient administration and the interests of beneficiaries, including, if appropriate, release of registration, removal of the trustee and appointment of a trustee in another state. Trust provisions relating to the place of administration and to changes in the place of administration or of trustee control unless compliance would be contrary to efficient administration or the purposes of the trust. Views of adult beneficiaries shall be given weight in determining the suitability of the trustee and the place of administration.

§ 7-306. [Personal Liability of Trustee to Third Parties.]

(a) Unless otherwise provided in the contract, a trustee is not personally liable on contracts properly entered into in his fiduciary capacity in the course of administration of the trust estate unless he fails to reveal his representative capacity and identify the trust estate in the contract.

(b) A trustee is personally liable for obligations arising from ownership or control of property of the trust estate or for torts committed in the course of administration of the trust estate only if he is personally at fault.

(c) Claims based on contracts entered into by a trustee in his fiduciary capacity, on obligations arising from ownership or control of the trust estate, or on torts committed in the course of trust administration may be asserted against the trust estate by proceeding against the trustee in his fiduciary capacity, whether or not the trustee is personally liable therefor.

(d) The question of liability as between the trust estate and the trustee individually may be determined in a proceeding for accounting, surcharge or indemnification or other appropriate proceeding.

§ 7-307. [Limitations on Proceedings Against Trustees After Final Account.]

Unless previously barred by adjudication, consent or limitation, any claim against a trustee for breach of trust is barred as to any beneficiary who has received a final account or other statement fully disclosing the matter and showing termination of the trust relationship between the trustee and the beneficiary unless a proceeding to assert the claim is commenced within [6 months] after receipt of the final account or statement. In any event and notwithstanding lack of full disclosure a trustee who has issued a final account or statement received by the beneficiary and has informed the beneficiary of the location and availability of records for his examination is protected after 3 years. A beneficiary is deemed to have received a final account or statement if, being an adult, it is received by him personally or if, being a minor or disabled person, it is received by his representative as described in Section 1-403(1) and (2).

ARTICLE VIII
EFFECTIVE DATE AND REPEALER

§ 8-101 [Time of Taking Effect; Provisions for Transition.]

(a) This Code takes effect on January 1, 19____.

(b) Except as provided elsewhere in this Code, on the effective date of this Code:

(1) the Code applies to any wills of decedents dying thereafter;

(2) the Code applies to any proceedings in Court then pending or thereafter commenced regardless of the time of the death of decedent except to the extent that in the opinion of the Court the former procedure should be made applicable in a particular case in the interest of justice or because of infeasibility of application of the procedure of this Code;

(3) every personal representative including a person administering an estate of a minor or incompetent holding an appointment on that date, continues to hold the appointment but has only the powers conferred by this Code and is subject to the duties imposed with respect to any act occurring or done thereafter;

(4) an act done before the effective date in any proceeding and any accrued right is not impaired by this Code. If a right is acquired, extinguished or barred upon the expiration of a prescribed period of time which has commenced to run by the provisions of any statute before the effective date, the provisions shall remain in force with respect to that right;

(5) any rule of construction or presumption provided in this Code applies to instruments

executed and multiple party accounts opened before the effective date unless there is a clear indication of a contrary intent;

(6) a person holding office as judge of the Court on the effective day of this Act may continue the office of judge of this Court and may be selected for additional terms after the effective date of this Act even though he does not meet the qualifications of a judge as provided in Article 1.

§ 8-102. [Specific Repealer and Amendments.]

(a) The following Acts and parts of Acts are repealed: (1) (2) (3)

(b) The following Acts and parts of Acts are amended: (1) (2) (3)

APPENDIX E

Internal Revenue Service Form 706

Form **706** (Rev. October 1991)
Department of the Treasury Internal Revenue Service

United States Estate (and Generation-Skipping Transfer) Tax Return

Estate of a citizen or resident of the United States (see separate instructions). To be filed for decedents dying after October 8, 1990, and before January 1, 1993. For Paperwork Reduction Act Notice, see page 1 of the instructions.

OMB No. 1545-0015
Expires 6-30-93

Part 1.—Decedent and Executor

1a Decedent's first name and middle initial (and maiden name, if any)	1b Decedent's last name	2 Decedent's social security no.
3a Domicile at time of death (county and state, or foreign country)	3b Year domicile established / 4 Date of birth	5 Date of death
6a Name of executor (see instructions)	6b Executor's address (number and street including apartment or suite no. or rural route; city, town, or post office; state; and ZIP code)	
6c Executor's social security number (see instructions)		
7a Name and location of court where will was probated or estate administered		7b Case number
8 If decedent died testate, check here ▶ ☐ and attach a certified copy of the will.	9 If Form 4768 is attached, check here ▶ ☐	
10 If Schedule R-1 is attached, check here ▶ ☐		

Part 2.—Tax Computation

Line	Description			Line	Amount
1	Total gross estate (from Part 5, Recapitulation, page 3, item 10)			1	
2	Total allowable deductions (from Part 5, Recapitulation, page 3, item 20)			2	
3	Taxable estate (subtract line 2 from line 1)			3	
4	Adjusted taxable gifts (total taxable gifts (within the meaning of section 2503) made by the decedent after December 31, 1976, other than gifts that are includible in decedent's gross estate (section 2001(b))			4	
5	Add lines 3 and 4			5	
6	Tentative tax on the amount on line 5 from Table A in the instructions			6	
7a	If line 5 exceeds $10,000,000, enter the lesser of line 5 or $21,040,000. If line 5 is $10,000,000 or less, skip lines 7a and 7b and enter -0- on line 7c	7a			
b	Subtract $10,000,000 from line 7a	7b			
c	Enter 5% (.05) of line 7b			7c	
8	Total tentative tax (add lines 6 and 7c)			8	
9	Total gift tax payable with respect to gifts made by the decedent after December 31, 1976. Include gift taxes by the decedent's spouse for such spouse's share of split gifts (section 2513) only if the decedent was the donor of these gifts and they are includible in the decedent's gross estate (see instructions)			9	
10	Gross estate tax (subtract line 9 from line 8)			10	
11	Maximum unified credit against estate tax	11	192,800 00		
12	Adjustment to unified credit. (This adjustment may not exceed $6,000. See instructions.)	12			
13	Allowable unified credit (subtract line 12 from line 11)			13	
14	Subtract line 13 from line 10 (but do not enter less than zero)			14	
15	Credit for state death taxes. Do not enter more than line 14. Compute the credit by using the amount on line 3 less $60,000. See Table B in the instructions and **attach credit evidence** (see instructions)			15	
16	Subtract line 15 from line 14			16	
17	Credit for Federal gift taxes on pre-1977 gifts (section 2012) (attach computation)	17			
18	Credit for foreign death taxes (from Schedule(s) P). (Attach Form(s) 706CE)	18			
19	Credit for tax on prior transfers (from Schedule Q)	19			
20	Total (add lines 17, 18, and 19)			20	
21	Net estate tax (subtract line 20 from line 16)			21	
22	Generation-skipping transfer taxes (from Schedule R, Part 2, line 10)			22	
23	Section 4980A increased estate tax (from Schedule S, Part I, line 17) (see instructions)			23	
24	Total transfer taxes (add lines 21, 22, and 23)			24	
25	Prior payments. Explain in an attached statement	25			
26	United States Treasury bonds redeemed in payment of estate tax	26			
27	Total (add lines 25 and 26)			27	
28	Balance due (or overpayment) (subtract line 27 from line 24)			28	

Under penalties of perjury, I declare that I have examined this return, including accompanying schedules and statements, and to the best of my knowledge and belief, it is true, correct, and complete. Declaration of preparer other than the executor is based on all information of which preparer has any knowledge.

Signature(s) of executor(s) Date

Signature of preparer other than executor Address (and ZIP code) Date

Cat. No. 20548R

Form 706 (Rev. 10-91)

Estate of:

Part 3.—Elections by the Executor

Please check the "Yes" or "No" box for each question.	Yes	No
1 Do you elect alternate valuation?		
2 Do you elect special use valuation? If "Yes," you must complete and attach Schedule A-1		
3 Do you elect to pay the taxes in installments as described in section 6166? If "Yes," you must attach the additional information described in the instructions.		
4 Do you elect to postpone the part of the taxes attributable to a reversionary or remainder interest as described in section 6163?		

Part 4.—General Information (Note: *Please attach the necessary supplemental documents.* **You must attach the death certificate.)**

Authorization to receive confidential tax information under Regulations section 601.502(c)(3)(ii), to act as the estate's representative before the Internal Revenue Service, and to make written or oral presentations on behalf of the estate if return prepared by an attorney, accountant, or enrolled agent for the executor:

Name of representative (print or type)	State	Address (number, street, and room or suite no., city, state, and ZIP code)

I declare that I am the ☐ attorney/☐ accountant/☐ enrolled agent (you must check the applicable box) for the executor and prepared this return for the executor. I am not under suspension or disbarment from practice before the Internal Revenue Service and am qualified to practice in the state shown above.

Signature	CAF number	Date	Telephone number

1 Death certificate number and issuing authority (attach a copy of the death certificate to this return).

2 Decedent's business or occupation. If retired, check here ▶ ☐ and state decedent's former business or occupation.

3 Marital status of the decedent at time of death:

☐ Married

☐ Widow or widower—Name, SSN, and date of death of deceased spouse ▶ ....

☐ Single

☐ Legally separated

☐ Divorced—Date divorce decree became final ▶

4a Surviving spouse's name	4b Social security number	4c Amount received (see instructions)

5 Individuals (other than the surviving spouse), trusts, or other estates who receive benefits from the estate (do not include charitable beneficiaries shown in Schedule O) (see instructions). For Privacy Act Notice (applicable to individual beneficiaries only), see the Instructions for Form 1040.

Name of individual, trust, or estate receiving $5,000 or more	Identifying number	Relationship to decedent	Amount (see instructions)
All unascertainable beneficiaries and those who receive less than $5,000 ▶			
Total			

(Continued on next page)

Form 706 (Rev. 10-91)

Part 4.—General Information *(continued)*

	Please check the "Yes" or "No" box for each question.	Yes	No
6	Does the gross estate contain any section 2044 property (qualified terminable interest property (QTIP) from a prior gift or estate) (see instructions)?		
7a	Have Federal gift tax returns ever been filed? If "Yes," please attach copies of the returns, if available, and furnish the following information:		
7b	Period(s) covered / **7c** Internal Revenue office(s) where filed		
	If you answer "Yes" to any of questions 8–16, you must attach additional information as described in the instructions.		
8a	Was there any insurance on the decedent's life that is not included on the return as part of the gross estate?		
b	Did the decedent own any insurance on the life of another that is not included in the gross estate?		
9	Did the decedent at the time of death own any property as a joint tenant with right of survivorship in which (a) one or more of the other joint tenants was someone other than the decedent's spouse, and (b) less than the full value of the property is included on the return as part of the gross estate? If "Yes," you must complete and attach Schedule E		
10	Did the decedent, at the time of death, own any interest in a partnership or unincorporated business or any stock in an inactive or closely held corporation?		
11	Did the decedent make any transfer described in section 2035, 2036, 2037, or 2038 (see the instructions for Schedule G)? If "Yes," you must complete and attach Schedule G		
12	Were there in existence at the time of the decedent's death:		
a	Any trusts created by the decedent during his or her lifetime?		
b	Any trusts not created by the decedent under which the decedent possessed any power, beneficial interest, or trusteeship?		
13	Did the decedent ever possess, exercise, or release any general power of appointment? If "Yes," you must complete and attach Schedule H		
14	Was the marital deduction computed under the transitional rule of Public Law 97-34, section 403(e)(3) (Economic Recovery Tax Act of 1981)? If "Yes," attach a separate computation of the marital deduction, enter the amount on item 18 of the Recapitulation, and note on item 18 "computation attached."		
15	Was the decedent, immediately before death, receiving an annuity described in the "General" paragraph of the instructions for Schedule I? If "Yes," you must complete and attach Schedule I		
16	Did the decedent have a total "excess retirement accumulation" (as defined in section 4980A(d)) in qualified employer plans and individual retirement plans? If "Yes," you must complete and attach Schedule S		

Part 5.—Recapitulation

Item number	Gross estate	Alternate value	Value at date of death
1	Schedule A—Real Estate		
2	Schedule B—Stocks and Bonds		
3	Schedule C—Mortgages, Notes, and Cash		
4	Schedule D—Insurance on the Decedent's Life (attach Form(s) 712)		
5	Schedule E—Jointly Owned Property (attach Form(s) 712 for life insurance)		
6	Schedule F—Other Miscellaneous Property (attach Form(s) 712 for life insurance)		
7	Schedule G—Transfers During Decedent's Life (attach Form(s) 712 for life insurance)		
8	Schedule H—Powers of Appointment		
9	Schedule I—Annuities		
10	Total gross estate (add items 1 through 9). Enter here and on line 1 of the Tax Computation		

Item number	Deductions	Amount
11	Schedule J—Funeral Expenses and Expenses Incurred in Administering Property Subject to Claims	
12	Schedule K—Debts of the Decedent	
13	Schedule K—Mortgages and Liens	
14	Total of items 11 through 13	
15	Allowable amount of deductions from item 14 (see the instructions for item 15 of the Recapitulation)	
16	Schedule L—Net Losses During Administration	
17	Schedule L—Expenses Incurred in Administering Property Not Subject to Claims	
18	Schedule M—Bequests, etc., to Surviving Spouse	
19	Schedule O—Charitable, Public, and Similar Gifts and Bequests	
20	Total allowable deductions (add items 15 through 19). Enter here and on line 2 of the Tax Computation	

Form 706 (Rev. 10-91)

Estate of:

SCHEDULE A—Real Estate

(For jointly owned property that must be disclosed on Schedule E, see the instructions for Schedule E.)

(Real estate that is part of a sole proprietorship should be shown on Schedule F. Real estate that is included in the gross estate under section 2035, 2036, 2037, or 2038 should be shown on Schedule G. Real estate that is included in the gross estate under section 2041 should be shown on Schedule H.)

(If you elect section 2032A valuation, you must complete Schedule A and Schedule A-1.)

Item number	Description	Alternate valuation date	Alternate value	Value at date of death
1				
Total from continuation schedule(s) (or additional sheet(s)) attached to this schedule . .				
TOTAL. (Also enter on Part 5, Recapitulation, page 3, at item 1.)				

(If more space is needed, attach the continuation schedule from the end of this package or additional sheets of the same size.)
(See the instructions on the reverse side.)

Form 706 (Rev. 10-91)

Instructions for Schedule A.— Real Estate

If the total gross estate contains any real estate, you must complete Schedule A and file it with the return. On Schedule A list real estate the decedent owned or had contracted to purchase. Number each parcel in the left- hand column.

Describe the real estate in enough detail so that the IRS can easily locate it for inspection and valuation. For each parcel of real estate, report the area and, if the parcel is improved, describe the improvements. For city or town property, report the street and number, ward, subdivision, block and lot, etc. For rural property, report the township, range, landmarks, etc.

If any item of real estate is subject to a mortgage for which the decedent's estate is liable, that is, if the indebtedness may be charged against other property of the estate that is not subject to that mortgage, or if the decedent was personally liable for that mortgage, you must report the full value of the property in the value column.

Enter the amount of the mortgage under "Description" on this schedule. The unpaid amount of the mortgage may be deducted on Schedule K. If the decedent's estate is NOT liable for the amount of the mortgage, report only the value of the equity of redemption (or value of the property less the indebtedness) in the value column as part of the gross estate. Do not enter any amount less than zero. Do not deduct the amount of indebtedness on Schedule K.

Also list on Schedule A real property the decedent contracted to purchase. Report the full value of the property and not the equity in the value column. Deduct the unpaid part of the purchase price on Schedule K.

Report the value of real estate without reducing it for homestead or other exemption, or the value of dower, curtesy, or a statutory estate created instead of dower or curtesy.

Explain how the reported values were determined and attach copies of any appraisals.

Schedule A Examples

In this example the alternate valuation is not adopted; the date of death is January 1, 1991.

Item number	Description	Alternate valuation date	Alternate value	Value at date of death
1	House and lot, 1921 William Street NW, Washington, DC (lot 6, square 481). Rent of $2,700 due at end of each quarter, February 1, May 1, August 1, and November 1. Value based on appraisal, copy of which is attached			108,000
	Rent due on item 1 for quarter ending November 1, 1990, but not collected at date of death			2,700
	Rent accrued on item 1 for November and December 1990			1,800
2	House and lot, 304 Jefferson Street, Alexandria, VA (lot 18, square 40). Rent of $600 payable monthly. Value based on appraisal, copy of which is attached			96,000
	Rent due on item 2 for December 1990, but not collected at date of death . . .			600

In this example alternate valuation is adopted; the date of death is January 1, 1991.

Item number	Description	Alternate valuation date	Alternate value	Value at date of death
1	House and lot, 1921 William Street NW, Washington, DC (lot 6, square 481). Rent of $2,700 due at end of each quarter, February 1, May 1, August 1, and November 1. Value based on appraisal, copy of which is attached. Not disposed of within 6 months following death	7/1/91	90,000	108,000
	Rent due on item 1 for quarter ending November 1, 1990, but not collected until February 1, 1991	2/1/91	2,700	2,700
	Rent accrued on item 1 for November and December 1990, collected on February 1, 1991	2/1/91	1,800	1,800
2	House and lot, 304 Jefferson Street, Alexandria, VA (lot 18, square 40). Rent of $600 payable monthly. Value based on appraisal, copy of which is attached. Property exchanged for farm on May 1, 1991.	5/1/91	90,000	96,000
	Rent due on item 2 for December 1990, but not collected until February 1, 1991 .	2/1/91	600	600

Form 706 (Rev. 10-91)

Checklist for Section 2032A Election—*If you are going to make the special use valuation election on Schedule A-1, please use this checklist to ensure that you are providing everything necessary to make a valid election.*

To have a valid special use valuation election under section 2032A, you must file, in addition to the Federal estate tax return, (a) a notice of election (Schedule A-1, Part 2), and (b) a fully executed agreement (Schedule A-1, Part 3). You must include certain information in the notice of election. To ensure that the notice of election includes all of the information required for a valid election, use the following checklist. The checklist is for your use only. Do not file it with the return.

1. Does the notice of election include the decedent's name and social security number as they appear on the estate tax return?

2. Does the notice of election include the relevant qualified use of the property to be specially valued?

3. Does the notice of election describe the items of real property shown on the estate tax return that are to be specially valued and identify the property by the Form 706 schedule and item number?

4. Does the notice of election include the fair market value of the real property to be specially valued and also include its value based on the qualified use (determined without the adjustments provided in section 2032A(b)(3)(B)?

5. Does the notice of election include the adjusted value (as defined in section 2032A(b)(3)(B)) of (a) all real property that both passes from the decedent and is used in a qualified use, without regard to whether it is to be specially valued, and (b) all real property to be specially valued?

6. Does the notice of election include (a) the items of personal property shown on the estate tax return that pass from the decedent to a qualified heir and that are used in qualified use and (b) the total value of such personal property adjusted under section 2032A(b)(3)(B)?

7. Does the notice of election include the adjusted value of the gross estate? (See section 2032A(b)(3)(A).)

8. Does the notice of election include the method used to determine the special use value?

9. Does the notice of election include copies of written appraisals of the fair market value of the real property?

10. Does the notice of election include a statement that the decedent and/or a member of his or her family has owned all of the specially valued property for at least 5 years of the 8 years immediately preceding the date of the decedent's death?

11. Does the notice of election include a statement as to whether there were any periods during the 8-year period preceding the decedent's date of death during which the decedent or a member of his or her family (a) did not own the property to be specially valued, (b) use it in a qualified use, or (c) materially participate in the operation of the farm or other business? (See section 2032A(e)(6).)

12. Does the notice of election include, for each item of specially valued property, the name of every person taking an interest in that item of specially valued property and the following information about each such person: (a) the person's address, (b) the person's taxpayer identification number, (c) the person's relationship to the decedent, and (d) the value of the property interest passing to that person based on both fair market value and qualified use?

13. Does the notice of election include affidavits describing the activities constituting material participation and the identity of the material participants?

14. Does the notice of election include a legal description of each item of specially valued property?

(In the case of an election made for qualified woodlands, the information included in the notice of election must include the reason for entitlement to the woodlands election.)

Any election made under section 2032A will not be valid unless a properly executed agreement (Schedule A-1, Part 3) is filed with the estate tax return. To ensure that the agreement satisfies the requirements for a valid election, use the following checklist.

1. Has the agreement been signed by each and every qualified heir having an interest in the property being specially valued?

2. Has every qualified heir expressed consent to personal liability under section 2032A(c) in the event of an early disposition or early cessation of qualified use?

3. Is the agreement that is actually signed by the qualified heirs in a form that is binding on all of the qualified heirs having an interest in the specially valued property?

4. Does the agreement designate an agent to act for the parties to the agreement in all dealings with the IRS on matters arising under section 2032A?

5. Has the agreement been signed by the designated agent and does it give the address of the agent?

Form 706 (Rev. 10-91)

Estate of: | **Decedent's Social Security Number**

SCHEDULE A-1—Section 2032A Valuation

Part 1.—Type of Election:

☐ **Protective election (Regulations section 20.2032A-8(b)).**—Complete Part 2, line 1, and column A of lines 3 and 4. (See instructions.)

☐ **Regular election.**—Complete all of Part 2 (including line 11, if applicable) and Part 3. (See instructions.)

Part 2.—Notice of Election (Regulations section 20.2032A-8(a)(3))

Note: *All real property entered on lines 2 and 3 must also be entered on Schedules A, E, F, G, or H, as applicable.*

1 Qualified use—check one ▶ ☐ Farm used for farming, or
▶ ☐ Trade or business other than farming

2 Real property used in a qualified use, passing to qualified heirs, and to be specially valued on this Form 706.

A Schedule and item number from Form 706	B Full value (without section 2032A(b)(3)(B) adjustment)	C Adjusted value (with section 2032A(b)(3)(B) adjustment)	D Value based on qualified use (without section 2032A(b)(3)(B) adjustment)
Totals			

Attach a legal description of all property listed on line 2.
Attach copies of appraisals showing the column B values for all property listed on line 2.

3 Real property used in a qualified use, passing to qualified heirs, but not specially valued on this Form 706.

A Schedule and item number from Form 706	B Full value (without section 2032A(b)(3)(B) adjustment)	C Adjusted value (with section 2032A(b)(3)(B) adjustment)	D Value based on qualified use (without section 2032A(b)(3)(B) adjustment)
Totals			

If you checked "Regular election," you must attach copies of appraisals showing the column B values for all property listed on line 3.

(Continued on next page)

Form 706 (Rev. 10-91)

4 Personal property used in a qualified use and passing to qualified heirs.

A Schedule and item number from Form 706	B Adjusted value (with section 2032A(b)(3)(B) adjustment)	A (continued) Schedule and item number from Form 706	B (continued) Adjusted value (with section 2032A(b)(3)(B) adjustment)
		"Subtotal" from Col. B, below left	
Subtotal		Total adjusted value	

5 Enter the value of the total gross estate as adjusted under section 2032A(b)(3)(A). ▶

6 Attach a description of the method used to determine the special value based on qualified use.

7 Did the decedent and/or a member of his or her family own all property listed on line 2 for at least 5 of the 8 years immediately preceding the date of the decedent's death? ☐ Yes ☐ No

8 Were there any periods during the 8-year period preceding the date of the decedent's death during which the decedent or a member of his or her family:

	Yes	No
a Did not own the property listed on line 2 above?		
b Did not use the property listed on line 2 above in a qualified use?		
c Did not materially participate in the operation of the farm or other business within the meaning of section 2032A(e)(6)?		

If "Yes" to any of the above, you must attach a statement listing the periods. If applicable, describe whether the exceptions of sections 2032A(b)(4) or (5) are met.

9 Attach affidavits describing the activities constituting material participation and the identity and relationship to the decedent of the material participants.

10 Persons holding interests. Enter the requested information for each party who received any interest in the specially valued property.

	Name	Address
A		
B		
C		
D		
E		
F		
G		
H		

	Identifying number	Relationship to decedent	Fair market value	Special use value
A				
B				
C				
D				
E				
F				
G				
H				

You must attach a computation of the GST tax savings attributable to direct skips for each person listed above who is a skip person. (See instructions.)

11 **Woodlands election.**—Check here ▶ ☐ if you wish to make a woodlands election as described in section 2032A(e)(13). Enter the Schedule and item numbers from Form 706 of the property for which you are making this election ▶

You must attach a statement explaining why you are entitled to make this election. The IRS may issue regulations that require more information to substantiate this election. You will be notified by the IRS if you must supply further information.

Form 706 (Rev. 10-91)

Part 3.—Agreement to Special Valuation Under Section 2032A

Estate of:	Date of Death	Decedent's Social Security Number

We (list all qualified heirs and other persons having an interest in the property required to sign this agreement)

____

____ ,

being all the qualified heirs and ____

____ ,

being all other parties having interests in the property which is qualified real property and which is valued under section 2032A of the Internal Revenue Code, do hereby approve of the election made by ______________________ ,
Executor/Administrator of the estate of ______________________ ,
pursuant to section 2032A to value said property on the basis of the qualified use to which the property is devoted and do hereby enter into this agreement pursuant to section 2032A(d).

The undersigned agree and consent to the application of subsection (c) of section 2032A of the Code with respect to all the property described on line 2 of Part 2 of Schedule A-1 of Form 706, attached to this agreement. More specifically, the undersigned heirs expressly agree and consent to personal liability under subsection (c) of 2032A for the additional estate and GST taxes imposed by that subsection with respect to their respective interests in the above-described property in the event of certain early dispositions of the property or early cessation of the qualified use of the property. It is understood that if a qualified heir disposes of any interest in qualified real property to any member of his or her family, such member may thereafter be treated as the qualified heir with respect to such interest upon filing a Form 706-A and a new agreement.

The undersigned interested parties who are not qualified heirs consent to the collection of any additional estate and GST taxes imposed under section 2032A(c) of the Code from the specially valued property.

If there is a disposition of any interest which passes or has passed to him or her or if there is a cessation of the qualified use of any specially valued property which passes or passed to him or her, each of the undersigned heirs agrees to file a **Form 706-A,** United States Additional Estate Tax Return, and pay any additional estate and GST taxes due within 6 months of the disposition or cessation.

It is understood by all interested parties that this agreement is a condition precedent to the election of special use valuation under section 2032A of the Code and must be executed by every interested party even though that person may not have received the estate (or GST) tax benefits or be in possession of such property.

Each of the undersigned understands that by making this election, a lien will be created and recorded pursuant to section 6324B of the Code on the property referred to in this agreement for the adjusted tax differences with respect to the estate as defined in section 2032A(c)(2)(C).

As the interested parties, the undersigned designate the following individual as their agent for all dealings with the Internal Revenue Service concerning the continued qualification of the specially valued property under section 2032A of the Code and on all issues regarding the special lien under section 6324B. The agent is authorized to act for the parties with respect to all dealings with the Service on matters affecting the qualified real property described earlier. This authority includes the following:

- To receive confidential information on all matters relating to continued qualification under section 2032A of the specially valued real property and on all matters relating to the special lien arising under section 6324B.
- To furnish the Service with any requested information concerning the property.
- To notify the Service of any disposition or cessation of qualified use of any part of the property.
- To receive, but not to endorse and collect, checks in payment of any refund of Internal Revenue taxes, penalties, or interest.
- To execute waivers (including offers of waivers) of restrictions on assessment or collection of deficiencies in tax and waivers of notice of disallowance of a claim for credit or refund.
- To execute closing agreements under section 7121.
- Other acts (specify) ▶ ______________________

By signing this agreement, the agent agrees to provide the Service with any requested information concerning this property and to notify the Service of any disposition or cessation of the qualified use of any part of this property.

Name of Agent	Signature	Address

The property to which this agreement relates is listed in Form 706, United States Estate (and Generation-Skipping Transfer) Tax Return, and in the Notice of Election, along with its fair market value according to section 2031 of the Code and its special use value according to section 2032A. The name, address, social security number, and interest (including the value) of each of the undersigned in this property are as set forth in the attached Notice of Election.

IN WITNESS WHEREOF, the undersigned have hereunto set their hands at ______________________ ,
this __________ day of __________ .

Qualified Heirs ____

____

Other Interested Parties

Instructions for Schedule A-1.—Section 2032A Valuation

The election to value certain farm and closely held business property at its special use value is made by checking "Yes" to line 2 of Part 3, Elections by the Executor, Form 706. Schedule A-1 is used to report the additional information that must be submitted to support this election. In order to make a valid election, you must complete Schedule A-1 and attach all of the required statements and appraisals.

For definitions and additional information concerning special use valuation, see section 2032A and the related regulations.

Part 1.—Type of Election

Estate and GST Tax Elections.—If you elect special use valuation for the estate tax, you must also elect special use valuation for the GST tax and vice versa.

You must value each specific property interest at the same value for GST tax purposes that you value it at for estate tax purposes.

Protective Election.—To make the protective election described in the separate instructions for line 2 of Part 3, Elections by the Executor, you must check this box, enter the decedent's name and social security number in the spaces provided at the top of Schedule A-1, and complete line 1 and column A of lines 3 and 4 of Part 2. For purposes of the protective election, list on line 3 all of the real property that passes to the qualified heirs even though some of the property will be shown on line 2 when the additional notice of election is subsequently filed. You need not complete columns B–D of lines 3 and 4. You need not complete any other line entries on Schedule A-1. Completing Schedule A-1 as described above constitutes a Notice of Protective Election as described in Regulations section 20.2032A-8(b).

Part 2.—Notice of Election

Line 10.—Because the special use valuation election creates a potential tax liability for the recapture tax of section 2032A(c), you must list each person who receives an interest in the specially valued property on Schedule A-1. If there are more than eight persons who receive interests, use an additional sheet that follows the format of line 10. In the columns "Fair market value" and "Special use value," you should enter the total respective values of all the specially valued property interests received by each person.

GST Tax Savings.—To compute the additional GST tax due upon disposition (or cessation of qualified use) of the property, each "skip person" (as defined in the instructions to Schedule R) who receives an interest in the specially valued property must know the total GST tax savings on all of the interests in specially valued property received. This GST tax savings is the difference between the total GST tax that was imposed on all of the interests in specially valued property received by the skip person valued at their special use value and the total GST tax that would have been imposed on the same interests received by the skip person had they been valued at their fair market value.

Because the GST tax depends on the executor's allocation of the GST exemption and the grandchild exclusion, the skip person who receives the interests is unable to compute this GST tax savings. Therefore, for each skip person who receives an interest in specially valued property, you must attach worksheets showing the total GST tax savings attributable to all of that person's interests in specially valued property.

How To Compute the GST Tax Savings.—Before computing each skip person's GST tax savings, you must complete Schedules R and R-1 for the entire estate (using the special use values).

For each skip person, you must complete two Schedules R (Parts 2 and 3 only) as worksheets, one showing the interests in specially valued property received by the skip person at their special use value and one showing the same interests at their fair market value.

If the skip person received interests in specially valued property that were shown on Schedule R-1, show these interests on the Schedule R, Parts 2 and 3 worksheets, as appropriate. Do not use Schedule R-1 as a worksheet.

Completing the Special Use Value Worksheets.—On lines 2–4 and 6, enter -0-.

Completing the Fair Market Value Worksheets.—*Lines 2 and 3, fixed taxes and other charges.*—If valuing the interests at their fair market value (instead of special use value) causes any of these taxes and charges to increase, enter the increased amount (only) on these lines and attach an explanation of the increase. Otherwise, enter -0-.

Line 6—GST exemption.—If you completed line 10 of Schedule R, Part 1, enter on line 6 the amount shown for the skip person on the *line 10 special use allocation schedule* you attached to Schedule R. If you did not complete line 10 of Schedule R, Part 1, enter -0- on line 6.

Total GST Tax Savings.—For each skip person, subtract the tax amount on line 10, Part 2 of the special use value worksheet from the tax amount on line 10, Part 2 of the fair market value worksheet. This difference is the skip person's total GST tax savings.

Part 3.—Agreement to Special Valuation Under Section 2032A

The agreement to special valuation by persons with an interest in property is required under section 2032A(a)(1)(B) and (d)(2) and must be signed by all parties who have any interest in the property being valued based on its qualified use as of the date of the decedent's death.

An interest in property is an interest that, as of the date of the decedent's death, can be asserted under applicable local law so as to affect the disposition of the specially valued property by the estate. Any person who at the decedent's death has any such interest in the property, whether present or future, or vested or contingent, must enter into the agreement. Included are owners of remainder and executory interests; the holders of general or special powers of appointment; beneficiaries of a gift over in default of exercise of any such power; joint tenants and holders of similar undivided interests when the decedent held only a joint or undivided interest in the property or when only an undivided interest is specially valued; and trustees of trusts and representatives of other entities holding title to, or holding any interests in the property. An heir who has the power under local law to caveat (challenge) a will and thereby affect disposition of the property is not, however, considered to be a person with an interest in property under section 2032A solely by reason of that right. Likewise, creditors of an estate are not such persons solely by reason of their status as creditors.

If any person required to enter into the agreement either desires that an agent act for him or her or cannot legally bind himself or herself due to infancy or other incompetency, or due to death before the election under section 2032A is timely exercised, a representative authorized by local law to bind the person in an agreement of this nature may sign the agreement on his or her behalf.

The Internal Revenue Service will contact the agent designated in the agreement on all matters relating to continued qualification under section 2032A of the specially valued real property and on all matters relating to the special lien arising under section 6324B. It is the duty of the agent as attorney-in-fact for the parties with interests in the specially valued property to furnish the IRS with any requested information and to notify the IRS of any disposition or cessation of qualified use of any part of the property.

Form 706 (Rev. 10-91)

Estate of:

SCHEDULE B—Stocks and Bonds

(For jointly owned property that must be disclosed on Schedule E, see the instructions for Schedule E.)

Item number	Description including face amount of bonds or number of shares and par value where needed for identification. Give CUSIP number if available.	Unit value	Alternate valuation date	Alternate value	Value at date of death
1					
	Total from continuation schedule(s) (or additional sheet(s)) attached to this schedule . . .				
	TOTAL. (Also enter on Part 5, Recapitulation, page 3, at item 2.)				

(If more space is needed, attach the continuation schedule from the end of this package or additional sheets of the same size.)

(The instructions to Schedule B are in the separate instructions.)

Form 706 (Rev. 10-91)

Estate of:

SCHEDULE C—Mortgages, Notes, and Cash

(For jointly owned property that must be disclosed on Schedule E, see the instructions for Schedule E.)

Item number	Description	Alternate valuation date	Alternate value	Value at date of death
1				
Total from continuation schedule(s) (or additional sheet(s)) attached to this schedule .				
TOTAL. (Also enter on Part 5, Recapitulation, page 3, at item 3.)				

(If more space is needed, attach the continuation schedule from the end of this package or additional sheets of the same size.)
(See the instructions on the reverse side.)

Instructions for Schedule C.—Mortgages, Notes, and Cash

If the total gross estate contains any mortgages, notes, or cash, you must complete Schedule C and file it with the return.

On Schedule C list mortgages and notes *payable to* the decedent at the time of death. (Mortgages and notes *payable by* the decedent should be listed (if deductible) on Schedule K. Also list on Schedule C cash the decedent had at the date of death.

Group the items in the following categories and list the categories in the following order:

1. Mortgages.—List: (a) the face value and unpaid balance; (b) date of mortgage; (c) date of maturity; (d) name of maker; (e) property mortgaged; and (f) interest dates and rate of interest. For example: bond and mortgage of $50,000, unpaid balance $24,000; dated January 1, 1980; John Doe to Richard Roe; premises 22 Clinton Street, Newark, N.J.; due January 1, 1992, interest payable at 10% a year January 1 and July 1.

2. Promissory notes.—Describe in the same way as mortgages.

3. Contract by the decedent to sell land.—List: (a) the name of the purchaser; (b) date of contract; (c) description of property; (d) sale price; (e) initial payment; (f) amounts of installment payment; (g) unpaid balance of principal; and (h) interest rate.

4. Cash in possession.—List separately from bank deposits.

5. Cash in banks, savings and loan associations, and other types of financial organizations.—List: (a) the name and address of each financial organization; (b) amount in each account; (c) serial number; and (d) nature of account, indicating whether checking, savings, time deposit, etc. If you obtain statements from the financial organizations, keep them for IRS inspection.

Form 706 (Rev. 10-91)

Estate of:

SCHEDULE D—Insurance on the Decedent's Life

You must attach a Form 712 for each policy.

Item number	Description	Alternate valuation date	Alternate value	Value at date of death
1				
Total from continuation schedule(s) (or additional sheet(s)) attached to this schedule .				
TOTAL. (Also enter on Part 5, Recapitulation, page 3, at item 4.)				

(If more space is needed, attach the continuation schedule from the end of this package or additional sheets of the same size.)
(See the instructions on the reverse side.)

Instructions for Schedule D.—Insurance on the Decedent's Life

If there was any insurance on the decedent's life, whether or not included in the gross estate, you must complete Schedule D and file it with the return.

Insurance you must include on Schedule D.—Under section 2042 you must include in the gross estate:

- Insurance on the decedent's life receivable by or for the benefit of the estate; and
- Insurance on the decedent's life receivable by beneficiaries other than the estate, as described below.

The term "insurance" refers to life insurance of every description, including death benefits paid by fraternal beneficiary societies operating under the lodge system, and death benefits paid under no-fault automobile insurance policies if the no-fault insurer was unconditionally bound to pay the benefit in the event of the insured's death.

Insurance in favor of the estate.—Include on Schedule D the full amount of the proceeds of insurance on the life of the decedent receivable by the executor or otherwise payable to or for the benefit of the estate. Insurance in favor of the estate includes insurance used to pay the estate tax, and any other taxes, debts, or charges that are enforceable against the estate. The manner in which the policy is drawn is immaterial as long as there is an obligation, legally binding on the beneficiary, to use the proceeds to pay taxes, debts, or charges. You must include the full amount even though the premiums or other consideration may have been paid by a person other than the decedent.

Insurance receivable by beneficiaries other than the estate.—Include on Schedule D the proceeds of all insurance on the life of the decedent not receivable by or for the benefit of the decedent's estate if the decedent possessed at death any of the incidents of ownership, exercisable either alone or in conjunction with any person.

Incidents of ownership in a policy include:

- The right of the insured or estate to its economic benefits;
- The power to change the beneficiary;
- The power to surrender or cancel the policy;
- The power to assign the policy or to revoke an assignment;
- The power to pledge the policy for a loan;
- The power to obtain from the insurer a loan against the surrender value of the policy;
- A reversionary interest if the value of the reversionary interest was more than 5% of the value of the policy immediately before the decedent died. (An interest in an insurance policy is considered a reversionary interest if, for example, the proceeds become payable to the insured's estate or payable as the insured directs if the beneficiary dies before the insured.)

Life insurance not includible in the gross estate under section 2042 may be includible under some other section of the Code. For example, a life insurance policy could be transferred by the decedent in such a way that it would be includible in the gross estate under section 2036, 2037, or 2038. (See the instructions to Schedule G for a description of these sections.)

Completing the Schedule

You must list every policy of insurance on the life of the decedent, whether or not it is included in the gross estate.

Under "Description" list:

- Name of the insurance company and
- Number of the policy.

For every policy of life insurance listed on the schedule, you must request a statement on **Form 712,** Life Insurance Statement, from the company that issued the policy. Attach the Form 712 to the back of Schedule D.

If the policy proceeds are paid in one sum, enter the net proceeds received (from Form 712, line 24) in the value (and alternate value) columns of Schedule D. If the policy proceeds are not paid in one sum, enter the value of the proceeds as of the date of the decedent's death (from Form 712, line 25).

If part or all of the policy proceeds are not included in the gross estate, you must explain why they were not included.

Form 706 (Rev. 10-91)

Estate of:

SCHEDULE E—Jointly Owned Property

(If you elect section 2032A valuation, you must complete Schedule E and Schedule A-1.)

PART 1.—Qualified Joint Interests—Interests Held by the Decedent and His or Her Spouse as the Only Joint Tenants (Section 2040(b)(2))

Item number	Description For securities, give CUSIP number, if available.	Alternate valuation date	Alternate value	Value at date of death
	Total from continuation schedule(s) (or additional sheet(s)) attached to this schedule			
1a	Totals			
1b	Amounts included in gross estate (one-half of line 1a)			

PART 2.—All Other Joint Interests

2a State the name and address of each surviving co-tenant. If there are more than three surviving co-tenants, list the additional co-tenants on an attached sheet.

	Name	Address (number and street, city, state, and ZIP code)
A.		
B.		
C.		

Item number	Enter letter for co-tenant	Description (including alternate valuation date if any) For securities, give CUSIP number, if available.	Percentage includible	Includible alternate value	Includible value at date of death
		Total from continuation schedule(s) (or additional sheet(s)) attached to this schedule			
2b		Total other joint interests			
3		**Total includible joint interests** (add lines 1b and 2b). Also enter on Part 5, Recapitulation, page 3, at item 5.			

(If more space is needed, attach the continuation schedule from the end of this package or additional sheets of the same size.)
(See the instructions on the reverse side.)

Instructions for Schedule E.—Jointly Owned Property

You must complete Schedule E and file it with the return if the decedent owned any joint property at the time of death, whether or not the decedent's interest is includible in the gross estate.

Enter on this schedule all property of whatever kind or character, whether real estate, personal property, or bank accounts, in which the decedent held at the time of death an interest either as a joint tenant with right to survivorship or as a tenant by the entirety.

Do not list on this schedule property that the decedent held as a tenant in common, but report the value of the interest on Schedule A if real estate, or on the appropriate schedule if personal property. Similarly, community property held by the decedent and spouse should be reported on the appropriate Schedules A through I. The decedent's interest in a partnership should not be entered on this schedule unless the partnership interest itself is jointly owned. Solely owned partnership interests should be reported on Schedule F, "Other Miscellaneous Property."

Part 1.—Qualified joint interests held by decedent and spouse.—Under section 2040(b)(2), a joint interest is a qualified joint interest if the decedent and the surviving spouse held the interest as:

- Tenants by the entirety, or
- Joint tenants with right of survivorship if the decedent and the decedent's spouse are the only joint tenants.

Interests that meet either of the two requirements above should be entered in Part 1. Joint interests that do not meet either of the two requirements above should be entered in Part 2.

Under "Description," describe the property as required in the instructions for Schedules A, B, C, and F for the type of property involved. For example, jointly held stocks and bonds should be described using the rules given in the instructions to Schedule B.

Under "Alternate value" and "Value at date of death," enter the full value of the property.

Note: *You cannot claim the special treatment under section 2040(b) for property held jointly by a decedent and a surviving spouse who is not a U.S. citizen. You must report these joint interests on Part 2 of Schedule E, not Part 1.*

Part 2.—Other joint interests.—All joint interests that were not entered in Part 1 must be entered in Part 2.

For each item of property, enter the appropriate letter A, B, C, etc., from line 2a to indicate the name and address of the surviving co-tenant.

Under "Description," describe the property as required in the instructions for Schedules A, B, C, and F for the type of property involved.

In the "Percentage includible" column, enter the percentage of the total value of the property that you intend to include in the gross estate.

Generally, you must include the full value of the jointly owned property in the gross estate. However, the full value should not be included if you can show that a part of the property originally belonged to the other tenant or tenants and was never received or acquired by the other tenant or tenants from the decedent for less than adequate and full consideration in money or money's worth, or unless you can show that any part of the property was acquired with consideration originally belonging to the surviving joint tenant or tenants. In this case, you may exclude from the value of the property an amount proportionate to the consideration furnished by the other tenant or tenants. Relinquishing or promising to relinquish dower, curtesy, or statutory estate created instead of dower or curtesy, or other marital rights in the decedent's property or estate is not consideration in money or money's worth. See the Schedule A instructions for the value to show for real property that is subject to a mortgage.

If the property was acquired by the decedent and another person or persons by gift, bequest, devise, or inheritance as joint tenants, and their interests are not otherwise specified by law, include only that part of the value of the property that is figured by dividing the full value of the property by the number of joint tenants.

If you believe that less than the full value of the entire property is includible in the gross estate for tax purposes, you must establish the right to include the smaller value by attaching proof of the extent, origin, and nature of the decedent's interest and the interest(s) of the decedent's co-tenant or co-tenants.

In the "Includible alternate value" and "Includible value at date of death" columns, you should enter only the values that you believe are includible in the gross estate.

Form 706 (Rev. 10-91)

Estate of:

SCHEDULE F—Other Miscellaneous Property Not Reportable Under Any Other Schedule

(For jointly owned property that must be disclosed on Schedule E, see the instructions for Schedule E.)
(If you elect section 2032A valuation, you must complete Schedule F and Schedule A-1.)

		Yes	No
1	Did the decedent at the time of death own any articles of artistic or collectible value in excess of $3,000 or any collections whose artistic or collectible value combined at date of death exceeded $10,000? . . . . If "Yes," submit full details on this schedule.		
2	Has the decedent's estate, spouse, or any other person, received (or will receive) any bonus or award as a result of the decedent's employment or death? . . . . If "Yes," submit full details on this schedule.		
3	Did the decedent at the time of death have, or have access to, a safe deposit box? If "Yes," state location, and if held in joint names of decedent and another, state name and relationship of joint depositor. If any of the contents of the safe deposit box are omitted from the schedules in this return, explain fully why omitted.		

Item number	Description For securities, give CUSIP number, if available.	Alternate valuation date	Alternate value	Value at date of death
1				
	Total from continuation schedule(s) (or additional sheet(s)) attached to this schedule. .			
	TOTAL. (Also enter on Part 5, Recapitulation, page 3, at item 6.)			

(If more space is needed, attach the continuation schedule from the end of this package or additional sheets of the same size.)
(See the instructions on the reverse side.)

Instructions for Schedule F.—Other Miscellaneous Property

You must complete Schedule F and file it with the return.

On Schedule F list all items that must be included in the gross estate that are not reported on any other schedule, including:

- Debts due the decedent (other than notes and mortgages included on Schedule C)
- Interests in business
- Insurance on the life of another (obtain and attach **Form 712,** Life Insurance Statement, for each policy)

Note for single premium or paid-up policies: *In certain situations, for example where the surrender value of the policy exceeds its replacement cost, the true economic value of the policy will be greater than the amount shown on line 56 of Form 712. In these situations, you should report the full economic value of the policy on Schedule F. See Rev. Rul. 78-137, 1978-1 C.B. 280 for details.*

- Section 2044 property
- Claims (including the value of the decedent's interest in a claim for refund of income taxes or the amount of the refund actually received)
- Rights
- Royalties
- Leaseholds
- Judgments
- Reversionary or remainder interests
- Shares in trust funds (attach a copy of the trust instrument)
- Household goods and personal effects, including wearing apparel
- Farm products and growing crops
- Livestock
- Farm machinery
- Automobiles

If the decedent owned any interest in a partnership or unincorporated business, attach a statement of assets and liabilities for the valuation date and for the 5 years before the valuation date. Also attach statements of the net earnings for the same 5 years. You must account for goodwill in the valuation. In general, furnish the same information and follow the methods used to value close corporations. See the instructions for Schedule B.

All partnership interests should be reported on Schedule F unless the partnership interest, itself, is jointly owned. Jointly owned partnership interests should be reported on Schedule E.

If real estate is owned by the sole proprietorship, it should be reported on Schedule F and not on Schedule A. Describe the real estate with the same detail required for Schedule A.

Line 1.—If the decedent owned at the date of death articles with artistic or intrinsic value (e.g., jewelry, furs, silverware, books, statuary, vases, oriental rugs, coin or stamp collections), check the "Yes" box on line 1 and provide full details. If any one article is valued at more than $3,000, or any collection of similar articles is valued at more than $10,000, attach an appraisal by an expert under oath and the required statement regarding the appraiser's qualifications (see Regulations section 20.2031-6(b)).

Form 706 (Rev. 10-91)

Estate of:

SCHEDULE G—Transfers During Decedent's Life

(If you elect section 2032A valuation, you must complete Schedule G and Schedule A-1.)

Item number	Description For securities, give CUSIP number, if available.	Alternate valuation date	Alternate value	Value at date of death
A.	Gift tax paid by the decedent or the estate for all gifts made by the decedent or his or her spouse within 3 years before the decedent's death (section 2035(c))	X X X X X		
B.	Transfers includible under section 2035(a), 2036, 2037, or 2038:			
1				
	Total from continuation schedule(s) (or additional sheet(s)) attached to this schedule . . .			
	TOTAL. (Also enter on Part 5, Recapitulation, page 3, at item 7.).			

SCHEDULE H—Powers of Appointment

(If you elect section 2032A valuation, you must complete Schedule H and Schedule A-1.)

Item number	Description	Alternate valuation date	Alternate value	Value at date of death
1				
	Total from continuation schedule(s) (or additional sheet(s)) attached to this schedule .			
	TOTAL. (Also enter on Part 5, Recapitulation, page 3, at item 8.).			

(If more space is needed, attach the continuation schedule from the end of this package or additional sheets of the same size.)
(The instructions to Schedules G and H are in the separate instructions.)

Form 706 (Rev. 10-91)

Estate of:

SCHEDULE I—Annuities

Note: *Generally, no exclusion is allowed for the estates of decedents dying after December 31, 1984 (see instructions).*

		Yes	No
A	Are you excluding from the decedent's gross estate the value of a lump-sum distribution described in section 2039(f)(2)? . . . . If "Yes," you must attach the information required by the instructions.		

Item number	Description Show the entire value of the annuity before any exclusions.	Alternate valuation date	Includible alternate value	Includible value at date of death
1				
	Total from continuation schedule(s) (or additional sheet(s)) attached to this schedule .			
	TOTAL. (Also enter on Part 5, Recapitulation, page 3, at item 9.)			

(If more space is needed, attach the continuation schedule from the end of this package or additional sheets of the same size.)
(The instructions to Schedule I are in the separate instructions.)

Form 706 (Rev. 10-91)

Estate of:

SCHEDULE J—Funeral Expenses and Expenses Incurred in Administering Property Subject to Claims

Note: *Do not list on this schedule expenses of administering property not subject to claims. For those expenses, see the instructions for Schedule L.*

If executors' commissions, attorney fees, etc., are claimed and allowed as a deduction for estate tax purposes, they are not allowable as a deduction in computing the taxable income of the estate for Federal income tax purposes. They are allowable as an income tax deduction on Form 1041 if a waiver is filed to waive the deduction on Form 706 (see the Form 1041 instructions).

Item number	Description	Expense amount	Total Amount
	A. Funeral expenses:		
1			
	Total funeral expenses		
	B. Administration expenses:		
1	Executors' commissions—amount estimated/agreed upon/paid. (Strike out the words that do not apply.)		
2	Attorney fees—amount estimated/agreed upon/paid. (Strike out the words that do not apply.)		
3	Accountant fees—amount estimated/agreed upon/paid. (Strike out the words that do not apply.)		
		Expense amount	
4	Miscellaneous expenses:		
	Total miscellaneous expenses from continuation schedule(s) (or additional sheet(s)) attached to this schedule		
	Total miscellaneous expenses		

TOTAL. (Also enter on Part 5, Recapitulation, page 3, at item 11.)

(If more space is needed, attach the continuation schedule from the end of this package or additional sheets of the same size.)
(See the instructions on the reverse side.)

Instructions for Schedule J.— Funeral Expenses and Expenses Incurred in Administering Property Subject to Claims

General.—You must complete and file Schedule J if you claim a deduction on item 11 of Part 5, Recapitulation.

On Schedule J itemize funeral expenses and expenses incurred in administering property subject to claims. List the names and addresses of persons to whom the expenses are payable and describe the nature of the expense. **Do not list expenses incurred in administering property not subject to claims on this schedule. List them on Schedule L instead.**

Funeral Expenses.—Itemize funeral expenses on line A. Deduct from the expenses any amounts that were reimbursed, such as death benefits payable by the Social Security Administration and the Veterans Administration.

Executors' Commissions.—When you file the return, you may deduct commissions that have actually been paid to you or that you expect will be paid. You may not deduct commissions if none will be collected. If the amount of the commissions has not been fixed by decree of the proper court, the deduction will be allowed on the final examination of the return, provided that:

- The District Director is reasonably satisfied that the commissions claimed will be paid;
- The amount entered as a deduction is within the amount allowable by the laws of the jurisdiction where the estate is being administered;
- It is in accordance with the usually accepted practice in that jurisdiction for estates of similar size and character.

If you have not been paid the commissions claimed at the time of the final examination of the return, you must support the amount you deducted with an affidavit or statement signed under the penalties of perjury that the amount has been agreed upon and will be paid.

You may not deduct a bequest or devise made to you instead of commissions. If, however, the decedent fixed by will the compensation payable to you for services to be rendered in the administration of the estate, you may deduct this amount to the extent it is not more than the compensation allowable by the local law or practice.

Do not deduct on this schedule amounts paid as trustees' commissions whether received by you acting in the capacity of a trustee or by a separate trustee. If such amounts were paid in administering property not subject to claims, deduct them on Schedule L.

Note: *Executors' commissions are taxable income to the executors. Therefore, be sure to include them as income on your individual income tax return.*

Attorney Fees.—Enter the amount of attorney fees that have actually been paid or that you reasonably expect to be paid. If on the final examination of the return the fees claimed have not been awarded by the proper court and paid, the deduction will be allowed provided the District Director is reasonably satisfied that the amount claimed will be paid and that it does not exceed a reasonable payment for the services performed, taking into account the size and character of the estate and the local law and practice. If the fees claimed have not been paid at the time of final examination of the return, the amount deducted must be supported by an affidavit, or statement signed under the penalties of perjury, by the executor or the attorney stating that the amount has been agreed upon and will be paid.

Do not deduct attorney fees incidental to litigation incurred by the beneficiaries. These expenses are charged against the beneficiaries personally and are not administration expenses authorized by the Code.

Form 706 (Rev. 10-91)

Estate of:

SCHEDULE K—Debts of the Decedent, and Mortgages and Liens

Item number	Debts of the Decedent—Creditor and nature of claim, and allowable death taxes	Amount unpaid to date	Amount in contest	Amount claimed as a deduction
1				
	Total from continuation schedule(s) (or additional sheet(s)) attached to this schedule			
	TOTAL. (Also enter on Part 5, Recapitulation, page 3, at item 12.)			

Item number	Mortgages and Liens—Description	Amount
1		
	Total from continuation schedule(s) (or additional sheet(s)) attached to this schedule	
	TOTAL. (Also enter on Part 5, Recapitulation, page 3, at item 13.)	

(If more space is needed, attach the continuation schedule from the end of this package or additional sheets of the same size.)
(The instructions to Schedule K are in the separate instructions.)

Form 706 (Rev. 10-91)

Estate of:

SCHEDULE L—Net Losses During Administration and Expenses Incurred in Administering Property Not Subject to Claims

Item number	Net losses during administration (**Note:** *Do not deduct losses claimed on a Federal income tax return.*)	Amount
1		
	Total from continuation schedule(s) (or additional sheet(s)) attached to this schedule	
	TOTAL. (Also enter on Part 5, Recapitulation, page 3, at item 16.)	

Item number	Expenses incurred in administering property not subject to claims (Indicate whether estimated, agreed upon, or paid.)	Amount
1		
	Total from continuation schedule(s) (or additional sheet(s)) attached to this schedule	
	TOTAL. (Also enter on Part 5, Recapitulation, page 3, at item 17.)	

(If more space is needed, attach the continuation schedule from the end of this package or additional sheets of the same size.)
(The instructions to Schedule L are in the separate instructions.)

Form 706 (Rev. 10-91)

Estate of:

SCHEDULE M—Bequests, etc., to Surviving Spouse

Election To Deduct Qualified Terminable Interest Property Under Section 2056(b)(7).—If a trust (or other property) meets the requirements of qualified terminable interest property under section 2056(b)(7), and

a. the trust or other property is listed on Schedule M, and

b. the value of the trust (or other property) is entered in whole or in part as a deduction on Schedule M,

then (unless the executor specifically identifies property to be excluded from the election) the executor shall be deemed to have made an election to have such trust (or other property) treated as qualified terminable interest property under section 2056(b)(7).

If less than the entire value of the trust (or other property) that the executor has included in the gross estate is entered as a deduction on Schedule M, the executor shall be considered to have made an election only as to a fraction of the trust (or other property). The numerator of this fraction is equal to the amount of the trust (or other property) deducted on Schedule M. The denominator is equal to the total value of the trust (or other property).

		Yes	No
1	Did any property pass to the surviving spouse as a result of a qualified disclaimer?		
	If "Yes," attach a copy of the written disclaimer required by section 2518(b).		
2a	In what country was the surviving spouse born? ____________		
b	What is the surviving spouse's date of birth? ____________		
c	Is the surviving spouse a U.S. citizen?		
d	If the surviving spouse is a naturalized citizen, when did the surviving spouse acquire citizenship? ____________		
e	If the surviving spouse is not a U.S. citizen, of what country is the surviving spouse a citizen? ____________		
3	Qualified Domestic Trust.—Do you elect under section 2056A(d) to treat any trusts reported on Schedule M as qualified domestic trusts? (identify in the description column on Schedule M below the trusts to which the QDT election applies) (see instructions).		
4	Election out of QTIP Treatment of Annuities.—Do you elect under section 2056(b)(7)(C)(ii) **not** to treat as qualified terminable interest property any joint and survivor annuities that are included in the gross estate and would otherwise be treated as qualified terminable interest property under section 2056(b)(7)(C)? (see instructions) .		

Item number	Description of property interests passing to surviving spouse	Amount
1		
	Total from continuation schedule(s) (or additional sheet(s)) attached to this schedule	

5	**Total** amount of property interests listed on Schedule M		5	
6a	Federal estate taxes (including section 4980A taxes) payable out of property interests listed on Schedule M	6a		
b	Other death taxes payable out of property interests listed on Schedule M . . .	6b		
c	Federal and state GST taxes payable out of property interests listed on Schedule M	6c		
d	Add items a, b, and c		6d	
7	Net amount of property interests listed on Schedule M (subtract 6d from 5). Also enter on Part 5, Recapitulation, page 3, at item 18		7	

(If more space is needed, attach the continuation schedule from the end of this package or additional sheets of the same size.)

Examples of Listing of Property Interests on Schedule M

Item number	Description of property interests passing to surviving spouse	Amount
1	One-half the value of a house and lot, 256 South West Street, held by decedent and surviving spouse as joint tenants with right of survivorship under deed dated July 15, 1937 (Schedule E, Part I, item 1)	$ 32,500
2	Proceeds of Gibraltar Life Insurance Company policy No. 104729, payable in one sum to surviving spouse (Schedule D, item 3)	20,000
3	Cash bequest under Paragraph Six of will	100,000

Instructions for Schedule M.—Bequests, etc., to Surviving Spouse (Marital Deduction)

General.—You must complete Schedule M and file it with the return if you claim a deduction on item 18 of Part 5, Recapitulation.

The marital deduction is authorized by section 2056 for certain property interests that pass from the decedent to the surviving spouse. You may claim the deduction only for property interests that are included in the decedent's gross estate (Schedules A through I).

Note: *The marital deduction is generally not allowed if the surviving spouse is **not** a U.S. citizen. The marital deduction is allowed for property passing to such a surviving spouse in a "qualified domestic trust" or if such property is transferred or irrevocably assigned to such a trust before the estate tax return is filed. The executor must elect qualified domestic trust status on this return. See the instructions for line 3 on the following page for details on the election.*

Line 1.—If property passes to the surviving spouse as the result of a qualified disclaimer, check "Yes" and attach a copy of the written disclaimer required by section 2518(b).

Property interests that you may list on Schedule M.—Generally, you may list on Schedule M all property interests that pass from the decedent to the surviving spouse and are included in the gross estate. However, you should not list any "Nondeductible terminable interests" (described below) on Schedule M unless you are making a QTIP election. The property for which you make this election must be included on Schedule M. See "Qualified Terminable Interest Property" on the following page.

For the rules on common disaster and survival for a limited period, see section 2056(b)(3).

You may list on Schedule M only those interests that the surviving spouse takes:

1. As the decedent's legatee, devisee, heir, or donee;

2. As the decedent's surviving tenant by the entirety or joint tenant;

3. As an appointee under the decedent's exercise of a power or as a taker in default at the decedent's nonexercise of a power;

4. As a beneficiary of insurance on the decedent's life;

5. As the surviving spouse taking under dower or curtesy (or similar statutory interest); and

6. As a transferee of a transfer made by the decedent at any time.

Property interests that you may not list on Schedule M.—You should not list on Schedule M:

1. The value of any property that does not pass from the decedent to the surviving spouse.

2. Property interests that are not included in the decedent's gross estate.

3. The full value of a property interest for which a deduction was claimed on Schedules J through L. The value of the property interest should be reduced by the deductions claimed with respect to it.

4. The full value of a property interest that passes to the surviving spouse subject to a mortgage or other encumbrance or an obligation of the surviving spouse. Include on Schedule M only the net value of the interest after reducing it by the amount of the mortgage or other debt.

5. Nondeductible terminable interests (described below).

6. Any property interest disclaimed by the surviving spouse.

Terminable interests.—Certain interests in property passing from a decedent to a surviving spouse are referred to as *terminable interests.* These are interests that will terminate or fail after the passage of time, or on the occurrence or nonoccurrence of some contingency. Examples are: life estates, annuities, estates for terms of years, and patents.

The ownership of a bond, note, or other contractual obligation, which when discharged would not have the effect of an annuity for life or for a term, is not considered a terminable interest.

Nondeductible terminable interests.—A terminable interest is *nondeductible,* and should not be entered on Schedule M (unless you are making a QTIP election) if:

1. Another interest in the same property passed from the decedent to some other person for less than adequate and full consideration in money or money's worth; and

2. By reason of its passing, the other person or that person's heirs may enjoy part of the property after the termination of the surviving spouse's interest.

This rule applies even though the interest that passes from the decedent to a person other than the surviving spouse is not included in the gross estate, and regardless of when the interest passes. The rule also applies regardless of whether the surviving spouse's interest and the other person's interest pass from the decedent at the same time. Property interests that are considered to pass to a person other than the surviving spouse are any property interest that: (a) passes under a decedent's will or intestacy; (b) was transferred by a decedent during life; or (c) is held by or passed on to any person as a decedent's joint tenant, as appointee under a decedent's exercise of a power, as taker in default at a decedent's release or nonexercise of a power, or as a beneficiary of insurance in the decedent's life.

For example, a decedent devised real property to his wife for life, with remainder to his children. The life interest that passed to the wife does not qualify for the marital deduction because it will terminate at her death and the children will thereafter possess or enjoy the property.

However, if the decedent purchased a joint and survivor annuity for himself and his wife who survived him, the value of the survivor's annuity, to the extent that it is included in the gross estate, qualifies for the marital deduction because even though the interest will terminate on the wife's death, no one else will possess or enjoy any part of the property.

The marital deduction is not allowed for an interest that the decedent directed the executor or a trustee to convert, after death, into a terminable interest for the surviving spouse. The marital deduction is not allowed for such an interest even if there was no interest in the property passing to another person and even if the terminable interest would otherwise have been deductible under the exceptions described on the following page for life estate and life insurance and annuity payments with powers of appointment. For more information, see Regulations sections 20.2056(b)–1(f) and 20.2056(b)–1(g), Example (7).

If any property interest passing from the decedent to the surviving spouse may be paid or otherwise satisfied out of any of a group of assets, the value of the property interest is, for the entry on Schedule M, reduced by the value of any asset or assets that, if passing from the decedent to the surviving spouse, would be nondeductible terminable interests. Examples of property interests that may be paid or otherwise satisfied out of any of a group of assets are a bequest of the residue of the decedent's estate, or of a share of the residue, and a cash legacy payable out of the general estate.

Example: A decedent bequeathed $100,000 to the surviving spouse. The general estate includes a term for years (valued at $10,000 in determining the value of the gross estate) in an office building, which interest was retained by the decedent under a deed of the building by gift to a son. Accordingly, the value of the specific bequest entered on Schedule M is $90,000.

Life Estate With Power of Appointment in the Surviving Spouse.—A property interest, whether or not in trust, will be treated as passing to the surviving spouse, and will not be treated as a nondeductible terminable interest if: (a) the surviving spouse is entitled for life to all of the income from the entire interest; (b) the income is payable annually or at more frequent intervals; (c) the surviving spouse has the power, exercisable in favor of the surviving spouse or the estate of the surviving spouse, to appoint the entire interest; (d) the power is exercisable by the surviving spouse alone and (whether exercisable by will or during life) is exercisable by the surviving spouse in all events; and (e) no part of the entire interest is subject to a power in any other person to appoint any part to any person other than the surviving spouse (or the surviving spouse's legal representative or relative if the surviving spouse is disabled. See Rev. Rul. 85-35 1985-1 C.B. 328). If these five conditions are satisfied only for a specific portion of the entire interest, see the section 2056(b) regulations to determine the amount of the marital deduction.

Life Insurance, Endowment, or Annuity Payments, With Power of Appointment in Surviving Spouse.—A property interest consisting of the entire proceeds under a life insurance, endowment, or annuity contract is treated as passing from the decedent to the surviving spouse, and will not be treated as a nondeductible terminable interest if: (a) the surviving spouse is entitled to receive the proceeds in installments, or is entitled to interest on them, with all amounts payable during the life of the spouse, payable only to the surviving spouse; (b) the installment or interest payments are payable annually, or more frequently, beginning not later than 13 months after the decedent's death; (c) the surviving spouse has the power, exercisable in favor of the surviving spouse or of the estate of the surviving spouse, to appoint all amounts payable under the contract; (d) the power is exercisable by the surviving spouse alone and (whether exercisable by will or during life) is exercisable by the surviving spouse in all events; and (e) no part of the amount payable under the contract is subject to a power in any other person to appoint any part to any person other than the surviving spouse. If these five conditions are satisfied only for a specific portion of the proceeds, see the section 2056(b) regulations to determine the amount of the marital deduction.

Charitable Remainder Trusts.—An interest in a charitable remainder trust will **not** be treated as a nondeductible terminable interest if:

1. The interest in the trust passes from the decedent to the surviving spouse; and

2. The surviving spouse is the only beneficiary of the trust other than charitable organizations described in section 170(c).

A "charitable remainder trust" is either a charitable remainder annuity trust or a charitable remainder unitrust. (See section 664 for descriptions of these trusts.)

Election To Deduct Qualified Terminable Interests (QTIP).—You may elect to claim a marital deduction for qualified terminable interest property or property interests. You make the QTIP election simply by listing the qualified terminable interest property on Schedule M and deducting its value. You are presumed to have made the QTIP election if you list the property and deduct its value on Schedule M. If you make this election, the surviving spouse's gross estate will include the value of the "qualified terminable interest property." See the instructions for line 6 of General Information for more details. **The election is irrevocable.**

If you file a Form 706 in which you do not make this election, you may not file an amended return to make the election unless you file the amended return on or before the due date for filing the original Form 706.

The effect of the election is that the property (interest) will be treated as passing to the surviving spouse and will not be treated as a nondeductible terminable interest. All of the other marital deduction requirements must still be satisfied before you may make this election. For example, you may not make this election for property or property interests that are not included in the decedent's gross estate.

Qualified Terminable Interest Property is property (a) that passes from the decedent, and (b) in which the surviving spouse has a qualifying income interest for life.

The surviving spouse has a *qualifying income interest for life* if the surviving spouse is entitled to all of the income from the property payable annually or at more frequent intervals, or has a usufruct interest for life in the property, and during the surviving spouse's lifetime no person has a power to appoint any part of the property to any person other than the surviving spouse. An annuity is treated as an income interest regardless of whether the property from which the annuity is payable can be separately identified.

The QTIP election may be made for all or any part of a qualified terminable interest property. A partial election must relate to a fractional or percentile share of the property so that the elective part will reflect its proportionate share of the increase or decline in the whole of the property when applying sections 2044 or 2519. Thus, if the interest of the surviving spouse in a trust (or other property in which the spouse has a qualified life estate) is qualified terminable interest property, you may make an election for a part of the trust (or other property) only if the election relates to a defined fraction or percentage of the entire trust (or other property). The fraction or percentage may be defined by means of a formula.

Line 3.—Qualified Domestic Trust Election.—The marital deduction is allowed for transfers to a surviving spouse who is not a U.S. citizen only if the property passes to the surviving spouse in a "qualified domestic trust" (QDT) or if such property is transferred or irrevocably assigned to a QDT before the decedent's estate tax return is filed.

A QDT is any trust:

1. That requires at least one trustee to be either an individual who is a citizen of the U.S. or a domestic corporation;

2. That requires that no distribution of corpus from the trust can be made unless such a trustee has the right to withhold from the distribution the tax imposed on the QDT;

3. That meets the requirements of any applicable regulations; and

4. For which the executor has made an election on the estate tax return of the decedent.

To make the election, you must answer "Yes" to the question on line 3. **Once made, the election is irrevocable.**

When listing property on Schedule M, identify that property for which the QDT election has been made. Include the employer identification number for each trust and the names and addresses of all trustees.

The determination of whether a trust qualifies as a QDT will be made as of the date the decedent's Form 706 is filed. If, however, judicial proceedings are brought before the Form 706's due date (including extensions) to have the trust revised to meet the QDT requirements, then the determination will not be made until the court ordered changes to the trust are made.

Line 4.—Section 2056(b)(7) creates an automatic QTIP election for certain joint and survivor annuities that are includible in the estate under section 2039. To qualify, only the surviving spouse can have the right to receive payments before the death of the surviving spouse.

The executor can elect out of QTIP treatment, however, by checking the "Yes" box on line 4. Once made, the election is irrevocable. If there is more than one such joint and survivor annuity, you are not required to make the election for all of them.

If you make the election out of QTIP treatment by checking "Yes" on line 4, you cannot deduct the amount of the annuity on Schedule M. If you do not make the election out, you must list the joint and survivor annuities on Schedule M.

How To Complete Schedule M.—List each property interest included in the gross estate that passes from the decedent to the surviving spouse and for which a marital deduction is claimed. This includes otherwise nondeductible terminable interest property for which you are making a QTIP election. Number each item in sequence and describe each item in detail. Describe the instrument (including any clause or paragraph number) or provision of law under which each item passed to the surviving spouse. If possible, show where each item appears (number and schedule) on Schedules A through I.

Enter the value of each interest before taking into account the Federal estate tax or any other death tax. The valuation dates used in determining the value of the gross estate apply also on Schedule M.

If Schedule M includes a bequest of the residue or a part of the residue of the decedent's estate, attach a copy of the computation showing how the value of the residue was determined. Include a statement showing:

- The value of all property that is included in the decedent's gross estate (Schedules A through I) but is not a part of the decedent's probate estate, such as lifetime transfers, jointly owned property that passed to the survivor on decedent's death, and the insurance payable to specific beneficiaries.
- The values of all specific and general legacies or devises, with reference to the applicable clause or paragraph of the decedent's will or codicil. (If legacies are made to each member of a class, for example, $1,000 to each of decedent's employees, only the number in each class and the total value of property received by them need be furnished.)
- The date of birth of all persons, the length of whose lives may affect the value of the residuary interest passing to the surviving spouse.
- Any other important information such as that relating to any claim to any part of the estate not arising under the will.

Lines 6a, b, and c.—The total of the values listed on Schedule M must be reduced by the amount of the Federal estate tax, the Federal GST tax, and the amount of state or other death and GST taxes paid out of the property interest involved. If you enter an amount for state or other death or GST taxes on lines 6b or 6c, identify the taxes and attach your computation of them. For additional information, see **Pub. 904,** Interrelated Computations for Estate and Gift Taxes.

Attachments.—If you list property interests passing by the decedent's will on Schedule M, attach a certified copy of the order admitting the will to probate. If, when you file the return, the court of probate jurisdiction has entered any decree interpreting the will or any of its provisions affecting any of the interests listed on Schedule M, or has entered any order of distribution, attach a copy of the decree or order. In addition, the District Director may request other evidence to support the marital deduction claimed.

Form 706 (Rev. 10-91)

Estate of:

SCHEDULE O—Charitable, Public, and Similar Gifts and Bequests

		Yes	No
1a	If the transfer was made by will, has any action been instituted to have interpreted or to contest the will or any of its provisions affecting the charitable deductions claimed in this schedule? . . . . If "Yes," full details must be submitted with this schedule.		
b	According to the information and belief of the person or persons filing this return, is any such action planned?. If "Yes," full details must be submitted with this schedule.		
2	Did any property pass to charity as the result of a qualified disclaimer? . . . . If "Yes," attach a copy of the written disclaimer required by section 2518(b).		

Item number	Name and address of beneficiary	Character of institution	Amount
1			

	Total from continuation schedule(s) (or additional sheet(s)) attached to this schedule		
3	Total	3	
4a	Federal estate tax (including section 4980A taxes) payable out of property interests listed above	4a	
b	Other death taxes payable out of property interests listed above	4b	
c	Federal and state GST taxes payable out of property interests listed above.	4c	
d	Add items a, b, and c.	4d	
5	Net value of property interests listed above (subtract 4d from 3). Also enter on Part 5, Recapitulation, page 3, at item 19	5	

(If more space is needed, attach the continuation schedule from the end of this package or additional sheets of the same size.)
(The instructions to Schedule O are in the separate instructions.)

Form 706 (Rev. 10-91)

Estate of:

SCHEDULE P—Credit for Foreign Death Taxes

List all foreign countries to which death taxes have been paid and for which a credit is claimed on this return.

If a credit is claimed for death taxes paid to more than one foreign country, compute the credit for taxes paid to one country on this sheet and attach a separate copy of Schedule P for each of the other countries.

The credit computed on this sheet is for the .... (Name of death tax or taxes)

.... imposed in .... (Name of country)

Credit is computed under the .... (Insert title of treaty or "statute")

Citizenship (nationality) of decedent at time of death

(All amounts and values must be entered in United States money)

1 Total of estate, inheritance, legacy, and succession taxes imposed in the country named above attributable to property situated in that country, subjected to these taxes, and included in the gross estate (as defined by statute)	
2 Value of the gross estate (adjusted, if necessary, according to the instructions for item 2)	
3 Value of property situated in that country, subjected to death taxes imposed in that country, and included in the gross estate (adjusted, if necessary, according to the instructions for item 3)	
4 Tax imposed by section 2001 reduced by the total credits claimed under sections 2010, 2011, and 2012 (see instructions)	
5 Amount of Federal estate tax attributable to property specified at item 3. (Divide item 3 by item 2 and multiply the result by item 4.)	
6 Credit for death taxes imposed in the country named above (the smaller of item 1 or item 5). Also enter on line 18 of Part 2, Tax Computation	

SCHEDULE Q—Credit for Tax on Prior Transfers

Part 1.—Transferor Information

	Name of transferor	Social security number	IRS office where estate tax return was filed	Date of death
A				
B				
C				

Check here ▶ ☐ if section 2013(f) (special valuation of farm, etc., real property) adjustments to the computation of the credit were made (see instructions).

Part 2.—Computation of Credit (see instructions)

Item	Transferor A	Transferor B	Transferor C	Total A, B, & C
1 Transferee's tax as apportioned (from worksheet, (line 7 ÷ line 8) × line 35 for each column)				
2 Transferor's tax (from each column of worksheet, line 20)				
3 Maximum amount before percentage requirement (for each column, enter amount from line 1 or 2, whichever is smaller)				
4 Percentage allowed (each column) (see instructions)	%	%	%	
5 Credit allowable (line 3 × line 4 for each column)				
6 TOTAL credit allowable (add columns A, B, and C of line 5). Enter here and on line 19 of Part 2, Tax Computation				

(The instructions to Schedules P and Q are in the separate instructions.)

Form 706 (Rev. 10-91)

SCHEDULE R—Generation-Skipping Transfer Tax

Note: *To avoid application of the deemed allocation rules, Form 706 and Schedule R should be filed to allocate the GST exemption to trusts that may later have taxable terminations or distributions under section 2612 even if the form is not required to be filed to report estate or GST tax.*

Part 1.—GST Exemption Reconciliation (Section 2631) and Section 2652(a)(3) (Special QTIP) Election

Check box ▶ ☐ if you are making a section 2652(a)(3) (special QTIP) election (see instructions)

1	Maximum allowable GST exemption	1	$1,000,000
2	Total GST exemption allocated by the decedent against decedent's lifetime transfers	2	
3	Total GST exemption allocated by the executor, using Form 709, against decedent's lifetime transfers	3	
4	GST exemption allocated on line 6 of Schedule R, Part 2	4	
5	GST exemption allocated on line 6 of Schedule R, Part 3	5	
6	Total GST exemption allocated on line 4 of Schedule(s) R-1	6	
7	Total GST exemption allocated to intervivos transfers and direct skips (add lines 2–6)	7	
8	GST exemption available to allocate to trusts and section 2032A interests (subtract line 7 from line 1)	8	

9 Allocation of GST exemption to trusts (as defined for GST tax purposes):

A Name of trust	B Trust's EIN (if any)	C GST exemption allocated on lines 2–6, above (see instructions)	D Additional GST exemption allocated (see instructions)	E Trust's inclusion ratio (optional—see instructions)
9D Total. May not exceed line 8, above		9D		

10	GST exemption available to allocate to section 2032A interests received by individual beneficiaries (subtract line 9D from line 8). You must attach special use allocation schedule (see instructions)	10	

(The instructions to Schedule R are in the separate instructions.)

Form 706 (Rev. 10-91)

Estate of:

Part 2.—Direct Skips Where the Property Interests Transferred Bear the GST Tax on the Direct Skips

Name of skip person	Description of property interest transferred	Estate tax value

1 Total estate tax values of all property interests listed above	1	
2 Estate taxes, state death taxes, and other charges borne by the property interests listed above	2	
3 GST taxes borne by the property interests listed above but imposed on direct skips other than those shown on this Part 2. (See instructions.)	3	
4 Total fixed taxes and other charges. (Add lines 2 and 3.)	4	
5 Total tentative maximum direct skips. (Subtract line 4 from line 1.)	5	
6 GST exemption allocated.	6	
7 Subtract line 6 from line 5	7	
8 GST tax due (divide line 7 by 2.818182).	8	
9 Enter the amount from line 8 of Schedule R, Part 3	9	
10 **Total GST taxes payable by the estate.** (Add lines 8 and 9.) Enter here and on line 22 of the Tax Computation on page 1	10	

Form 706 (Rev. 10-91)

Estate of:

Part 3.—Direct Skips Where the Property Interests Transferred Do Not Bear the GST Tax on the Direct Skips

Name of skip person	Description of property interest transferred	Estate tax value

1 Total estate tax values of all property interests listed above	1	
2 Estate taxes, state death taxes, and other charges borne by the property interests listed above	2	
3 GST taxes borne by the property interests listed above but imposed on direct skips other than those shown on this Part 3. (See instructions.)	3	
4 Total fixed taxes and other charges. (Add lines 2 and 3.)	4	
5 Total tentative maximum direct skips. (Subtract line 4 from line 1.)	5	
6 GST exemption allocated	6	
7 Subtract line 6 from line 5	7	
8 GST tax due (multiply line 7 by .55). Enter here and on Schedule R, Part 2, line 9.	8	

SCHEDULE R-1 (Form 706) (October 1991) Department of the Treasury Internal Revenue Service	**Generation-Skipping Transfer Tax** Direct Skips From a Trust Payment Voucher	OMB No. 1545-0015 Expires 6-30-93

Executor: File one copy with Form 706 and send two copies to the fiduciary. Do not pay the tax shown. See the separate instructions.
Fiduciary: See instructions on following page. Pay the tax shown on line 6.

Name of trust		Trust's EIN
Name and title of fiduciary	Name of decedent	
Address of fiduciary (number and street)	Decedent's SSN	Service Center where Form 706 was filed
City, state, and ZIP code	Name of executor	
Address of executor (number and street)	City, state, and ZIP code	
Date of decedent's death	Filing due date of Schedule R, Form 706 (with extensions)	

Part 1.—Computation of the GST Tax on the Direct Skip

Description of property interests subject to the direct skip	Estate tax value

1	Total estate tax value of all property interests listed above	1	
2	Estate taxes, state death taxes, and other charges borne by the property interests listed above	2	
3	Tentative maximum direct skip from trust. (Subtract line 2 from line 1.)	3	
4	GST exemption allocated	4	
5	Subtract line 4 from line 3	5	
6	**GST tax due from fiduciary** (divide line 5 by 2.818182) **(See instructions if property will not bear the GST tax.)**	6	

Under penalties of perjury, I declare that I have examined this return, including accompanying schedules and statements, and to the best of my knowledge and belief, it is true, correct, and complete.

Signature(s) of executor(s) ____________________ Date ________

____________________ Date ________

Signature of fiduciary or officer representing fiduciary ____________________ Date ________

Instructions for Fiduciary

Purpose of Schedule R-1

Code section 2603(a)(2) provides that the Generation-Skipping Transfer (GST) tax imposed on a direct skip from a trust is to be paid by the trustee. Schedule R-1 (Form 706) serves as a payment voucher for the trustee to remit the GST tax to the IRS. See the instructions for Form 706 as to when a direct skip is from a trust.

How To Pay the GST Tax

The executor will compute the GST tax, complete Schedule R-1, and give you two copies. You should pay the GST tax using one copy and keep the other copy for your records.

The GST tax due is the amount shown on line 6. Make your check or money order for this amount payable to "Internal Revenue Service," write "GST tax" and the trust's EIN on it, and send it and one copy of the completed Schedule R-1 to the IRS Service Center where the Form 706 was filed, as shown on the front of the Schedule R-1.

When To Pay the GST Tax

The GST tax is due and payable 9 months after the decedent's date of death (entered by the executor on Schedule R-1). Interest will be charged on any GST taxes unpaid as of that date. However, you have an automatic extension of time to file Schedule R-1 and pay the GST tax due until 2 months after the due date (with extensions) for filing the decedent's Schedule R, Form 706. This Schedule R, Form 706 due date is entered by the executor on Schedule R-1. Thus, while interest will be due on unpaid GST taxes, no penalties will be charged if you file Schedule R-1 by this extended due date.

Signature

You, as fiduciary, must sign the Schedule R-1 in the space provided.

Form 706 (Rev. 10-91)

Estate of:

SCHEDULE S—Increased Estate Tax on Excess Retirement Accumulations

(Under section 4980A(d) of the Internal Revenue Code)

Part I Tax Computation

1 Check this box if a section 4980A(d)(5) spousal election is being made. . . . . ▶ ☐
You must attach the statement described in the instructions.

2 Enter the name and employer identification number (EIN) of each qualified employer plan and individual retirement account in which the decedent had an interest at the time of death:

	Name	EIN
Plan #1		
Plan #2		
Plan #3		
IRA #1		
IRA #2		
IRA #3		

	A Plan #1	B Plan #2	C Plan #3	D All IRAs
3 Value of decedent's interest				
4 Amounts rolled over after death				
5 Total value (add lines 3 and 4)				
6 Amounts payable to certain alternate payees (see instructions)				
7 Decedent's investment in the contract under section 72(f)				
8 Excess life insurance amount.				
9 Decedent's interest as a beneficiary.				
10 Total reductions in value (add lines 6, 7, 8, and 9) . . .				
11 Net value of decedent's interest (subtract line 10 from line 5)				

12 Decedent's aggregate interest in all plans and IRAs (add columns A–D of line 11) . . . . . ▶			12	
13 Present value of hypothetical life annuity (from Part III, line 4)	13			
14 Remaining unused grandfather amount (from Part II, line 4)	14			
15 Enter the greater of line 13 or line 14			15	
16 Excess retirement accumulation (subtract line 15 from line 12).			16	
17 Increased estate tax (multiply line 16 by 15%). Enter here and on line 23 of the Tax Computation on page 1			17	

(The instructions to Schedule S are in the separate instructions.)

Form 706 (Rev. 10-91)

Part II **Grandfather Election**

1 Was a grandfather election made on a previously filed Form 5329? . . . . ▶ ☐ Yes ☐ No
If "Yes," complete lines 2–4 below. **You may not make or revoke the grandfather election after the due date (with extensions) for filing the decedent's 1988 income tax return.** If "No," enter -0- on line 4 and skip to Part III.

2 Initial grandfather amount	2	
3 Total amount previously recovered	3	
4 Remaining unused grandfather amount (subtract line 3 from line 2). Enter here and on Part I, line 14, on page 37	4	

Part III **Computation of Hypothetical Life Annuity**

1 Decedent's attained age at date of death (in whole years, rounded down)	1	
2 Applicable annual annuity amount (see instructions).	2	
3 Present value multiplier (see instructions)	3	
4 Present value of hypothetical life annuity (multiply line 2 by line 3). Enter here and on Part I, line 13, on page 37	4	

Form 706 (Rev. 10-91) (Make copies of this schedule before completing it if you will need more than one schedule.)

Estate of:

CONTINUATION SCHEDULE

Continuation of Schedule ____________________
(Enter letter of schedule you are continuing.)

Item number	Description For securities, give CUSIP number, if available.	Unit value (Sch B or E only)	Alternate valuation date	Alternate value	Value at date of death or amount deductible
TOTAL. (Carry forward to main schedule.)					

See the instructions on the reverse side.

Instructions for Continuation Schedule

The Continuation Schedule on page 39 provides a uniform format for listing additional assets from Schedules A, B, C, D, E, F, G, H, and I and additional deductions from Schedules J, K, L, M, and O. Use the Continuation Schedule when you need to list more assets or deductions than you have room for on one of the main schedules.

Use a separate Continuation Schedule for each main schedule you are continuing. For each schedule of Form 706, you may use as many Continuation Schedules as needed to list all the assets or deductions to be reported. Do not combine assets or deductions from different schedules on one Continuation Schedule. Because there is only one Continuation Schedule in this package, you should make copies of the schedule before completing it if you expect to need more than one.

Enter the letter of the schedule you are continuing in the space provided at the top of the Continuation Schedule. Complete the rest of the Continuation Schedule as explained in the instructions for the schedule you are continuing. Use the *Unit value* column only if you are continuing Schedules B or E. For all other schedules, you may use the space under the *Unit value* column to continue your description.

To continue Schedule E, Part 2, you should enter the *Percentage includible* in the *Alternate valuation date* column of the Continuation Schedule.

To continue Schedule K, you should use the *Alternate valuation date* and *Alternate value* columns of the Continuation Schedule as *Amount unpaid to date* and *Amount in contest* columns, respectively.

To continue Schedules J, L, and M, you should use the *Alternate valuation date* and *Alternate value* columns of the Continuation Schedule to continue your description of the deductions. You should enter the amount of each deduction in the *amount deductible* column of the Continuation Schedule.

To continue Schedule O, you should use the space under the *Alternate valuation date* and *Alternate value* columns of the Continuation Schedule to provide the *Character of institution* information required on Schedule O. You should enter the amount of each deduction in the *amount deductible* column of the Continuation Schedule.

Carry the total from the Continuation Schedule(s) forward to the appropriate line of the main schedule.

☆ U.S. GOVERNMENT PRINTING OFFICE: 1991 618-783/41242

GLOSSARY

A-B trust (also called bypass trust, credit-shelter trust, or exemption-equivalent trust) Trust under which a deceased spouse's estate passes to a trust rather than to the surviving spouse, thereby reducing the possibility of the surviving spouse's estate being taxable.

abate Reduce, lessen, or diminish.

adeem Extinguish; take away.

ademption Extinction; not being owned.

administering an estate Settling and distributing the estate of a deceased person.

administrator Male appointed to administer the estate of an intestate decedent.

administrator ad litem Person appointed by a court to furnish a necessary party to a lawsuit in which a deceased has an interest.

administrator cum testamento annexo (also called administrator c.t.a. or administrator with the will annexed [administrator w.w.a]) Person appointed to administer a testate estate in which no executor is nominated or the named executor declines the nomination or is deceased or disqualified.

administrator de bonis non (also called administrator d.b.n or administrator of goods not administered) Person appointed to succeed to the office of an administrator who did not fully perform the task of settling the estate.

administrator de bonis non cum testamento annexo (also called administrator d.b.n.c.t.a or administrator of goods not administered with the will annexed) Person appointed to succeed to the office of an executor or an administrator c.t.a. who did not fully perform the task of settling the estate.

administrator of goods not administered (also called administrator de bonis non [administrator d.b.n]) Person appointed to succeed to the office of an administrator who did not fully perform the task of settling the estate.

administrator of goods not administered with the will annexed (also called administrator de bonis non cum testamento annexo [administrator d.b.n.c.t.a]) Person appointed to succeed to the office of an executor or an administrator c.t.a. who did not fully perform the task of settling the estate.

administrator pendente lite Temporary administrator appointed before the adjudication of testacy or intestacy to preserve the assets of an estate.

administrator with the will annexed (also called administrator w.w.a or administrator cum testamento annexo [administrator c.t.a.]) Person appointed to administer a testate estate in which no executor is nominated or the named executor declines the nomination or is deceased or disqualified.

administratrix Female appointed to administer the estate of an intestate decedent.

advance directives Written statements in which individuals specify whether they want life-sustaining medical treatment if they become desperately ill.

affinity Related by marriage.

agent One appointed to act in place of another.

alternate valuation method Method that allows property to be valued as of a date other than the date of death for estate tax purposes.

ambulatory Movable or subject to change.

anatomical gift Donation of all or part of a human body, to take effect upon or after death.

ancillary administration Administration of an estate in a state other than where the decedent was domiciled where the decedent owns property.

annuity Right to receive fixed, periodic payments either for life or for a term of years.

antilapse statutes Statutes that minimize the effects of lapse in a will. Typically, they provide that gifts in a will made to relatives who die before the testator but leave issue surviving the testator pass to the relative's issue.

appearance Formal, written entry submitting a person to the court's jurisdiction.

appointee Person for whose benefit a power of appointment is made.

appointive property Property subject to a power of appointment.

appointment Act of executing a power of appointment.

attest To see a signature or take note mentally that the signature exists as fact.

attestation clause Clause in a will that follows the testator's signature and precedes the witnesses' signatures.

attorney-in-fact An agent; one who is authorized to act on another's behalf.

bastard Child born out of wedlock.

beneficial title (also called equitable title) Right to the beneficial enjoyment of trust property.

beneficiary Person who receives a gift under a will; person holding equitable or beneficial title of a trust (also called cestui que trust).

bond Written promise by a fiduciary to pay a sum of money to the court if the fiduciary's duties are not faithfully performed.

bypass trust (also called A-B trust, credit-shelter trust, or exemption-equivalent trust) Trust under which a deceased spouse's estate passes to a trust rather than to the surviving spouse, thereby reducing the possibility of the surviving spouse's estate being taxable.

caveat Formal notice or warning to the court to prevent the proving of a will or the grant of administration of an estate.

cestui que trust Beneficiary of a trust.

charitable remainder annuity trust Trust in which a fixed amount of income is given to a beneficiary at least annually, and the entire remainder is given to charity.

charitable remainder trust Trust in which the settlor or a beneficiary retains the income from the trust for a period of time (usually for life), after which the trust principal is given to a charity.

charitable remainder unitrust Trust in which a percentage—not less than 5%—of the value of the trust property is determined annually and given to a beneficiary, with the entire remainder going to charity.

charitable trust (also called public trust) Trust in which the property held by the trustee must be used for public charitable purposes.

chose in action (also called intangible personal property) Personal right not reduced to possession but recoverable by a suit at law.

citation Written order of the court commanding the petitioner to appear on a day named and do something mentioned therein.

codicil Separate instrument with new provisions that change a will in some way.

collateral consanguinity Relationship between people who have the same ancestors but who do not ascend or descend from each other, such as one's brothers and sisters, aunts and uncles, nieces and nephews, and cousins.

community property Property (except a gift or inheritance) acquired by the personal efforts of either spouse during marriage and which, by law, belongs to both spouses equally. Community property is recognized in Arizona, California, Idaho, Louisiana, Nevada, New Mexico, Texas, Washington and Wisconsin.

consanguinity Kinship; blood relationship.

conservator Person appointed to care for the property of another person who, by reason of advanced age, mental weakness, or physical incapacity, is unable to do so himself or herself, but who is not mentally ill.

constructive trust Trust created by operation of law when someone obtains legal title to property through fraud or other wrongdoing.

conveyance in trust Trust created by a settlor transferring legal title to trust property to a trustee for the benefit of either the settlor or someone else.

court of chancery (also called orphan's court, probate court, or surrogate court) Court with probate jurisdiction.

credit-shelter trust (also called A-B trust, bypass trust, or exemption-equivalent trust) Trust under which a deceased spouse's estate passes to a trust rather than to the surviving spouse, thereby reducing the possibility of the surviving spouse's estate being taxable.

Crummey powers Powers in a life-insurance trust that give one or more beneficiaries the right to withdraw each year the money that is contributed to the trust.

curtesy Under English law, a right that a widower had, upon the death of his wife—but only if issue of the marriage were born alive—to a life estate in all real property owned by the wife during the marriage.

CUSIP number (Committee on Uniform Security Identification Procedure) Nine-digit number assigned to all stocks and bonds traded on major exchanges and many unlisted securities.

custodian Person who is entrusted with property that belongs to a minor.

cy pres ("as near as possible") Doctrine which dictates that, if a charity receiving trust funds discontinues existence and the court finds that the settlor had a general charitable intent, the trust fund will be turned over to another closely related charity; otherwise, the trust fund will revert to the settlor's estate.

declaration of trust Trust in which a settlor transfers equitable title to trust property to someone else and retains legal title.

demonstrative legacy A gift in a will of a certain sum of money with a direction that it be paid out of a particular fund.

descent Passage of real property by inheritance from an intestate.

devise A gift of real property in a will.

disclaimer Formal renunciation of a gift under a will, a trust, or the law of intestate succession.

discretionary trust (also called spray trust or sprinkling trust) Trust that gives the trustee the power to determine how the trust's income or principal or both are to be allocated among a group or class of beneficiaries.

disinterred Unearthed.

dispositive provisions Provisions of a will that dispose of the testator's property.

distribution Passage of personal property by inheritance from an intestate.

divest Take away.

domicile One's principal place of abode to which, whenever one is absent, one has the present intent of returning with no present purpose to depart.

donee Person who receives a gift or who has the right to exercise a power of appointment.

donor Person who makes a gift or creates a power of appointment; person who establishes a trust (also called settlor, trustor, or grantor).

dower Under English law, a right that a widow had, upon the death of her husband, to a one-third life estate in all real property owned by the husband during the marriage.

durable power of attorney Power of attorney with language indicating that the power is to survive incapacity or become effective when the principal becomes incapacitated.

elective share (also called forced share) Share of a deceased spouse's estate which a surviving spouse may elect instead of inheriting under the terms of the deceased spouse's will.

employer identification number Number beginning with "04" that is assigned by the IRS to identify an estate; used in place of a Social Security number.

endowment insurance Kind of insurance providing protection for a stated time—20 to 30 years. The face value of the policy is paid to the insured at the end of the agreed period, or, if the insured dies during that period, the face value is paid to the beneficiary.

equitable title (also called beneficial title) Right to the beneficial enjoyment of trust property.

escheat Passing of property to the state.

estate planning Arrangement of a person's property and estate in the manner best calculated to maintain and protect the family, both during the client's lifetime and after the client's death.

executor Male nominated in the will of a decedent to carry out the terms of the will.

executor de son tort Person who performs tasks of a personal representative and intermeddles with the property of a decedent without authority.

executrix Female nominated in the will of a decedent to carry out the terms of the will.

exempt property Certain property of a decedent that passes to the surviving spouse or children without being subject to the claims of general creditors.

exemption-equivalent trust (also called A-B trust, bypass trust, or credit-shelter trust) Trust under which a deceased spouse's estate passes to a trust rather than to the surviving spouse, thereby reducing the possibility of the surviving spouse's estate being taxable.

exordium clause (also called publication clause) Opening paragraph of a will.

express trust (also called voluntary trust) Trust that is created in explicit terms, either oral or written.

extinction Act of extinguishing or putting to an end.

fair market value Price at which property would change hands between a willing buyer and a willing seller if neither one is under any compulsion to buy or sell and if both have reasonable knowledge of all relevant facts.

family allowance (also called widow's allowance) Allowance from a decedent's estate to a widow or widower and surviving children to provide for their immediate needs after the death of the decedent.

fiduciary Person who is appointed to serve in a position of trust, including an executor, administrator, guardian, or trustee.

fiduciary capacity A position of trust.

fiduciary relationship A relationship of trust and confidence requiring the exercise of a high degree of honesty and good faith.

filius nullius Child of nobody.

forced heir Surviving spouse who elects to renounce the provisions of a deceased spouse's will and, instead, to take a forced share.

forced share (also called elective share) Share of a deceased spouse's estate which a surviving spouse may elect instead of inheriting under the terms of the deceased spouse's will.

formal proceedings Proceedings conducted before a judge with notice to interested persons (UPC § 1-201(15)).

general legacy A gift of money from the general assets of an estate.

general power of appointment Power of appointment that gives the donee the right to appoint the property to any desired appointee, including the donee or the donee's estate.

generation-skipping transfer tax Federal tax imposed when property exceeding $1 million is transferred to a person who is two or more generations below the donor or decedent, thereby skipping the generation directly below the transferor.

grantor (also called donor, settlor, or trustor) Person who establishes a trust.

gross estate All property owned by a decedent that is subject to the federal estate tax. It includes individually owned property, jointly owned property, property held in trust, life insurance, pensions and annuities, and certain gifts made over the decedent's lifetime.

gross estate tax Tentative estate tax computed by applying the unified rate schedule to the sum of the taxable estate and all taxable gifts.

group term life insurance Term life insurance protection provided under a master policy, or group of individual policies, which form part of a plan of group insurance as defined by U.S. Treasury Regulations.

guardian Person appointed to care for and manage the person, property, or both of a minor or incompetent.

guardian of the person One who has the care and custody of a child.

guardian of the property One who has the responsibility of caring for a child's property until the child becomes an adult.

half blood Relation between persons having only one parent in common.

head of household (also called householder) Person who is entitled to the homestead exemption.

health care proxy Written statement authorizing an agent or surrogate to make medical treatment decisions for a principal in the event of the principal's incapacity.

heirs Persons, including the surviving spouse, who are entitled under the statutes of intestate succession to the property of a decedent. In its broadest sense, persons who inherit property from a decedent's estate.

heirs at law Persons who would have inherited had the decedent died intestate.

holographic will (sometimes spelled olographic) Will written entirely in the handwriting of the testator(-trix) and signed by the testator(-trix) but not witnessed.

homestead exemption Law that places the family residence beyond the reach of creditors, allowing the head of a family to keep the family home regardless of the amount of family debt.

householder (also called head of household) Person who is entitled to the homestead exemption.

illegitimate children Children born out of wedlock.

implied trust (also called involuntary trust) Trust that comes about by operation of law rather than by the express terms of the settlor.

in personam jurisdiction Jurisdiction over the person.

in rem proceedings Proceedings directed against property rather than against persons.

in terrorem clause (also called no-contest clause) Provision in a will eliminating a will contestant from being a beneficiary under the will.

incidents of ownership Indications of ownership of life insurance, such as the power to change the beneficiary, surrender or cancel the policy, assign the policy, revoke an assignment, pledge the policy for a loan, or obtain a loan against the policy's cash surrender value.

income in respect of the decedent All gross income that a decedent would have received, had death not occurred, that was not properly includable on the decedent's final income tax return.

incorporation by reference Reference in a will to another existing document that makes the other document a part of the will itself.

independent probate Informal probate proceedings.

informal proceedings Proceedings conducted without notice to interested persons by an officer of the court acting as a registrar for probate of a will or appointment of a personal representative (UPC § 1-201(19)).

insolvent Unable to pay debts because of insufficient assets.

intangible personal property (also called chose in action) Personal right not reduced to possession but recoverable by a suit at law.

inter vivos trust (also called living trust) Trust that becomes effective during the settlor's lifetime.

intestacy The state of dying without having made a valid will.

intestate To die without a will. Also, a person who dies without a will.

intestate succession Process of an heir's becoming beneficially entitled to the property of one who dies without a will.

inventory Detailed list of property owned by the decedent together with its estimated value as of the decedent's date of death.

involuntary trust (also called implied trust) Trust that comes about by operation of law rather than by the express terms of the settlor.

irrevocable Cannot be taken back.

irrevocable living trust Living trust that cannot be revoked or amended by the settlor once it has been established.

issue Lineal descendants; all persons who have descended from a common ancestor.

joint tenants (also called joint tenants with the right of survivorship) Two or more persons holding one and the same interest, accruing by one and the same conveyance, commencing at one and the same time, and held by one and the same undivided possession.

joint will One instrument that serves as the will of two or more persons.

jurisdiction Power or authority that a court has to hear a case and to make a decision.

lapsed devises (also called lapsed legacies) Gifts of personal or real property in a will that fail because the legatee predeceased the testator.

lapsed legacies (also called lapsed devises) Gifts of personal or real property in a will that fail because the legatee predeceased the testator.

legal title Full, absolute ownership without a beneficial interest.

letters of administration Certificate of appointment of a personal representative in an intestate estate, or a testate estate in which someone other than the person nominated as executor(-trix) in the will is appointed.

letters testamentary Certificate of appointment of a personal representative in a testate estate.

life estate Ownership interest that is limited in duration to either the life of the owner or the life of another person.

limited-payment life insurance Insurance for which premiums are paid only for the limited period required by the policy, such as 10, 20, or 30 years. After that period, the policy is paid up.

lineal consanguinity Relationship between people who are related in a direct line, either downward, as between child, grandchild, and great-grandchild, or upward, as between parent, grandparent, and great-grandparent.

living trust (also called inter vivos trust) Trust that becomes effective during the settlor's lifetime.

living will Written expression of one's wishes to be allowed to die a natural death and not be kept alive by heroic measures or artificial means.

marital deduction Under federal estate tax law, property passing from a decedent to a surviving spouse. It is not taxable.

marital deduction trust Trust that is designed to make optimal use of the marital deduction.

marshaling of assets Legal principle that ranks estate assets in a certain order for the payment of debts.

model acts (also called uniform laws) Laws that have been proposed by the National Conference of Commissioners on Uniform State Laws for adoption by state legislatures.

mutual wills (also called reciprocal wills) Separate, identical wills by two testators containing reciprocal provisions and accompanied by an agreement that neither testator will change his or her will after the death of the other.

net estate tax Amount of estate tax that must be paid to the government; determined by deducting certain allowable credits, including a unified credit of $192,000, from the gross estate tax.

next of kin Persons nearest of kindred to the decedent; those most nearly related by blood.

no-contest clause (also called in terrorem clause) Provision in a will eliminating a will contestant from being a beneficiary under the will.

nonmarital children Children born out of wedlock.

nuncupative will An oral will.

olographic will (also called holographic will) Will that is entirely in the handwriting of the testator(-trix) and signed by the testator(-trix) but not witnessed.

ordinary life insurance (also called straight life or whole life) Insurance that gives lifetime protection and builds up a cash surrender value, with the payment of premiums continuing for the insured's life.

organ-tissue donor's card Document, signed by a donor in the presence of two witnesses, donating all or part of the donor's body; the donation takes effect upon or after death.

orphan's court (also called court of chancery, probate court, or surrogate court) Court with probate jurisdiction.

parol Oral.

pay-on-death (POD) account (also called Totten trust) Savings account in the name of the depositor as trustee for another person.

pecuniary bequest A gift of money in a will.

per capita By the heads.

per stirpes By right of representation.

personal property Everything that can be owned that is not real property.

personal representative Person who carries out the terms of a will or administers an estate; an executor or administrator.

petition for administration Written application by one or more heirs, next of kin, or creditors asking the court to appoint the petitioner as administrator(-trix) of the estate.

petition for administration with the will annexed Written application by someone other than the person nominated as personal representative in a will, asking the court to prove and allow the will and to appoint the petitioner as administrator(-trix).

petition for probate Formal, written application asking the court to prove and allow the will and to appoint the petitioner, who is nominated in the will, as executor(-trix) thereof.

posthumous issue Issue conceived before the decedent's death but born afterwards.

post-mortem planning Estate planning after a person dies.

pour-over trust Provision in a will in which the testator(-trix) leaves a gift to the trustee of an existing living trust.

power of appointment Right created in a will, trust, or other instrument that allows the holder to direct the disposition of property.

power of attorney Written instrument authorizing another person to perform certain specified acts on one's behalf.

precatory trust Trust created by words of entreaty, request, desire, or recommendation rather than by direct command.

preliminary letters testamentary Certificate, used in some states, giving a preliminary executor the same powers that are given to an ordinary executor, with some limitations, when a delay in probate is anticipated.

pretermitted child Child omitted from a parent's will.

principal One who authorizes another to act on one's behalf.

probate To prove and allow by the court.

probate court (also called court of chancery, surrogate court, or orphan's court) Court with probate jurisdiction.

probate estate (also called probate property) Property belonging to the decedent that is subject to administration by the executor or administrator.

probate in common form Informal probate proceedings.

probate in solemn form Formal probate proceedings.

probate jurisdiction Authority to probate wills and to administer estates.

probate property (also called probate estate) Property belonging to the decedent that is subject to administration by the executor or administrator. Among other things, it includes real and personal property that was owned either solely by the decedent or with others as a tenant in common.

probating a will Process of proving or establishing before the probate court that the document being offered for official recognition as the will of the decedent is in fact genuine.

proponent One who proposes or offers something.

public administrator(-trix) Official appointed to administer the estate of an intestate decedent when no one appears who is entitled to act as administrator.

public trust (also called charitable trust) Trust in which the property held by the trustee must be used for public charitable purposes.

publication clause (also called exordium clause) Opening paragraph of a will.

purchase money mortgage Mortgage given to purchase the property on which the mortgage is placed.

QTIP trust (qualified terminable interest property trust) Trust that gives all trust income to the surviving spouse for life, payable at least annually, and which meets the requirements of I.R.C. § 2056(b)(7).

qualified disclaimer Under federal tax law, an irrevocable and unqualified refusal by a person to accept an interest in property. It is effective only if it is in writing, received within a specified time, received prior to the acceptance of any benefits, and legally effective to pass the disclosed interest to another person without direction from the person making the disclaimer.

real property The ground and anything permanently affixed to it.

reciprocal wills (also called mutual wills) Separate, identical wills by two testators containing reciprocal provisions and accompanied by an agreement that neither testator will change his or her will after the death of the other.

Registry of Deeds Office where deeds, mortgages, and other instruments affecting title to real property are kept.

Registry of Probate Office where the records of all probate activities are kept.

republish Reestablish.

residuary clause Clause in a will that distributes all of the testator's property not disposed of in other clauses of the will.

resulting trust Trust that is implied from the intentions of the parties that the person holding legal title to property is holding it for another's benefit.

revocable living trust Living trust in which the settlor retains the right to alter, amend, or revoke the trust during the settlor's lifetime.

revoke Cancel.

right-to-die laws Cases and statutes that deal with the right of a dying person to refuse extraordinary treatment to prolong life.

rule against perpetuities Rule providing that every interest in property is void unless it must vest, if at all, not later than 21 years after some life in being at the time of creation of the interest.

satisfaction The giving by a testator, while alive, of property or money that was provided by will, with the intent that the gift or payment be in lieu of the legacy.

self-proof clause Clause in a will containing affidavits of the testator and witnesses that allow a will to be proved without testimony.

settlor (also called donor, grantor, or trustor) Person who establishes a trust.

severally Apart from others; solely.

signature clause (also called testimonium clause) Clause in a will that falls immediately before the testator's signature.

skip person Person receiving the property in a generation-skipping transfer.

slayer statutes State laws providing that one who is convicted of murdering another cannot inherit from the victim's estate.

sound mind Having the ability to make a will.

special administrator(-trix) Person appointed to handle the affairs of an estate for a limited time for a special purpose.

special power of appointment Power of appointment that limits appointment of the property to a specified class of persons named by the donor.

specific bequest (also called specific legacy) A gift in a will of an identifiable item of property other than real estate.

specific devise A gift in a will of an identifiable parcel of real property.

specific legacy (also called specific bequest) A gift in a will of an identifiable item of property other than real estate.

spendthrift Person who spends money profusely and improvidently.

spendthrift trust Trust containing restrictions on the voluntary and involuntary alienation of the trust's principal and interest.

split-dollar insurance policy Insurance policy in which the employee pays only that part of the annual premium which is the difference between the annual increase in the cash surrender value of the policy and the annual premium. The employer pays that part of the premium which is equal to the annual increase in the cash surrender value. If the employee dies, the employer receives the amount of the cash surrender value which the employer has paid, and the employee's beneficiary receives the balance of the maturity value.

split-gift provision Provision in the Internal Revenue Code under which spouses may consent to treat gifts of one spouse as if made one-half by each spouse, thereby doubling the amount that may be given away tax-free each year.

spray trust (also called discretionary trust or sprinkling trust) Trust that gives the trustee the power to determine how the trust's income or principal or both are to be allocated among a group or class of beneficiaries.

springing power Power in a durable power of attorney that does not become effective unless and until the principal becomes incapacitated.

sprinkling trust (also called discretionary trust or spray trust) Trust that gives the trustee the power to determine how the trust's income or principal or both are to be allocated among a group or class of beneficiaries.

straight life insurance (also called ordinary life and whole life) Insurance that gives lifetime protection and builds up a cash surrender value, with the payment of premiums continuing for the insured's life.

subscribe To write beneath, below, or following.

successor personal representative Personal representative, other than a special administrator, who is appointed to succeed a previously appointed personal representative (UPC § 1-201(41)).

supervised administration Process in which an estate is settled under the continuing surveillance of the court from beginning to end.

surety One who stands behind a fiduciary by agreeing to pay the amount of the bond in the event the fiduciary becomes liable to pay it.

surrogate An agent; one appointed to act in place of another.

surrogate court (also called court of chancery, orphan's court, or probate court) Court with probate jurisdiction.

tangible personal property Personal property that has substance and can be touched.

taxable estate Under federal estate tax law, the gross estate minus administration and funeral expenses, claims against the estate, outstanding obligations, casualty and theft losses, the marital deduction, and the charitable deduction.

tenants by the entirety A husband and wife who hold title as joint tenants, modified by the common law doctrine that gives the husband the exclusive rights of possession and profits with protection against attachment and alienation by one spouse alone.

tenants in common Two or more persons who own an undivided interest in property in such a way that each owner's interest passes to his or her heirs upon death rather than to the surviving co-owners.

tenants in partnership Form of co-ownership of property belonging to members of a partnership.

term insurance Type of insurance that furnishes maximum protection at minimum cost but has no cash surrender value and offers no protection after expiration of the term.

testament Under early English law, a will of personal property.

testamentary capacity Having the ability to make a will; being of sound mind.

testamentary trust Trust within the body of a will.

testator Male who has made a will.

testatrix Female who has made a will.

testimonium clause (also called signature clause) Clause in a will that falls immediately before the testator's signature.

Totten trust (also called a pay-on-death (POD) account) Savings account in the name of the depositor as trustee for another person.

trust Arrangement under which title to property is divided into two parts, legal title and equitable title.

trust res (also called trust corpus, trust fund, trust principal, trust property) Property that is held in trust.

trustee Person who holds legal title in trust for the benefit of a beneficiary.

trustor (also called donor, grantor, or settlor) Person who establishes a trust.

Uniform Anatomical Gifts Act (UAGA) (See appendix B) Uniform law that provides a simplified manner of making a testamentary donation of vital organs for medical research or transplant.

Uniform Gifts to Minors Act (UGMA) Uniform law that provides an inexpensive, easy mechanism for transferring property to minors.

uniform laws (also called model acts) Laws that have been proposed by the National Conference of Commissioners on Uniform State Laws for adoption by state legislatures.

Uniform Probate Code (UPC) Uniform law designed to modernize and standardize the laws relating to the affairs of decedents, minors, and certain other persons who need protection. (See appendix D.)

Uniform Simultaneous Death Act (See appendix A) Uniform law, adopted by most states, that sets forth rules to be followed when the passage of property depends upon the time of one's death, and there is no sufficient evidence that the persons died other than at the same time.

Uniform Transfers to Minors Act (UTMA) (See appendix C) Uniform law that revised and restated the Uniform Gifts to Minors Act.

unsupervised administration Method of administering an estate, under the Uniform Probate Code, without court action unless it is requested by an interested person.

vest Accrue to.

voluntary administrator(-trix) Person who undertakes the informal administration of a small intestate estate.

voluntary executor(-trix) Person who undertakes the informal administration of a small testate estate.

voluntary trust (also called express trust) Trust that is created in explicit terms, either oral or written.

whole life insurance (also called ordinary life and straight life) Insurance that gives lifetime protection and builds up a cash surrender value, with the payment of premiums continuing for the insured's life.

widow's allowance (also called family allowance) Allowance from a decedent's estate to a widow or widower and surviving children to provide for their immediate needs after the death of the decedent.

will Under early English law, a will of real property.

will and testament Under early English law, a will of real and personal property.

INDEX

NOTE: Italicized page numbers refer to non-text material. Italicized page numbers following the word "defined" refer to definitions placed in the margins of the pages referred.

J

K

L

M

N

V

W